TELEVISION VIOLENCE AND THE ADOLESCENT BOY

Television violence and the adolescent boy

WILLIAM A. BELSON
BA, PhD

Reader in Research Methods

North East London Polytechnic

British Library Cataloguing in Publication Data

Belson, William Albert
Television violence and the adolescent boy.
1. Television and youth 2. Violence in Television 3. Adolescent boys
4. Television - United States - Psychological aspects
I. Title
301.16'2 HQ799.2.T4

ISBN 0-566-00211-6

Published by
Saxon House, Teakfield Limited,
Westmead, Farnborough, Hampshire, England

ISBN 0 566 00211 6

Printed in Great Britain by
Biddles Limited, Guildford, Surrey

CONTENTS

INTRODUCTION

Origins

This enquiry was financed by the Columbia Broadcasting System of the United States of America.

In March 1969, I attended a meeting of social scientists called together by the Columbia Broadcasting System under the chairmanship of Dr J.T. Klapper, Director of the Office of Social Research of that organisation. The purpose of this meeting was to discuss ways and means of securing realistic estimates of the different effects of exposure to television violence.

Subsequently I was invited to put forward a proposal for research based upon certain of my suggestions at the CBS meeting. Following discussions and further meetings, a grant was made in June 1970 for carrying through this proposal. The grant was to be administered by the London School of Economics and Political Science and the work was to be done by the Survey Research Centre under my direction. The total value of the grant was approximately £157,000.

Real life 'cause and effect' phenomena

The emphasis in the proposal had been upon the assessment of the effects of *real life* exposure to television violence and upon *real life* effects. This approach is to be contrasted with laboratory-type studies involving experimentation with simulated factors and situations. Furthermore it was fully recognised that any meaningful real life study of the effects of exposure to television violence would have to go well beyond simply establishing the level of correlation between amount of exposure to television violence and whatever form of behaviour or attitude was being investigated as possibly affected by exposure to television violence.

The real life or naturalistic approach raises major difficulties for research conducted at this advanced stage in television's growth and establishment. There was a period, when television was a new phenomenon in Britain and the world, when there was still major scope for naturalistic studies of the long-term influence of television violence. Ideally, such investigation called for a sophisticated application of a long-term 'before and after' design, and it is most unfortunate that so little of this class of work has been carried out. Certainly it was feasible in country after country as these entered the television age. Instead, what tended to happen was that the necessarily expensive and complex research process was not financed and initiated prior to the country's television experience. And later on, when alarm began to be expressed about the possible effects of television violence, it was assumed by many that it was too late to do anything effective through the naturalistic approach.

However, though the opportunity to apply the *ideal* methodology to the study of the real life influence of television violence was largely lost, there is available another potentially powerful approach, namely a development of the Hypothetico-Deductive method. This is a strategy well known in certain of the physical sciences but which has much to offer to the social scientist attempting to study cause and effect processes in the real-life situation — a situation in which any one cause-effect process may be catalysed or damped down by the multi-determinant context in which it naturally occurs. The application of this approach in such a setting calls for the testing of multiple (deduced) propositions and the use of advanced forms of matching technology of an empirical kind. In practice, the workability of this approach depends to a large extent upon computer usage.

In the present — or in any other — context, this method will not provide *proof* that some hypothesised causal connection exists. But it can be used to determine the degree to which highly relevant evidence is supportive of such an hypothesis. The more rigorously the deduction system is applied, the firmer will be the basis of evidence for reaching conclusions.

This approach, which is relatively simple in principle, but complex and costly in application, is summarised in chapter 1, is described in working detail in chapter 3 and is referred to in each of chapters 12 and 14-19. It is hoped that the reader will be interested in the Hypothetico-Deductive method in its own right, that is as a means for dealing with naturalistic hypotheses about cause and effect.

Tool making

Another feature of the proposal was that it specified the construction of all necessary measuring instruments as an important and extensive preliminary to the data gathering phase of the enquiry. Indeed, this approach was a standard one for the Survey Research Centre with its extensive background in methodological research and development. There are many investigations for which such an approach is essential and the failure to adopt it is often the reason why vital social investigations are not made.

USA sponsorship of the London enquiry

The reader may well have noted that though the study was conducted in London and relates specifically to the London scene, the sponsor was a USA broadcasting organisation. This situation arose because the methods put forward in my proposal were not at that time established in the USA whereas the Survey Research Centre in London had already had much experience in using them. It was for this reason that the present investigation was based on London. At the same time it is noteworthy that many of the programmes investigated were of USA origin (which is, of course, a feature of the UK output) and that I have suggested in my conclusions (chapter 20), that I would in general expect my findings to be relevant to similar city cultures with a similar television output with respect to violent content.

Several important by-products of the enquiry

Whereas the principal purpose of this enquiry was to investigate the nature and extent of the effects of exposure to television violence, steps were taken, through the formulation of sub-hypotheses, to further our understanding of *what sorts of television violence* were the more likely to produce violence by boys and what sorts were least likely to do so. In the event, the findings with regard to these sub-hypotheses were of a kind that could be used to generate provisional guidelines for use in making decisions about the presentation of violence on television. Similarly, it was by no means a principal purpose to develop classes of data sufficient to generate hypotheses about the nature of the psychological processes underlying such changes as television violence produces in boys. Nonetheless, the enquiry did yield data that appears to give strong support to an hypothesis about one such process and a degree of support to the limited operation of others.

The effects of the other media on violence by boys

From the outset it had been intended that the investigation of hypotheses about the effects of *television* should be paralleled by the investigation of similar hypotheses about the effects of other of the mass media. This part of the enquiry was not taken anywhere near as far as that for television, but what was done was sufficient to indicate the relative potentials of the different media for producing change. Chapter 12 provides the principal results for this part of the study, and additional details are given in chapters 14-19.

Acknowledgements

The completion of this enquiry was made possible by the receipt of facilities and help of many kinds. I am very glad to record my indebtedness and my gratitude:

To the Columbia Broadcasting System of the USA for providing the grant through which the investigation was financed.

To Joseph Klapper, Head of the Office of Social Research of CBS, through whom the grant was secured.

To the London School of Economics and Political Science for administration of research funds and for the provision of facilities for part of the huge volume of computer processing required for the project.

To Purdue and George Washington Universities for the rest of the computer processing.

To the British Broadcasting Corporation and the Independent Broadcasting Authority for facilities and ready discussion whenever these were required.

To George Brosan, Director of the North East London Polytechnic, for his help in providing facilities during the later stages of the investigation.

To Phil Wirtz for his major contribution to computer processing.

To Susannah Brown, Ira Cisin, Graham Dossett, Brian Emmett, Ian Haldane, Frank Land, Richard Maisel, Richard Martin, Harold Mendelsohn, Vernon Thompson, Walter Weiss, Lee Williams for highly productive discussion of technical aspects of the investigation.

To the following members of the research staff of the Survey Research Centre, for their substantial participation in the project – Michael Couzens, Graham Hankinson, Richard Kitney, Peter Southgate, Carol Wain, Barbara Williams, Gil Williams.

To members of the administrative and clerical staff of the Survey Research Centre, particularly Jean Carr, Joan Rowat and her coding staff, Margaret Bradgate, Inetta Capsey, Joanna Chubb, Joy Dixon, Brian Silk, Doris Toms.

To several thousand London boys and their parents for their participation in the enquiry.

To the members of my team of interviewing and testing officers who took part in the main data collection phase of the investigation in the period from mid July 1972 to early 1973.

The availability of a summary of the enquiry

For some, the large size of this report may be forbidding. I felt it necessary to present it at this length partly to enable social scientists to make critical examinations of methods and findings, partly because the results of the enquiry seem to call for major changes in programme policy and therefore should be fully documented, and partly because the results could hardly be condensed more than they have been without loss of important evidence. However, the reader with little time to spare may limit himself to chapter 1 of this volume which is an extended summary of the enquiry along with recommendations.

William Belson
Project Director

August 1978

CHAPTER 1

AN EXTENDED SUMMARY OF THE INVESTIGATION AND RECOMMENDATIONS FOR ACTION

Contents

1 AN EXTENDED SUMMARY OF THE INVESTIGATION AND RECOMMENDATIONS FOR ACTION

THE AIMS OF THE INVESTIGATION

(see chapter 2 for details)

1 The purpose of the investigation described in this report was to investigate the tenability of a number of hypotheses about the effects, on male adolescents, of long term exposure to television violence. The tenability of an hypothesis was to be gauged in terms of the degree to which it was supported by the evidence brought to bear on it.

There were 22 principal hypotheses of this kind, all of them developed through exploratory work, and of these the two key hypotheses were:

(1) 'High exposure to television violence increases the degree to which boys engage in violent behaviour of a serious kind'.

(2) 'High exposure to television violence increases the degree to which boys engage in violent behaviour considered generally'. [1] [2]

For the purposes of this enquiry, and of these hypotheses in particular, 'violence' had been defined as 'physical or verbal activity of a kind that produces or is likely to produce hurt or harm of any kind for the object on the receiving end. This object could be animate or inanimate and the hurt or harm could be physical or psychological'.

The other principal hypotheses took the following forms.

(a) '*High exposure to television violence increases the degree to which boys:*

- are violent in the company of other boys;
- engage in irritating, argumentative or annoying behaviour;
- engage in aggressive behaviour in sport or play;
- use bad language or swear.'

(b) '*High exposure to television violence increases the degree to which boys:*

- are preoccupied with the forms of violence shown on television;
- feel like committing the forms of violence shown on television;
- 'feel willing' to commit the different forms of violence shown on television;
- are callous in relation to violence being committed in their own vicinity;
- are callous in relation to more distant violence about which they hear through the mass media;
- find the prospect of violence attractive;
- object to the idea of violence in the world;

· see violence as a basic part of human nature and therefore as inevitable;
· accept violence as a way to solve problems;
· are involved in problems over sleep;
· are made anxious or nervous;
· have angry or bitter feelings about people.'

(c) *'High exposure to television violence decreases the degree to which boys:*

· are considerate towards others;
· have respect for authority.'

The enquiry was also designed to allow the investigation of various sub-hypotheses (84 in all) linked to the principal hypotheses. Each of these sub-hypotheses linked some class of television violence to one or more of the hypothesised effects of exposure, as detailed in 1 (a), (b) and (c) above. For example:

'High exposure to fictional violence of a realistic kind increases the degree to which boys engage in serious violence;'

'High exposure to programmes in which violence is presented as being in a good cause increases the degree to which boys find violence attractive.'

Twenty-five different types of exposure were featured in the sub-hypotheses as follows:

No.	TYPES OF PROGRAMME VIOLENCE STUDIED
2*	Programmes containing fictional violence of a realistic kind
3	Programmes where violence is performed by basically 'good guy' types who are also rebels or 'odd-men-out'
4	Programmes in which much of the violence takes place in a domestic or family setting
5	Programmes that feature defiance or rudeness towards authority figures
6	Programmes where violence is shown as glorified, romanticised, ennobling
7	Programmes where violence is presented as fun and games or like a game or as something to entertain.
8	Programmes in which the violence is presented as being in a good cause
9	Programmes where the physical or mental consequences of violence, for the victim, are shown in detail
10	Programmes where the violence is related to racial or minority strife
11	Programmes where the violence is performed by basically 'good guy' types or heroes who are also tough (i.e. who can endure physical violence and fight on)
12	Programmes where the violence is of a verbal kind
13	Programmes in which the violence is just 'thrown in' for its own sake or is not necessary to the plot
14	Programmes in which the violence is gruesome, horrific or scary
15	Fictional programmes about the English police at work which also feature the kinds of violence that go on in society
16	A selection of (5) cartoon programmes in which the characters are violent to each other (i.e. Boss Cat, Popeye, Pugwash, Yogi Bear, Tom and Jerry)
17	Tom and Jerry
18	Plays or films in which personal relationships are a major theme and which feature verbal abuse (e.g. swearing, quarrelling) or physical violence.
19	Violence through the News or newsreel programmes
20	Comedy programmes which feature slapstick violence and/or verbal abuse between characters
21	Science fiction programmes involving violence (e.g. where creatures destroy people, where humans use super weapons to destroy men)

22 Westerns which include violence, for example, as between Cowboys and Indians

23 A selection of (3) sporting programmes which present violence by competitors or spectators (i.e. Sportsview, Grandstand, Saturday Sportstime)

24 Wrestling and boxing

25 Films or series featuring gangs/gangsters in organised violent crime

26 Programmes in which the violence is performed by adults.

*Type 1 = television violence generally.

The various linkages between types of exposure and hypothesised effects are included in table 2.8, chapter 2 and are shown diagrammatically on pages 369-70 of chapter 12.

3 The enquiry was designed to allow also the investigation of a number of hypotheses about the effects of exposure to certain mass media, namely newspapers, violent films, comics. For each of these, the investigation was in terms of the 22 different dependent variables listed on pages 1 and 2. For example:

'High exposure to violent films increases the degree to which boys engage in serious violence'.

'High exposure to newspapers increases the degree to which boys are callous in relation to the spectacle of violence'.

Here, too, see table 2.8, chapter 2 and pages 369-70 of chapter 12 for the different hypotheses of this kind.

THE METHODS OF INVESTIGATION USED

(for details, see chapters 2-9 of this volume and the General Appendix)

From the outset it was planned that in this investigation every effort would be made to avoid certain methodological features that had characterised a number of earlier studies of the influence of television violence. More specifically, the enquiry was *not* to be of the laboratory type involving the simulation of key variables and it was *not* to be limited to a simple correlational approach.

The enquiry was conducted in two stages:

1 A preparatory stage for the development of relevant hypotheses (see chapter 2), for the design of the strategy of investigation (see chapter 3) and for the construction of the necessary measuring techniques (see chapters 4-8).

2 An investigation in which the yield from the preparatory work was used in a study of 1565 London boys in the age range 12-17 years.

It was a condition of the granting arrangement that funds for carrying the study into its second stage would be made available only if in the opinion of CBS's scientific advisors the first stage had been satisfactorily completed.

THE PREPARATORY STAGE

Work on the preparatory stage of the enquiry took approximately 16 months, ending in

July 1972. In this summary, I have presented only the principal features of these different preparatory operations, but they are described very fully in chapters 2-8.

Hypothesis development (see chapter 2)

The development of hypotheses about the effects on boys of exposure to television violence was based upon (i) an extensive and critical study of the published literature on the subject; (ii) group discussions with boys (in the age range 12-17 years) and (separately) with their parents; (iii) individual interviews with boys and with parents; (iv) interviews with people who, through the press or television, had expressed views about the influence of television on young people; (v) interviews with production staff in the television industry; (vi) a study of collections of press clippings going back to 1950. The number of individuals interviewed under (ii)-(v) was 143.

The yield from these different sources was content analysed to produce a large and heterogeneous array of hypotheses. These were then subjected to critical scrutiny by the research team with the purpose of eliminating those that were hopelessly vague or which were beyond the financial or the temporal scope of the enquiry.

The final array of hypotheses thus set up for investigation is referred to under AIMS and is presented in diagrammatic form in table 2.8, chapter 2 and on pages 369-70 of chapter 12.

Construction of the measuring instruments (see chapters 4-8)

The construction of the necessary measuring instruments for use in the enquiry was closely guided by the hypotheses, in that the hypotheses defined the variables in terms of which measurements would have to be made. The variables to be measured included the following.

1. Measures for assessing the degree to which boys have been exposed to presentations of violence through television and the extent to which they have been exposed to *different sorts* of television violence. These were the independent (or 'causal') variables.
2. Measures for assessing the extent to which boys engage in violent behaviour of different degrees of seriousness (see hypotheses 1-4).
3. Measures of the extent to which boys are involved in specific forms of violent behaviour, i.e. swearing, violence in sport or play, violence in the company of other boys, irritating or annoying behaviour (see hypotheses 5-8).
4. Measures of 'state of mind' in relation to a range of TV-type acts of violence (see hypotheses 9-11).
5. Measures of various attitudes, opinions and reactions, e.g. extent of liking violence, consideration for others, respect for authority (see hypotheses 12-16, 20-22).
6. Measures of callousness in relation to the spectacle of violence in the news or going on around them (see hypotheses 18 and 19).
7. Assessment devices for registering the incidence of problems over sleep (see hypothesis 17).

The methods used for constructing these measures, and the final form of such measures, are given in detail in chapters 4-8. The summary which follows deals principally with two key measures which were both complex in form and central to the total enquiry, namely those referred to under 1 and 2 above.

1 *Measuring exposure to television violence (see chapter 4)*

The extent of a boy's exposure to television violence was defined in terms of his viewing of a sample of the television violence broadcast in the period 1959-1971.

The drawing of this sample was a major task which included the following steps: (i) a 'universe' of the possibly violent output of that period was compiled; (ii) from this universe a representative sample of programmes was drawn, with stratification in terms of year of output, station of origin, size of audience.

Score for exposure to television violence was based jointly upon extent of exposures to each of the sampled programmes in the period up to the interview and the rated level of violence of each of them. The ratings for level of violence had been made by a panel of approximately fifty experienced viewers (ex-members of the BBC's viewing panel) who made their ratings on an illustrated scale (see chapter 4) running from 'not violent at all' to 'completely violent'. Frequency of exposure to the sample of programmes was determined through (i) a lengthy self-completion operation by boys working at home; (ii) follow-up questioning at the Centre involving the use of visual and other aids, and the persistent challenging of frequency claims. A boy's score was the sum of the products of number of exposures (up to a limited ceiling to protect the enquiry from distortion through extreme cases) to sampled programme on the one hand and its violence rating on the other.

A complication in the development of this measuring system was that the sample of programmes was to be used *also* to provide measures of the *different kinds of programme violence* to which boys were exposed. To this end, each of the programmes in the sample had been rated (by the same set of judges) in terms of various of the 25 different types of programme violence being investigated (see chapters 2 and 4). For example, the judges rated the programme 'The Untouchables' in terms of how much of its violence was of the 'realistic fiction' kind, how much of its violence was presented as being in a good cause, how much of its violence seemed to be unnecessary to the plot, and so on. Similarly for the other programmes in the sample. On this system, each programme in the sample had attributed to it a whole series of weights – in fact, up to a maximum of 25 of them – and these weights are presented in table 4.6, chapter 4. Given these weights, the overall violence rating and the number of exposures for each of the programmes in the sample, it was possible to calculate a boy's score for exposure to violence of any of the 25 different kinds under investigation.

Programme	Times seen	Violence rating	Rating of its violence as		Contribution of these programmes to total score for exposure to violence of	
			Realistic fiction	of good-cause kind	the realistic fiction kind	the good-cause kind
A	50	4.89	0.67	0.48	50 x 4.89 x 0.67	50 x 4.89 x 0.48
B	35	5.17	0.68	0.46	35 x 5.17 x 0.68	35 x 5.17 x 0.46
C	0	6.82	0.48	0.67	0 x 6.82 x 0.48	0 x 6.82 x 0.67
D	15	7.25	0.88	0.56	15 x 7.25 x 0.88	15 x 7.25 x 0.56

The total number of programmes in the final sample of violent programmes was 68 and the system was used to generate 26 different exposure scores, one for violence in general and 25 for exposure to specific kinds of violence. For further details of the construction process and for illustration of the scoring systems used, see chapter 4.

The completed measure was subjected to a test with status somewhere between a reliability and a validity measure and this test yielded coefficients of 'reproducibility' ranging from .87 to .93 according to the type of television exposure being measured.

2 *Measuring involvement in violent behaviour* [3] *(see chapter 6)*

The general approach with this measure was based closely upon that used in the writer's earlier work in measuring involvement in stealing [4] – the problem of getting boys to give accurate information in this case being broadly of a similar kind. The precise form of the violence measure had, however, to be geared to the subtleties of the violence phenomenon and the construction process was lengthy and demanding. The method of Progressive Modification was used in the sense that each new version of the developing method was subject to test and then to modification on the basis of the results of that test. This process was continued until an acceptable level of efficiency had been achieved. The number of respondents used in this particular construction process was 203.

In its final form (as used in the enquiry proper), this measuring device had the following features, full details of which are given in chapter 6.

(a) The interview was administered to boys on Centre premises under conditions of stressed anonimity and privacy. Each boy had a false name for the interview and had been through preparatory processing with the same interviewer.

(b) In the first of the two stages of the eliciting procedure, the boy and interviewer sat on opposite sides of a sorting screen, the boy being required to process 53 cards on each of which was printed a 'violence category'. The 53 categories were of three kinds: somewhat generalised references to acts of violence (e.g. 'I have smashed up things or places'); situational (e.g. 'I have been violent at school'); motivational (e.g. 'I have been violent in self-defence'). As a collection, they were *not* meant to be a list of specific acts but simply a *web of stimuli* sufficient (i) to define violence as featured in this enquiry; (ii) help the boy recall his own acts *without there being gaps* in the recall aid system. Working under certain rules, the boy was required to sort each card according to whether he had or had not done what was printed on it in the last six months.

In the second stage of the eliciting technique the boy went through a procedure designed to bring out any resistances he had to making truthful statements about his violent behaviour and to condition him against resistance to so doing. He then re-sorted all the cards previously sorted as 'not in the last six months'.

In stage three of the sorting procedure, the boy was asked a series of questions about each of his 'yes' cards with the intention of establishing: (i) all the different sorts of acts on the basis of which the card had been sorted as 'yes'; (ii) the frequency of occurrence of each of these specific acts in the last six months; (iii) for each of these acts, the nature of the act, the object of the acts, the implement if any, the circumstances of the act, what led the boy to commit the act. Steps were taken to avoid counting any one act more than once (i.e. in developing a total score).

(c) The whole of the extraction procedure was controlled by a booklet of instructions within which the 53 cards were inserted at appropriate places in relation to the instructions. This administration involved: rule teaching (for card sorting); reminders of important points and distinctions; challenging; probing; periodic reconditioning against making false claims. The whole process was tape recorded for quality control in relation to interviewer performance, quality control being conducted daily and on a continuing basis by quality control staff.

(d) In developing aggregate scores, a ceiling of 50 was placed on the number of times any one category of act could be counted, the reason for this being to reduce the danger (for the study as a whole) of massive claims from some limited number of boys.

(e) The interviewers were given lengthy training in administering this technique.

3 *Measuring the other dependent variables (see chapters 7 and 8)*

(a) For each of the different attitudinal variables, the principal construction method was the Thurstone Equal Appearing Interval Method, though some variations away from the strict Thurstone Method were desirable where the scales were for use on boys. This process yielded a separate scale or measure for each attitudinal variable. Each such scale consisted of a set of evaluative statements about matters directly relating to its attitudinal variable. For example, two of the statements making up the measure of 'respect for authority' were:

- 'most policemen are decent people';
- 'cheeking the teacher at school is OK if done in fun'.

Boys could accept or reject these statements, each of which had linked to it an empirically derived value which would contribute to the boy's 'score' if he endorsed it.

The attitudes so measured related to:

- level of attractiveness of violence for the boy;
- degree of boy's objection to the occurrence of violence in the world generally;
- degree to which violence is regarded as basic to human nature and hence inevitable;
- degree of acceptance of violence as a way to solve problems;
- level of consideration for others;
- level of respect for authority.

(b) Three of the measures constructed dealt with how boys felt about some 20 acts of violence of the sort presented on television (see chapter 8).

(i) One of these measures was 'feeling of willingness' to commit such acts. For each of these acts (e.g. 'stabbing someone with a knife'), boys examined a series of circumstances in which they might or might not be 'willing to commit' such an act (e.g. 'if my life was threatened'/'if my girl friend was insulted by someone'), and endorsed each of those circumstances as 'yes' or 'no'. Each 'circumstance' had linked to it an empirically derived index of willingness, and a boy's score for a given act was the sum of the indices of the circumstances he had endorsed.

(ii) For each of the 20 acts, boys used scaling devices to indicate: how often this sort of act came into their thinking (i.e. for use as an index of preoccupation); how often they 'felt like committing it'.

For each of these three measures, 16 of the 20 'scores' (4 were deleted as being unusable) were accumulated into a single measure.

(c) Two of the other measures were concerned with callousness in relation to (i) violence going on in one's own vicinity and (ii) violence as reported in the news. For each of these, the measure was geared to a set of pictures presenting violence, those for reported violence being pictures reproduced from the national press. Reactions to the pictures were assessed through a Thurstone-type rating scale designed to measure callousness (see chapter 7).

(d) The identification of sleep problems was linked to four questions, two to the boy and two to one or the other of his parents, dealing with different sorts of sleep problems (see chapter 8).

The strategy used for investigating the causal hypotheses (see chapter 3)

From the outset, it was planned that this enquiry would be based upon *normal* long term exposure to television violence, upon behaviour as it *normally* occurs and upon attitudes as they *normally* develop. This meant that there could be no question of the enquiry being a controlled experiment. It had to be based upon processes as they normally occur in the long term working of a multi-dimensional and changeful society.

It is not unusual, in situations like this, for researchers to make do with correlational studies, for example, assessments of the level of the correlation between violent behaviour by boys and the extent of their exposure to different sorts of television violence. But this investigation had to be taken beyond the obvious ambiguities of such an approach. What was needed was an investigation of causal-type hypotheses – not mere calculation of correlations. To this vital end, the following strategies were used. What follows is of course no more than a summary, the full details of the research strategy being set out in chapters 3 and 10.

The basic problem to be overcome

The research strategy used is best described through an actual hypothesis, say the hypothesis that 'high exposure to television violence increases the degree to which boys engage in serious violence'.

(a) This strategy *begins* with the comparison of 2 groups of boys, namely the Qualifiers and the Controls. The Qualifiers are the higher scoring half of the sample in terms of exposure to television violence and the Controls are the lower scoring half.

(b) Any difference between the Qualifiers and Controls (in terms of violent behaviour by boys) can be attributed to one or more of the following:

(i) the differential effect of the greater exposure of the Qualifiers to television violence;

(ii) differences between the Qualifying and the Control samples in terms of characteristics or background factors that are associated with level of violent behaviour (as distinct from differential exposure to television violence);

(iii) a tendency for the more violent boys to watch a greater amount of television violence just because of their greater involvement in violence (i.e. a tendency for the hypothesis to be working *in reverse*).

The steps taken to disentangle the ambiguities of a straightforward comparison of Qualifiers and Controls

1 If the difference in violence level of Qualifiers and Controls is due simply to original differences between them, then the close matching of those two samples in terms of all the correlates of violent behaviour, should, in principle, tend to eliminate the difference between them in terms of level of violent behaviour.

Hence a key step in this study was to search for a composite of predictors of the dependent variable and to equate the Controls to the Qualifiers in terms of this composite of predictors. To this end a pool of 227 possible predictors of violent behaviour was developed and this pool was used, within the Stable Correlate Technique, [5] to equate the Controls to the Qualifiers. As a new feature of the Stable Correlate Technique, the composite of predictors was chosen against a double criterion, namely the correlation of each trial variable with *both* the dependent and the independent variables, [6] the joint index of matching power being the product of those two predictive indices.

The Controls could now be thought of as Modified Controls and the matching process was almost certain to have changed the assessed violence levels. If there still remained a meaningful difference between this modifed violence level and the violence level of the Qualifiers, we could conclude that the initial hypothesis is still intact. The larger the residual difference and the greater its statistical significance, the greater would the tenability of the hypothesis be judged to be.

2 There is still the possibility, however, that the hypothesis is true *in reverse* – i.e. 'being violent causes boys to watch more violence on television'. So the same challenge through matching was applied to the reverse form of the hypothesis.

3 (a) If the *forward form* of the hypothesis is not supported by the results of the matching operation, the results for its reversed form are irrelevant: whatever the situation for the reverse phenomenon, the forward form of the hypothesis is not tenable.

(b) If *both* the forward and the reversed forms of the hypothesis are supported by the tests made, then we face a possibility that the forward test is in part supported by the hypothesis working in reverse. There are of course other possible explanations: (i) that the whole process is circular, with television leading to greater violence and greater violence leading to more watching of television violence, and so on; (ii) that for some boys, the forward form of the hypothesis is true while for others the reverse form of the hypothesis is true. In the circumstances, we must conclude that the evidence supports the hypothesis but that this support is not as firm as it would have been if the reverse hypothesis had gone unsupported.

(c) If the forward form of the hypothesis is supported by the evidence and the reverse form is not, then we have the firmest sort of evidence of the tenability of the hypothesis in its forward form.

4 This is the kind of investigatory strategy which was applied to all the causal hypotheses and sub-hypotheses in this enquiry. With 22 principal hypotheses and 150 sub-hypotheses being investigated, [7] it became necessary to develop 344 matching composites and to carry out 344 associated matching operations. Some additional composite development and some further matching were necessary for additional hypothesis testing in connection with a secondary control system.

THE ENQUIRY FOR WHICH THE PREPARATORY WORK WAS DONE

(see chapter 9)

The completion of the preparatory phase of the enquiry opened the way for conducting the enquiry proper. [8] A summary follows and details are given in chapter 9.

Sampling methods

The sampling of the boy population of London is a complicated matter because no complete list of them exists – and certainly there is no such list for boys aged 12-17 years. Against this background, a stratified random sampling system involving drawing a sample of 'random starting points' was used to derive a random sample of 2,001 boys qualifying for interview. Under rigorously applied controls, this sample yielded 1,650 home interviews with boys and their mothers. [9] Of the 1,650 boys so interviewed, 1,565 subsequently completed the (essential) second interview on Survey Research Centre premises (a 78 per cent success rate for the double interview).

The information extraction strategies

The collection of the large amount of information that was required for the overall testing strategy necessitated an extended form of contact with each boy in the sample. In fact three stages of data collection were required for each boy.

(a) An at-home interview with the boy and his mother [9].

(b) A phase of at-home information provision by the boy and his parents on a self-completion basis (requiring the input of a lot of time by the boy and some by his parents).

(c) An extended and intensive interview with the boy at the Survey Research Centre lasting three and a half hours on average and involving the administration of various eliciting and measuring procedures under conditions of complete privacy.

Full details of each of these three stages in the data collection procedure are given in the report (chapter 9) and what follows is a summary of key elements of the enquiry.

1 In securing the co-operation of boys and parents, the interviewer explained: that she was from the University and that this enquiry was about the ways in which young people are influenced by various things – their reading, the films they see, the schooling they get and so on; that the interview was strictly confidential; that we were going to pay a fee of £2.00 [10] for a home interview plus a follow-up interview at the Survey Research Centre.

2 At the 'home interview' the mother [11] went through an interview dealing principally with the rearing of the boy, with her own and her husband's background and with the sort of person the boy was when under four years of age. The *boy* was set going on several self-completion tasks which related to his own general background, tastes, education, interests, ambitions and to aspects of his media usage. This self-completion task was lengthy and allowed for help by parents.

At the end of this home interview, the interviewer made an appointment for the boy to be collected by car and brought to the Survey Research Centre for his second interview in about a week's time. Most of these Centre interviews were arranged for evening sessions but afternoon and weekend interviews were also arranged where necessary.

3 Some 95 per cent of all boys interviewed at home eventually went through the interview at the Centre, though this involved a major follow-up effort, with second and third and even further appointments sometimes being necessary to get a boy to the Centre. On arrival at the Centre, boys were allowed to choose a false name and were then passed on to an interviewer for an extended testing/questioning sequence, details of which are given in chapter 9.

4 Most of the interviewers working at the Centre had university backgrounds. Many of them were employed as teachers, so that they not only had experience in dealing with boys, but were free for evening work on 3-5 evenings a week. All interviewers went through an extended initial training period.

5 The whole interviewing operation was spread over a period of six months which ran from July to February and spanned both hot and cold weather. Quality control on all aspects of interviewing was an integral feature of the operation.

FINDINGS

A vast amount of data processing was completed and the results of this are presented in detail in (i) two Technical Appendices and (ii) this report, chapters 11-19. The results are presented in two sections, namely (i) results relating to the extent and nature of such violence as goes on amongst London boys and (ii) the tenability of the hypotheses that were investigated. The findings about the extent and nature of violence were simply a by-product of the investigation and they *have already been reported in their own right.* [12]

The nature and extent of violence by London boys (Chapter 11 for details)

In chapter 11 are details of violence carried out by boys. These are presented under the following headings.

- The frequency of endorsement of each of the 53 stimulus items (consisting of acts of violence, situations in which violence has occurred, reasons for being violent) used in the elicitation procedure.
- The incidence of violence (over a six month period) at each of six levels of intensity/seriousness.

The characteristics of boys in relation to the level of their violence.

The principal findings were as follows:

1 Violence by boys ranges all the way from a rough form of mischief which is done on a major scale, to violence of a serious kind. Illustrative details are given in chapter 11.

2 At the *serious* level, about half the boys (54 per cent) had committed no such acts in the last six months. But 12 per cent had done so 10 times or more in that period and of these at least 4 per cent were committing violence at this serious level with high frequency. For the sample as a whole, the average per boy for the six month period was about 6 (serious) acts of violence.

3 Violence of the more serious kind is quite strongly associated with: frequent truancy from school (positively); disliking school (positively); lower occupational level of father (positively). There is a tendency for grammar school boys and for boys from small families to be less violent than others. Also, older boys (ages 16-17 years) were somewhat less violent than those in the 12-15 year range.

4 In spite of these and other tendencies, serious violence tends to occur in all the different social sectors.

The investigation of causal hypotheses

The nature of the hypotheses

A great array of hypotheses and sub-hypotheses was investigated in the course of this enquiry and these can be classified into the following groups.

1 Principal hypotheses linking some form of behaviour or some attitude or opinion or state of mind to exposure to television violence. There were 22 of these hypotheses.

2 Sub-hypotheses linking some form of behaviour or attitude or opinion or state of mind to exposure to some particular form of television violence (e.g. fictional violence of a realistic kind). There were 84 of these sub-hypotheses.

3 Sub-hypotheses which had been postulated and investigated solely for control purposes. There are 44 of these.

4 Sub-hypotheses which were postulated and investigated solely to look into the possibility that 'outlyer' phenomena were 'responsible' for the findings about the effects of mass media violence upon the level of serious violence by boys. There are 62 of these.

5 Hypotheses dealing with the effects of 3 different media upon the behaviour, the attitudes, opinions and 'state of mind' of boys. There are 66 of these hypotheses.

For each of these hypotheses and sub-hypotheses, both its forward and its reversed forms were investigated, in line with the investigatory strategy set out in chapter 3. [13] There was thus a target of 2 x 278 (= 556) hypotheses and sub-hypotheses to be investigated, though 2 x 106 of these were included for methodological checks only.

The results of the investigation of these many hypotheses and sub-hypotheses are set out in working detail in the technical appendices to this report (available in microfich form) and in report form in chapters 12-19. Furthermore, the principal findings are brought together in chapter 20. The following summary of the findings includes but goes beyond the presentation in chapter 20.

Investigation results

1 The evidence gathered through this investigation is very strongly supportive of the hypothesis that high exposure to television violence increases the degree to which boys engage in serious violence. Thus for serious violence by boys: (i) heavier viewers of television violence commit a great deal more serious violence than do lighter viewers of television violence who have been closely equated to the heavier viewers in terms of a wide array of empirically derived matching variables; (ii) the reversed form of this hypothesis is *not* supported by the evidence.

2 Broadly the same type of result emerged for many of the 25 sub-hypotheses of hypothesis 4, namely sub-hypotheses about the effects, on involvement in serious violence, of high exposure to certain kinds of television output. On the evidence of this enquiry, five types of television violence appear to be the more potent in releasing serious violence by boys, namely:

(a) plays or films in which violence occurs in the context of close personal relations;

(b) violent programmes in which the violence appears to have been 'just thrown in for its own sake or is not necessary to the plot';

(c) programmes presenting fictional violence of a realistic kind;

(d) programmes in which the violence is presented as being in a good cause;

(e) Westerns of the violent kind.

By contrast, there was but little or no support for the hypotheses that the following kinds of programme output increases serious violence by boys.

(a) sporting programmes presenting violent behaviour by competitors or spectators (excluding programmes on boxing and wrestling);

(b) violent cartoons including Tom and Jerry;

(c) science fiction violence;

(d) slapstick comedy presenting violence or verbal abuse.

3 Hypotheses 1, 2 and 3 dealt with the effects of high exposure to television violence upon violent behaviour (principally) of the 'less than serious' kind. All three hypotheses were supported by the evidence to a 'moderate' degree. However, in each case the reverse hypothesis also got a degree of support from the evidence, and so we cannot rule out the possibility that the support given the forward form of each hypothesis is to some extent simply a reflection of a reverse process being in operation.

4 The evidence gave a 'fairly large' degree of support to two other behavioural hypotheses, namely that high exposure to television violence increases the degree to which boys: (i) are aggressive in sport or play (hypothesis 7); (ii) swear or use bad language (hypothesis 8). Here too, however, the evidence does not allow us to

rule out the possibility that the support given to the forward forms of the hypotheses is to some extent simply a reflection of a reverse process being in operation.

5 On the other hand, the evidence gives no meaningful support to the hypotheses that exposure to television violence increases the degree to which boys: (i) are irritating, annoying or argumentative; (ii) are violent in the company of other boys.

6 At a more generalised level, the evidence indicated that certain broad categories of violent behaviour were more likely (than were other categories) to be produced by high exposure to television violence, namely violent behaviour that is unskilled, spontaneous, unplanned; television-type acts of violence that offer scope for *easy* imitation. The opposite applied with acts that appeared to carry their own deterrents or where deterrents were 'in the offing' (e.g. picking a fight).

7 On the basis of a major set of purely correlational data (see figure 12.1, chapter 12) it appears that the association between involvement in serious violence and extent of exposure to television violence is of an irregular kind – with the level of serious violence tending to increase only after quite a lot of television violence had been seen. Such evidence raises questions concerning margins of safety and long term effects (see later for discussion). On the other hand, for less serious forms of violence by boys, the association is more regular in character, being suggestive of a rising curve.

8 There is a major difference in the character of the findings in going from the behavioural to the attitudinal hypotheses: the evidence gives very little support indeed to the various hypotheses dealing with attitudes or outlook or states of mind.

More specifically:

(a) The evidence gave no meaningful support to the hypotheses that high exposure to television violence
   (i) leads to preoccupation with acts of violence frequently shown on television,
   (ii) leads boys to feel more willing to commit such acts.

(b) The evidence gave no meaningful support to the hypothesis that high exposure to television violence 'hardens boys' (i.e. makes them more callous) in relation to violence in the world around them.

(c) Similarly there was no meaningful support for the hypotheses that high exposure to television violence
   (i) causes boys to see violence as a basic part of human nature;
   (ii) causes boys to accept violence as a way to solve their problems;
   (iii) leads in general to sleep disturbances; [14]
   (iv) leads to a reduction in boys' consideration for others or in boys' respect for authority.

9 Some of the hypotheses investigated dealt with the influence of high exposure to comics, violent films and newspapers.

(a) *Concerning violence considered generally* [15]. For all three media, the evidence gives a fairly large degree of support to the hypotheses that high exposure increases boys' involvement in violence considered generally [15] – though for each it remains possible (because of the evidence of reverse hypothesis testing) that this support is to some extent the reflection of a process, opposite in character to that hypothesised, being in operation.

(b) *Concerning serious violence.* The evidence gives no meaningful support to the hypothesis that high exposure to newspapers increases boys' involvement in serious violence. With respect to exposure to comics/comic books and violent films, the index of effect is in both cases large (34.51 per cent and 26.16 per cent respectively). We must exercise scientific wariness in our interpretation of these indices because of the joint indications of the statistical significance levels and of the reverse hypothesis test results. However, scientific wariness does not mean that we should disregard the positive indications of those large indices of effect. The case for wariness does not provide grounds for disregarding either hypothesis.

SOME COMMENTS ON THE FINDINGS

In chapters 13 and 20 I have put forward a commentary on certain of the findings. The principal points in that commentary are presented here in summary form. As a commentary, this section of my report does of course take us beyond what are strictly *findings* to an *interpretation* of findings.

Comments about the general applicability of the findings

Strictly speaking, the findings relate to adolescent boys of London and they do not necessarily apply anywhere else. However, I would be willing to hypothesise a similar outcome in other big cities where the nature of television programming and the general cultural situation are similar to those of London. This issue is taken further in chapter 20.

Comments about the psychological processes that appear to underlie changes induced by television violence

1 On the total body of the evidence of this enquiry, I have *hypothesised* that a major operating mechanism of television violence is to reduce or break down those inhibitions against being violent that parents and other socialising agencies have been building up in boys. I have referred to this process as 'disinhibition'.

2 As this break-down or erosion goes on, boys slip more easily and spontaneously than formerly into violent forms of behaviour in response to their environment. Moreover the disinhibition process occurs without evidence of any parallel changes in boys' (conscious) attitudes towards violence.

3 The evidence tends to support the presence of a limited 'imitation' process as well, namely imitation where a television production makes some particular act of violence relatively easy for boys to adopt. This is not to say that the occasional

individual does not pick up some quite complex form of violence from a television presentation. It may well be that imitation is facilitated by a disinhibition process.

4 The findings militate against the operation of any generalised 'catharsis' process. However certain parts of the findings do not rule out the operation of a catharsis process working on a limited and special-situation basis – though equally they might support a 'displacement' hypothesis.

5 The evidence gives no support to the 'desensitisation' hypothesis – that is, as a conscious process.

Comments about the indications of the findings for the control of the presentation of violence on television

For the control of the overall amount of violence presented. The findings of this enquiry support the case for making a substantial cut-back in the total amount of television violence being made available to the adolescent viewer. It would doubtless make it easier to do this if the programme staff concerned could regard violence first and foremost as potentially damaging rather than regarding it as potential entertainment. On the present appearance of programme output, it is difficult to resist the view that those two criteria are often applied in reverse.

For the control of the different kinds of violence that are presented on television. The findings provide a basis for setting up provisional guidelines for the control of violence presentations. These guidelines were put forward in chapter 13 and are represented hereunder. As guidelines they are provisional in the sense that further study should be carried out as soon as possible to examine, to tighten up, to extend and generally to develop their guideline detail and function.

Programme features *more* likely to stimulate serious violence in boys

1 Programmes where violence of a nasty kind appears to be sanctioned by showing it being done in a good cause or with seeming legality. Though this point arises out of the detail of table 13.3, it should also be linked up with the finding of a strong tendency by boys to regard their own violent acts (and those of others) as somehow not violent if those acts were 'justified'.

2 Programmes that make it easy for boys to identify with the person or persons being violent.

3 Programmes where the subject matter is of a kind which tends to demand that the constituent violence be on a large scale, possibly with mass killings. Westerns have tended to be of this kind, as have many programmes (usually films) of the epic variety.

4 Programmes where the law enforcer, in order to defeat the villains, does himself commit considerable violence, perhaps of a kind that is tougher and nastier than that used by the villains.

5 Programmes in which violence is presented in a context where personal relationships are a major theme. In real life, priority has been given, through training and sanctions, to the protection of our working relationships with other people against the outbreak of serious violence. Presumably the presentation by television of nastiness and violence as a normal element in such relationships tends to reduce in boys such barriers as

society has built up in them against being seriously violent in the personal relations context.

6 Programmes where violent television of a serious kind is taken out of its developmental context (as when it is just 'thrown in') (i) so that it can be made more violent than its developmental background would warrant it being and (ii) so that boys are not in a position to regard that developmental background as unlikely to apply to them.

7 Programmes where the violence is presented with such realism that it is unlikely to be rejected as mere fiction, but instead is given the weight of believability and of normality.

Programme features *less* likely to stimulate serious violence in boys

1 Programmes where the violence shown is obviously far beyond the capabilities and/or the opportunities of the viewer, as are many forms of science fiction and cartoon programmes.

2 Programmes where the violence shown is so ridiculous or far fetched that it is passed off by boys as having nothing to do with real life.

3 Where the programme is humorous – in that a humorous presentation or theme is likely to make it harder for the programmer to introduce into it really nasty violence. This is not the same thing as saying that a humorous context somehow lessens the effects of such violence as is inherent in it.

4 Programmes where the violence presented is of the purely verbal kind rather than being all or partly of the physical kind. Such programmes are less likely to stimulate serious violence. (At the same time, the evidence indicates that they do produce violence of the *less serious* kind, particularly swearing and the use of bad language.)

5 Programmes where the television experience leaves the boy satisfied and good tempered – as distinct from tense or irritated or bored (see also chapter 18).

6 Actuality programmes where the televised violence is, as it were, closely contained within a special environment – as for the sporting event where the televised violence is in fact an accurate representation of the specialised violence that is intrinsic to that particular sport.

7 Programmes where the process of watching a televised event is likely to keep boys out of a situation in which violence is likely to occur (for example, a televised soccer match).

8 In actuality broadcasting, provided it is not markedly selective and is not edited to highlight its more violent elements. This is mainly because actuality tends to put a limit upon the excesses of the occasional producer who has an innovative fixation on the production of nasty or epic violence.

RECOMMENDATIONS

The enquiry as presented in this report forms the basis for the following recommendations. These recommendations relate particularly to the London region but they may be relevant also to other large cities with a similar form of television output and with similar cultural characteristics.

1 Steps should be taken as soon as possible to achieve a substantial reduction in the total amount of violence being presented on television. This cutback should be guided in the first instance by a policy which evaluates violent output first and foremost as potentially damaging and only secondly as desirable for the attainment of high audience figures.

2 In the long term, a set of empirically established guidelines is necessary for reaching decisions about the type of violence that should be most avoided. In this chapter I have presented a set of provisional guidelines of such a kind. They have an empirical background and I suggest that they be used, on a provisional basis, *now.* As soon as possible, research should be conducted to challenge, to tighten up and to extend their guideline detail and capabilities. The necessary form of such research is set out on very broad lines under 4 below.

3 It is further recommended that a continuing monitoring system be set up to provide periodic analyses of the kind and the amount of violence being presented on television. *However, it is essential that such analyses be made in terms of those features of television violence which research shows to be associated with the stimulation of violence in the viewer and, of course, in terms of those features of programmes that research shows to be associated with the containment or reduction of violence amongst viewers.* The present guideline system should be regarded as constituting provisional criteria for such analyses. However it is vital that in the long term research be undertaken to tighten up and to extend them as the criteria in terms of which programme content should be monitored. The resulting reports should be made widely available as material for formulating factually based appraisals of television output.

4 The research reported in this document was principally concerned with identifying the effects on boys of long-term exposure to television violence. Action should be taken now on the basis of its findings/indications. But it is essential that while this is going on, certain further enquiries of the following kinds be set going.

(a) The present body of research data should be subject to further analyses:

(i) to examine further the correlation-type evidence that serious violence does not occur until the accumulated input has gone beyond a certain level and to secure operatively useful evidence as to what that level is;

(ii) to extend the analysis of 'effects by programme types' to produce additional guidelines for the control of television presentations of violence.

(b) Experimental studies of changes and development in boy's mental content following exposure to specific forms of television violence. Such work would be geared to the further development of guidelines for the control of television violence.

(c) Experimental studies designed to increase understanding of the psychological processes involved when boys are influenced in some way by television violence.

5 It was impossible, for financial reasons, to extend this enquiry to girls as well as boys. Whereas I consider that the recommendations made here would be helpful with respect to girls, it is obviously of importance that a parallel study of adolescent girls be made.

I need no telling that research of the kind proposed in 2, 3, 4 and 5 could be costly. But such costs seem likely to be small in relation to the cost to society of the damage that the evidence of this enquiry has indicated is being done.

In considering costs, it is well to remember too, that the present expensive enquiry has cost the British taxpayer *nothing* for it was fully funded by the Columbia Broadcasting System of the United States of America.

Notes

[1] Violent behaviour, whether serious or not, was expressed as a weighted sum, with serious violence being heavily weighted and marginally violent behaviour being lightly weighted (see chapter 6 for details). Nonetheless, because of the great preponderance of the minor forms of violence, this weighted score was principally reflective of those minor forms of violence.

[2] Two other indices of violence level were used in two further hypotheses, namely total number of acts irrespective of how violent; total number of acts, less those of a trivial kind.

[3] For the purposes of this enquiry, 'violence' had been defined as 'physical or verbal activity of a kind that produces or is likely to produce hurt or harm of any kind for the object on the receiving end. This object could be animate or inanimate and the hurt or harm could be either physical or psychological.

[4] *Juvenile Theft: The Causal Factors*, W.A. Belson, Harper & Row Ltd., London 1975.

[5] 'Matching and prediction on the principle of biological classification', W.A. Belson, *Applied Statistics*, vol.8 (2), 1959.

[6] On the principle that matching in terms of any correlate of the dependent variable is warranted only if there exists a difference between the two groups in terms of that correlate.

[7] Exclusive of the hypotheses and sub-hypotheses postulated either as a secondary control system (44) or as a check on the operation of an 'outlyer' effect (62).

[8] CBS's scientific advisers had accepted the results of the preparatory stage as adequate and CBS had then agreed to provide the funds for the second stage.

[9] If mother dead or gone away or persistently not available, the father was interviewed instead of mother.

[10] The development and testing of the technique for securing information about violent behaviour was carried out with this payment system included in the procedure. In this context, boys had been asked to resist any tendency to let this payment affect what they said about their behaviour — though in fact the evidence from the construction process argues strongly against there being any significant tendency to do so in any case.

[11] As note [9].

[12] At the Annual Conference of the National Association for Maternal and Child Welfare, June 1975.

[13] This strategy was summarised on page 78 of chapter 3.
[14] See comment in chapter 20.
[15] A weighted score in which the 'less than serious' violence dominates the weighted total.

TABLE 1

SUMMARY OF RESULTS OF INVESTIGATING HYPOTHESES

VARIABLES FEATURED IN HYPOTHESES

DEPENDENT VARIABLES ARE LISTED ACROSS

INDEPENDENT VARIABLES ARE LISTED BELOW

HIGH EXPOSURE TO	1 Violent behaviour: weighted total of all acts	2 Violent behaviour: all-in total of acts	3 Violent behaviour: all-in total less trivia	4 Violent behaviour: total of serious acts	5 Violent behaviour: in company with boys	6 Violent behaviour: in form of irritating, arguing, annoying	7 Violent behaviour: in form of aggression in sport or play	8 Use of bad language, swearing	9 Preoccupation with different forms of violence shown on television	10 Feels like committing different sorts of violence shown on television	11 Feels willing to use different forms of violence shown on television	18 Degree of acceptance of 'near' violence	19 Degree of acceptance of 'distant' violence	12 Finds the idea of violence attractive	20 Degree of objection to violence in world generally	21 Sees violence as inevitable	22 Degree of acceptance of violence as way to solve problems	17 Extent of sleep disturbance	13 Level of consideration for others	14 Level of respect for authority
1. Violence on television generally.	□	□	□	◇	⏢+ M̄	⏢ M̄	□+	□+	○	○ M̄	○ M̄	○	○	⏢	○ M̄	○ M̄	○ M̄	○	○V ??	○
2. Programmes containing fictional violence of a realistic kind.	□+			◇					○ M̄											
3. Programmes where violence is performed by basically 'good guy' types who are also rebels or 'odd-men-out'.	□ ?			◇							○ M̄						○ M̄			
4. Programmes in which much of the violence occurs in a domestic or family setting.	□			◇																
5. Programmes which feature defiance of or rudeness towards authority figures.	⏢+ ?			◇																○
6. Programmes where violence is shown as glorified, romanticised, idealised or ennobling.	□			◇										○V ??	○					
7. Programmes where violence is presented as 'fun and games' or like a game or as something to entertain.	□			□ ??							⏢ ??			○V ???						
8. Programmes in which the violence is presented as being in a good cause.	□			◇							○						○ M̄			
9. Programmes where the physical or mental consequences of violence, for the victim, are shown in detail.	□+			◇					○ M̄		⏢+ ?			⏢				○		
10. Programmes where the violence is related to racial or minority group strife.	□			◇	⏢ M̄															
11. Programmes where the violence is performed by basically good guy types or heroes who are also tough.	⏢+ ?			◇							⏢ ???									
12. Programmes where the violence is of a verbal kind.	□+			◇ ?				□++												
13. Programmes in which the violence is just thrown in for its own sake or is not necessary to the plot.	□			◇												○				
14. Programmes in which the violence is gruesome, horrific, scary.	□+			◇														○		
15. Fictional programmes about the English police at work which also feature the kinds of violence that go on in society.	⏢+ ???			◇ ?												○V ?				
16. Five cartoon programmes in which characters are violent to each other (Boss Cat, Popeye, Pugwash, Yogi Bear, Tom & Jerry).	□			□+ M̄																
17. Tom and Jerry (considered alone).	□ ?			⏢+ M̄										○ M̄						
18. Plays or films in which personal, relationships are a major theme and which feature verbal abuse or physical violence.	□			◇				◇												
19. Violence through the news or newsreel programmes.	□			◇							⏢+ ?	○	○		○	○ M̄				
20. Comedy programmes which feature 'slap-stick' violence and/or verbal abuse between the characters.	□			□++ ???																
21. Science fiction programmes involving violence.	⏢+ ???			⏢+ M̄																
22. Westerns that include violence, for example between cowboys and Indians.	□			◇			□										○V ??			
23. Three sporting programmes which present violence by competitors/spectators (Sportsview, Grandstand, Sat Sportstime).	⏢+ ?			○			□++													
24. Wrestling and Boxing.	○ M̄			◇			□													
25. Films or series which feature gangs or gangsters in violent organised crime.	□			◇																
26. Programmes in which the violence is performed by adults.	□			◇																
28. Comic books and comics.	□+	⏢ ??	□+	◇ ?	□	○	⏢+ ??	⏢+ ??	○ M̄	⏢+ ?	□ ?	○	○	⏢	○ M̄	○	○V ?	⏢+ ?	○	○V ??
29. Violent films.	□+	□+	□++	□++ ??	□++	□++	□+	□ ??	⏢ ??	□	○ M̄	○V	○ M̄	○V	○	○V ??	○	○	⏢	○V ???
30. Newspapers.	□+	□+	□+	○	⏢ M̄	○	□	□+	○ M̄	⏢+ ?	○ M̄	○V ???	○	⏢	○	○ M̄	○ M̄	○	○ M̄	○V ???

SYMBOLS USED IN CHART

Symbol	Level of support from evidence	Index of effect %	P - value of difference	Symbol	Level of support from evidence	Index of effect %	P - value of difference	Symbol	Degree of confidence warranted	P - value of difference
○	None	0 or less	.05 or less	□	A moderate amount	10⁺ - 15	.05 or less	?	Slightly uncertain	.05⁺ - .10
○V	Virtually none	0⁺ - 3	.05 or less	□+	A fairly large amount	15⁺ - 20	.05 or less	??	Uncertain	.10⁺ - .15
⏢	Very little	3⁺ - 5	.05 or less	□++	A large amount	20⁺ - 30	.05 or less	???	Very uncertain	.15⁺ - .20
⏢+	A small amount	5⁺ - 10	.05 or less	◇	A very large amount	30⁺	.05 or less	M̄	Not meaningful	.20⁺

CHAPTER 2

THE DEVELOPMENT OF HYPOTHESES FOR INVESTIGATION

Contents

2 THE DEVELOPMENT OF HYPOTHESES FOR INVESTIGATION

It was considered essential that the hypotheses investigated through this enquiry be both broad in their coverage and realistic in their foundations. Accordingly it was planned that the first step in their derivation should involve (i) a study of available literature relating to television's effects; (ii) discussion with individuals professionally or otherwise involved with television output; (iii) intensive interviews with members of the viewing public, both boys and their parents; (iv) a close scrutiny of statements presented in the Press.

On these bases, initial hypotheses would be formulated and there would then follow a number of developmental stages designed to render these initial hypotheses properly reflective of the evidence collected, precisely stated and unambiguous in meaning. There were in all four of these developmental stages.

STAGE 1: THE COLLECTION AND SORTING OF IDEAS ABOUT THE EFFECTS OF EXPOSURE TO TELEVISION VIOLENCE

Interviews with boys and their parents

Reasons for conducting interviews with boys

In developing hypotheses about the influence of some form of exposure, it is essential to secure the views of those directly subject to such exposure. This is not to say that these people will necessarily be aware of all that this exposure is doing to them. Nor is it suggested that *other* sources should not be explored as well. But it is reasonable to expect that people who are constantly exposed to some phenomenon will have much that is well grounded to say about the possible influences of that exposure. Accordingly a considerable effort was made to secure from boy-viewers their ideas about what television was doing to them (and to other boys). A parallel effort was made to secure ideas from boys' *parents* because the parents of boys are in some ways well positioned to observe the relevant behaviour of their sons and to speculate about any connection between that behaviour and the viewing the observed boys have done.

A summary of the methods used to secure the views of boys and parents

Groups of boys and groups of parents met under controlled conditions and (i) *wrote down*, in response to a series of questions, their views about the effects of television violence and about related matters; (ii) *discussed* their views about how television violence affects boys.

Origin of boys and parents taking part

The parents and boys taking part had been recruited through a special survey carried out for the project by Audits of Great Britain Limited. The recruitment survey was carried out in six wards, of varied social level, located within eight miles of Central London. Working to a quota control system, the recruiter in each ward was to locate homes in which there was at least one boy in the age range 12-17 years. At each such home she was to invite a boy and one of his parents to take part in a meeting of viewers at a Central London location. She was to explain that the purpose of the meeting was to find out from them what they thought might be the effects of television on young people and she was to persuade the boy and one of his parents to attend. Invitees were told that they were to receive payment for attendance, return of fares and that there would be light refreshment on arrival at the meeting. The quota controls were designed to secure participants who were realistically varied in terms of social class, ages of boys, sex of accompanying parent. Those accepting the invitation received a letter of confirmation of their invitation along with printed details to help them get to the meeting place.

A total of 67 boys and 61 parents, with characteristics as set out in table 2.1, took part in the exploratory sessions.

Obviously this system of recruitment is liable to introduce bias of some kind into the recruiting process and it is clear from table 2.1 that it has done so. However, the purpose of the proposed sessions was to secure ideas and leads from the attenders and certainly not to provide distribution figures purporting to be representative of the views of the general population. For the purely exploratory purposes of this phase of the enquiry, the system used was viable.

Information gathering procedures in relation to boys

Typically, those taking part were seated round a large conference table, with the Group Administrator at one end. As a preliminary to discussion of the possible effects of television, group members spent about five minutes writing down what they thought were the effects on boys of watching programmes with a lot of violence in them. Subsequently, they discussed this issue using their written notes as an aid, but being encouraged to go beyond those notes. Throughout this discussion, the views of boys were clarified, challenged and elaborated. The discussion period on this central issue lasted for about one hour.

Other questions were also asked and the pattern of action with these was the same, namely: boys wrote down their replies and then went on to general discussion. These other questions dealt with related aspects of the issue and the ideas derived through them were to be used in other related aspects of the enquiry. The full set of 7 questions is presented below. [1]

Q.1 'Do you watch any programmes on television that have violence in them?'

IF YES: 'Write down the names of all the programmes you see that have violence in them.'

IF NO: 'Write down the names of all the television programmes you think have violence in them.'

Table 2.1
Characteristics of those who attended the exploratory sessions

Boys (67 in all)		Parents (61 in all)	
Age	n	Age	n
12	14	30-35	9
13	20	36-40	21
14	8	41-45	18
15	9	46-50	9
16	7	51+	4
17+	9		
		Sex	
Social class*		Male	25
AB	13	Female	36
C1	12		
C2	31	Social class*	
DE	11	AB	12
		C1	8
		C2	30
		DE	11

*The social class distributions of boys and of parents (both based on householder's job) differ because some boys came alone

Q.2 'Just suppose boys watch a lot of television programmes with violence in them. What sorts of effects do you think these programmes might have on boys? In working out your answer, go by what you have noted about its effect on *you* and about the way it seems to have affected other boys.'

Q.3 'What sorts of boys are most affected by seeing violence on television? I mean how do those boys differ from other boys?'

Q.4 'In your opinion, what sorts of boys go in for a lot of violence? Write down what it is about them that makes them different from other boys — everything that is different about these violent boys.'

Q.5 'What sorts of boys watch a lot of violence on television? I want all your ideas about what sorts of boys they are.'

Q.6 'Write down all the different sorts of violence you have seen going on around you, or that you have heard about going on around you.'

Q.7 'Write down all the things that you think cause a boy to be violent.'

Table 2.2
The views of boys and parents about the effects on boys of long term exposure to television violence (see Appendix 1 for further details) †

Respondent claims 'no effect' or makes qualified claim of 'no effect'		54*
No effect at all	14	
No effect (where the claim is a form of elaborated denial rather than an argument or reason)	7	
No effect because (reason given)	13	
No effect on majority/usually/in the long term	3	
No effect on certain kinds of boys (i.e. older boys, stable, normal, happy, intelligent, rational, those who have no opportunity to be violent, those who do not go around in gangs or groups	13	
No effects when certain conditions prevail (if good triumphs over bad on the screen; if bad guy loses in the end; if the violence shown is not part of the boy's 'everyday' life; if told by parents or at school that television violence is bad; if other television material is watched as well; if television violence is treated as a joke)	9	
Seeing violence on television acts as a deterrent		8
Seeing violence on television may make you opposed to it		21
Watching violence on television leads to boys sympathising with the victims		2
Watching violence on television changes children's play patterns		9
Watching violence on television allows you to release your pent-up feelings		3
Watching violence on television puts violent ideas into boys' heads		26
Watching violence on television causes boys to want to imitate the ways of the bad characters depicted		2
Watching violence on television makes boys copy what they see		46
Watching violence on television causes boys to behave violently/more violently		35
Watching violence on television reinforces existing tendencies towards violence		17
Watching violence on television makes boys more boisterous in behaviour/speech		4
Watching violence on television causes boys to join gangs		2
Watching violent war films may produce prejudice against some nationals		2
Watching violence on television gives boys the impression that violence can be used as a means to one's ends		12
Watching violence on television reduces respect for other people and for people in authority		7
Watching violence on television makes boys take pleasure in seeing violence		4
Watching violence on television may give boys the impression that violence is not harmful		6
Seeing glorified violence on television makes violence desirable		15
Watching violence on television leads boys to regard violence as a good thing		3
Watching violence on television makes boys less sensitive to violence		10
Watching violence on television leads boys to accept violence as normal behaviour		12
Watching violence on television upsets children		9
Watching violence on television frightens children		20
Watching violence on television causes boys to have nightmares/disturbed sleep		10
Miscellaneous statements at least marginally relevant to the impact of television violence		18

† See fuller analysis in Appendix

* Some of the Constituent sub-groups within this broad category overlap and so the gross total for all such sub-groups is more than the total of cases involved.

Information gathering in relation to parents

Parents of boys went separately through a very similar procedure, the purposes of which were closely similar.

The yield of information from boys and their parents

The information secured from the groups was large in quantity and of highly varied content. Details are set out in full in Appendix 1 and are summarised in table 2.2.

Analysis of statements presented in the Press

Over the years, the British Press has carried a great many statements about the effects of television violence. These statements have been made by critics, by feature writers and by newsmen reporting on the statements of experts and others. Without entering into discussion of the validity or otherwise of these statements and views, it was regarded as essential that they be considered, along with other views, in formulating initial hypotheses. Accordingly, a search was made for relevant statements in a wide range of publications, starting in 1950. [2]

As must be expected, comment in the Press is wide ranging in its coverage, with a great deal of it referring to people in general rather than to boys in particular. Also, only part of it relates to the *effects* of television violence. The results of analysing relevant comments are presented in summary form in table 2.3 and in full in Appendix 2.

There is a sizeable minority rejection in the Press of the view that television violence increases the incidence of violence. Where explanatory references are given for this view, they tend to be in terms of a 'catharsis process' and/or of an anti-reaction to the violence shown.

However, the majority of the Press comments involve some degree of support for the view that television violence increases the likelihood of young viewers becoming violent. The more commonly offered explanations are in terms of: television makes violence more normal and acceptable; viewers copy the violence shown to them on television; the portrayal of television violence disturbs the viewer's sense of reality by making violence seem more dominant than it is; television violence seems to harden the viewers; television violence exaggerates existing predispositions to be violent.

Of course this is not a listing of the actual effects of exposure to television – it is simply an appraisal of the different opinions presented in the British Press.

Study of the published literature

Publications dealing with the effects of exposure to television violence were given detailed study. The purpose of this study was to extract the different views put forward in the literature about the possible effects of exposure to television violence.

It was understood at the outset that these views were of varying status. Thus at one extreme would be hypotheses that had been carefully developed from specific findings or from a close consideration of the facts of viewing behaviour. At the other extreme would be views that would have to be rated as no more than speculation. However, at this point in the

Table 2.3
Classes of claims made in the British Press about the effects of television violence

	Frequency of claims
	n
Violence on television does not cause violence by children or it has only a minor effect on them	27
Television violence does not affect normal people	2
Television violence does not affect people if they are warned beforehand	2
Certain types of television violence do not do any harm/do less harm than others	15
Television violence creates anti-violence feelings	9
Television violence has a cathartic effect	13
There are other, stronger, influences than television in producing violence	8
TV violence exaggerates existing predispositions	9
TV violence has a bad influence (no explanation of 'bad')	29
Television violence leads to copying/imitation	25
Television violence causes/encourages crime and violence	29
Television has bad psychological effects	18
Through television, violence becomes acceptable or normal	26
Through television, violence comes to be seen as an acceptable means to an end	4
Through television, people become hardened to violence	13
TV violence gives children a premature/distorted view of life	5
Viewers' sense of balance/of values becomes blurred	4
Disturbs sense of reality by making violence seem more dominant than it is	15
TV violence gives children ideas that they would not normally have	4
Some types of violence are more harmful than others (see table A2 for details)	40

derivation of hypotheses, the emphasis was upon collecting them as a body of postulations.

The articles and papers consulted at this stage of the inquiry are included in Appendix 3. The main groups of hypotheses/speculations derived from them and relevant to this study are set out in table 2.4.

One thing that must be kept in mind in considering the content of table 2.4 is the overall purpose of the present enquiry – namely to assess the degree to which and in what ways exposure to television violence had in fact influenced boys. Thus to establish that exposure to violent spectacles under specific laboratory conditions leads to certain forms of violent behaviour does not necessarily establish television violence as a determinant under *normal* exposure and living conditions. On the other hand, the listed hypotheses (table 2.4) must be taken very seriously because they do provide us with the close and reasoned thinking of many different social scientists and in some cases with results that have been supported under laboratory conditions.

Within the list of references to reports and papers (A3), the reader will see a number of reports that were published *after* the completion of the hypothesis development work reported here, but which were considered in the analysis and report writing stages of the enquiry.

Table 2.4
Hypotheses drawn from the literature and possibly relating to the effects of exposure to violent television*

Hypotheses postulating an increase in aggressive behaviour/ideas

- Boys imitate the aggression of aggressive models.
- Aggressive stimulus models have a facilitating and modelling influence on children.
- Exposure to cartoon violence increases aggressive behaviour in a subsequent 'permissive' situation.
- Beginning with the idea that consummatory behaviour is drive reducing (i.e. cathartic) and antecedent cues are drive arousing, vicarious experience which is passively received (such as TV) is of the latter variety and hence fosters aggressive behaviour.
- Television persuades the mind that violence is an acceptable mode of conduct.

Hypotheses postulating an increase in violence under certain conditions

- Viewing aggressive film material leads to aggression, but it varies as a function of contextual variables such as 'justification' and 'type of aggression' (physical/verbal).
- The effectiveness of perceived violence in eliciting subsequent aggression is a function of similarity of cues in the viewing situation and the situation in which the viewer finds himself.
- Justified fantasy aggression particularly is likely to lead to a greater volume of open aggression to the appropriate stimuli.
- The showing of familiar objects such as weapons may increase a child's urge to imitate.
- Violence presented in isolation for its own sake desensitizes viewers and appeals to their aggressive passions, thus stimulating violence.
- An aggressor punished immediately stimulates less aggressive behaviour in children than an aggressor who is punished after the completion of his aggressive behaviour.

Hypotheses postulating a reduction in aggressiveness of behaviour or outlook

- Viewing fantasy aggression reduces the propensity for aggressive behaviour.
- Television violence can be cathartic for viewers who would otherwise act out their excitement dangerously.
- Violence presented in the context of human experience and 'character identification' causes people to reject violence as acceptable behaviour.

Hypotheses postulating a reduction of conditions possibly associated with being violent

- Viewing fantasy aggression reduces the anxiety associated with the performance of aggressive behaviour.
- Television serves as an escape mechanism for children whose peers prevail over the family as the dominant reference group.

Hypotheses postulating that the direction of the effect depends upon certain pre-conditions

- The effect of vicariously experienced aggression is dependent on the child's emotional state prior to exposure (i.e. the effect is cathartic for children made hostile, and stimulating for non-hostile children).

Views suggesting that present violence of boys controls the degree to which boys become exposed to television violence (i.e. possibly the reverse of the view that television violence affects the amount of violence committed)

- The violent content in children's favourite programmes varies directly with the amount of aggressive behaviour indulged in by the child.
- The amount of television watched varies inversely with the amount of aggressive behaviour indulged in by the child.
- Children with peer reference groups watch more action and violence on television than children whose reference group is the family.

Suggested correlation (only) between exposure to television and delinquency

- Degree of identification with 'hero figures' in fictional series is related (in boys) to: delinquency; low respect for father; rejection of middle class norms of competition and achievement; a high need for immediate gratification and stimulation; apathy towards school and educational material in the mass media.
- A preference for 'exciting and aggressive' fictional series is associated with delinquency in boys.

Hypotheses postulating that exposure to television violence changes attitudes or state of mind in some way

- Children's preference for adult programmes (e.g. westerns and crime) give children a premature and stereotyped glimpse of adulthood.
- Television violence contributes to a disenchantment with the older generation.
- Television violence produces a sharper comprehension of the problems of the adult world.
- Viewing visual material which involved 'superforce' fosters a belief in man's inability to control his destiny.
- High exposure to television leads to greater stereotyped thought.
- Television produces an earlier intellectual awareness of the complexity and essential unfairness of life.
- Watching adult television plays leaves few of the comforting, black and white philosophies of childhood intact.

*Available at this preparatory stage of the project.

Interviews with those with a specialist interest in television

In the search for well grounded ideas about the effects of exposure to television violence, special interviews were conducted with individuals each of whom had a specialist interest in television. These people included: two drama producers, two heads of television departments, four audience research practitioners, a script writer; a member of the British Board of Film Censors, a campaigner for the modification of mass media content; feature writers, television and film critics associated with newspapers. In addition, conferences and seminars dealing with the influence of the media were also attended and pertinent statements were noted. The interviews were for the most part lengthy and intensive. The yields from the different interviews were variable, with people in UK television production being relatively unforthcoming. A content analysis of the ideas secured from the range of people interviewed in this way provided the following categories of ideas and suggestions.

Table 2.5
Views of a range of specialists

Whatever is shown teaches something.

Television violence has increased awareness of how to injure people: new techniques have replaced the old playground fisticuffs.

Children copy the techniques of violence shown on television.

People have copied television portrayals of methods of robbery (e.g. 'Rififi').

Hanging scenes have led to instances of children hanging themselves.

Television violence has contributed to the increase in crime.

The news highlights the revolutionary aims of a very few people and is thus responsible for the current widespread student revolt.

Realistic violence on television (e.g. as in 'Big Breadwinner Hogg') shows how bad violence is and thus deters people from it.

Scenes of horror in television drama make children nervous and frightened, and may cause bedwetting or nightmares.

Sensitive children are most affected by television violence.

Adult interpretations of violence can be an assault on the minds of children who watch (e.g. 'Dr Who', the beheading of Mary Queen of Scots).

Television violence, particularly news which shows deaths, killings, executions, leads to desensitisation, acceptance of violence, loss of shock.

The continuing watching of television violence reduces viewer's capacity to be shocked.

Television violence makes boys think that there is really nothing to violence: you don't feel anything.

Television violence leads to the acceptance of violence as normal.

Some cartoons (especially 'Tom and Jerry') encourage people to laugh at violence and sadism.

Seeing sadism (e.g. detailed portrayal of holding a man's head under water to drown him) coarsens boys and can damage their personalities.

Television violence leads to anxiety and frustration which may lead to different types of violent behaviour.

News condenses the decision making process, making it seem simpler and quicker than it really is, thereby frustrating people who don't find decision making quick or simple. Such viewers thereafter resort to violence to secure their desired quicker decision.

Films, particularly war films, put across prejudiced and stereotyped pictures of foreign groups.

People use media to reinforce prejudices and attitudes.

The effects of the medium itself can be greater than the effects of its contents – people become drugged and can lose the ability to react to violence on the screen. Television in this sense is hypnotic.

The large pool of propositions brought together in Stage 1 was now content analysed in preparation for the selection from it of some more limited but appropriate set that could be developed into hypotheses for investigation.

STAGE 2 IN HYPOTHESIS DEVELOPMENT

Stage 2 was to be concerned principally with the identification of the different sorts of effects that might be investigated as stemming from the exposure of boys to television violence. (Later stages were to be concerned with the detailed specification of the different causal aspects of that exposure and with rendering more relevant and specific the postulated 'effects').

Four considerations were brought to bear upon the selection of effects for investigation.

1. The agreed purpose of this enquiry had been to determine the extent to which exposure to television violence influenced boys. This objective is to be contrasted with studies of the psychological mechanisms whereby such changes may have come about – e.g. imitation, conditioning, catharsis, triggering, inhibition and so on. Certainly such studies have been and will continue to be very important. And in all probability, the results of the planned investigation would throw further light upon them, possibly calling for the formulation of hypotheses about them. But the specification of this particular project quite rightly ruled them out as principal objectives. Accordingly such hypotheses are not amongst those selected for investigation through this enquiry.
2. On the other hand, there was every intention that the study of change (produced by television violence) should be linked to the different kinds of television violence (e.g. cartoons, realistic violence, violence in the News).
3. Propositions that were logically inconsistent within themselves or which were majorly confused, were given low priority as subjects for investigation.
4. Low priority was also given to propositions that called for the expenditure of finances beyond those available or which involved a research design basically different from that required for the central core of the investigation.

Against this background, 26 different 'effects' were tentatively selected as targets for investigation. They are listed in table 2.6. At this stage, the reference to 'causal' factors was limited to the broad and unspecific terms set out at the top of table 2.6, namely:

> 'A high degree of/extensive exposure to some aspect of television violence'

Table 2.6
The initial forms of the dependent variables selected for inclusion in causal hypotheses

A HIGH DEGREE OF/EXTENSIVE* EXPOSURE TO SOME ASPECTS OF TELEVISION VIOLENCE:

1	Reduces the strength of the urge to be violent oneself.
2/3	Increases/decreases the relative potency and the operative pervasiveness of anti-violence in their value systems.
4	Increases the strength of the urge to be violent oneself.
5	Increases the appeal of violence to boys.
6	Increases boys' willingness to take part in volence seen on television/to use the weapons shown on television.
7	Increases the degree to which they themselves engage in volent acts.
8	Increases the degree to which they themselves engage in acts of delinquency/crime.
9	Leads boys to copy certain of the forms of violence and its techniques as seen on television.
10	Leads to the formation or joining of gangs whose activities include delinquent behaviour.
11	Raises the level and/or frequency of aggressive activity in play behaviour.
12	Fosters verbal aggression and poor speech habits.
13	Produces immediate shock, distress, tension, fear.
14	Produces long-term symptoms of emotional distress or psychological disturbance.
15	Increases awareness of the techniques and opportunities for violence.
16	Leads to an incomplete understanding of the consequences of violence.
17	Makes violence seem more attractive.
18	Leads to war and riots seeming more attractive.
19	Leads to violence being seen as a legitimate means of coping with inter-personal and economic problems.
20	Increases the degree to which boys perceive violence as inevitable and as a natural way to behave.
21	Hardens them so that when they perceive real violence going on in the real world around them, they are desensitised and more likely to accept it without shock or horror.
22	Gives young people the impression that there are no happy families.
23	Gives them rigid and fixed ideas about adult life.
24	Causes a lowering of respect and consideration for other human beings.
25	Causes a lowering of respect for various forms of authority.
26	Leads boys to think critically of the causes of violence in the world.

*As indicated by an examination of extent of exposure over a long period.

STAGE 3 IN HYPOTHESIS DEVELOPMENT

Stage 3 in hypothesis development was concerned with: specifying causal factors; rendering more relevant and specific the postulated 'effects'.

During the group discussion sessions with boys and with parents, it had become clear that people postulating a given 'cause—effect' sequence (e.g. exposure to television violence leads boys to *copy* what they see') could have in mind rather different 'causal' factors and rather different 'effects'. It was thought that many of the propositions gathered through other of the means described in Stage 1 might be involved in a similar problem.

Accordingly the development of hypotheses was now taken through a challenging procedure designed to define the 'cause' and 'effect' variables as specifically as possible.

Boys and parents at the discussion sessions had been asked if they were willing to take part in a follow-up interview for a further fee and the majority had agreed. Home-interviews were conducted with 34 of these volunteers.

In preparation for these interviews, the 26 broad propositions presented in table 2.6 were translated into common language forms and respondents were asked to indicate any that they disagreed with, any they agreed with and any they *strongly* agreed with. *For all agreed with, starting with the most strongly supported, the respondent was taken through the following questioning procedure.*

1. He was asked to say precisely *what kind* of effect he had in mind for that proposition.
2. He was asked to say what sort of programme material he thought led to such an effect. Whereas the respondent might begin by naming a programme or a series of programmes, the interviewer was to press for whatever characteristic the respondent thought to be common to those programmes (e.g. programmes showing weapons, programmes that show a good guy being violent, and so on).

This questioning system may perhaps have yielded a specific single 'causal factor' and a specific single 'effect' (for a given respondent). But even so it would be necessary to ascertain that the respondent really was linking the two in a single proposition (e.g. 'Are you saying that X causes Y?').

More likely, however, the questioning process would have yielded a small group of 'causal factors' and a small group of 'effects' and in this case it was essential to find out precisely *what* was being said to cause *what*. It might emerge that all in the small group of 'causal factors' were examples of some one variable (e.g. horror violence) and that *all* in the small group of 'effects' were examples of one variable (e.g. fear of going to bed). But on the other hand, 2-3 rather different effects might be included and several rather different causes, and it was the interviewer's task in that case to sort out *what* was being said to cause *what*. Take as an example the proposition:

> 'Seeing television violence hardens boys so that when they see real violence they are likely to accept it without shock or horror.'

For a given respondent, this challenging procedure might have produced the following range of 'cause—effect' definitions and linkages.

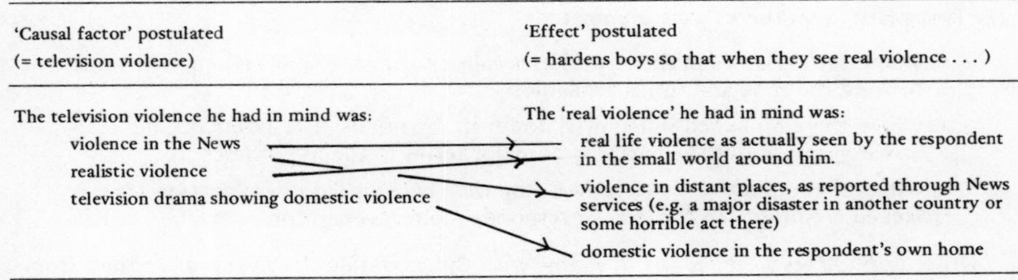

The analysis of the data from these interviews produced results of considerable importance to the further development of the hypotheses.

(a) The *independent* variable (i.e. exposure to television violence) proliferated into a large number of much more specific variables (e.g. fictional violence of a realistic kind, violence by good guys versus violence by bad guys, violence in news programmes, cartoon violence).

(b) The dependent variable (i.e. the variable in terms of which effect was postulated) also broke into a number of specifics.

(c) Some of the new (and more specific) independent variables were linked to a wide array of the dependent variables and others to only a few.

The developing complex of hypotheses could now be set out in grid form on the following pattern.

Type of postulated 'causal factor' (i.e. programme type)	Type of postulated 'effect'								
	1	2	3	4	5	6	7	8	→
High exposure to programmes containing fictional violence of a realistic kind									
High degree of exposure where violence is performed by basically good guys									
High exposure to programmes in which much of the violence occurs in a domestic or family setting									
↓					↓				

STAGE 4 OF THE DEVELOPMENT OF HYPOTHESES

Other considerations now came into play in finalising the grid or matrix of hypotheses. In the first place, hypotheses were eliminated:

- where the variables in the hypotheses called for instrument making that went beyond the time and funds available;
- where there remained substantial doubt in the minds of respondents and investigators about the meaning of major terms in the hypotheses;
- where the hypothesis *both* lacked empirical backing (in its origination) *and* lacked credibility in the eyes of respondents or investigator.

Other hypotheses were *modified* in line with these considerations (i.e. as distinct from being discarded).

In addition, several hypotheses were added to the matrix for control or for comparison purposes. In these hypotheses, the causal factors were respectively:

(a) the extent of television exposure considered generally;

(b) the extent of exposure to non-violent television;

(c) the extent of exposure to newspapers;

(d) the extent of exposure to cinema violence;

(e) the extent of exposure to comic violence.

THE FINAL SET OF HYPOTHESES FORMULATED FOR INVESTIGATION

These four stages of development had led to the selection/development of a large number of hypotheses for investigation, many of them sharing independent variables.

In table 2.7 are listed all the independent variables and all the dependent variables included in the different hypotheses. In table 2.8 are shown the different linkages between independent and dependent variables.

In the process of analysis, further linkages were specified for investigation and each of these is marked with an asterisk in table 2.8. In addition, some further dependent variables were specified for special analyses [3] and these are marked with a double asterisk in table 2.8.

Table 2.7

The dependent and independent variables in their final forms

Independent variables

1 High exposure to violence on television generally

2 High exposure to programmes containing fictional violence of a realistic kind

3 High exposure to programmes where violence is performed by basically 'good guy' types who are also 'rebels' or 'odd-men out'

4 High exposure to programmes in which much of the violence occurs in a domestic or family setting

5 High exposure to programmes which feature defiance of, or rudeness toward, authority figures

6 High exposure to programmes where violence is shown as glorified, romanticised, idealised or enobling

7 High exposure to programmes where violence is presented as 'fun and games' or like a game or a something to entertain

8 High exposure to programmes in which the violence is presented as being in a good cause

9 High exposure to programmes where the physical or mental consequences of violence, for the victim, are shown in detail

10 High exposure to programmes where the violence is related to racial or minority group strife

11 High exposure to programmes where the violence is performed by basically 'good guy' types or heroes who are also tough (i.e. who can endure physical violence and fight on)

12 High exposure to programmes where the violence is of a verbal kind

13 High exposure to programmes in which the vioience is just thrown in for its own sake, or is not necessary to the plot

14 High exposure to programmes in which the violence is gruesome, horrific or scary

15 High exposure to fictional programmes about the English police at work which also feature the kinds of violence which go on in society

16 High exposure to a selection of 5 cartoon programmes in which the characters are violent to each other (i.e. Boss Cat, Popeye, Pugwash, Yogi Bear, Tom and Jerry)

17 High exposure to Tom and Jerry

18 High exposure to plays or films in which personal relationships are a major theme and which feature abuse (e.g. swearing, quarrelling) or physical violence

19 High exposure to violence through the news or newsreel programmes

20 High exposure to comedy programmes which feature 'slapstick' violence and/or verbal abuse between characters

21 Science fiction programmes involving violence (e.g. where creatures destroy people, where humans use super weapons to destroy men)

22 High exposure to 'Westerns' which include violence, for example, as between cowboys and Indians

23 High exposure to a selection of 3 sporting programmes which present violence by competitors or spectators (i.e. Sports View, Grandstand, Saturday Sports Time).

24 High exposure to wrestling and boxing

25 High exposure to films or series which feature gangs or gangsters engaged in violent organised crime

26 High exposure to programmes in which the violence is performed by adults

27 High exposure to television generally

28 High exposure to violent comic books

29 High exposure to violent films

30 High exposure to newspapers

31 High exposure to non-violent programmes

Dependent variables

1 Violent behaviour, weighted total of all acts from Level 1 to Level 6*

2 Violent behaviour, all-in total, no weighting*

3 Violent behaviour, total of L2, L3, L4, L5, L6 entries*

4 Violent behaviour, total of L4, L5, L6 entries*

5 Violent behaviour, in company of other boys

6 Violent behaviour, in form of being irritating, argumentative, annoying to others

7 Violent behaviour, in form of aggressive behaviour in sport or play

8 Use of bad language/swearing

9 Preoccupation with different forms of violence on television

10 Feels like committing different forms of violence shown on television

11 Willingness to use forms of violence presented on television

12 Degree to which boy finds violence attractive

13 Degree of consideration for other people

14 Degree of respect for authority

15 Degree of anxiety, nervousness, emotional instability

16 Extent of angry and bitter feelings

17 Sleep disturbance

18 Acceptance of near violence

19 Acceptance of distant violence

20 Degree of objection to violence in world generally

21 See violence as inevitable

22 Degree of acceptance of violence as way to solve problems

**23 Number of acts of serious violence, with ceiling of 70 acts per boy

**24 Number of acts of serious violence, with ceiling of 40 acts per boy

*See chapter 6 for definition of the different levels of violence.
**Added for checking the extent of any 'outlyer' effect (see chapter 12 for details)

Table 2.8
Linkages between independent and dependent variables

The different independent variables (IV) in the different groups of hypotheses		The different dependent variables (DVs) in the different groups of hypotheses
Group 1	IVs 1-31 . . . each separately linked to	DV 1
Group 2	IVs 1,27-31 . . . each separately linked to	DV 2
Group 3	IVs 1,27-31 . . . each separately linked to	DV 3
Group 4	IVs 1,2,3-8*,9,10*,11*,12-14,15*,16,17*,18*, 19,20,21*,22,23*,24*,25,26*,27-31	DV 4
Group 5	IVs 1,10,27-31	DV 5
Group 6	IVs 1,27-31	DV 6
Group 7	IVs 1,22-24,27-31	DV 7
Group 8	IVs 1,12,18,27-31	DV 8
Group 9	IVs 1,2,9,27-31	DV 9
Group 10	IVs 1,27-31	DV 10
Group 11	IVs 1,3,7,8,9,11,19,27-31	DV 11
Group 12	IVs 1,6,7,9,17,27-31	DV 12
Group 13	IVs 1,27-31	DV 13
Group 14	IVs 1,5,27-31	DV 14
Group 15	IVs 1,4,14,21,27-31	DV 15
Group 16	IVs 1,27-31	DV 16
Group 17	IVs 1,9,14,27-31	DV 17
Group 18	IVs 1,19,27-31	DV 18
Group 19	IVs 1,19,27-31	DV 19
Group 20	IVs 1,6,19,27-31	DV 20
Group 21	IVs 1,13,15,19,27-31	DV 21
Group 22	IVs 1,3,8,22,27-31	DV 22
Group 23**	IVs 1-31	DV 23
Group 24**	IVs 1-31	DV 24

*Added for extension of analysis

**Analyses introduced for challenging the existence of an 'outlyer' effect (see chapter 12 for details)

Notes

[1] Question 1 was intended both to orient boys to the issue of television violence and to provide research staff with an early impression of the kinds of programmes that boys regard as having violent content. Question 3 was intended to provide ideas – and possibly guide lines – relevant to the cross analysis of the findings. Thus if boys with characteristic 'X' tended to be thought of as especially subject to television's influence, then it could well be desirable to analyse the results of the investigation in such a way as to bring out television's influence upon that group in particular. Question 4 was intended to provide ideas for the development or discovery of predictors of violence. Such predictors were highly relevant in that one of the important elements in the research strategy to be used involved the matching of heavy and light viewers (of violence) in terms of the correlates of violence. Question 5 was intended to provide ideas for the development or the discovery of predictors of exposure to television violence – for a purpose closely similar to that for which Q.4 was asked. Question 6 was intended to guide thinking in relation to *what* boys regarded as violence, and also to yield ideas and items for the construction of a reminder/stimulus system for assessing the degree to which boys had been involved in violence. Question 7 was intended to provide part of a basis for speculation about factors other than television violence that might enter into the development of juvenile violence.

[2] This search was facilitated by the availability of the press clipping file of the Independent Broadcasting Authority. This file contained the contributions of a very wide range of publications for the greater part of the search period.

[3] These were based on existing data and were introduced for challenging the possibility that the findings for a particular hypothesis were the result mainly of an 'outlyer' phenomenon (see chapter 12 for details).

APPENDICES TO CHAPTER 2

Appendix 1	The views of boys and parents about the effects on boys of long-term exposure to television violence.
Appendix 2	Classes of claim made in the British Press about the effects of television violence.
Appendix 3	A list of articles, papers, books examined (i) in the development of hypotheses about the effects of exposure to television violence and (ii) during analysis and report writing.

Appendix 1

The views of boys and parents about the effects on boys of long-term exposure to television violence (67 boys and 61 parents)

	n	n
Claim of 'no effect' or qualified claims of 'no effect' (54 claimants)*		
No effect at all		14
No effect (where claim is in a form of elaborated denial rather than an argument or reason) It won't make him a bully/he sees it and enjoys it but does not practice it/ Westerns don't affect him/before TV it was the pictures and before that something else		7
No effect because:		
Television violence is too obvious/television violence is not true to life/ television violence is not the real thing	3	
The violence shown is just entertainment	1	
The real violence is shown later in the evening	1	
Not enough is shown to make him violent	1	13
The violent boys are out in the street and so are not watching television violence	2	
Television shows only old methods of crime	1	
Boys were violent before television/without television	3	
The character of a boy will predominate	1	
No effect on majority/usually/in the long-term		3
No effect on certain kinds of boys, i.e. Older boys/stable/normal/happy/intelligent/rational/those who have no opportunity to be violent/those who do not go around in gangs or groups		13
No effect under certain conditions, i.e.		
If good triumphs over bad/if bad guy loses in the end	4	
If violence shown is not part of his 'everyday' life	1	
If told by parents or at school that television violence is bad	1	9
If other television material is watched as well	1	
If television violence is funny/is treated as a joke	2	
Seeing violence on television acts as a deterrent (8 claimants)*		
Seeing a bad guy punished has a steadying effect upon boys		4
Showing violence being punished could deter		1
Seeing police catch up with murderers might teach kids crime does not pay/seeing police win/seeing Z cars where cops usually catch criminals		7
Seeing real violence (e.g. Vietnam war) can show you violence is not so great – could act as a deterrent/news can act as a deterrent		2
Television can teach them right from wrong		4
Seeing violence on television may make you opposed to it (21 claimants)*		
Seeing close-up of real violence might put boys off it/realistic violence shows how dreadful it is/if it is horrific, it can turn you away from violence		6
Seeing war films makes young people anti-war		5
Seeing violence on television could set an example to stop boys getting into fights/ would add to feeling that peace is best and should be aimed for/may warn boys against violence/could teach them to oppose violence as wrong/may lead boys to withdraw from such activities		14
Seeing injustice in the form of violence may lead boys to oppose violence		1
Seeing animals hunted might make boys want to do something about it (i.e. oppose it)		2

	n	n
Watching violence on television leads to boys sympathising with the victims (2 claimants)		
Makes you sorry for the victims		1
War films can make you sorry for the underdog		1
Watching violence on television changes children's play patterns (9 claimants)*		
It creates or channels play patterns (i.e. towards violence		2
They play more games like those shown on television/play aggressive games like those on television		4
The play of maladjusted children is often a copy of what is shown on television		1
They copy war films in their play		1
Some may do real injury when playing in imitation of television violence (e.g. hitting head, throwing stones, using knife/may not know where to 'draw the line'		2
Watching violence on television allows you to release your pent-up feelings (3 claimants)		
Television functions in part to release emotions and feelings held in by inhibitions		1
Television violence gives boys an outlet for pent-up feelings		1
Television violence is cathartic		1
Watching violence on television puts violent ideas into boys' heads (26 claimants)		
It puts ideas (of violence) into their heads, e.g.		
– types of violence not thought of yet	1	
– the idea of fighting at football matches	2	
– the idea of mediaeval torture	1	
– effective techniques of crime and violence/of violence for use in fights	2	11
– modern methods of breaking in	2	
– could teach them the way to become violent and bad	3	
Highly strung boys may get ideas from television		1
It encourages them to do things not normally in their heads		2
It gives boys an urge to try out what they see		2
It could make them become violent in nature/violent		4
It makes them think they can hurt people and get away with it/makes it look easy		6
Watching violence on television causes boys to want to imitate the ways of the bad characters depicted (2 claimants)		2
Watching violence on television makes boys copy what they see (46 claimants)		
They try to copy things on TV/try to copy violence shown/try to imitate the actions they see/try to do it themselves/it could make them do what they see on TV/in a play/the occasional boy might try out the violence seen/boys pick up bad habits from it		13
TV shows them how to commit certain kinds of violence/how to do it		2
They might try to copy the stunts shown on TV/might try kicking a boy/ twisted boys may be tempted to copy sadistic violence		3
Boys might try it to see what happens/might be tempted to experiment with things they see/might experiment with weapons or bombs or chemistry sets (after seeing it on TV)		7

	n
They will want to experiment with things they see to find out if they will be punished	2
Specially likely to copy if good guy does the violence/children like to copy heroes/stars	6
Batman has caused fatal accidents	1
They want to be like the tough guys on TV/they want to seem big	2
They think it big to copy adults	4
Romanticised violence can lead to copying/thrillers for entertainment likely to influence them	2
Weak willed boys copy it to cover up their own weaknesses	2
Less brainy kids might see a lot of violence and go and try it out/are more easily led (by TV)	2
Child who lacks loving parents might copy TV violence just for something to 'grab' at	1
They might copy it because they don't realise that TV violence is just pretending	1
Watching violence on television causes boys to behave violently/more violently (35 claimants)	
It could make boys violent/encourage people to be violent (e.g. unstable people, those with opportunity to be violent/it would make boys aggressive if provoked	12
It may make them dangerous/attack people/rob with violence/become bullies	7
It may make them create a lot of fuss/bother	3
It may make them re-live a television action in a playful but dangerous way	1
It causes them to fight more/fight more in school sports/go in for kicking	4
It causes them to fight with knives/commit arson/rob banks/use guns	4
It causes football hooligans to chase/beat up the opposition	2
It makes them think they are tough/makes them big-headed	2
Watching violence on television reinforces existing tendencies towards violence (17 claimants)	
It may strengthen existing tendencies in psychopathic types/in those who are already psychologically disturbed/maladjusted/unstable/insecure	8
It triggers off aggressive individuals or tendencies/latent aggressiveness is stimulated/it gives the violent more ideas	5
It influences those who are of low I.Q./are bullies	3
No effect if boy is already violent	1
Watching violence on television makes boys more boisterous in behaviour/speech (4 claimants)	
Television violence makes boys more boisterous and noisy	1
Television violence makes boys more quarrelsome (in the short term)	1
Television violence produces bad language/slang speech	2
Watching violence on television causes boys to join gangs (2 claimants)	2
Watching violent war films may produce prejudice against some nationals (2 claimants)	
War films may make boys prejudiced against Germans (e.g. make them see them as aggressive, torturers)	2

	n	n
Watching violence on television gives boys the impression that violence can be used as a means to one's ends (12 claimants)*		
It leads them to think of violence as a means to an end/as an acceptable means to an end/to use it to their advantage		3
It leads boys to think that violence is the only way to get what they want		1
It leads boys to think of violence as an answer to their problems		2
It leads boys to resort to violence when in a tight spot		1
It may lead them to use violence to make them seem more important/to get glamour/to impress girls		5
If the violence is used by authority figures to solve problems, boys will think it is OK to do the same		1
Watching violence on television reduces respect for other people and for people in authority (7 claimants)		
It causes a general lowering of respect for other people		1
It may be the reason for children behaving badly towards their parents		2
It reduces respect for the police/for law and order		3
It reduces discipline amongst boys		1
Watching violence on television makes boys take pleasure in seeing violence (4 claimants)		
It gives them an opportunity for violence		1
It can give a boy a warped sense of humour		1
Killing is regarded as 'fun and games'		2
Watching violence on television may give boys the impression that violence is not harmful (6 claimants)		
Seeing violence on television without showing its effects will make boys think that the victims don't feel anything/don't get hurt		4
They don't think first about the effects of being violent		1
It might make them think there is no harm in copying		1
Seeing glorified violence on television makes violence desirable (15 claimants)		
Showing violence as pleasurable or in glorified form encourages violence		2
It could create a feeling of 'glory of power'		1
War films glorify war and so make violence desirable to boys		8
War films make boys want to fight in wars/join army		4
Watching violence on television leads boys to regard violence as a good thing (3 claimants)		
It makes violence seem less of a bad thing		1
It makes younger boys/boys think violence is a good thing to commit/do		2
Watching violence on television makes boys less sensitive to violence (10 claimants)		
It has a desensitising effect on boys/makes them less sensitive to the pain of others/dulls the senses of boys		4

	n	n
It is so prevalent on television that you shrug it off and so don't react to it in real life/Vietnam war has been seen so often that there is now no reaction to it/there is so much news of violence that you feel you have seen it all before		5
Shooting in Vietnam is like shooting by cowboys so it produces no feelings of concern		1
Watching violence on television leads boys to accept violence as normal behaviour (12 claimants)*		
Television violence leads boys to accept violence as normal behaviour/gives impression that violence is normal and acceptable/violence is taken for granted as normal behaviour/makes children think this is the normal way to behave/makes violence seem a normal part of life		8
It makes violence seem acceptable/makes for a casual attitude towards violence		3
Gives boys a bad idea about today's world (i.e. it is presented as violent)		1
It makes violence more acceptable only if television plays a big part in the child's life		2
A boy's sense of values is distorted		1
Watching violence on television upsets children (9 claimants)		
The injustice of violence in the news is upsetting for a while (only)/makes son want to cry		2
It is 'disheartening'		1
It makes you go 'all funny'/scared		2
It may lead to mental disturbance/some may be disturbed or deranged		4
Watching violence on television frightens children (20 claimants)*		
It frightens children/frightens smaller boys/produces bad nerves/they grow up terrified of all violence/it shocks them		13
It makes them scared to go to bed		2
It makes them scared to stay in the house alone/it makes them 'look over their shoulders'/it stimulates an unhealthy imagination/it makes them scared of dark alleys and of silent streets at night		6
They fear they may one day become victims		1
It's frightening when you see the blood colour/when you see a head chopped off		2
When violent scenes are cut, children might guess at what was left out and be scared		1
Watching violence on television causes boys to have nightmares/disturbed sleep (10 claimants)*		
It gives them nightmares		3
Gruesomeness gives them nightmares		1
Makes them afraid when in bed		3
Has a bad effect on sleep		2
Makes them wet the bed		1
Miscellaneous statements at least marginally relevant to the impact of television violence (18 claimants)		
Justified and unjustified violence have similar adverse effects		1

Appendix 1 (cont.)

	n	n
It depends on a boy's nature: it could make him more brave		1
It might ruin their lives if tempted		1
It could have bad effect on younger children		1
Reactions depend upon the similarity between television material and one's own experience		1
It conditions people to authoritarian ways of leadership		1
Boys are only influenced by seeing murders		1
The violence of television advertising divests boys of moral and personal opinions		1
It improves the instinct for survival		1
Television and the press highlight riots, making football crowd violence seem worse than it is		1
Realistic violence (news) will affect sensitive children more		1
Documentaries (e.g. bombing Vietnam) makes children realise that this is 'real life'		1
Seeing news hour after hour is the only way to put something in a child's mind		1
News is known to be real: this causes antagonism to those responsible for keeping the peace		1
Seeing policemen hurt in demonstrations can stop boys wanting to become policemen		1
Newspaper details of violence are more upsetting than television violence		1
Children will want to experiment with weapons irrespective of what they see on television		1

*Less than total in accumulated sub-groups because of overlap between constituent sub-groups.

Appendix 2

Classes of claim made in the British Press about the effects of television violence

	n
Violent television does not cause violence by children or has only a minor effect on them (27 claimants)	
No effect	
Harmless/favourite programmes are not polluting minds/not a cause of delinquency or hooliganism/no effect/not connected with street violence/violence existed before TV or films were invented/crime rates are independent of TV/nothing to show that TV violence leads to real-life violence/no proof	10
Minor effect only	
It is not a major determinant of delinquency/has only a minor role in delinquency/not conclusively shown to lead to violence by the young/TV is the least effective persuader/TV violence is unlikely to have a 'seductive' effect	5
Affects adults/adults rather than children	
Blunting of adult sensibilities/shooting and fighting affect adults/children are less vulnerable than are adults to its' bad influence	3
TV violence does not worry people	
There is little cause for concern/people may be shocked but they like TV violence/television violence is a political issue and is not of general public concern/viewers are less worried by violence than by sex and swearing on TV/viewers don't see violence on TV as harmful	9
TV violence does not affect normal people	2
TV violence does not affect people if they are warned beforehand	2
Certain types of television violence do not harm/less harm	
Types listed were: stylised/symbolic violence/'clean-cut' action/fist fights and bloody gun battles/Westerns/violence in an historical setting/where the violence is justified/violence shown as moral/if the 'goodies' win	15
TV violence creates anti-violence feelings (9 claimants)	
Realistically presented dramatic violence/brutal realism/bloody, brutal murders . . . are a deterrent to violent behaviour	5
Realistic violence in crime series deters by showing how bad violence is/showing realistic violence makes viewers anti-violent	3
Seeing guns and knives creates an inner resistance to using them	1
Television violence has a cathartic effect	
Television violence creates a release of tension/cathartic for everybody/reduces real-life violence/cathartic for viewers who would otherwise act out their excitement dangerously/creates sublimation of violent feelings	13
There are other/stronger influences than violence in producing violence	
These include: bad social conditions/poor parents/lack of education/existing social tradition of violence/growing willingness to accept violence/rigid social institutions and customs/violent toys/violent comics/violent films/peer group influences	8
TV violence exaggerates existing pre-dispositions	
TV violence reinforces existing (aggressive) attitudes or dispositions/it exaggerates existing deviance/it causes crime in those already so involved/it acts as a catalyst for normally well-hidden violent emotions	9

	n
TV violence has a bad influence (no explanation of 'bad') (29 claimants)	
TV violence has a bad influence on society in general	6
TV violence has a bad influence on young people	17
TV violence is most likely to have a bad affect with disturbed people/working class children/middle class children/small children/children from depressed homes	6
TV violence leads to copying/imitation (25 claimants)	
Children mimic what they see on television/imitation effect/teaches violence	6
TV violence is more likely to be copied if dramatically enacted/if it beautifies violence/if it shows aggressive instincts/if it is dangerous/if it is realistic/if it is villainous/if it shows a violent demonstration	13
TV violence is more likely to be copied by impressionable youths/younger boys/small children/children of low I.Q./children with a background of trauma	6
Television violence causes/encourages crime and violence (29 claimants)	
It causes violence/contributes to violence/invites violence/may increase probability of violence/stimulates aggressive behaviour/causes murder/is responsible for the increase in crime/increases youth crime	15
TV violence causes crime by psychopaths	1
TV violence causes an increase in civil disorder and violence/is related to anti-social behaviour/fosters anti-social behaviour/is responsible for skinhead violence	7
Persistent portrayal of violence on TV encourages use of weapons for fighting rather than use of fists	2
Violence seen in ones formative years causes an increase in crime	4
TV violence has had psychological effects (18 claimants)	
TV violence has a deplorable affect on the adolescent mind/bad affect especially if child identifies with TV violence/TV violence produces disturbance, anxiety, fear/punch-ups on television are upsetting/brutality in close-ups can cause disturbance to children/sadistic violence of any kind including cartoons can be terrifying	11
Bad psychological affects are caused by television that is in colour/that is realistic/that is presented in a familiar setting/if the violence is in an old feature film/if the child is already unsettled or disturbed or unstable	7
Through television, violence becomes acceptable or normal	
Seeing TV violence leads the child to see violence as normal, as everyday, as acceptable/it accustoms people to violence/it leads to toleration of violence/it leads to acceptance of gang attacks as normal/brutality and sadism on television leads to the belief that these are part of real-life/it can cause an indifference to violence on the news/violence in police programmes increases people's acceptance of murder	26
Violence comes to be seen as an acceptable means to an end	
Violence becomes an acceptable means to an end/justified killing makes the child think that he can get away with anything	4
People become hardened to violence	
TV creates lack of compassion/lack of regret for immoral behaviour/lack of contrition/callousness in small children/hardening of the senses/reduction of revulsion at violence/violence in the news produces insensitivity in children	13

	n
Television violence gives children a premature and distorted view of life	
Leads to premature (harmful) learning about adult world/subjects children to the full force of the outside world and inflicts on them sick fantasies of adult minds/causes boys to grow up too early/presents a part of adult life that children later seek out/it provides the child with a most accessible back door to the adult world	5
Sense of balance/values become blurred	
It blurs children's sense of values/destroys sense of values/leads to lack of responsibility/lowers respect for sanctity and dignity of human life	4
Disturbs the sense of reality by making violence seem more dominant than it is	
Affects sense of reality/gives idea that violence is wonderful, that life is more violent than it is/gives idea that there are no happy families/horror in the news makes it hard for children to distinguish between fact and fiction/makes violence seem painless/people do not learn from TV violence the consequences of violence/selective coverage of American riots has led to distorted viewer response	15
TV violence gives children ideas they would not normally have	
Introduces something foreign to the individual/it is harmful because it is the child's only 'experience' of violence/it makes people dissatisfied with the peaceful quality of their lives	4
Some types of violence are more harmful than others (40 claimants)	
News and drama have the worst effect: plays and newsreels/unnecessary violence in news and drama/news features/sadistic violence in close-ups	4
Real violence (new news) is more harmful/bad/traumatic	5
Well produced violence in drama is more harmful	4
Television violence which is gratuitous or out of context or over-emphasised is more harmful	9
Violence that shows police in a bad light (i.e. this is more harmful)	4
Programmes showing civil disorder are more harmful: coverage of demonstrations/riots/showing civil disorder	8
Verbal aggression on television is as harmful as/more harmful than physical aggression on television	6
More specific types of TV violence that are harmful	
American violent spy series/glamorised violence/Westerns/vicious short episodes of violence/the 'Saint'/hangings/using weapons/police continually beaten by thugs/use of guns, knives, strangling/violence shown without retaliation/heroes who glorify violence/equally unpleasant heroes and villains/casual violence/professional boxing/violence in the news/sadistic close-ups/violence 'in action' rather than 'static'/violence in slow motion	21
Miscellaneous comments on television violence (30 claimants)	
It has the same conditioning effect as advertising and people only see it as harmful when this proposition is put to them	1
Television is used by the delinquent to rationalise his behaviour	2
Television has a brutalising effect	3
It leads to suicide	1

	n
Offensiveness to viewers is a sign of a good quality production	1
Television violence is justified if integral to the programme	2
Viewers attitudes are the main cause of a disturbed response to social violence on television	1
Television is a scapegoat for our social ills	2
Television's effect depends upon the predispositions of the child	1
Criminals don't watch TV and are not influenced by it	1
It causes boredom but not harm	1
It is not a deterrent to violent behaviour	1
Television violence is not cathartic	2
Violence on television is more harmful than sex (on television)	3
People do not imitate violence seen on television	5
Seeing pain and suffering leads to compassion	1
Television makes people more aware of violence/it defines it as a social problem	2
Of television in general (9 claimants)	
Television has a more immediate (close) affect than other media in putting ideas across	2
The trivial content of television does more harm than violence	4
Exciting programmes can lead to heart failure	1
Factual news coverage and documentaries are needed to educate and inform about the real world	1
Plays that are immoral and didactic are harmful to the simple and ignorant viewer	1

Appendix 3

A list of articles, papers, books examined (i) in the development of hypotheses about the effects of exposure to television violence and (ii) during the analysis and report writing

Albert, R.S. (1957) 'The role of mass media and the effect of aggressive film content upon children's aggressive responses and identification choices', *Genetic Psychology Monographs*, vol.55, p.221.

Arendt, H. (1970) *On Violence*, Allen Lane, London.

Arnold, A. (1969) *Violence and Your Child*, Henry Regnery, Chicago.

Association for Childhood Education International (1967) *Children and TV: Television's Impact on the Child*, Association for Childhood Education International, Washington DC.

Atkin, C.K., Murray, J.P. and Nayman, O.B. (eds) (1971) *Television and Social Behaviour*, National Institute of Mental Health, Washington DC.

Bailyn, L. (1959) 'Mass media and children: a study of exposure habits and cognitive effects', *Psychological Monographs*, vol.73, p.1.

Baker, R.K. and Ball, S.J. (eds) (1969) *Mass Media and Violence. Staff Report to the National Commission on the Causes and Prevention of Violence*, United States Government Printing Office, Washington DC.

Bakewell, J. and Garnham, N. (1970) *The New Priesthood: British Television Today*, Allen Lane, London.

Baldwin, T.F. and Lewis, C. (1971) *Violence in Television: the Industry Looks at Itself*, report of the Department of Communication, Michigan State University.

Bandura, A., Ross, D. and Ross, S.A. (1961) 'Transmission of aggression through imitation of aggressive models', *Journal of Abnormal and Social Psychology*, vol.63, p.575.

Bandura, A. and Huston, A.C. (1961) 'Identification as a process of incidental learning', *Journal of Abnormal and Social Psychology*, vol.63, p.311.

Bandura, A., Ross, D. and Ross, S.A. (1963) 'Vicarious reinforcement and imitative learning', *Journal of Abnormal and Social Psychology*, vol.67, p.601.

Bandura, A. and Menlove, F.L. (1968) 'Factors determining vicarious extinction of avoidance behaviour through symbolic modelling', *Journal of Personality and Social Psychology*, vol.8, p.99.

Bauchard, P. (1952) *The Child Audience – A Report on Press, Film and Radio for Children*, UNESCO, Paris.

Belson, W.A. (1956) 'A technique for studying the effects of a television broadcast', *Applied Statistics*, vol.5, no.3, p.195.

Belson, W.A. (1956) 'Learning and attitude changes resulting from viewing a television series "Bon Voyage" ', *British Journal of Educational Psychology*, vol.26, p.31.

Belson, W.A. (1958) 'Selective perception in viewing a television broadcast', *Audio-Visual Communication Review*, vol.6, p.23.

Belson, W.A. (1967) *The Impact of Television*, Crosby Lockwood & Sons, London.

Berelson, B. and Janowitz, M. (eds) (1966) *Reader in Public Opinion and Communication* (2nd ed.), Free Press, New York.

Berger, S.M. (1962) 'Conditioning through vicarious instigation', *Psychological Review*, vol.69, p.405.

Berkowitz, L. (1962) *Aggression: a Social Psychological Analysis*, McGraw-Hill, New York, London.
Berkowitz, L. and Rawlings, E. (1963) 'Effects of film violence on inhibitions against subsequent aggression', *Journal of Abnormal and Social Psychology*, vol.66, p.405.
Berkowitz, L. (1964) 'The effects of observing violence', *Scientific American*, vol.210, no.2, p.35.
Berkowitz, L. (1965) 'Some aspects of observed aggression', *Journal of Personality and Social Psychology*, vol.2, p.359.
Berkowitz, L. (1965) 'The concept of aggressive drive: some additional considerations' in Berkowitz, L. (ed.) *Advances in Experimental Social Psychology*, vol.II, Academic Press, New York.
Berkowitz, L. and Geen, R.G. (1966) 'Film violence and the cue properties of available targets', *Journal of Personality and Social Psychology,* vol.3, no.5, p.525.
Berkowitz, L. and Geen, R.G. (1967) 'The stimulus qualities of the target of aggression: a further study', *Journal of Personality and Social Psychology*, vol.5, no.3, p.364.
Berkowitz, L. (1968) 'The frustration-aggression hypothesis revisited' in Berkowitz, L., *Roots of Aggression: a Restatement of the Frustration-Aggression Hypothesis*, Atherton Press, New York.
Berkowitz, L. (1970) 'The contagion of violence: an S-R mediational analysis of some effects of observed aggression', *Nebraska Symposium on Motivation*, vol.18, p.95.
Berkowitz, L. (1971) 'Sex and Violence: we can't have it both ways', *Psychology Today*, vol.5, no.7, p.18.
Blizard, J. (1972) *Individual Differences and Television Viewing Behaviour*, Business Consultants and Finance Pty. Ltd., Sydney.
Blumenthal, M.D., Kahn, R.L., Andrews, F.M. and Head, K.B. (1972) *Justifying Violence: Attitudes of American Men*, Institute for Social Research, University of Michigan.
Bogart, L. (1972) *The Age of Television* (3rd ed.), Frederick Ungar, New York.
Bogart, L. (1972) 'Warning: The Surgeon General has determined that TV violence is moderately dangerous to your child's mental health', *Public Opinion Quarterly*, vol.36, no.4, p.491.
Bramel, D. and Blum, B. (1968) 'An observer's reaction to the suffering of his enemy', *Journal of Personality and Social Psychology*, vol.8, p.384.
British Broadcasting Corporation (1950) *Dick Barton and Juvenile Delinquency*, LR/50/958. An unpublished report of the Audience Research Department, British Broadcasting Corporation, London.
British Broadcasting Corporation (1971) *In the Public Interest: a Six-Part Explanation of BBC Policy*, British Broadcasting Corporation: London.
British Broadcasting Corporation Audience Research Department (1972) *Violence on Television: Programme Content and Viewer Perception*, British Broadcasting Corporation, London.
British Broadcasting Corporation (1972) *British Broadcasting 1922-1972: a Select Bibliography*, British Broadcasting Corporation, London.
BBC and ITA Joint Committee (1960) *Children and Television Programmes*, British Broadcasting Corporation, London.
British Medical Journal (1969) 'Violence on TV', *British Medical Journal,* 1969, vol.3, p.125.
Brock, A. (1970) *Violence and Responsibility of the Media*, UNESCO, Department of Mass Communication, Paris.

Burnet, M. (ed.) (1971) *The Mass Media in a Violent World*, UNESCO, Department of Mass Communication, Paris.

Buss, A.H. (1961) *The Psychology of Aggression*, Wiley, London, New York.

Cameron, P. and Janky, C. (1971) 'The effects of TV violence upon children: a naturalistic experiment', *Proceedings of the Annual Convention of the American Psychological Association*, vol.6, no.1, p.233

Chaffee, S.H., McLeod, J.M. and Atkin, C.K. (1971) 'Parental influences on adolescent media use', *American Behavioural Scientist*, vol.14, no.3, p.323.

Chaney, D.C. (1966) 'Television dependency and family relationships amongst juvenile delinquents in the United Kingdom', *Sociological Review*, vol.18, no.1, p.103.

Chaney, D.C. (1970) 'Involvement, realism and the perception of aggression in television programmes', *Human Relations*, vol.23, no.5, p.373.

Chaney, D.C. (1972) *Processes of Mass Communication*, MacMillan, London.

Clayre, A. (1973) *The Impact of Broadcasting or Mrs Buckle's Wall is Singing*, Compton Russell, Salisbury, England.

Cline, V.B., Croft, R.G. and Courrier, S. (1973) 'Desensitization of children to television violence', *Journal of Personality and Social Psychology*, vol.27, no.3, p.360.

Comstock, G.A. (1972) *Television Violence: Where the Surgeon General's Study Leads*, The Rand Corporation, Washington DC.

Cole, B.G. (1970) *Television: a Selection of Readings from TV Guide Magazine*, Free Press, New York.

De Fleur, M.L. (1970) *Theories of Mass Communication* (2nd ed.), David McKay, New York.

Edgar, P.M. and Edgar, D.E. (1971) 'Television violence and socialization theory', *Public Opinion Quarterly*, vol.35, no.4, p.608.

Eguchi, H. and Ichinohe, H. (eds) (1971) *International Studies in Broadcasting*, NHK Radio and TV Culure Research Institute, Tokyo.

Elliott, P. (1972) *The Making of a Television Series: a Case Study in the Sociology of Culture*, Constable, London.

Ellis, G. and Sekyra, F. (1972) 'The effect of aggressive cartoons on the behaviour of first grade children', *Journal of Psychology*, vol.81, p.37.

Emery, F.E. (1959) 'Psychological effects of the Western Film: a study in television viewing. I – the theoretical study: working hypotheses on the psychology of television', *Human Relations*, vol.12, no.3, p.215.

Emery, F.E. (1959) 'Psychological effects of the Western Film: a study in television viewing. II – the experimental study', *Human Relations*, vol.12, no.3, p.215.

Eron, L.D., Walder, L.O. and Lefkowitz, M.M. (1971) *Learning of Aggression in Children*, Little, Brown, Boston.

Eron, L.D. Huesmann, L.R. Lefkowitz, M.M. and Walder, L.O. (1972) 'Does television violence cause aggression?', *American Psychologist,* vol.27, no.4, p.253.

Fechter, J.V. (1971) 'Modelling and environmental generalisation by mentally retarded subjects of televised aggressive or friendly behaviour', *American Journal of Mental Deficiency*, vol.76, no.2, p.266.

Feshbach, S. (1961) 'The stimulating versus cathartic effects of a vicarious aggressive activity', *Journal of Abnormal and Social Psychology*, vol.63, p.381.

Feshbach, S. and Singer, R.D. (1971) *Television and Aggression*, Jossey-Bass, San Francisco.

Feshbach, S. (1971) 'Reality and fantasy in filmed violence' in *Television and Social Behaviour, Vol.2: Television and Social Learning*, (eds) Murray, J.P., Rubenstein, E.A. and Comstock, G.A., US Government Printing Office, Washington DC.

Furu, T. (1971) *The Function of Television for Children and Adolescents*, Sophia University, Tokyo.

Geen, G. and Berkowitz, L. (1966) 'Name-mediated aggressive cue properties', *Journal of Personality*, vol.34, p.456.

Geen, R.G. and Berkowitz, L. (1967) 'Some conditions facilitating the occurrence of aggression after the observation of violence', *Journal of Personality*, vol.35, p.666.

Geen, R.G. (1968) 'Effects of frustration, attack, and prior training in aggressiveness on aggressive behaviour', *Journal of Personality and Social Psychology*, vol.9, no.4, p.316.

Geen, R.G. and O'Neal, E. (1969) 'Activation of cue-elicited aggression by general arousal', *Journal of Personality and Social Psychology*, vol.11, p.289.

Gerbner, G. (1971) 'Violence in television drama: trends and symbolic functions' in *Television and Social Behaviour, Vol.1: Content and Control*, (eds) Comstock, G.A. and Rubenstein, E.A., US Government Printing Office, Washington DC.

Glucksman, A. (1971) *Violence on the Screen*, British Film Institute, London.

Goranson, R. (1969) 'The catharsis effect: two opposing views' in *Mass Media and Violence*, (eds) Baker, R. and Ball, S.J., US Government Printing Office, Washington, DC.

Goranson, R. (1969) 'A review of recent literature on psychological effects of media portrayals of violence' in *Mass Media and Violence*, (eds) Baker, R.K. and Bell, S.J. US Government Printing Office, Washington DC.

Green, T. (1972) *The Universal Eye: World Television in the Seventies*, Bodley Head, London.

Greenberg, B.S. (1973) 'Viewing and listening parameters among British youngsters', *Journal of Broadcasting*, Spring 1973, p.173.

Greenberg, B.S. (1973) *British Children and Televised Violence*, Paper given at the Annual Convention of the Association for Education in Journalism, Colorado State University.

Groombridge, B. (1972) *Television and the People: a Program for Democratic Participation*, Penguin, London.

Halloran, J.D. and Elliot, P. (1970) *Television for Children and Young People*, European Broadcasting Union, Geneva.

Halloran, J.D., Elliot, P. and Murdoch, G. (1970) *Demonstrations and Communications: a case study*, Penguin, London.

Halloran, J.D., Brown, R.L. and Chaney, D.C. (1970) *Television and Delinquency*, Leicester University Press, Leicester.

Halloran, J.D. (1970) 'The effects of media portrayal of violence and aggression' in Tunstall, J. (ed.), *Media Sociology*, Constable, London.

Halmos, P. (ed.) (1969) 'The Sociology of Mass Media Communicators', *Sociological Review Monograph*, no.13, University of Keele, Keele.

Hammond, S.B. and Gleser, H. (1971) *Mass Media Preference in Adolescence,* Australian Broadcasting Council, Melbourne.

Hapkiewicz, W. and Roden, A. (1971) 'The effect of aggressive cartoons on children's interpersonal play', *Child Development*, vol.42, p.1583.

Harper, D., Munro, J. and Himmelweit, H.T. (1970) 'Social and personality factors associated with children's taste in television viewing' in Tunstall, J. (ed.) *Media Sociology,* Constable, London.

Hartley, R. (1964) *The Impact of Viewing Aggression*, Office of Social Research, CBS, New York.

Hartmann, D.P. (1969) 'Influence of symbolically modelled instrumental aggression and pain cues on the disinhibition of aggressive behaviour', *Journal of Personality and Social Psychology*, vol.11, no.3, p.280.

Hartmann, D.P. and Husband, C. (1974) *Racism and the Mass Media*, Davis-Poynter, London.

Haskins, J.B. (1968) *How to Evaluate Mass Communications: the Controlled Field Experiment*, Advertising Research Foundation, New York.

Head, S.W. (1972) *Broadcasting in America* (2nd ed.), Houghton Mifflin, Boston.

Heller, M.S. and Polsky, S. (1971) 'Television violence: guidelines for evaluation', *Archives of General Psychiatry*, vol.24, no.3, p.279.

Hicks, D. (1965) 'Imitation and retention of film-mediated aggressive peer and adult models', *Journal of Personality and Social Psychology*, vol.2, p.97.

Hicks, D. (1968) 'Short and long term retention of affectively varied modelled behaviour', *Psychonomic Science*, vol.11, p.369.

Himmelweit, H., Oppenheim, A. and Vance, P. (1958) *Television and the Child: an Empirical Study of the Effect of Television on the Young*, Oxford University Press, London.

Hood, S. (1972) *The Mass Media*, Macmillan, London.

Howitt, D. and Cumberbatch, G. (1975) *Mass Media Violence and Society*, Elek Science, London.

Independent Television*Authority (1970) *Violence on Television: Control of the Portrayal of Violence in the Programmes of Independent Television (ITA Notes, no.20)*, Independent Television Authority, London. *Later, Independent Broadcasting Authority.

Independent Television* Authority (1971) *Violence in Television Programmes: the ITV Code*, Independent Television Authority, London. *Later, Independent Broadcasting Authority.

Kay, H. (1972) 'Weaknesses in the television-causes-aggression analysis by Eron et al', *American Psychologist*, vol.27, p.970.

Katz, E. (1972) *Research on Televised Violence: Some Notes for a Dialogue with Policy Makers*, lecture at the Special Television Seminar, University of Leeds.

Klapper, J.T. (1954) *Children and Television: A Review of Socially Prevalent Concerns*, Bureau of Applied Social Research, Columbia University, New York.

Klapper, J.T. (1957) *The Effects of Mass Communication*, Free Press, Glencoe, Illinois.

Kline, F.G. and Tichenor, P.J. (1972) *Current Perspectives in Mass Communication Research*, Sage Publications, Beverly Hills.

Klineberg, O. and Klapper, J.T. (1960) *The Mass Media: Their Impact on Children and Family Life*, Television Information Office, New York.

Kuhn, D.Z., Madsen, C.H. and Becker, W.C. (1967) 'Effects of exposure to an aggressive model and "frustration" on children's aggressive behaviour', *Child Development*, vol.38, no.3, p.739.

Larsen, O. (1968) *Violence and the Mass Media*, Harper and Row, New York.

Larsen, O., Gray, L. and Fortas, J. (1968) 'Achieving goals through violence on television' in Larsen, O. (ed.) *Violence in the Mass Media*, Harper and Row, New York.

Lazarsfeld, P.F. (1955) 'Why is so little known about the effects of television on children and what can be done', *Public Opinion Quarterly*, vol.19, no.3, p.243.

Lefcourt, H.M., Barnes, K., Parke, R. and Schwartz, F. (1966) 'Anticipated social censure and aggression-conflict as mediators of response to aggression induction', *Journal of Social Psychology*, vol.70, p.251.

Leibert, R.M. and Baron, R.A. (1972) 'Some immediate effects of televised violence on children's behaviour', *Developmental Psychology*, vol.6, no.3, p.469.

Liebert, R.M., Neale, J. and Davidson, E.S. (1973) *The Early Window: the Effects of Television on Children and Youth*, Pergamon, Oxford.

Linne, O. (1971) *Reactions of Children to Violence on TV*, Report of the Audience and Programme Research Department, Swedish Broadcasting Corporation.

Long, B.H. and Henderson, E.H. (1973) 'Children's use of time: some personal and social correlates', *Elemental School Journal*, vol.73, no.4, p.193.

Lovaas, O.I. (1961) 'Effect of exposure to symbolic aggression on aggressive behaviour', *Child Development*, vol.32, p.37.

MacCoby, E.E. (1964) 'Effects of Mass Media' in Hoffman, M.L. and Hoffman, L.W. (eds) *Review of Child Development Research*, Russell Sage Foundation, New York.

McLuhan, M. (1970) *Counterblast*, Rapp and Whiting, London.

McLuhan, M. (1964) *Understanding Media: the extensions of man*, Sphere Books (1969 reprint), London.

McQuail, D. (1969) *Towards a Sociology of Mass Communications*, Collier-Macmillan, London.

Mayer, T.P. (1972) 'Effects of viewing justified and unjustified real film violence on aggressive behaviour', *Journal of Personality and Psychology*, vol.23, p.21.

Melody, W. (1973) *Children's Television: the Economics of Exploitation*, Yale University Press, New Haven.

Mendelsohn, H. (1966) *Mass Entertainment*, College and University Press, New Haven.

Milgram, S. and Shotland, R.L. (1973) *Television and Anti-Social Behaviour: Field Experiments*, Academic Press, New York.

Murray, R.L.,Cole, R.R. and Felder, F. (1970) 'Teenagers and TV violence: how they rate and view it', *Journalism Quarterly*, vol.47, no.2, p.247.

Murray, J.P. (1973) 'Television and violence: implications of the Surgeon General's Research Program', *American Psychologist*, vol.28, no.6, p.472.

National Association of Broadcasters (1969) *The Television Code (14th ed.)*, National Association of Broadcasters, Washington DC.

National Commission on the Causes and Prevention of Violence (1969) *Commission Statement on Violence in Television Entertainment Programs*, United States Government Printing Office, Washington DC.

National Commission on the Causes and Prevention of Violence (1970) *To Establish Justice to Insure Domestic Tranquility: the Final Report of the National Commission on the Causes and Prevention of Violence*, Bantam Books, New York.

Noble, G. (1970) 'Discrimination between different forms of televised aggression by delinquent and non-delinquent boys', *British Journal of Criminology*, vol.11, no.3, p.230.

Noble, G. (1970) 'Film mediated creative and aggressive play', *British Journal of Social and Clinical Psychology*, vol.9, p.1.

Noble, G. (1971) 'Some comments on the nature of delinquents' identification with television heroes, fathers and best friends', *British Journal of Social and Clinical Psychology*, vol.10, p.172.

Noble, G. (1973) 'Effects of different forms of filmed aggression on children's constructive and destructive play', *Journal of Personality and Social Psychology*, vol.26, p.54.

Osborn, D.K. and Endsley, R.C. (1971) 'Emotional reactions of young children to TV violence', *Child Development*, vol.42, no.1, p.321.

Pinderhughes, C.A. (1972) 'Televised violence and social behaviour', *Psychiatric Opinion*, vol.9, no.2, p.28.

Pool, I., Schramm, W., Frey, F.W., MacCoby, N. and Parker, E.B. (eds) (1973) *Handbook of Communications*, Rand McNally, Chicago.
Rabinovitch, M.S. (1972) 'Violence perception as a function of entertainment value and TV violence', *Psychonomic Science*, vol.29, no.6A, p.360.
Rivers, W.L. and Schramm, W. (1969) *Responsibility in Mass Communication*, Harper and Row, New York.
Rosenthal, S.P. (1962) 'Crime and violence in television programmes – their impact on children and adolescents', *Visual Aids Review*, December.
Schramm, W., Lyle, J. and Parker, E.B. (1961) *Television in the Lives of our Children*, Stanford University Press, Stanford.
Schramm, W. (1968) *Motion Pictures and Real-Life Violence: What the Research Says*, Institute for Communications Research, Stanford, California.
Sears, R., MacCoby, E. and Levin, H. (1957) *Patterns of Child Rearing*, Harper, New York.
Siegal, A. (1956) 'Film mediated fantasy aggression and strength of aggressive drive', *Child Development*, vol.27, p.365.
Shaw, C. and Baker, R. (1972) 'Violence on television', *Medicine, Science and the Law*, vol.12, no.4, p.248.
Shulman, M. (1973) *The Ravenous Eye: the Impact of the Fifth Factor*, Cassell, London.
Siegel, A.E. (1958) 'The influence of violence in the mass media upon children's role expectations', *Child Development*, vol.29, no.1, p.35.
Small, W. (1970) *To Kill a Messenger: Television News and the Real World*, Hastings House, New York.
Social Morality Council (1974) *The Future of Broadcasting*, Eyre Methuen, London.
Stephens, D. (1967) 'The electronic whipping boy', *Mental Health*, vol.26, no.4, p.12.
Surgeon General's Scientific Advisory Committee on Television and Social Behaviour (1972) *Television and Growing Up: the Impact of Televised Violence*, United States Government Printing Office, Washington DC.
Surgeon General's Scientific Advisory Committee on Television and Social Behaviour (1972) *Television and Social Behaviour, volumes I-V*, US Government Printing Office, Washington DC.
Television Research Committee (1966) *Problems of Television Research: a Progress Report*, Leicester University Press, Leicester.
Television Research Committee (1969) *Second Progress Report and Recommendations*, Leicester University Press, Leicester.
Thomas, S.A. (1972) 'Violent content in television: the effect of cognitive style and age in mediating children's aggressive responses', *Proceedings of the Annual Convention of the American Psychological Association*, vol.7, no.1, p.97.
Tunstall, J. (ed.) (1970) *Media Sociology*, Constable, London.
Turner, W.C. and Berkowitz, L. (1972) 'Identification with film aggressor and reactions to film', *Journal of Personality and Social Psychology*, vol.23, p.21.
UNESCO (1970) *Mass Media in Society: the Need of Research*, UNESCO, Department of Mass Communications, Paris.
United States Senate (1973) *Hearings before the Subcommittee on Communications of the Committee on Commerce, United States Senate, on the Surgeon General's Report by the Scientific Advisory Committee on Television and Social Behaviour*, United States Government Printing Office, Washington DC.

Walters, R. and Willows, D. (1968) 'Imitative behaviour of disturbed and non-disturbed children following exposure to aggressive and non-aggressive models', *Child Development*, vol.39, p.79.
Walters, R., Thomas, E. and Acker, C. (1962) 'Enhancement of punitive behaviour by audio-visual displays', *Science*, vol.136, p.872.
Wedell, E.G. (1968) *Broadcasting and Public Policy*, Michael Joseph, London.
Weigel, R.H. and Jessor, R. (1973) 'Television and adolescent conventionality: an exploratory study', *Public Opinion Quarterly*, vol.37, no.1, p.76.
Weiss, W. (1969) 'Effects of mass media on communication' in *Handbook of Social Psychology*, Lindzey, G. and Aronson, E. (eds), Addison-Wesley Press, Boston.
Whitehouse, M. (1967) *Cleaning-up TV: from Protest to Participation*, Blandford Press, London.
Zillman, D. and Johnson, R. (1973) 'Motivated aggressiveness perpetuated by exposure to aggressive films and reduced by non-aggressive films', *Journal of Research in Personality*, vol.7, p.261.

CHAPTER 3

THE RESEARCH STRATEGY FOR INVESTIGATING CAUSAL HYPOTHESES

Contents

3 THE RESEARCH STRATEGY FOR INVESTIGATING CAUSAL HYPOTHESES

The investigation of the *essentially causal* hypotheses of this enquiry involved the joint use of specialised research strategies of two kinds: (a) a form of massive empirical matching based upon the author's Stable Correlate Technique [1] and modelled on the application of that method in an earlier enquiry [2] ; (b) the investigation of each hypothesis in both its forward and its reversed forms.

AN OVERVIEW OF THE INVESTIGATORY STRATEGY USED

The nature of this double strategy and the reasons for using it are best illustrated through an example. Suppose we are seeking to investigate the tenability of the following hypothesis:

> 'High exposure to television violence causes boys to increase the amount of their violent behaviour'.

Suppose also that we have established the following measures or indices of violent behaviour for the heavier exposees (the Qualifying group in terms of the hypothesis) and for the lighter exposees (the Control group in the present context):

57.76 : 46.79

Then we might reasonably conclude that the difference between those two indices might be explained in one or more of the following three ways.

1. It is an effect of the higher level of exposure of the Qualifiers to television violence.
2. It is a reflection of the Qualifying and the Control groups being different in terms of their personal characterstics and background and experiences.
3. The difference in violence level between the Qualifiers and the Controls is not an effect of exposure to television violence at all; rather it reflects a tendency for the more violent boys to seek out violent television.

If we are to reduce the ambiguity of this situation, one thing we must do is to eliminate the second possibility, namely the possibility that the difference between the two samples in terms of violent behaviour is due to those two samples being different in terms of characteristics and background factors that are themselves associated with violence level. Such an elimination is attempted in this enquiry through the matching of the Control sample to the Qualifying sample, *on a massive basis*, in terms of the empirically selected correlates of violent behaviour (i.e. of the dependent variable). If after such matching, the amount of violence being committed by the Qualifiers is still meaningfully [3] greater than the amount being committed by the Modified Controls, then the forward form of the hypothesis may be regarded as being given support by the evidence.

However, this still leaves us with the third possibility listed above, namely that the difference in violence levels between the Qualifiers and the Controls is not an effect of exposure to television violence, but that it represents a tendency for the hypothesis to operate in reverse, i.e.

> 'Violent boys, just because they are violent, [4] seek out violent television programmes to a greater degree than do boys who are less violent.'

If we are to investigate *this* as a possible explanation of the postulated difference in violence level of the heavier and the lighter exposees (i.e. 56.76 : 46.79), then we must subject that *reverse* form of the hypothesis to as rigorous a form of test or challenge as we did its forward form. [5]

Such a test or challenge likewise involves massive empirical matching. In this case, the matching of the less violent boys to the more violent boys will be in terms of the empirically derived correlates of exposure to television violence. If after such matching, the amount of violence viewed is still meaningfully [6] greater for the more violent boys, then the reverse form of the hypothesis is regarded as being given support by the evidence.

This strategy of challenging the tenability of both the forward and the reverse forms of the hypothesis is likely to leave us with one or another of the following sets of results.

1 *Possibility 1.* The residual difference between Qualifiers and Controls, in terms of the dependent variable, is meaningful [6] for the *forward* test but *not* for the reverse test: such a combination of findings would give support of a relatively unambiguous kind to the forward form of the hypothesis.

2 *Possibility 2.* The residual difference between Qualifiers and Controls, in terms of the dependent variable, is meaningful [6] for the hypothesis in reverse but not for the forward form of the hypothesis: such a combination of findings would give no support to the forward form of the hypothesis (irrespective of what it meant for the reverse form).

3 *Possibility 3.* The residual difference between Qualifiers and Controls, in terms of the dependent variable, is meaningful [6] for *both* the forward and the reversed forms of the hypothesis. Such a situation would in general give support to the forward form of the hypothesis, but it would leave open several possibilities: (i) that for some parts of the sample the forward form of the hypothesis applies while its reverse form applies for other parts of the sample; (ii) that both the forward and the reversed hypotheses are operative in a circular form or relationship; (iii) that the forward form of the hypothesis is partly supported by the working of the hypothesis in reverse.

4 *Possibility 4.* The residual difference between Qualifiers and Controls, in terms of the dependent variables, is not meaningful [6] for either the forward or the reverse forms of the hypothesis: such a combination of findings would give no support to the forward form of the hypothesis (irrespective of what it means for the reverse form).

In considering the research strategy used here, it is relevant to see it as an application of the hypothetico-deductive method and not in terms of laboratory or agricultural models. The latter strategies can be used where one can exercise tight control over the factors in the situation. In the present class of study, no such control is feasible and the hypothetico-deductive method is the appropriate strategy to use.

INTRODUCTION TO THE MATCHING TECHNIQUE USED

Clearly, empirical matching is central to the research strategy used in this enquiry, whether in relation to forward or to reversed forms of hypotheses. Accordingly, a considerable part of this chapter is given over to a detailed description of how this matching was carried out. However there is an advantage in beginning this description with a short outline of the principal steps in the procedure.

THE MATCHING PROCEDURE – IN BRIEF

1 As a first step in achieving matching of Controls to Qualifiers, at the level and on the lines proposed, a large pool of over 200 potential matching variables was developed. These variables were drawn as likely to be: correlated with one or more of the dependent and independent variables involved in the study; relatively independent of each other; stable in relation to the independent variable in the hypothesis under investigation.

2 From this pool of potential matching variables a composite was drawn in such a manner as to maximise the correlation of that total composite with the dependent variable in the hypothesis under investigation, provided such variables are also a source of difference between the Control and the Qualifying samples. The final pool for use in the investigation of any single hypothesis was expected to be composed of up to 25 different variables. The technique used for their derivation was the Stable Correlate Technique.

3 The Qualifying and the Control samples were then *each* split into the 30-40 sub-groups defined by the matching composite and a weighting method was used to equate the number of Control cases in each sub-group to the number of Qualifiers in it. This method yielded a modified 'score' on the dependent variable for the Control group and the difference between this score and the Qualifier score was used in computing an 'index of effect' (of the independent variable).

Extra points about the matching operation that are worthy of special note are the following: (i) a separate matching composite had to be developed for *each* forward and *each* reverse hypothesis due for investigation (over 400 different composites in all); each such composite was then to be used in a separate matching operation; (ii) the whole of the composite development and the matching for each hypothesis were computerised.

THE MATCHING METHODS USED – IN DETAIL

The pool of variables formulated for matching purposes

The requirements of the pool of matching variables. The development of a pool of matching variables was an integral part of the matching operation used in the investigation of each hypothesis. From this pool we would aim to draw a set of matching variables which, taken together, would have a large multiple correlation with the dependent variable in the hypothesis concerned. To be effective, this pool would have to meet the following requirements.

(a) Its variables would have to be very mixed in the sense of being relatively independent of each other: only if this was so could a high multiple correlation be built up.

(b) The total number of pool variables would have to be very large. This is simply to increase the chances of accounting for a large amount of the variability of score on the *dependent* and on the independent variables. It is one of the facts of prediction science that our ability to volunteer or intuitively 'pick' the principal correlates of some variable is at present low. Accordingly, one's only chance of success lies in developing a big array which will turn out to have in it the many different, but fairly unrelated, dimensions that are needed.

(c) The variables in the pool should tend to call for fairly simple questioning and the offering of a simple response system: only if this were so would it be possible to collect information about the necessarily large number of variables in the pool.

(d) The pool variables must be 'stable' in character – in the sense that they are not themselves open to being changed by the independent variable. If they are *unstable* in this sense, then the use of them in the matching process could affect (misleadingly) the residual difference between the higher and the lower exposure groups. [7]

(e) It is one of the complexities of matching technology that matching two samples in terms of a powerful predictor of a dependent variable may *in certain circumstances* make no difference at all to the size of the residual difference between the Qualifying and the modified Control groups. This could occur when the Qualifying and the Control groups were in fact already equal in terms of that particular matching variable. In other words, *there was no difference to be matched out by that powerful matching variable*. In that particular case it would be better to match in terms of a variable with a somewhat lower correlation with the dependent variable and which is a source of difference between the Qualifying and the Control groups. The upshot of all this is that the pool of variables must have in it also *a large number of variables which are expected to be sources of difference between the Qualifying and the Control groups.*

These, then, are the criteria which surround the development of a pool of possible matching variables.

The formulation and the content of the initial pool of matching variables. A complication in developing the 'pool' was that it became desirable for the pool to be *general* in its purposes, in the sense that it should serve matching needs in investigating a large number of somewhat different hypotheses – in fact, over 400 of them (including both forward and reverse formulations).

Over and above this, the pool came together through several cycles of development which at one stage or another drew upon a fairly wide range of sources and source material. These sources were as follows.

1 Variables which the author had in the past found to be usefully predictive of deviant behaviour were fed into the pool. Many of these were drawn directly from his study (using very similar techniques) of causal factors in the development of juvenile stealing.

2 The views of boys and parents (as expressed in the hypothesis development sessions) about what sorts of boys are violent. These views were examined with the purpose of detecting any underlying variables.

3 The literature was closely examined for leads, either in the form of correlational results or of speculations by theorists.

4 A study was made of press cuttings relating to violence in television programmes.

5 Team members, working both at an experiential and at an imaginative level, developed further leads.

6 Finally, a limited number of items was added to the pool with the purpose of extending the heterogeniety of the items within it. Some of these items came out of a 'think-tank' situation, some were tenuously intuitive, and some were sharply out of line with traditional thinking. This sixth category was included to increase the possibility of lifting the multiple correlation of the composite of variables that would be used for matching purposes. It has been the writer's experience that this category can yield variables with useful correlations with the dependent variable, and, more important, which add to the overall or combined predictive power inherent in a large pool (of potential matching variables).

Sources (5) and (6) were seen also as filling gaps that were felt, intuitively, to exist in the total pool. Their principal purpose, however, was to expand the list or pool of possible matching variables to make it as complete and as heterogeneous as possible.

The several cycles in the development of the pool of potential matching variables. In the first stage of development of potential matching variables, no attempt was made to formulate questions in the form in which they would be put to respondents. Rather, a list of 'variables' or 'issues' was compiled, with the compilers taking careful note of the nature of the dependent variable in each hypothesis.

These variables/issues numbered 122 at this first stage and their range was wide as is shown in the following selection from the full list. Some examples follow.

> Socio-economic class, slum environment, number of parks and playgrounds in the area, . . . broken home, family size, amount of parental love or attention given to the boy, frequency of parental absences, frequency of family rows, amount of help he gives at home, . . . drinking/drug-taking by parents, any criminal record for parents, difference in parents' ages, . . . a range of variables featuring the early history of the boy and how he was 'handled' by parents, . . . age, intelligence, physical strength, academic performance, truancy by boy, . . . nervousness, depression, sadism, pre-disposition to be violent, whether easily bored, sense of humour, extraversion, rigidity, . . . gang membership, place of birth, is the home multi-occupied, number of close friends boy has, . . . ratio of indoor to outdoor activities, number of hobbies and interests, interest in pop music, literary interests, sports played, . . . moral development, religion, attitudes towards being caught by police, . . . ambitions (if any) of boy, any spare time jobs by boy, number of holidays spent abroad, . . .

Beyond this first and very exploratory listing of items came a series of modifications. Through them:

1 The items in the pool were increased in number through consideration of the different dependent variables involved in the inquiry and with a view to filling

apparent gaps in the pool.

2 The items were made more specific and the requisite measuring procedures were entered against them where the nature of such measures seemed clear enough.

3 Some of the proposed pool items were modified or dropped where the available measures seemed to be beyond the financial scope of the project, or to raise risks at the public relations level.

4 Pool items which involved self-reporting by boys or parents were tentatively given question forms both to assess their appropriateness for self-reporting and to gauge the quantity of questioning involved.

5 An assessment was made, particularly in the fifth cycle of modification, of the stability of the pool items, a process which led wherever possible to substitute items being introduced but in some cases to the discarding of the pool item concerned.

6 The items remaining the pool were expressed either as questions for the respondent or in the form of instructions to interviewers to gather information of some specified kind (e.g. measure boy's height to nearest centimetre).

The nature of the changes made under (3) and (5) is important and is illustrated below.

(a) Where the measurement of the proposed pool item did not seem viable, the following kinds of steps were taken.

(i) In some cases, a related measure calling for less time or less equipment was made (e.g. a measure of chest expansion with tape measure was used instead of a balloon or machine test; speed of running was assessed through a form of comparative self-report instead of a direct test; a chromosome eount was dropped, but parental testimony of violence by the boy when under four was expected to provide some indication of violent disposition (if there was one).

(ii) In other cases, a known correlate of some complex variable was included instead (e.g. 'stealing sweets from a shop' was found in an earlier project [8] to be usefully predictive of overall theft level and so was used in lieu of the very demanding and time-consuming measure of theft behaviour itself).

(iii) There were some proposed measures which, while not very promising as predictors, would together have added quite substantially to what already looked like a very long interview, for example: an eyesight test; reaction-time test using a button-pressing device with automatically recorded response lag; an endurance test. Some of these tests were dropped.

(b) The scrutiny of the pool items for possible instability [9] was considered a very important process and it led to the following modifications.

(i) For some suspect items, an attempt was made to go back to the time or circumstance where the independent variable could not reasonably be thought to be exerting an influence on the variable concerned. Thus for assessment of certain personality traits of the boy, questions were asked of his mother about him when he was under four years of age, e.g. 'When your son was under four years of age how often did he break up his toys or break up anything else?'; 'When your son was under four years of age, did he often get bored?' 'When he was under four, was he highly strung or nervous?' This tactic can be usefully thought of as a search for '*precedence*'. I should add at this point that the search for 'precedence' was not the only reason for developing items that went well back in the life of the child. Many items could not reasonably apply to anything but the early years of the child (e.g. 'When he was under four, did you pet him or cuddle him when he cried?' / 'When he was under four, did he get anyone up a lot in the night?').

(ii) For other items suspected of instability, a seemingly related item of a more fixed or stable kind was sought.

(iii) For others again, a stable *correlate of the suspect item* was sought.

The items in the pool that were to be used for investigating the 'forward' hypothesis and the pool items to be used for investigating the hypothesis in 'reverse'. The pool described above was for use in investigating the hypotheses in their *forward forms*. Automatically that pool was considered for incorporation into another pool, namely one that was to be used for investigating the hypotheses in their *reversed* forms. Most of the items in the forward pool were considered as possibly correlated with one or more of the dependent variables in the reversed forms of the hypotheses and so were retained for the reverse pool. However, some were dropped on the grounds that they might well be unstable (in relation to one or more of the new independent variables [10]). On the other hand, twenty new items were added to the reverse pool (as possible correlates of the new dependent variables). The forward and reverse pools are shown in full in the Appendix to this chapter. The forward-pool items that were not carried over into the reverse pool are shown with an asterisk (*) and those that were brought in solely for the reverse pool are shown with a double asterisk (**).

The pool items were distributed through the different parts of the questioning procedure as follows.

1 A self-completion questionnaire filled in by the boy approximately a week before his main interview at the Survey Research Centre. The pool items in this questionnaire were of a straightforward kind, suitable for this form of administration. They included: questions about the type of music in which the boy is interested; many personal details including age, place of birth, aspects of school performance and school life, . . . sports available at school, religion, separation from parents, performance (relative to other boys) at running and at swimming; sleeplessness, general level of health, membership of various clubs or associations, pet ownership, ...

2 A questionnaire delivered to the boy's mother and dealing with a wide range of variables including: her son's characteristics and behaviour when under four years of age; her own handling of him (when he was a baby and when a small child) in a range of situations; her training of him when he was very small; the number and kind of his illnesses; her own age and aspects of her own and her husband's educational and occupational background; her own and her husband's religion; place of birth; number of markets and of playgrounds in the area.

3 A questionnaire sequence towards the end of an extended interview at the Survey Research Centre where pool information of the following kind was collected: family composition and household size; number of houses lived in;

household facilities of various kinds; family ownership of a range of items; extent of violence in the district; various aspects of family life; aspects of his own personality, outlook and experiential background; aspects of school life and facilities.

4 In addition, boys went through physical checks at the centre which included measurements of 'grip strength', height, weight, chest size and expansion, cranial size. Interviewers also rated boys in terms of behaviour and appearance at the Centre interviews.

The full set of questionnaires is shown in the General Appendix to this report and the full set of pool items is presented in the Appendix to this chapter. In the latter, the predictive powers of each pool item (i.e. power to predict the dependent variable and power to predict the independent variable) are also entered. [11] It must be noted however, that the relative predictive power of pool items tended to change for each dependent and each independent variable to which it was specially linked during hypothesis investigation.

Problems relating to error in the information about variables in the pool. Naturally, one needs to avoid error in the information collected with respect to potential matching variables. At the same time, errors in this sort of information constitute a type of problem which is different in kind from errors in data wanted in its own right (e.g. measures of the dependent and the independent variables).

Suppose for instance that a mother under-rates the frequency with which her son had tantrums when under the age of four years. If in fact frequency of tantrums is a correlate of the dependent variable (e.g. 'present-day violence'), then errors in that frequency measure may serve to reduce the value of that frequency data as a predictor. If the error is great enough, *all* the predictive power of the 'tantrum' data may be lost, though in practice, the loss is a matter of degree and generally of small degree. Be that as it may in a particular case, the outcome of error in the predictive variable is *loss of matching power* – but no more than that. In particular, the frequency data for that matching variable is not for use in its own right – and of course must never be used in that way unless we are confident about its accuracy.

For the above reason, a *potentially* good predictor will sometimes take second place to one with less potential predictive power. From this point of view it is best to see predictive variables not as absolute measures but as the responses one gets in reply to particular questions.

The selection of the composite of matching variables

The principles behind the selection of the matching composite are simple enough but the selection process itself is tedious and calls for computer processing and analysis.

The strategy of variable selection is set out below and it is described in terms of the investigation of the forward test of hypothesis 1.

Reducing the pool of potential matching variables to workable size. The very first step in developing a matching composite is to reduce the large pool of potential matching items (227 of them in the case of the 'forward pool') to a smaller size, so that computer processing will be technically and financially feasible. The reduced number sought was 100 items. To reduce or 'slim' the pool in this way a computer program (called 'the slimming program') was developed. It would calculate the power of each of the 227 items in the Forward pool to predict the value of the dependent variable (i.e. amount of violent behaviour in the case of the forward test of hypothesis 1). The top 100 in this respect were carried over into the rest of the analysis, the other 127 being discarded. The results of this slimming program, applied to hypothesis 1 (Forward Test), are shown in Appendix 2 to this chapter. The 'slimming' program would automatically list all 227 in order according to predictive power. They take the form shown in table 3.1.

Table 3.1
Yield from the 'slimming' program

Items in the matching pool	Predictive* index
Have you ever stolen sweets from a shop?	86.64
In your district, how many of the boys are violent?	64.96
Do you often act first and think after?	60.91
....	
....	
How often do/did your parents go out together?	45.47
Did the boy come to the interview wearing a tie?	43.89
In your childhood, how often were you teased or hurt?	42.96
When under four years did he lose his temper easily? (mother's questionnaire)	42.14
....	
Grip strength (best of three) in kilograms	40.44
....	
....	

*See page 70 for details of calculation.

The selection process. The first predictor or matching variable in the proposed matching composite for use in investigating a given hypothesis was selected in the following way.

(i) For each of the 100 variables remaining in the pool, two calculations were made, namely the extent of its association with the dependent variable and with the independent variable. In the case of hypothesis 1, these were: the extent of the respondent's involvement in violent behaviour and the extent of his exposure to television violence.

(ii) In each case, the calculation of predictive power was on the following pattern (table 3.2).

The index of 86.6 is to be interpreted as providing a direct indication of variable K's predictive power: the higher this index, the higher the predictive power of variable K. Similarly for any other variable.

Table 3.2
Assessing predictive power of pool item 'K'

Dependent variable score (= violent behaviour in this case)		Pool variable K Yes	Not yes	All
Higher score for violence		434	355	789
Lower score for violence		255	521	776
	Totals	689	876	1565
Expected number in lower group if no statistical association		341.64	434.36	
Expected-actual in lower group		+86.64	- 86.64	
Hence 'predictive power' = 86.64				

(iii) Each variable in the (now) '100 item' pool thus had set against it two predictive powers or indices, one for the dependent variable and the other for the independent variable. These were multiplied together to yield a product. All 100 were then compared for size of this product and the top ten in terms of product size were printed in numerical order as in the following example drawn from the investigation of hypothesis 1 (forward test).

Table 3.3
Showing best 10 on basis of product of two predictive powers

Position	Pool variables	Displacement on IV	DV	Product (IV x DV)
1st	Has the boy ever stolen sweets from a shop?	43.72	86.64	3787.90
2nd	Age at interview (years)	94.30	39.07	3684.30
3rd	Grip strength (average of best right and left hand)	87.69	40.44	3546.18
4th	Height to nearest centimetre	90.25	35.74	3225.54
5th	Grip strength, best of 3, right hand	85.24	34.28	2922.03
6th	Grip strength, best of 3, left hand	82.23	33.96	2792.53
7th	Weight to nearest kilogram	93.23	26.98	2515.35
8th	Still at school and has spare time job	55.22	39.65	2189.47
9th	Under 15 years and has reached puberty	93.19	23.40	2180.65
10th	In his district, proportion of boys who are violent	32.78	64.96	2129.39

(iv) At this early stage in the selection process, the top variable in the list of ten was selected as the first element in the matching composite (i.e. variable 42 = stealing sweets from a shop). [12]

(v) The total sample of 1565 was now split into two groups, those who had said 'no' (group 2) to the question about stealing sweets from a shop at some time in their lives and those who had said 'yes' (group 3). The splitting pattern was as follows:

Figure 3.1 Splitting on the first predictor

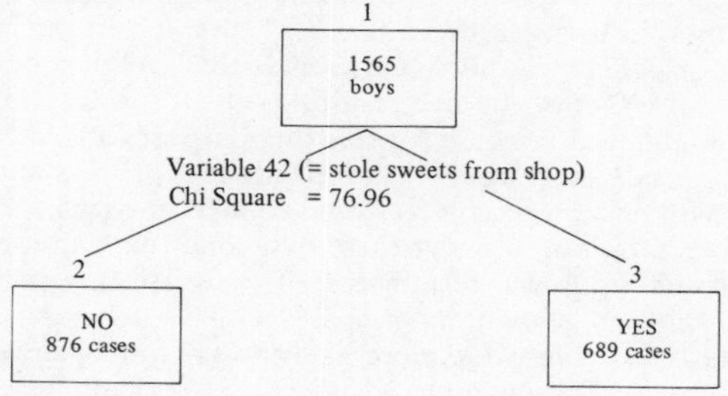

(vi) The selection process was now applied separately to group 2 ('no') and in this case variable 190 (= age of boy) emerged as the top predictor, leading to the splitting of group 2 into groups 4 and 5, namely the younger and the older boys. That same process was now applied, separately, to group 3 ('yes'), leading to the selection of V65 (= average grip strength) as the top predictor and to the splitting of group 3 into groups 6 and 7.

Figure 3.2 Second level of sample splitting

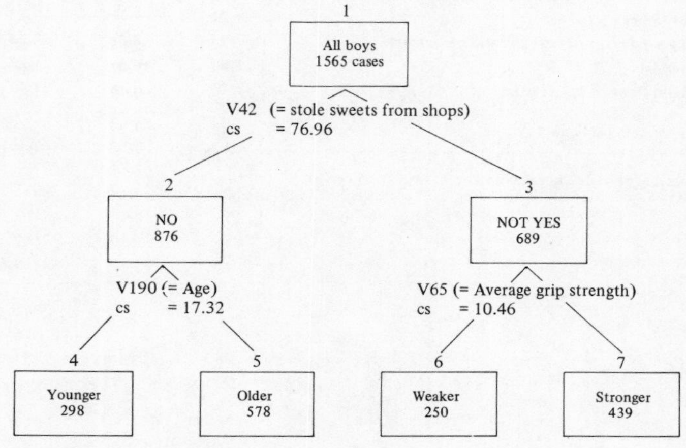

(vii) The whole process was continued in this way to the limits of statistical viability, leading to the emergence of the splitting composite shown in figure 3.3.

(viii) The splitting process had one other important feature. At each splitting stage, a statistical control was placed upon the selection of the splitting variable. If the relationship between the *dependent variable* and the *item at the top of the list of ten products* was not significant at the level of 5 per cent (P = 0.05), or if the size of either of the two resulting sub-groups was less than 30, that 'top of ten' variable was rejected for splitting purposes and the 'next in the list of ten' was considered as a substitute for it. This process was continued till a variable within the top ten was found to meet the two conditions imposed. If no variable in the top ten met these two conditions, the splitting of that particular sub-group was terminated. The significance figures for all the accepted splits are shown in figure 3.3.

Obviously variables were more likely to fail one or the other test as the splitting process became more advanced. Two examples of the failure of items in the top ten are shown in tables 3.4 and 3.5.

Table 3.4
Example of 1st predictor being rejected
(from hypothesis 1, featuring DV1 and IV1)

Total cases in the group being examined for viable predictors = 75

		Displacement on		Product
		IV	DV	(IV x DV)
1	What is his father's job	6.77	4.32	29.25
2	Grip strength (average of best left and best right)	5.25	5.28	27.72
3	District number	5.80	4.52	26.22
4	Grip strength (best of 3, left hand)	3.84	6.36	24.42
10	Do/did enjoy being at school	5.11	4.32	22.08

1st predictor gives a split with Chi-square value of only 3.15 (=NS)
2nd predictor gives a split with CS of 4.89 (Sig) and is chosen splitting variable

Figure 3.3 Showing a composite of predictors of a dependent variable and the scores in terms of this variable for each of the terminal sub-groups defined by the composite.

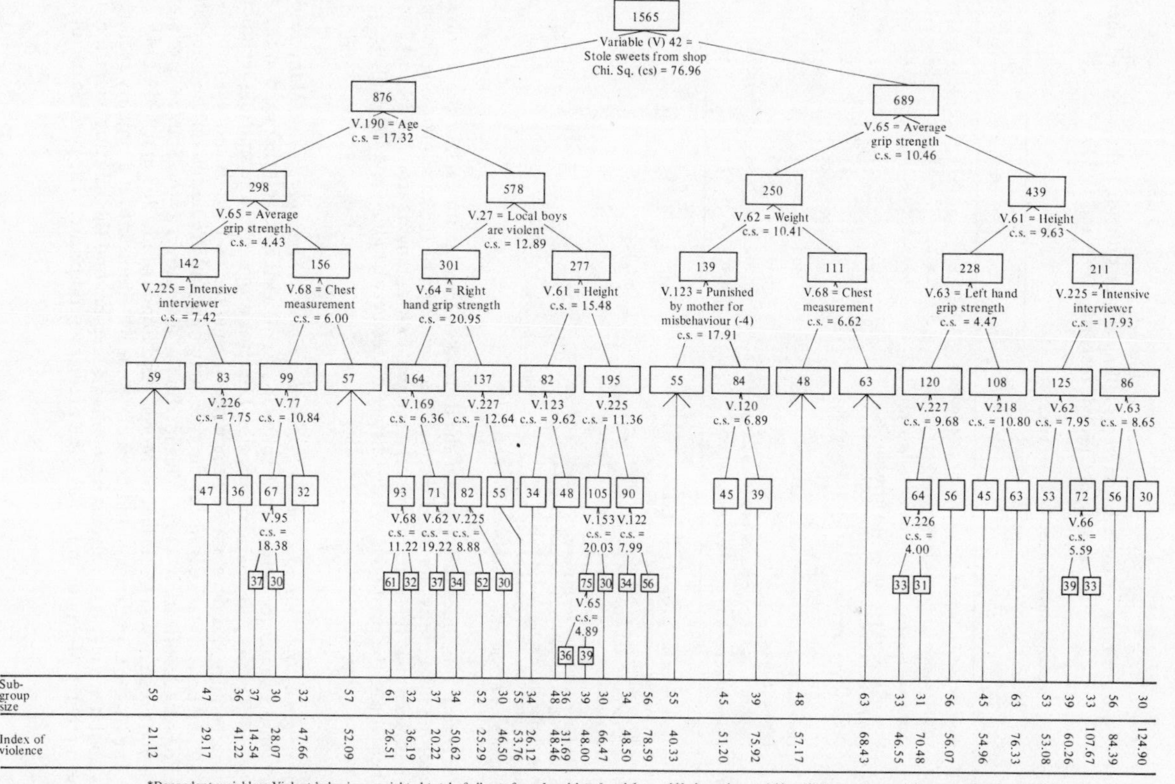

*Dependent variable = Violent behaviour, weighted total of all acts from Level 1 to Level 6: **Independent variable = High exposure to violence on television generally.

Table 3.5
Example of each of the top ten items failing and of splitting being stopped thereafter (from hypothesis 4, featuring DV4 and IV31)

Total cases in group being examined for viable predictor = 62

		Displacement on IV	Displacement on DV	Product (IV x DV)
1	When he lost his temper did mother try to calm him?	5.00	5.71	28.55
2	Was he punished when he misbehaved?	5.50	4.71	25.91
3	How many jobs has husband had since marriage?	5.50	4.58	25.19
4	How often were privileges taken from boy as punishment (when under four years)?	4.50	5.23	23.54
5	Grip strength (average of best left and best right)	6.50	3.45	22.43
6	Date of intensive interview	5.00	4.29	21.45
7	How many of listed sports were available at school?	4.50	4.26	19.17
8	District number	4.50	4.26	19.17
9	How often did he have tantrums when under four?	7.00	2.68	18.76
10	Did mother reward him when he was good?	4.50	4.13	18.59

1st predictor yields sub-group of only 25 cases
2nd predictor yields sub-group of only 25 cases
3rd predictor yields sub-group of only 19 cases
4th predictor yields sub-group of only 16 cases
5th predictor gives a split with the Chi-square value of only 2.27 (=NS)
6th predictor yields sub-group of only 25 cases
7th predictor yields sub-group of only 26 cases
8th predictor yields sub-group of only 26 cases
9th predictor yields sub-group of only 17 cases
10th predictor yields sub-group of only 18 cases

This group (of 62) therefore becomes TERMINAL.

Figure 3.3 includes the mean for the dependent variable for each of the terminal matching sub-groups identified through the derivation of the total matching composite. It will be seen that these means are very variable in size, ranging from 14.54 to 124.90. In other words, the predictive system differentiates between high and low violence scores.

The origin of the method used for developing the matching composite. Many readers will recognise a similarity between the splitting system used here and that used in the AID program (i.e. the Automatic Interaction Detector program). The splitting technique used in this enquiry was developed by the writer during the mid-1950s and was published in 1959 in *Applied Statistics* under the title 'Matching and Prediction on the Principle of Biological Classification' [13]. This method is also known as the Stable Correlate Method. The AID system was published by Morgan and Sonquist in 1963 and 1964 [14].

The Stable Correlate method does of course have built into it a stability requirement in its pool items and it has always been taken a step beyond the splitting operation, namely to the matching of groups in terms of the predictive composite. The *present* use of the method involves one further feature, namely the use of a *double* criterion for the selection of each matching variable in the matching composite.

The use of the predictive composite for equating the Control to the Qualifying group

The matching (through re-weighting) strategy. The next step in the matching operation called for the use of the matching composite for the matching of the Control group to the Qualifying group.

The total sample is split into Qualifiers and Controls. Each of these is then separately split into the many different matching sub-groups as defined by the terminal groups in the matching composite (see figure 3.3). A typical outcome of such a process is shown in columns (2) and (3) of table 3.6.

A weighting system is now applied to the sub-groups in the Control sample with the sole purpose of equating the numbers in those sub-groups to their equivalent sub-groups in the Qualifying sample. This can be illustrated through table 3.6. Here there were 31 cases in sub-group 1 of the Control sample and only 28 cases in sub-group 1 of the Qualifying sample. Hence sub-group 1 is over-represented in the Control group. The mean score on the dependent variable for group 1 (i.e. 18.81) is therefore given the weight of 28. The same thing is done with respect to each of the other sub-groups in the matching system, as shown in table 3.6. The result of this sequence of re-weightings is that the Control group and the Qualifying group are made equivalent with regard to *their composition in terms of the matching sub-groups*. The matching process in its entirety can be seen in table 3.6: the effect of matching has been to raise the Control group average from 46.79 to 51.01, with a partial closing of the original gap between the Qualifiers and the Controls.

56.76 : 46.79 --------→ 51.01

Another way of describing this outcome is to say that the Modified Control group now (after matching) yields us an estimate of what the Controls *would* have 'scored' if they had been the same kind of people as the Qualifiers.

The number of matching operations completed on this system. The development of a matching composite and its application in a matching operation was called for with regard to *each* hypothesis in the grid shown in table 2.8 of chapter 2 – separately for both the forward and the reverse versions of each hypothesis. That grid would therefore entail 556 matching operations. This was a major enterprise and it called for a very considerable outlay in computer time and money.

The matching composite for each forward and each reverse hypothesis test, is shown in detail in the two technical appendices to this report. So are the matching operations based on those composites.

A preliminary comment on the meaningfulness of the findings yielded by the matching technique. Much can be said in appraising the adequacy of the research strategy used in this inquiry for investigating essentially *causal* hypotheses. I think it desirable that I set out here what I believe to be the major limitation of the system.

The central question in using any empirically derived matching system is 'to what extent is the matching complete?' If, for instance, a matching composite yielded a multiple

Table 3.6
Showing the matching of Controls to Qualifiers in terms of the matching composite. This example of the method relates to the forward version of hypothesis 1.

(1) Matching sub-groups	(2) Sub-group means for qualifiers†		(3) Sub-group means for controls†		(4) Weighting the controls (C) to the Qualifiers (Q)	
	No. of cases	Index	No. of cases	Index	Cases in Q group (f)	Means of C group (M)
1	28	23.68	31	18.81	28	18.81
2	22	30.59	25	27.92	22	27.92
3	23	39.78	13	43.77	23	43.77
4	9	15.67	28	14.18	9	14.18
5	9	38.22	21	23.71	9	23.71
6	9	41.00	23	50.26	9	50.26
7	28	60.14	29	44.31	28	44.31
8	29	35.10	32	18.72	29	18.72
9	19	42.26	13	27.31	19	27.31
10	14	13.14	23	24.52	14	24.52
11	13	54.31	21	48.33	13	48.33
12	18	33.83	34	20.76	18	20.76
13	15	38.53	15	54.47	15	54.47
14	29	62.55	26	43.96	29	43.96
15	10	23.70	24	27.12	10	27.12
16	23	44.00	25	52.56	23	52.56
17	20	38.10	16	26.69	20	26.69
18	21	39.86	18	57.50	21	57.50
19	12	90.00	18	50.72	12	50.72
20	21	56.81	13	35.08	21	35.08
21	22	92.41	34	69.65	22	69.65
22	26	51.08	29	30.69	26	30.69
23	28	54.61	17	45.59	28	45.59
24	23	65.43	16	91.00	23	91.00
25	26	58.65	22	55.41	26	55.41
26	28	75.36	35	62.89	28	62.89
27	20	50.35	13	40.69	20	40.69
28	20	82.70	11	48.27	20	48.27
29	32	62.31	24	47.75	32	47.75
30	26	52.73	19	58.00	26	58.00
31	33	75.33	30	77.43	33	77.43
32	31	52.32	22	54.14	31	54.14
33	22	60.05	17	60.53	22	60.53
34	19	89.84	14	131.86	19	131.85
35	35	91.74	21	72.14	35	72.14
36	19	124.42	11	125.73	19	125.73
Totals	782		783		782	
Means*		56.76		46.79		51.01 ††

†Qualifying group = those who have been exposed to a relatively large amount of television violence as defined by Independent variable.
Control group = those who have been exposed to relatively little television violence as defined by Independent variable.

*All scores are in terms of 'violence score' for last six months.

††Sub-group means were taken to 4 decimal places for computer calculation of the weighted mean.

correlation with the dependent variable of +0.70, we have to ask if this is really as far as we can or should go in securing matching power. After all, it would appear, with a multiple correlation of 0.70, to have left unexplained a large part of the variability of score on the dependent variable.

What variables, then, are missing? And what can we do about missing predictive elements? And how much does it matter that they are missing?

In the first place, there are some omissions from the predictive composite that we will ordinarily know about.

(a) Thus on the present method, we will have thrown out some predictive variables because they are not the source of any appreciable difference between the Qualifying and the Control groups (and because their rejection allows room for the introduction of predictors that *are* a source of such difference). Whereas this particular loss does not matter to the adequacy of the matching operation, we must ask in the present context if it involves any substantial reduction in overall predictive power? One of the interesting things about variables that are cast out in this way is that almost always they are overlapped quite substantially by the retained variables. That is one of the realities of multivariate prediction. However it may still be that some moderate amount of predictive power has been lost irretrievably in this way.

(b) Variables were also rejected where they were thought to be *unstable*. Ordinarily one would seek to replace these with their possible correlates, provided the latter are stable. Also, the overlap phenomenon should protect the system from any major loss. However, all in all, I would expect some moderate loss in predictive power to result from the loss of the 'unstables'. What is more important in this case is the possibility that the loss is biased in character – that the Qualifiers are different from the Controls in terms of the unstable element in the discarded predictive variables.

There are two other possible explanations of missing predictive power that call for comment.

(a) The first of these is that one or more major predictors have been omitted altogether from the pool – that is, variables whose predictive power is largely unrelated to that already accumulated within the composite. Strong as this argument may seem at the speculative level, experience is strongly against it. It is the researcher's experience that once one has a large and heterogeneous pool to choose from, the addition of even bizarre and 'way out' variables does not appreciably affect overall predictive power. This, in spite of 'brain storming' sessions to originate or discover new variables. There is a simple reason for such an outcome: variables overlap each other, some of them appreciably so, and it becomes increasingly difficult to find some largely *new* element as the predictive composite builds up. Such is the degree of overlap between variables that the discovery of one that is largely independent of a big and varied pool of them is very hard to conceive of. We must not rule out or take lightly the possibility of such a discovery, but the case against it is really quite considerable.

(b) There is one other explanation of 'missing predictive power' which I believe should be taken seriously. It is that the missing predictive power is distributed very widely – indeed scattered – among a wide range of variables that are specific to individuals or to very small groups: a fixation on knives on the part of one boy, produced by a traumatic experience in early childhood; a mother's absence for several months from the home; a hospital experience by a small boy; a psychopathic tendency on the part of a few; parental indoctrination about getting revenge for harm done to one; fear of the dark engendered by parents or siblings; father's imprisonment; and so on *by the thousand*. Together, they might account for no small part of the missing predictive power.

Unfortunately, one cannot, *on the present model*, [15] go on with more and more splits, that is, irrespective of how small the final sub-groups become. And even if one *could* do so, there would not be in the pool all those individual factors or variables that would be necessary for distinguishing between individuals.

All of this would matter but little if one could be sure that the Qualifying and the Control groups were closely similar in terms of such variables – i.e. that they were 'randomly distributed', as it were. But this we do not at present know and in my view it is both the weakness and the key issue for further research in the technology of matching. On this particular score, my overall impression, based on earlier analyses that have gone beyond the present cut-out system, is that we are here involved with up to twenty per cent additional coverage of score variability and that the predictive factors concerned are near-individual in character. Whether they are biased in their distribution between Qualifying and Control groups, we do not – but should – know.

Having said this, let me try to restore general balance in appraising the evidence that the technique can provide us with. We are concerned with the general tenability of the hypotheses under investigation – not with finally proving or disproving them. The matching technique used here is certainly capable of providing evidence which contributes strongly to an appraisal of hypothesis tenability.

A RESTATEMENT OF THE LOGIC OF THE INVESTIGATORY STRATEGY, WITH SPECIAL REFERENCE TO THE FORWARD AND THE REVERSE TESTS

Interpretation of the results of the forward and the reverse checks calls for a careful weighing of the evidence on the following general lines. (See pages 61-2 for an earlier statement of the same interpretative principles).

1 If the forward version of the hypothesis is not given meaningful [16] support by the evidence, then that forward version of the hypothesis may be regarded as being rendered *less* tenable by the evidence. This applies irrespective of the finding for the check on the hypothesis in its *reversed* form.

2 If *both* the forward and the reversed forms of the hypothesis are supported by the evidence to a meaningful [16] degree, then the forward version of the hypothesis may be regarded as being rendered more tenable by the evidence, though the possibility exists that this positive finding for the forward version of the hypothesis is supported, to some degree at least, by the working of the hypothesis in reverse. Where this type of finding emerges, it is also possible that: (a) there is in operation a circular process in which television violence leads to greater violence by boys, that when boys become more violent they elect to watch a greater amount of violent television, that this in turn makes them more violent,

and so on; (b) that for *some* boys the forward hypothesis is true and that for others the reverse hypothesis is true.

3 If the evidence gives meaningful [16] support to the forward version of the hypothesis but not the reverse form of the hypothesis, then that forward version of the hypothesis may be regarded as being rendered more tenable by the evidence – and there is very little possibility that the positive finding for the forward hypothesis is simply a reflection of the hypothesis being true in its reverse form. In this case the support given to the forward form of the hypothesis is appreciably firmer.

4 These three arguments apply equally to the tenability of the reversed form of the hypothesis.

The special character of the problem investigated through this enquiry does not allow us to conclude in terms of an hypothesis being proved or disproved. To do so would be scientifically improper. The problem is, after all, one of evaluating social cause and effect in the multi-determinant context of the ongoing social scene. I have already referred, in this chapter, to the technical problems and limiting factors principally involved. However, the research design used *does* allow us to reach conclusions in terms of the degree to which the evidence increases or decreases the tenability of an hypothesis or in terms of the extent to which an hypothesis gets support from the evidence. Furthermore, markedly increased tenability for an hypothesis, combined with no adverse indications, certainly could emerge from the research design used – and in fact this is the case for a principal hypothesis – and in that event it would be scientifically improper to reject such an hypothesis and socially irresponsible to give its implications anything less than careful attention.

Notes

[1] Belson, W.A. 'Matching and prediction on the principle of biological classification', *Applied Statistics*, vol.8 (2), 1959.
[2] Belson, W.A., *Juvenile Theft: the Causal Factors*, Harper and Row Ltd., London 1975.
[3] The term 'meaningful' is used here in a specialised way. It involves taking into consideration two elements of evidence: (a) the statistical significance of the difference between the means for the Qualifiers and the Modified Controls; (b) the numerical size of that difference expressed as a percentage of the mean of the Modified Controls and referred to in this report as the 'index of effect'.

For a residual difference between the means of Qualifiers and Modified Controls to be 'meaningful', it is necessary for that difference to be not only statistically significant, but to be of appreciable numerical size. The *degree* of 'meaningfulness' of a difference is a function of the *size* of that difference *and* the *level* of its statistical significance. Working details of the interpretative system involved are given in table 10.1 of chapter 10 and the outcome is expressed in terms of the degree to which the forward form of the hypothesis is supported by those two elements of the evidence.
[4] For the measure used as an index of this variable, see chapter 12.

[5] If the relationship between exposure to TV violence and involvement in violent behaviour is of a tightly straight-line kind, one could expect the challenging of the forward and the reversed forms of an hypothesis to yield similar results. But where that relationship is irregular or scattered, the outcome for those two forms of an hypothesis could be quite different. See chapter 12.

[6] See note [3]

[7] Though there can be exceptions, the usual result of matching in terms of an unstable variable is to reduce (in a misleading way) the evidence of any effect that the independent variable may have on the dependent variable.

[8] Belson, W.A., *Juvenile Stealing: Causal Factors*, Harper & Row Ltd., London 1975.

[9] The following classes of variables were amongst those considered as being more likely to be stable in relation to the independent variables:

(a) conditions that existed before the boy could become exposed to any appreciable amount of television violence;

(b) present physiological characteristics;

(c) past and present environments (i.e. locality, home conditions);

(d) facilities available for letting off steam (e.g. sporting facilities, proximity of swimming pool);

(e) abilities;

(f) aspects of personality, i.e. temperament;

(g) parental background in terms of a wide array of characteristics.

However, the question of probable stability must be considered for each question or variable in its own right.

[10] 'New' in the sense that in the forward forms of hypotheses they had been dependent variables, whereas in the reversed hypotheses they became the independent variables.

[11] See page 70 for methods of calculation.

[12] See chapter 12 for assessment of results with this variable excluded from the matching composite.

[13] Belson, W.A., 'Matching and prediction on the principle of biological classification', *Applied Statistics*, vol.8 (2), 1959.

[14] Morgan, J.N. and Sonquist, J.A. (1963), 'Problems in the analysis of survey data, and a proposal', *Journal of the American Statistical Association*, vol.58 (302); Sonquist, J.A. and Morgan, J.N. (1964), *The detection of interaction effects: a report on a computer program for the selection of optimal combinations of explanatory variables,* Ann Arbor, Michegan, University of Michegan.

[15] I said 'on the present model'. However, there is another way of thinking about the search for predictors in the present case. Strictly speaking, all we are doing in the current matching operation is equating one sample to another in terms of the variables which, *in this particular sample*, are predictive of the dependent variable and the independent variable. In particular, we are not seeking to generalise about any one of the associations found to exist in this sample – *only to operate on this particular sample in terms of its particular inner dynamics.* At this 'inner adjustment' level we would thus seem to be beyond the special demands of sampling theory as it applies to 'generalising to other samples'. We do, however, re-enter this issue of the validity of generalisation once we ask if the residual difference

between Qualifiers and Modified Controls would have been the same in some alternative sample.

In the present matching operation, I have *not* worked on the principles implied above, but have, for safety, worked to the conventional and accepted standards. The upshot of this is that no sub-groups have been split into anything smaller than 30-person groups (i.e. sub-groups consisting of both Qualifiers and Controls) and no predictors have been selected below the 0.05 level of significance.

[16] See note [3].

APPENDICES TO CHAPTER 3

Appendix 1	The items in the two pools of potential matching variables
Appendix 2	The application of the 'slimming run' to hypothesis 1, yielding estimates of the predictive power of each pool item in relation to 'total amount of violence' committed

The items in the two pools of potential matching variables

	Shortened version of items in pool of potential matching variables	(For Hypothesis 1 variables) Predictive power on‡	
		Dependent variable	Independent variable
1	Number of people in his household (boy)†	19.43	33.21
	Number of siblings living in his household (boy)	19.67	28.24
	Number of his brothers living in his household (boy)	17.76	26.72
	His birth order (boy)	9.42	23.90
	One or more grandparents present in household (boy)	2.03	4.46
	Either parent missing from household (boy)	3.77	6.56
	Lodger present in his household (boy)	5.09	4.47
	Landlord or landlady present in his household (boy)	2.04	0.50
	Mother or mother-substitute present in household (boy)	1.88	2.01
	Father or father-substitute present in household (boy)	0.53	4.54
	Number of bedrooms in his home (boy)	14.18	46.84
	How many homes has he lived in (boy)	33.91	17.68
	Is his lavatory or bathroom shared with any other family (boy)	5.33	2.97
	Does he have a bedroom to himself (boy)	2.78	9.29
	Is there a garden or play area at his home (boy)	20.44	12.04
	Do any of his relations live within one mile (boy)	20.82	8.24
	Is there a workshop in his home (boy)	1.51	4.66
	Is there a refrigerator in his home (boy)	1.22	5.98
	Is there a washing machine in his home (boy)	3.74	6.13
20	Is there a dishwasher in his home (boy)	6.62	19.47
	Is there a record player in his home (boy)	8.84	3.97
	Is there a sewing machine in his home (boy)	7.41	6.65
	Is there a telephone in his home (boy)	3.67	1.13
	Is there a bookcase in his home (boy)	0.98	1.88
	Is there a desk in his home (boy)	23.73	20.71
	Is there a family picture on wall in his home (boy)	20.79	17.86
	*In his district how many of the boys are fairly violent (boy)	64.96	
	Financial status of family (boy)	2.02	18.38
	Do/did parents usually talk over family problems (boy)	6.40	18.85
	Do/did parents share interests with each other (boy)	10.68	17.32
	How often do/did his parents go out together (boy)	45.47	14.24
	When little, how often teased or hurt (boy)	42.96	20.81
	*Were punishments from his parents usually fair/reasonable (boy)	7.70	
	When he was smaller did family usually have a Christmas tree (boy)	5.42	13.97
	Does he go away with family for holidays each year (boy)	7.66	16.72
	*When small, was his mother always at home after school (boy)	12.18	
	Is he shy (boy)	37.52	23.27
	Has he got a quick temper (boy)	40.87	11.75
	Does he often act first and think after (boy)	60.91	11.26
40	Has he got a steady girlfriend at present (boy)	36.10	15.11
	Are his close friends mostly older than him (boy)	16.37	5.87
	*Has he ever stolen sweets from a shop (boy)	86.64	
	*Has he ever stolen money (boy)	47.04	
	Does he do very well at anything (boy)	8.30	1.50
	Does he feel the cold very much (boy)	5.38	33.34
	Is he still at school (intensive int.) (boy)	3.78	29.56
	If he has left school, is he in a job (boy)	6.44	32.05
	If he has left school, what is his job (boy)	7.79	28.04
	If still at school, has he a spare-time job (boy)	39.65	55.22

	Shortened version of items in pool of potential matching variables	(For Hypothesis 1 variables) Predictive power on‡ Dependent variable	Independent variable
	*At school did anyone teach him to settle differences by discussion (boy)	31.33	
	*Do/did he enjoy being at school (boy)†	38.65	
	At school are/were there any subjects he especially enjoyed (boy)	0.47	4.96
	Is/was his school playground overcrowded (boy)	2.95	13.70
	At school is/was playground supervised by teacher (boy)	5.45	7.31
	*At school is/was his punishment usually fair (boy)	30.01	
	It is difficult to get out of what mates are doing (boy)	5.00	22.85
	*How often does he 'bunk off' from school (boy)	45.53	
	Are his hands or nails dirty (interviewer)	3.16	10.14
	He came to interview wearing a tie (interviewer)	43.89	28.91
60	Any of his clothes too large or too small for him (interviewer)	2.27	3.02
	Height to nearest centimetre	35.74	90.25
	Weight to nearest kilogram	26.98	93.23
	Grip strength – left hand (kilogram)	33.96	82.23
	Grip strength – right hand (kilogram)	34.28	85.24
	Grip strength – average of left and right (kilogram)	40.44	87.69
	Grip strength – difference between left and right hands (kilogram)	25.40	27.24
	Cranial circumference to nearest centimetre	14.09	49.70
	Chest measurement to nearest centimetre – expanded	26.70	72.70
	Chest measurement – difference between expanded and deflated (centimetres)	14.32	30.28
	His skin colour	14.17	15.45
	When under 4, how often did he laugh (mother)†	16.33	11.31
	When under 4, how often was he ill (mother)	10.30	10.88
	*When under 4, how often did he break toys or anything else (mother)	34.85	
	*When under 4, how often did he lose his temper (mother)	42.14	
	*When under 4, how often did he have tantrums (mother)	16.37	
	When under 4, how often did he cry for long periods (mother)	10.42	23.35
	When under 4, how often did he yell when hurt (mother)	16.78	25.72
	*When under 4, how often did he hurt animals or insects (mother)	5.24	
	When under 4, how often did he show off (mother)	24.56	8.94
80	When under 4, how often did he try to get attention (mother)	16.32	25.33
	When under 4, how often did he exaggerate (mother)	14.48	13.17
	After age 2, did he suck thumb or fingers (mother)	14.86	16.92
	When under 4, how often did he get bored (mother)	22.07	14.21
	*When under 4, was he calm (mother)	15.15	
	When under 4, was he shy (mother)	25.83	11.75
	When under 4, was he highly strung or nervous (mother)	18.81	33.82
	When under 4, was he sulky (mother)	8.38	22.90
	*When under 4, was he noisy (mother)	18.86	
	*When under 4, was he gentle (mother)	17.55	
	*When under 4, was he kind to others (mother)	11.88	
	When under 4, was he cheerful (mother)	6.15	14.81
	*When under 4, was he friendly towards strangers (mother)	15.66	
	When under 4, was he generous (mother)	11.97	6.77
	When under 4, was he jealous (mother)	9.87	30.31
	*When under 4, was he competitive (mother)	33.73	

	Shortened version of items in pool of potential matching variables	(For Hypothesis 1 variables) Predictive power on ǂ Dependent variable	Independent variable
	When under 4, was he determined (mother)	21.34	18.93
	*When under 4, was he bossy (mother)	19.40	
	*When under 4, was he tough (mother)	22.72	
	When under 4, was he cheeky (mother)	25.07	19.34
100	*When under 4, was he obedient (mother)	17.61	
	*When under 4, did he lash out if teased/angry (mother)	12.30	
	When under 4, was he shy about playing with other children (mother)	23.74	11.87
	When under 4, did he often lack confidence (mother)	28.53	20.79
	When under 4, was he keen on making things (mother)	3.96	4.49
	When under 4, was his mother in a job (mother)	10.47	15.12
	Was he a breast fed baby (mother)	1.17	2.99
	As a baby, was he fed according to a strict timetable (mother)	7.31	13.72
	When under 4, was he fed when he cried for/demanded food (mother)	2.62	15.18
	When under 4, how often did mother cuddle him (mother)	14.24	19.82
	When under 4, how often did parents read to him at bedtime (mother)	20.46	31.88
	When under 4, how often did mother have to tell him to eat food (mother)	18.46	16.72
	When under 4, how often did mother go to him if he cried (mother)	14.02	16.77
	When under 4, how often did mother pet/cuddle him when he cried (mother)	22.08	24.38
	When under 4, how often did mother get angry when he cried (mother)	26.60	12.38
	*When under 4, how often did mother ignore his tantrums (mother)	15.39	
	*When under 4, how often did mother punish his tantrums (mother)	6.29	
	*When under 4, how often did mother try to calm when lost temper (mother)	13.21	
	*When under 4, how often did mother give in when he rebelled (mother)	13.98	
	*When under 4, how often did mother get angry when lost temper (mother)	17.02	
120	*When under 4, how often did mother punish him when he rebelled (mother)	24.98	
	*When under 4, how often did mother ignore him when he rebelled (mother)	30.69	
	*When under 4, how often punished when violent/destructive (mother)	33.45	
	*When under 4, how often did mother punish him when misbehaved (mother)	17.02	
	When under 4, how often did mother reward him when good (mother)	8.11	26.34
	When under 4, was mother 'strict but loving' with him (mother)	18.00	14.24
	When under 4, did he get anyone up in the night (mother)	1.88	12.38
	When under 4, was there a lot of affection between him and mother (mother)	1.72	5.98
	When under 4, was there a lot of affection between him and his father (mother)	6.39	7.94

	Shortened version of items in pool of potential matching variables	(For Hypothesis 1 variables) Predictive power on‡ Dependent variable	Independent variable
	When under 4, was a lot of religious instruction given at home (mother)	10.63	8.12
	When under 4, was he taught to say prayers at night (mother)	13.62	21.28
	*When under 4, did mother teach him not to be violent (mother)	16.33	
	When under 4, did he go to nursery school or day nursery (mother)	13.18	15.86
	When under 4, was he taken regularly to place of worship (mother)	1.97	7.85
	Was he ever big for his age (mother)	4.49	18.19
	Was he ever a fat boy (mother)	0.32	12.59
	If under 15, has he reached puberty (mother)	23.40	93.19
	Over last year has he been frequently ill (mother)	3.55	2.02
	Has he had whooping cough (mother)	5.28	6.64
	Has he had chicken pox (mother)	8.58	7.40
140	Has he had mumps (mother)		
	Has he had scarlet fever (mother)	4.98	11.54
	Has he had diptheria (mother)	1.02	3.00
	Has he had measles (mother)	8.14	9.46
	Has he had glandular fever (mother)	4.21	5.52
	Has he had pneumonia (mother)	2.56	2.97
	Has he had tuberculosis (mother)	1.96	2.51
	Has he had tonsilitis (mother)	1.07	7.30
	Has he had bronchitis (mother)	3.33	19.63
	Has he had influenza (mother)	17.73	23.79
	Has he had rheumatic fever (mother)	1.43	0.49
	Has he had gastritis (mother)	5.85	3.87
	Has he had polio (mother)	1.05	1.00
	Number of illnesses he has had (mother)	24.14	21.84
	Was he often absent from school through illness (mother)	4.55	1.49
	Is he a generous boy (mother)	10.78	17.91
	When under 10, was he in hospital for a week or more (mother)	13.99	13.70
	If in hospital under 10, did mother visit him lots (mother)	20.18	15.70
	Mother's age (mother)	8.45	30.28
	Is his mother widowed/separated/divorced (mother)	8.60	10.55
160	If mother is widowed/divorced/separated, how long ago (mother)	7.64	11.04
	If father now missing, what was his job (mother)	6.79	7.53
	Occupation of his father (mother)	20.89	34.72
	Does father's job take him away from home a lot (mother)	4.87	9.46
	Does father do evening shift work (mother)	7.49	14.65
	How many jobs has father had since marriage (mother)	11.04	90.76
	Does his mother go out to a job (mother)	11.49	34.25
	How many years was mother in a job since marriage (mother)	23.69	28.70
	Difference between parents' ages (years) (mother)	8.49	23.22
	Terminal education age of his mother (mother)	28.08	44.70
	Terminal education age of his father (mother)	30.14	48.76
	Difference of 2 or more years between parents' terminal education ages	7.11	8.97
	Religion of his mother (mother)	8.06	25.83
	Religion of his father (mother)	21.78	30.84
	Do his parents share the same religion	3.71	9.60
	Country of birth of his mother (mother)	15.05	18.92

	Shortened version of items in pool of potential matching variables	(For Hypothesis 1 variables) Predictive power on‡ Dependent variable	Independent variable
	Country of birth of his father (mother)	18.19	21.91
	Street market within a quarter of a mile of his home (mother)	23.30	2.13
	Park or big playground within quarter mile of his home (mother)	6.39	2.95
	Number of siblings he has (mother)	18.15	23.19
180	One or more grandparents living in his household (mother)	5.65	1.95
	*When under 4, how often was he scolded (mother)	31.90	
	*When under 4, how often was he spanked or slapped (mother)	32.24	
	*When under 4, how often put in a room, not allowed to leave (mother)	27.46	
	*When under 4, how often punished being kept indoors (mother)	32.07	
	*When under 4, how often sent to bed without supper (mother)	27.46	
	*When under 4, how often was privilege removed as punishment (mother)	33.17	
	*When under 4, how often was he punished (mother)	29.93	
	*When under 4, how severely was he punished (mother)	31.06	
	*When under 4, did he ever have to be physically restrained (mother)	27.99	
	Age at interview (years)	39.07	94.30
	Country of birth of boy (boy)	8.47	16.46
	Is he still at school (home completion) (boy)	4.81	28.55
	If he has left school, at what age was this (boy)	7.11	30.05
	Number of schools attended since age 5 (boy)	16.52	21.95
	His religion (boy)	9.10	36.32
	*At what age was he away from family for over 2 months (boy)	6.48	
	Size of his school class (boy)	20.10	21.85
	Left or right handed (boy)	5.33	5.57
	Level of school last attended (boy)	17.63	41.42
200	Can/could special projects be done at his school (boy)	5.91	4.49
	Has he ever been in a school sports team (boy)	32.36	35.36
	*Is/was discipline tough at any of his schools (boy)	2.77	
	Can football be played at his school (boy)	10.99	6.46
	Can rugby be played at his school (boy)	2.60	3.65
	Can gym be played at his school (boy)	11.11	4.04
	Can athletics be played at his school (boy)	2.53	9.96
	Can boxing be played at his school (boy)	2.53	9.60
	Can fencing be played at his school (boy)	5.75	6.63
	Can judo be played at his school (boy)	11.97	11.16
	Can cricket be played at his school (boy)	10.04	5.46
	How many sports can be played at his school (boy)	18.02	21.79
	Does he run faster or slower than other boys (boy)	11.34	11.94
	How far can he swim (boy)	39.29	21.93
	Does he shave yet (boy)	15.02	66.12
	How would he describe his health (boy)	4.21	20.43
	Colour of hair (boy)	12.96	10.89
	Are most of his friends older or younger (boy)	9.93	18.97
	Proportion of coloured people in his neighbourhood	22.44	29.74
	Economic level of his street	24.00	34.73
220	Was he keen to take part in placement interview	5.76	2.48

Shortened version of items in proof of potential matching variables	(For Hypothesis 1 variables) Predictive power on‡ Dependent variable	Independent variable
Was he keen to come to intensive interview	6.69	4.49
Was parent keen to take part in placement interview	3.74	6.57
Was parent keen to have boy come to intensive interview	4.74	3.01
Placement interviewer	36.31	34.24
Intensive interviewer	53.46	20.25
District of residence	34.73	45.75
Date of intensive interview (week number)	39.11	31.17
**Is there something interesting if he brings friends home (boy)		2.00
**Does he ever laugh at himself (boy)		37.86
**Does he laugh a lot (boy)		27.39
**Does he often get the miseries (boy)		16.32
**Has he got a lot of close friends (boy)		5.51
**Does he smoke at all (boy)		25.62
**Did he often play in streets when younger (boy)		36.27
**How many evenings does family eat together (boy)		28.87
**Does he bite his nails		4.14
**Was he ever a bed wetter after age six (mother)		2.50
**Does he have similar interests to those of his parents (mother)		14.22
**When under 4, did mother say 'Go outside and play' (mother)		18.88
**When under 4, did mother say 'Go and meet your friends' (mother)		20.39
**How many evenings does he have homework set (boy)		29.83
**How tired does he feel after school/work (boy)		24.74
**How often does he bite his nails (boy)		13.83
**Does he belong to a youth club (boy)		10.63
**Has he ever taken first aid lessons (boy)		21.14
**How often does he buy records (boy)		48.25
**Does he own any pets (boy)		4.21

‡See page 70 for calculation of this index.
†(boy) = questions asked of the boy himself
†(mother) = questions asked of the boy's mother
*in the Forward pool only . . .
**in Reverse pool only

The application of the 'slimming run' to hypothesis 1, yielding estimates of the predictive power of each pool item in relation to 'total amount of violence' committed

Item No.	Pool items	Displacement on dependent variable*
(a) The best 100 predictors		
42	Has he ever stolen sweets from a shop (according to boy)	86.64
27	In his district how many of the boys are fairly violent (acc. boy)	64.96
39	Does he often act first and think after (acc. boy)	60.91
225	Intensive interviewer	53.46
43	Has he ever stolen money (acc. boy)	47.04
57	How often does he 'bunk off' from school (acc. boy)	45.53
31	How often do/did his parents go out together (acc. boy)	45.47
59	He came to interview wearing a tie	43.89
32	When little how often teased or hurt (acc. boy)	42.96
74	When under 4, how often did he lose his temper (mother)	42.14
38	Has he got a quick temper (acc. boy)	40.87
65	Grip strength – average of left and right (kilograms)	40.44
49	If still at school, has he a spare-time job (acc. boy)	39.65
213	How far can he swim (acc. boy)	39.29
227	Date of intensive interview (week number)	39.11
190	Age at interview (years)	39.07
51	Do/did he enjoy being at school (acc. boy)	38.65
37	Is he shy (acc. boy)	37.52
224	Placement interviewer	36.31
40	Has he got a steady girlfriend at present (acc. boy)	36.10
61	Height to nearest centimetre	35.74
73	When under 4, how often did he break toys or anything else (mother)	34.85
226	District of residence	34.73
64	Grip strength – right hand (kilograms)	34.28
63	Grip strength – left hand (kilograms)	33.96
12	How many homes has he lived in (acc. boy)	33.91
95	When under 4, was he competitive (mother)	33.73
122	When under 4, how often punished when violent/destructive (mother)	33.45
186	When under 4, how often was privilege removed as punishment (mother)	33.17
201	Has he ever been in a school sports team (acc. boy)	32.36
182	When under 4, how often was he spanked or slapped (mother)	32.24
184	When under 4, how often punished by being kept indoors (mother)	32.07
181	When under 4, how often was he scolded (mother)	31.90
50	At school did anyone teach him to settle differences by discussion (acc. boy)	31.33
188	When under 4, how severely was he punished (mother)	31.06
121	When under 4, how often did mother ignore him when he rebelled (mother)	30.69
170	Terminal education age of his father (mother)	30.14
55	At school is/was his punishment usually fair (acc. boy)	30.01
187	When under 4, how often was he punished (mother)	29.93
103	When under 4, did he often lack confidence (mother)	28.53
169	Terminal education age of his mother (mother)	28.08
189	When under 4, did he ever have to be physically restrained (mother)	27.99
98	When under 4, was he tough (mother)	27.72
183	When under 4, how often put in a room, not allowed to leave (mother)	27.46
185	When under 4, how often sent to bed without supper (mother)	27.40
62	Weight to nearest kilogram	26.98
68	Chest measurement to nearest centimetre – expanded	26.70
114	When under 4, how often did mother get angry when he cried (mother)	26.60

Item No.	Pool items	Displacement on dependent variable*
85	When under 4, was he shy (mother)	25.83
66	Grip strength – difference between left and right hands (kilograms)	25.40
99	When under 4, was he cheeky (mother)	25.07
120	When under 4, how often did mother punish him when he rebelled (mother)	24.98
79	When under 4, how often did he show off (mother)	24.56
153	Number of illnesses he has had (mother)	24.14
219	Economic level of his street	24.00
102	When under 4, was he shy about playing with other children (mother)	23.74
25	Is there a desk in his home (acc. boy)	23.73
167	How many years was mother in a job since marriage (mother)	23.69
136	If under 15, has he reached puberty (mother)	23.40
177	Street market within a quarter mile of his home (mother)	23.30
218	Proportion of coloured people in his neighbourhood	22.44
113	When under 4, how often did mother pet/cuddle him when he cried (mother)	22.08
83	When under 4, how often did he get bored (mother)	22.07
173	Religion of his father (mother)	21.78
96	When under 4, was he determined (mother)	21.34
162	Occupation of his father (mother)	20.89
16	Do any of his relations live within one mile (acc. boy)	20.82
26	Is there a family picture on wall in his home (acc. boy)	20.79
110	When under 4, how often did parents read to him at bedtime (mother)	20.46
15	Is there a garden or play area at his home (acc. boy)	20.44
157	If in hospital under 10, did mother visit him lots (mother)	20.18
197	Size of his school class (acc. boy)	20.10
2	Number of his siblings living in his household (acc. boy)	19.76
1	Number of people in his household (acc. boy)	19.43
97	When under 4, was he bossy (mother)	19.40
88	When under 4, was he noisy (mother)	18.86
86	When under 4, was he highly strung or nervous (mother)	18.81
111	When under 4, how often did mother have to tell him to eat food (mother)	18.46
176	Country of birth of his father (mother)	18.19
179	Number of siblings he has (mother)	18.15
211	How many sports can be played at his school (acc. boy)	18.02
125	When under 4, was mother 'strict but loving' with him (mother)	18.00
3	Number of his brothers living in his household (acc. boy)	17.76
149	Has he had influenza (mother)	17.73
199	Level of school last attended (acc. boy)	17.63
100	When under 4, was he obedient (mother)	17.61
89	When under 4, was he gentle (mother)	17.55
119	When under 4, how often did mother get angry when lost temper (mother)	17.02
123	When under 4, how often did mother punish him when misbehaved (mother)	17.02
77	When under 4, how often did he yell when hurt (mother)	16.78
194	Number of schools attended since age 5 (acc. boy)	16.52
41	Are his close friends mostly older than him (acc. boy)	16.37
75	When under 4, how often did he have tantrums (mother)	16.37
131	When under 4, did mother teach him not to be violent (mother)	16.33
71	When under 4, how often did he laugh (mother)	16.33
80	When under 4, how often did he try to get attention (mother)	16.32
92	When under 4, was he friendly towards strangers (mother)	15.66

Item No.	Pool items	Displacement on dependent variable*
115	When under 4, how often did mother ignore his tantrums (mother)	15.39
84	When under 4, was he calm (mother)	15.15
175	Country of birth of his mother (mother)	15.05

*These figures do not indicate whether the correlation between a pool item and violent behaviour is positive or negative – they indicate only the strength of the correlation.

(b) The remaining 127 variables tried out as predictors

For the remaining 127 pool items, only the number of the item and its predictive power are given. The reader will be able to identify the numbered items by referring to the full list of items in the final pool as given in Appendix 1 of this chapter.

Item No.	Predictive power	Item No.	Predictive power	Item No.	Predictive power	Item No.	Predictive power
214	15.02	94	9.87	151	5.85	14	2.78
82	14.86	4	9.42	139	5.85	202	2.77
81	14.48	195	9.10	220	5.76	108	2.62
69	14.32	21	8.84	208	5.75	204	2.60
109	14.24	159	8.60	180	5.65	145	2.56
11	14.18	168	8.49	54	5.45	206	2.53
70	14.17	191	8.47	34	5.42	207	2.53
67	14.09	158	8.45	45	5.38	60	2.27
112	14.02	87	8.38	13	5.33	8	2.04
156	13.99	44	8.30	198	5.33	5	2.03
118	13.98	143	8.14	138	5.28	28	2.02
130	13.62	124	8.11	78	5.24	133	1.97
117	13.21	172	8.06	7	5.09	146	1.96
132	13.18	48	7.79	56	5.00	126	1.88
216	12.96	33	7.70	141	4.98	9	1.88
101	12.30	35	7.66	163	4.87	127	1.72
36	12.18	160	7.64	192	4.81	140	1.62
209	11.97	164	7.49	223	4.74	17	1.51
93	11.97	22	7.41	154	4.55	150	1.43
90	11.88	107	7.31	134	4.49	18	1.22
166	11.49	193	7.11	215	4.21	106	1.17
212	11.34	171	7.11	144	4.21	147	1.07
205	11.11	161	6.79	104	3.96	152	1.05
165	11.04	221	6.69	46	3.78	142	1.02
203	10.99	20	6.62	6	3.77	24	0.98
155	10.78	196	6.48	222	3.74	10	0.53
30	10.68	47	6.44	19	3.74	52	0.47
129	10.63	29	6.40	174	3.71	135	0.32
105	10.47	128	6.39	23	3.67		
76	10.42	178	6.39	137	3.55		
72	10.30	116	6.29	148	3.33		
210	10.04	91	6.15	58	3.16		
217	9.93	200	5.91	53	2.95		

CHAPTER 4

THE CONSTRUCTION OF A TECHNIQUE FOR MEASURING THE EXTENT AND NATURE OF BOYS' EXPOSURE TO TELEVISION VIOLENCE

Contents

4 THE CONSTRUCTION OF A TECHNIQUE FOR MEASURING THE EXTENT AND NATURE OF BOYS' EXPOSURE TO TELEVISION VIOLENCE

INTRODUCTION

Every one of the 22 hypotheses had a primary form and at least one subsidiary form. In the primary form of the hypothesis, the independent variable was always:

- total amount of exposure to television violence (irrespective of *type* of violence)

But in the secondary form of the hypothesis, the independent variable was always amount of exposure to some particular form of television violence, for example

- fictional violence of a realistic kind,
- violence presented in a good cause,
- violence of a verbal kind.

For all 22 hypotheses taken together, a total of 25 [1] types of television violence was involved (as subsidiary independent variables), along with 'violence in general' (as the primary independent variable), and all 26 are enumerated in list 4.1. In terms of a measuring tool, therefore, what was required was a technique that would assess the extent of a boy's exposure to each and every one of these 26 categories of violence. In this chapter is presented a description of the development of such a technique.

THE BASIC PRINCIPLES OF THE TECHNIQUE

One possible approach to this task might have been to attempt long-term record-keeping of the viewing behaviour of a sample of boys. However, this was out of the question in the present enquiry. In the first place it was intended that the enquiry should be based upon a boy's whole lifetime of viewing — and record-keeping could hardly be maintained over that period for each of the large sample of boys to be included in the enquiry. Secondly, it was essential that the viewing should be entirely natural — as would hardly be the case if the boy's viewing had been under observation all the time. *The technique had in fact to be one resting upon a carefully developed form of aided recall.* This and other requirements of the situation automatically influenced the necessary form of the measuring procedure. Thus:

1 The *aiding* of recall, absolutely essential in this case, automatically put a limit on the number of programmes for which adequate memory aids could be developed and administered. At the same time, those programmes would have to be sufficient in number and in kind to be properly representative of each boy's viewing of violence.

List 4.1
The dependent and independent variables in their final form*

Independent variables

1 High exposure to violence on television generally
2 High exposure to programmes containing fictional violence of a realistic kind
3 High exposure to programmes where violence is performed by basically 'good-guy' types who are also 'rebels' or 'odd-men out'
4 High exposure to programmes in which much of the violence occurs in a domestic or family setting
5 High exposure to programmes which feature defiance of, or rudeness toward authority figures
6 High exposure to programmes where violence is shown as glorified, romanticised, idealised or ennobling
7 High exposure to programmes where violence is presented as 'fun and games' or like a game or as something to entertain
8 High exposure to programmes in which the violence is presented as being in a good cause
9 High exposure to programmes where the physical or mental consequences of violence, for the victim, are shown in detail
10 High exposure to programmes where the violence is related to racial or minority group strife
11 High exposure to programmes where the violence is performed by basically 'good-guy' types or heroes who are also tough (i.e. who can endure physical violence and fight on)
12 High exposure to programmes where the violence is of a verbal kind
13 High exposure to programmes in which the violence is just thrown in for its own sake, or is not necessary to the plot
14 High exposure to programmes in which the violence is gruesome, horrific or scary

(Dichotomous items)

15 High exposure to fictional programmes about the English police at work which also feature the kinds of violence which go on in society
16 High exposure to a selection of 5 cartoon programmes in which the characters are violent to each other (i.e. Boss Cat, Popeye, Pugwash, Yogi Bear, Tom and Jerry)
17 High exposure to Tom and Jerry
18 High exposure to plays or films in which personal relationships are a major theme, and which feature verbal abuse (e.g. swearing, quarrelling) or physical violence
19 High exposure to violence through the news or newsreel programmes
20 High exposure to comedy programmes which feature 'slapstick' violence and/or verbal abuse between characters
21 Science fiction programmes involving violence (e.g. where creatures destroy people, where humans use super weapons to destroy men)
22 High exposure to 'Westerns' which include violence, for example, as between cowboys and Indians
23 High exposure to a selection of 3 sporting programmes which present violence by competitors or spectators (i.e. Sports View, Grandstand, Saturday Sports Time)
24 High exposure to wrestling and boxing
25 High exposure to films or series which feature gangs or gangsters engaged in violent organised crime
26 High exposure to programmes in which the violence is performed by adults
27 High exposure to television generally
28 High exposure to violent comic books
29 High exposure to violent films
30 High exposure to newspapers

Dependent variables

1 Violent behaviour, weighted total of all acts from Level 1 to Level 6
2 Violent behaviour, all-in total, no weighting
3 Violent behaviour, total of L2, L3, L4, L5, L6 entries
4 Violent behaviour, total of L4, L5, L6 entries
5 Violent behaviour, in company of other boys
6 Violent behaviour, in form of being irritating, argumentative, annoying to others
7 Violent behaviour, in form of aggressive behaviour in sport or play
8 Use of bad language/swearing
9 Preoccupation with different forms of violence on television
10 Feels like committing different forms of violence shown on television
11 Willingness to use forms of violence presented on television
12 Degree to which boy find violence attractive
13 Degree of consideration for other people
14 Degree of respect for authority
15 Degree of anxiety, nervousness, emotional instability
16 Extent of angry and bitter feelings
17 Sleep disturbance
18 Acceptance of near violence
19 Acceptance of distant violence
20 Degree of objection to violence in world generally
21 See violence as inevitable
22 Degree of acceptance of violence as way to solve problems

*In final form at the end of the construction of measuring techniques

2 The required measure of exposure would have to be standardised in the sense that it would have to yield strictly comparable assessments, from boy to boy, in terms of exposure to television violence in general and in terms of the many different kinds of television violence.

It was against this background that the approach decided upon was given the following basic features.

1 A large and broadly representative sample would be drawn of the violent programmes available to London boys within their lifetime.

2 Each of these programmes would be rated by a large number of judges in terms of (i) the degree to which it was violent (irrespective of what sort of violence was involved); (ii) the degree to which the violence it presented was of one or another *kind* [2], for example, fictional violence of the realistic kind, violence performed by a good guy, Western type violence, cartoon type violence, violence when its consequences are shown in detail, and so on for each of the types of violence featured in the secondary forms of the 22 hypotheses. Initially there were 30 of these *types* of violence, as shown on pages 105-6 but this total was reduced to 25 in the course of technique development.

3 As a result of such a rating operation, it would be possible, using empirical methods, to develop *up to* 26 ratings for any of the sampled programmes, one for general level of violence (irrespective of *type* of violence) and one for each of the 25 subsidiary forms of violence included in the complex of hypotheses. As an example, let us imagine the following set of ratings, each of them relating to a scale running from 0-10.

Table 4.1

Programme	How violent is it? (= amount of violence) *	What kind of violence is it?			
		Fictional violence of the realistic kind †	The glorified kind of violence †	Where the consequences are shown in detail †	25 dimensions in all
(1)	4.1	8.3	3.1	3.2	
(2)	3.4	4.7	2.1	5.2	
(3)	7.3	8.8	6.6	0.5	
(4)	3.1	0.8	3.5	3.1	
(50)	8.2	0.4	4.2	1.1	

*Irrespective of type of violence
†See page 94 for list of the dimensions of violence featured in the enquiry

For programme (1): a single viewing experience will contribute 4.1 units of exposure to violence in general 4.10

8.3/10.0 of its 4.1 units of violence is of the realistic fictional kind, so that a single viewing of this programme will contribute 0.83 x 4.1 units of violence of the realistic/fictional kind to the viewer's exposure experience 3.40

3.1/10.0 of its 4.1 units of violence is of the *glorified* kind, so that a single viewing of this programme will contribute evidence of 0.31 x 4.1 units of violence of the glorified kind to the viewer's exposure experience 1.27

3.2/10.0 of its 4.1 units of violence is of the kind where the consequences of violence are shown in detail, so that a single viewing of this programme would contribute evidence of 0.32 x 4.1 units of violence of the 'consequences shown' kind to the viewer's exposure experience 1.31

Each programme in the final list is dealt with in this way, thereby yielding a grid of weights of the kind shown in table 4.2.

Table 4.2

The programme (series)	How violent is it?	How many units of violence of the specified kind will accrue from each exposure to the programme			
		Fictional violence of the realistic kind	The glorified kind of violence	Where the consequences are shown in detail	25 dimensions in all
(1)	4.1	3.40	1.27	1.31	
(2)	3.4	1.60	0.71	1.77	
(3)	7.3	6.42	4.82	0.37	
(4)	3.1	0.25	1.09	0.96	
(50)	8.2	0.33	3.44	0.90	

4 From such data it becomes possible to derive aggregate indices of exposure to television violence of the 26 different kinds being investigated. For instance, suppose there were 50 programme series in the rated sample and that we knew how many times in a given period a specific boy had viewed those different programmes. Then we could, for example, calculate an index of aggregate exposure (a) to television violence considered generally and (b) to fictional violence of the realistic kind, in the following way.

(a) *For exposure to violence considered generally*

Table 4.3

Programme series (50 in all)	How often seen (f)	Violence rating (v)	Product (fv)
(1)	20	4.1	82.0
(2)	0	3.4	00.0
(3)	3	7.3	21.9
(4)	1	3.1	3.1
(50)	7	8.2	57.4
All			f.v

For this boy, the index of aggregate exposure to television violence (considered generally) = Σ f.v.

(b) *For exposure to realistic fictional violence*

Table 4.4

Programme series (50 in all)	How often seen (f)	Programme rating for amount of fictional violence of the realistic kind (v)	Product (fv)
(1)	20	3.40	68.00
(2)	0	1.60	0.00
(3)	3	6.42	19.26
(4)	1	0.25	0.25
(50)	7	0.33	2.31
All			Σf.v.

(c) *For exposure to other forms of television violence*

The same multiplication and adding process would be used for developing aggregate scores for a boy in each of the other programme dimensions.

5 For any one of the 31 dimensions here involved, it would thus be possible to give each respondent an overall exposure score and hence to compare boys on the dimensions concerned. They are of course always compared *within* a single dimension and never *between* dimensions.

A single sample of programmes could in this way be made to yield scores for each of the 31 exposure variables for which measures were required. The development of such a procedure, simple enough in concept, was expected to be – and was – extremely demanding and tedious. The several steps in its development are set out in this chapter.

THE DIFFERENT STAGES OF DEVELOPMENT OF THE TECHNIQUE

In the account that follows, the construction and use of the procedure are dealt with under the following headings:

A developing a large and broadly representative sample of television programmes that present violence;

B having the sample of programmes rated for degree and type of violence involved in them;

C selecting the final composite of programmes to be used in the measurement system;

D deriving basic exposure scores;

E the control system.

A: DEVELOPING A LARGE AND BROADLY REPRESENTATIVE SAMPLE OF TELEVISION PROGRAMMES THAT PRESENT VIOLENCE

This part of the developmental work called (i) for the setting-up of something approximating to a 'universe' of violent programmes presented by the BBC and the ITA services in the period 1958-1971; (ii) the drawing from these of a sample of violent programmes.

Setting-up a near universe of programmes presenting violence

For each year in the period 1958-1969 [3], a study was made of the programmes listed in the TV Times and the Radio Times [4] for a single week in each of six different months [5] Separately for BBC and ITA, a list was made up of all the *possibly violent programmes* broadcast in the periods examined for that year. From 1965, the BBC programme list included possibly violent programmes shown on BBC 2. For the years 1958-1960, programmes shown after 9.00 pm were not included because even the older boys to be interviewed in 1972 would have been very young in the period 1958-1960.

This process led to the listing of approximately 100 BBC and 100 ITA programmes per year throughout the period 1958-1969. For each of these programmes, a record was made of *time of showing*, of *subject matter* and of its *duration over time.*

Drawing a sample of possibly violent programmes

Stratified random sampling methods were used to select from the list for each year a total of 9 BBC programmes (including one or two BBC 2 programmes as indicated above) and a total of 9 ITA programmes, in each case with a control over size of audience to ensure that the selection was representative in that respect. BBC programmes from 1965 and 1966 would include one 'BBC 2' programme and from 1967, two 'BBC 2' programmes. The selection procedure was as follows. For *all the BBC 1 programmes* in the list for a given year, the programmes were set out in order according to size of audience [6], with low percentages at the top of the list and large percentages at the bottom of it, on the following pattern.

Table 4.5

	Programme name	Audience size %	Cumulative %
1	Spotlight	1	1
2	'To be or not to be'	1	2
3	Pepe Moreno	1	3
4	The Thin Man	1	4
5	The Machine Breakers	2	6
6	The Silver Sword	2	8
44	Steve Allen Show	8	226
45	'Stranger Left no Card'	9	235
46	The Sky Larks	9	244
70	'Tonight'	20	566
71	Hancock's Half Hour	22	588
72	Dixon of Dock Green	22	610
77	FA Cup Final	46	755

The total of the percentages was progressively made out and entered to the right of the audience percentage figures. The overall total was divided by 8 for years 1965 and 1966 (allowing for the addition of one BBC 2 programme yet to be selected), and by 7 for 1967 onwards (allowing for two BBC 2 programmes yet to be selected) to derive sampling intervals and to allow the total list to be cut into 7/8 equal sections according to the cumulative percentage figures. Within the first of these 7/8 sections, a random number was used to identify the first programme to be chosen and thereafter 6/7 more, separated by the sampling interval.

For BBC 2 programmes, the 'universe' was listed separately (for each year) and random methods were used to draw one from each of the 1965 and 1966 lists and two from each of the lists for the other years.

The total number of BBC programmes (of the possibly violent kind) drawn for each year was thus 9.

For ITA [7] programmes, the same selection principles (as illustrated through table 4.5 and the paragraph immediately following it) were used to draw 9 (possibly violent) programmes per year.

In activating this pattern of selection, the different years were dealt with in random order. Whenever a programme was selected that had already been drawn for another year, it was substituted for by drawing in its stead the programme nearest to it in the cumulative frequency list. [8] The reason for dealing with years in random order was to avoid a situation where the, say, 1958 selection of programmes tended to have in it most of the long-running programmes and the, say, 1969 selection had in it most of the short-running programmes.

The list of 'possibly violent programmes' selected in this way thus numbered 9 x 2 x 12 (= 216) programmes. Eight of the 216 were rejected on the grounds that:

(a) the total list included too many 'one-off' (single) programmes;

(b) some of the programmes in the list were closely similar.

The remaining 208 programmes were now ready for the proposed rating operation referred to on page 95 and described in detail later in this chapter. However, before it was appropriate to do this, two other steps had to be taken, namely:

(i) a small sample of seemingly non-violent programmes had to be drawn with a view to dealing with them in the same rating process as the possibly violent programmes;

(ii) the 1970-71 programmes had also to be sampled for the selection of programmes to be included in the rating operation.

The first of these extra steps is described hereunder and the other in the section called 'Constructing an illustrated scale for rating programmes'. The full list of 231 programmes of 1958-1969 origin is given in Appendix 1 to this chapter.

Sampling non-violent programmes

It had initially been intended that a small sample of non-violent programmes be included in the proposed rating operation for what might broadly be called 'control' purposes. Thus it was thought that (i) their presence in the large pool of 'possibly violent programmes' would allow raters to use *all* parts of the rating scales on which they would be grading programmes for degree or type of violence (the zero positions in particular); (ii) they would give greater variability to the total list of programmes being rated; (iii) they might be used as control material in the sense of providing for a test of an hypothesis that being exposed to a *lot* of non-violent programme material affected violent behaviour in much the same way as being exposed to a lot of violent programme material. [9]

The non-violent programmes drawn *at this particular stage* were selected in two steps. In the first step a list was compiled of seemingly non-violent programmes. This list, which included quiz shows, pop music, religious programmes, consisted of 15-20 programmes for each of the years 1958-1969 and was equally split between BBC and ITA output. From each BBC list for each year, one programme was drawn at random. Similarly for the ITA programmes. The total of the non-violent programmes selected in this way was 23 (after the exclusion of one programme as unsuitable for this purpose), and these are identified in the total list of 231 programmes in Appendix 1 at the end of this chapter.

B: HAVING JUDGES RATE THE SAMPLED PROGRAMMES FOR EXTENT AND NATURE OF THE VIOLENCE PRESENT IN THEM

The rating of the sampled programmes was planned to go ahead in two stages. The *first* stage would involve the construction of 31 [10] specialised rating scales. These included one scale for grading programmes in terms of *how* violent they are; one for grading them in terms of the degree to which their violence was of the realistic fiction kind; one for grading programmes in terms of whether they present violence in the context of Westerns; and so on, as indicated on pages 105 and 106 of this chapter. In the second stage, each of the 231 programmes in the 1958-1969 samples was to be graded on each of the 31 specialised rating scales. This arrangement does, of course, fit into the measurement strategy outlined at the beginning of this chapter: thus if we had details of a boy's viewing of fifty or so programmes which had been graded in this way, we would be able to calculate for the boy a weighted score for each of the 31 independent variables (i.e. type of violence to which boys are exposed). Each of these two stages was very important in the development of the measuring procedure and they are dealt with separately hereunder.

Stage I: Constructing the specialised (or 'illustrated') rating scales

It would have been a simple matter to have set up numerical rating scales, of the kind shown in diagram 4.1, for the rating process.

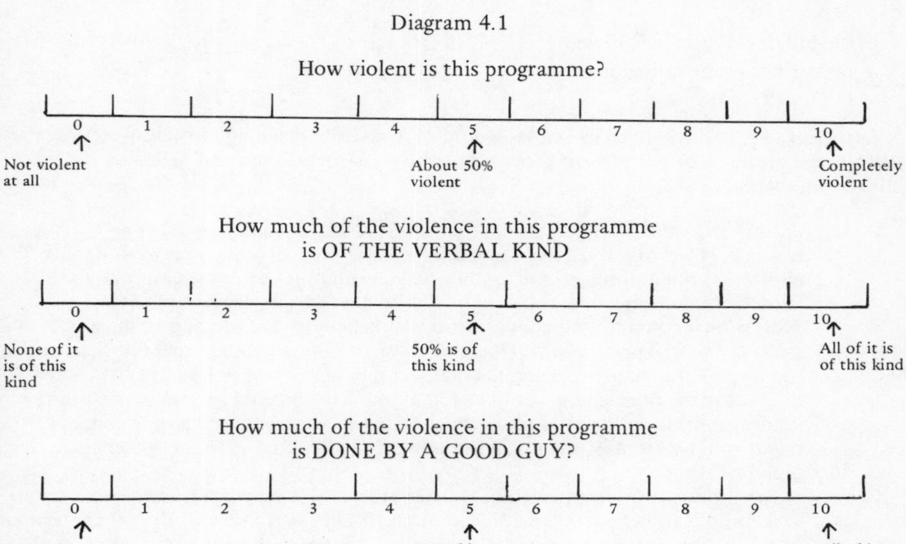

The weakness of this system, however, is that it gives the rater too little guidance in an operation which he is almost certain to find unusual and vague. It is common experience among research technologists that in rating operations of this general kind (i) the one individual may on different occasions place the one item at significantly different points on the scale, the scale sectors being less than meaningful in their own right; (ii) the ratings of a single term or concept or thing on a purely numerical scale of the kind shown above can vary considerably in going from one rater to another.

For a reliable and discriminating rating system, each of the scalar sections has to be given fairly specific meaning, either through some verbal description or through *carefully developed* examples of the kinds of things that should be placed or graded within them. In the present case, it would have been extremely difficult – probably impossible – to derive, for each scale, another nine descriptive terms equally spaced along the scale. Nor did it seem that this approach, even if possible, would be as effective as the placement in each scalar section, *as examples*, of programmes featuring the degree of violence *appropriate to* that particular scalar sector.

The stipulation 'appropriate' is of course the key requirement in this approach and it was met by drawing on the combined judgements of a panel of 30 teachers with extensive viewing experience. The methods used to do this, and the results of it, are set out under the headings:—

- the number and origin of the teachers in the panel;
- the programmes to be judged as potential examples for placement on the (illustrated) scale;
- the judging or grading process;
- the results of the rating process;
- the illustrated scales.

In the sense that the derived examples would illustrate the meaning of the different scalar sectors, the products of the present process of scale construction were to be called 'illustrated scales'.

1 *The number and origin of the teachers in the panel*

It was decided to use *teachers* as judges. There were two main reasons for this choice: (i) the judgement and grading tasks would inevitably be complex so that people of good intellectual ability would be needed; (ii) because of their professional contact with children and young people, the teachers' concepts of violence were expected to be closer to those of young people generally than might be the case for some other intellectually competent set of judges; (iii) it seemed likely that many teachers would at some time have taken a special interest in the kinds of television material to which their pupils were exposed and in this case might well be usefully analytical in their appraisals of programme materials in the present case.

Advertisements were placed in teacher journals for teachers to serve on a (paid) Television Rating Panel, and a selection of 30 [11] was made from 200 applicants. The selection criteria were: (i) residence in London or the Home Counties area; (ii) availability for the rating assignment during a specified two-week period; (iii) a minimum viewing time of 7 hours a week and regular viewing on both the BBC and ITA channels; (iv) familiarity with at least 14 out of 28 well known current television programmes. The judges had to do their grading and rating work entirely at the Survey Research Centre and under continuing supervision and instruction. [12]

2 *The programmes to be judged or graded as potential examples for placement in the illustrated scale*

It was important that the derivation of examples with which to illustrate scales should be free from any unnecessary sources of error. It was for this reason that the programmes to be considered for selection were all of fairly recent origin – 1970 and 1971 in fact; it would have served no good purpose at all to work with programmes broadcast so long ago that the judges were somewhat hazy about them. Nor would an illustrated scale made up of half forgotten programmes have been of much use as a rating system.

The selection of 1970-1971 programmes for use in this way was made as follows:

(a) The selection process began with the listing of (i) all 1970 programmes broadcast in a single week in alternate months of that year; (ii) the listing of all 1971 programmes broadcast in a single week in alternate months in 1971 up to July. This produced a pool of about 150 programmes.

(b) What was required of this pool of 150 programmes was that it should provide a sufficient number of examples of each of the types of programme defined by the 31 independent variables. In the end, this would only be determined by the considerations of the grading panel. But as a preliminary step, members of the research team intuitively graded programmes to see if there was enough of each type in the pool. Programmes were eliminated (i) on grounds such as shortness of 'run' and probable unfamiliarity to judges and (ii) when it seemed that in their absence there would be a sufficient number of each type of programme left in the pool (e.g. slapstick comedy, Westerns) to meet the needs of scale construction. This left 119 of the 1970-1971 programmes in the pool. Seemingly 'non-violent' programmes broadcast in the period 1970-1971 were also drawn systematically and from these 20 varied examples were chosen for inclusion in the pool of programmes to be used in scale construction.

There was thus a maximum of 139 programmes in the pool of programmes that would be used for the construction of the required illustrated rating scales. Some examples from the list follow and the full set of 139 programmes is given in table A2.1 of Appendix 2.

List 4.2
Examples from the 139 programmes used for developing the illustrated scale

1	Budgie	104	Star Trek
2	Shadows of Fear	105	Ryan International
3	Man at the Top		
4	Bless this House	124	Softly, Softly
5	Cilla	125	Cartoon Time
6	Troubleshooters		
		129	The Expert
36	Panorama	130	Dustbin Men
37	Education Programme	131	Talk Back
38	Take Three Girls		
		134	Tom and Jerry
73	World of Sport		
74	Z-Cars	139	The Baron

3 *The judging or grading process*

The judging or the grading of the 139 programmes by the 30 judges proceeded as follows:

1 The 30 judges attended rating sessions at the Survey Research Centre in groups of 4-6 at a time and there worked on the grading task under supervision. They were paid hourly for their work and any one judge might have attended between two and five times to complete his or her grading task.

2 The different stages of the grading process were set out on an instruction form passed to each judge.

(a) Each judge was given a set of 139 small cards on each of which was the title of one of the 139 programmes to be judged. These cards were numbered 1-139.

(b) After general orientation and a practice session, each judge sorted his pile of cards into two heaps, one for programmes with which he was familiar and one for programmes with which he was unfamiliar. The latter were put to one side on the grounds that the judge concerned could not be expected meaningfully to grade them.

(c) The grading process differed according to the type of independent variable with respect to which the grading was to be done. Thus in some cases it was necessary to decide *how much* of the violence in a given programme was of a specified kind (e.g. fictional violence of a realistic kind; violence featuring defiance of, or rudeness towards authority figures; violence presented as being in a good cause). There were 15 of these ratings to be completed for each programme and 16 if we include the rating of each programme for the degree to which it presented violence (irrespective of the type or kind of violence concerned). For these 16 ratings of each programme, 11-point rating scales were to be used. But there were also 15 independent variables with respect to which all that judges could be expected to say was whether a given programme was or was not a specified type (e.g. 'a fictional programme about the English police at work, including violence going on in society'; 'a cartoon in which the characters are violent to each other'; 'a Western involving violence by, for example, cowboys and Indians'). These two classes of rating are referred to hereunder as 'continuous' and 'dichotomous' respectively.

In the one case, we were concerned with the *degree* to which certain programmes had in them certain *kinds* of violence. In the others, we were concerned with whether or not a given programme was of a specified kind.

(d) Judges dealt first with the dichotomous ratings. For each programme with which he [13] was familiar, he was required to answer 'Yes' or 'No' to questions phrased and set out as follows.

For each question, put a tick in either the 'yes' or 'no' column, whichever comes closest to your opinion about the programme being considered.

Name of programme ______________________________

IS THIS PROGRAMME		Yes	No
1	A 'Western' which includes violence?		
2	A cartoon in which the characters are violent to each other?		

There was a total of 15 questions of this sort, with coverage as follows:

'IS THIS PROGRAMME ....':-

1 A fictional programme about the English police at work, and showing violence going on in society?
2 A cartoon in which the characters are violent to each other?
3 A series, a play or a film in which personal relationships are a major theme, and which features verbal abuse (e.g. swearing, quarrelling) or physical violence?
4 A programme intended for adults?
5 A play, film or drama series, portraying conflict(s) between individuals, and where it would be difficult for the average boy to decide who is right and who is wrong?
6 A fictional programme where spies use unusual forms of violence, e.g. torture, novel weapons, or individual unarmed combat?
7 A programme which includes newsreel film of the violence of war, or its aftermath?
8 A comedy programme featuring 'slapstick' violence and/or verbal abuse between the characters?
9 A science fiction programme in which non-human fantasy creatures (e.g. monsters) ruthlessly fight with or destroy people?
10 A 'Western' involving violence by, for example, cowboys and Indians?
11 A fictional programme in which the violence tends to go unpunished?
12 A programme showing violence by competitors or spectators at sporting events?
13 A programme which includes real violence (not acted) as it happened, or is happening?
14 A film or part of a series/serial featuring gangs or gangsters engaged in violent, organised crime?
15 A science fiction programme in which humans use bizarre forms of violence, which may involve super-human powers?

Each judge was required to deal with a given programme in terms of *all* these 15 questions before dealing with the next programme in the same way, and then the next in the same way, and so on for all of the 139 programmes with which he was familiar.

This process provided evidence on the basis of which it was possible to select programmes which judges tended to regard as being of the kind asked about. There were 3 sets of rating questionnaires, each set being in a different order as a means of reducing 'order effects'.

(e) After this, the judges used the *continuous* scales to indicate *to what extent* each of the 139 programmes (to be rated) had in it violence *of a particular kind.* These different kinds of violence, 15 in all, were as follows.

Fictional violence of the realistic kind (that is, like what really happens).

Violence performed by a basically 'good guy' hero, who is also a rebel or 'odd man out' type.

Violence in a domestic or family setting (that is, a quarrel between members of a family).

Violence committed by adults (that is, not by children or young people below the age of majority).

Violence featuring defiance of or rudeness towards authority figures (for example, public officials like the police, school or medical staff, the fire-brigade, clergymen, parents).

Violence shown as glorified, romanticised, idealised or ennobling.

Violence presented as if it is 'fun and games', like a game or something to entertain.

Violence presented as being in a good cause.

Violence showing the physical or mental consequences for the victim in detail.

Violence related to racial or minority-group strife.

Violence committed by children or young people (that is, by persons apparently below the age of twenty-one.

Violence performed by a basically 'good guy' type of hero, who is also tough (that is, he can take physical violence and fight on).

Violence of the verbal kind (for example, abuse, threats, quarrelling, cheekiness, insult, rudeness, disrespect, swearing at people or animals or objects).

Violence just thrown in for its own sake, or not necessary to the plot.

Violence which is gruesome, horrific or scary.

The fifteen were arranged in 3 basic orders, so that different judges dealt with the ratings in different orders (as a means of reducing possible 'order effects').

For any one set of ratings or judgements (of familiar programmes amongst the 139 programmes), the physical process of rating was to place the cards along a giant-sized scale of the following kind, the nature of the rating dimensions being specified (e.g. 'Fictional violence of the realistic kind').

How much of the violence in this programme is
'FICTIONAL VIOLENCE OF THE REALISTIC KIND'

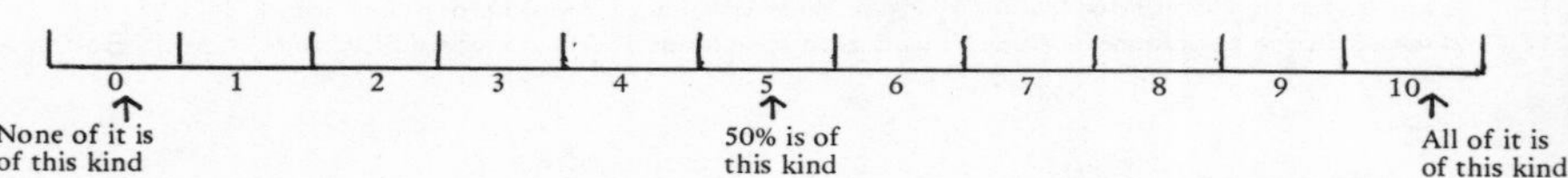

The judge could re-sort any programme as he worked through his total pack of (familiar) cards. When all had been placed or graded, the judge entered his grading results on a record sheet. After this, the process was repeated with the same set of 'familiar-programme' cards, but in terms of the next programme dimension (e.g. violence performed by basically 'good guy' type of hero, who is also a rebel or 'odd-man-out').

Just as with the dichotomous gradings, this process provided evidence on the basis of which it would be possible to identify programmes that could reliably be placed in the different scalar sections of each of the 15 different scales.

(f) Finally, each judge rated his familiar programmes on a further 11-point scale, but this time in terms of 'How violent' he thought the programme to be. The scale used in this case took the following form.

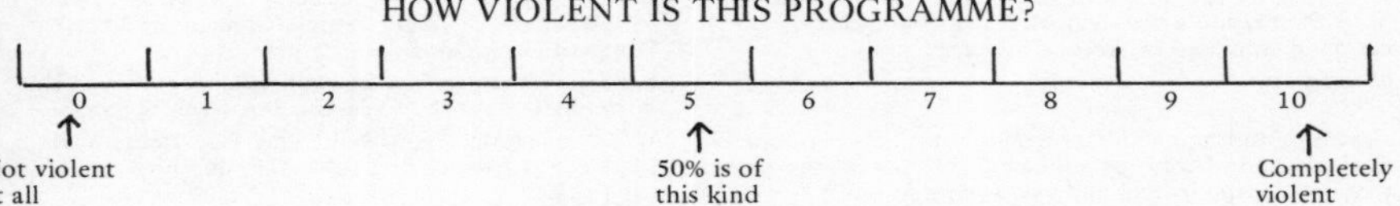

These ratings provided a basis for the selection of programmes to illustrate different scalar sections in the above scale.

4 *The results of the judging process*

(a) *For dichotomous type ratings*, what was sought in relation to each dimension were programmes which the majority of judges had rated as 'Yes'. A ratio of 2 'Yes' : 1 'No' was regarded as a minimum qualification for retaining a programme as an example of the type of programme concerned (e.g. as an example of, say a 'Western' involving violence). Programmes with gradings based on the opinions of less than 10 judges were also rejected. Findings are presented in list 4.3 and details of the ratings for all 139 programmes (as they relate to two programme categories) are given in Appendix 3, table A3.1.

(b) *For the continuous-type ratings*, the choice of programmes for illustrating the continuous-type scales was constrained by the following considerations.

(i) Programmes were assigned to scale sectors on the basis of median scores and 5-6 programmes which were satisfactory in this sense were to be chosen for illustrative purposes in each sector.

(ii) To be chosen, a programme: would need to have been familiar to at least 10 of the 30 judges (and to have been graded by them); would need to have achieved a distribution of judgements with relatively low scatter (in this case, a low semi-interquartile range). Where a choice still remained after the application of these criteria, final selection was to be made on the basis of: smallness of semi-interquartile range in combination with 'largeness' of number of judges familiar with that programme; contribution to diversity of subject matter of the set of programmes illustrating the scalar sector concerned.

List 4.3
The programmes which emerged as examples of different kinds of violent programmes

Programme types	Qualifying examples
A fictional programme about the English police at work, including violence going on in society	Z-Cars/Softly, Softly/Dixon of Dock Green
A cartoon in which characters are violent to each other	Tom and Jerry/Pink Panther/Thunderbirds
A series, play or film in which personal relationships are a major theme, and which feature verbal abuse (e.g. swearing, quarrelling) or physical violence	Z-Cars/Steptoe and Son/Softly, Softly/ Henry VIII (Six Wives of . . .)/Paul Temple/Coronation Street/ Dixon of Dock Green
A programme intended for adults	Panorama/News at Ten/24 Hours/9 o'clock News/ The Wednesday Play/The Avengers/This Week/Callan
A play, film or drama series, portraying conflicts between individuals, and where it would be difficult for the average boy to decide who is right and who is wrong	W. Somerset Maugham/Wednesday Play/Henry VIII/ Elizabeth R./Armchair Theatre/Troubleshooters/Play for Today
A fictional programme where spies use unusual forms of violence, e.g. torture, novel weapons, or individual unarmed combat	Avengers/Mission Impossible/Dr Who/Callan/ Paul Temple/Doomwatch
A programme which includes newsreel film of the violence of war, or its aftermath	Panorama/News at Ten/9 o'clock News/24 Hours/ World in Action/All our Yesterdays/This Week
A comedy programme featuring 'slapstick' violence and/or verbal abuse between the characters	Steptoe and Son/Dad's Army/Monty Python/Tom and Jerry/Please, Sir!/Laurel and Hardy
A science fiction programme in which non-human fantasy creatures (e.g. monsters) ruthlessly fight with or destroy people	Dr Who/Lost in Space/Star Trek/Thunderbirds/ Doomwatch/Captain Scarlett
A 'Western' involving violence, for example, cowboys and Indians	The Virginian/Bonanza/Wayne in Action/Gunsmoke/ Legend of Jesse James/Last of the Mohicans
A fictional programme in which the violence tends to go unpunished	Callan
A programme showing violence by competitors or spectators at sporting events	Match of the Day/Grandstand/Professional Wrestling/ Sportsnight with Coleman
A programme which includes real violence (not acted) as it happened, or is happening	Panorama/9 o'clock News/24 Hours/World in Action/ Professional Wrestling/All our Yesterdays/Match of the Day
A film or part of a series/serial featuring gangs or gangsters engaged in violent organised crime	The Avengers/Z-Cars/Hawaii 5-0/Paul Temple
A science fiction programme in which humans use bizarre forms of violence, which may involve super-human powers	Dr Who/Star Trek/Lost in Space

(iii) For the scales dealing with the degree to which programmes present different types of violence, all programmes with a general-violence rating of less than 0.5 were rejected.

In this way, illustrations for the 16 continuous-type scales were developed. The illustrations for two of them are shown as examples, in scalar form, in list 4.4, while table 4.6 gives numerical details for all sixteen of them.

5 *What has now been achieved* [14]

We have now reached the point where we can illustrate each grading system with programmes empirically derived for that purpose. There are 31 of these systems in all, 15 of them being dichotomous in character and 16 being 11-point (continuous) rating scales. These illustrated grading systems were

List 4.4
Two examples of the selection of programmes to illustrate the scales*

HOW VIOLENT IS THIS PROGRAMME?		How much of this violence is FICTIONAL VIOLENCE OF A REALISTIC KIND	
Median of judgements to nearest whole number	Programmes selected to illustrate the different scalar sectors	Median of judgements to nearest whole number	Programmes selected to illustrate the different scalar sectors
0 (=not violent at all)	Opportunity Knocks Magic Roundabout This is Your Life The Weatherman University Challenge	0 (= none of it is of this kind)	Match of the Day Yogi Bear World in Action News at Ten Panorama
1	Match of the Day Crossroads Coronation Street Doctor at Large Never Mind the Quality	1	Laurel and Hardy Never Mind the Quality Feel the Width Star Trek Monty Python's Flying Circus
2	All Our Yesterdays Sherlock Holmes Yogi Bear W. Somerset Maugham Please, Sir! Steptoe and Son	2	Please, Sir! Dad's Army Dr Who Lost in Space
3	Twenty-four Hours Armchair Theatre Cinema Dixon of Dock Green This Week	3	Out of the Unknown The Tuesday Film
4	Softly, Softly Z-Cars Doomwatch Robin Hood The Wednesday Play	4	Playhouse
5	A Man called Ironside Star Trek Dr Who Gunsmoke Six Wives of Henry VIII	5	The Avengers Cinema Mission Impossible Midnight Movie
6	The Last of the Mohicans The Borderers Mission Impossible	6	The Sunday Adventure Film Wayne in Action Saturday Thriller Randall & Hopkirk Dec'd
7	The Avengers The Callan Saga	7	The High Chaparral Man at the Top Bonanza Play for Today The Virginian
8	The Legend of Jesse James Wayne in Action (films) Tom and Jerry Hawaii Five-0	8	The Troubleshooters Gunsmoke Brett
9	The FBI Fight of the Week The Untouchables	9	The Expert A Man called Ironside Hawaii Five-0 Z-Cars The Untouchables
10 (= completely violent)		10 (= all of it is of this kind)	Budgie Softly, Softly Callan

*Based on the ratings of 30 teachers. See median indices and scatter figures, Appendix 3, for these two programme categories.

now made up for use in Stage II of the rating procedure, namely the rating of programmes shown in the period 1958-1971. The forms of two of the illustrated rating scales (11-point) are shown in diagram 4.2 as examples. All 31 systems are shown in the context of table 4.6.

Stage II: Rating a sample of programmes on the illustrated grading system

The illustrated grading systems having been constructed, it was now possible to use those systems to derive sets of gradings or ratings for each of the 231 programmes that had been selected for potential use in the measurement system described on pages 94-97.

With such values linked to each of the programmes in the sample and with information about the extent of boys' exposure to each of these programmes, it would be possible to compare boys in terms of their exposure to any of the kinds of television violence under investigation.

This important rating process is described under the following headings.

1 The sample of programmes to be rated on the illustrated grading system.

2 The grading or rating process.

3 The results of the grading process.

The sample of programmes to be rated or graded

A description has already been provided of the sampling of 'possibly violent' programmes broadcast in the period 1958-1969, of the drawing of a small sample of non-violent programmes for contrast purposes, and of the sampling of programmes broadcast in the period 1970-1971. These programmes, numbering 231 in all, were now ready for grading in terms of the 31 dimensions of television violence. They are listed in full in Appendix 1.

The grading or rating process

The judges. The grading of the 231 programmes (broadcast in the period 1958-1971) was done by 52 persons who had previously served on the BBC's Television Panel. As panel members they had for some time acted as raters of a wide range of television programme output – and this background served to increase the likelihood of their being (a) familiar with many programmes and (b) experienced in the judging process.

Invitations to act as judges or graders were limited to persons who had been educated to the age of 16 or over – the view being taken that the rating task was intellectually demanding and hence likely to be better done by people with more advanced education behind them. Of the 70 persons who agreed to take part, 52 actually did so. They knew that they would be paid for completing the task. The 52 judges attended in groups of up to 20 each at instruction sessions held at the offices of the ITA [15] in London. At these sessions they were instructed for about two hours in the rating procedure and given a practice session. They then took the rating materials home and completed the rating task there, posting in the completed forms about a week later.

The rating operation: the rating dimensions. Following Stage I work, certain changes had been made with respect to the rating dimensions.

(a) Two of the continuous-type dimensions of television violence had been reclassified as dichotomous in character. These were: 'violence committed by

Diagram 4.2

Showing the form of two 11-point rating scales of the illustrated kind

RATING SCALE FOR:
HOW VIOLENT IS THIS PROGRAMME?*

Opportunity Knocks The Magic Roundabout This is Your Life The Weatherman University Challenge	Match of the Day Crossroads Coronation Street Doctor at Large Never Mind the Quality	All Our Yesterdays Sherlock Holmes Yogi Bear W. Somerset Maugham Please, Sir! Steptoe & Son	24 Hours Armchair Theatre Cinema Dixon of Dock Green This Week	Softly, Softly Z-Cars Doomwatch Robin Hood The Wednesday Play	A Man called Ironside Star Trek Dr Who Gun Smoke Six Wives of Henry VIII	The Last of the Mohicans The Borderers Mission Impossible	The Avengers The Callan Saga	Legend of Jesse James Wayne in Action Tom and Jerry Hawaii Five-0	The FBI Fight of the Week The Untouchables	
0	1	2	3	4	5	6	7	8	9	10
NOT VIOLENT AT ALL					ABOUT 50% VIOLENT					COMPLETELY VIOLENT

RATING SCALES FOR:
HOW MUCH OF THE VIOLENCE IN THIS PROGRAMME IS FICTIONAL VIOLENCE OF THE REALISTIC KIND?*

Match of the Day Yogi Bear The World in Action News at Ten Panorama	Laurel and Hardy Never Mind the Quality Star Trek Monty Python's Flying Circus	Please, Sir! Dad's Army Dr Who Lost in Space	Out of the Unknown The Tuesday film	Playhouse	The Avengers Cinema Mission Impossible The Midnight Movie	Sunday Adventure film Wayne in Action The Saturday Thriller Randall and Hopkirk, dec'd	The High Chaparral Man at the Top Bonanza Play for Today The Virginian	The Trouble Shooters Gunsmoke Brett	The Expert A Man called Ironside Hawaii Five-0 Z-Cars The Untouchables	Budgie Softly, Softly The Callan Saga
0	1	2	3	4	5	6	7	8	9	10
NONE OF IT IS OF THIS KIND					50% IS OF THIS KIND					ALL OF IT IS OF THIS KIND

*See Appendix 3 for full details of this scale.

children or young people' and 'violence committed by adults'. This was done because in Stage I the programmes tended for each of them to be grouped at the extreme ends of the 11-point scale, indicating that respondents were in fact treating the scale as dichotomous.

(b) The wording of some of the dichotomous dimensions was changed slightly to make their meanings clearer.

(c) The continuous-type dimensions were otherwise left as they were in Stage I.

The rating operation: the way the ratings were to be made. Just as in Stage I, the judges each had a pile of cards, 231 this time, one for each of the programmes to be rated. As a recall aid, each judge was provided with a booklet of programme details. For each of the 231 programmes to be rated, this booklet contained a programme description giving details of plot, times of showing, actors and characters, the television service on which shown. Furthermore, wherever possible a photograph was shown of some relevant element in the programme concerned (mostly of the central character(s) or of some recognisable scene). The 124 photographs obtained were provided free of charge by the BBC and by many of the commercial programme companies. The photographs and programme details were printed on facing pages of the booklet and were numbered to correspond with the numbers on the programme cards. A single set of programme details of this kind is presented in Appendix 5 to this chapter. Judges were instructed to examine the programme details with respect to any programmes about which they were uncertain in any way.

Each judge began by sorting all 231 programme cards into two heaps, one for programmes he/she *could* remember and the other for programmes he/she could *not* remember. If *not sure*, the judge was to look up the programme details in the recall aid booklet. If still unsure he/she was to put the card into a 'do not remember' heap. The programmes in the 'don't remember' and the 'not sure' heaps were put aside and not rated at all by that particular judge (though obviously they would be in the 'remember' heaps of *other* judges). The programmes in the 'remember' heap were now sorted by the judge into two heaps, one for '*un*familiar with it' and one for 'familiar with it'. If only 'slightly unfamiliar', the card was to go into the 'unfamiliar' heap. All ratings by a judge were limited to the cards with which that judge was 'familiar'.

Judges then rated familiar programmes on the 17 dichotomous dimensions and after that rated the same set of programmes on all 14 of the continuous dimensions, working to printed instructions (following the briefing and practice sessions).

The rating operation: rating programmes on the continuous dimensions. In principle, the rating system used in Stage II was closely similar to that used in Stage I — with the important exception that this time the judge was aided by illustrations along his rating scale, as shown in diagram 4.2. The 14 continuous dimensions were as follows:

1. Fictional violence of the realistic kind (that is, like what really happens).
2. Violence performed by a basically 'good guy' hero, who is also a rebel or 'odd man out' type.
3. Violence in a domestic or family setting (that is, a quarrel between members of a family).
4. Violence featuring defiance of or rudeness towards authority figures (for example, public officials like the police, school or medical staff, the fire-brigade, clergymen, parents).
5. Violence shown as glorified, romanticised, idealised or ennobling.
6. Violence presented as if it is 'fun and games', like a game or something to entertain.

7. Violence presented as being in a good cause.
8. Violence showing the physical or mental consequences for the victim in detail.
9. Violence related to racial or minority-group strife.
10. Violence performed by a basically 'good guy' type of hero, who is also tough (that is, he can take physical violence and fight on).
11. Violence of the verbal kind (for example, abuse, threats, quarrelling, cheekiness, insult, rudeness, disrespect, swearing at people or animals or objects).
12. Violence just thrown in for its own sake, or not necessary to the plot.
13. Violence which is gruesome, horrific or scary.
14. The degree to which the programme is violent (irrespective of type of violence).

In their instructions about how to use the illustrated rating scales, the judges were told that the illustrations were meant to help them in deciding where on the scale to rate or grade a given programme. The judges were told that they did not necessarily have to accept the positionings of any illustrations – though they were not *encouraged* to disregard or disagree with them. In general, the illustrations were presented to the judges as *guides*.

Judges were told they could change any of their ratings while still working on a given dimension. They then entered the numbers of all their graded cards on a master list to show *where* they had graded them. They then went to work on the next scale, once again with all the *familiar* programme cards.

Separately for each scale, the ratings from the judges [16] were then analysed to provide, for each programme, the total number of boys, the *median* value of all its ratings, the *semi-interquartile range* of all these ratings. Details for several such analyses are set out in Appendix 4A.

The rating operation: rating programmes on the dichotomous dimensions. The judge took the topmost of the programmes in the 'familiar' heap and entered its name on a rating sheet. Thereunder he indicated, for each of the 17 dichotomous dimensions, whether he thought the programme was of that kind. In fact, with a few changes, the form used was the same as that used for the dichotomous ratings in Stage I.

There were 17 of these ratings to be completed with respect to that first programme, the full 17 being as follows:

1. A fictional programme about the English police at work, including violence going on in society?
2. A cartoon in which the characters are violent to each other?
3. A series, a play or a film in which personal relationships are a major theme, and which features verbal abuse (e.g. swearing, quarrelling) or physical violence?
4. A violent programme intended, by the producers, for adults.
5. A play, film or drama series, portraying conflict(s) between individuals, and where it would be difficult for the average boy to decide who is right and who is wrong?
6. A fictional programme where spies use unusual forms of violence, e.g. torture, novel weapons, or individual unarmed combat?
7. A programme which includes newsreel film of the violence of war, or its aftermath?
8. A comedy programme featuring 'slapstick' violence and/or verbal abuse between the characters?
9. A science fiction programme in which non-human fantasy creatures (e.g. monsters) ruthlessly fight with or destroy people?
10. A 'Western' involving violence by, for example, cowboys and Indians?
11. A fictional programme in which the violence tends to go unpunished?
12. A programme showing violence by competitors or spectators at sporting events?
13. A programme which includes real violence (not acted) as it happened, or is happening?
14. A film or part of a series/serial featuring gangs or gangsters engaged in violent, organised crime?

15. A science fiction programme in which humans use bizarre forms of violence, which may involve super-human powers?

16. A programme where the violence is mostly carried out by children or young people (under 18)?

17. A programme where adults use violence?

After this, a second rating pad was used for the second of the programmes in the judge's 'familiar' pack, a third for his third programme, and so on.

There were three basic orders of dichotomous dimensions, with a third of the judges doing their ratings in terms of one order, a third of them in terms of the next order and a third in terms of the remaining order.

C: SELECTING THE FINAL SET OF PROGRAMMES TO BE USED IN THE MEASUREMENT SYSTEM AND DERIVING THE MANY DIFFERENT EXPOSURE SCORES FROM THESE

Summing up on the present position

Through Stage II of the construction process, a large number of programmes had been graded on each of 31 dimensions of exposure to television violence. These programmes were conceptually of three kinds:

(a) 208 possibly violent programmes drawn from the broadcast years 1958-1969 and spread evenly between those years and evenly between ITV and BBC as origins.

(b) 23 non-violent programmes drawn from the broadcast years 1958-1969 and included as contrast material.

(c) 139 programmes drawn from the broadcast years 1970 and 1971, initially used for the development of illustrated rating scales, but contributing in their own right to the pool of programme materials from which the required measuring technique would be constructed. Inevitably there was much overlap between the programmes in this group and those in group (a) (in that programmes in that earlier period continued on into 1970-71).

Programme groups (a) and (b) had been rated by 50 judges (ex-BBC panel members) while programmes in group (c) had been rated (during Stage I) by a panel of teachers.

Some seventeen of the dimensions in terms of which the programmes had been rated were dichotomous in character and fourteen were continuous. The 17 dichotomous and 13 of the continuous dimensions related to *kinds* of violence in programmes. The 14th of the continuous dimensions related to the degree to which programmes were violent (irrespective of kind of violence) and it was a key dimension in the selection process described hereunder.

The reader will find: the names of all 208 possibly violent programmes for 1958-1969 and of all 23 non-violent programmes for this period in Appendix 1; the names and the origins of all 139 of the 1970-71 programmes in Appendix 2.

The methods used to select the total composite of programmes used in the measuring procedure (including some modifications to the programme dimensions being studied)

The object in this phase of the development of the technique was to select from the great array of material available some single set of programmes, limited in number, through which to develop discriminating measures of exposure (a) to TV violence in general and (b) to different sorts of TV violence.

The general strategy of selection was as follows:

1. To the 231 programmes of 1958-69 was added a 40-programme sample of the 139 programmes (of 1970-71) which had been used in the development of the illustrated scales.

2. Selection was initially restricted to the HOW VIOLENT dimension, as follows.
   - (a) The programme ratings in terms of HOW VIOLENT IS IT? were grouped by scalar sections, i.e. 0-1, 1-2, 2-3, 3-4, . . . 9-10 after the preliminary exclusion of those for which (a) the number of ratings was less than 10 and (b) the semi-interquartile range of ratings was 2.00 or more.
   - (b) All the violence ratings of less than 1.00 were set aside as being virtually non-violent.
   - (c) The others were scanned and selectively eliminated on one or another of the grounds that: they added too little to the variety of the programmes in the sample; their periods of showing were broken and hence likely to lead to confusion; they had been shown only once or briefly; between them they led to an under-representation of short-running series in certain years; the number of judges, though in excess of 10, was relatively small. Part of one scalar sector of the residual list is shown as an example below.

Scalar Sector 5-6

Programme number	Name of programme	Channel	Duration**	Median rating	S I R †	Number of raters††
53	The Informer	ITV	1966-67	5.00	1.17	16
61	Crane	ITV	1963-65	5.25	1.03	20
103	Dr Who	BBC 1	1965-72	5.14	1.47	40

**Principal broadcasting period at time of sampling
† Semi-interquartile range
††Out of 50 – the others being unfamiliar with the programme concerned

3 The total array of the programmes left after this initial sorting and screening was then examined in terms of programme ratings on the other 30 dimensions of programme violence, with a view to seeing that each of those other dimensions was adequately represented by programmes. This body of data could be thought of as forming a large grid, such that against each of the programmes being considered for selection there were 30 entries, one for each of the 30 other ratings.

The criteria for deciding which programmes to bring together as representing a given violence dimension were as follows;

(a) For a given dimension, the programmes to be considered were those with the lower semi-interquartile ranges (for the continuous type of ratings) or the higher proportion of 'Yes' gradings (for the dichotomous variables).

(b) Where competition between two programmes existed, priority was to be given to that which had been rated by the *larger* number of judges.

(c) The programmes selected to represent a given dimension should together be varied in character and should provide for a fairly even spread of broadcast output over the period 1958-71.

(d) For a given scale, the selected programmes should together provide a wide array of rating values in terms of violence considered generally and, for the continuous type dimensions, a wide array of rating values in terms of the dimension itself.

4 For certain of the dichotomous dimensions, the number of clearly relevant programmes (i.e. 'clear' in the sense that they had been rated by a large number of judges and that the ratings of these judges had been predominantly 'Yes') was not quite sufficient to constitute a stable measurement base. To meet this difficulty, several additional programmes (already rated on the system described above) were brought into use as additional examples of the under-represented categories of TV violence). See table 4.8 for details. These added programmes were *not* included in the existing sample of 'violent programmes in general' but were used solely for establishing exposure scores for specific categories of television violence.

5 For other of the dichotomous dimensions, this process still left the number of examples below four and these dimensions were therefore dropped. They were:

- a violent programme intended for adults . . .
- a fictional programme where spies use unusual forms of violence . . .
- a fictional programme in which the violence tends to go unpunished
- a programme where the violence is mostly carried out by children or young people
- a play, film or drama series, portraying conflict(s) . . . and where it would be difficult for the average boy to decide who was right and who was wrong.

6 Certain other changes were made on the basis of appraisal and discussion of the sets of programmes representing different types of programme violence.

(a) The cartoon programme Tom & Jerry, which had been included as one amongst five programmes representing cartoon programmes generally, was taken out as a separate category for the investigation of an hypothesis that exposure to Tom & Jerry contributed to violent behaviour by boys. The reason for doing this was the recurrent reference, during hypothesis development, to Tom & Jerry as a 'cause of violence amongst boys'. At the same time, Tom & Jerry continued to be included amongst the five programmes representing cartoon violence and it did not contribute in its own right to the overall score for exposure to television violence. On the other hand, it was used to strengthen the measurement of exposure to different categories of TV violence (see table 4.8 for details).

(b) The two science fiction dimensions were represented by almost the same programmes and were therefore combined into a singie dimension called 'Science fiction programmes involving violence (e.g. where creatures destroy people, where humans use super weapons to destroy men').

(c) The original category 'programmes which include newsreel film of the violence of war or its aftermath' was represented by four programmes presenting news and one dealing with the 1914-18 war ('The Great War'). The suggestions that had led to this hypothesis being set up had been principally concerned with the presentation of actual violence through the news (thereby (i) showing the real thing more or less at the time of its happening and (ii) catching many viewers unaware). Since 'The Great War' was a composite of edited and broadly expected violence, the latter series was cut out of the composite of five and the hypothesis was re-stated in terms of violence 'presented through the news and newsreel programmes'.

(d) The category 'programmes showing violence by competitors or spectators at sporting events' originally included professional wrestling but (because of rating problems) not professional boxing. This was an unsatisfactory situation (i) because of the exclusion of boxing and (ii) because of the seeming difference between wrestling and the other sporting programmes in the composite of programmes representing 'violence in sporting programmes', namely 'Sportsview', 'Grandstand', 'Saturday Sportstime'. Accordingly these three programmes were regarded as representing the original dimension of television violence and the wrestling and boxing programmes were grouped as involving a separate dimension of violence.

(e) The category programmes showing *real* violence depended upon the same programmes as appeared in the 'news programmes' category, along with 'wrestling', so that its retention as part of a separate hypothesis seemed wasteful. The category was therefore dropped.

The various modifications made meant that in the end the measurement of exposure to violence was limited to:

(i) a measure of the extent of exposure to television violence (irrespective of *type* of violence);

(ii) measures of 13 different types of violence where the type was a matter of degree (and hence measurable as a continuous-type variable);

(iii) measures of twelve different types of violence where the type or property was either present or absent (and hence measurable as a dichotomous-type variable).

These 26 variables are detailed in list 4.1, page 94.

The programmes selected for inclusion in the measure of exposure to television violence

In the final count, the programmes selected for use in measuring exposure to television, in terms of the 26 different dimensions of television violence numbered 117, made up as follows:

1 Programmes constituting *the sample of violent TV output* (68 programmes in all)

2 Programmes making up *the sample of control TV output* (60 in all but with 15 of them in the violent programme sample as well)

3 Some additional programmes in neither of the above samples but used for strengthening the assessment of amount of exposure to specific categories of TV violence (4 extra programmes)

All the 117 programmes had been broadcast within the period 1959-1971 and the 117 were distributed fairly evenly over that period. Numerical details are given in table 4.12 on page 135.

Table 4.6, dealing with the continuous dimensions only, presents the first set of (68) programmes in full. Table 4.7, dealing only with the dichotomous dimensions, similarly includes all 68 programmes, but also the nine additions referred to on page 116 and listed separately in table 4.8 as well. For these nine, the 'How Violent?' ratings are shown in brackets to indicate that they were not used for developing overall scores for exposure to television violence.

One feature of tables 4.6 and 4.7 is the marking of some programmes with the letter (C). This means that such programmes are part of the *control* sample as well as being in the composite of programmes to be used in measuring different sorts of violence. Since the control sample consists of programmes generally – irrespective of whether they are violent or not – such overlap between samples is both inevitable and basic to the research strategy as outlined in chapter 3. There is a special section later in this chapter dealing with the control system.

The reader will see many gaps in tables 4.6 and 4.7, that is, in moving horizontally across it. The reason for the gaps is that each of the 25 subsidiary measures of exposure to television was 'pruned' of items that were inadequate as discriminants on grounds such as the following: inadequate number of raters who 'knew' the programme; large scatter of ratings; near zero rating for this characteristic.

Table 4.6

Sixty eight (68) programmes, presenting violence in different degrees, and of different kinds, to be used in measuring degree of exposure to (a) television violence in general and (b) thirteen kinds of television violence

PROGRAMME	HOW VIOLENT	TYPE OF TELEVISION VIOLENCE* (13 continuous dimensions)												
		Realistic fiction	By a good guy, rebel	Domestic setting	Rudeness, defiance to authority	Glorified, romanticised	As fun and games	In a good cause	Consequences shown	Racial or minority strife	Good guy, tough	Verbal	Not necessary to plot	Gruesome, horrific
Dr Finlay	1.11				1.00			1.20				1.94		
Grandstand (c)	1.12													
The Rag Trade	1.13	1.00												
Marty	1.14				2.00									
Tonight	1.15								1.12	2.20				1.00
Army Game	1.16	1.95				1.20			1.06					
Coronation Street (c)	1.25			7.58	1.97			1.33	1.55					
Sports View	1.25						1.10					1.17		
Yogi Bear (c)	1.42							1.38						
Billy Bunter	1.71	1.14						1.00				1.06		
Please Sir!	2.10	2.17			7.17		8.53	1.39	1.05			7.22	1.22	
Human Jungle	2.17		1.43	2.50		1.58					1.00			
Whacko	2.25	1.25						1.28	1.06				1.87	
The Defenders	2.25		1.66	2.18					3.50	1.72				1.40
News Summary (c)	2.25				1.12				2.06	3.75				1.75
The Power Game	2.32					2.50	1.08	2.75	2.50	1.10	1.30			
Steptoe and Son	2.39	2.28		9.68			7.64		1.23			8.89		
The Main Chance	2.50					2.30		2.80			1.25	3.50		
Mr Rose	2.71						2.60				2.00			
Panorama (c)	2.81				1.25			2.61		3.97		1.67		2.60
Lone Ranger (c)	3.00				2.08		1.75	6.20	1.71			1.50		
Sherlock Holmes	3.04		2.25	1.28		3.50		3.58	3.08		2.58	1.91	1.02	2.27
News at 10 (c)	3.07				1.06			1.77	2.27	4.05				2.26
Dixon of Dock Green	3.10	7.82	1.02	2.96	4.80			4.13	3.22	2.04	2.29	3.05	1.26	1.18
Thunderbirds	3.25						4.56	4.57					2.07	
Probation Officer	3.17					1.75					1.00			
Wednesday Play	3.36	4.70	1.75	5.25	3.62	2.07		2.20	5.17	2.21	1.79	4.58		

Table 4.6 (cont.)

PROGRAMME	HOW VIOLENT	TYPE OF TELEVISION VIOLENCE* (13 continuous dimensions)												
		Realistic fiction	By a good guy, rebel	Domestic setting	Rudeness defiance to authority	Glorified, romanticised	As fun and games	In a good cause	Consequences shown	Racial or minority strife	Good guy, tough	Verbal	Not necessary to plot	Gruesome, horrific
World in Action (c)	3.36				1.00			2.79		4.65		1.06		3.00
Perry Mason	3.55		1.75	1.45	3.50				3.95	1.79		3.08	1.90	1.80
Sergeant Cork	3.57					3.12		3.50			3.00			
Invisible Man	3.60	2.25				3.62						1.42		
Maigret	3.73			2.36	3.78	3.50		4.73	3.95	1.20	3.31	2.36	1.27	1.83
Till Death us do Part	3.87			9.83								9.10		
Z-Cars (c)	3.95	9.00	1.25	2.87		2.54	1.02	4.67	4.72	2.17	3.25	3.70	1.35	2.00
Robin Hood	4.00	2.21	7.00		6.93	8.57	6.88	7.31	1.42		7.25	2.27	1.45	
Out of the Unknown	4.00	2.25				1.00					1.17	1.33		6.40
Wells Fargo (c)	4.00	6.00	3.21		2.00	5.50	1.50	5.05	2.04		6.25		2.05	
Bonanza	4.11	5.92		2.83	2.00		2.83	5.14	2.39	1.63	6.25	2.94	2.06	
No Hiding Place	4.14	8.30	1.45	1.39		3.08	1.15	4.91	3.15	1.46	3.08		1.91	2.00
Virginian	4.22	6.56	3.86	2.09	2.44	5.96	2.00	4.94	2.42	1.37	6.50	2.77	1.91	1.10
Cinema	4.37	4.56	2.22		2.33	4.20	3.50	3.40	4.25	3.25	4.10	4.17	3.60	3.45
Mystery and Imagination	4.37	2.50	1.20	1.35										6.33
Adam Adamant	4.44	3.87	5.00		2.05						6.57	1.92		2.75
Cheyenne	4.50	5.75	4.25			4.37				2.00				
Wyatt Earp	4.67		4.25		4.37	5.00		5.20			6.50			
Ironside (c)	4.72	8.44	2.19	1.91	5.73	4.11	1.16	5.53	4.61	2.05			2.09	2.12
Rawhide	4.86		3.37			5.50						5.17		
High Chaparral	4.89	6.69	3.77	2.83		5.83		4.83	2.83	1.58	6.25	2.61	2.00	1.00
Highway Patrol (c)	5.00											3.00		
The Informer	5.00	8.68				3.50			5.17			3.20		
High Adventure	5.10	4.25	3.33		3.25	6.50	4.50		4.00					
Dr Who	5.14	1.94			1.69			3.92	2.81		4.00	1.73	3.08	
Gunsmoke	5.17	6.81	3.00	1.28		5.80	2.06	4.60	2.28	1.89	7.00	2.56	2.28	1.04
Crane	5.25	6.50				5.17	2.20							1.38

Table 4.6 (cont.)

PROGRAMME	HOW VIOLENT	TYPE OF TELEVISION VIOLENCE* (13 continuous dimensions)												
		Realistic fiction	Be a good guy, rebel	Domestic setting	Rudeness, defiance to authority	Glorified, romanticised	As fun and games	In a good cause	Consequences shown	Racial or minority strife	Good guy, tough	Verbal	Not necessary to plot	Gruesome, horrific
77 Sunset Strip	5.70		2.37			4.50		5.00				5.50	3.70	
Danger Man	5.75		5.16			6.75		5.92			8.00		3.92	3.61
The Saint	5.77	5.36	5.00	1.07	4.00	7.50		6.71	3.60		8.00	2.79	3.27	2.00
Late Night Horror	6.67	2.90										1.17		2.66
The Avengers	6.82	4.75				7.82	7.61	6.67		1.17	7.86	2.78	5.24	3.91
Man from UNCLE	7.03					7.05		6.00			7.18		5.21	3.30
Hawaii Five-0	7.25	8.75		1.20	4.33	6.60	1.21	5.63		2.10	6.36	2.81	3.67	3.75
Professional Boxing	7.33													
The Great War	7.62													
ADDITIONAL PROGRAMMES FROM 1970-71 SAMPLE														
Softly, Softly	4.45	9.12		1.22								1.49	1.08	1.50
Star Trek (c)	4.78				1.10			5.21				1.92		
Last of the Mohicans (c)	5.30							4.96				1.75		
Wayne in Action	6.83	5.92		1.00		8.00			4.64		8.13	3.25	4.50	1.15
The Untouchables	8.38	8.69						5.00				3.17		

*See page 94 for a full naming of these dimensions of television violence. Scale 0-10 used (In Appendix, converted to 1-11).

(c) = Programmes also usable for control purposes, as detailed later in this chapter. The (c) programmes listed in table 4.6 do not constitute the full control sample – only those programmes amongst the control programmes which occur in both the violence sample and the control sample.

Table 4.7

Sixty four (64) programmes, presenting violence in different degrees, and of different kinds, to be used in measuring degree of exposure to twelve dichotomously defined types of television violence

PROGRAMME	HOW VIOLENT	IS IT A PROGRAMME THAT PRESENTS VIOLENCE IN CONTEXT OF											
		English police	Cartoons	Tom and Jerry	Personal relation-ships	News or News-reels	Slap-stick comedy	Science fiction	Westerns	Sporting events	Wrestling and boxing	Gangs in organised crime	Adults' behaviour
Dad's Army	(0.85)						✓						
Captain Pugwash	(1.08)		✓										
Grandstand (c)	1.12									✓			
The Rag Trade	1.13						✓						
Marty	1.14						✓						
Army Game	1.16						✓						
Coronation Street (c)	1.25				✓								
Sports View	1.25									✓			
Yogi Bear (c)	1.42		✓										
Billy Bunter	1.71						✓						
Saturday Sports-time	(1.75)									✓			
Please Sir!	2.10						✓						
Whacko	2.25						✓						
The Human Jungle	2.17				✓								
News Summary (c)	2.25					✓							
The Power Game	2.32				✓								
The Boss Cat	(2.35)		✓										
Steptoe and Son	2.39				✓		✓						
Mr Rose	2.71	✓											
Panorama (c)	2.81					✓							
Lone Ranger (c)	3.00								✓				
News at 10	3.07					✓							
Dixon of Dock Green (c)	3.10	✓			✓								
Probation Officer	3.17				✓								
Wednesday Play	3.36				✓								
World in Action (c)	3.36					✓							
Quatermass and the Pit	(3.50)							✓					

Table 4.7 (cont.)

PROGRAMME	HOW VIOLENT	IS IT A PROGRAMME THAT PRESENTS VIOLENCE IN CONTEXT OF											
		English police	Cartoons	Tom and Jerry	Personal relation-ships	News or News-reels	Slap-stick comedy	Science fiction	Westerns	Sporting events	Wrestling and boxing	Gangs in organised crime	Adults' behaviour
Lost in Space	(3.50)							✓					
Popeye	(3.50)		✓										
Sergeant Cork	3.57	✓										✓	✓
Maigret	3.73												✓
Till Death Us Do Part	3.87				✓		✓						
Z-Cars	3.95	✓			✓							✓	
Wells Fargo (c)	4.00								✓				✓
Out of the Unknown	4.00							✓					
Bonanza	4.11								✓				✓
No Hiding Place	4.14	✓										✓	
The Virginian	4.22								✓				✓
*Softly, Softly (c)	4.45	✓			✓							✓	
Cheyenne	4.50								✓				
Wyatt Earp	4.67								✓				✓
Ironside (c)	4.72											✓	✓
*Star Trek (c)	4.78							✓					
Rawhide	4.86								✓				
High Chaparral	4.89								✓				
The Informer	5.00	✓										✓	✓
Highway Patrol (c)	5.00											✓	✓
Dr Who	5.14							✓					
Gunsmoke	5.17								✓				
Crane	5.25				✓							✓	
*Last of the Mohicans (c)	5.30								✓				
77 Sunset Strip	5.70											✓	
Danger Man	5.75											✓	✓
The Saint	5.77											✓	✓

Table 4.7 (cont.)

PROGRAMME	HOW VIOLENT	English police	Cartoons	Tom and Jerry	Personal relation-ships	News or News-reels	Slap-stick comedy	Science fiction	Westerns	Sporting events	Wrestling and boxing	Gangs in organised crime	Adults' behaviour
		IS IT A PROGRAMME THAT PRESENTS VIOLENCE IN CONTEXT OF											
Late Night Horror	6.67							✓					
The Avengers	6.82											✓	
*Wayne in Action (c)	6.83				✓				✓				✓
The Man from UNCLE	7.03											✓	✓
Hawaii Five-0	7.25											✓	✓
Professional Boxing	(7.33)										✓		
The Great War	7.62												✓
Tom and Jerry	(7.75)			✓			✓						
Professional Wrestling	7.83										✓		
*The Untouchables (c)	8.38											✓	✓
Total in sample	56	7	5	1	12	4	11	6	11	3	2	16	16

✓ = an example of the class of programme violence set out across the top of the table

( ) = a programme included only for the dichotomous variables (and not for the continuous variables)

(c) = programmes also usable for control purposes, as detailed later in this chapter. The (c) programmes listed in table 4.6, do not constitute the full control sample – only those programmes amongst the control programmes which occur in both the violence sample and the control sample

*These are all programmes added from the 1970-71 sample.

Table 4.8
Nine programmes used to provide additional bases for estimating the extent of exposure to certain types of programme violence: showing overall ratings for level of violence *and how rated for specific categories of programme violence*

PROGRAMME	HOW VIOLENT	Whether it presents specific types of programme violence				
		Cartoon violence	Wrestling/ boxing violence	Violence in other types of sport	Science fiction violence	Slapstick comedy violence
Dad's Army (C)	0.85	–	–	–	–	✓
Captain Pugwash (C)	1.08	✓	–	–	–	–
Saturday Sportstime (C)	1.75	–	–	✓	–	–
The Boss Cat (C)	2.35	✓	–	–	–	–
Popeye*	3.50	✓	–	–	–	–
Lost in Space (C)	3.50	–	–	–	✓	–
Quatermass and the Pit*	3.50	–	–	–	✓	–
Tom and Jerry†	7.75	✓	–	–	–	✓
Professional Wrestling†	7.83	–	✓	–	–	–

(C) programmes drawn from the control sample (five in all)

*Programmes which had already been rated for violent content both generally and in terms of specific types of TV violence but which had been dropped in the course of the selection process. Used here only as basis for strengthening the measurement of extent of exposure to specific categories of TV violence and not for contributing to the measurement of exposure to TV violence in general

†Brought into the enquiry because of a late decision to study the effects of two further categories of television violence: boxing and wrestling violence; Tom and Jerry violence.

D: DERIVING TWENTY SIX (26) DIFFERENT EXPOSURE SCORES FOR EACH BOY

An account of the weighting system to be used for scoring amount of exposure to each class of television violence was given on pages

Very briefly, if a programme had an overall rating of, say, 4.1 (out of 10.0) for 'degree to which it was violent' – that is, irrespective of its *type* of violence – and if it had a rating of 8.3/10.0 for degree to which its violence is of the Realistic Fictional kind, then we may say that a single viewing of this programme would contribute $\frac{8.3}{10.0} \times 4.1$ (= 3.40) units of violence of the Realistic Fictional kind to that viewer's exposure experience. Tables 4.1 and 4.2 developed this point fairly fully.

A different type of calculation was required for derivation of equivalent figures for programmes which involved measurements in terms of dichotomous variables. A ✓ in table 4.7 against a particular programme on a particular dimension means that the programme concerned *qualifies* in terms of that dimension. A rating of 0 is given to all programmes that don't qualify in this way . . . and a rating of 1 when they do. If we read '1' in all the cells in table 4.7 that have a ✓ in them, then the relevant unit of exposure to be written into this cell is 1 x the 'How Violent' rating.

The units of exposure (per single viewing of a programme) have been entered in (for all programmes) tables 4.9 and 4.10. These units are extremely important: they represent the different weights to be given to each programme in calculating the extent of a boy's exposure to each of the 26 different classes of violence specified in the hypotheses.

E: SAMPLES OF CONTROL PROGRAMMES

An internal control system involving amount of exposure to television output considered generally

As part of an internal challenging or control system, it was hypothesised that:

> Any increase in violent behaviour produced by seeing a lot of television *output* (considered generally) will be just as large as any increase produced by seeing a lot of television *violence*.

This is what one might expect if exposure to television as such was just as potent in producing violent behaviour as was exposure to television violence. There is, of course, an assumption within this challenging device that a high score for exposure to television output, considered generally, includes a greater degree of exposure to non-violent television material than does a high score for exposure to *violent* television material. [17]

The investigation of this challenging or control hypothesis called for the selection and the use of a sample of television programmes in general, that is, a randomly selected sample of television programmes, drawn without reference to whether they seemed violent or not. To this end, using a random number drawing system, two ITV and two BBC 1 programmes were drawn from the programme schedules for each of the years in the period 1958-1971.

Table 4.9

Sixty-eight (68) programmes used in the measuring technique, each scored for its presentation of violence of different kinds

PROGRAMME	HOW VIOLENT	TYPE OF TELEVISION VIOLENCE*												
		Realistic fiction	By a good guy, rebel	Domestic setting	Rudeness, defiance to authority	Glorified, romanticised	As fun and games	In a good cause	Consequences shown	Racial or minority strife	Good guy, tough	Verbal	Not necessary to plot	Gruesome, horrific
Dr Finlay	1.11				0.11			0.13				0.22		
Grandstand (c)	1.12													
The Rag Trade	1.13	0.11												
Marty	1.14				0.23									
Tonight	1.15								0.13	0.25				0.12
Army Game	1.16	0.23				0.14			0.12					
Coronation St (c)	1.25			0.95	0.25			0.17	0.19					
Sports View	1.25						0.14					0.15		
Yogi Bear	1.42							0.20						
Billy Bunter	1.71	0.20						0.17				0.18		
Please Sir!	2.10	0.46			1.51		1.79	0.29	0.22			1.52	0.26	
Human Jungle	2.17		0.31	0.54		0.34					0.22			
Whacko	2.25	0.28						0.29	0.24				0.42	
The Defenders	2.25		0.37	0.49					0.79	0.39				0.32
News Summary (c)	2.25				0.25				0.46	0.84				0.39
The Power Game	2.32					0.58	0.25	0.64	0.58	0.26	0.30			
Steptoe and Son	2.39	0.55		2.31			1.83		0.29			2.13		
The Main Chance	2.50					0.58		0.70			0.31	0.88		
Mr Rose	2.71						0.71				0.54			
Panorama	2.81				0.35			0.73		1.12		0.47		0.73
Lone Ranger (c)	3.00				0.62		0.53	1.86	0.51			0.45		
Sherlock Holmes	3.04		0.68	0.39		1.06		1.09	0.94		0.78	0.58	0.31	0.69

Table 4.9 (cont.)

PROGRAMME	HOW VIOLENT	TYPE OF TELEVISION VIOLENCE*												
		Realistic fiction	By a good guy, rebel	Domestic setting	Rudeness, defiance to authority	Glorified, romanticised	As fun and games	In a good cause	Consequences shown	Racial or minority strife	Good guy, tough	Verbal	Not necessary to plot	Gruesome, horrific
News at 10 (c)	3.07				0.33			0.54	0.70	1.24				0.69
Dixon of Dock Green	3.10	2.42	0.32	0.92	1.49			1.28	1.00	0.63	0.71	0.95	0.39	0.37
Thunderbirds	3.25						1.48	1.49					0.67	
Probation Officer	3.17					0.56					0.32			
Wednesday Play	3.36	1.58	0.59	1.76	1.22	0.70		0.74	1.74	0.74	0.60	1.54		
World in Action (c)	3.36				0.34			0.94		1.56		0.36		1.01
Perry Mason	3.55		0.62	0.52	1.24				1.40	0.64		1.09	0.68	0.64
Sergeant Cork	3.57					1.11		1.25			1.07			
Invisible Man	3.60	0.81				1.30						0.51		
Maigret	3.73			0.88	1.41	1.31		1.76	1.47	0.45	1.24	0.88	0.47	0.68
Till Death us do Part	3.87			3.80								3.39		
Z-Cars (c)	3.95	3.56	0.49	1.13		1.00	0.40	1.85	1.86	0.86	1.28	1.46	0.53	0.79
Robin Hood	4.00	0.88	2.80		2.77	3.43	2.75	2.92	0.57		2.90	0.91	0.58	
Out of the Unknown	4.00	0.90				0.40					0.47	0.53		2.56
Wells Fargo (c)	4.00	2.40	1.28		0.80	2.20	0.60	2.02	0.82		2.50		0.82	
Bonanza	4.11	2.43		1.16	0.82		1.16	2.11	0.98	0.67	2.57	1.21	0.85	
No Hiding Place	4.14	3.44	0.60	0.58		1.28	0.48	2.03	1.30	0.60	1.28		0.79	0.83
Virginian	4.22	2.77	1.63	0.88	1.03	2.52	0.84	2.09	1.02	0.58	2.74	1.17	0.81	0.46
Cinema	4.37	1.99	0.97		1.02	1.84	1.53	1.49	1.86	1.42	1.79	1.82	1.57	1.51
Mystery and Imagination	4.37	1.09	0.52	0.59										2.77
Adam Adamant	4.44	1.72	2.22		0.91						2.92	0.85		1.22
Cheyenne	4.50	2.89	1.91			1.97				0.90				
Wyatt Earp	4.67		1.99		2.14	2.34		2.43			3.04			

Table 4.9 (cont.)

PROGRAMME	HOW VIOLENT	TYPE OF TELEVISION VIOLENCE*												
		Realistic fiction	By a good guy, rebel	Domestic setting	Rudeness, defiance to authority	Glorified, romanticised	As fun and games	In a good cause	Consequences shown	Racial or minority strife	Good guy, tough	Verbal	Not necessary to plot	Gruesome, horrific
Ironside (c)	4.72	3.98	1.03	0.90	2.71	1.94	0.55	2.61	2.18	0.97			0.99	1.00
Rawhide	4.86		1.64			2.67						2.51		
High Chaparral	4.89	3.27	1.84	1.38		2.85		2.36	1.38	0.77	3.06	1.28	0.98	0.49
Highway Patrol (c)	5.00											1.50		
The Informer	5.00	4.34				1.75			2.89			1.60		
High Adventure	5.10	2.17	1.70		1.66	3.32	2.25		2.04					
Dr Who	5.14	1.00			0.87			2.02	1.44		2.06	0.89	1.58	
Gunsmoke	5.17	3.52	1.56	0.66		3.00	1.07	2.38	1.18	0.98	3.62	1.32	1.18	0.54
Crane	5.25	3.41				2.71	1.16							0.73
77 Sunset Strip	5.70		1.35			2.57		2.85				3.14	2.11	
Danger Man	5.75		2.97			3.88		3.40			4.60		2.25	2.08
The Saint	5.77	3.09	2.89	0.62	2.31	4.33		3.87	2.08		4.62	1.61	1.89	1.15
Late Night Horror	6.67	1.93										0.78		1.77
The Avengers	6.82	3.24				5.33	5.19	4.55		0.80	5.36	1.90	3.57	2.67
Man from UNCLE	7.03					4.96		4.22			5.05		3.66	2.32
Hawaii Five-0	7.25	6.34		0.87	3.14	4.79	0.88	4.08		1.52	4.61	2.04	2.66	2.72
Professional Boxing	7.33													
The Great War	7.62													
ADDITIONAL PROGRAMMES FROM 1970-71 SAMPLE														
Softly, Softly	4.45	4.06		0.54								0.66	0.48	0.67
Star Trek (c)	4.78				0.53			2.49				0.92		
Last of the Mohicans (c)	5.30							2.63				0.93		
Wayne in Action	6.83	4.04		0.68		5.46			3.17		5.55	2.22	3.07	0.79
The Untouchables	8.38	7.28						4.19				2.66		

(c) = programmes making up part of the control sample as well as being part of the violence sample.
*For full naming of these dimensions of television violence, see p.94

Table 4.10

Sixty-four (64) programmes used in the measuring technique, each scored for its presentation of violence of different kinds (12 dichotomous variables)

PROGRAMME	HOW VIOLENT	IS IT A PROGRAMME THAT PRESENTS VIOLENCE IN CONTEXT OF											
		English police	Cartoons	Tom and Jerry	Personal relation-ships	News or News-reels	Slap-stick comedy	Science fiction	Westerns	Sporting events	Wrestling and boxing	Gangs in organised crime	Adults' behaviour
Dad's Army	(0.85)						0.85						
Captain Pugwash	(1.08)		1.08										
Grandstand (c)	1.12									1.12			
The Rag Trade	1.13						1.13						
Marty	1.14						1.14						
Army Game	1.16						1.16						
Coronation St (c)	1.25				1.25								
Sports View	1.25									1.25			
Yogi Bear (c)	1.42		1.42										
Billy Bunter	1.71						1.71						
Saturday Sportstime	(1.75)									1.75			
Please Sir!	2.10						2.10						
Whacko	2.25						2.25						
The Human Jungle	2.17				2.17								
News Summary (c)	2.25					2.25							
The Power Game	2.32				2.32								
The Boss Cat	(2.35)		2.35										
Steptoe and Son	2.39				2.39		2.39						
Mr Rose	2.71	2.71											
Panorama (c)	2.81					2.81							
Lone Ranger (c)	3.00								3.00				
News at 10	3.07					3.07							
Dixon of Dock Green (c)	3.10	3.10			3.10								
Probation Officer	3.17				3.17								
Wednesday Play	3.36				3.36								
World in Action (c)	3.36					3.36							
Quatermass and the Pit	(3.50)							3.50					

Table 4.10 (cont.)

PROGRAMME	HOW VIOLENT	IS IT A PROGRAMME THAT PRESENTS VIOLENCE IN CONTEXT OF											
		English police	Cartoons	Tom and Jerry	Personal relation-ships	News or News-reels	Slap-stick comedy	Science fiction	Westerns	Sporting events	Wrestling and boxing	Gangs in organised crime	Adults' behaviour
Lost in Space	(3.50)							3.50					
Popeye	(3.50)		3.50										
Sergeant Cork	3.57	3.57										3.57	3.57
Maigret	3.73												3.73
Till Death us do Part	3.87				3.87		3.87						
Z-Cars	3.95	3.95			3.95							3.95	
Wells Fargo (c)	4.00								4.00				4.00
Out of the Unknown	4.00							4.00					
Bonanza	4.11								4.11				4.11
No Hiding Place	4.14	4.14										4.14	
The Virginian	4.22								4.22				4.22
**Softly, Softly (c)	4.45	4.45			4.45							4.45	
Cheyenne	4.50								4.50				
Wyatt Earp	4.67								4.67				4.67
Ironside (c)	4.72											4.72	4.72
**Star Trek (c)	4.78							4.78					
Rawhide	4.86								4.86				
High Chaparral	4.89								4.89				
The Informer	5.00	5.00										5.00	5.00
Highway Patrol (c)	5.00											5.00	5.00
Dr Who	5.14							5.14					
Gunsmoke	5.17								5.17				
Crane	5.25				5.25							5.25	
**Last of the Mohicans (c)	5.30								5.30				
77 Sunset Strip	5.70											5.70	
Danger Man	5.75											5.75	5.75
The Saint	5.77											5.77	5.77

Table 4.10 (cont.)

PROGRAMME	HOW VIOLENT	IS IT A PROGRAMME THAT PRESENTS VIOLENCE IN CONTEXT OF											
		English police	Cartoons	Tom and Jerry	Personal relation-ships	News or News-reels	Slap-stick comedy	Science fiction	Westerns	Sporting events	Wrestling and boxing	Gangs in organised crime	Adults' behaviour
Late Night Horror	6.67							6.67					
The Avengers	6.82											6.82	
**Wayne in Action (c)	6.83				6.83				6.83				6.83
The Man from UNCLE	7.03											7.03	7.03
Hawaii Five-0	7.25											7.25	7.25
Professional Boxing	(7.33)										7.33		
The Great War	7.62												7.62
Tom and Jerry	(7.75)		7.75	7.75			7.75						
Professional Wrestling	7.83										7.83		
**The Untouchables (c)	8.38											8.38	8.38
Total in sample	56	7	5	1	12	4	11	6	11	3	2	16	16

*For a full naming of these dimensions of television violence, see p.94.

(c) = programmes making up part of the control sample as well as being part of the violence sample

( ) = a programme included only for the dichotomous variables (and not for the continuous variable

**These are all programmes added from the 1970-71 sample

Table 4.11

Nine programmes used to provide additional bases for estimating the extent of exposure to certain types of programme violence: showing overall ratings for level of violence and the weighted values of these nine programmes with respect to different types of programme violence

PROGRAMME	HOW VIOLENT	Whether it presents specific types of programme violence				
		Cartoon violence	Wrestling/ boxing violence	Violence in other types of sport	Science fiction violence	Slapstick comedy violence
Dad's Army (c)	0.85	–	–	–	–	0.85
Captain Pugwash (c)	1.08	1.08	–	–	–	–
Saturday Sportstime (c)	1.75	–	–	1.75	–	–
The Boss Cat (c)	2.35	2.35	–	–	–	–
Popeye*	3.50	3.50	–	–	–	–
Lost in Space (c)	3.50	3.50	–	–	3.50	–
Quatermass and the Pit*	3.50	–	–	–	3.50	–
Tom and Jerry †	7.75	7.75	–	–	–	7.75
Professional Wrestling †	7.83	–	7.83	–	–	–

(c) = programmes drawn from the control sample (five in all)

*Programmes which had already been rated for violent content both generally and in terms of specific types of TV violence but which had been dropped in the course of the selection process. Used here only as basis for strengthening the measurement of extent of exposure to specific categories of TV violence and not for contributing to the measurement of exposure to TV violence in general.

†Brought into the enquiry because of a late decision to study the effects of two further categories of television violence: boxing and wrestling violence; Tom and Jerry violence.

For each of the years 1968-1971 inclusive, a randomly drawn BBC 2 programme was added, bringing the total number of selected programmes to sixty. Of these, eleven were programmes already included in the violence sample, and a further seven were replaced by such programmes. The decision to replace the seven was based on one or both of the following reasons: (a) too little information about the programme could be found for use as a memory aid in the coming survey investigation; (b) the programme concerned was closely similar to one already in the violence sample. This replacement might of course have been made through programmes altogether outside of the violence sample, but it was desirable to keep down as much as possible the already large number of programmes about which boys were to be questioned. Accordingly, all seven replacements were of programmes already in the violence sample which were closely similar to them in terms of general and apparent violence level.

The full set of 60 Control programmes is shown in Appendix 6. It consists of 18 programmes already in the violence sample (and identified as such in the Appendix item) and 42 more which were quite new.

A second challenging or control system, involving amount of exposure to non-violent television

A further and more direct internal control or challenging system was vested in the hypothesis that:

> Any increase in violent behaviour produced by exposure to a lot of non-violent television material will be just as large as any increase produced by exposure to violence on television. [18]

For the investigation of this hypothesis, a total of 40 programmes was compiled from the 117 already in the testing system. The choice of the 40 was dominated by the aim of bringing together a set of non-violent programmes, but in fact this aim was approached rather than fully achieved.

For presentation in the survey investigation, the selected programmes were to be integrated into the violence sample. The total number of programmes to be used in the assessment of the nature and extent of exposure to television material was 117, made up as shown in table 4.12.

The full set of 117 programmes, set out in order of presentation within various test materials, is given in Appendix 7 to this chapter.

Table 4.12
The different groupings of the 117 programmes used in the enquiry as bases for exposure scores

The different groupings of the TV programmes included in the enquiry		Number of programmes in each of four groupings	Number of programmes in the 2 samples: Violent programmes sample	Number of programmes in the 2 samples: Control programmes sample
(V)	Programmes included only in the sample of violent programmes	53	68	
(C)	Programmes included only in the sample of control programmes	45		60
(V, C)	Programmes included in both the violence sample and the control sample	15		
(N)	Programmes included in neither sample – used only for assessment of extent of exposure to specific categories of TV violence	4		
	All programmes dealt with in the enquiry	117		

FREQUENCY OF EXPOSURE TO THE SAMPLED PROGRAMMES

THE SCORING SYSTEM ONCE FREQUENCY IS ESTABLISHED

Complex survey methods were used to derive information about the frequency with which a representative sample of London boys had, since 1958, viewed the programmes in the violence (and the control) samples. However, it will aid the description of the scoring system if we leave until later the description of those methods and concentrate now upon the ways in which the frequencies were used to calculate scores for exposure to the different sets of television violence and to TV material generally.

A ceiling upon the claims made about exposure to the sample of TV violence

It had been planned (see pages 95-97 and table 4.4) that if a programme with a unit score of 3.40 (say) for realistic but fictional violence was seen by a boy 20 times, then he would thereby be allotted a score of 20 x 3.40 (= 68.00) towards his total score for exposure to violence of the realistic fictional kind.

But a special problem arises when the total number of times a boy says he ever saw a given programme is very large – e.g. 1,500 viewings of the 9 o'clock news. Such a degree of exposure to one class of programme (even if quite true) would partly or even largely swamp out much of the discriminative power of the rest of that boy's viewing. Furthermore, the acceptance (and integration into score) of unlimited numbers of exposures to given programmes would require an assumption that the say, 100th exposure to the News was just as effective as the 1st or 2nd or 3rd exposure . . . or that the 1,000th was just as effective as the 100th exposure. An assumption was made that this was not so, and that the impact, generally speaking, of exposure to a series falls off beyond a certain point as more and more programmes in that series are seen. [19] In effect, this meant that *a ceiling* was set upon the number of exposures that could be counted with respect to any one programme series.

However, the main reason for setting some moderate ceiling was to protect the overall findings from distortion through some boys making massive claims/overclaims.

For the calculation of total score on any of the exposure dimensions, the ceiling set was 100 exposures per programme series. The reasons for setting this *particular* ceiling rather than a higher or a lower one, were as follows.

(a) A ceiling of 100 affected less than 10 per cent of all the 75 exposure estimates available per boy.

(b) The correlation between total number of exposures (over all programmes in the violence sample) in going from *no ceiling* to a ceiling of 100 was + 0.94, compared with + 0.96 in going from a ceiling of 100 to a ceiling of 50.

Calculating indices of exposure to specified forms of television violence

As a result of data collection through two interviews, estimates of exposure to each of the 117 programmes were derived for each boy (see the information collection phase, below). These estimates were coded with a ceiling of 999 per programme series. [20] From here on the estimates of exposure to different kinds of television violence were derived through computerised processes and the resultant scores for each boy were then fed into his total data set for computer processing in the context of the many hypothesis tests being carried out. The arithmetic of the scoring system was, however, quite simple and was described at the beginning of this chapter (see pages 95-97). To recapitulate, taking into account the imposition of the ceiling of 100 exposures per programme series, the method was as illustrated through table 4.13.

Calculating indices of exposure to television output generally

The calculation of an index of exposure to television output generally was a much simpler operation. Thus it involved a straightforward count of the total number of exposures (after the imposition of a ceiling of 100 per programme) without any other form of weighting. This too was done through a computer process and the indices of exposure to television output generally were fed into the data set for each boy and thence through the programme for testing the control hypothesis.

THE INFORMATION COLLECTION PHASE

The collection of information about the exposure of boys to different programmes in the list of 117 was complex and demanding.

To this end, and stated in summary form: (i) all 117 programmes were built into a self-completion booklet, with one programme to a single page of the booklet; (ii) through this booklet, the boy provided information, with respect to each programme, about whether he had ever seen it and his ages on first and last seeing it; (iii) at a subsequent interview at the Survey Research Centre a questioning sequence was used to develop an approximate estimate of how many times in that period of viewing the boy had seen the programme concerned. These three stages and the equipment involved in them are detailed as follows.

Table 4.13
Calculating the index† of an individual boy's exposure to *fictional* violence of the *realistic* kind

Programme Name	Estimated frequency of exposure	Frequency used* (f)	Units of this sort of violence accruing per single exposure (v)	Product of f and v (f.v)
The Rag Trade	10	10	0.11	1.10
The Army Game	0	0	0.23	0.00
Billy Bunter of Greyfriars School	0	0	0.20	0.00
Please, Sir!	80	80	0.46	36.80
Whacko!	4	4	0.28	1.12
Steptoe and Son	0	0	0.55	0.00
Dixon of Dock Green	85	85	2.42	205.70
The Wednesday Play	0	0	1.58	0.00
The Invisible Man	0	0	0.81	0.00
Z-Cars	120	100	3.56	356.00
Robin Hood	30	30	0.88	26.40
Out of the Unknown	25	25	0.90	22.50
Wells Fargo	15	15	2.40	36.00
Bonanza	90	90	2.43	218.70
No Hiding Place	20	20	3.44	68.80
The Virginian	70	70	2.77	193.90
Cinema	25	25	1.99	49.75
Mystery and Imagination	0	0	1.09	0.00
Adam Adamant Lives!	7	7	1.72	12.04
Cheyenne	15	15	2.89	43.35
A Man called Ironside	70	70	3.98	278.60
The High Chaparral	5	5	3.27	16.35
The Informer	3	3	4.34	13.02
High Adventure	10	10	2.17	21.70
Dr Who	115	100	1.00	100.00
Gunsmoke	75	75	3.52	264.00
Crane	0	0	3.41	0.00
The Saint	40	40	3.09	123.60
Late Night Horror	0	0	1.93	0.00
The Avengers	85	85	3.24	275.40
Hawaii Five-0	29	29	6.34	183.85
Softly, Softly	120	100	4.06	406.00
Wayne in Action	0	0	4.04	0.00
The Untouchables	35	35	7.28	254.80
Aggregate of f x v (=Index* of exposure to this sort of television violence) =				3209.48

*After ceiling applied

†'Index' in the sense that the total of the products is simply a discriminant for differentiating between degrees of exposure to the specified kinds of television violence.

The form and the functions of the self-completion method

The self-completion booklet was of octavo size, with its 137 pages lightly bound to facilitate easy tear-out of each. For each of 117 programmes, there was a single page on the front of which were printed programme details giving: name of the programme, its general character and coverage, its main actors, its station of origin, the period(s) during which it was broadcast. On its back were two questions, one asking the respondent how old he was when he first viewed this programme, and the other asking how old he was when he last viewed it (see diagram 4.6 (a)).

The 117 programme sheets were introduced with a short series of *instruction* sheets which between them (i) told the boy what he was first required to do with the booklet, namely to sort its pages into three heaps to indicate whether he had *definitely* seen the programme concerned, had definitely not seen it, was unsure whether he had seen it or not (see diagram 4.6 (b)); (ii) told him about certain important rules of procedure; (iii) told him that at the end of his work at home and a further interview at the Centre he would receive £2, and would have a chance to win one of 20 large cash prizes (see diagram 4.6 (c)).

The instruction sheets were white and the programme sheets were in various colours. Further white sheets, in the form of reminders and instructions, were strategically placed throughout the booklet (see diagram 4.6 (d)).

After the sorting process had been completed for all 117 programme sheets, a further instruction sheet told the boy: to pack away (in 2 of the 3 envelopes that were provided) all programmes he was unsure about (envelope 3) or definitely had not seen (envelope 2); to turn over the heap of programmes he had sorted as 'definitely seen' and to deal with these as instructed on the next white sheet in the booklet. On this and the subsequent instruction sheets (see diagram 4.6 (e)), the boy was instructed to answer the two questions on the back of each of these programme sheets asking him what was his age on first watching programmes in this series and his age when he last watched it; to get help as necessary from his parents in doing this and to use certain other memory aids that would have been explained to him by his interviewer; to put the completed programme sheets into envelope 1 and to bring all three envelopes with him to his interview at the Survey Research Centre.

Preparing boys to use the self-completion booklet at home

The interviewing techniques which were used to locate and to make effective contact with the sampled boys in their homes are described in detail in chapter 9 under 'Sampling'.

Before starting her interview with the boy, the interviewer would have told him that (i) this was a university study, (ii) he could earn £2 for a double interview – this one and a further one at the Survey Research Centre later on; (iii) his first job was to provide information about his past viewing of television; (iv) he would be called for by car to go to his second interview at the Centre.

Demonstrating the sorting process [21]

The interviewer began by using a demonstration copy of the programme pack in order to show the boy what he would have to do with his own programme pack later on. The boy was asked to read through the first (instructional) page of the booklet (see diagram 4.6 (c)) and was urged to ask questions about anything that was not clear. He was asked to take out of a large package three 8 in. x 12 in. envelopes labelled respectively:

Diagram 6(a)

No.28.

TOM AND JERRY

A series of ten-minute cartoons, about the adventures of Tom the cat and Jerry the mouse.

STARRING:

Tom (cartoon cat)

Jerry (cartoon mouse)

SHOWN

On BBC 1, on various evenings, from 1967 to 1972.

37

No.28.

TOM AND JERRY

1. How OLD were you when you FIRST watched it?

(write in) years

2. How old were you when you LAST watched it?

(write in) years

If you find you are getting bored or tired, take a break for a few minutes.

WHAT YOU HAVE TO DO

In this booklet there are some WHITE pages that are mostly rules and there are COLOURED pages with the names of TV programmes on them.

Go through the booklet page by page.

Each time you come to a WHITE sheet, read it carefully and tick it at the bottom to show you have read it.

Each time you come to a COLOURED sheet, tear it out and sort it into one of three heaps.

- HEAP 1 is for programmes you definitely HAVE seen at some time.
- HEAP 2 is for programmes you definitely have NOT seen.
- HEAP 3 is for programmes you are NOT SURE about.

You will find the names of your 3 heaps on the 3 envelopes that come with your kit. Lay the three envelopes out on a table to mark where your 3 HEAPS will go.

So your job is to read the WHITE pages and to sort all the COLOURED pages into 3 heaps. DO THIS RIGHT TO THE VERY END OF THE BOOKLET.

Put a tick in the box when you have read these rules. Then read them through once more. ☐

1

Diagram 6(b)

YOUR PAYMENT
FOR HELPING US

Bring this page with you when you come for your interview.

If the work you are doing for us at home is complete, it will entitle you to a fee of:

TWO POUNDS

at the end of your interview.

2

Diagram 6(c)

TWENTY CASH PRIZES

This page gives you a chance of winning a cash prize if you complete the tasks you kindly agreed to do for us.

THERE ARE TWENTY CASH PRIZES
RANGING FROM

£5 – £20

Bring this page with you to the Centre and pass it to your interviewer. He or she will sign it and give it a number if you have completed your task properly. When he or she has signed it, you will have a chance of winning one of the prizes.

Signature of
Interviewer ______________

Ticket Number: ______________

3

Diagram 6(c)

REMEMBER

Use the big envelope to mark out your three heaps. Pile each heap on top of its envelope in the square marked out for it.

Put a tick in the box when you have read this rule. ☐

4

Diagram 6(c)

PLEASE NOTE
CAREFULLY

When you are sorting the coloured sheets into 3 heaps, DON'T ANSWER THE QUESTIONS ON THE BACKS OF THEM. That will come later.

Sort them all before you bother with the backs.

Put a tick in the box when you have read this rule. ☐

5

Diagram 6(c)

ONE MORE IMPORTANT RULE
BEFORE YOU START

You can get help from your parents if you are puzzled about what we want you to do.

But don't ask them to do this job for you. It is your own viewing we are interested in.

Put a tick in the box when you have read this rule. ☐

6

Diagram 6(c)

Diagram 6(d)

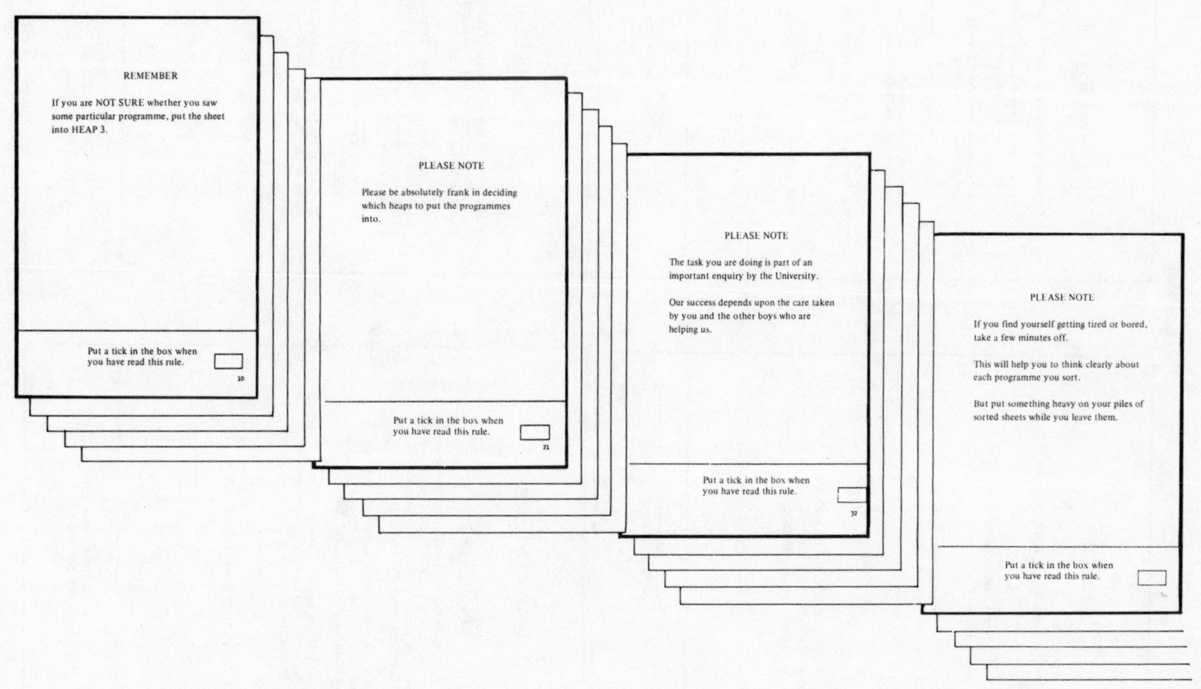

REMEMBER
If you are NOT SURE whether you saw some particular programme, put the sheet into HEAP 3.
Put a tick in the box when you have read this rule.
10
PLEASE NOTE
Please be absolutely frank in deciding which heaps to put the programmes into.
Put a tick in the box when you have read this rule.
21
PLEASE NOTE
The task you are doing is part of an important enquiry by the University.
Our success depends upon the care taken by you and the other boys who are helping us.
Put a tick in the box when you have read this rule.
32
PLEASE NOTE
If you find yourself getting tired or bored, take a few minutes off.
This will help you to think clearly about each programme you sort.
But put something heavy on your piles of sorted sheets while you leave them.
Put a tick in the box when you have read this rule.

Diagram 6(e)

NEXT STEPS

Now that you have sorted all the coloured cards into 3 heaps, there is something new to do.

Put all the Heap 3 lot inside the Heap 3 envelope, and put it to one side.

Put all the Heap 2 lot inside the Heap 2 envelope, and put it to one side.

BUT

JUST PICK UP THE HEAP 1 LOT AND READ ON THE NEXT WHITE PAGE WHAT YOU HAVE TO DO WITH THEM.

Put a tick in this box when you have read this rule. ☐

134

THE NEXT STEP

Turn over the whole set of Heap 1 cards.

On every one of these there are 2 questions that we want you to answer. They are about

how old you were when you first watched the programmed named on it.

how old you were when you last watched it.

We want you to answer these questions on the back of every one of your Heap 1 cards.

It is quite all right to ask your parents to help if you don't quite know what to do. But it is YOUR viewing we are asking about.

NOW TURN TO THE NEXT WHITE SHEET

Put a tick in this box when you have read this rule. ☐

135

IMPORTANT REMINDER

Instructions for Using Your Personal time-scale Sheet

To help answer the two questions on the back of your Heap 1 cards you should check when each series of programmes started and finished. This is printed on the fronts of the cards.

THEN, check these dates against your Personal Time-Scale Sheet and you will see how old you were when the series started and finished.

You should now be able to answer Questions 1 and 2 more easily. REMEMBER, you can use all the information on your Personal Time-Scale Sheet to help you.

NOW TURN TO THE LAST WHITE SHEET

Put a tick in this box when you have read this rule. ☐

136

THE NEXT AND LAST STEP

Now sort into numerical order all the sheets in your Heap 1. You will find the number of each sheet at its top right hand corner.

When this is done, your lowest Programme Number will be on top of the Heap 1 sheets and the highest Programme Number will be at the bottom of the Heap 1 sheets.

Put a rubber band round the pile of sheets and put them into the Heap 1 envelope.

Then seal up the Heap 1 envelope and have it ready for the interviewer when he or she calls at the agreed time.

Put a tick in the box when you have read this instruction. ☐

137

Diagram 7

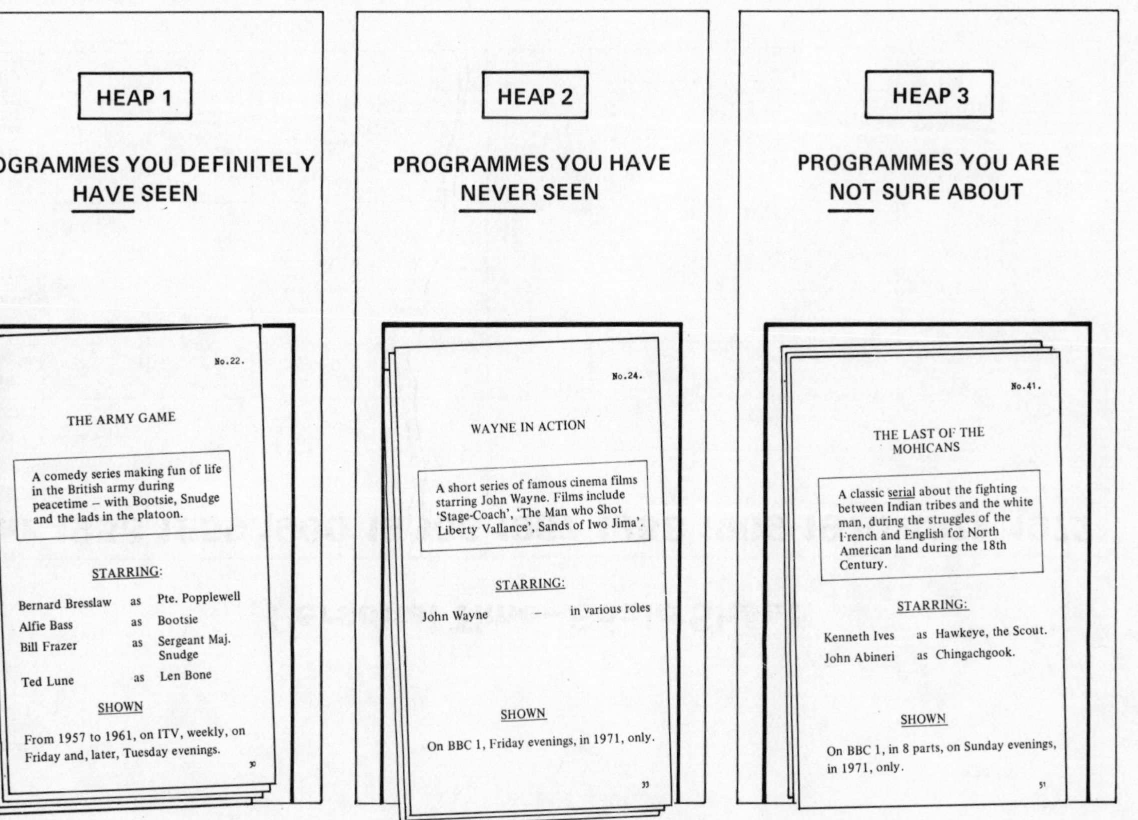

HEAP 1
PROGRAMMES YOU DEFINITELY HAVE SEEN
No.22.
THE ARMY GAME
A comedy series making fun of life in the British army during peacetime – with Bootsie, Snudge and the lads in the platoon.
STARRING:
Bernard Bresslaw as Pte. Popplewell
Alfie Bass as Bootsie
Bill Frazer as Sergeant Maj. Snudge
Ted Lune as Len Bone
SHOWN
From 1957 to 1961, on ITV, weekly, on Friday and, later, Tuesday evenings.
30
HEAP 2
PROGRAMMES YOU HAVE NEVER SEEN
No.24.
WAYNE IN ACTION
A short series of famous cinema films starring John Wayne. Films include 'Stage-Coach', 'The Man who Shot Liberty Vallance', Sands of Iwo Jima'.
STARRING:
John Wayne – in various roles
SHOWN
On BBC 1, Friday evenings, in 1971, only.
33
HEAP 3
PROGRAMMES YOU ARE NOT SURE ABOUT
No.41.
THE LAST OF THE MOHICANS
A classic serial about the fighting between Indian tribes and the white man, during the struggles of the French and English for North American land during the 18th Century.
STARRING:
Kenneth Ives as Hawkeye, the Scout.
John Abineri as Chingachgook.
SHOWN
On BBC 1, in 8 parts, on Sunday evenings, in 1971, only.
51

Diagram 8

Personal Time-Scale Sheet

Year	1958	1959	1960	19 ... 66	1967	1968	1969	1970	1971	1972
YOUR AGE										
YOUR SCHOOLS										
YOUR CLASSES										
SOME PERSONAL EVENTS IN YOUR LIFE										
SOME WORLD EVENTS BETWEEN 1958-1972	FIRST BAN THE BOMB (C.N.D.) MARCH IN NORFOLK STREET BATTLES IN CUBA BETWEEN CASTRO'S REBELS AND BATISTA BEGINNINGS OR NOTTINGHILL GATE 'RACE RIOTS'	BRIAN LONDON vs HENRY COOPER BRITISH TITLE FIGHT WOLVERHAMPTON WANDERERS TOP DIV. 1	BELGIANS PULL OUT OF CONGO. POWER STRUGGLE AND CIVIL WAR LED TO MASS STARVATION BRITISH AID SENT TO CONGO	CONGO STARVATI... ORLD AT ITS PEAK FOOD AID REQUIR... ER USA PUT CHIMP INTO ... D SPACE ... T RUSSIANS SEND FIRST MAN INTO SPACE (YURI GAGARIN) ... TH ... CR	QE 2 LAUNCHED ABERFAN DISASTER THE BREATHALYSER WAS BROUGHT IN FIRST HEART TRANS-PLANT BY DR. BARNARD DONALD CAMPBELL KILLED IN 'BLUEBIRD' SENATOR ROBERT KENNEDY ASSASSINATED	NIXON BECAME PRESIDENT OF U.S.A. BIAFRAN CRISIS BEGAN SOLDIERS FIRST SENT TO IRELAND	HANGING ABOLISHED IN GREAT BRITAIN FIRST MEN LAND ON MOON FIRST OF THE SKINHEADS EMERGED	EDWARD HEATH BECAME PRIME MINISTER ROLLS ROYCE CRASHES LILLIAN BOARD TREATED FOR CANCER	INDIA/PAKISTAN WAR POST OFFICE TOWER BOMBED ROBERT CARR'S HOME BOMBED CONCORDE'S FIRST FLIGHT	INDUSTRIAL RELATIONS BILL BECAME LAW BEA TRIDENT CRASHED NEAR STAINES DUKE OF WINDSOR DIED

Programmes you definitely *have* seen
Programmes you have *never* seen
Programmes you are not sure about

These (see diagram 4.6 (b)) were laid out in a row as sorting bases for the programme sheets. The interviewer tore out the first programme sheet and asked the boy to sort it onto one of the envelopes as appropriate; she then challenged his placement of it, looking for and correcting any evidence of misunderstanding. This was repeated for nine more programme sheets and the basic rules of sorting were then repeated to the boy. After this, the boy dealt in the same way, under supervision, with the next ten programme sheets. He was now told that there were about 100 of these sheets in his pack that needed to be dealt with in this way.

Introducing the boy to (i) the task of recalling his age on first and on last viewing a given programme series, (ii) two memory aids

The interviewer next told the boy that at the end of this sorting job he would find a further instruction sheet telling him what to do next (see diagram 4.6 (e) p.135). He was shown this sheet and asked to read it out aloud. In effect, it told him that for each of the programmes he had said *he had definitely seen*, he was to answer the two questions on the back of the programme sheet, namely:

'How old were you when you *first* watched it?'

'How old were you when you *last* watched it?'

When he had done this, he was told that there were several ways of making things easier for him and he was asked to read about these on the next instruction sheet in his programme booklet (see diagram 4.6 (e) p.136). These were (a) the information on the front of each programme sheet about the time period during which that programme was broadcast; (b) a personal time-scale which he would be asked to fill in.

The personal time-scale. The boy was introduced to the personal time-scale (see diagram 4.8) which in general terms was a device meant to increase his consciousness of time and of the passage of time. The time-scale gave and asked for certain information for each year in the past back to that in which the boy was only five years old. Thus under 1972 (the date of the enquiry) he was asked to write his present age; under 1971, his age the year before, and so on across the sheet. Then, for each year (and age), he was asked what school and class he was in at that time *and* for one event in his life that he recalled happening that year. The interviewer could help him by giving him some of the public events of the period and by prompting with different sorts of things that happen to boys (e.g. holiday, got a bike, had an operation). The boy's mother was not excluded from giving help, but the recall task had to be the boy's own as much as possible.

At the end of this, the boy was asked to look again at his answers on the back of the programme sheet he had filled in. He was asked to note from his time-scale what was happening in his life the year the programme was first shown, what was happening in the year he had said he first watched it . . . and he was encouraged to make any changes he now thought necessary.

Providing the 'age' details. The boy now worked through the same two questions on the backs of each of the (say) 20 programmes he had sorted as being seen at some time, with the interviewer urging throughout that he make use of the two aid-systems explained to him, and helping him to do so wherever this seemed necessary.

After trying to clear up any doubts expressed by the boy or suspected by the interviewer, the interviewer took back all her demonstration sheets and gave the boy a fresh programme pack for completion on his own. He was asked to have it with him, completed, when he came for his second interview. The interviewer fixed a time at which a car would call for him on a particular day approximately a week hence. He should bring the completed materials with him (along with the other papers completed during that period by the boy and his parents).

Continuing the extraction of programme exposure information at the Survey Research Centre

At the Survey Research Centre, the boy underwent an intensive interview which, with rest pauses and refreshment breaks, lasted for three and a half hours for most boys. Early in this interview the intensive interviewer (a separate person from the one who had conducted the at-home interview) went through the following steps.

(a) He/she checked through the content of each envelope to make sure that the boy had understood what he was required to put into each.

(b) He/she took out the programme sheets in the 'definitely have seen' envelope and studied them for completeness.

(c) For each of these programme sheets he/she: (i) noted the period of viewing claimed (e.g. two years); (ii) calculated from a guide sheet the maximum number of viewings which that period would, on average, allow the boy (e.g. two years of a programme shown on average 15 times a year indicates a maximum possible exposure of 30 times); (iii) told the boy that there were that many (i.e. 30) broadcasts of the programme in the total period he had claimed; (iv) asked him to say how many of that total he had actually viewed; (v) entered that number on the back of the programme sheet concerned.

(d) This process was guarded by certain other steps, taken as deemed necessary by the interviewer; (i) the interviewer had with him/her a book of visual aids providing programme details (including pictures for many of the programmes) which were used to help clear up doubts on the part of the boy or interviewer about whether a given programme had in fact been seen by the boy; (ii) the boy was challenged from time to time about the claims he had made concerning his age on first and last seeing the programme, and especially about the number (out of the maximum possible) of times the boy had viewed the given programme; this applied particularly to boys who claimed the maximum or something near the maximum (e.g. 'You mean you saw just about every episode that was shown when you were a viewer of . . . ?')

The instructions to which the interviewer worked are set out in full in Appendix 8 to this chapter.

Completing the collection of data

At the end of this process, the interviewer returned all programme sheets from the 'definitely saw' envelope back to that envelope – but now with the boy's frequency estimates for the different programmes entered on them. At a later stage this information was entered on transfer sheets for coding and was used for the calculation of indices of exposure as described in earlier pages of this chapter.

THE RELIABILITY AND VALIDITY OF THE METHOD

With a procedure of the complex kind described in this chapter, it is highly desirable to carry out any available check on its adequacy. Ideally this means a validating check and in the present case this means that one needs to find out to what extent the discriminations achieved through the survey data are in fact true discriminations. More specifically, if we classify a boy as being in the top 10 per cent or the top 25 per cent or the top 50 per cent as far as exposure to TV violence is concerned, is that his true position?

Methods used

The nature of the detail being gathered ruled out any possibility of a full validation test being made. Nonetheless a useful degree of challenge to the adequacy of the data gathered could be carried out and this took the following form. [22] All interviewing was conducted by specialist interviewers trained to carry out the rather demanding forms of elicitation involved.

I A sample of 76 boys was interviewed at home and processed through the self-completion methods as described above (to yield initial sorting of programme sheets and age details).

II A week later (by appointment) an interviewer called at the boy's home and took him through the type of interview which ordinarily would take place at the Centre (to yield frequency data for each programme sorted as 'seen').

III Once this was done, the interviewer changed role and began a process designed to challenge the details collected through stages I and II. This challenging process was conducted as follows.

1 The boy was told that the purpose of his interview was in fact to allow us to test our own methods – to see if 'the methods we are using are in fact working' He was told that this meant we would be asking him to go back over some of the sorting he did during the past week. He was assured that this was *not* a test of him but of the method. He was asked to try to forget all about what he did the first time, to think of himself as starting afresh and to try at all times for the greatest possible accuracy.

2 He was then asked to work through a fresh booklet of the test programmes, sorting them into heaps 1, 2 and 3 as before – but 'this time I will be giving you some extra information about them'. Envelopes 1, 2 and 3 were laid out in the usual way and their meanings were re-stated and stressed to the boy.

3 The boy was then passed the first of the programme sheets and told: 'Read out for me what is on the front of the sheet'.

Pause while he reads *all* of it. Then say: 'Can you remember anything at all you ever saw in a programme in that series?'

The interviewer then helped the boy with pictorial and verbal aids relevant to that particular series, the verbal aids being extended descriptions of the programme series concerned. After this, the boy was asked to sort that programme sheet onto one of the three envelopes as appropriate.

4 (a) If the boy sorted that sheet into heap 1, that choice was challenged with the following questions:

'When was the last time you ever saw a programme in that series?'

'How can you be sure you ever saw a programme in that series?'

He was also pressed for some of the things he saw in it at some time or other. If there was any doubt at all after this, he was asked to think again about where he had sorted the programme sheet.

(b) If he sorted the programme sheet into heap 2, he was challenged with the question: 'Do you mean *never* in your whole life?'/'How can you be sure of that?' If there was evidence of doubt or uncertainty, the interviewer was to take the respondent through the recall aids again and to ask the boy to think again about where the programme sheet should go.

(c) If the boy sorted the programme sheet into heap 3 (i.e. 'not sure'), the boy was to be asked: 'Why did you put it into *that* heap?' (the right answer being 'don't know') / 'What in particular makes you doubtful?' Here too, the boy would be asked to reconsider his original sorting if the interviewer felt, on the basis of the boy's replies, that the 'don't know' response was possibly wrong.

5 This process was repeated for each of the first six sheets sorted into heap 1, the first six sorted into heap 2, the first six sorted into heap 3. It was also repeated for the eighth, the ninth, the eleventh and so on according to the following pattern: fourteenth, seventeenth, twentieth, twenty-first, twenty-third, twenty-seventh, and thereafter for every fifth sheet. The reason for this irregular system was that the respondent should not be able to predict when his sorting would be challenged again.

6 After this, the interviewer began extracting information about the *frequency of viewing* programmes sorted by the boy into heap 1. This was a lengthy and rather demanding process lasting in many cases for well over an hour. During it, the boy was taken through the following processes.

(a) The intensive interviewer began with several steps designed to re-acquaint the boy with the sorting process and, above all, to induce in him a heightened awareness of the need for care.

(i) The interviewer told the boy that he now wanted to get details from him of his age when he viewed certain programmes and of the number of times certain programmes were viewed by him.

(ii) The interviewer told the boy that everything depended on his taking care and why it was necessary to take care. The interviewer warned the boy that the checking process to be done would involve some repetition of questions and that he (the interviewer) hoped that the boy would excuse this.

(iii) The topmost of the heap 1 programme sheets was used to show the boy what was wanted and to teach him how to go about his task. He was reminded of that programme by means of the visual and verbal aids and was asked for his earliest memory of what happened in that programme. Its starting date was linked, through the 'personal time scale' to the boy's own age and to his personal events at that time. He was then told:

'Now I want to get your age when you first watched programmes in the . . . (*name it*) series. *I need you to be very careful about this*. I want you to be as accurate as possible in telling me how old you were when you first watched this programme. It would be easy for you to guess wildly, but that would only spoil our research. So please try hard for an accurate answer.' (*pause*). 'Let's use your time chart for this.'

The interviewer now worked with the boy to establish his use of the time chart for this task, commenting on the following general lines.

- 'You were about eight when this one first started . . . that was when you were at St Martin's School and when you took a holiday at Billy Butlin's . . . '
- 'Going by that, how old were you when you first started to watch . . . (*name it*).'

On getting his estimate of his age when he first viewed this programme, the boy was challenged with: 'How did you work out it was *that* age?' When he settled for a 'first saw it' age, this was entered against question 1 on the back of the programme sheet. The interviewer next took up the question of the boy's *last* viewing of the programme, using the following verbal leads.

- 'That programme was last shown in 19 . . , when you were aged . . . / is still showing.
- 'What do you remember about the last programme in that series you watched?'
- 'Look at your time chart and try to work out for me how old you were the last time you watched it.'

Here too, the boy was challenged with: 'How did you work out it was that age?'

(iv) The boy was next challenged with regard to the duration of his viewing as implied by the period between his first and last viewing ages: 'That makes it seem that you were watching it for about . . . years in all. Is that about right, or was it more or less than that period that you were watching it?'

(v) The boy was now told that the interviewer wanted to know *how many times* he had watched programmes in the . . . series. He was reminded of his *period* of viewing, was told how many times the programme was broadcast in that period. He was then asked to take his time in thinking about how many of those . . . programmes he actually saw. When he offered a number he was challenged with: 'How did you arrive at that number?' / 'What makes you think it was that many times?' / 'Do you mean you saw just about all of them?' The number finally settled on was entered on the back of the programme sheet.

(b) The interviewer now took the boy through virtually the same procedure for the second to the sixth of the programme sheets in the boy's heap 1, still aiming to engender care in the boy.

(c) From here on, a shortened procedure (but one involving quite a lot of challenging of the boy's replies) was used with the rest of the boy's heap 1 programme sheets, but with a randomised return to the full checking procedure. In the randomised system the following programmes were subject to the full treatment: 13th in order in the heap 1 set, 17th, 20th, 24th, 28th, 34th, 38th, 44th, 46th, 50th, 55th, 57th, 62nd, 65th.

7 In the next step in the checking process, the interviewer attempted to find out if the boy's parents disagreed with his sortings and estimates. The procedure was broadly as follows.

(a) The boy was told that the interviewer now wanted to check his information with the boy's parents.

(b) The parent(s), after an introduction to the process, was/were asked to go through the full set of the boy's sortings and estimates, pointing out any disagreements.

(c) After this, any such disagreements were made the subject of discussion between parent(s) and boy and interviewer. If the boy agreed that the parent was correct, an appropriate change was made. If not, the boy's evidence was allowed to stand. Long wrangling over differences was discouraged.

8 The last stage in the present check involved a *confrontation* phase. The boy sorted all his sheets into numerical order and a sheet by sheet comparison of the boy's evidence in the first and the second extraction processes was made. The comparison in each case was in terms of heap number, age interval, frequency of viewing claimed. For any differences the interviewer said: 'I see we have different answers for the question about . . .'

The interviewer defined the difference and asked the boy to talk about it, giving his reasons for the difference. The 'reasons' were entered on the backs of the programme sheets concerned. The boy was then asked to say which of the differing estimates was correct and it was this estimate that was finally fed into the comparison with the first interview results.

Findings

The findings from this enquiry are set out in table 4.14. They tend quite markedly to support the general adequacy of the measuring technique. At the same time, one must remember that this test of the method is not a thorough-going validity test but probably falls between such a test and one of reliability.

Table 4.14
The comparability of the original and the challenged exposure scores (75 cases)

The different indices of exposure	Correlation co-efficient (product-moment) based on full scores	Number changing position on a 50 : 50 split	Number changing position on a quartile split		
			by 1 place	by 2 places	by 3 places
	r	n	n	n	n
Total number of exposures to the 68 programmes in the violence sample	0.93	8	14	1	0
Index of exposure to violence of a realistic fictional kind	0.93	8	16	2	0
Index of exposure to violence by a 'good guy' who is also a rebel	0.87	9	18	1	1
The News	0.87	7	15	3	0

Notes

[1] There were 25 types at the *end* of the construction process, though at the beginning there were 30. Reasons for the deletions are given in the later pages of this chapter.
[2] For about half the programme types or kinds, the rating of degree was simply in terms of whether or not the programme violence was of that kind.
[3] At this stage, and for reasons connected with the preparation of an 'illustrated rating scale', programmes for the period 1970 and 1971 were temporarily left out. It may be taken however, that they were in fact dealt with in very similar style later in the sampling procedures.
[4] These two publications are the principal guides to broadcast television programmes available in the United Kingdom.
[5] The week chosen was usually the first week in the month and the months were usually January, March, May, July, September, November.
[6] The figure used was that for a random day of broadcast (or *the* day of broadcast) in the week from which the programme was drawn. Audience figures were provided by the BBC.
[7] Then ITA; now IBA.
[8] i.e. that programme for which the mid-point of its cumulative frequency count was nearest to the cumulative frequency figure on the basis of which the *first* selection was made.
[9] See chapters 3 and 12 for details.
[10] See later for cut-back to 26 programme types.

[11] The results were virtually the same when, in response to challenge, this number was increased to 93 – see notes [12] and [14].

[12] Subsequently 63 *more* teachers were chosen from the original 200 with a view to challenging the adequacy of judgements based on only 30 persons. These teachers tended to be people whose period of availability was relatively short, so that different working arrangements had to be devised for them. These arrangements are described in note [14]. It should be noted at this point, however, that such differences as would have resulted in the illustrated scale, had the larger panel been used, would *not* appreciably have changed the form of that illustrated scale. Some examples are given in tables A3.1, A3.2 and A3.3 in Appendix 3.

[13] For brevity, the word 'he' is used, when in fact the reference should always be to 'he or she'.

[14] *A challenge to the meaningfulness of the illustrative programmes used in the scale.* In discussion with the sponsor and with others, it was suggested that the use of a panel of only 30 judges may have left the illustrated scales less stable than was desirable and it was agreed that a check be made by having a further panel of judges of equivalent background repeat the rating process. By this time, stage II of the grading process had been completed, but it had been agreed that if the repeat of stage I with the larger sample produced substantially different results, then stage II would have to be repeated.

For this purpose an additional 63 teachers were chosen from the 200 teachers who had originally applied for such work. The additional 63 tended to be people whose period of availability was relatively short, so that different working arrangements had to be devised for them. Thus they met in groups of about 20 at a time in large-group sessions at which they were introduced to the rating procedure and given practice in using it. They then went home with the rating equipment to complete the rating task there. They posted the results to the Centre. Apart from this, they rated the same programmes as the original 30, on the same scales, under the same conditions.

For the continuous variables, the ratings of the extra 63 judges were combined with those of the first 30, to yield ratings from 93 judges. A comparison could then be made of the results yielded by the first 30 judges and those yielded by all 93 judges. More specifically, this comparison was made to find out if the various scalar positions of the programmes selected through the first 30 judges changed appreciably when based upon the ratings of all 93 judges.

The results of this comparison were as follows:

(1) A majority of the programmes did not shift in scale position at all (59 per cent of the 499 placements).

(2) Where programmes shifted, the shift tended to be *one* scalar position (31 per cent of the 499 placements).

(3) There were, however, cases of shifts by two positions (7 per cent of the 499 placements) and by 3 positions (3 per cent of the 499 placements). The scales most subject to large shifts were those concerned with programmes that present: violence as fun and games; fictional violence of the realistic kind.

(4) The average of the correlation coefficients between placements was + 0.95.

For the dichotomous variables, the ratings of only two of the three groups of extra judges (making up 44 of the 63) could be used because of incomplete returns. Hence the comparison with respect to the dichotomous variables was based on the original 30 judges on the one hand and a total of 74 judges on the other. The selection of illustrative programmes based on the first 30 judges was supported by the gradings made by all 74 judges, the average of the correlations between the two sets of decisions being + 0.98.

In these circumstances, the selections based on the judgements of the 30 teacher-judges were allowed to stand, as were the results of using those illustrated scales in stage II of the development of the technique for measuring exposure to violence generally and to different forms of television violence.

[15] Now IBA (Independent Broadcasting Authority).

[16] Of the 52 raters, two had not carried out instructions as required, and their gradings were discarded. The panel of effective judges was thus reduced to 50.

[17] As it turns out those who had been highly exposed to television output (i.e. disregarding its level of violence) were also markedly exposed to television violence as well. In fact a comparison of the more and the less exposed to television output considered generally was very nearly equivalent to a comparison of the more and the less exposed to television *violence*. What was done in that situation was to equate the less exposed to television output to those more exposed, this equation or matching being in terms of level of exposure to television *violence*. In other words, what was done was to compare the violence level of those who saw a lot of television with the violence level of those who saw less television, any difference between them in amount of exposure to television *violence* being partialled out of the comparison. The results of doing this are shown in chapter 12.

[18] See note [17].

[19] In fact, the findings of this enquiry threw some doubt on that assumption. See chapters 12 and 20.

[20] *Not* used in developing aggregate exposure scores, but so coded to provide a record of the claims actually made (up to that limit).

[21] Unavoidably involving some degree of repetition of points already presented in this report.

[22] Boys were told, at the time of agreeing to the first interview, that they would receive a fee of £2.00 for this and the follow-up interview. The boys were drawn from ten polling districts of London, widely spaced in terms of location. In each polling district the interviewer was given a series of randomly drawn starting addresses linked to a controlled-route follow-up system.

APPENDICES TO CHAPTER 4

Appendix 1	The 231 programmes used for grading in stage II of technique development
Appendix 2	The 1970-71 programmes from which the illustrative scales were to be made
Appendix 3	Comparing the results of programme gradings with (a) 30 judges only and (b) that 30 plus 63/44 more judges
Appendix 4	The gradings or ratings attributed to (231) programmes in stage II of the technique construction process
Appendix 5	An example of the programme guide used to aid raters' recall of programmes
Appendix 6	The sample of control programmes
Appendix 7	The full set of 117 programmes used in the research materials for measurement of boys' exposure to different types of television output
Appendix 8	Instructions to intensive interviewers for establishing how often certain programmes had been seen.

Table A1.1
The 231 programmes used for grading in stage II of technique development

Those programmes marked with an asterisk (*) are included for contrast purposes, *being classed as non-violent in character. For each of the 231, details are entered of station of origin and of audience size on a randomly selected broadcasting occasion within the period 1958-69. Note that for the 1970-71 'sample', the audience size given was that of a randomly selected broadcasting occasion, but within the period 1970-71.

Programme	Station	Size of audience per cent	Programme	Station	Size of audience per cent
1 Hugh and I	BBC 1	13	56 The Money Man	BBC 1	13
2 The Desperate People	BBC 1	15	57 No Hiding Place	ITV	30
3 Top Cat	BBC 1	7	58 Echo Four-Two	ITV	25
4 Perry Mason	BBC 1	17	59 The Dickie Henderson Show	ITV	35
5 Hector Heathcote	BBC 1	10	60 Sanctuary	ITV	4
6 Benny Hill	BBC 1	37	61 Crane	ITV	30
7 Club Night	BBC 1	13	62 Boyd Q.C.	ITV	.17
8 Moonstrike	BBC 1	10	63 The Defenders	BBC 1	15
9 The Telegoons	BBC 1	18	64 The Man from UNCLE	BBC 1	24
10 Steptoe & Son	BBC 1	35	65 The Prior Commitment	BBC 1	11
11 Top of the Pops*	BBC 1	24	66 Marty	BBC 2	3
12 Sportsview	BBC 1	14	67 Sherlock Holmes	BBC 1	22
13 Travellers Tales (Mecca Holy City)	BBC 1	14	68 The British Film Comedy	BBC 1	28
14 The Great War	BBC 1	26	69 The Great Stars (Movies)	BBC 1	25
15 Detective	BBC 1	16	70 (1968) F.A. Cup Final	BBC 1	33
16 Z-Cars	BBC 1	28	71 Out of the Unknown	BBC 2	3
17 The Old Curiosity Shop	BBC 1	22	72 The Monkees	BBC 1	17
18 The Ken Dodd Show	BBC 1	14	73 This Man Craig	BBC 2	1
19 Your Life in their Hands	BBC 1	22	74 A Game of Murder	BBC 1	17
20 Compact	BBC 1	26	75 High Chaparral	BBC 2	10
21 Phil Silvers Show	BBC 1	25	76 The Revenue Men – the Waiting Game	BBC 2	0.6
22 Outbreak of Murder	BBC 1	11	77 Play of the Month	BBC 1	9
23 It's a Square World	BBC 1	15	78 Tom and Jerry	BBC 1	18
24 Carry Halliday	BBC 1	6	79 A Man called Ironside	BBC 1	13
25 Sykes and a (Salesman)	BBC 1	33	80 All Gas and Gaiters	BBC 1	23
26 The Hidden Truth	BBC 1	20	81 The Army Game	ITV	40
27 Look	BBC 1	8	82 Nearest and Dearest	ITV	16
28 What's My Line*	BBC 1	14	83 Counterstrike	BBC 1	14
29 Overland Trail	BBC 1	12	84 Late Night Horror	BBC 2	2
30 Silent Evidence	BBC 1	17	85 Stories of D.H. Lawrence	ITV	16
31 Criminal Capers of Bonehead	BBC 1	9	86 University Challenge*	ITV	13
32 Six more Faces of Jim	BBC 1	31	87 Blood and Thunder	ITV	13
33 Billy Bunter of Greyfriars School	BBC 1	8	88 Professional Wrestling/International All Star Wrestling	ITV	19
34 Dixon of Dock Green	BBC 1	29	89 Cinema	ITV	15
35 Afterthought	BBC 1	19	90 Maupassant	ITV	14
36 Grandstand	BBC 1	13	91 Knight Errant '60	ITV	36
37 Tonight	BBC 1	21	92 What the Papers Say*	ITV	8
38 Juke Box Jury*	BBC 1	30	93 Spot the Tune*	ITV	25
39 Wells Fargo	BBC 1	28	94 Coronation Street	ITV	21
40 Quatermass and the Pit	BBC 1	32	95 Junior Showtime*	ITV	8
41 Private Investigator	BBC 1	17	96 The Main Chance	ITV	12
42 Charlie Drake's Boxing Day Show	BBC 1	15	97 Survival	ITV	9
43 Good Wives*	BBC 1	3	98 Great Expectations	BBC 1	12
44 Panorama	BBC 1	18	99 The Virginian	BBC 2	7
45 Charlie Chester Show	BBC 1	25	100 The Likely Lads	BBC 2	1
46 The Jack Benny Spectacular	BBC 1	12	101 This is Your Life*	BBC 1	15
47 Bleak House	BBC 1	14	102 Adam Adamant Lives	BBC 1	21
48 The Young Lady from London	BBC 1	3	103 Dr Who	BBC 1	11
49 Whack-0!	BBC 1	20	104 Dr Kildare	BBC 1	14
50 Thin Man	BBC 1	7	105 Tom Tom*	BBC 1	7
51 The Lone Ranger	BBC 1	9	106 Gilda	BBC 1	28
52 The Ted Ray Show	BBC 1	27	107 Pinky and Perky's Island	BBC 1	9
53 The Informer	ITV	15	108 The Count of Monte Cristo	BBC 1	5
54 Arsenic and Old Lace	BBC 1	22			
55 The Perry Como Show*	BBC 1	19			

Table A1.1 (cont.)

No.	Programme	Channel	Score
109	The World of Wooster	BBC 1	23
110	The Frost Report	BBC 1	29
111	Dr Finlay's Casebook	BBC 1	19
112	Les Miserables	BBC 1	8
113	Blue Peter*	BBC 1	14
114	Dombey and Son	BBC 1	7
115	All Our Yesterdays	ITV	19
116	Mr Rose	ITV	7
117	Rupert of Hentzau	BBC 1	8
118	Please, Sir!	ITV	15
119	Maigret	BBC 1	31
120	The Rag Trade	BBC 1	18
121	BBC TV Puppet Theatre	BBC 1	4
122	Burns and Allen	BBC 1	6
123	O Henry Playhouse	BBC 1	8
124	Billy Cotton	BBC 1	10
125	The Big Game	ITV	21
126	The Main News	BBC 1	24
127	The Saturday Film	BBC 1	19
128	Interpol Calling	ITV	32
129	Riverboat	ITV	38
130	Ghost Squad	ITV	21
131	Whiplash	ITV	3
132	Somerset Maugham Hour	ITV	5
133	Hawaii Five-0	ITV	7
134	The Avengers	ITV	10
135	News at Ten	ITV	17
136	Songs of Praise*	BBC 1	11
137	International Football	ITV	18
138	Shadow Squad	ITV	29
139	The Wednesday Play	BBC 1	19
140	Yogi Bear	ITV	13
141	77 Sunset Strip	ITV	24
142	Hancock	ITV	22
143	African Patrol	ITV	12
144	The Grey Ghost	ITV	6
145	Wyatt Earp	ITV	31
146	The Arthur Haynes Show	ITV	32
147	Jango	ITV	19
148	The Magic Roundabout*	BBC 1	13
149	The Man from Interpol	ITV	6
150	Cimarron City	ITV	34
151	Murder Bag	ITV	35
152	The News (summary)	BBC 1	20
153	Sergeant Cork	ITV	17
154	Saturday Sportstime	ITV	2
155	Captain Pugwash	BBC 1	7
156	The Lucy Show	ITV	25
157	The Littlest Hobo	ITV	3
158	Crossroads	ITV	3
159	Nine o'clock (main) News	ITV	20
160	The Larkins	ITV	31
161	Tree House Family*	ITV	11
162	Morecombe and Wise Show	ITV	14
163	The Americans	ITV	15
164	Half Hour Story	ITV	8
165	Star Soccer	ITV	12
166	Playhouse	ITV	22
167	The Friday Film	ITV	3
168	Tyranny	ITV	45
169	Target Luna	ITV	11
170	Film Festival	ITV	14
171	A Family at War		
172	The Space Explorers	BBC 1	2
173	The Invisible Man	ITV	8
174	Highway Patrol	ITV	28
175	Mary Britten, MD	ITV	15
176	Adventure	BBC 1	21
177	Double Your Money*	ITV	30
178	The Adventures of Noddy	ITV	4
179	Cannonball	ITV	12
180	White Hunter	ITV	20
181	Cheyenne	ITV	31
182	Sea War	ITV	7
183	Oh Boy!*	ITV	18
184	Educating Archie	ITV	7
185	Sea Hunt	ITV	27
186	Lorna Doone	ITV	5
187	World Heavyweight Boxing Championship	BBC 1	26
188	G.S.5	ITV	13
189	San Francisco Beat	ITV	19
190	The Sunday Night Play	BBC 1	17
191	Robin Hood	ITV	23
192	The Cruel Sea	ITV	10
193	Tonight with Dave Allen	ITV	22
194	The Power Game	ITV	19
195	Sunday Playhouse	ITV	18
196	Out of this World	ITV	9
197	Professional Boxing	ITV	21
198	The Warning Voice	ITV	6
199	Rawhide	ITV	25
200	International Zone	ITV	4
201	Ready, Steady, Go!*	ITV	12
202	Court Martial	ITV	4
203	Plays of Action	ITV	5
204	Danger Man	ITV	9
205	Mystery and Imagination	ITV	16
206	The Saint	ITV	25
207	Opportunity Knocks*	ITV	20
208	Hope and Keen	ITV	16
209	Cilla (Black) at the Savoy*	ITV	21
210	Route '66'	ITV	17
211	Emergency Ward 10	ITV	23
212	Play of the Week	ITV	12
213	Escape	ITV	13
214	The Criminal	ITV	6
215	Thunderbirds	ITV	3
216	Gunsmoke	ITV	5
217	Felony Squad	ITV	6
218	This Week	ITV	18
219	Take Your Pick*	ITV	15
220	World in Action	ITV	7
221	Drama '64	ITV	15
222	Love Story (TV Series)	ITV	19
223	Intrigue	ITV	6
224	The Big Valley	ITV	7
225	Bonanza	ITV	21
226	Sunday Night at the London Palladium*	ITV	44
227	The Human Jungle	ITV	21
228	Probation Officer	ITV	19
229	Popeye	ITV	9
230	Till Death Us do Part	BBC 1	15
231	High Adventure	BBC 1	22

*Mainly non- violent programmes provided (a) to give the raters items to put into the 0-1 scale of positions (and so protect other items from mis-rating); (b) to break the 'sameness' of the list (i.e. all violent).

Appendix 2

Table A2.1
The 1970-71 programmes from which the illustrative scales were to be made

Programme name	Service	Audience size* per cent
1 Budgie	ITV	24
2 Shadow of Fear	ITV	19
3 Man at the Top	ITV	26
4 Bless this House	ITV	4
5 Cilla		
6 Trouble Shooters	BBC 1	16
7 Crossroads	ITV	10
8 The FBI	ITV	3
9 Steptoe & Son	BBC 1	39
10 High Chaparral	BBC 2	13
11 Question of Sport		
12 This Week	ITV	9
13 Mannix	ITV	4
14 Atom Ant	ITV	1
15 Thunderbirds	ITV	1
16 Dear Mother - Love Albert	ITV	19
17 Tuesday Film	ITV	4
18 University Challenge		
19 Stars on Sunday		
20 Professional Wrestling	ITV	10
21 Me Mammy	BBC 1	17
22 On the Ball	ITV	1
23 Wednesday Play	BBC 1	17
24 Elizabeth R.	BBC 2	9
25 Midnight Movie	BBC 2	8
26 Freewheelers	ITV	11
27 Hine	ITV	16
28 Captain Scarlet	ITV	0.2
29 On the Buses	ITV	35
30 Roads to Freedom	BBC 2	5
31 Peyton Place	ITV	4
32 Nearest & Dearest	ITV	5
33 Monday Film		
34 News Review		
35 Dixon of Dock Green	BBC 1	28
36 Panorama	BBC 1	14
37 Education Programme		
38 Take Three Girls	BBC 1	11
39 W. Somerset Maugham	BBC 1	7
40 Robin Hood	ITV	2
41 Mission Impossible	BBC 1	16
42 Doctor at Large	ITV	27
43 Golden Goose	BBC 1	7
44 Bonanza	ITV	3
45 Randall & Hopkirk deceased		
46 Lost in Space	ITV	3
47 Disappearing World	ITV	8
48 Callan Saga	ITV	4
49 Copper's End	ITV	4
50 Zingalong		
51 Seeing Stars		
52 Magpie		
53 Survival	ITV	2
54 Forest Rangers	ITV	0.4
55 Weatherman		
56 Grandstand	BBC 1	6
57 Kindly leave the Kerb	ITV	2
58 The Untouchables	ITV	0.2
59 Catweazle	ITV	11
60 Yogi Bear	BBC 1	4
60 Coronation Street	ITV	30
62 Hogan's Heroes		
63 Music Room		
64 Garden Indoors		
65 This is Your Life		
66 Blue Peter		
67 Confession	ITV	11
68 Doomwatch	BBC 1	21
69 Gunsmoke	ITV	2
70 Fight of the Week	BBC 1	6
71 Sportsnight with Coleman	BBC 1	18
72 Sherlock Holmes	ITV	5
73 World of Sport	ITV	4
74 Z-Cars	BBC 1	19
75 Here's Lucy	BBC 1	18
76 News at Ten	ITV	24
77 All our Yesterdays	ITV	1
78 Opportunity Knocks		
79 The Borderers	BBC 2	2
80 The Virginian	BBC 1	20
81 Sunday's Adventure Film		
82 Impact	BBC 2	7
83 Playhouse	ITV	8
84 World about Us	BBC 2	3
85 Dr Who	BBC 1	16
86 Six Wives of Henry VIII	BBC 2	16
87 Saturday Thriller		
88 Magic Roundabout		
89 Today	ITV	13
90 Hawaii Five-0	ITV	10
91 Ivanhoe	BBC 1	14
92 Viewpoint	BBC 1	1
93 Come Dancing		
94 Misfit	ITV	14
95 Cinema	ITV	13
96 Huckleberry Finn	ITV	2
97 World in Action	ITV	14
98 Family at War	ITV	26
99 That's your Funeral	BBC 1	11
100 Match of the Day	BBC 1	20
101 Brett	BBC 1	14
102 Dad's Army	BBC 1	28
103 Man in the News	ITV	0.4
104 Star Trek	BBC 1	21
105 Ryan International	BBC 1	16
106 Out of the Unknown	BBC 2	5
107 Pink Panther	BBC 1	13
108 Laurel & Hardy	BBC 1	9
109 Play for Today	BBC 1	15
110 Both Sides of Europe	BBC 1	2
111 The Avengers	ITV	2
112 Never mind the Quality ...	ITV	6
113 Last of the Mohicans	BBC 1	16
114 Armchair Theatre	ITV	10
115 Circus Boy		
116 Chingachook	BBC 1	5
117 Mind of Mr J.G. Reeder	ITV	17
118 9 o'clock News	BBC 1	15
119 Marine Boy	BBC 1	8
120 Wayne in Action	BBC 1	20

Table A2.1 (cont.)

Programme name	Service	Audience size* per cent	Programme name	Service	Audience size* per cent
121 Queenie's Castle	ITV	15	130 Dustbin Men	ITV	15
122 Monty Python	BBC 1	6	131 Talkback	BBC 1	2
123 A Man Called Ironside	BBC 1	23	132 Living Writers		
124 Softly, Softly	BBC 1	27	133 Paul Temple	BBC 1	14
125 Cartoon Time	ITV	0.2	134 Tom & Jerry	BBC 1	18
126 Man Alive	BBC 2	3	135 Oh! Brother	BBC 1	14
127 Codename	BBC 2	3	136 Please, Sir!	ITV	3
128 Rugby Special	BBC 2	3	137 24 Hours	BBC 1	9
129 The Expert	BBC 2	6	138 Legend of Jesse James	ITV	1
			139 The Baron		

*Audience size for a randomly drawn programme in the series at that time

Appendix 3

Comparing the results of programme gradings with (a) 30 judges only and (b) that 30 plus 63/44 more judges

A. Dichotomous gradings

At this stage of the project, 15 of the 31 measures of exposure to television violence related to *types* of programmes (e.g. a cartoon in which the characters are violent to each other), as distinct from the nature of *programme content* (e.g. defiance of or rudeness towards authority; presentation in detail of the consequences of violence). For the former measure, the selection of programmes for illustrative purposes required simply that the judges grade such programmes in terms of whether they are or are not of that type (e.g. Is this a Western involving violence?). These are the dichotomous gradings.

Comparison of the gradings based on the views of the first 30 judges and of those based on that 30 plus an additional 44 judges are given in table A3.1.

B. Continuous gradings

At this stage of the project, 16 of the 31 measures of exposure to television violence related to the nature of programme content (e.g. defiance of or rudeness towards authority; presentation in detail of the consequences of violence). For these measures, the selection of programmes for illustrative purposes required that the judges grade such programmes on an 11-point scale to indicate to what extent the programmes concerned contained some specified type of violent content. Each of the programmes in the pool drawn upon was, provided it was familiar to the judge, separately graded on each of the sixteen dimensions concerned.

Comparisons of the gradings based on the views of the first 30 judges and the ratings based on the views of the 30 plus an additional 63 judges are given in tables A3.2 and A3.3.

Table A3.1
Comparing dichotomous gradings of programmes using (a) 30 judges, (b) an additional 63/44 judges

Programme type	Initially selected illustrative programmes (based on gradings of 30 judges)*	'Yes' : 'No' ratios	
		of original 30	of all-in 74
A fictional programme about the English police at work, including violence going on in society	Z-Cars	28 : 0	50 : 0
	Softly, Softly	26 : 1	65 : 1
	Dixon of Dock Green	26 : 2	47 : 0
A cartoon in which the characters are violent to each other	Tom and Jerry	26 : 1	44 : 2
	Pink Panther	12 : 4	26 : 6
	Yogi Bear	11 : 7	14 : 7
A series, a play or a film in which personal relationships are a major theme and which features verbal abuse (e.g. swearing, quarrelling) or physical violence	Z-Cars	26 : 2	34 : 17
	Steptoe & Son	25 : 3	45 : 5
	Softly, Softly	24 : 3	52 : 13
	Henry VIII (Six Wives of)	21 : 2	51 : 4
	Paul Temple	21 : 4	†
	Coronation Street	20 : 6	25 : 6
	Dixon of Dock Green	20 : 8	32 : 15
A programme intended for adults	Panorama	25 : 3	
	News at Ten	24 : 5	
	24 Hours	24 : 5	
	9 o'clock News	23 : 4	**
	The Wednesday Play	20 : 1	
	The Avengers	20 : 8	
	This Week	20 : 4	
	Callan	19 : 1	
A play, film or drama series, portraying conflict(s) between individuals, and where it would be difficult for the average boy to decide who is right and who is wrong	W. Somerset Maugham	18 : 0	38 : 3
	The Wednesday Play	18 : 3	13 : 3
	Henry VIII	17 : 6	42 : 11
	Elizabeth R	15 : 6	35 : 15
	Armchair Theatre	14 : 5	30 : 6
	Trouble Shooters	14 : 5	39 : 6
	Play for Today	13 : 2	30 : 6
A fictional programme where spies use unusual forms of violence, e.g. torture, novel weapons or individual unarmed combat	The Avengers	26 : 2	34 : 2
	Mission Impossible	16 : 2	29 : 4
A programme which includes newsreel film of the violence of war or its aftermath	Panorama	28 : 0	41 : 2
	News at Ten	28 : 1	40 : 2
	9 o'clock News	27 : 0	32 : 2
	24 Hours	26 : 3	63 : 1
	World in Action	22 : 1	20 : 3
	All our Yesterdays	22 : 1	28 : 3
	This Week	21 : 3	19 : 3
A programme featuring slapstick violence and/or verbal abuse between the characters	Steptoe & Son	26 : 2	45 : 6
	Dad's Army	25 : 3	52 : 13
	Monty Python	23 : 2	56 : 5
	Tom and Jerry	21 : 8	33 : 13
	Please, Sir!	19 : 7	32 : 8
	Laurel & Hardy	19 : 0	45 : 3
A science fiction programme in which non-human fantasy creatures (e.g. monsters) ruthlesslessly fight with or destroy people	Dr Who	28 : 0	39 : 3
	Lost in Space	14 : 3	25 : 4
	Star Trek	14 : 4	34 : 13

Table A3.1 (cont.)

A 'Western' including violence by, for example, cowboys and Indians	The Virginian	23 : 1	42 : 1
	Bonanza	18 : 0	26 : 1
	Wayne in Action	14 : 0	20 : 4
	Gunsmoke	13 : 0	23 : 0
	Legend of Jesse James	10 : 2	12 : 0
	Last of the Mohicans	10 : 2	20 : 6
A fictional programme in which the violence tends to go unpunished	Callan	13 : 7	28 : 13
A programme showing violence by competitors or spectators at sporting events	Match of the Day	22 : 3	51 : 9
	Grandstand	20 : 8	26 : 5
	Professional Wrestling	18 : 3	26 : 4
	Sportsnight with Coleman	17 : 6	43 : 9
A programme which included violence as it happened or is happening	Panorama	26 : 2	40 : 3
	9 o'clock News	26 : 1	40 : 2
	24 Hours	24 : 5	61 : 2
	World in Action	22 : 1	21 : 2
	Professional Wrestling	20 : 1	22 : 8
	Match of the Day	18 : 7	†
A film or part of a series/serial featuring gangs or gangsters engaged in violent, organised crime	The Avengers	25 : 3	25 : 11
	Z- Cars	22 : 6	40 : 11
	Hawaii Five-0	21 : 0	31 : 1
	Paul Temple	20 : 5	43 : 17
A science fiction programme in which humans use bizarre forms of violence, which may include super-human powers	Dr Who	24 : 4	38 : 4
	Star Trek	16 : 2	†
	Lost in Space	16 : 1	†

*Criteria selection were: Yes/No must be 2/1 or more; there must have been more than 10 ratings.

**The question was changed to 'a violent programme intended (by the producer) for adults'. The comparison of results is therefore not meaningful.

†Data not available from second sample.

Table A3.2
Comparing gradings based on first 30 judges and all 93 judges: *How violent is this programme?*

Dimension in terms of which the gradings were made	Initially selected illustrated programmes (based on original 30 judges)		Original 30 judges			All-in 93 judges		
	Programmes	Scale sector	n*	Median†	Range††	n*	Median†	Range ††
	Opportunity Knocks	0	22	0.00	0.25	70	0.03	0.27
HOW	Magic Roundabout		26	0.02	0.26	80	0.01	0.26
	This is your Life		26	0.07	0.28	78	0.05	0.27
VIOLENT	The Weatherman		28	0.00	0.25	73	0.01	0.25
	University Challenge		29	0.06	0.28	86	0.03	0.27
IS THIS								
	Match of the Day	1	25	1.29	0.74	75	1.37	0.85
PRO-	Crossroads		15	0.58	0.59	51	0.84	0.61
	Coronation Street		25	0.96	0.54	74	1.17	0.83
GRAMME?	Doctor at Large		17	0.58	0.63	52	0.50	0.68
	Never Mind the Quality		16	0.67	0.63	49	0.82	0.74
(i.e.								
	All our Yesterdays	2	22	2.50	3.17	65	2.43	2.08
irres-	Sherlock Holmes		21	2.38	1.56	65	2.39	1.43
	Yogi Bear		18	2.00	1.85	49	1.57	2.00
pective	W. Somerset Maugham		19	2.00	1.06	41	2.25	1.07
	Please, Sir!		25	1.75	1.94	81	2.21	1.71
of type	Steptoe and Son		28	2.50	2.18	90	2.92	2.29
of	24 Hours	3	28	3.36	1.67	84	2.89	1.81
	Armchair Theatre		18	3.33	0.71	40	3.30	1.00
violence)	Cinema		24	3.17	1.83	67	3.28	1.61
	Dixon of Dock Green		28	3.25	1.57	89	2.63	1.21
	This Week		24	3.07	1.83	67	2.82	1.67
	Softly, Softly	4	26	4.50	1.22	84	4.45	1.53
	Z-Cars		28	4.50	1.38	90	4.38	1.42
	Doomwatch		20	4.21	0.80	65	3.64	1.96
	Robin Hood		23	4.33	1.56	65	3.94	1.68
	The Wednesday Play		22	4.00	1.02	58	3.63	1.10
	A Man called Ironside	5	25	4.67	1.70	81	4.59	1.58
	Star Trek		18	4.93	1.50	64	4.78	1.78
	Dr Who		28	5.25	2.50	90	5.36	2.14
	Gunsmoke		13	4.75	2.13	29	5.20	1.77
	Six Wives of Henry VIII		23	4.75	2.34	57	4.29	2.41
	The Last of the Mohicans	6	12	6.17	1.50	34	5.30	1.74
	The Borderers		13	6.40	1.56	25	6.08	2.08
	Mission Impossible		18	6.50	2.21	43	6.25	2.06
	The Avengers	7	27	7.20	1.93	78	6.50	1.95
	The Callan Saga		20	7.50	2.25	53	7.45	1.74
	Legend of Jesse James	8	10	8.17	1.63	13	7.67	2.06
	Wayne in Action		14	7.90	1.25	26	6.83	1.79
	Tom and Jerry		25	7.92	2.17	83	7.54	3.33
	Hawaii Five-0		21	7.63	1.94	58	7.10	1.81
	The FBI	9	15	8.60	1.49	46	7.21	1.99
	Fight of the Week		11	9.25	1.85	29	9.37	2.03
	The Untouchables		15	8.88	1.44	35	8.38	1.45
	None graded here	10						

Overall correlation between scalar positions indicated by the two sets of judges r = + 0.98

* n = number of judges actually rating the programme (the others, out of 30 or 93, were not familiar with the programme and so did not rate it)
† Median value (i.e. that value above and below which fall 50 per cent of the ratings)
††Range = semi-interquartile range (i.e. a measure of the scatter of the ratings).

Table A3.3
Comparing gradings based on first 30 judges and all 93 judges:
Fictional violence of the realistic kind

Dimension in terms of which the gradings were made	Initially selected illustrated programmes (based on original 30 judges)		Original 30 judges			All-in 93 judges		
	Programmes	Scale sector	n*	Median†	Range††	n*	Median†	Range††
FICTIONAL VIOLENCE OF THE REALISTIC KIND	Match of the Day	0	24	0.07	0.29	73	0.04	0.27
	Yogi Bear		16	0.17	0.33	44	0.09	0.30
	World in Action		23	0.02	0.26	57	0.03	0.26
	News at Ten		30	0.04	0 27	88	0.02	0.26
	Panorama		28	0.02	0.26	84	0.04	0.27
	Laurel and Hardy	1	18	1.00	1.66	59	0.48	1.38
	Never Mind the Quality		15	0.75	1.36	46	0.50	1.83
	Star Trek		18	1.50	2.26	61	1.46	2.37
	Monty Python		24	1.25	1.50	77	0.40	1.10
	Please, Sir!	2	22	1.83	2.29	76	1.75	2.55
	Dad's Army		27	1.80	2.33	77	0.91	2.09
	Dr Who		28	2.50	1.71	84	1.83	1.98
	Lost in Space		17	1.67	1.58	37	1.14	1.29
	Out of the Unknown	3	10	3.50	2.17	18	2.50	2.20
	The Tuesday Film		12	3.50	1.00	38	3.25	1.67
	Playhouse	4	12	3.83	1.75	23	3.67	2.97
	The Avengers	5	27	4.75	2.43	77	4.13	2.32
	Cinema		23	5.38	2.09	64	4.70	2.45
	Mission Impossible		18	5.10	1.75	40	5.10	2.39
	Midnight Movie		17	5.33	1.59	42	4.79	1.84
	The Sunday Adventure Film	6	12	5.38	2.25	33	5.43	1.75
	Wayne in Action		14	6.10	0.88	27	5.92	1.39
	Saturday Thriller		19	6.00	2.24	39	6.25	2.00
	Randall & Hopkirk Deceased		15	6.25	2.19	42	3.30	2.56
	The High Chaparral	7	11	6.63	2.53	43	6.73	2.38
	Man at the Top		11	6.75	2.42	28	7.00	3.06
	Bonanza		18	6.75	1.94	54	4.67	2.71
	A Play for Today		14	7.00	2.81	45	5.19	2.67
	The Virginian		24	6.83	1.80	71	4.78	2.92
	The Trouble Shooters	8	18	8.50	2.25	62	5.50	3.06
	Gunsmoke		13	8.00	2.03	29	6.00	2.17
	Brett		17	8.00	1.53	40	7.00	2.85
	The Expert	9	18	9.50	2.38	38	7.70	3.27
	A Man called Ironside		25	8.86	1.55	77	7.71	2.26
	Hawaii Five-0		20	9.10	1.19	55	8.57	2.28
	Z-Cars		29	9.00	1.17	90	8.68	1.88
	The Untouchables		15	8.88	1.44	33	8.69	1.52
	Budgie	10	11	9.58	2.31	26	7.17	2.56
	Softly, Softly		25	9.54	1.05	81	9.12	1.63
	The Callan Saga		20	9.67	0.96	51	8.31	1.99

Overall correlation between scalar positions indicated by the two sets of judges r = + 0.96

* n = number of judges actually rating the programme (the others, out of 30 or 93, were not familiar with the programme and so did not rate it).
† Median value (i.e. that value above and below which fall 50 per cent of the ratings).
††Range = semi-interquartile range (i.e. a measure of the scatter of the ratings).

Appendix 4

The gradings or ratings attributed to (231) programmes in stage II of the technique construction process

A. *Gradings in terms of 14 continous variables*

Thirteen of the dimensions referred to in the subsidiary or supporting hypotheses were *continuous* in character, in the sense that they called for the grading of programmes on an 11-point scale to indicate *to what extent* they had certain specified characteristics. All 231 programmes were to be graded in terms of each of the thirteen which were as follows.

1 Fictional violence of the realistic kind (that is, like what really happens).
2 Violence performed by a basically *'good guy' hero*, who is also a *rebel or 'odd man out' type.*
3 Violence in a domestic or family setting (that is, a quarrel between members of a family).
4 Violence featuring *defiance/or rudeness towards authority figures* (for example, public officials like the police, school or medical staff, the Fire Brigade, clergymen, parents).
5 Violence shown as *glorified, romanticised, idealised or ennobling.*
6 Violence presented *as if it is 'fun and games', like a game or something to entertain.*
7 Violence presented as being *in a good cause.*
8 Violence showing the *physical or mental consequences for the victim in detail.*
9 Violence *related to racial or minority group strife.*
10 Violence performed by a basically *'good guy' type of hero*, who is also *tough* (that is, he can take physical violence and fight on).
11 Violence of the *verbal kind* (for example, abuse, threats, quarrelling, cheekiness, insult, rudeness, disrespect, swearing at people or animals or objects.)
12 Violence *just thrown in for its own sake or not necessary to the plot.*
13 Violence which is *gruesome, horrific or scary.*

The fourteenth of the continuous variables involved the degree to which the programmes (being rated) were violent (that is, irrespective of *kind* of violence).

The results of rating all 231 programmes on one of the 14 scales is given as an example in tables A4A.1 and A4A.2 in this Appendix.

Table A4A.1
Programmes rated in terms of how much of their violence is: *Fictional violence of the realistic kind*

	Name of programme	n (a)	SIR (b)	Med (c)	PBP (d) 19..
1	Hugh and I	32	0.5	1.3	63-68
3	Top Cat	30	0.7	1.3	63-67
4	Perry Mason	45	2.0	8.7	61-67
5	Hector Heathcote	11	0.3	1.1	65-67
6	Benny Hill	32	0.5	1.3	58-68;71/2
9	The Telegoons	13	0.3	1.1	63-64
10	Steptoe and Son	48	1.6	3.3	62-71/2
11	Top of the Pops	38	0.3	1.0	64-71/2
12	Sportsview	35	0.3	1.1	58-68
14	The Great War	17	0.3	1.1	64-65
16	Z-Cars	49	0.9	10.0	62-71/2
17	The Old Curiosity Shop	10	1.8	2.5	62-63
18	The Ken Dodd Show	20	0.3	1.1	59-63
19	Your Life in their Hands	30	0.3	1.1	61-64
20	Compact	30	0.7	1.3	62-65
21	Phil Silvers Show	28	0.8	2.1	58-60,1,6,7
23	It's a Square World	32	0.6	1.4	61-65
24	Garry Halliday	10	1.5	5.5	59-63
25	Sykes (and a Salesman)	23	0.7	1.7	60-4;66;71
27	Look	31	0.3	1.1	55-69
28	What's My Line	35	0.3	1.0	55-63
32	Six More Faces of Jim	13	0.8	2.0	62-63
33	Billy Bunter of Greyfriars School	19	0.8	2.1	58-62
34	Dixon of Dock Green	47	1.8	8.8	58-71/2
36	Grandstand	32	0.3	1.1	59-71/2
37	Tonight	34	0.3	1.1	58-65
38	Juke Box Jury	38	0.3	1.0	61-67
39	Wells Fargo	30	1.5	7.0	57-64
40	Quatermass & the Pit	21	1.3	2.8	58-60
42	Charlie Drake's Boxing Day Show	19	0.7	1.6	60
44	Panorama	39	0.3	1.1	58-71/2
49	Whack-O!	31	0.8	2.3	58-60;71/2
51	The Lone Ranger	25	2.4	4.9	58-63
53	The Informer	17	1.0	9.7	66-67
54	Arsenic and Old Lace	15	2.2	2.4	66;67;71
55	The Perry Como Show	20	0.3	1.1	58-61
57	No Hiding Place	30	1.3	9.3	59-67
59	The Dickie Henderson Show	24	0.4	1.2	60/5;68-71
60	Sanctuary	14	0.5	1.3	67-68
61	Crane	22	1.2	7.5	63-65
62	Boyd QC	17	2.5	6.6	57-61;63
63	The Defenders	30	2.1	8.3	62/4;66/7
64	The Man from UNCLE	45	2.4	6.1	65-68
66	'Marty'	28	0.9	1.8	68-70
67	Sherlock Holmes	39	2.1	5.4	65-70
68	British Film Comedy – ('Nearly a Nasty Accident')	13	1.2	1.8	69
70	(1968) F.A. Cup Final	17	0.3	1.1	68
71	Out of the Unknown	15	1.0	3.3	65-71
72	The Monkees	26	0.6	1.5	67-69
73	This Man Craig	12	1.8	2.8	66-67
75	The High Chaparral	25	1.0	7.7	67-71/2
76	The Revenue Men – 'The Waiting Game'	10	3.5	8.0	67-68
77	Play of the Month	18	0.8	4.9	67-71/2
78	Tom and Jerry	43	0.6	1.3	67-71/2
79	A Man called Ironside	43	1.1	9.4	68-71
80	All Gas and Gaiters	39	0.5	1.3	67;69-71
81	The Army Game	25	1.0	3.0	57-61
82	Nearest and Dearest	16	0.9	2.1	68-71
84	(No such thing as a Vampire) Late Night Horror	12	1.5	3.9	69-70
86	University Challenge	40	0.3	1.0	62-71/2
88	Professional Wrestling/ International All-Star Wrestling	25	0.8	1.3	69-71
89	'Cinema'	25	0.8	5.6	65-71/2
92	What the Papers Say	21	0.3	1.1	61-71/2
93	Spot the Tune	11	0.3	1.0	56-62
94	Coronation Street	31	2.8	3.1	60-71/2
95	Junior Showtime	18	0.3	1.0	69-72
96	The Main Chance	14	2.9	6.5	69-70
97	Survival	19	0.3	1.1	63-71
98	Great Expectations	25	2.0	3.3	67
99	The Virginian	42	1.3	7.6	65-71/2
100	The Likely Lads	30	1.0	1.8	65-69
101	This is Your Life	35	0.3	1.0	55-64;69-72
102	Adam Adamant Lives	27	1.2	4.9	66-67;69
103	Dr Who	42	1.2	2.9	65-71/2
104	Dr Kildare	38	2.1	2.0	61-66
105	Tom Tom	22	0.3	1.0	65-71
107	Pinky and Perky's Island	33	0.3	1.1	65-68;69+
108	Count of Monte Cristo	16	1.0	5.7	64-66
109	World of Wooster	36	0.6	1.3	65-67
110	The Frost Report	33	0.3	1.2	66-69
111	Dr Finlay's Casebook	41	2.0	2.8	65-69
113	Blue Peter	34	0.3	1.0	58-71/2
114	Dombey and Son	14	0.6	1.5	69
115	All Our Yesterdays	30	0.3	1.1	58-71
118	Please, Sir!	39	0.9	3.2	68-71/2
119	Maigret	39	2.1	8.8	60-64
120	The Rag Trade	31	0.8	2.0	61-63
124	Billy Cotton	31	0.3	1.1	58-69
126	The (main) News	41	0.3	1.1	daily
131	Whiplash	12	2.2	7.2	60/4;68
132	Somerset Maugham Hour	16	1.6	3.5	60-62
133	Hawaii Five-0	28	1.1	9.8	69-71
134	The Avengers	39	1.7	5.8	61-69
135	News at Ten	40	0.3	1.0	68-71/2
136	Songs of Praise	29	0.3	1.0	61-71/2
139	The Wednesday Play	16	0.9	5.7	64-70
140	Yogi Bear	20	0.3	1.1	63-65;71
141	77 Sunset Strip	20	2.3	6.5	60-63
142	Hancock	38	0.7	1.5	66-67;63
145	Wyatt Earp	14	2.0	7.7	56-60
146	The Arthur Haynes Show	15	0.4	1.2	58-66
148	The Magic Roundabout	41	0.3	1.0	65-71
152	The News (summary)	33	0.3	1.1	daily
153	Sergeant Cork	16	3.0	7.8	63-64
155	Captain Pugwash	14	0.3	1.1	58-66
156	The Lucy Show	34	0.5	1.4	58-71
158	Crossroads	18	0.6	2.1	65-71/2
159	Nine o'clock News (main)	35	0.3	1.0	56-67
160	The Larkins	12	0.7	2.5	58-61;64

Table A4A.1 (cont.)

161	Tree House Family	12	0.3	1.0	68
162	Morecambe and Wise Show	44	0.6	1.4	62-67;68,69
171	A Family at War	20	2.8	7.0	69-72
173	The Invisible Man	15	1.6	3.3	60-65
174	Highway Patrol	14	2.6	6.5	57-60
176	Adventure	13	1.7	1.3	59-61
177	Double your Money	31	0.3	1.0	58-68
178	The Adventures of Noddy	11	0.3	1.1	58-59
179	Cannonball	15	2.3	4.0	59-61
181	Cheyenne	18	1.5	6.8	58-63
186	Lorna Doone	11	2.9	2.4	68
191	Robin Hood (Adventures of)	33	1.2	3.2	56-71
192	'The Cruel Sea'	22	1.9	9.5	67
193	Tonight with Dave Allen	24	0.6	1.3	67;69
194	The Power Game	27	2.7	4.9	66;69
197	Professional Boxing	21	0.3	1.2	58-71/2
199	Rawhide	20	2.0	7.1	59-64
201	Ready, Steady, Go!	18	0.3	1.1	63-67
204	Danger Man	30	2.1	8.8	60-69
205	Mystery and Imagination	16	1.2	3.5	66;68
206	The Saint	40	1.7	6.4	62-69
207	Opportunity Knocks	25	0.3	1.0	64-71
211	Emergency Ward 10	28	1.7	2.4	56-67
215	Thunderbirds	29	0.7	1.7	65/6;69-7
216	Gunsmoke (Gun Law)	23	1.6	7.8	57-67;71
218	This Week	23	0.3	1.1	57-71/2
219	Take Your Pick	26	0.3	1.0	58-68
220	World in Action	23	0.3	1.1	63-71
222	Love Story	12	0.8	1.4	63-66
225	Bonanza	27	1.4	6.9	60/4;69-7
226	Sunday Night at the London Palladium	30	0.3	1.0	58-64
227	The Human Jungle	19	2.9	6.0	63;65-7
228	Probation Officer	11	2.4	6.3	59-62
229	Popeye	28	0.6	1.2	59-62;6,8
230	Till Death Us Do Part	44	2.1	3.9	66-69
231	High Adventure	12	1.0	5.3	66-71/2

(a) n = Total number of judges who rated the programme on this variable. If less than 10, the programme is omitted.
(b) SIR = Semi-interquartile range (= a measure of scatter of the ratings of judges).
(c) Med = median = score at which 50 per cent of ratings are higher and 50 per cent are lower. On scale of 1-11. Note that tables 4.6 and 4.9 in text are based on scale of 0-10.
(d) PBP = Principal broadcast period.

Table A4A.2

Programmes rated in terms of how much of their violence is:

Violence performed by a basically 'good guy' hero who is also a rebel or 'odd man out' type

Name of programme	n (a)	SIR (b)	Med (c)	PBP (d) 19..
1 Hugh and I	32	0.3	1.1	63-68
3 Top Cat	28	2.5	3.0	63-67
4 Perry Mason	44	1.0	2.8	61-67
5 Hector Heathcote	12	0.8	1.3	65-67
6 Benny Hill	32	0.3	1.2	58-68;71/2
9 The Telegoons	12	0.3	1.0	63-64
10 Steptoe and Son	48	1.5	1.5	62-71/2
11 Top of the Pops	38	0.3	1.0	64-71/2
12 Sportsview	35	0.3	1.1	58-68
14 The Great War	18	0.3	1.1	64-65
16 Z-Cars	48	0.8	2.3	62-71/2
17 The Old Curiosity Shop	10	0.6	1.5	62-63
18 The Ken Dodd Show	20	0.3	1.1	59-63
19 Your Life in their Hands	28	0.3	1.0	61-64
20 Compact	30	0.3	1.2	62-65
21 Phil Silvers Show	29	1.3	2.0	58-60,1,6,7
23 It's a Square World	32	0.3	1.1	61-65
24 Garry Halliday	10	1.6	2.8	59-63
25 Sykes (and a Salesman)	24	0.5	1.3	60-4;66;71
27 Look	29	0.3	1.0	55-69
28 What's my Line	33	0.3	1.0	55-63
32 Six more Faces of Jim	12	0.6	1.3	62-63
33 Billy Bunter of Greyfriars School	21	0.9	1.8	58-62
34 Dixon of Dock Green	46	0.8	2.0	58-71/2
36 Grandstand	31	0.3	1.1	59-71/2
37 Tonight	34	0.3	1.0	58-65
38 Juke Box Jury	40	0.3	1.0	61-67
39 Wells Fargo	32	1.3	4.2	57-64
40 Quatermass & the Pit	18	0.8	1.8	58-60
42 Charlie Drake's Boxing Day Show	19	1.2	2.2	60
44 Panorama	41	0.3	1.1	58-71/2
49 Whack-O!	31	1.3	1.8	58-60;71/2
51 The Lone Ranger	26	2.7	5.7	58-63
53 The Informer	17	2.1	5.0	66-67
54 Arsenic and Old Lace	15	1.0	1.9	66;67;71
55 The Perry Como Show	20	0.3	1.0	58-61
57 No Hiding Place	29	0.8	2.5	59-67
59 Dickie Henderson Show	24	0.3	1.1	60/5;68-71
60 Sanctuary	15	0.3	1.0	67-68
61 Crane	21	2.2	6.2	63-65
62 Boyd QC	17	0.6	1.6	57-61;63
63 The Defenders	29	1.0	2.7	62/4;66/7
64 The Man from UNCLE	44	1.9	5.4	65-68
66 'Marty'	26	1.5	1.4	68-70
67 Sherlock Holmes	38	0.9	3.3	65-70
68 British Film Comedy – 'Nearly a Nasty Accident'	13	0.9	1.4	69
70 (1968) F.A. Cup Final	18	0.3	1.1	68
71 Out of the Unknown	16	1.0	2.5	65-71
72 The Monkees	27	0.5	1.3	67-69
73 This Man Craig	11	0.9	1.8	66-67
75 The High Chaparral	24	0.8	4.8	67-71/2
76 The Revenue Men – 'The Waiting Game'	10	1.6	2.8	67-68
77 Play of the Month	17	0.6	2.2	67-71/2
78 Tom and Jerry	44	0.8	1.3	67-71/2
79 A Man called Ironside	43	0.8	3.2	68-71
80 All Gas and Gaiters	40	0.3	1.1	67;69-71
81 The Army Game	26	1.3	1.8	57-61
82 Nearest and Dearest	16	0.7	1.4	68-71
84 (No such thing as a Vampire) Late Night Horror	13	1.0	1.8	69-70
86 University Challenge	42	0.3	1.0	62-71/2
88 Professional Wrestling/ International All-Star Wrestling	23	1.1	1.3	69-71
89 'Cinema'	25	1.4	3.2	65-71/2
92 What the Papers Say	22	0.3	1.0	61-71/2
93 Spot the Tune	11	0.3	1.0	56-62
94 Coronation Street	29	1.0	1.6	60-71/2
95 Junior Showtime	18	0.3	1.0	69-72
96 The Main Chance	14	1.0	2.3	69-70
97 Survival	20	0.3	1.0	63-71
98 Great Expectations	25	2.2	1.9	67
99 The Virginian	42	1.1	4.9	65-71/2
100 The Likely Lads	29	0.7	1.4	65-69
101 This is Your Life	37	0.3	1.0	55-64;69-72
102 Adam Adamant Lives	27	1.3	6.0	66-67;69
103 Dr Who	42	2.1	3.9	65-71/2
104 Dr Kildare	36	0.6	1.4	61-66
105 Tom Tom	25	0.3	1.0	65-71
107 Pinky and Perky's Island	32	0.3	1.0	65-68;69+
108 Count of Monte Cristo	14	1.8	3.5	64-66
109 The World of Wooster	34	0.3	1.1	65-67
110 The Frost Report	33	0.4	1.2	66-69
111 Dr Finlay's Casebook	42	0.6	1.3	65-69
113 Blue Peter	34	0.3	1.0	58-71/2
114 Domey and Son	16	1.0	1.5	69
115 All Our Yesterdays	33	0.3	1.1	58-71
118 Please, Sir!	38	0.6	1.9	68-71/2
119 Maigret	38	1.0	2.8	60-64
120 The Rag Trade	32	0.8	1.3	61-63
124 Billy Cotton	34	0.3	1.0	58-69
126 The (main) News	42	0.3	1.1	daily
131 Whiplash	12	1.1	3.5	60/4;68
132 Somerset Maugham Hour	15	0.9	2.2	60-62
133 Hawaii Five-O	30	1.7	3.3	69-71
134 The Avengers	39	1.7	5.8	61-69
135 News at Ten	39	0.3	1.1	68-71/2
136 Songs of Praise	30	0.3	1.0	61-71/2
139 The Wednesday Play	16	0.6	2.8	64-70
140 Yogi Bear	22	0.3	1.1	63-65;71
141 77 Sunset Strip	19	1.3	3.4	60-63
142 Hancock	38	0.7	1.4	66-67;63
145 Wyatt Earp	14	1.0	5.3	56-60
146 Arthur Haynes Show	16	0.8	1.2	58-66
148 The Magic Roundabout	43	0.3	1.0	65-71
152 The News (summary)	33	0.3	1.1	daily
153 Sergeant Cork	15	1.1	2.6	63-64
155 Captain Pugwash	17	0.3	1.1	58-66
156 The Lucy Show	36	0.3	1.1	58-71
158 Crossroads	19	0.5	1.2	65-71/2
159 9 o'clock News (main)	35	0.3	1.0	56-67
160 The Larkins	14	0.6	1.4	58-61;64
161 Tree House Family	11	0.3	1.0	68
162 Morecambe and Wise Show	47	0.3	1.1	62-67;68,69

Table A4A.2 (cont.)

171	A Family at War	19	1.1	2.2	69-72
173	The Invisible Man	15	1.8	3.9	60-65
174	Highway Patrol	14	1.2	2.5	57-60
176	Adventure	14	0.3	1.1	59-61
177	Double your Money	32	0.3	1.0	58-68
178	Adventures of Noddy	10	0.3	1.1	58-59
179	Cannonball	15	1.2	2.1	59-61
181	Cheyenne	18	1.2	5.3	58-63
186	Lorna Doone	11	1.9	1.4	68
191	Robin Hood (Adventures of)	31	1.7	8.0	56-71
192	'The Cruel Sea'	23	1.7	2.3	67
193	Tonight with Dave Allen	25	0.3	1.2	67;69
194	The Power Game	26	1.7	2.1	66;69
197	Professional Boxing	21	0.5	1.2	58-71/2
199	Rawhide	19	1.6	4.4	59-64
201	Ready, Steady, Go!	17	0.3	1.0	63-67
204	Danger Man	30	1.5	6.2	60-69
205	Mystery & Imagination	15	1.2	2.2	66;68
206	The Saint	39	1.5	6.0	62-69
207	Opportunity Knocks	27	0.3	1.0	64-71
211	Emergency Ward 10	29	0.6	1.4	56-67
215	Thunderbirds	30	1.6	2.5	65/6;69-71
216	Gunsmoke (Gun Law)	22	1.4	4.0	57-67;71
218	This Week	23	0.3	1.1	57-71/2
219	Take Your Pick	28	0.3	1.0	58-68
220	World in Action	24	0.3	1.1	63-71
222	Love Story	11	0.6	1.4	63-66
225	Bonanza	25	1.7	3.4	60/4;69-70
226	Sunday Night at the London Palladium	32	0.3	1.0	58-64
227	The Human Jungle	17	0.7	2.4	63;65-7
228	Probation Officer	11	0.9	2.0	59-62
229	Popeye	26	2.2	2.2	59-62;6,8,
230	Till Death Us Do Part	44	1.3	1.5	66-69
231	High Adventure	11	1.1	4.3	66-71/2
116	Mr Rose	17	0.9	2.3	67-68

(a) n = Total number of judges who rated the programme on this variable. If less than 10, the programme is omitted.
(b) SIR = Semi-interquartile range (= a measure of scatter of the ratings of judges).
(c) Med = median = score at which 50 per cent of ratings are higher and 50 per cent are lower. On scale of 1-11. Note that tables 4.6 and 4.9 in text are based on scale of 0-10.
(d) PBP = Principal broadcast period.

B Classification in terms of seventeen dichotomous variables

Seventeen of the variables referred to in the subsidiary or supporting hypotheses were dichotomous in character, in the sense that they tended to produce a grading response of either 'yes' or 'no' (e.g. Is this programme a cartoon in which the characters are violent to each other?).

The 17 variables of this kind were as follows.

1. A fictional programme about the English police at work, including violence going on in society.
2. A cartoon in which the characters are violent to each other.
3. A series, a play or a film in which personal relationships are a major theme, and which features verbal abuse (e.g. swearing, quarrelling) or physical violence.
4. A violent programme intended, by the producers, for adults.
5. A play, film or drama series, portraying conflict(s) between individuals, and where it would be difficult for the average boy to decide who is right and who is wrong.
6. A fictional programme where spies use unusual forms of violence, e.g. torture, novel weapons, or individual unarmed combat.
7. A programme which includes newsreel film of the violence of war, or its aftermath.
8. A comedy programme featuring slapstick violence and/or verbal abuse between the characters.
9. A science fiction programme in which non-human fantasy creatures (e.g. monsters) ruthlessly fight with or destroy people.
10. A Western involving violence by, for example, cowboys and Indians.
11. A fictional programme in which the violence tends to go unpunished.
12. A programme showing violence by competitors or spectators at sporting events.
13. A programme which includes real violence (not acted) as it happened or is happening.
14. A film or part of a series/serial featuring gangs or gangsters engaged in violent organised crime.
15. A science fiction programme in which humans use bizarre forms of violence which may involve superhuman powers.
16. A programme where the violence is mostly carried out by children or young people.
17. A programme where adults use violence.

The results of classifying the 231 programmes in terms of several of the variables listed above are given as examples in table 4B.1 in this Appendix.

Table A4B.1

Programmes graded in terms of 17 dichotomous variables
(ratings by 50 judges* except for 1970-71 where there were 74)

Classifying variable		Programme name**	Classified as yes	no	?
1 Fictional programmes about the English police at work, including violence going on in society.	16	Z-Cars	50	0	0
	34	Dixon of Dock Green	47	0	3
	53	The Informer	14	2	34
	57	No Hiding Place	30	2	18
	76	The Revenue Men	8	2	40
	116	Mr Rose	13	4	33
	153	Sergeant Cork	16	0	34
	1970-71*				
		The Mind of Mr J.G. Reeder	16	7	51
		Softly, Softly	65	1	8
		The Expert	34	6	34
2 A cartoon in which the characters are violent to each other.	3	The Boss Cat (Top Cat)	29	2	29
	5	Hector Heathcote	10	3	37
	78	Tom and Jerry	44	2	4
	140	Yogi Bear	14	7	29
	155	Captain Pugwash	13	6	31
	229	Popeye	24	4	22
	1970-71*				
		Atom Ant	8	3	63
		Captain Scarlet	9	3	62
		The Pink Panther	26	6	42
		Marine Boy	13	5	56
		Cartoon Time	25	1	48
3 A series in which personal relationships are a major theme and which feature verbal abuse or physical violence.	10	Steptoe and Son*	45	5	0
	16	Z-Cars*	34	17	0
	34	Dixon of Dock Green*	32	15	3
	61	Crane	14	5	29
	94	Coronation Street*	25	6	19
	108	Count of Monte Cristo	12	3	35
	171	A Family at War*	15	6	29
	227	The Human Jungle	13	5	32
	230	Till Death Us Do Part	42	3	5
	1970-71*				
		Budgie	20	2	52
		Man at the Top	24	0	50
		Troubleshooters	39	0	35
		Crossroads	26	13	35
		Tuesday Film	25	9	40
		Me Mammy	30	4	40
		Wednesday Play	43	3	28
		Elizabeth R	43	7	24
		On the Buses	39	14	21
		Roads to Freedom	15	3	56
		Peyton Place	31	4	39
		Monday Film	14	4	56
3 (cont.)		W. Somerset Maugham	33	9	32
		Bonanza	29	14	31
		Callan Saga	36	5	33
		Hogan's Heroes	15	7	52
		Gunsmoke	18	6	50
		The Virginian	42	17	15
		Playhouse	14	5	55
		Henry VIII	51	4	19
		Saturday Thriller	31	4	39
		The Misfit	8	4	62
		Brett	33	4	37
		Play for Today	30	8	36
		Armchair Theatre	31	8	35
		Wayne in Action	17	6	51
		Queenie's Castle	12	3	59
		Softly, Softly	52	13	9
		Dustbin Men	14	7	53
		Please, Sir!	42	20	12
4 A violent programme intended, by the producers, for adults.	14	The Great War	12	5	33
	84	Late Night Horror	11	2	37
	1970-71*				
		Man at the Top	22	2	50
		The FBI	26	7	41
		The Wednesday Play	33	14	27
		Midnight Movie	31	6	37
		Hine	13	4	57
		Roads to Freedom	16	2	56
		Callan Saga	35	6	33
		The Untouchables	25	7	42
		The Borderers	16	6	52
		Playhouse	14	5	55
		Brett	26	11	37
		Man in the News	14	11	37
		Play for Today	25	12	37
		Armchair Theatre	26	12	36
		Man Alive	24	12	38
		The Expert	28	12	34
5 A play, film or drama, portraying conflict between individuals and where it would be difficult for the average boy to decide who is right and who is wrong.	139	Wednesday Play*	13	3	34
	171	A Family at War*	14	7	29
	194	The Power Game	20	6	24
	1970-71*				
		Budgie	18	4	42
		Man at the Top	22	2	50
		Troubleshooters	39	9	26
		Elizabeth R	35	15	24

Table A4B.1 (cont.)

Classifying variable	Programme name**	Classified as yes	no	?	Classifying variable	Programme name**	Classified as yes	no	?
5 (cont.)	Hine	15	1	57	7 A programme that includes newsreel film of the violence of war or its aftermath.	14 The Great War	16	0	34
	Roads to Freedom	17	1	56		44 Panorama*	41	2	7
	Peyton Place	25	9	40		115 All Our Yesterdays*	28	3	19
	W. Somerset Maugham	38	3	33		126 Main News (BBC 1, 9 pm)*	40	3	7
	Playhouse	12	5	57		135 News at Ten*	40	2	8
	Henry VIII (Six Wives of)	42	11	21		152 News Summary	32	2	16
	Brett	25	12	37		159 Main 9 o'clock News (ITV)	33	2	15
	Play for Today	30	6	38		218 This Week*	19	3	28
	Armchair Theatre	27	12	35		220 World in Action*	20	3	27
6 Fictional programmes where spies use unusual forms of violence (eg torture, novel weapons, individual unarmed combat).	64 The Man from UNCLE	42	2	6		1970-71*			
	134 The Avengers*	34	2	14		News Review	30	2	42
	204 Danger Man	23	7	20		Today	31	15	28
	1970-71*					24 Hours	63	1	10
	Mission Impossible	29	4	41					

* For convenience, the 1970-71 programmes, rated by 74 judges in all, have been included here. Where 1970-71 programmes duplicate those rated by the 50 judges dealing with the 1958-69 programmes, they are not repeated under the 1970-71 head, but the 1958-69 entry is marked with an (*).

** Excluding all programmes for which the total number of ratings is less than 10 and all programmes where the yes:no ratio is less than 2 : 1.

Two examples from the Programme Guide used to aid raters' recall of programmes seen

Used by judges in stage II of the construction process

---

1 Programme title: DR WHO 103

2 *Main characters:* *Acted by:*
Dr Who — William Hartnell

3 *Description:*
Serial about the exploits of a time travelling doctor.

4 *When shown:*

Year:	From 1965 till 1971
Frequency:	Weekly
Time:	5.15 pm
Night:	Saturday

5 *Channel:*
BBC 1

---

1 Programme title: DR KILDARE 104

2 *Main character:* *Acted by:*
Dr Kildare — Richard Chamberlain

3 *Description:*
Series. A story about the life and work of a young doctor.

4 *When shown:*

Year:	From 1965 till 1966
Frequency:	Weekly – some stories are continued to the following week, others are complete in themselves.
Time:	Evening, about 8.00 pm
Night:	Friday

5 *Channel:*
BBC 1

PROGRAMME GUIDE

Used by Judges in Stage II of the construction process

The sample of control programmes

The following programmes were derived by principally random methods for use as a control system in the investigation of hypotheses. It consists of 60 programmes broadly representative of programmes broadcast in the period 1958-71. It was intended that it be used as a basis for testing the (control) hypothesis that exposure to a lot of television output (irrespective of the degree to which its content is violent) has the same effect on boys' violent behaviour as a lot of exposure to *violence* in television.

In the following list, 18 of the programmes coincide with programmes already in the violence list and these are marked as 'also used as control programmes'. The other 18 may be regarded as 'for control purposes only'. In this list, the selected programmes are set out in terms of the year for which sampled and the station of origin. The order in which the years were sampled was randomly determined.

Table A6.1

Broadcasting year from which sampled	Station of origin	Programmes in the Control sample
1958	BBC 1	The Thrilling Adventures of Captain Pugwash
		*6.00 pm News (summary)
	ITV	Hawkeye
		Play of the Week
1959	BBC 1	*The Lone Ranger
		The Young Lady from London
	ITV	White Hunter
		The Four Just Men
1960	BBC 1	*Wells Fargo
		All Your Own
	ITV	Mickey Mouse Club
		†Pathfinders to Mars
1961	BBC 1	The Singing Years
		This is Your Life
	ITV	Supercar
		Deadline Midnight
1962	BBC 1	Junior Points of View
		Travellers' Tales
	ITV	Sir Francis Drake
		Lassie
1963	BBC 1	Moonstrike
		†Deputy Dawg
	ITV	Close-Up
		†Quick-Draw McGraw
1964	BBC 1	Compact
		Clapperboard
	ITV	Roving Report
		National Velvet
1965	BBC 1	The Danny Kaye Show
		Robinson Crusoe
	ITV	†Captain of Detectives
		†Sing a Song of Sixpence
1966	BBC 1	King of the River
		*Grandstand
	ITV	David Jacobs' Words & Music
		George and the Dragon
1967	BBC 1	The Engineer in Wonderland
		†Association Football
	ITV	The Song Break
		*World in Action
1968	BBC 1	Farming
		*A Man called Ironside
	ITV	Zoo Time
		*News at Ten
	BBC 2	The Hollywood Musical
1969	BBC 1	*Dad's Army
		*Star Trek
	ITV	Junior Showtime
		Lost in Space
	BBC 2	The French Cinema
1970	BBC 1	*Z-Cars
		†24 Hours
	ITV	*Coronation Street
		Tales of Edgar Wallace
	BBC 2	Newsroom
1971	BBC 1	The Doctors
		It's Cliff Richard
	ITV	The Golden Shot
		Albert and Victoria
	BBC 2	Yesterday's Witness

Broadcasting year from which originally sampled	Station of origin	Programmes used to replace unsatisfactory items in the original control sample (marked † in the above listings)
1960	ITV	††Highway Patrol
1963	ITV	††Yogi Bear
1963	ITV	††The Boss Cat
1964	ITV	††Saturday Sportstime
1965	BBC 1	††Sportsview
1960	BBC 1	††Panorama
1971	BBC 1	††The Last of the Mohicans

* These programmes are also included in the violence sample.
† Programmes which were dropped either because they were unsatisfactory for this purpose or because they were closely similar to programmes in the original control sample.
†† These programmes were substituted, from the violence programmes, for the 'dropped' items, marked with †.

Table A7.1
The full set of 117 programmes used in the research materials for measurement of boys' exposure to different types of television output

Programme number	Station of origin	Which sample *	Name of programme
1	BBC 1	V	The Rag Trade
2	BBC 1	N	Captain Pugwash
3	ITV/BBC	V	Professional Boxing
4	BBC 2	V	The Late Night Horror
5	BBC 1	V	Dr Finlay's Casebook
6	ITV	C	Junior Showtime
7	BBC 1	V	Tonight
8	ITV/BBC 1	V, C	Yogi Bear
9	BBC 1	V	Billy Bunter of Greyfriars School
10	BBC 2	V	The Great War
11	BBC 1/ITV	C	This is Your Life
12	BBC 1	C	The Young Lady from London
13	ITV	V	The Avengers
14	ITV	V	Danger Man
15	ITV	V	The Saint
16	BBC 1	C	Moonstrike
17	BBC 1	C	Travellers' Tales
18	ITV	C	Play of the Week
19	ITV	V, C	Coronation Street
20	BBC 1	C	Compact
21	BBC 1	V	The Man from UNCLE
22	ITV	V	The Army Game
23	ITV	V	The Untouchables
24	BBC 1	V	Wayne in Action
25	BBC 1/2 ITV	V	Marty
26	ITV	C	White Hunter
27	BBC 1	V, C	Sportsview
28	BBC 1	N	Tom and Jerry
29	BBC 1	V, C	Grandstand
30	ITV	V	Hawaii Five-0
31	BBC 1	V, C	The Lone Ranger
32	ITV	V	The Adventures of Robin Hood
33	BBC 1	V	Whack-0!
34	ITV	V	No Hiding Place
35	BBC 1	C	The Singing Years
36	ITV	V	Wyatt Earp
37	ITV	C	Zoo Time
38	ITV	C	Close-Up
39	BBC 1	C	The Engineer in Wonderland
40	ITV	V	The Informer
41	BBC 1	V, C	The Last of the Mohicans
42	ITV	C	David Jacobs' Words and Music
43	BBC 2	C	The Hollywood Musical
44	BBC 1	C	Farming
45	BBC 1	C	Clapperboard
46	BBC 1	V	Dixon of Dock Green
47	BBC 1	V	High Adventure
48	BBC 1	C	King of the River
49	BBC 1/2	V	Sherlock Holmes
50	ITV	V	Gunsmoke (or Gun Law)
51	BBC 1	V	Adam Adamant Lives
52	BBC 1	V, C	Z-Cars
53	ITV	V, C	Highway Patrol
54	ITV	C	Lost in Space
55	ITV	V	The Human Jungle
56	BBC 1	V, C	5.50/6.00 pm News Summary
57	ITV	C	Saturday Sportstime
58	ITV	N	Professional Wrestling
59	ITV	V	Bonanza
60	ITV	V	Sergeant Cork
61	BBC 1	C	It's Cliff Richard
62	BBC 1	V, C	A Man called Ironside
63	BBC 2	C	The French Cinema
64	BBC 1	V	Till Death us do Part
65	BBC 2/1	V	The Virginian
66	BBC 1	V, C	Panorama
67	BBC 2	C	Yesterday's Witness
68	ITV	V	Cinema
69	BBC 1	V, C	Wells Fargo
70	ITV	C	George and the Dragon
71	BBC 2	C	Newsroom
72	BBC 1	V	Dr Who
73	BBC 1	C	Junior Points of View
74	BBC 2	V	Out of the Unknown
75	ITV	V	Cheyenne
76	BBC 1	N	Quatermass and the Pit
77	ITV	C	Supercar
78	ITV	C	The Four Just Men
79	ITV	C	Roving Report
80	ITV	V	The Invisible Man
81	BBC 1	V, C	Star Trek
82	ITV	C	The Song Break
83	ITV	N	Popeye
84	ITV	C	Albert and Victoria
85	BBC 1	V	The Wednesday Play
86	BBC 1	C	The Doctors
87	BBC 1	C	Robinson Crusoe
88	BBC 1	V	Perry Mason
89	ITV	C	National Velvet
90	BBC 2	V	The High Chaparral
91	ITV	V	Mystery and Imagination
92	ITV	C	Sir Francis Drake
93	ITV	V	Please, Sir!
94	BBC 1	V	The Defenders
95	ITV	V, C	The News at Ten
96	ITV	V	Thunderbirds
97	ITV	V, C	World in Action
98	ITV	C	Tales of Edgar Wallace
99	BBC 1	V	Steptoe and Son
100	ITV	V	Crane
101	ITV	C	Deadline Midnight
102	ITV	C	Lassie
103	BBC 1	C	The Boss Cat (Top Cat)
104	ITV	C	The Golden Shot
105	ITV	C	Hawkeye
106	ITV	V	Mister Rose
107	BBC 1	V	Maigret
108	BBC 1	C	All your Own
109	ITV	C	Mickey Mouse Club
110	ITV	V	Probation Officer
111	BBC 1	V	Softly, Softly
112	ITV	V	The Main Chance
113	ITV	V	The Power Game
114	BBC 1	C	Dad's Army
115	ITV	V	Rawhide
116	BBC 1	C	The Danny Kaye Show
117	ITV	V	77 Sunset Strip

*
V only = a programme in only the sample of violent programmes
C only = a programme in only the sample of control programmes
V, C = a programme in both the violent programme sample and the control programme sample
N = a programme in neither sample (used only in assessment of exposure to specific categories of television violence)

Appendix 8

INSTRUCTIONS TO INTENSIVE INTERVIEWER FOR ESTABLISHING HOW OFTEN CERTAIN PROGRAMMES HAD BEEN SEEN

GETTING NUMBER OF TIMES HE SAW THE PROGRAMMES IN HIS HEAP 1 PACK

1 TAKE UP HEAP 1 ENVELOPE AND SAY:

'I am going to go through all the programmes you put into this envelope.'

TAKE OUT ITS CONTENTS

SAY:

'Are these *all* programmes you have seen at some time?'

IF NO, CLEAR UP AND IF NECESSARY HAVE SORTING DONE AGAIN'

SAY:

2 'There is something else I need to know about each of the programmes in this pack (HOLD UP). I will show you what I mean with the first of them. It's . . . ' (NAME IT).

NOTE, ON THE BACK OF THE SHEET, THE AGE RANGE BETWEEN THE FIRST AND THE LAST VIEWING OF IT.

SAY:

'You said you first watched . . . (NAME IT) when you were aged . . . and last when you were aged . . . . So you watched it over a period of about . . . (GIVE INTERVAL) years. Is that right?'
PAUSE.

SAY:

'In that . . . year period, there were about . . . episodes of . . . (NAME IT).

'*I want you to tell me just how many of these . . . episodes you think you saw.* BUT before you answer, I want to say that it is very important for you to make a real effort to remember how many times it was. If you answer carelessly, then our work will be wasted. It's very important for you to really try to remember how many times it was. Will you really try hard for me?
WAIT FOR HIS REPLY.

EMPHASISE WITH:

'Thank you. Your careful reply is absolutely necessary if our research is to be of any use.'

3 SAY:

'So you watched . . . (NAME THE PROGRAMME) over a period of . . . years. In that time, there were . . . (GIVE NUMBER) episodes of . . . ' (NAME THE PROGRAMME).

WRITE NUMBER JUST UNDER NAME OF PROGRAMME AND LET BOY SEE IT. SAY:

'How many of those . . . episodes do you think you saw?'

WRITE HIS NUMBER IN THE SPACE JUST BELOW Q.2. ON THE BACK OF THE SHEET.

IF THE BOY SEEMS TO BE IN DIFFICULTY WITH THE QUESTIONS OR TO BE ANSWERING CARELESSLY, HELP HIM IN ONE OR MORE OF THE FOLLOWING WAYS:

Use your visual and verbal aids.

Tell him the time of day it was on.

Remind him of how it differs from some other programmes.

ALSO BE PREPARED TO CHALLENGE SLIPSHOD OR OBVIOUSLY ERRONEOUS REPLIES, SAYING THINGS SUCH AS:

You mean you saw just about every episode that was shown when you were a viewer of . . . .

But that's more than were shown.

So you saw only very few of the episodes of . . . that were broadcast in the period you were a viewer of it. Is that right? Only . . . (GIVE HIS FIGURE)?

SAY:

'So you see I do need you to be careful about your answer. Think carefully before you give me the number of times. Now let's do the others.'

4 NOW DEAL WITH THE SECOND SHEET AS FOLLOWS:
PUT IT DOWN IN FRONT OF HIM, BACK UPPERMOST.

'Let's take the next programme in your heap 1. It is . . . . You said you viewed that one from age . . . to . . . . That's . . . years you were a viewer of it.

'In those . . . years, there were . . . episodes of . . . .'

ENTER THIS NUMBER ON HIS CARD JUST BELOW THE TITLE OF THE PROGRAMME.

'How many of those . . . episodes do you think you saw?'

ENTER REPLY.

5 NOW PROCEED AS FOR ITEM 4 FOR EACH OF THE REST OF THE VIOLENCE SHEETS.

*IF BOY SEEMS TO BE GETTING CARELESS, DELIVER THE CHALLENGE SYSTEM SET OUT IN ITEM 3 ABOVE.

ALSO HELP AS NECESSARY.

6 CLIP YOUR PROGRAMME SHEETS TOGETHER AND PUT INTO THE HEAP 1 ENVELOPE.

7 NOW TAKE OUT HIS HEAP 3 SHEETS AND USE YOUR VISUAL AND VERBAL AIDS TO TRY TO CLEAR UP HIS UNCERTAINTIES.

8 MARK ALL ENVELOPES WITH HIS SERIAL NUMBER.

CHAPTER 5

DEVELOPING INDICES OF EXPOSURE TO THE OTHER MEDIA: NEWSPAPERS, COMICS, VIOLENT FILMS

Contents

5 DEVELOPING INDICES OF EXPOSURE TO THE OTHER MEDIA: NEWSPAPERS, COMICS, VIOLENT FILMS

INTRODUCTION

Whereas this enquiry is focussed upon the influence of *violence on television*, it was intended that the enquiry should also yield assessments of the influence of other media presentations of violence, namely violence in films, comics, newspapers. The rationale of this decision is set out in chapter 2.

The assessment of exposure to violence in films was relatively straightforward in the sense that films are small units that can be graded in terms of whether they are in general violent or not violent. That situation makes it feasible to derive a sample of violent films.

However, for both newspapers and comics, the situation is different. Boys' comics of the sort that are generally available (excluding small children's comics) all tend to present some degree of violence. Similarly for newspapers in that all seek to present the news, some of which is violent. Accordingly, for these two media the hypotheses about effects were formulated in terms of exposure to the media as such, namely:

> 'High exposure to comics leads boys to . . . '

and

> 'High exposure to newspapers leads boys to . . . '

The third hypothesis (about the influence of other mass media) was of course more specific, namely:

> 'High exposure to *violent* films leads boys to . . . '

AN INDEX OF EXPOSURE TO VIOLENT FILMS

The general strategy of measurement of exposure to violent films was as follows:

1. A large number of the more popular films screened in Britain between 1958 and 1971 was brought together, being made up of an approximately equal number of them for each year.
2. From this collection or pool, steps were taken to select first 50 and then 22 relevant films of a violent kind.
3. In the main survey, each boy was questioned to find out how many of the 22 films he had ever seen in the cinema, the total out of 22 being regarded as an index of his exposure to violent films.

The large pool of popular films for the period 1958-1971

The Motion Picture Herald lists (in its Almanack) the top 10-20 money-making films on general release for each year (from 1956). Also, where the information is available, the Almanack gives the top 2 or 3 'hard ticket special presentations' which are spectacular type films shown for long periods in big urban cinemas in London and other centres before being generally released.

Against each of the listed films was entered its certificate grading as an 'A' or 'U' or 'X' or 'AA'. [1]

The great majority of the Certificate gradings in the Almanack lists were 'A' or 'U', meaning among other things that these were films to which young people were easily or readily admitted. Because of this and because box office successes were more likely than other films to have been seen by large numbers of Londoners, the annual listings of the Almanack for 1958-71 were adopted as the 'pool' of films from which the proposed selection of violent films would be made.

As a further guide to the selection that had to be made from the full list or pool of films, the records of the British Film Institute were consulted and for each film the following additional details were obtained: country of origin, the main actors, indication of the plot and (usually) the name of the director or producer.

Consideration of plot, grading, cast and of any other available evidence about these films led to their categorisation by research staff as

V or VV = much violent content (e.g. fighting, battles, deaths)
V? = some violent content or possible violent content
C = a comedy film, either slapstick or sophisticated
C/V = comedy plus violence
Others = apparently non-violent

Reducing the full list to the 50 for rating by judges

From the long list, 50 films were selected according to the following criteria:

1. All films with X or AA ratings or which were shown before 1958 were eliminated from the full list on the grounds that relatively few of the boys in the sample would have seen them. 'Romances' and 'musicals' were also excluded (on the grounds that they contained little or no violence). Films graded as 'comedy' (i.e. 'C' as distinct from 'C/V') were also excluded.
2. The selection of the 50 films from the remaining films was made by research staff with a view to maintaining (a) representativeness in terms of year of listing; (b) a wide range in terms of type of violence. The selected 50 included many that were classifiable as war films, epics, spy films, westerns.

The final list (22) of films for use in assessing relative exposure to film violence

Fifteen members of the research and interviewing staff of the Survey Research Centre were given a list of the 50 films so far selected and were asked to grade those of them which they had seen on the following 4-point scale:

0 = not violent
1 = low (level of) violence
2 = medium (level of) violence
3 = highly violent

In getting from the 50 (on the basis of the ratings of the judges), films were excluded if given any zero ratings and if they seemed unlikely to appeal to boys. Beyond this and in general, selection of films was made on the basis of the frequency of their being rated as 3 or 2. Within this system an attempt was made to maintain variety in terms of film content. The final selection of 22 films is set out in table 5.1.

Table 5.1
The final selection of 22 violent films

Dr No	Goldfinger	The Green Berets
Spartacus	Zulu	Planet of the Apes
From Russia with Love	The Long Ships	Where Eagles Dare
The Great Escape	The Fall of the Roman Empire	The Battle of Britain
The Longest Day	Thunderball	On Her Majesty's Secret Service
How the West was Won	Nevada Smith	Butch Cassidy & the Sundance Kid
Lawrence of Arabia	You Only Live Twice	Cromwell
		Little Big Man

This selection of films included spy films, westerns, epic 'historical' adventures, a science fiction film, war films. In general, they had not been shown on television.

Assessing the relative degree of boys' exposure to violent films

The 22 violent films were to be presented to boys in the form of a checklist. The boy would be required to mark with a tick (✓) each of them he had ever seen at the cinema and with a cross (X) each of them that he had *not* seen at the cinema.

The form of this check list (used in the survey) is given in Appendix 1. It was delivered to boys as part of a self-completion booklet to which they were to be introduced during a home interview and which they were to complete at home prior to being brought to the Centre for a second (intensive) interview.

Total score for a boy was the number out of the 22 programmes which he claimed to have seen.

AN INDEX OF EXPOSURE TO COMICS

The general strategy of measurement of exposure to violent forms of comic material was similar in some ways to that employed in relation to exposure to film violence.

1 A preliminary study was made of the level of violence in comics available to boys through newsagents' shops and station bookstalls.

2 Boys were asked to volunteer all the comics read by or known to them.

3 The more frequently named 21 were selected as a basis for developing a comparative measure of boys' exposure to comics.

4 Information about the extent of exposure to such comics was collected in the main survey by means of a self-completion booklet.

A preliminary study of the comics available and of the level of violence presented in them

In defining the type of comic reading to be investigated, it was decided to rule out girls' comics, small childrens' comics and cheap adult comics. This left the weekly comics aimed by their publishers at boys and school children of both sexes and the American style comic books issued monthly or fortnightly. Boys' football comics were also to be included.

For general preparatory purposes, visits were then made to newsagents' shops and to station bookstalls in order to secure as many as possible of the different comics (within the above definition) as were available. This search yielded 45 different comics and comic books.

An examination was made of the contents of these 45 comics, with the following conclusions.

1 They presented between them a great variety of forms of violence. At the same time, practically all of them tended to have in them one or more forms of violence so that it did not seem possible readily to classify them as either violent or non-violent.

2 The 45 presented very little of what might be regarded as horror or sadism. Whereas the latter type of content may perhaps have been available 'under the counter', it appears that it did not constitute the comic material generally available to boys.

On this evidence, it was decided to treat comics *generally* rather than stratifying them by degrees or type of violence presented in them.

Selecting 21 comics for use in discriminating between boys in terms of amount of comic reading done

Boys (39) in a secondary modern school in London were asked to write down the names of all the comics or comic books known to them. They listed 70 titles between them. The more frequently named of them were included in the set of comics in terms of which the comparison of boys was to be made. The selected 21 are listed in table 5.2.

Table 5.2
The comics (21) selected for use in the assessment of exposure to comics

Dandy	Smash	Wizard
Hornet	Hotspur	Goal (magazine)
Batman with Robin (comic book)	Beezer	Scorcher
Beano	Score	Valiant (and TV 21)
Topper	Superman (comic book)	Shoot
Victor	Tiger (and Jag)	Buster (and Jet)
Sparky	Cor!!	Lion (and Thunder)

Assessing the relative degree of exposure to comics

The 21 comics listed above were to be presented in the form of a check-list. Boys were required to put a tick (✓) against each of the listed comics they had 'ever regularly read or regularly looked through'. The form of the check list and the instructions about what to tick are given in Appendix 2. It was presented in the context of a self-completion booklet, along with questions about the films seen and newspapers read, for completion by boys in the at-home part of the investigation.

Total score for a boy was the number of comics (out of 21) with ticks (✓) entered against them.

AN INDEX OF EXPOSURE TO NEWSPAPERS

All the different newspapers available to boys in London present violence – in that they report violent events as news. The possibility of distinguishing between them, in terms of degree to which violence is presented, is both difficult and unrealistic.

The publications selected as a basis for questioning were the national daily papers, the two London evening papers, the national Sunday papers and three popular weekly publications. All 21 are listed below in table 5.3

Table 5.3
The publications (21) selected for use in the assessment of exposure to newspapers

Daily Telegraph	The Morning Star	Sunday Express
The Sun	Financial Times	Sunday Telegraph
Daily Mirror	Evening Standard	Observer
Daily Express	Evening News	Sunday Times
The Guardian	Weekend	News of the World
Daily Mail	Reveille	The People
The Times	Tit Bits or Sat. Tit Bits	Sunday Mirror

Assessing the relative degree of exposure to newspapers

All 21 were to be presented in the form of a check list, the respondents being required to tick each of them that they had '*ever regularly read or regularly looked through*'. The form of the list and the instructions that were with it are set out in Appendix 3. This material was part of a self-completion questionnaire in which were presented the comic and the film check-lists.

Total score for a boy was the number of publications (out of 21) that he ticked. The nature of the questions it was possible to ask in the situation available was such that their readership scores must be interpreted relatively and not as absolutes.

Notes

[1] These are the certificate gradings used by the film industry. They have the following designations.

Category U	Passed for general exhibition.
Category A	Passed for general exhibition but parents or guardians are advised that the film contains material they might prefer children under 14 years not to see.
Category AA	Passed as suitable only for 14 years and over. When a programme includes an AA film no person under 14 years can be admitted.
Category X	Passed as suitable for exhibition to adults. When a programme includes an X film no person under 18 years can be admitted.

APPENDICES TO CHAPTER 5

Appendix 1

THE FILMS YOU HAVE SEEN

1 Which of the following films have you seen at the cinema?

PUT A TICK (LIKE THIS ✓) IN THE BOX OPPOSITE THE NAME OF EACH FILM YOU HAVE SEEN AT THE CINEMA. PUT A X AGAINST EACH YOU HAVE NOT SEEN AT THE CINEMA.

	✓or X here
Dr No	
Spartacus	
From Russia with Love	
The Great Escape	
The Longest Day	
How the West was Won	
Lawrence of Arabia	
Goldfinger	
Zulu	
The Long Ships	
The Fall of the Roman Empire	
Thunderball	
Nevada Smith	
You Only Live Twice	
The Green Berets	
Planet of the Apes	
Where Eagles Dare	
The Battle of Britain	
On Her Majesty's Secret Service	
Butch Cassidy & the Sundance Kid	
Cromwell	
Little Big Man	

2 These days, how often do you go to the cinema?

PUT A TICK (✓) AGAINST THE ANSWER THAT IS NEAREST TO HOW OFTEN YOU GO TO THE CINEMA THESE DAYS.

Two or more times a week	
About once a week	
About once a fortnight	
About once a month	
About once in two months	
Less often	
Not at all	

3 Who is your favourite film star?

WRITE YOUR ANSWER HERE ____________________

4 Describe the sort of film you like seeing most.

____

____

____

THE COMICS YOU HAVE EVER READ

1 Which of the following comics or magazines have you EVER *regularly read* or *regularly looked through*?

PUT A TICK (✓) IN THE BOX OPPOSITE THE NAME OF EACH OF THE FOLLOWING COMICS THAT YOU HAVE EVER READ REGULARLY OR EVER LOOKED THROUGH REGULARLY. PUT A X OPPOSITE ALL THE OTHERS.

	✓ or X here
Dandy	
Hornet	
Batman with Robin (comic book)	
Beano	
Topper	
Victor	
Sparky	
Smash	
Hotspur	
Beezer	
Score	
Superman (comic book)	
Tiger (and Jag)	
Cor!!	
Wizard	
Goal (magazine)	
Scorcher	
Valiant (and TV 21)	
Shoot	
Buster (and Jet)	
Lion (and Thunder)	

2 These days how often do you read a comic?

PUT A (✓) AGAINST THE ANSWER THAT IS NEAREST TO WHAT YOU DO.

Once a week	
Once a fortnight	
Once a month	
Less often	

THE PAPERS YOU HAVE READ

1 Which of the following papers have you EVER *regularly read* or *regularly looked through*?

PUT A TICK (LIKE THIS ✓) IN THE BOX OPPOSITE THE NAME OF EACH NEWSPAPER THAT YOU HAVE <u>EVER</u> REGULARLY READ OR REGULARLY LOOKED THROUGH. PUT A X AGAINST ALL THE OTHERS.

	✓ or X here
Daily Telegraph	
The Sun	
Daily Mirror	
Daily Express	
The Guardian	
Daily Mail	
The Times	
The Morning Star	
Financial Times	
Evening Standard	
Evening News	
Weekend	
Reveille	
Tit Bits or Sat. Tit Bits	
Sunday Express	
Sunday Telegraph	
Observer	
Sunday Times	
News of the World	
The People	
Sunday Mirror	

2 These days, how often do you read a daily newspaper?

PUT A (✓) OPPOSITE THE ANSWER THAT IS NEAREST TO WHAT YOU DO

Every day	
Most days	
Once or twice a week	
Once a month	
Less often	

3 These days, how often do you read a Sunday paper?

PUT A (✓) OPPOSITE THE ANSWER THAT IS NEAREST TO WHAT YOU DO.

Every Sunday	
About one Sunday in two	
About once a month	
Less often	

CHAPTER 6

THE CONSTRUCTION OF A TECHNIQUE FOR MEASURING THE EXTENT AND NATURE OF BOYS' INVOLVEMENT IN VIOLENT BEHAVIOUR

Contents

6 THE CONSTRUCTION OF A TECHNIQUE FOR MEASURING THE EXTENT AND NATURE OF BOYS' INVOLVEMENT IN VIOLENT BEHAVIOUR

INTRODUCTION

In this chapter is a description of the methods used to derive a measure principally [1] of the dependent variable in the hypothesis:

> 'High exposure of boys to television violence increases/reduces the degree to which they are involved in acts of violence.'

In more specific terms, this dependent variable was *the extent of violence done by boys over some specified and relevant period*. The development of a technique to measure it was undertaken as a project of some difficulty and complexity.

Certain difficulties were expected from the outset, namely:

1 variability, from person to person, in what is meant or understood by 'violence';
2 unwillingness by boys to admit involvement in violence, especially major acts committed recently [2] ; a tendency by some boys to invent or exaggerate;
3 inaccuracy in the recall processes of boys;
4 uncertainty about the duration of the period to which to refer boys in seeking information about acts of violence they had committed.

On the basis of past work in the area of deviant behaviour, it was expected that further problems would emerge as work progressed.

TWO BASIC DEFINITIONS

Before the construction of a measure of violence could proceed very far, it was necessary that the key term 'violence' be defined. Another matter that called for initial definition or specification (at least on a provisional basis) was the duration of the period within which a boy's violent behaviour was to be 'counted' or measured.

The definition of violence

In the present case, the definition of 'violence' could be achieved on pragmatic lines, for it was both possible and necessary to define 'violence' in terms of whatever it was that people had in mind when they said that television violence and youth violence might be causally linked. If, for example, the people making such suggestions had ruled out *psychological* violence and had referred only to physical violence, then any hypothesis representing the views of these people would be bound to define violence in terms of only *physical* violence. In fact, no such limitation was evident in the views of the people questioned, or in the literature consulted, in the hypothesis development stage of the enquiry. Rather, violence (as something that seemed likely to be affected by television) was conceived very broadly indeed. *Thus it appeared to relate to activity of a kind that produces or is likely to produce hurt or harm of any kind to the object on the receiving end. The object on the receiving end could be animate or inanimate and the hurt or harm to animate objects could be either physical or psychological.* This breadth of the concept of 'violence' had to be maintained or safeguarded in the development of the procedure that was to be used to measure the incidence of 'violence'.

The period within which violence was to be assessed

Another important aspect of the measure to be made was the period within which boys' violence had to be assessed. It had to be long enough for differences between boys to show up and for the assessment to extend well beyond a boy's very recent acts. But at the same time, the qualifying period could not be so long as to raise serious memory problems – or to produce too many acts for the interviewer to be able to collect the necessary detail about each.

In fact, this period or interval was provisionally set at 6 months – and was maintained at that level in the final form of the procedures [3] in spite of it generating a very large volume of acts for many boys.

THE BASIC APPROACH TO BE USED

It was possible to short-cut what would have been a major and lengthy construction process by modelling the required measuring technique, where possible, upon a similar technique developed several years previously at the Survey Research Centre, namely a procedure for assessing the extent of a boy's involvement in stealing. [4] The serious problems facing that project were very similar to the ones expected in the present case and are listed in the introduction to this chapter. In the face of these problems, it had taken a year, much thought and a lot of money to develop the measure of theft to the point at which it was considered to be a viable tool. There was thus a strong case for drawing upon the form and tactics of that earlier procedure where possible and appropriate, in constructing the required measure of violence. On the other hand, much original construction work had also to be done.

It was against this background that the procedure eventually took the following general form and features. The procedure is presented in full working detail at the end of this chapter and details of original construction work are given in the next section.

1 Boys were interviewed on Centre premises under conditions of stressed anonymity and privacy, with each boy having a fictitious name for the occasion. Prior to this they had already been through lengthy questioning on a quite innocuous issue with the same interviewer.

2 A central feature of the present procedure involved the sorting, by the boys, of many cards on each of which was a different statement about violence and which together made up what has been called a 'web of stimuli' [5]. Many of the statements referred to a form of violent behaviour in general or in specific terms (e.g 'I have thrown something at someone'; 'I have given someone a head butt'), but

others referred to *situations* in which violence occurred (e.g. 'I have been violent at a football match') and others again referred to *reasons* for being violent (e.g. 'I have done something to get my own back on somebody', 'I have been violent just for fun or for a laugh or for a dare'). These carded statements (the development of which is described in this chapter) together constituted a 'web of stimuli' [5] sufficiently comprehensive in coverage to refer to virtually the whole range or 'universe' of the behaviour defined as violent in this enquiry.

3 The basic requirement in sorting was that the boy should look at each card in turn and put it into a bag labelled 'yes' if he had done what was on it in the last six months and into one labelled 'no' if he had *not* done so. The two bags were fixed to a screen which separated the boy from the interviewer in order to give the boy a sense of privacy, the cards being passed to the boy one at a time through a slot at the bottom of the screen (see diagram in the appendix to this chapter).

4 The sorting requirement had been preceded by an introductory phase in which the boy was told what the next set of questions would be about, was told that it was essential that he be completely frank and was reminded that he had a false name. There was then a reading test and a period of fairly intensive teaching of the rules for sorting. These rules were principally that:

- the period being asked about was 'the last six months' and anything done earlier than that would not count;
- an act was to be counted even if the boy considered it was not serious, even if accidental, even if done in self-defence;
- the boy was to ask the interviewer for help whenever he was uncertain about anything;
- the boy should place face down in front of him any cards about which he was unable to make a decision (even after seeking clarification through the interviewer).

For marker purposes, the interviewer was to set the boy thinking of public and personal events six months ago. During sorting, there were spaced reminders of rules and especially of the requirement that the boy be completely frank. For some cards, there were special introductory or clarifying statements.

5 After the 53 carded statements (i.e. constituting the 'web of stimuli') had been sorted, the interviewer came out from behind the screen and tried to help the boy to clear up any 'don't know' cards. He then put the boy through what has been called the 'pretending game' [6]. In this 'game' the interviewer was required to ask the respondent to imagine that he had used violence on some other boy and that this had damaged the boy very badly. He then asked the respondent if he would have admitted such an act to the interviewer.

If the boy said 'yes', the interviewer was required to ask 'why' and to reinforce the boy's willingness to tell all, by (a) repeating the boy's reasons back to him, (b) delivering certain additional arguments (for telling 'all') as detailed in the interviewer's instructions (e.g. 'What you say is absolutely private' / 'There's no name connected with it – in fact you've got a false name'). The interviewer then proceeded to seek certain details about each card sorted as 'yes', using the system detailed in (6) below.

If the boy said 'no', in the pretending game, the interviewer was required to find out 'why' and to discuss with the boy his reasons for *not* being willing to admit that act – the interviewer's purpose being to identify any general or specific reticence about making admissions and the reasons for such reticence. The interviewer sought to overcome that reticence or resistance both by clearing up any basic misunderstanding on the part of the boy and by delivering certain standard 'counter arguments' proposed for such purposes and presented in the interviewer's instructions. For example, if the boy had said he was ashamed to tell, the interviewer would say, amongst other things: 'I'm not *judging* anyone – I'm just finding out' / 'You don't know me, I don't know you, and I don't suppose we will ever meet again'. After this, the boy was asked to re-sort all the cards previously sorted as 'No'.

6 The interview now proceeded into its final stage. The sorting screen was taken down and the boy was questioned with respect to each of the statements or acts he had sorted into the 'Yes' box. Thus for a given statement (e.g. 'I have thrown something at someone'), the interviewer asked the boy for:

(a) the total number of times he had done what was on the card over the last six months [7].
(b) the different sorts of things he had done (in relation to what was on the card.
(c) for each of these different sorts of things,
    (i) the nature of the act (e.g. kicked, punched, pushed, cut),
    (ii) the object of the act (e.g. another boy, the cat),
    (iii) the implement if any (e.g. knife, stick),
    (iv) what led him to do it (e.g. the other boy was rude to him, for fun) [8],
    (v) the circumstances of the act (e.g. at football),
    (vi) how many times he had done that sort of thing in the last six months.

Responses to questions (i) – (vi) were entered on the cards themselves as part of the record of the interview and subsequently were used to derive 'violence scores' for the boys [9].

7 The whole of the extraction procedure was controlled by a booklet which detailed what the interviewer had to do and say throughout, with the exception of the discussional stage of the 'pretending game'. The 53 statements were interlaced with the pages of the instruction booklet, because many of the instructions were geared to what was written on specific cards. The booklet and the statements on the 53 cards are presented in diagrammatic and verbal form at the end of this chapter.

THE DEVELOPMENT OF ASPECTS OF THE PROCEDURE SPECIFIC TO THE MEASUREMENT OF VIOLENCE [10]

Though the elicitation strategy used was drawn from that developed for an earlier study (see statement under 'The Basic Approach to be Used'), converting that strategy into a working tool called for a great deal of original construction work. For a start, it was necessary to develop an appropriate 'web of stimuli' for evoking comprehensive recall of acts of violence. In addition, special attention had to be given to: the specification of sorting rules relevant to the violence cards; the formulation of a questioning sequence for securing relevant information about the acts or cards sorted as 'Yes'; the formulation of a procedure for going from the details collected in the interview to the different scores required for the investigation of the hypothesis here concerned; the incorporation of challenging and checking tactics.

The remaining sections of this chapter are principally concerned with these processes, namely the construction of a relevant web of stimuli; the formulation of rules for the sorting process; the formulation of questions about the acts committed; the development of a scoring procedure.

DEVELOPING THE WEB OF STIMULI

The rationale and functions of the 'web of stimuli'

The statement in the next three paragraphs is an elaboration, involving some necessary degree of repetition, of an earlier statement about the nature of the 'web of stimuli'.

Of the 53 carded statements sorted by boys, 50 [11] were central to the measurement of the total amount of a boy's violence and constituted the 'web of stimuli'. Typically, these stimuli were designed both as memory aids for the boy and as a means of drawing his attention to all the different parts of the wide-ranging universe of violent behaviour.

The 50 statements were not offered as 50 distinct types or categories of violence. Rather they were stimuli designed to evoke comprehensive recall in the boy of all his violent behaviour in the period asked about. As stimuli, they took several different forms. (i) Some of the statements referred to *broad classes of behaviour* like 'I have thrown something at someone', 'I have tried to torment someone', 'I have hurt an animal'. Their purpose was to evoke recall at a broad level, as a preliminary to further questioning (in a later stage of the interview) designed to elicit details. (ii) Other of the 50 statements were about *fairly specific acts*, for example, 'I have given someone a head butt', 'I have twisted someone's arm. (iii) A third category of statements presented *situations* in which boys might be violent, for example, 'I have been violent at a football match', 'I have been violent during sport', 'I have been violent at school or work'. Their purpose was to provide another opportunity for recall, in the sense that boys will on occasions be reminded by a *situation* rather than directly recalling an act. (iv) Then again, there were statements that dealt with *motivation* or with *reasons* for committing an act of violence, for example, 'I have been violent just for fun or for a laugh or for a dare', 'I have been violent to impress my mates or girls or other people'.

This criss-cross of stimuli, this *web* of stimuli, increased very much the likelihood of any one act being recalled and that was its main function as a web. In principle, the web technique involves the use of overlapping broad stimuli, with specific stimuli added where the broader stimuli tend to fail to evoke recall of fairly specific types of acts or where some particular act is so common as to justify a statement of its own. Inevitably, this system leads to some act being reported more than once and in the present case this required that special steps be taken to identify (and then to discount) repeat mentions. To this aspect of the procedure attention will be given later in this chapter and in the next chapter.

One other matter should be noted at this point and returned to later. It is that *the sorting of the web items as 'yes' or 'no' does not end the eliciting procedure.* It was intended that each statement sorted as 'yes' would be used as a starting point for detailed questioning about each of the acts subsumed under it.

The construction of the 'Web of Stimuli'

The 'Web of Stimuli' was constructed through three cycles, using the method of Progressive Modification developed by Belson [12]. In the present context, progressive modification involves progressively modifying a research procedure on the basis of evidence about its viability. Typically, the method proceeds through several stages. Cycle 1 usually involves the setting up of a tentative form of the procedure based on a study of the eliciting problems it must overcome. Cycle 2 consists of a test of the first form of the procedure followed by a modification of it on the basis of the results of that test. Cycle 3 consists of a test of the procedure in its modified form, followed by such modifications of it as the new set of test results indicate are necessary. And so on till the procedure tests out at some satisfactory level.

Cycle 1: a first approximation to the required 'web of stimuli'

The source of web items. A first approximation to the required web of stimuli was generated on the basis of a large collection of acts of violence said to go on amongst London boys. The main sources of these acts were boys aged 12-17 years who met in large groups under test room conditions. They were asked, amongst other things [13], to write down 'all the different sorts of violence that you see boys going in for. Include your own violence as well . . . '. The total yield from the 71 who took part was very large, lurid, and highly varied. [14] Parents of some of these boys (tested in another group in another room) also volunteered information about the nature of any violence they had seen boys committing, but in fact their submissions added very little to the kinds of violence volunteered by the boys. To the total list of 'acts' generated in this way, were added the results of scanning the relevant academic literature and newspaper articles, and of interviews with persons professionally associated with television.

Whereas the majority of the acts detailed by the respondents were fairly specific, there were some that were global in character, some that referred to the conditions under which the violence occurred, some that involved justification for an act or motivation for it, and some were simply types of weapon used.

The object in generating the first list of *web items* was to construct statements which would between them include or pertain to all the different kinds of violence listed by the boys, parents or others, but at the same time keep the proposed 'web' items both meaningful and relatively limited in number. It was also the object to overlap such items with statements relating to situations, motivations, justifications.

The first list of web items. The first list generated in this way consisted of the following 45 items.

1 I have kicked somebody
2 I have twisted someone's arm
3 I have set a 'booby trap' of some kind
4 I have been violent in order to look big
5 I have sworn at somebody
6 I have been violent in a gang
7 I have been violent to impress my mates/friends/girls
8 I have tripped someone up
9 I have bullied another boy
10 I have taken part in boxing/wrestling/judo/karate
11 I have smashed up things/places
12 I have been violent at or on the way to football matches
13 I have given someone a 'head butt'
14 I have given someone a 'deadleg'
15 I have been violent just for kicks/fun
16 I have been violent in self defence
17 I have tried to torture someone
18 I have been violent at a demonstration
19 I have kicked someone 'where it hurts most'
20 I have threatened somebody
21 I have been in something like a protection racket
22 I have been violent while doing sport
23 I have played violent games as a kid/child
24 I have hit somebody with a bottle/brick/hammer/metal bar/stick/brolly/chain
25 I have smashed up trains/buses/shops/cars/old houses/phone boxes
26 I have been violent at school
27 I have been in fights with boys from other schools
28 I have been rude to people in authority (police, teachers, parents)
29 I have been violent to people in authority (police, teachers, parents)
30 I have hit someone with something (or used something on somebody)
31 I have shot an airgun/catapult/arrow at someone or something
32 I have thrown something at someone
33 I have hurt an animal
34 I have beaten someone up
35 I have beaten up a Pakistani/Jew/Negro/queer/teacher/policeman/old person
36 I have interfered with a girl in some way
37 I have tried to make girls do things they don't want to
38 I have broken into parking meters/gas meters/electric meters
39 I have deliberately tried to frighten someone
40 I have thrown a firework at someone
41 I have set something on fire
42 I have been violent because I have been excited or upset about something
43 I have cut someone with a knife or razor
44 I have been in a gang which has picked on somebody
45 I have been violent when I really didn't want to be

Cycle 2: testing and modifying the first web of stimuli

The likely weaknesses of the first list of web items. It was expected that the first list of items would suffer from several defects, namely:

(a) misinterpretation of the statements themselves;

(b) gaps in the list such that a substantial number of relevant acts of violence would not fall under any of the 45 heads in the list – or at least would not be picked up through the list;

(c) unnecessary duplication of web items – such that two of them tended to bring out the same acts;

(d) a range of unexpected difficulties of various kinds either in the sorting process or concerned with the web items.

The form of the test made. In cycle 2, a test was made to assess the adequacy of the list from these four standpoints. The testing procedure took the following form.

1 Thirty-five boys who had taken part in the test room session referred to in connection with Cycle 1, and whose composition as a small sample was subject to control with respect to age and social class, came to the Centre in small groups.

2 At the Survey Research Centre, using a fictitious name, each boy sorted 45 cards on which were the 45 web items developed through Cycle 1. All sorting as 'yes' or 'no' was related to the last 4 weeks [15]. At this stage, the boy was told to consult the interviewer if he met difficulty with any card, but that if the help given was not sufficient to enable him to sort the card concerned, he was to place that card face down in front of him to indicate that he was 'not sure' about it. At the same time, the interviewer was to 'turn back' to the boy all queries concerning what did or did not constitute violence. The interviewer noted any such difficulties and the numbers of the cards concerned.

3 At the end of sorting, the interviewer attempted to find out, for each card in the 'not sure' category, the nature of the difficulty that had led to the card being categorised in this way.

4 Following this, an attempt was made to identify any of the boy's acts that had *not* been elicited by the web of stimuli being tried out. To this end, the boy was asked to tell the interviewer of any of his acts of violence, committed in the last four weeks [15], that he felt had not been covered by the statements on the cards. The boy's responses were subject to probing. To aid in this eliciting process, a long list of acts of violence that had been presumed covered by the web items was offered to the boy as a prompt system. For each act thereby established as having been missed, the boy was questioned to find out why, and in particular which if any of his omissions he felt were not covered by any of the web items.

5 Following this, the interviewer dealt with those cards which, though sorted, had been noted at the time as causing the respondent trouble. He sought to understand what the difficulties were.

6 Finally, the interviewer took a sample of the sorted cards, both those endorsed and those denied, and attempted to get from the boy his understanding of what was typed on them.

This work was done by three interviewers who had received training in the methods of probing and challenging. Their work with the boys was tape-recorded both to secure responses in full and to allow the quality of the interview to be checked and controlled.

The results of the tests made in Cycle 2. An analysis of the evidence provided by the testing of the web indicated that certain kinds of acts were on occasions being omitted, that some items were subject to misunderstanding and that there were in addition difficulties connected with certain of the items.

1 The evidence indicated that *omissions* were occurring with respect to:

(a) violence committed in retaliation or to get revenge on someone;

(b) generally harassing people;

(c) a variety of activities occurring while boys were in *groups* (not necessarily gangs).

2 The interpretation by some boys of certain of the items in the web was especially noteworthy.

(a) 'I have kicked somebody' (card 1): apparently 'kicking' can include 'punching'.

(b) 'I have been violent at or on the way to football matches' (card 12): this was sometimes interpreted as meaning one or the other but not both.

(c) 'I have been violent just for kicks/fun' (card 15): boys tended to include 'for a dare'.

(d) 'I have played violent games as a kid/child' (card 23): there was varied interpretation of what was meant by 'violent games'.

(e) 'I have hurt an animal' (card 33): a great variety of methods of hurting was considered.

(f) 'I have interfered with a girl in some way' (card 36): for the older boys, 'interfered' tended to mean 'hurt' in some way, whereas for younger boys it could mean things like 'interrupting a conversation'.

(g) 'I have cut someone with a knife or razor' (card 43): some boys thought this included cutting *themselves* whilst shaving.

3 Some of the carded statements tended to coincide or to overlap each other in their coverage of acts, for example:

(a) 'I have been violent in order to look big' and 'I have been violent in order to impress my mates/friends/girls'.

(b) Acts referred to on card 25 ('I have smashed up trains, buses, shops, cars, old houses, phone boxes') tended to be referred to under card 11 ('I have smashed up things/places').

(c) Acts referred to under card 35 ('I have beaten up a Pakistani, Jew, Negro, queer, teacher, policeman, old man') tended to be offered under card 34 ('I have beaten someone up').

(d) Acts referred to under card 21 ('I have been in something like a protection racket') tended also to be the ones evoked by card 20 ('I have threatened somebody').

4 In addition, boys expressed difficulties of various kinds, including:

(a) 'I have tried to torture someone': (Was 'teasing' a form of torture?);

(b) 'I have kicked somebody' and 'I have kicked someone where it hurts most' (Would 'kicking' include punching?);

(c) 'I have been in something like a protection racket' (What is a 'protection racket'?);

(d) 'I have played violent games' (What games would be considered 'violent'? Football?).

5 Other problems emerged, for example:

(a) Items 26 and 27 ('I have been violent at school' and 'I have been in fights with boys from other schools') seemed between them to cover a great many of the boys' acts of violence.

(b) Boys differed in terms of *how* violent an act had to be for them to regard it as violent. Furthermore, this threshold appeared to vary with the circumstances under which the act was committed.

(c) Many boys were puzzled over what to do if they had intended to commit some act of violence but had not succeeded in bringing it off (e.g. he had tried to trip someone up but had failed to do so).

(d) There was also uncertainty about what to do over violent acts that were *accidental* (e.g. he had accidentally smashed crockery or had accidentally kicked someone at football).

(e) There was an extremely low endorsement of card 18 ('I have been violent at a demonstration') – raising the question of its value in the web.

(f) There was also the question of how honest were boys in responding to certain of the carded statements. In this connection, the very low frequency of endorsement of card 33, 'I hurt an animal', seemed suspicious (only three boys out of the thirty-five actually endorsed it).

Modifying the web items on the basis of the test results. On the basis principally of the foregoing evidence, certain changes were made in the web items and in their positioning. The principal changes in the web items themselves are shown in table 6.1.

Cycle 3: testing and modifying the second form of the web

In Cycle 3, the check made was closely similar to that made in Cycle 2. The 25 boys tested were recruited from a London Comprehensive boys' school.

Results of testing the second form of the web. Generally speaking, there was evidence of fewer difficulties now than had emerged through the Cycle 2 tests.

1 The general level of omissions was lower. Where they occurred, they were of the kind:

(a) making rude finger signs at someone;

(b) just larking around while out with your mates,

(c) lying to get one's own ends,

(d) teasing or taking the mickey out of someone,

(e) provoking people or setting up a fight.

2 There was relatively little misinterpretation of the statements on the cards, the main exception being the item: 'I have kicked someone where it hurts most'. The range of places that boys thought 'would hurt most' was considerable and it seemed that acts covered by the item in its present form would adequately

Table 6.1
Detail of the changes made in the Cycle 1 web items

ORIGINAL FORM OF ITEMS THAT PROVED TO BE UNSATISFACTORY		THE MODIFIED ITEMS	
Item		Item	
4 7	I have been violent in order to look big I have been violent to impress my mates/friends/girls	8	I have been violent to impress my mates/girls/other people
6 44	I have been violent in a gang I have been in a gang which has picked on somebody	7 9 10	I have been violent while I was with some of my mates/friends My mates and I have picked on or set about other people/boys I have got my mates to get other people
8	I have tripped someone up	4	I have deliberately tried to trip someone up
11 25	I have smashed up things I have smashed up trains/buses/shops/cars/old houses/phone boxes)	18	I have deliberately damaged things or places (like trains, buses, shops, cars, old houses, phone boxes, parking meters, electric meters, gas meters, etc.)
12	I have been violent at or on the way to football matches	11 12	I have been violent on the way to watch a football match I have been violent while at a football match
15	I have been violent just for kicks/fun	15	I have been violent just for fun or a laugh, or for a dare
18	I have been violent at a demonstration		(dropped altogether)
23	I have played violent games	23	I have played violent games (like slaps, knuckles, bulldog, murder ball, etc.)
26 27	I have been violent at school I have been in fights with boys from other schools	24 25 26 27	I have been violent at school/work I have been violent on the way to/from school/work I have been violent during the break at school/work (lunchtime or breaks) I have been in fights with boys from other schools
33	I have hurt an animal	33	(No change in the item, but interviewer instructed to reassure boys by saying that he – the interviewer – was not there to judge the boy)
34 35	I have beaten someone up I have beaten up a Pakistani/Jew/Negro/queer/teacher/policeman/old person	34	I have beaten someone up
40	I have thrown fireworks at someone	40	I have larked around with fireworks in some way
43	I have cut someone with a knife or razor	43	I have cut someone else with a knife or a razor
	(new items ⟶)	21 35 38 44	I have irritated/annoyed/teased or played people up I have had an argument with somebody I have been violent to get my own back on somebody I have lost my temper with somebody

be covered by the rather general statement on card 1 (i.e. 'I have kicked somebody').

3 Several boys expressed difficulty with the item: 'I have beaten someone up', being unsure as to how badly the other person had to be hurt before one could say he had been 'beaten up'.

Modifying the web on the basis of the test results. The changes made were principally as follows.

1 Item 19 ('I have kicked someone where it hurts most') was dropped.

2 Five new items (as set out below) were added on the basis of the evidence of omissions:

- I have lied to someone
- I have made finger signs at someone
- I have teased or taken the mickey out of someone
- I have fooled or larked about while I was out with some of my mates
- I have tried to start a fight in some way.

3 Another item was added on researcher initiative: 'I have been violent while I was bunking off from school or lessons'.

4 In addition, some changes were made in the order of the web items.

TRIMMING THE WEB AND MODIFYING OTHER ASPECTS OF THE PROCEDURE

Identifying weaknesses in the technique

Beyond the end of Cycle 3, certain further steps in the development of the eliciting procedure were taken, namely: (1) the full eliciting procedure was piloted under conditions approaching those to be used in the final survey; (2) a critical and constructive appraisal was made of all aspects of the procedure, both before and after the piloting operation.

1 *Piloting the full procedure.* Piloting was based upon trials with boys who had been recruited through personal interviews in London suburbs in the context of preparatory work closely similar to that which would take place in the full enquiry. A total of 30 boys arrived at the Centre by car between 5 pm and 6 pm and there, during a session lasting up to 3 hours, they were individually and privately put through most of the procedures to be used in the full enquiry.

Within this piloting check, boys went through the full *eliciting procedure.* The purpose of this trial of the eliciting procedure was principally to assess the general workability of that procedure as a whole, with special reference to: how long it took to administer; the quality of rapport in relation to the whole procedure and its different parts; the emergence of any special difficulties; the derivation of ideas, in the staff administering the tests, about ways in which the procedure might be tightened up or otherwise improved.

The results of the piloting operation were as follows.

(a) Generally speaking, the eliciting procedure was administratively workable and boys appeared to accept it.

(b) For the majority of the boys, the total eliciting procedure took between an hour and 1¼ hours to deliver. The greater part of that time was spent in probing for detail connected with the cards sorted as 'yes'. In the opinion of one administrator, this part of the sequence was tiring for boys, raising the possibility of a reducing yield of acts in working through the 'yes' cards.

(c) Some boys appeared to be averse to sorting cards as 'yes' when the act concerned had been accidental or in response to violence from others.

(d) Boys seemed to accept, as a working definition of violence, the expression 'some of the arguments, pranks, larks, fights or destruction that boys get into'. On the other hand, some boys seemed to be upset or annoyed at the constant stressing of the confidentiality of the interview [16] (in that it seemed to imply that they were not already being completely frank).

(e) It was also felt by the interviewers that the re-sorting of the 'no' cards seemed on the evidence of sorting to serve little purpose in cases where the respondent had already indicated (through the 'pretending game') that he was being completely frank. Also such boys tended to become resentful.

2 *Critical appraisal of the method and related suggestions for changes.* A number of people participated in critical appraisal of (i) the wording and the coverage of the web items and (ii) other features of the eliciting procedure. This was done before, during and after the piloting of the technique.

The changes made

On the basis of (1) and (2) above, further changes were made in the procedure. Several of these preceded piloting and others followed that operation.

Changes in the web of stimuli. The principal changes made in the web of stimuli were as follows.

1 Certain of the web items were changed in minor ways to increase comprehensibility, for example:

'I have taken part in Wrestling/Boxing/Judo or Karate'

became

'I have taken part in Wrestling or Boxing or Judo or Karate'

and

'I have been rude to people in authority (police, teachers, parents)'

became

'I have been rude to people in authority (like police, teachers, parents)'.

2 Some of the items were widened in coverage to make them more inclusive, for example:

'I have sworn at someone' had added to it 'or used bad language on them'.

'I have set my mates onto other people' had added to it 'or boys'.

3 In one item the word 'torture' was changed to 'torment' as being broader and more in line with what boys do.

4 One item was dropped because of its seasonal character, namely:

'I have larked about with fireworks in some way'.

5 Three new items were added, none strictly part of the web of stimuli, but still usable in the event of their evoking further evidence of violence. Two of them were inserted to provide evidence about certain forms of violence commonly featured in the news, namely:

'I have damaged someone's car (but not in a road accident)'

'I have done some damage to a train'.

The third new item was to provide a fairly direct basis for investigating one of the other hypotheses set up for investigation [17], this item being:

'I have been rough or tough or violent in sport or play'.

6 The order of presentation of some of the web items was changed.

The 'web of stimuli' in its final form is given on page 207.

Changes in other aspects of the eliciting procedure. Wherever practical and not in conflict with other evidence, recommended changes in other aspects of the procedure were adopted. These were principally as follows:

1 The instructions presented to respondents were made to include the rules that:

- an act counts even if it was done by accident;
- an act counts even if it was done in self-defence.

2 The acts on the cards were at the outset described as 'Some of the rough or violent things that boys sometimes get up to – some of the arguments, pranks or fights they get into .... '.

3 After the 'pretending game', the re-sorting of 'no' cards had originally been required of *all* boys, irrespective of response in the pretending game. Re-sorting was now limited to those boys who had said, in the course of that 'game', that they would *not* admit the serious act concerned. Previously, re-sorting was required whether the boy said 'yes' or 'no' in the 'pretending game'. The modified procedure for the 'pretending game' is given on page 220.

4 In collecting details from boys about the acts they had committed, the procedure used in the *pilot* interviews had been to ask for the following details with respect to *each web item sorted as 'yes'*:

(i) the number of times or occasions the general class of act on the card had been done in the last six months;

(ii) *what* it was the boy did on that (or those) occasion(s) [18];

(iii) whether the act(s) referred to had been volunteered already through another of the boy's 'yes' cards (in which case it was marked with a minus (-) sign).

This procedure was initially modified on the basis of a critical appraisal of it and that modification was itself subject to further change after experience in using it through interviewers during their training period. That latter experience brought out very clearly (i) the multiplicity of acts of a closely similar kind that an individual might commit and (ii) *the need to specify closely the kinds of detail that the interviewer must collect about each act.* In its final form, this part of the procedure had the following features.

(a) As already detailed elsewhere in this chapter, for each of the cards sorted as 'yes' the interviewer:

(i) asked 'Exactly how many times did you do that in the last six months?';

(ii) asked the respondent to tell him the different things he did on those occasions;

(iii) asked the respondent to specify, for each such occasion,

- the nature of the act (e.g. kicked, punched, pushed, cut, . . .),
- the object of the act (e.g. another boy, a cat, . . .),
- the implement if any (e.g. knife, stick, . . .),
- what led him to do it (e.g. the boy was rude to him, for fun, . . .),
- the circumstances if not already given (e.g. in football);

(iv) asked the respondent 'How many times did you do that sort of thing in the last six months?';

(v) entered a minus sign just after the number if the act concerned was a repeat of one volunteered earlier.

(b) The same form of questioning was applied to the next 'yes' card, and so on.

(c) The interviewer was required to give special attention to getting the detail of the act – its nature – and to avoid being given only *why* the boy did it.

(d) There was provision for exercising continuing quality control (through the recording of the interview) over the type of information that interviewers were collecting about each act.

Not all the information gathered through the questions a(i)-(v) was needed in its own right. Thus the overall total asked for through question a(i) was wanted solely to alert interviewers when it (that overall total) was still substantially higher than the sum of all the frequencies attached to the acts subsumed under it. Where this was the case, the interviewer had strong grounds for pressing the boy for further acts and, if necessary, for challenging him to explain the discrepancy. This technique did in practice quite frequently uncover further acts. It served also to put a 'damper' on extravagant or careless claiming.

Another requested detail, not actually needed for scoring, was 'why' the boy had committed any given act. It had emerged quite strongly during the period of interviewer training that boys were more likely to admit to acts of violence if they were allowed to justify those acts. It also emerged that the interviewers, however much they seemed to accept at an intellectual level that justification was not relevant to the assessment of *how much* violence had been done, did nonetheless find it hard to resist asking for it. Hence it seemed desirable to arrange for its collection – but within a system which specified all the *other* information that was needed.

Using the foregoing procedure, a typical entry on a web card could take the following form.

I have tried to torment someone

12 times

I held down my brother and kept on tickling him until he cried; just for fun; at home when my parents were out	2
I twisted the ear of a boy who sits in front of me in class; because I dislike him	3
While with other boys I have rung doorbells and run off; for fun and because it's a posh block	10
I booted a boy on the behind, because he had been rude to me; at school	1(-)

I have tried to torment someone

A NOTE ON THE TOTAL ARRAY OF INFORMATION NOW AVAILABLE AND ITS INTERPRETATION

The information secured from a boy through the eliciting procedure, and entered on his 'Yes' cards in the manner illustrated, was now available for making the several numerical assessments of his involvement in violence required for investigating Hypothesis 1. These, it will be remembered, were (a) an overall score reflecting both the frequency of a boy's acts of violence and the degree of violence involved in those acts; (b) the total number of boy's acts that exceed given levels or degrees of violence (e.g. How many acts had he committed that were at least 'quite' violent? How many acts, excluding only the 'slightly' violent ones? How many acts irrespective of how violent they were?). To the methods of making these assessments we will come in the next chapter.

Another important issue is the viability of the eliciting procedure in its final form. This is discussed in some detail towards the end of this chapter, just after the presentation of the full procedure in diagrammatic and verbal form.

SOME OTHER MEASURES CARRIED BY THE WEB OF STIMULI

The web of stimuli in its final form (see page 209) and the questions subsequently asked about the web items sorted as 'Yes' were together intended to serve a secondary function, namely to provide the bases for deriving measures of the dependent variables in certain *other hypotheses.* These were the dependent variables in the hypotheses dealing with the influence of television violence upon:

(a) the degree to which boys commit violence in the company of gangs or groups of boys (Hypothesis 5);

(b) the degree to which boys are argumentative or are irritating or annoying to others (Hypothesis 6);

(c) the degree to which boys are aggressive or violent in sport or play (Hypothesis 7);

(d) the degree to which boys use various forms of bad language (Hypothesis 8).

At the end of Cycle 3 in the development of web items, it was clear that the items then included in the web were sufficient to yield the necessary basic information with respect to the dependent variables in Hypotheses 5, 6 and 8. Quite possibly they would have similarly served Hypothesis 7, but for safety a further item, relating specifically to its dependent variable, was added. This was item 53 (page 209):

'I have been rough or tough or violent in sport or play'.

The scoring system to be used with respect to dependent variables (a)-(d) will be described in the next chapter, but it will be useful to note here *which* web items were expected to contribute principally to *which* dependent variables:

(a) *violence in the company of gangs or groups of boys*

- I have been violent while I was with some of my mates or friends (Item 21 – no other item used in this case)

(b) *argumentativeness, irritating or annoying behaviour*

- I have made finger signs at someone (Item 9)
- I have teased or taken the 'mickey' out of someone (Item 13)
- I have irritated, annoyed or played people up (Item 25)
- I have been rude to people in authority (like police, teachers, parents) (Item 38)
- I have had an argument with somebody (Item 40).

(c) *aggressiveness in sport or play*

- I have been rough or tough or violent in sport or play (Item 53 – no other items included)

(d) *use of bad language*

- I have sworn at somebody or used bad language on them (Item 7 – no other item included).

THE FINAL AND COMPLETE FORM OF THE PROCEDURE

DEVELOPED FOR ELICITING FROM BOYS COMPREHENSIVE DETAILS OF THEIR INVOLVEMENT IN VIOLENT BEHAVIOUR

The full procedure, which is available as a package to the serious technical enquirer, is presented hereunder in diagrammatic and verbal form. More specifically, what follows consists of a full set of instructions, rules and reminders contained in the control booklet, with the web items interspersed between them as in the actual eliciting procedure. For clarity, this presentation is preceded by an unbroken list of the items in the 'web of stimuli' in its final form.

The items in the 'Web of Stimuli'

In the following list of items that made up the web of stimuli used in the final survey, the extra items included for other purposes are marked with an asterisk.

1 I have kicked somebody
2 I have tried to torment someone
3 I have set a 'booby trap' of some kind
4 I have tried to trip someone up
5 I have had a fight
6 I have hurt an animal
7 I have sworn at somebody or used bad language on them
8 I have taken part in Wrestling or Boxing or Judo or Karate
9 I have made finger signs at someone
10 I have given someone a 'head butt'
11 I have been violent on the way to watch a football match
12 I have been violent while at a football ground
13 I have teased or taken 'the mickey' out of someone
14 I have given someone a 'deadleg'
15 I have been violent just for fun or for a laugh or for a dare
16 I have lied to somebody
17 I have fooled or larked around while I was out with some of my mates
18 I have been violent to impress my mates or girls or other people
19 My mates and I have picked on or set about other people or boys
20 I have set my mates onto other people or boys
21 I have been violent while I was with some of my mates or friends
22 I have damaged things or places (like trains, buses, shops, cars, old houses, phone boxes, parking meters, electric meters, gas meters, etc.)
23 I have twisted someone's arm
24 I have threatened somebody
25 I have irritated, annoyed, or played people up
26 I have been violent while doing sport
27 I have tried to start a fight in some way
28 I have played violent or dangerous games (like slaps, knuckles, bulldog, murder ball, splits, chicken, etc.)
29 I have hit someone with something (like bottle, hammer, stick, brolly, etc.)
30 I have been violent at school or at work
31 I have been violent on the way to or from school or work
32 I have been violent during the breaks at school or at work (lunchtime or breaks)
33 I have been in fights with boys from other schools
34 I have been violent while I was 'bunking off' from school or lessons
35 I have shot an airgun or catapult or arrow at someone or something
36 I have thrown something at someone
37 I have beaten someone up
38 I have been rude to people in authority (like police, teachers, parents)
39 I have been violent to people of authority (like police, teachers, parents)
40 I have had an argument with somebody
41 I have done something to get my own back on somebody
42 I have tried to frighten someone
43 I have been violent in self defence
44 I have set something on fire
45 I have hurt a girl in some way
46 I have tried to make girls do things they don't want to
47 I have been violent because I have been excited or upset about something
48 I have cut someone with a knife or a razor or glass
49 I have lost my temper with somebody
50 I have been violent when I really didn't want to be
*51 I have damaged someone's car (but not in a road accident)
*52 I have done damage to a train
*53 I have been rough or tough or violent in sport or play

WEB OF STIMULI BOOKLET

THE SORTING OF THE VIOLENCE CARDS AS 'YES' OR 'NO'

(Part D of the Intensive Interview Procedure)

Through this booklet, the 53 violence cards are sorted into two boxes, 'YES' and 'NO'. This sorting process is governed by various rules and definitions which are to be taught through the earlier parts of the booklet and thereafter re-inforced (through instructions built into the booklet).

Through an earlier part of the evening's procedure, the boy had been told that his £2 fee was just a small repayment for his time on the project and that it was essential that this should not upset the accuracy of what he said in answer to our questions. Our role as researchers was explained, especially that it was essential for us to get really frank and honest replies to all our questions.

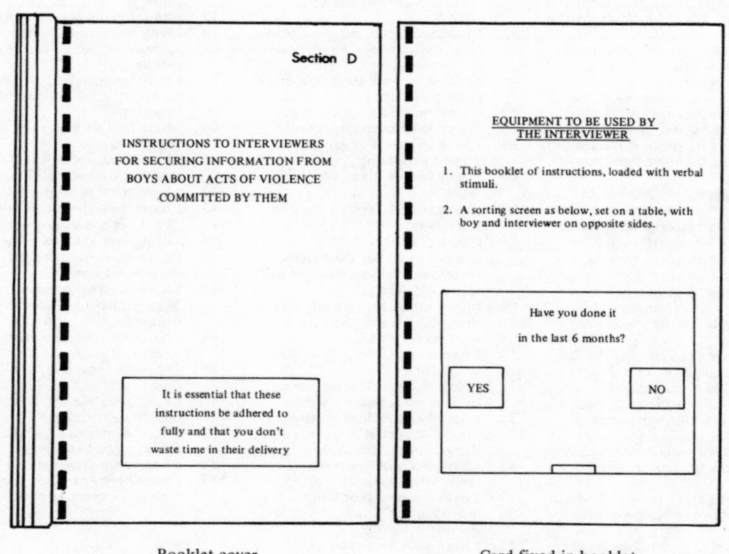

Booklet cover

Card fixed in booklet

INSTRUCTION TO INTERVIEWERS

Tell boy you are now ready for the next step, which will involve using 'this sorting screen'. Set it up.

What follows is a demanding procedure that will call for faithful but speedy work by the interviewer.

1a

BASIC INSTRUCTIONS

1. Tell boy we want him to sort some cards and that on each card is a description of one of the things that boys may get up to in their spare time.
2. Show him green Card 1 as an example. Ask him to read out what is on it. (If he can't read, you will have to read all cards for him).
3. Tell him that you have about 50 more cards and that you need to know if he has done these things in the last six months. Say 'we' will be using 'this' screen and 'these' sorting boxes in the interview.
4. Explain that:
   - if he did it in the last six months, he should put the card in the YES box;
   - if he did NOT do it in the last six months he should put the card in the NO box;
   - if he is not sure he should put it face down in front of the screen.
5. Also explain:
   - where you will sit and he will sit;
   - the use of the slot at the bottom of the screen.
6. Check his grasp of instructions by asking him:
   - what goes into the YES box;
   - what goes into the NO box;
   - what to do if NOT SURE.

1b

INITIAL SORTING TO TEACH THE RULES

TELL BOY YOU WILL SOON BE GOING BEHIND THE SCREEN AND WILL PASS HIS CARDS TO HIM ONE AT A TIME THROUGH THE SLOT. TELL HIM THE FIRST FEW WILL BE PRACTICE CARDS.

SEAT YOURSELF BEHIND SCREEN. SAY:

"You will see that the cards I pass you are about some of the rough and violent activities that boys sometimes get up to – some of the arguments, pranks or fights they get into. This is something a lot of boys do. We want to know how much of it you yourself do."

"In your case it is only the last six months we are interested in. We want to know about things you did in the last six months."

"Remember, you have got a false name and I don't want to know your real name. That is so that you can tell us everything. Is that all right?"

"We need to know everything if our research is going to be useful. If you hold back anything then we will both be just wasting our time. Is that O.K.?"

"And remember you have a false name. I will be calling you . . . . (give false name)."

"I don't know you, you don't know me, and I don't suppose we will ever meet again. And everything you say is absolutely private."

1c

SAY:

"Just before we start, I want you to think back to a time that was six months ago . . . That will be back in . . . ." (NAME THE MONTH).

PAUSE

"Round about that time . . . ."

NAME 3 - 4 MAJOR NEWS ITEMS

THEN SAY:

"Can you remember anything you were doing round about that time?"

PAUSE AND ENCOURAGE HIM TO FIX SOME PERSONAL EVENTS.

THEN SAY:

"So when I ask you if you did something in the last six months, I mean the six months since (NAME THE MONTH) last when you were . . . ." (NAME HIS PERSONAL EVENTS OR, IF THERE WERE NOT ANY, THE PUBLIC EVENTS OF THAT TIME).

"Once you've sorted them all, I'll want to ask you some questions about some of them, so try to sort them carefully."

1d

Above cards fixed in booklet

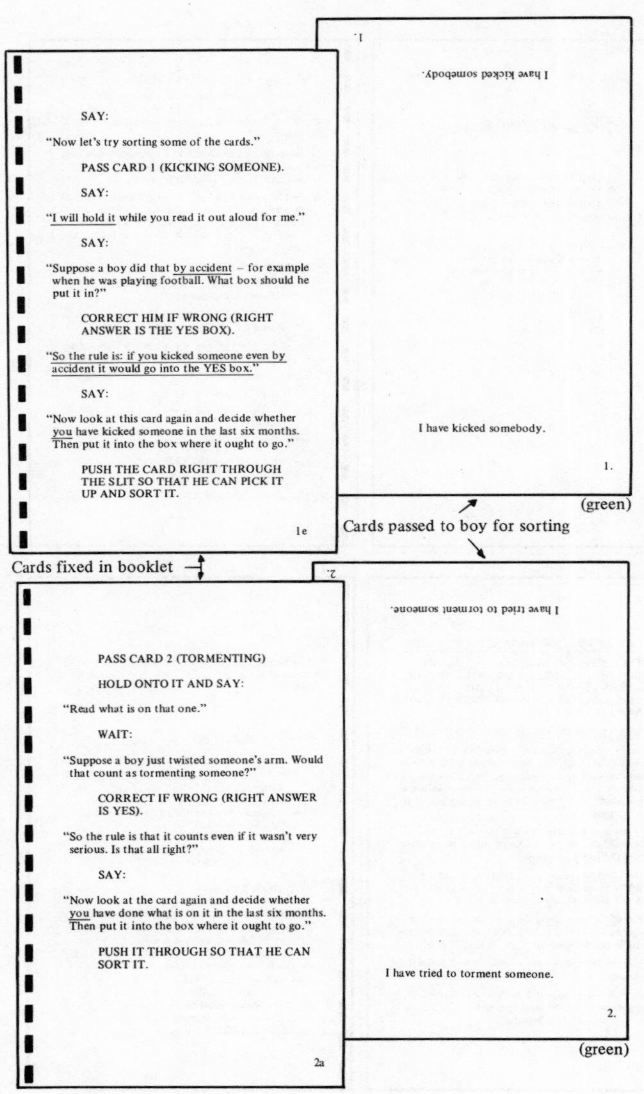
SAY:
"Now let's try sorting some of the cards."
PASS CARD 1 (KICKING SOMEONE).
SAY:
"I will hold it while you read it out aloud for me."
SAY:
"Suppose a boy did that by accident – for example when he was playing football. What box should he put it in?"
CORRECT HIM IF WRONG (RIGHT ANSWER IS THE YES BOX).
"So the rule is: if you kicked someone even by accident it would go into the YES box."
SAY:
"Now look at this card again and decide whether you have kicked someone in the last six months. Then put it into the box where it ought to go."
PUSH THE CARD RIGHT THROUGH THE SLIT SO THAT HE CAN PICK IT UP AND SORT IT.
1e
1.
I have kicked somebody.
I have kicked somebody.
1.
(green)
Cards passed to boy for sorting
Cards fixed in booklet
2.
I have tried to torment someone.
PASS CARD 2 (TORMENTING)
HOLD ONTO IT AND SAY:
"Read what is on that one."
WAIT:
"Suppose a boy just twisted someone's arm. Would that count as tormenting someone?"
CORRECT IF WRONG (RIGHT ANSWER IS YES).
"So the rule is that it counts even if it wasn't very serious. Is that all right?"
SAY:
"Now look at the card again and decide whether you have done what is on it in the last six months. Then put it into the box where it ought to go."
PUSH IT THROUGH SO THAT HE CAN SORT IT.
2a
I have tried to torment someone.
2.
(green)

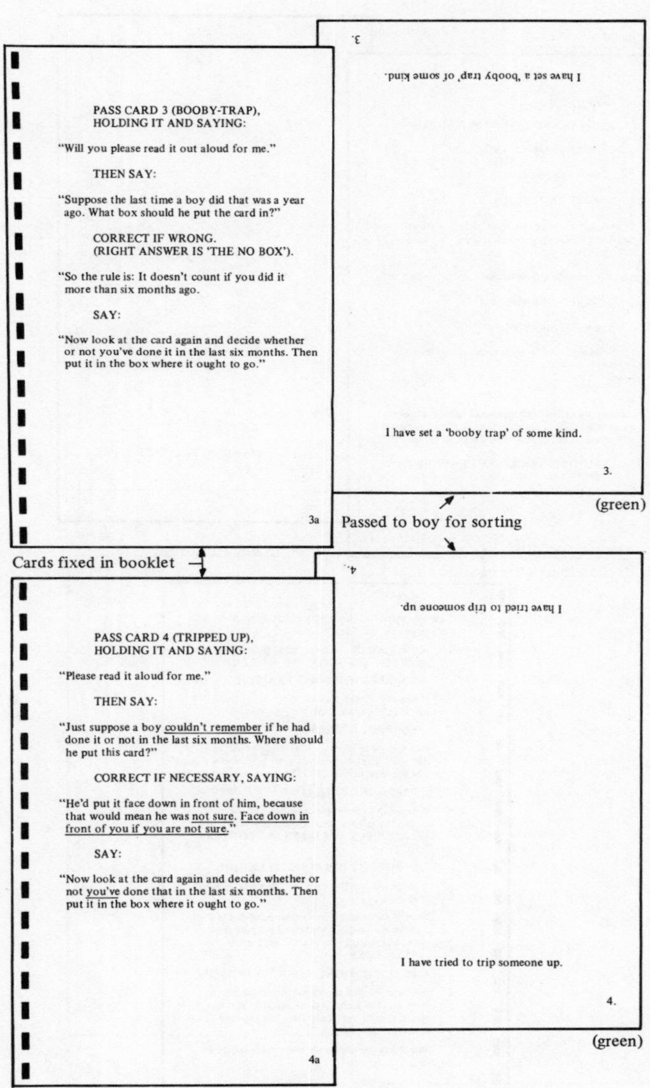

PASS CARD 3 (BOOBY-TRAP),
HOLDING IT AND SAYING:
"Will you please read it out aloud for me."
THEN SAY:
"Suppose the last time a boy did that was a year ago. What box should he put the card in?"
CORRECT IF WRONG.
(RIGHT ANSWER IS 'THE NO BOX').
"So the rule is: It doesn't count if you did it more than six months ago.
SAY:
"Now look at the card again and decide whether or not you've done it in the last six months. Then put it in the box where it ought to go."
3a
3.
I have set a 'booby trap' of some kind.
I have set a 'booby trap' of some kind.
3.
(green)
Passed to boy for sorting
Cards fixed in booklet
4.
I have tried to trip someone up.
PASS CARD 4 (TRIPPED UP),
HOLDING IT AND SAYING:
"Please read it aloud for me."
THEN SAY:
"Just suppose a boy couldn't remember if he had done it or not in the last six months. Where should he put this card?"
CORRECT IF NECESSARY, SAYING:
"He'd put it face down in front of him, because that would mean he was not sure. Face down in front of you if you are not sure."
SAY:
"Now look at the card again and decide whether or not you've done that in the last six months. Then put it in the box where it ought to go."
4a
I have tried to trip someone up.
4.
(green)

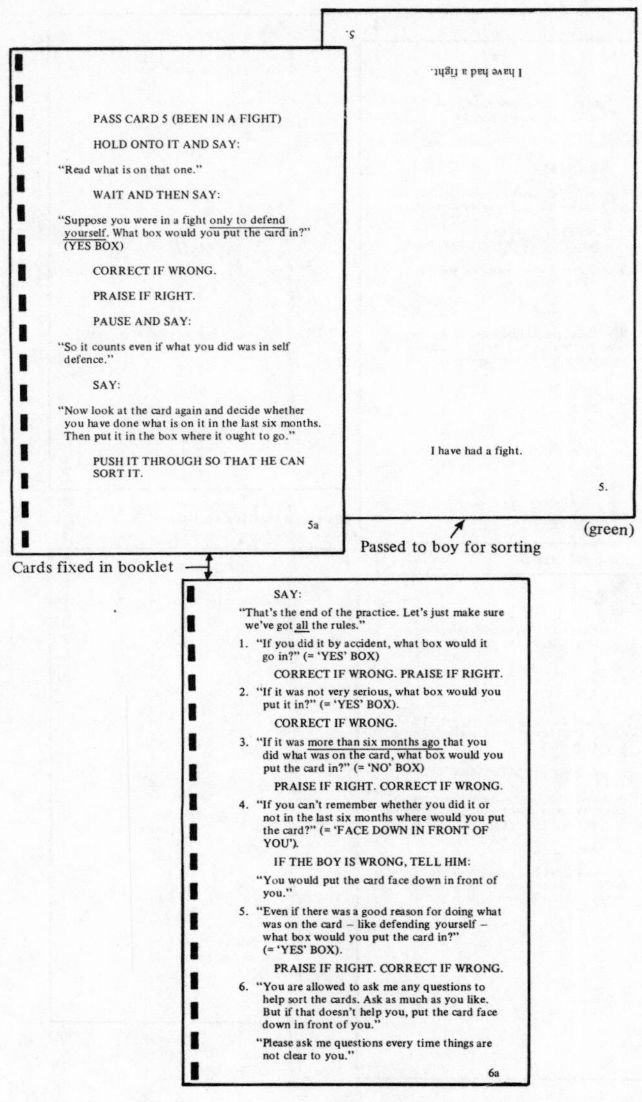

PASS CARD 5 (BEEN IN A FIGHT)

HOLD ONTO IT AND SAY:

"Read what is on that one."

WAIT AND THEN SAY:

"Suppose you were in a fight only to defend yourself. What box would you put the card in?" (YES BOX)

CORRECT IF WRONG.

PRAISE IF RIGHT.

PAUSE AND SAY:

"So it counts even if what you did was in self defence."

SAY:

"Now look at the card again and decide whether you have done what is on it in the last six months. Then put it in the box where it ought to go."

PUSH IT THROUGH SO THAT HE CAN SORT IT.

5a

I have had a fight.

5.

I have had a fight.

5.

SAY:

"That's the end of the practice. Let's just make sure we've got all the rules."

1. "If you did it by accident, what box would it go in?" (= 'YES' BOX)

   CORRECT IF WRONG. PRAISE IF RIGHT.

2. "If it was not very serious, what box would you put it in?" (= 'YES' BOX).

   CORRECT IF WRONG.

3. "If it was more than six months ago that you did what was on the card, what box would you put the card in?" (= 'NO' BOX)

   PRAISE IF RIGHT. CORRECT IF WRONG.

4. "If you can't remember whether you did it or not in the last six months where would you put the card?" (= 'FACE DOWN IN FRONT OF YOU').

   IF THE BOY IS WRONG, TELL HIM:

   "You would put the card face down in front of you."

5. "Even if there was a good reason for doing what was on the card – like defending yourself – what box would you put the card in?" (= 'YES' BOX).

   PRAISE IF RIGHT. CORRECT IF WRONG.

6. "You are allowed to ask me any questions to help sort the cards. Ask as much as you like. But if that doesn't help you, put the card face down in front of you."

   "Please ask me questions every time things are not clear to you."

6a

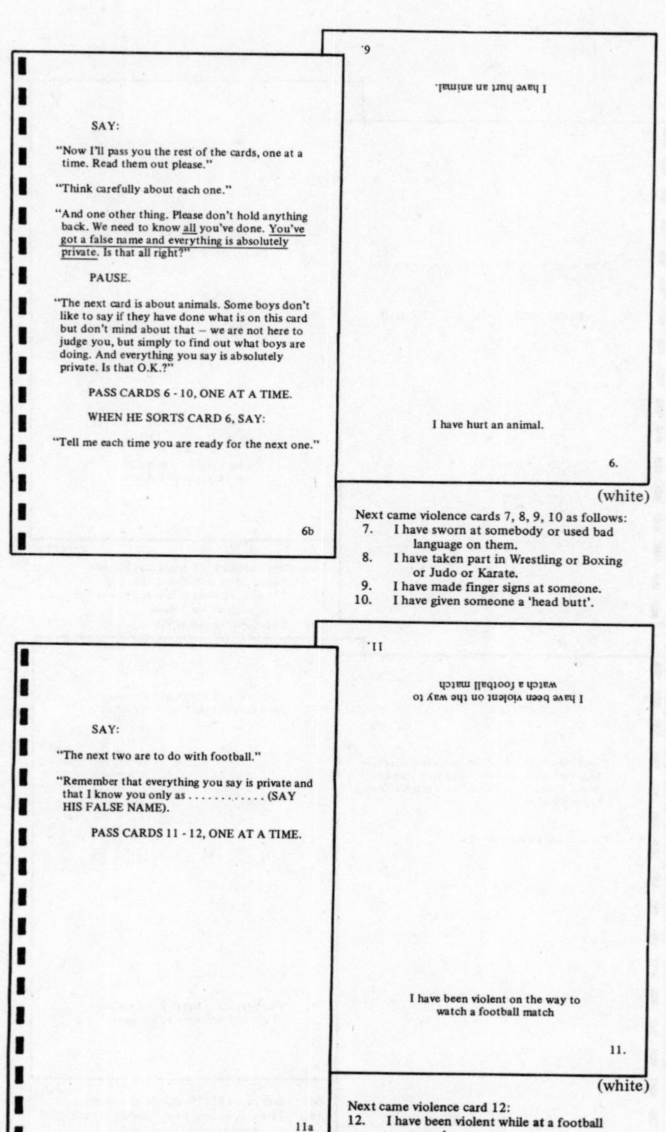

SAY:

"Now I'll pass you the rest of the cards, one at a time. Read them out please."

"Think carefully about each one."

"And one other thing. Please don't hold anything back. We need to know all you've done. You've got a false name and everything is absolutely private. Is that all right?"

PAUSE.

"The next card is about animals. Some boys don't like to say if they have done what is on this card but don't mind about that – we are not here to judge you, but simply to find out what boys are doing. And everything you say is absolutely private. Is that O.K.?"

PASS CARDS 6 - 10, ONE AT A TIME.

WHEN HE SORTS CARD 6, SAY:

"Tell me each time you are ready for the next one."

6b

6.

I have hurt an animal.

I have hurt an animal.

6.

(white)

Next came violence cards 7, 8, 9, 10 as follows:

7. I have sworn at somebody or used bad language on them.
8. I have taken part in Wrestling or Boxing or Judo or Karate.
9. I have made finger signs at someone.
10. I have given someone a 'head butt'.

SAY:

"The next two are to do with football."

"Remember that everything you say is private and that I know you only as . . . . (SAY HIS FALSE NAME).

PASS CARDS 11 - 12, ONE AT A TIME.

11a

11.

I have been violent on the way to watch a football match

I have been violent on the way to watch a football match

11.

(white)

Next came violence card 12:

12. I have been violent while at a football ground.

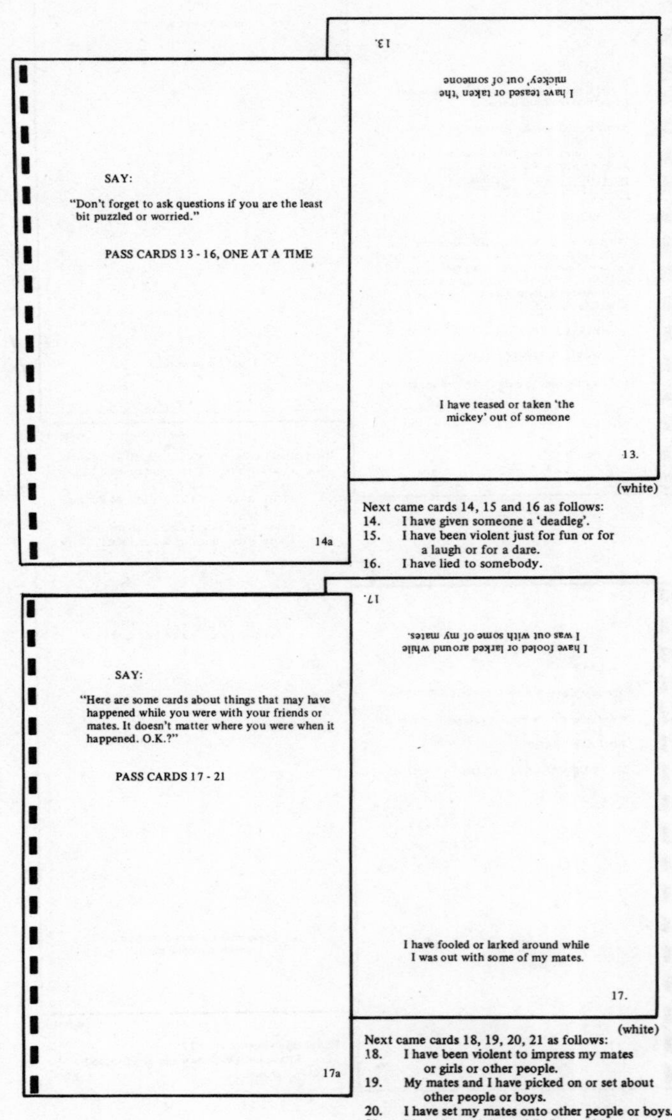

13.

I have teased or taken 'the mickey' out of someone

SAY:

"Don't forget to ask questions if you are the least bit puzzled or worried."

PASS CARDS 13 - 16, ONE AT A TIME

14a

I have teased or taken 'the mickey' out of someone

13.

(white)

Next came cards 14, 15 and 16 as follows:

14. I have given someone a 'deadleg'.
15. I have been violent just for fun or for a laugh or for a dare.
16. I have lied to somebody.

17.

I have fooled or larked around while I was out with some of my mates.

SAY:

"Here are some cards about things that may have happened while you were with your friends or mates. It doesn't matter where you were when it happened. O.K.?"

PASS CARDS 17 - 21

17a

I have fooled or larked around while I was out with some of my mates.

17.

(white)

Next came cards 18, 19, 20, 21 as follows:

18. I have been violent to impress my mates or girls or other people.
19. My mates and I have picked on or set about other people or boys.
20. I have set my mates onto other people or boys.
21. I have been violent while I was with some of my mates or friends.

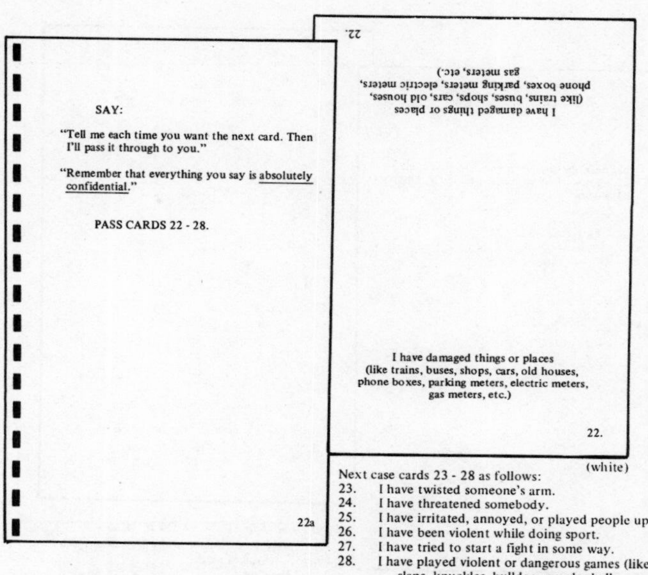

SAY:

"Tell me each time you want the next card. Then I'll pass it through to you."

"Remember that everything you say is <u>absolutely confidential</u>."

PASS CARDS 22 - 28.

22a

I have damaged things or places (like trains, buses, shops, cars, old houses, phone boxes, parking meters, electric meters, gas meters, etc.)

22.

(white)

Next case cards 23 - 28 as follows:

23. I have twisted someone's arm.
24. I have threatened somebody.
25. I have irritated, annoyed, or played people up.
26. I have been violent while doing sport.
27. I have tried to start a fight in some way.
28. I have played violent or dangerous games (like slaps, knuckles, bulldog, murder ball, splits, chicken, etc.)

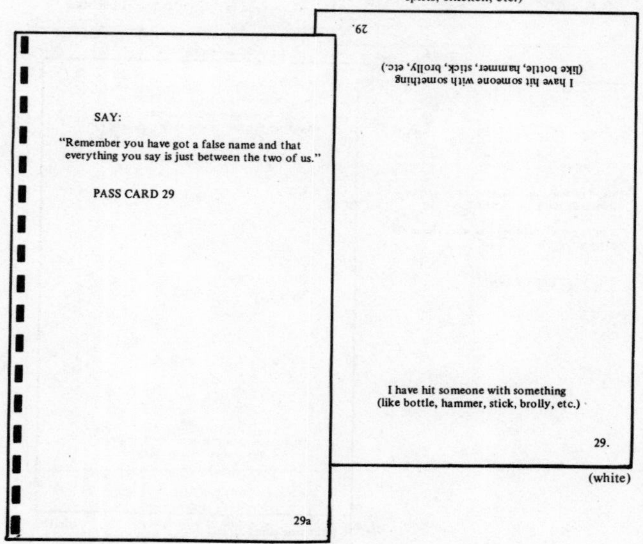

SAY:

"Remember you have got a false name and that everything you say is just between the two of us."

PASS CARD 29

29a

I have hit someone with something (like bottle, hammer, stick, brolly, etc.)

29.

(white)

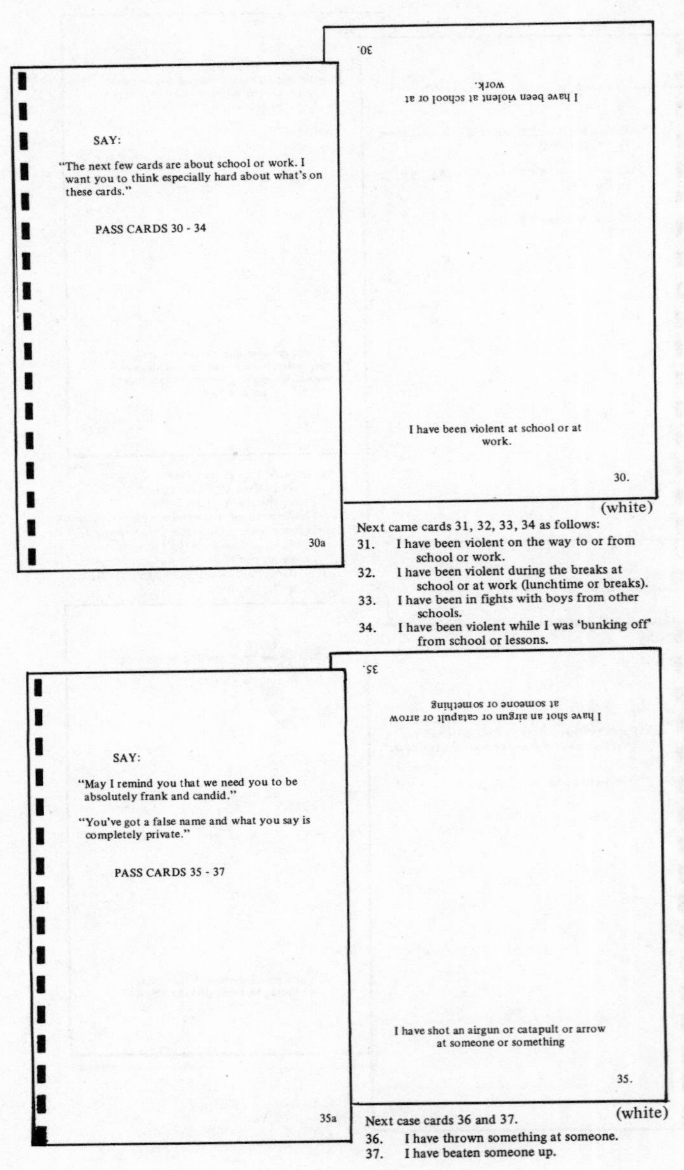

SAY:

"The next few cards are about school or work. I want you to think especially hard about what's on these cards."

PASS CARDS 30 - 34

30a

I have been violent at school or at work.

30.

(white)

Next came cards 31, 32, 33, 34 as follows:

31. I have been violent on the way to or from school or work.
32. I have been violent during the breaks at school or at work (lunchtime or breaks).
33. I have been in fights with boys from other schools.
34. I have been violent while I was 'bunking off' from school or lessons.

SAY:

"May I remind you that we need you to be absolutely frank and candid."

"You've got a false name and what you say is completely private."

PASS CARDS 35 - 37

35a

I have shot an airgun or catapult or arrow at someone or something

35.

(white)

Next case cards 36 and 37.

36. I have thrown something at someone.
37. I have beaten someone up.

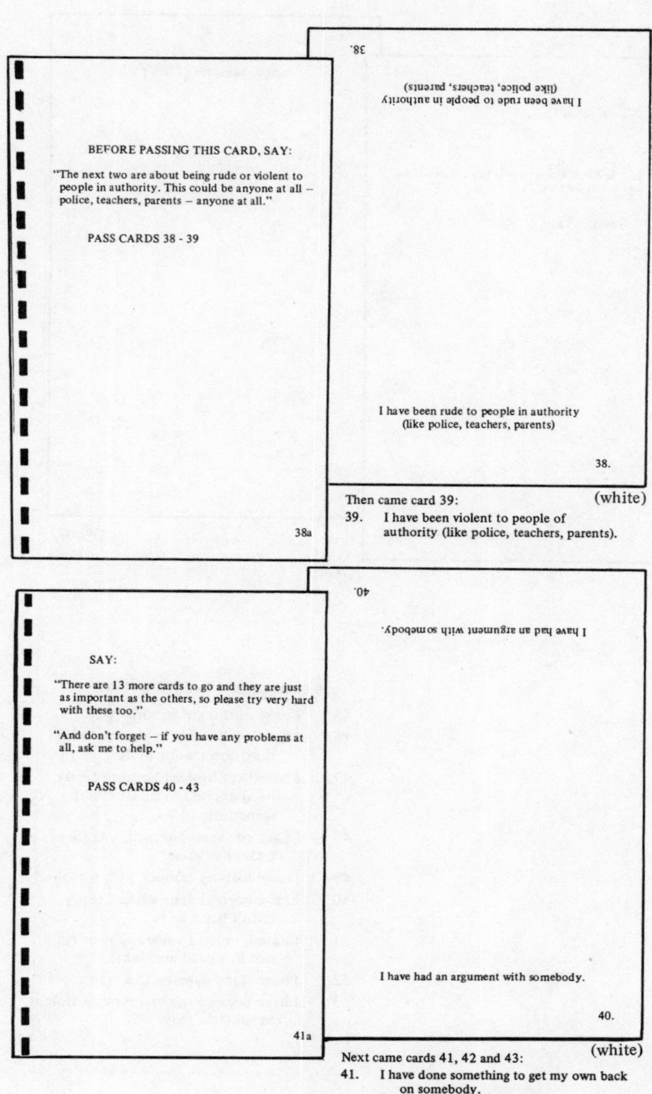

BEFORE PASSING THIS CARD, SAY:

"The next two are about being rude or violent to people in authority. This could be anyone at all – police, teachers, parents – anyone at all."

PASS CARDS 38 - 39

38a

38.

I have been rude to people in authority
(like police, teachers, parents)

I have been rude to people in authority
(like police, teachers, parents)

38.

(white)

Then came card 39:

39. I have been violent to people of authority (like police, teachers, parents).

SAY:

"There are 13 more cards to go and they are just as important as the others, so please try very hard with these too."

"And don't forget – if you have any problems at all, ask me to help."

PASS CARDS 40 - 43

41a

40.

I have had an argument with somebody.

I have had an argument with somebody.

40.

(white)

Next came cards 41, 42 and 43:

41. I have done something to get my own back on somebody.
42. I have tried to frighten someone.
43. I have been violent in self defence.

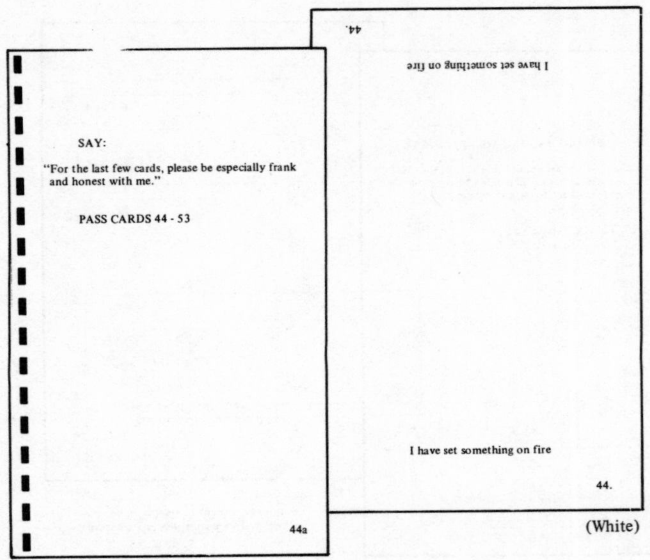

Then came cards 45 - 53 as follows:

45. I have hurt a girl in some way.
46. I have tried to make girls do things they don't want to do.
47. I have been violent because I have been excited or upset about something.
48. I have cut someone with a knife or a razor or glass.
49. I have lost my temper with somebody.
50. I have been violent when I really didn't want to be.
51. I have damaged someone's car (but not in a road accident).
52. I have done damage to a train.
53. I have been rough or tough or violent in sport or play.

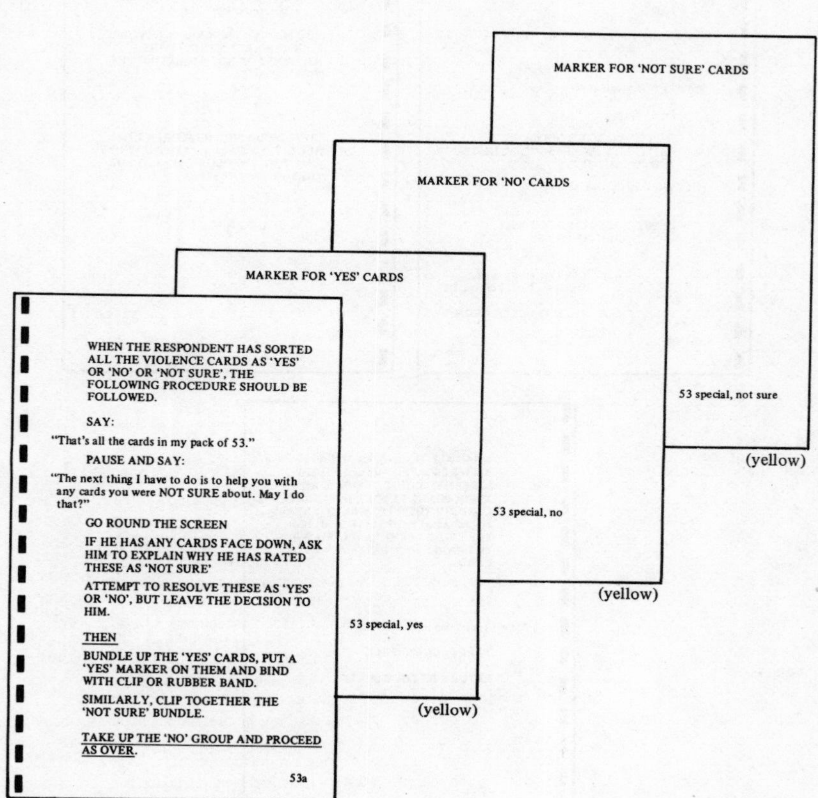
MARKER FOR 'NOT SURE' CARDS
53 special, not sure
(yellow)
MARKER FOR 'NO' CARDS
53 special, no
(yellow)
MARKER FOR 'YES' CARDS
53 special, yes
(yellow)
WHEN THE RESPONDENT HAS SORTED ALL THE VIOLENCE CARDS AS 'YES' OR 'NO' OR 'NOT SURE', THE FOLLOWING PROCEDURE SHOULD BE FOLLOWED.
SAY:
"That's all the cards in my pack of 53."
PAUSE AND SAY:
"The next thing I have to do is to help you with any cards you were NOT SURE about. May I do that?"
GO ROUND THE SCREEN
IF HE HAS ANY CARDS FACE DOWN, ASK HIM TO EXPLAIN WHY HE HAS RATED THESE AS 'NOT SURE'
ATTEMPT TO RESOLVE THESE AS 'YES' OR 'NO', BUT LEAVE THE DECISION TO HIM.
THEN
BUNDLE UP THE 'YES' CARDS, PUT A 'YES' MARKER ON THEM AND BIND WITH CLIP OR RUBBER BAND.
SIMILARLY, CLIP TOGETHER THE 'NOT SURE' BUNDLE.
TAKE UP THE 'NO' GROUP AND PROCEED AS OVER.
53a

INSTRUCTIONS FOR NEXT STAGE

SAY:

"Now I want you to imagine something for me. I want you to imagine that you have used violence on a boy and that this has damaged him very badly."

PAUSE.

"Just imagine you had done that."

PAUSE.

"Would you have admitted it to me?"

PAUSE.

IF 'YES', FIND OUT WHY AND CAPITALIZE ON REASONS, AS INSTRUCTED ON FOLD OUT.

← THEN GO TO PAGE 53e.

IF 'NO'
(i) FIND OUT WHY
(ii) DISCUSS
(iii) USE COUNTER ARGUMENTS AS ON FOLD OUT PAGE 53g
(iv) THEN PROCEED AS ON 53c.

53b

NEXT

SAY:

"I want you to go through all your 'NO' cards just once more in case there is any card amongst them that should have gone into the 'YES' box. But before you start, remember . . . ."

YOU SHOULD THEN RESTATE YOUR COUNTER-ARGUMENTS TO HIS REASONS FOR NOT ADMITTING THE VIOLENT ACT.

THEN:

GO TO YOUR SIDE OF SCREEN WITH ALL HIS 'NO' CARDS. PASS THESE ONE AT A TIME THROUGH THE SLOT FOR SORTING BY THE BOY.

53c

WHEN ALL THE 'NO' CARDS HAVE BEEN RESORTED, GO ROUND THE SCREEN TO COLLECT THEM FROM THEIR BOXES, PLACE THE RESORTED CARDS IN THE 'YES' AND 'NOT SURE' PACKS AS APPROPRIATE, AND USE THE LOOSE SHEET LABELLED 'NO' TO BUNDLE UP THE RESIDUAL 'NO' CARDS.

SAY:

"May I take down the screen now?"

TAKE IT DOWN IF O.K.

RETURN TO YOUR SEAT.

53d

THEN:

Tell boy that you are going to ask him some questions about the cards he sorted as 'YES'.

Say that you are doing this to try to learn in greater detail what it was he did.

Explain that this is where we will depend on him to be very honest with us.

Remind him that the interview is strictly confidential and that you don't know his name.

53e

53f

ESTABLISHING FREQUENCY OF COMMITTING THE ACTS

1) SAY:

"Let's take the first card you sorted as 'YES'. It is . . . ."

READ IT OUT AND HOLD IT IN FRONT OF BOY

"Exactly how many times did you do that in the last 6 months?"

FORCE A NUMERICAL ANSWER AND ENTER ON FRONT OF CARD.

2) THEN SAY:

"Tell me the different things you did on those occasions/that occasion."

*FOR EACH OF THEM, GET ENOUGH INFORMATION TO BE ABLE TO SPECIFY:

- The nature of the act (e.g., kicked, punched, pushed, cut, ...)
- The object of the act (e.g., another boy, a cat, ...)
- The implement if any (e.g., knife, stick, ...)
- What led him to do it (e.g., the boy was rude to him, 'for fun', ...)
- The circumstances (e.g., in football)

3) *THEN ASK

"How many times did you do that sort of thing?"

ENTER NUMBER AFTER THE SPECIFIED ACT.

4) IF THE ACT SOUNDS LIKE A REPEAT OF A PREVIOUS ONE, CHECK THAT THIS IS SO AND IN THAT EVENT ENTER A MINUS SIGN AFTER IT.

5) *NOW GO ON, GETTING HIM TO SPECIFY THE OTHER ACTS AND GETTING A NUMBER FOR EACH.
MARK AS MINUS IF THE ACT HAS BEEN SPECIFIED ALREADY.

KEEP IT UP WHILE HIS OVERALL TOTAL IS STILL GREATER THAN THE SUM OF HIS SPECIFICS.

> I have been violent just for fun or for a laugh or for a dare.
>
> 5 times
>
> gave boy a head butt just for fun (2)
>
> smashed a shop window for a dare (3)
>
> kicked a boy on the behind for a dare (1)

6) NOW DEAL WITH ALL OTHER 'YES' SHEETS IN THE SAME WAY.

BUT WORK QUICKLY.

page 53g

THE COUNTER ARGUMENTS USED IN THE PRETENDING GAME

I IF A BOY IS ASHAMED OF HIS ACT

SAY:

1. "I'm not judging anyone. I'm just finding out."
2. "You don't know me . . . I don't know you . . . and I don't suppose we'll ever meet again."

II YOU MIGHT TELL SOMEONE

SAY:

1. "Do you really think this is so?"

WHATEVER HE REPLIES, TELL HIM:

2. "If we did a thing like that, boys would not help us any more . . . we'd be finished. If we talked, other boys in your area would get to know and we'd be finished."
3. "Anyhow there were several boys who came in together. I don't know their names. Even if I did, I wouldn't know which one you were."

IF HE HAS DOUBTS STILL, SAY:

4. "I wouldn't do a thing like that. Anyhow, it would only be my word against yours . . . And you could deny the whole thing."

III

(a) THEY REALLY KNOW MY NAME

SAY:

"I don't know your name. There were several boys came this evening. Even if I knew any names, I wouldn't know which one you were. You've got a false name. I don't know who you are."

(b) THE LADY KNOWS MY NAME

SAY:

"Yes, but she didn't tell the receptionist who was who, did she. And nobody's told me."
"There will be no leak. You've got my word for that. It's private."

IV IT'S GOING DOWN IN A BOOK

Explain that there are no real names in this sort of book. Explain that it is all figures.

SAY ALSO:

"You could just deny it and you could sue me. Anyway, nobody is allowed to give names in this sort of book. That's one of the rules. The people who publish these books don't allow it because they know they'd be sued."

V HE DOES NOT BELIEVE IT IS FOR A BOOK

Show him the cover of a criminological book.
Show him pages of tables.

VI IT'S ON THAT TAPE

SAY:

"Yes, but your name is not on it . . . it's just . . . (e.g. Ringo)."

SAY ALSO:

"If you really want me to, I'll wipe it off the tape at the end. I hope you won't ask me to do that, but I will if you really want me to. That's a promise."

VII SOME GENERAL ARGUMENTS

1. "Nobody knows who you did it to, do they? So they couldn't do anything about it, could they?"
2. "Nobody will find out – it's just between the two of us."

SUPPORTING ARGUMENTS

IF A BOY SAYS SOMETHING TO THE EFFECT THAT HE WOULD ADMIT TO SUCH AN ACT OF VIOLENCE, SAY:

"Why would you have admitted it to me?"

WHATEVER REASON IS GIVEN, SAY:

"Yes, that's right, you . . . (REPEAT THE REASON)

ADD OTHER ARGUMENTS OF THE FOLLOWING KIND, DECIDING WHICH IS APPROPRIATE TO THE SITUATION.

"What you say is absolutely private."
"There's no name connected with it . . . in fact, you've got a false name."
"In our report, all this will come out as tables, with lots of figures and absolutely no names."

AND SO ON.

EVALUATING THE PROCEDURE

The form of the eliciting procedure described in this chapter closely resembles that developed by the Centre for its Theft Study and it is reasonable to consider that those of its features that were *both* taken over from the theft study *and* intensively challenged in that earlier context for their contribution to accurate responses, will stand up to similar challenge in the present context. Moreover, the web itself was developed in an empirical context involving challenge to the adequacy of the web's coverage and eliciting power. At the same time, it has not been subject to a reliability check in the full sense of that term and because of this the following comments about it should be made.

1 It is reasonable to expect some boys to exaggerate, not only in terms of the degree of violence committed in a given instance, but in terms of the number of times they did certain kinds of things. Other boys will tend to hold back, especially with regard to serious activities committed recently.

2 Nor can we *rely* upon being able to detect all the *repeat* admissions – arising because of the overlap of some of the stimulus items in the web. So much depends upon the alertness of the interviewer in picking up duplications.

3 Another common problem in gathering information of this memory-dependent kind is a tendency for respondents to extend the qualifying period to include acts falling outside of it – that is if the respondent has the desire to 'score'. On the other hand, sheer forgetting of some acts is likely to occur to some appreciable degree.

In most sample studies these different kinds of errors will cancel out each other *to some degree* – but it would be quite unrealistic to expect them to do so totally. In the circumstances, while we may take the *quantities* of violence derived through this study as approximating to reality, it would be wiser to regard them as *indices* – as providing a basis for the comparison of sub-samples rather than as providing 'absolute' measures. It is as indices that the violence scores derived from the eliciting procedure are best seen in this enquiry – indices that are meant to *differentiate or discriminate* between boys in terms of the *degree* to which they are involved in violence.

In the next section of this chapter there is a fairly detailed description of the complex procedures used for deriving 'violence scores' or indices from the violence data collected through the eliciting technique.

THE DERIVATION OF 'SCORES' FOR VIOLENCE COMMITTED

THE FOUR MEASURES OR SCORES

It had been planned that four assessments of involvement in violence be derived from the survey data.

Three of them were to constitute a combination, each one of which would contribute to an understanding of the other. These three were:

(a) Total number of acts of violence, irrespective of whether the constituent acts were *extremely violent* in character or violent only to some small degree: this measure was called V_{L1+}, meaning violence score (V) made up of all acts from the lowest level up (L1+).

(b) Total number of acts of violence, excluding acts involving only a minor degree of violence: this measure was called V_{L2+}, meaning total acts of violence from level 2 upwards, when level 2 is clearly defined as involving violence in excess of L1-type acts.

(c) Total number of acts of violence of the more violent kind: this measure was called V_{L3}, meaning total number of acts of violence done above the L2 level. In fact – and jumping ahead of the explanation yet to be made – the three levels were distributed along a continuum of violence in the following manner.

ACTS GRADED AS

Only very slightly violent	L1
A bit violent *Fairly* violent	L2
Quite violent *Very* violent *Extremely* violent	L3

No one of these measures used alone could, in the context of an hypothesis, provide sufficient information about the influence of television exposure on violence, for any one of them suffers from either or both (i) being extremely mixed in terms of level of violence, (ii) being incomplete as a record of the total violence committed by a boy.

It was intended, however, that the hypothesis here involved should be investigated in terms of all three levels, namely:

- long-term exposure to television violence increases the frequency of boys' involvement in violence at level 1 and above (= L1+);
- long-term exposure to television violence increases the frequency of boys' involvement in violence at level 2 and above (= L2+);
- long-term exposure to television violence increases the frequency of boys' involvement in violence at level 3 (= L3).

Thus it could possibly be that this class of hypothesis was verified or made more tenable at L1+ but not at L2+ or L3.

This system has the advantage of requiring no assumptions about how many acts of the L1 type equal one of the L2 type and so on. But it does require the use of a grading system sufficient to determine, in a reliable fashion, the *level* of violence of each of a boy's acts.

The *fourth* of the planned measures was to be a *weighted* total of all the acts of the boy concerned. Thus it was planned that for a given boy:

(a) each of his acts of violence was to be classified (reliably) on the 6-point scale set out above;

(b) all acts at a specific scale point would be given an empirically derived weight to represent the degree to which it was violent;

(c) subject to certain safety measures designed to reduce the effects (on sample scores) of extravagant or massive claims by individuals – subject to such safety measures, the allotted weights representing the boy's accumulation of acts of violence of different kinds, should be added to yield an *index* of total involvement in violent behaviour.

For a preview of this system in operation the reader may turn to page 235 of this chapter.

This fourth measure does of course require the use of an empirically developed classifying or grading system, just as do the L1 and the L2 systems. In addition, it requires that *weights* be derived for the quantification of acts of widely different degrees of violence.

This fourth measure was built into an hypothesis in the form

> long term exposure to television violence increases the extent of a boy's involvement in violent behaviour.

Both the 'levels system' of measurement and the 'index of total involvement' system required the prior development of a grading or classification system of a reliable kind. In addition, the index system required that each scale or point in the grading system should be convertible into a value or weight, as is ordinarily possible with any well constructed rating scale. What follows is primarily a description of how the rating system was set up and how the numerical values of the scalar points were established.

THE DEVELOPMENT OF A RELIABLE GRADING OR CLASSIFICATION SYSTEM

Defining 'How violent'

One feature of the classification or grading system was of prime importance: in grading an act of violence, no account whatever was to be taken of the *justification* for committing that act. Thus, for grading purposes,

> 'hitting a boy hard in the mouth with my fist'

was to be considered *no less violent* just because the victim had been tormenting the boy who therefore hit him. Nor, for grading purposes, would the act of

> 'scratching the paint on a new car'

be considered any less violent just because its owner was a local show-off, or because the owner refused to give the boy concerned the paid job of cleaning it, or because he had previously clouted that boy, or because the boy resented the wealth of the owner.

Grading was to be in terms of *how* violent the act was. The following instructions concerning this point were issued.

'In rating an act in terms of *how violent it is*, make the rating in terms of the amount of hurt or harm that is done to the person or thing on the receiving end. In judging this act of violence, keep in mind the following three conditions:

(i) The hurt or harm may not be directly and immediately involved in the act itself, but may nonetheless follow as a very probable consequence of the act (e.g. I dropped a bottle down onto a football crowd; I threw a brick at a boy). But this inclusive or extended thinking does not extend to purely fortuitous aftermaths of the act (e.g. I punched a boy *who then got beaten by his mother for being in a fight*).

(ii) The hurt or harm may be physical or psychological and it may be inflicted on an animate or an inanimate object. All these kinds of hurt or harm count in making your rating.

(iii) To count at all, the act has to be other than purely accidental. But beware of the boy for whom everything is "an accident".' (The rule for sorting had of course been that 'it counts even if it was accidental'. But if on questioning that act appeared to have been *pure accident*, it was not counted.)

The grading scale

An existing grading scale was adopted for classifying acts of violence according to *how* violent they were. This was the scale:

Scale items	Scale value
Not the least bit violent	0
Only very slightly violent	9
A bit violent	26
Fairly violent	44
Quite violent	63
Very violent	87
Extremely violent	100

The verbal part of this scale (the words in italics) had been developed by the Survey Research Centre for other work and its seven items had emerged then as being usefully spaced for discrimination purposes and as having workably low semi-interquartile ranges [19].

Subsequent work on this project (in the context of violence), yielded the scale values, on a continuum running from 0 – 100, set out on the right of the scale. The derivation of these figures will be described later in this section.

Analysis staff were given trials in using this scale, along with repeated instructions about how to use it and especially about the exclusion of considerations of 'justification', but it quickly emerged that the one act was being given widely different gradings by different coders. Thus the act

'I made a six inch scratch on the paint of a new car, using my pocket knife'

was graded all the way from *Just a bit* violent to *Extremely* violent by eight analysts and a very wide range of judgements was forthcoming for many of the other acts they graded. Intensive interviewers working on the project were brought into the grading and the same type of variability was apparent in *their* ratings. Discussion with them made it clear that their individual views about how much harm was done or was likely to be done by the act . . . differed markedly. They were also differentially allowing the intrusion into their ratings of considerations of *justification* for the act. Indeed, there was clear evidence of a *strong reluctance* on the part of these people to exclude justification from their ratings.

The use of illustrations at each point along the grading scale

Accordingly it was deemed necessary to illustrate the grading scale with quite specific examples of violence in order to establish in coders a common reference and judgement system. For example:

A BIT violent

Examples

I deliberately broke a school window with a stone
I shoved people out of the way to get into a bus
I called a girl a slut
I irritated a boy at school by jabbing him with a stick

...... and so on

However, such a system could not be *arbitrarily* set up because it would then mirror the limitations of the individuals setting it up. *What was needed was a form of consensus or population average* and steps were taken to develop the examples (on the illustrated scale) on that basis. The reader wanting to see the outcome of this work as an aid to understanding this description of it will find the illustrated scale itself in the Appendix to this chapter. The construction process involved several steps as detailed below.

Bringing together a large number of acts from which to develop examples. At the time this construction work was begun, many boys in the survey sample had already been interviewed, so that numerous examples of acts of violence were available for making up a large pool of possible examples or illustrations. As a first step, therefore, these acts were scanned and an initial pool of acts, varying in kind and degree of violence, was developed.

Clarifying the examples. All these acts were then modified in such a way as clearly to specify the *nature* of the act and the *object* of the act. The modification was always minimal but obviously any acts used to illustrate the grading scale would have to be as clear and as unambiguous as possible [20]. For example, the vague statement 'I cut someone with a knife' was converted into 'I deliberately cut a boy's face with a penknife' [20]. Similarly, the vague statement 'I was rude to someone from a vehicle' was converted to 'I made rude finger signs at someone in the street from the back of a school bus'. [20]

The reason for doing this was that the illustrated scale would have to be as unambiguous and as specific as possible. There would never be any question of modifying in any way whatsoever the acts of violence that would eventually be graded on the scale or through it, and the very acts used as starting points in this present process would eventually be graded just as they were recorded on the record sheet prepared by the interviewer. But it was essential that the measuring tool itself be as unambiguous and specific and reliable as possible. To take this explanation one point further, it will be seen that the initial scanning of boys' statements about what they had done was intended solely to yield ideas or starting points for the specification of a clearly defined pool of items from which the illustrated scale could be made.

The pool of acts to be considered as examples. This form of selection and modification was combined with certain other evidence and experience [21] to produce a pool of 116 acts of violence. These, it must be emphasised, were yet to be subject to certain types of scrutiny and test to determine both their suitability as examples and their scalar positions. Sections of this list are shown in list 6.1 and the full list is available in Appendix 2.

List 6.1
The general character of acts in the list of 116 violent acts from which the illustrated scale was to be developed

---

1 I deliberately hit a boy across the back with my school bag while we were waiting for the bus
2 I threw pieces of brick at a girl
3 I swung a crowbar around to threaten someone
4 I deliberately cut a boy's face with a penknife
5 I tripped my brother with a rope that I put across his path at ankle level

---

18 I threatened to kill my father
19 I told a boy I would set my mates on him if he went on trying to go out with my girl friend

---

42 I slashed the tyres of half a dozen cars in a car park
43 I let down the tyres on a parked car
44 I set a letter box on fire
45 I deliberately tipped a cart full of groceries onto its side on the floor of a supermarket

---

74 I gave a boy a head butt
75 I loosened the screws on the handlebars of a bike of one of the boys at school so that he would have a crash
76 I deliberately booted a boy in the stomach
77 I practised Judo at a youth club

---

91 I deliberately cut someone with a razor
92 I deliberately trod on a cat's paw

---

96 I kept throwing stones in the water while my friends were fishing
97 I told a teacher who grabbed me by the shoulder to 'fuck off'

---

107 I deliberately dropped a lighted cigarette into a shopper's bag
108 I broke open a parking meter
109 I kicked over a whole line of 'No Parking' signs
110 I chopped down a young tree that had just been planted in the park

---

116 I set fire to the contents of a rubbish bin that was standing against a shop door

Between them, these acts ranged over the following types: psychological hurt to a person including swearing, insult, deprivation; physical hurt to a person with hand, foot, head, . . . ; physical hurt to a person through an implement; hurt to an animal; damage to property.

Having members of the public rate the acts in terms of how violent they thought them to be

These 116 acts were next prepared for presentation to a sample of members of the public using the rating scale already presented in this section (i.e. not the least bit violent/only very slightly violent/a bit violent/fairly violent/quite violent/very violent/extremely violent). Members of the public went through fairly elaborate procedures in making these ratings.

The sources of the members of the public who made the ratings. Some 43 members of the public took part in the rating of the acts. They were all drawn from samples previously participating in research being carried out by Midas Research Ltd. [22] at the Commonwealth Institute in London. These sessions are normally attended by approximately 250 males and females aged 16 and over and drawn from the general population of the Greater London conurbation on a random sample basis. In the course of such a session a letter from the Survey Research Centre had been delivered to session members, inviting them to take part in a further meeting on either of two evenings. A fee for attendance and a repayment of fares were offered. Of those who agreed to attend, a selection was made and invitations were issued for the Survey Research Centre test sessions with a view to processing two groups of about 30 each. The 43 who subsequently took part in the SRC session were not appreciably dissimilar from the general adult public in terms of age, sex and social class [23].

The test materials. Three items of test material were prepared. The first was a list of eleven acts of violence which were to be rated in a *preliminary (practice) session*, e.g. 'I hit a boy hard on the nose with my fists'; 'I twisted a boy's arm till he cried out with pain'; 'I threw stones at a car on the motorway'. These acts were to be rated on the second item of equipment, namely a set of seven terms presented in bold print on a 5 inch x 8 inch card on which was also printed a set of rules or instructions for making the ratings. The third item of equipment prepared for the session was the list of 116 acts, well spread over eight coloured pages, and with a space for entering a rating (from 0–6) after each act. The first two of these items of equipment are presented in Appendix 3 to this chapter. The third item is in the general form of the first item and its content is shown in Appendix 2.

The administration of the rating session. On arrival, respondents were given light refreshment and were introduced to the task to be done. From the beginning, they operated under three rules: (a) that they should *not*, while actually rating acts, have any discussion at all with any other member of the group; (b) that they were required to be completely frank in all their ratings (they did in fact remain nameless throughout the session and much was made of this); (c) that what they were being asked to do called for constant thought and hard work.

In preparing the raters for the task in hand, great stress was laid upon the need to *exclude* considerations of how justified or otherwise the act of violence might seem to be . . . or might conceivably be. Indeed, right from the beginning the exclusion of justification as a rating dimension or consideration was regarded as of prime importance and as calling for major effort on the part of respondent and test administrator. The Centre's earlier experience on this score had shown how insidious was the tendency to allow 'justification' to creep into the rating process.

At the end of the practice session, the raters were invited to work in pairs, to identify any acts that they had rated in substantially different ways and then to discuss such differences with a view to discovering what lay behind them. This proved to be a contentious and very lively process with evidence not only of major differences in ratings but of sharp division over the grounds for differences. The session administrator talked to each pair with a view to understanding the reasons for difference, particularly any that involved misunderstanding of the instructions. Again and again it emerged that raters were allowing into their judgements the possibility that the act was justified in some way (e.g. that the victim possibly deserved it). But they were also (i) arguing that the act concerned was really quite normal or common (and so rating the act as less violent because of this); (ii) differing markedly over whether hurt or harm to an *animal* or harm to inanimate *objects* were in the same realm or dimension as hurt or harm to a human. There were also differences over how much hurt or harm might result from an act which had delayed consequences (e.g. 'I threw an empty beer bottle down at a football crowd').

The session administrator then brought the group back under his control and used the evidence from the discussion to re-emphasise the rules. Thus he (i) re-emphasised the importance of excluding considerations of possible *justifications* for acts; (ii) stressed that the commonness of some act mattered only if its commonness reduced (or increased) the extent of the hurt or harm done; (iii) stated that it was the act and its possible direct consequences (in the form of hurt or harm) that was to be rated. On the other hand, no attempt was made to settle disagreements about how violent an act was provided the basic rules were being applied.

After this session, the respondents were asked to go ahead and rate the first page of 116 acts, working quite independently once more. At the end of this, individuals were moved round the room to work with new partners in the same way as before: they compared ratings with the partner and discussed differences. The session staff moved round the room listening in and correcting once again any misunderstandings of the rules. At the end of this process, each member was invited to reconsider his or her ratings and to make any changes which he or she thought were called for in view of previous misunderstanding of the rules.

The session chairman then reminded the group of the continuing misunderstandings that were occurring, gave examples of these, and then had the group work through the *next* page of acts. After this, the same process was repeated (with a further change of partners).

This whole process was repeated through four cycles in the course of the rating session, with increases in the number of pages of ratings to be done in each cycle. Experience showed that this rather heavy control over the rating operation was necessary principally because of the persistence with which respondents brought into the rating process considerations of the unwarranted kind already referred to, especially considerations of how *justified* the act of violence could possibly have been.

The results of the rating session: anomalies. It may nonetheless come as a surprise to some readers to learn that the ratings of specific acts in the list were subject to quite considerable variations, as exemplified in the following table.

The full set of ratings for all acts is given in Appendix 2 and will serve to confirm the general pattern shown. This outcome appears to be of considerable importance because it means that *there is in society a very considerable tendency for people to differ – and to differ quite markedly – in their judgements of the DEGREE to which acts are violent.* As a phenomenon it seems to call for investigation in its own right.

The act to be rated	How violent is the act?						
	Not the least bit	Only slightly	A bit	Fairly	Quite	Very	Extremely
	n	n	n	n	n	n	n
I chopped down a young tree that had just been planted	3	9	9	12	6	3	1
I scratched the paint on a new car with a knife	0	3	6	15	11	7	1
I slashed the tyres of half a dozen cars in a car park	0	1	1	9	9	16	7
I pulled the wings off flies at school	7	7	7	7	6	6	3
I spat on a boy's suit	1	10	18	5	9	0	0
I punched someone in the eye	0	2	8	10	14	6	3
I deliberately cut someone with a razor	0	0	0	2	5	17	19
I broke open a parking meter	2	7	15	8	5	5	1

The results of the rating session: the items selected

Once the ratings were completed, several steps were taken to assess the relative suitability of the different acts for inclusion in the illustrated scale.

(a) For each act, the approximate *mean* of its distribution of ratings was identified and a count made of the number of responses (out of the 43) that fell more than one scalar position away from that mean. The second count or measure is referred to here as an *index* of scatter. For example, for the following distribution:

Scale position	0	1	2	3	4	5	6
Distribution	2	4	10	15	8	4	0

the approximate mean is 3 and the index of scatter is 10.. What this means is that if a choice has to be made amongst items with approximate means at 3, the smaller the index of scatter, the greater should be the case for selecting that item as part of the illustrated scale.

(b) All 116 acts were now sorted according to approximate mean values, their distribution being as follows, and the index of scatter varying markedly within each *scalar* group.

Scalar points	Number of acts with approximate means at this point	Number selected
	n	n
0	2	2
1	17	12
2	28	12
3	31	12
4	19	12
5	16	12
6	3	2
	All 116	

(c) All the acts with means at a given scalar point were listed in order, with the one with the smallest index of scatter first and that with the biggest index last.

(d) Within each of these groups, the acts with lower indices of scatter were selected up to a total of 12. In a few cases, this meant the inclusion of two or more very similar acts and in these cases the one with the larger index of scatter was dropped and was replaced with the next act down the list provided that this one, too, did not virtually duplicate another item amongst those already selected. In the '0' group and the '6' group there were only two and three acts available for selection.

The first version of the illustrated scale and its general effectiveness

The resulting scale was regarded as very tentative in form and content and was prepared for use by intensive interviewers (acting as coders) on a trial basis. It was issued to the specialised coders with a set of instructions and these, along with the first form of the illustrated scale, are shown in Appendix 4A.

In line with initial plans for the scoring of a boy's violent behaviour, the coders were required first of all to write out, in a single list, all the acts of violence admitted by the boy, with the exception of any marked with a minus sign (i.e. indicating that these acts appeared more than once amongst his admissions). In writing out an act, the coder was required to specify its essential elements, namely:

who did it (e.g. 'I');

what was the nature of the act;

who or what was the object of the act.

In order to separate out that part of the elicited detail which was in fact no more than justification or motivation – something which boys insisted on providing and which the intensive interviewers were resistant to omitting – the coders were also required to enter such detail in brackets after the description of the act itself.

The number of times committed was to be entered after this entry and the illustrated scale was then to be used to grade the act on the 6-point rating scale.

It quickly emerged that a very large amount of time was being used in writing out the different acts in the manner required and that a continuance of this practice would lead not only to substantial expense, but to a failure to complete this part of the data processing on time. The bracketed entries (i.e. concerning justification or motivation) were then dropped, but this reduced the task only marginally and it became necessary for the grading of each act to be entered directly onto the interview report sheet itself (using a new colour of ink to avoid confusion with the original interview entries). At the same time, a 100 per cent check on the grading of acts was set up.

It also became clear that there were many gaps in the illustrated scale, in the sense that the coders frequently asked what to do about certain recurrently admitted acts of violence that were not in the scale and which the scale gave too little help in placing, for example:

> deliberately killing insects/threatening to give a boy a hiding/graffiti in its various forms/telling lies in order to tease someone/head butting/playing bulldog/ deliberate kicking in a game/getting into premises and smashing things up/ . . .

There were also complaints that there were insufficient examples for the 'not violent at all' grade and similarly for the 'extremely violent' grade.

There was quite a lot of disagreement (amongst the intensive interviewers doing the grading work) with the placement of certain of the examples already on the scale and for several of these the graders or coders were closely in agreement, for example:

(i) there seemed no good reason for having both the items 'I deliberately cut someone with a razor' and 'I deliberately cut somebody's face with a penknife' – they seemed much alike;

(ii) similarly for the examples: 'I hit a boy with an iron bar' and 'I attacked someone in the street with an iron bar'.

The modified illustrated scale (in final form)

The illustrated scale was modified in various ways to overcome its weaknesses.

1 Apparent gaps in the examples at different scalar points were filled in
   (a) by bringing back into the scale some of the acts among the total 116 that had previously been excluded;
   (b) by having a small number of new items defined and placed through a discussion session with coders and in the context of the existing illustrations.

2 Commonly committed acts not on the scale in the form of examples were graded in a meeting with coders and in the context of the existing scale and then were added to the scale itself.

3 Several ambiguous and disputed acts were dropped from the scale altogether.

The scale then went into general use but was subject to a limited number of additions (i.e. of further examples) as the grading operation proceeded.

The illustrated scale in its final form, along with instructions for using it, is shown in Appendix 4B. The outcome of using it was the entry, on each of the 53 cards of the Web of Stimuli, of a grading for each act written thereon. These entries had still to be transferred to a general score sheet, but that was a fairly straightforward operation.

DEVELOPING VALUES OR WEIGHTS FOR THE SCALAR ITEMS

The grading operation which has just been described was sufficient to classify a boy's violent acts into six grades, for example:

	f
Grade 1 (*only very slightly* violent)	198
Grade 2 (*a bit* violent)	131
Grade 3 (*fairly* violent)	42
Grade 4 (*quite* violent)	10
Grade 5 (*very* violent)	0
Grade 6 (*extremely* violent)	0

This in turn made it possible to derive scores within the levels system described on pages 224-5, as follows.

L1+ = 381
L2+ = 183
L3+ = 10

But to derive a *weighted* total score, as for the fourth of the planned measures, it was necessary to derive values for each of the six grades defined by the rating scale.

There is a standard way of doing this, namely of asking a set of competent judges to place each of the terms on a continuum (e.g. from 0–100) in such a position as to indicate its weight or value in relation to all the other items or terms. The weight for any one item is the mean or, better, the median of the distribution of the ratings of the different judges. In the present case, this rating or evaluation was carried out through three different sets of judges, with much the same result each time.

(a) A panel of 45 adult members of the public rated the scalar terms on a continuum running from 0–100 where the value 0 was given to the scale item 'not the least bit violent' and the value 100 was given to the scale item 'extremely violent'. Each respondent took each intermediate item and said at which point on the 0–100 point continuum it should be placed to best represent its relationship to the end items and to the other intermediate items. For each of the intermediate items, the following mean scores were derived:

	(fixed)						(fixed)
Scale items	0	1	2	3	4	5	6
Means	0	10.8	29.0	45.4	62.9	84.6	100

(b) A further panel of 43 adult members of the public rated the scalar terms on the same rating system, and produced the following mean values.

	(fixed)						(fixed)
Scale items	0	1	2	3	4	5	6
Means	0	11.7	23.8	43.5	63.8	86.7	100

(c) A small panel (25) of intensive interviewers who had been using the illustrated scale for some time were asked to help rate *not* just the scalar terms in isolation, but each of the illustrated scalar sections. In other words, each intensive interviewer was to consider each scalar item defined in terms of the acts illustrating it. The rating instructions given to them are presented in Appendix 5. The means derived from these ratings were as follows.

	(fixed)						(fixed)
Scale items	0	1	2	3	4	5	6
Means	0	9.4	25.7	44.1	63.1	86.7	100

In the circumstances, the third set of values was adopted in that (i) it did not depart appreciably from the ratings of the other panels and (ii) it was based on the judgements of people who had made extensive use of the illustrated scale for grading purposes and who in this present context had weighted the scalar terms or items in the context of the various acts coming under the individual scalar items.

Transferring gradings from the survey sheets to a transfer and summary sheet

The details now entered on the Web of Stimuli cards were transferred to a summary sheet in the following form.

Act No. (= 1-53)	All Acts Claimed (= Total Number)	HOW VIOLENT WAS IT? Not least bit 0	Only very slightly 1	A bit 2	Fairly 3	Quite 4	Very 5	Extremely 6
1	4			4				
1	2				2			
5	1				1			
5	1			1				
7	60		50					
15	26					26		
15	4				4			
22	3			3				
27	6		6					
31	2							

Act No. (= 1-53)	All Acts Claimed (= Total Number)	HOW VIOLENT WAS IT? Not least bit 0	Only very slightly 1	A bit 2	Fairly 3	Quite 4	Very 5	Extremely 6
42	2			2				
42	2				2			
44	1		1					
47	3			3				
49	1						1	
51	2					2		
53	6			6				

Thus for *each act*, the details to be transferred were: the number of times the act was said to be committed and the grade of that act. A ceiling of 50 times was imposed on each act in entering it under its 'grade'.

Acts marked with a minus sign (-) were omitted from the transfer sheet. It was then possible to add all the '0' grade acts (i.e. not violent at all), all grade '1' acts, all grade '2' acts and so on for each grade on the following pattern.

	0	1	2	3	4	5	6	All
All								
Cols	7-9	10-12	13-15	16-18	19-21	22-24	25-27	28-31

These accumulations then made it possible to calculate all four violence scores for each boy. These scores were to be derived through a computer programme and then entered on tape (and on cards for a permanent record).

Notes

[1] This measure also provided measures of the dependent variables in several other hypotheses, namely the dependent variables: 'committing violence in the company of gangs or groups of boys' (Hypothesis 2), 'being argumentative or irritating or annoying to others' (Hypothesis 3), 'being aggressive or violent in sport or play' (Hypothesis 4), 'using bad language' (Hypothesis 5).

[2] See *Causal Factors in the Development of Stealing by London Boys*, W.A. Belson, P.J. Didcott, G.L. Millerson, J.G. Cleland, V.R. Thompson, Survey Research Centre, 1972.

[3] The *survey period* was planned to extend over a calendar period of six months and in the event was extended over a period of five and a half months, with the result that the calendar period to which the sample's behaviour could be referred was six months + five and a half months (= eleven and a half months) in fact from end February 1972 to mid-January 1973.

[4] See *The Development of a Technique for Eliciting Information about Stealing by London Boys*, W.A. Belson, G.L. Millerson, P.J. Didcott, Survey Research Centre, 1968.

[5] The concept 'web of stimuli' was developed during a Centre study of stealing. (see [4] above). It was of course necessary that the statements on the cards be developed empirically for the present enquiry, but the rationale and the strategy of the method were the same.

[6] See *The Development of a Procedure for Eliciting Information from Boys about the Nature and Extent of their Stealing*, W.A. Belson, G.L. Millerson, P.J. Didcott, Survey Research Centre, 1968.

[7] This particular item of information was required solely as a means of alerting the interviewer to the possibility that there were still more acts to be reported (i.e. as when the sum total of acts enumerated through (c) (vi) still fell below the number claimed through (a)).

[8] Items (iv) and (v) were not required for the scoring system. But it had become very clear during the interviewer-training period that boys were more able to admit acts if allowed to justify them. It emerged too that the interviewers also wanted to secure such information and felt frustrated if not allowed to do so. See later for further comment.
[9] See page 235 for details of how such scores were derived.
[10] That is, aspects of the procedure that were not simply adaptations of procedures used in the theft study.
[11] Two of the other three were added to provide information required for other purposes, namely 'I have damaged someone's car (not in a road accident)' and 'I have done damage to a train'. The third statement, 'I have been rough or tough or violent at sport or play', was added as an additional basis for investigating Hypothesis 4 (see the master list of hypotheses in chapter 1).
[12] See *Studies on Readership*, W.A. Belson, Oakwood Press, 1962. See also *The Development of a Technique for Eliciting Information about the Extent and Nature of Stealing by Boys*, W.A. Belson, G.L. Millerson, P.J. Didcott, Survey Research Centre, 1968.
[13] For example, what they *thought* the effects on boys might be of viewing a lot of television violence (for use in *formulating* hypotheses).
[14] Thus one boy listed: street fights/football-stand fights/shop windows being smashed/revenge/gang fights/trains being wrecked/personal property being thrown and taken/demonstrations/scratching cars.

Another listed: fighting (one against one)/gang fighting/bullying (one boy to another)/a group of boys on to a smaller number or one person/picking on some race of people who would not fight back/kicking/stabbing/pellet guns and sling shots, etc./violence at a football match.

Another listed: beatings up/damaging cars, motor cycles, etc./cruelty to animals and birds/damaging property (houses, shops, etc.)/smashing meters/holding someone under water.
[15] For this particular purpose (i.e. checking the web of stimuli), the whole process was geared to the last four weeks in order to cut down recall problems.
[16] This reaction had been encountered in constructing the web of stimuli in the theft study, but the evidence from that latter study showed that the rate of admissions increased with the use of 'confidentiality' references.
[17] This hypothesis was: 'Long term exposure to television violence makes boys more aggressive in sport or play'.
[18] This was intended to mean that details were wanted with respect to every single act referred to by the stimulus cards sorted as 'yes'.
[19] See the scale construction methods of Thurstone in chapters 4 and 7.
[20] There was no question of interfering with the survey data – the acts used in this construction process would, *for scoring purposes*, remain exactly as provided and described by respondents. This point is extremely important.
[21] An earlier attempt at deriving such a list and at having members of the public rated, had been less successful and had indicated both ambiguity in the wording of acts and misunderstanding by the raters about the task they were to do. The list was subsequently modified and the tests re-run.
[22] At that time the Group was known as Market Decisions Ltd.
[23] Obviously the 43 people who took part were self-selected in that they had volunteered to take part in the Survey Research Centre session. Bias in this situation is

known to operate in favour of the more skilled, of those with more formal education, of those with greater sociability. At the same time, the rating operation required of them was one (a) that did not call for strictly representative sampling and (b) that would gain from having the more intelligent people carry it through. The distribution of the 43 persons taking part (in terms of age, sex, social class and marital state) was as follows.

Sex:	Male	20	*Age:*	20-39	13	*Marital status:*	
	Female	23		40-49	21	Married	33
				50 and over	9	Single	8
Social Class:						Divorced/ separated	3
	AB	16					
	C_1 C_2	25					
	DE	2					

APPENDICES TO CHAPTER 6

Appendix 1	Diagrams of the equipment used
Appendix 2	A full set of all 116 acts, each with the distribution of responses against it
Appendix 3	Practice sheets and rating criteria for use in developing an illustrated scale
Appendix 4A	First form of illustrated rating scale and instructions for using it
Appendix 4B	Final form of the illustrated rating scale
Appendix 5	Weighting the scale items in the illustrated scale

Diagrams of the Equipment Used

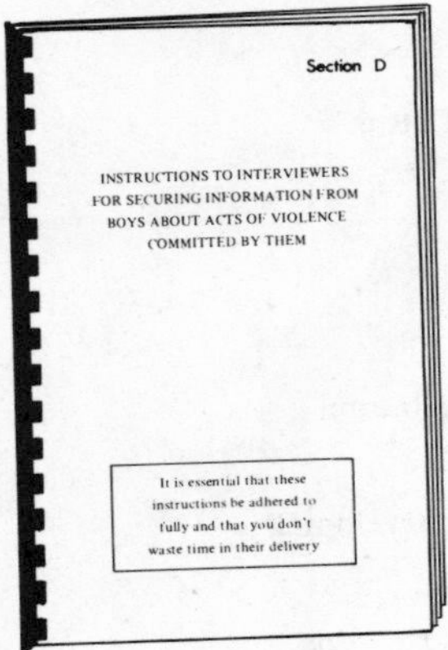

Section D

INSTRUCTIONS TO INTERVIEWERS
FOR SECURING INFORMATION FROM
BOYS ABOUT ACTS OF VIOLENCE
COMMITTED BY THEM

It is essential that these
instructions be adhered to
fully and that you don't
waste time in their delivery

The booklet of instructions
with 53 web-cards inserted

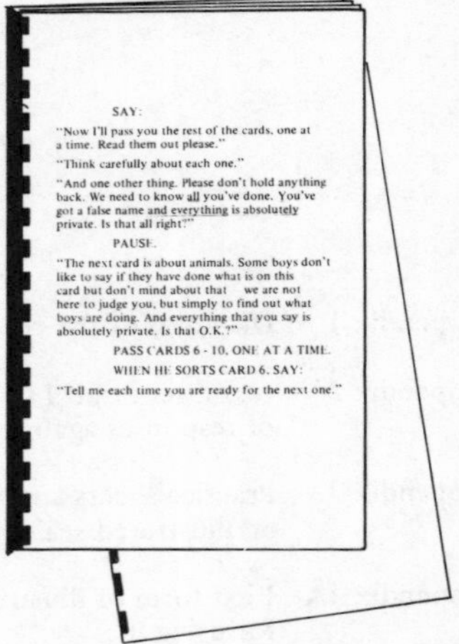

SAY:

"Now I'll pass you the rest of the cards, one at a time. Read them out please."

"Think carefully about each one."

"And one other thing. Please don't hold anything back. We need to know all you've done. You've got a false name and everything is absolutely private. Is that all right?"

PAUSE.

"The next card is about animals. Some boys don't like to say if they have done what is on this card but don't mind about that   we are not here to judge you, but simply to find out what boys are doing. And everything that you say is absolutely private. Is that O.K.?"

PASS CARDS 6 - 10, ONE AT A TIME.

WHEN HE SORTS CARD 6, SAY:

"Tell me each time you are ready for the next one."

The booklet of instructions
open at an illustrative page
with web-card ready for sorting

A boy accepting a web-card
through slot in preparation
for sorting it into the 'yes' or
the 'no' box on his side of the
screen.

After sorting all web-cards for first time, the interviewer administers the 'pretending' game

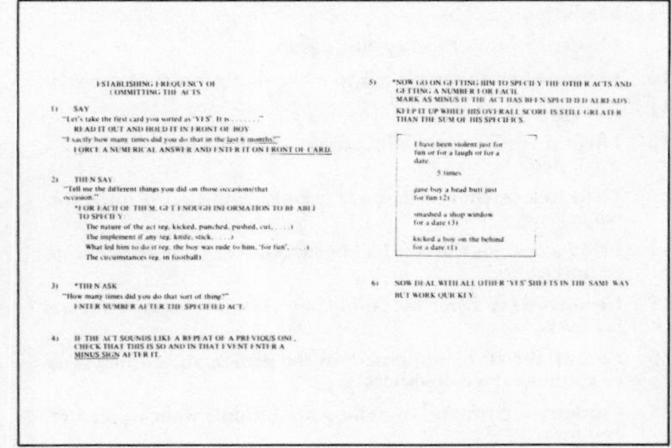

ESTABLISHING FREQUENCY OF COMMITTING THE ACTS

1) SAY
"Let's take the first card you sorted as 'YES'. It is . . . ."
READ IT OUT AND HOLD IT IN FRONT OF BOY
"Exactly how many times did you do that in the last 6 months?"
FORCE A NUMERICAL ANSWER AND ENTER IT ON FRONT OF CARD.

2) THEN SAY
"Tell me the different things you did on those occasions/that occasion."
*FOR EACH OF THEM, GET ENOUGH INFORMATION TO BE ABLE TO SPECIFY:
The nature of the act (eg. kicked, punched, pushed, cut, ...)
The implement if any (eg. knife, stick, ...)
What led him to do it (eg. the boy was rude to him, 'for fun', ...)
The circumstances (eg. in football)

3) *THEN ASK
"How many times did you do that sort of thing?"
ENTER NUMBER AFTER THE SPECIFIED ACT.

4) IF THE ACT SOUNDS LIKE A REPEAT OF A PREVIOUS ONE, CHECK THAT THIS IS SO AND IN THAT EVENT ENTER A MINUS SIGN AFTER IT.

5) *NOW GO ON GETTING HIM TO SPECIFY THE OTHER ACTS AND GETTING A NUMBER FOR EACH.
MARK AS MINUS IF THE ACT HAS BEEN SPECIFIED ALREADY.
KEEP IT UP WHILE HIS OVERALL SCORE IS STILL GREATER THAN THE SUM OF HIS SPECIFICS.

I have been violent just for fun or for a laugh or for a dare.
5 times
gave boy a head butt just for fun (2)
smashed a shop window for a dare (3)
kicked a boy on the behind for a dare (1)

6) NOW DEAL WITH ALL OTHER 'YES' SHEETS IN THE SAME WAY BUT WORK QUICKLY.

In the final phase of the eliciting procedure the boy is asked for details of the acts of violence committed (and admitted through the sorting procedure.

Appendix 2

A fuli set of 116 acts examined in preparing the illustrated rating scale, each act with its distribution of responses set against it

Public ratings of the degree to which certain acts are violent

	The acts rated by the public	Not the least bit violent (0)	Only very slightly violent (1)	A bit violent (2)	Fairly violent (3)	Quite violent (4)	Very violent (5)	Extremely violent (6)
		How violent is it?						
1	I deliberately hit a boy across the back with my school bag while we were waiting for the bus	7	15	13	6	2	0	0
2	I threw pieces of brick at a girl	0	2	4	11	16	8	2
3	I swung a crowbar around to threaten someone	0	2	6	6	14	12	3
4	I deliberately cut a boy's face with a penknife	0	0	0	0	6	10	27
5	I tripped my brother with a rope that I put across his path at ankle height	4	10	12	10	6	1	0
6	I hid behind a door and when my sister came in I hit her over the head with a pillow	18	20	4	0	1	0	0
7	One day after gym, I kept flicking my towel at my brother after he came out of the shower	19	12	9	1	2	0	0
8	I deliberately hit my sister on the head with an umbrella handle	2	4	9	12	10	5	1
9	I bashed a boy's head against a wall	0	0	0	3	11	18	11
10	I stamped on the dog's tail to make him get out of the way	0	6	4	8	10	11	4
11	I flogged the dog	0	0	2	2	6	14	19
12	I kept hitting a horse with stones when the horse was in a small pen	0	0	4	2	7	12	18
13	I lied to a teacher so that my friends would get blamed for what I did	5	8	10	8	7	4	1
14	I told a boy his mother had been killed in a car accident just to upset him	0	1	1	6	8	7	20
15	I annoyed my sister by calling her 'Dumbo' because she has big ears	16	10	9	4	3	1	0
16	I set up the Hi-Fi equipment in the garden and turned it up to torment the neighbours	10	16	12	3	1	1	0
17	I upset my girlfriend by telling her I didn't want to see her any more	19	11	4	8	1	0	0
18	I threatened to kill my father	0	3	2	5	12	15	6
19	I told a boy I would set my mates on him if he went on trying to go out with my girlfriend	6	4	10	11	7	5	0
20	I rang someone up and just made breathing noises in the speaker. I did this four times in a row	4	7	10	8	11	2	1

The acts rated by the public	How violent is it?						
	Not the least bit violent (0)	Only very slightly violent (1)	A bit violent (2)	Fairly violent (3)	Quite violent (4)	Very violent (5)	Extremely violent (6)
21 I called a girl a slut	8	16	9	8	1	1	0
22 I told a policeman to 'Piss off and leave me alone'	9	21	7	4	1	1	0
23 I made rude finger signs at people in the street from the back of a school bus	23	16	2	1	1	0	0
24 I have teased boys by calling them nasty names	22	16	4	0	1	0	0
25 I teased a Greek boy by saying insulting things about Greeks.	8	15	8	10	1	1	0
26 I knocked a boy off his bicycle as he rode past me	0	2	2	9	17	12	1
27 I tormented my brother by holding him down and tickling him for about ten minutes	16	10	5	6	3	3	0
28 I tried to force a girl to have sexual intercourse with me	0	0	1	1	10	16	15
29 I deliberately kicked a boy on the leg during a football match	2	6	8	11	9	7	0
30 I deliberately kicked a boy in the crutch	0	0	1	2	8	16	16
31 I have wrestled with friends in the park	31	6	4	1	1	0	0
32 I punched a boy in the stomach	2	6	6	13	11	4	1
33 I threatened to give a boy a hiding	11	16	10	5	1	0	0
34 I had a fight with someone using bare fists and I hit him many times	1	10	16	15	1	0	0
35 I bashed up an old woman	1	0	0	0	1	10	31
36 I deliberately broke a school window with a stone	1	8	19	10	3	2	0
37 I threw the radio against the wall smashing it to bits	4	4	12	10	10	2	1
38 I broke open an electricity meter to get money	3	4	11	11	9	4	1
39 I wrote in big letters on the wall of a building	17	18	6	2	0	0	0
40 I deliberately ran into a parked car with a milk float	0	1	3	12	17	10	0
41 I scratched the paint on a new car with a knife	0	3	6	15	11	7	1
42 I slashed the tyres of half a dozen cars in a car park	0	1	1	9	9	16	7
43 I let down the four tyres on a parked car	2	5	10	9	12	5	0
44 I set a letter box on fire	2	3	0	6	13	13	6
45 I tipped a cart full of groceries onto its side on the floor of a supermarket	1	10	10	10	9	2	1
46 I kicked and banged a cigarette machine to get money out of it	4	4	15	11	4	4	1
47 On the way home from school I smashed some bottles on the pavement leaving the broken bits lying there	0	5	9	9	15	5	0
48 I fired a .22 rifle at bottles in the local rubbish dump	13	12	10	3	3	1	1

The acts rated by the public

		How violent is it?						
		Not the least bit violent (0)	Only very slightly violent (1)	A bit violent (2)	Fairly violent (3)	Quite violent (4)	Very violent (5)	Extremely violent (6)
49	I shot hairpins at a boy from an elastic band	2	6	9	13	9	2	2
50	I threw a metal dart at a boy's foot	0	1	5	11	10	11	5
51	I kept poking my brother with a ruler to make him say he was sorry	4	14	14	8	1	2	0
52	I irritated a boy at school by jabbing him with a stick	5	16	12	9	1	0	0
53	I deliberately hit a boy on the face with a broken bottle	0	0	0	0	3	21	19
54	I attacked someone in the street with an iron bar	0	0	0	0	2	17	24
55	I threw slates off the roof of an old house, making them fall into the street below	0	3	3	5	16	9	7
56	I put a book on top of a door so it would fall on whoever came through the door	4	21	11	5	1	1	0
57	I fired an airgun at boys passing in the street outside my home	0	1	2	3	13	17	7
58	I pulled the wings off flies at school	7	7	7	7	6	6	3
59	I shot a cat with a pellet from an air rifle	0	1	2	7	14	12	7
60	I shot a pigeon with a .22 rifle	5	5	5	11	9	5	3
61	I lied to my mother about where I had been one night, because I didn't want to get into trouble	21	13	6	3	0	0	0
62	I told lies about someone to make him look bad	3	12	7	10	8	3	0
63	With my mates, I teased and shouted at meths. drinkers and other old blokes in the park	6	7	12	12	6	0	0
64	I made my little sister cry by pretending I had a handful of 'creepy crawlies'	1	17	16	4	3	2	0
65	I turned my back and just walked away when the teacher told me to do something I didn't want to	19	15	7	2	0	0	0
66	I deliberately annoyed my parents by asking a neighbour for money	9	14	11	7	2	0	0
67	I took the mickey out of a new teacher by making fun of him in front of the rest of the class	7	12	10	11	1	2	0
68	I told my parents to get stuffed	7	12	11	5	6	2	0
69	I teased another boy by saying his girlfriend was an ugly brute	14	7	12	7	2	1	0
70	I busted the telephone in a telephone box	2	1	3	6	17	10	4
71	I sent obscene letters to someone	1	4	6	8	16	8	0
72	I spat on a boy's suit	1	10	18	5	9	0	0
73	I shoved people out of the way in order to get onto a bus	1	14	11	12	4	1	0
74	I gave a head-butt to a boy	1	5	13	12	8	3	1

The acts rated by the public

		How violent is it?						
		Not the least bit violent (0)	Only very slightly violent (1)	A bit violent (2)	Fairly violent (3)	Quite violent (4)	Very violent (5)	Extremely violent (6)
75	I loosened the screws on the handlebars of a bike of one of the boys at school so that he would have a crash	0	0	0	5	5	24	9
76	I deliberately booted a boy in the stomach	0	0	1	3	9	23	7
77	I deliberately kicked a policeman in the face during a rough-up at a football match	0	0	0	3	5	20	15
78	I practised judo at a Youth Centre	33	5	4	1	0	0	0
79	I hurt a girl by twisting her ear and punching her	0	1	7	8	18	7	2
80	I had a fist fight with an Indian boy to show him our kind are better than his	1	3	6	15	10	5	3
81	I punched someone in the eye	0	2	8	10	14	6	3
82	I tramped through the flower garden of an old man down the street	1	3	8	11	12	7	1
83	I deliberately broke a mirror on the wall in a train	0	5	9	16	9	3	1
84	I broke off the radio aerial on someone's car	0	5	12	12	10	4	0
85	I stuck matches in a parking meter so it wouldn't work	5	17	14	4	2	0	1
86	I deliberately ripped a seat in a bus	2	3	14	9	8	7	0
87	I hit my cousin on the face with a heavy stick	0	0	2	4	15	16	6
88	I dug a hole about 3 feet deep and covered it over so my friends would fall into it	0	1	9	16	8	5	4
89	While my mates held him down, I burned a boy on the chest with a cigarette	0	0	2	0	9	14	18
90	I threw eggs at other spectators at a football match	0	8	9	17	6	3	0
91	I deliberately cut someone with a razor	0	0	0	2	5	17	19
92	I deliberately trod on the cat's paw	0	2	11	8	9	8	5
93	I began to strangle the cat with my hands	0	1	2	5	8	12	15
94	Although it wasn't true, I told my older sister that I saw her boyfriend drive past in his car with another girl sitting very close to him	4	10	13	11	2	3	0
95	My mates and I frightened a boy by pretending we were going to throw him over a balcony	1	1	7	7	14	10	3
96	I kept throwing stones in the water while my friends were fishing	20	13	6	3	1	0	0
97	I told a teacher who grabbed me by the shoulder to 'fuck off'	10	11	11	7	2	2	0
98	I made a rude finger sign at the woman next door	13	13	9	6	2	0	0
99	I played up a boy at school by throwing his shoes and case out of the window	2	12	16	13	0	0	0

The acts rated by the public

		How violent is it?						
		Not the least bit violent (0)	Only very slightly violent (1)	A bit violent (2)	Fairly violent (3)	Quite violent (4)	Very violent (5)	Extremely violent (6)
100	I called a boy a bastard while playing rugby	23	14	3	3	0	0	0
101	I called a coloured boy a 'wog'	9	11	14	5	3	1	0
102	I tripped a boy by putting my feet out when he was walking along the school corridor	4	13	14	11	1	0	0
103	I kicked my brother on the backside fairly hard	3	15	12	10	2	1	0
104	I kicked a teacher in the seat of the pants in front of the class, while he was writing on the board	1	2	15	14	9	2	0
105	I picked a fight with a boy and then, as arranged, I called for my mates who joined in against the other boy	0	0	6	8	11	12	6
106	I cut the tyres on a boy's bike	0	3	6	15	12	4	3
107	I deliberately dropped a lighted cigarette into a shopper's bag	0	0	3	17	8	12	3
108	I broke open a parking meter	2	7	15	8	5	5	1
109	I kicked over a whole line of plastic 'No Parking' signs	11	15	10	3	2	2	0
110	I chopped down a young tree that had just been planted in the park	3	9	9	12	6	3	1
111	I hit a boy with an iron bar	0	0	0	1	12	17	13
112	I deliberately cut a friend's thumb with a knife during a school row	0	0	0	14	10	11	8
113	I threw mudballs at another boy	5	14	12	10	1	1	0
114	I twisted a boy's arm until he yelled with pain	1	4	5	14	13	5	1
115	I fired air gun pellets at empty parked cars	3	4	10	14	9	3	0
116	I set fire to the contents of a rubbish bin that was standing against a shop door	1	0	9	12	16	3	2

Practice sheet and rating criteria for use in developing an illustrated scale

How violent is the act?

An act is considered to be violent if it could cause *hurt or harm of any kind* at all to the person on the receiving end. The hurt or harm may be physical or it may be mental or psychological. Both kinds of hurt or harm count when you are making your ratings of how violent the act is.

When you decide *how* violent the act is, we want you to think about the *amount* of hurt or harm that the act is intended to do or is likely to do, whichever is the worst.

In deciding *how* violent the act is, please choose your answer from the ones listed below. Pick the one that comes nearest to *how* violent you think the act was. Then put its number on to your rating sheet in the place shown for it.

6 – EXTREMELY VIOLENT
5 – VERY VIOLENT
4 – QUITE VIOLENT
3 – FAIRLY VIOLENT
2 – A BIT VIOLENT
1 – ONLY VERY SLIGHTLY VIOLENT
0 – NOT THE LEAST BIT VIOLENT

Your list of acts of violence	Your rating of how violent the act is (0 – 6)
I hit a boy hard on the nose with my fist	
I deliberately smashed up a boy's go-kart	
I threw an empty beer bottle down into a football crowd	
I teased my sister by calling her 'Spotty'	
I deliberately kicked a boy in the stomach	
I broke 2 windows in a neighbour's house by throwing stones at the windows when the neighbour was out	
I twisted a boy's arm until he cried out with pain	
I prodded a boy with my knife to make him do as I told him	
I drowned a litter of kittens	
I threw a giant cracker at a car driving along the main road	
I threw stones at cars on the motorway	

First form of illustrated rating scale and instructions for using it*

Instructions for rating acts of violence

1 *The total rating operation*

The purpose of this operation is to rate each of the acts of violence elicited from the boys. The rating is to be in terms of *HOW violent that act is.* The first step will be to write down an adequate (but brief) description of the act. The second step will be to use an 'illustrated rating scale' to allot ratings to each of the listed acts.

2 *Writing down a description of the act*

You are to enter a description of each act on the transfer sheet, seeing that the description has in it the following essential elements.

- Who did the act (e.g. 'I')?
- Who or what was the object of the act?
- What was the nature of the act?

Here are some examples of such a description:

- I bashed a boy's head against a wall
- I hit my sister over the head with a pillow
- I teased a boy by calling him a 'bastard'
- I knocked a boy off his bicycle as he rode past me
- I scratched the paint on a new car with a knife
- I hit a boy hard in the mouth with my fist
- I sent an obscene letter to someone
- I stuck match sticks into a parking meter so that it would not work

The class of information we need entered has to be such as will allow our coders to rate the acts in terms of:

> *the amount of intended or very probable hurt or harm that may be involved in the act itself or result directly from the act.* The hurt or harm I have in mind may be physical or psychological. And physical violence may of course be done to inanimate objects as well as to animate things.

You must enter the sort of information that will allow such a rating to be made.

So far I have not referred to the question of motivation or justification because these can have very little to do with the hurt or harm done. They matter to this project *but not to this particular rating.* In this instance what I want you to do is to enter the reason or justification *in brackets* just after your description of the act itself. Put it in brackets just after the description of the act. And keep it short. *This* way, the coders or raters will be helped to avoid the confusion inherent in a statement that is a mixture of an act *and* justification.

In writing out the nature of the act (and the bracketed motivation or justification), don't

*Replaced by modified form – see Appendix 4B

try to avoid the request for brevity by squeezing a lot of words into the space available on the Transfer Sheet. Keep your statement brief. You can do this by following the form set out in the example. You will also be helped by studying the set of further examples which make up the 'illustrated rating scale' that will be used by our coders and which is attached.

3 *What to do with acts that are given more than once (i.e. they have your minus sign against them)?*

You will of course go on entering a minus sign against any repeats that you get from the boy. But for this particular task, do not enter on the Transfer Sheet any items that have a minus against them. To do so would mean entering them twice on this cumulative Transfer Sheet and this is something we want to avoid.

W.A. Belson
17th November, 1972.

The first form of the illustrated rating scale

HOW VIOLENT IS THE ACT?

Judge degree of violence in terms of the amount of hurt or harm that was intended or what would result from the act. The hurt or harm may be physical or psychological or it may involve damage to an inanimate object. In making your ratings, be guided to a marked degree by the illustrated rating scale.

0 NOT VIOLENT AT ALL

I practised judo at a youth centre.

I have wrestled with friends in the park.

I had a friendly argument with someone.

1 ONLY VERY SLIGHTLY VIOLENT

I hid behind a door and when my sister came in I hit her over the head with a pillow.

I have teased boys by calling them nasty names.

I made rude finger signs at people in the street from the back of a school bus.

I wrote in big letters on the wall of a building .

I turned my back and just walked away when the teacher told me to do something I didn't want to.

One day after gym, I kept flicking my towel at a boy after he came out of the shower.

I lied to my mother about where I had been one night, because I didn't want to get into trouble.

I called a boy a bastard while playing rugby.

I kept throwing stones in the water while my friends were fishing.

I set up the Hi-Fi equipment in the garden and turned it up to torment the neighbours.

I told a policeman to 'Piss off and leave me alone'.

I threatened to give a boy a hiding.

2 A BIT VIOLENT

I had a fight with someone using bare fists and I hit him many times.

I played up a boy at school by throwing his shoes and case out of the window.

I tripped a boy by putting my foot out when he was walking along the school corridor.

I deliberately broke a school window with a stone.

I irritated a boy at school by jabbing him with a stick.

I put a book on top of a door so it would fall on whoever came through the door.

I made my little sister cry by pretending I had a handful of 'creepy crawlies'.

I shoved people out of the way in order to get onto a bus.

I kept poking my brother with a ruler to make him say he was sorry.

I deliberately hit a boy across the back with my school bag while we were waiting for the bus.

I stuck matches in a parking meter so it wouldn't work.

I spat on a boy's suit.

3 FAIRLY VIOLENT

I kicked a teacher in the seat of the pants in front of the class, while he was writing on the board.

I set fire to the contents of a rubbish bin that was standing against a shop door.

I deliberately broke a mirror on the wall in a train.

I gave a head-butt to a boy.

I cut the tyres on a boy's bike.

I fired air gun pellets at empty parked cars.

I threw the radio against the wall smashing it to bits.

I scratched the paint on a new car with a knife.

I twisted a boy's arm until he yelled with pain.

I shot hairpins at a boy from an elastic band.

I tramped through the flower garden of an old man down the street.

I deliberately ripped a seat in a bus.

4 QUITE VIOLENT	5 VERY VIOLENT	6 EXTREMELY VIOLENT
I knocked a boy off his bicycle as he rode past me.	I deliberately hit a boy on the face with a broken bottle.	I attacked someone in the street with an iron bar.
I deliberately ran into a parked car with a milk float.	I hit a boy with an iron bar.	I deliberately cut a boy's face with a penknife.
I deliberately dropped a lighted cigarette into a shopper's bag.	I tried to force a girl to have sexual intercourse with me.	
I broke off the radio aerial on someone's car.	While my mates held him down, I burned a boy on the chest with a cigarette.	
I threw pieces of brick at a girl.	I deliberately cut someone with a razor.	
I slashed the tyres of half a dozen cars in a car park.	I bashed a boy's head against a wall.	
I shot a cat with a pellet from an air rifle.	I deliberately kicked a boy in the crutch.	
I busted the telephone in a telephone box.	I deliberately kicked a policeman in the face during a rough-up at a football match.	
I swung a crowbar around to threaten someone.	I flogged the dog.	
I set a letter box on fire.	I deliberately booted a boy in the stomach.	
I threw a metal dart at a boy's foot.	I loosened the screws on the handlebars of a bike of one of the boys at school so that he would have a crash.	
My mates and I frightened a boy by pretending we were going to throw him over a balcony.	I kept hitting a horse with stones when the horse was in a small pen.	

The final form of the illustrated rating scale

HOW VIOLENT IS THE ACT?

In rating an act in terms of HOW VIOLENT it is, make the rating in terms of the amount of hurt or harm that is done to the person or thing or object on the receiving end. In judging this amount of violence keep in mind the three conditions set out on the right under (a), (b), (c).

1 ONLY VERY SLIGHTLY VIOLENT	2 A BIT VIOLENT	3 FAIRLY VIOLENT
Lying: I lied to my mother about where I had been one night, because I didn't want to get into trouble. Insult to authority: I turned by back and just walked away when the teacher told me to do something I didn't want to do. Swearing (and visual equivalent): I made rude finger signs at people in the street from the back of a school bus. I called a boy a bastard while playing rugby. I told a boy to: 'Piss off and leave me alone'. Verbal abuse, teasing, torment: I have teased boys by calling them nasty names. I annoyed my sister by calling her 'Dumbo' because she has big ears. I set up the Hi-Fi equipment in the garden and turned it up to torment the neighbours. I kept throwing stones in the water while my friends were fishing. Hurt to creatures (other than man): I stamped on some insects in the garden. Threat: I threatened to give a boy a hiding. Damage to property: I deliberately kicked over a line of plastic 'No Parking' signs. I fired a .22 rifle at bottles in the local rubbish dump. I wrote in big letters on the wall of a building. Physical teasing, torment, assault: I hid behind a door and when my sister came in I hit her over the head with a pillow. One day after gym, I kept flicking my towel at a boy after he came out of the shower. I squirted another boy with water, wetting his clothes. Slaps. Knuckles. Arguments (unspecified) Losing temper (unspecified)	Malicious lying: Although it wasn't true, I told my older sister that I saw her boyfriend drive past in his car with another girl sitting very close to him. Swearing: I told my parents to get stuffed. I told a teacher who grabbed me by the shoulder to 'fuck off'. Verbal abuse: I called a girl a slut. I called a coloured boy a 'wog'. I teased a Greek boy by saying insulting things about Greeks. With my mates, I teased and shouted at meths. drinkers and other old blokes in the park. Teasing, tormenting, without touching the person or recipient: I deliberately annoyed my parents by asking a neighbour for money. I took the mickey out of a new teacher by making fun of him in front of the rest of the class. I played up a boy at school by throwing his shoes and case out of the window. Damage to property: I deliberately broke a school window with a stone. I stuck matches in a parking meter so it wouldn't work. I spat on a boy's suit. Physical teasing, torment, assault, conflict (practised on another person) I put a book on top of a door so it would fall on whoever came through the door. I irritated a boy at school by jabbing him with a stick. I kept poking my brother with a ruler to make him say he was sorry. I tripped a boy by putting my foot out when he was walking along the school corridor. I threw mudballs at another boy. I deliberately hit a boy across the back with my school bag while we were waiting for the bus. I had a fight with someone using bare fists. I shoved people out of the way in order to get onto a bus. Bulldog. Chicken. Boxing.	Abuse/Torment without touching person: I sent obscene letters to someone. I rang someone up and just made breathing noises in the speaker. I did this four times in a row. Threat: I told a boy I would set my mates on him if he went on trying to go out with my girlfriend. Damage to property: I kicked and banged a cigarette machine to get money out of it. I broke open an electricity meter to get money. I scratched the paint on a new car with a knife. I let down the four tyres on a parked car. I cut the tyres on a boy's bike. I deliberately ripped a seat in a bus. I deliberately broke a mirror on the wall in a train. I set fire to the contents of a rubbish bin that was standing against a shop door. I tramped through the flower garden of an old man down the street. I chopped down a young tree that had just been planted in the park. Violence to creatures other than human: I shot a pigeon with a .22 rifle. I pulled the wings off flies at school. Physical violence to a person: I punched a boy in the stomach. I had a fist fight with an Indian boy to show him our kind are better than his. I kicked a teacher in the seat of the pants in front of the class, while he was writing on the board. I deliberately kicked a boy on the shin during a football match. I twisted a boy's arm until he yelled with pain. I gave a hard head-butt to a boy. I dug a hole about 3 feet deep and covered it over so my friends would fall into it. I shot hairpins at a boy from an elastic band. Splits. Deadleg.

NOTE

(a) The hurt or harm may not be directly and immediately involved in the act itself, but may nonetheless follow as a very probable consequence of the act (e.g. I dropped a bottle down onto a football crowd; I threw a brick at a boy). But this inclusive or extended thinking does not extend to purely fortuitous aftermaths of the act (e.g. I punched a boy who then got beaten by his mother for being in a fight).
(b) The hurt or harm may be physical or psychological and it may be inflicted on an animate or inanimate object. All these kinds of hurt or harm count in making your rating.
(c) To count at all the act has to be other than purely accidental. But beware of the boy for whom everything is an accident.

4 — QUITE VIOLENT

Threat:
My mates and I frightened a boy by pretending we were going to throw him over a balcony.
I swung a crowbar around to threaten someone.
I threatened to kill my father.

Damage to property:
I deliberately ran into a parked car with a milk float.
I broke off the radio aerial on someone's car.
I slashed the tyres of half a dozen cars in a car park.
I set a letter box on fire.
I busted the telephone in a telephone box.

Hurt to animal:
I stamped on the dog's tail to make him get out of the way.
I deliberately trod on the cat's paw.
I shot a cat with a pellet from an air rifle.

Action likely to harm some person:
I threw slates off the roof of an old house, making them fall into the street below.
I deliberately dropped a lighted cigarette into a shopper's bag.

Physical violence to a person:
I knocked a boy off his bicycle as he rode past me.
I picked a fight with a boy and then, as arranged, I called for my mates who joined in against the other boy.
I threw a metal dart at a boy's foot.
I deliberately cut a friend's thumb with a knife during a school row.
I threw pieces of brick at a girl.

5 — VERY VIOLENT

Malicious lying:
I told a boy his mother had been killed in a car accident just to upset him.

Damage to property:
I broke into a house and smashed up everything I could find.
I took a hammer to a car and laid into it.

Hurt to animals:
I flogged the dog.
I kept hitting a horse with stones when the horse was in a small pen.
I began to strangle the cat with my hands.

Action likely to severely harm a person:
I loosened the screws on the handlebars of a bike of one of the boys at school so that he would have a crash.

Physical assault to a person:
I deliberately kicked a boy in the crutch, as hard as I could.
I deliberately booted a boy in the stomach.
I bashed a boy's head against a wall.
I deliberately kicked a policeman in the face during a rough-up at a football match.
While my mates held him down, I burned a boy on the chest with a cigarette.
I deliberately hit a boy on the face with a broken bottle.
I tried to force a girl to have sexual intercourse with me.
I fired an airgun at boys passing in the street outside my home.
I hit my cousin on the face with a heavy stick.

6 — EXTREMELY VIOLENT

Malicious lying:
I rang the airport to pretend there was a bomb on an aircraft.

Extreme damage to property:
I set fire to a large building.

Extreme physical damage to a person:
I fired a revolver at someone.

Weighting the scale items in the illustrated scale

We have over the past month or so been using an illustrated scale as a means of rating different acts of violence in terms of HOW violent they are.

As a final step in the scoring system, I need your help in giving weights to each of the six classes of violence set out on the illustrated scale. We have allotted the score of 0 to the group at present labelled 'not the least bit violent' (0) and a weight of 100 to the list labelled' extremely violent' (6).

Your job is to consider what weights should be given to each of the intermediate lists. In doing this, have in mind the standard or criterion you used in rating the individual acts, namely the amount of hurt or harm or damage that is caused by the act concerned or is likely to be caused by it.

It does not follow at all that the weights you allocate will be spread at equal intervals along the scale from 0 – 100. Consider each list in its own right and decide where *on average* it should go on the scale running from 0 – 100, giving 0 and 100 the values specified above. If you feel that a single list (e.g. all those under 'very violent') is made up of acts of very different degrees of violence, consider what that range is but work towards an *average* for the whole list under that term. Enter your allotted average in the relevant box below.

Above all DON'T DISCUSS THE WEIGHTS YOU ALLOT WITH ANYONE ELSE.

Not the least bit violent	0
Only very slightly violent	
A bit violent	
Fairly violent	
Quite violent	
Very violent	
Extremely violent	100

CHAPTER 7

THE CONSTRUCTION OF MEASURES OF BOYS' ATTITUDES TOWARDS VIOLENCE AND TOWARDS THEIR SOCIAL ENVIRONMENT

Contents

7 THE CONSTRUCTION OF MEASURES OF BOYS' ATTITUDES TOWARDS VIOLENCE AND TOWARDS THEIR SOCIAL ENVIRONMENT

INTRODUCTION

This chapter is concerned with the development of measures of the attitudinal and reactive variables featured in the following hypotheses.

High exposure to television violence

1 reduces the degree to which boys are considerate towards other people (e.g. a reduction in courtesy and good manners, a tendency not to care about other people);

2 reduces the degree to which boys respect various forms of authority (e.g. police, teachers, football referees, parents);

3 makes violence generally more attractive to boys;

4 makes boys less likely to object to the idea of violence in the world generally;

5 leads boys to accept violence as a normal part of human nature ('normal part of human nature' was later changed to 'an intrinsic or inevitable part of human nature');

6 leads boys to accept violence as a means of solving their problems (e.g. use of violence to get what they want);

7 hardens boys (i.e. renders them more callous) in relation to directly experienced 'near' violence such as occurs in the home, street, areas which boys frequent;

8 hardens boys (i.e. renders them more callous) in relation to indirectly experienced 'distant' violence — mediated by a form of mass media such as the press, television;

9 increases the degree to which boys have angry and bitter feelings towards their social environment;

10 produces symptoms of anxiety, nervousness and emotional instability in boys.

The developmental work connected with the dependent variables in hypotheses 1-6, 9 and 10 is described on pages 257-64. That connected with the dependent variables in hypotheses 7 and 8 involved certain differences in developmental procedure and is described separately on pages 267-71.

In referring to the dependent variables in hypotheses 1-6, 8 and 9, there is a semantic problem in that some of them, hypothesis 10 especially, are more 'emotional states' than attitudes. Ordinarily one might have dealt with them separately, but they were brought together here because measurement of any one of them calls for an identical construction procedure. This however raises the question of how one refers to them all with any sort of brevity. The practice adopted here has been to refer to them as 'attitudes' but the reader is asked to interpret this usage of the term as convenient shorthand for 'attitudes and/or emotional states'.

Certain other hypotheses relating broadly to attitudes and outlook were considered for investigation, but were not proceeded with for various reasons as set out in chapter 2.

SUMMARY OF CONSTRUCTION TECHNIQUES USED

The procedures used in developing the required measuring techniques were principally those of Thurstone's Equal Appearing Interval Technique [1], though some variations were introduced where deemed necessary. The construction steps used were as follows. Thus, *separately for each attitude:*

1. Many statements were brought together, each thought to reflect or embody some degree of that attitude.
2. Relevant judges rated these statements on a continuum to indicate the degree to which they thought the statements embodied or reflected the attitude.
3. Analytical methods were used to identify those 12 to 15 of the statements about which the judges tended to agree with regard to their ratings and which, taken together, were fairly evenly spread along the rating continuum.
4. Each of the selected statements was given the value of the scalar point at which the median of its distribution of ratings fell.
5. In *using* the selected statements to measure the attitude in a given boy, that boy would be asked to endorse each of the statements with which he agreed and his attitude score would be the arithmetical average of the scalar values of all the statements endorsed.

The construction strategy outlined in 1-4 above was used with respect to each of the 8 attitudinal type variables specified in the hypotheses listed as 1-6 and 9, 10 in the introduction. Similarly for the variables in hypotheses 7 and 8 but reported later in this chapter.

THE TECHNIQUES IN DETAIL

Originating the statements for each attitudinal dimension

Initial challenging of concepts. As a preliminary to originating statements, each of the attitudinal or reactive dimensions referred to in the hypotheses was closely examined to ensure that its meaning properly reflected the views which led to its formulation. For example, a critical appraisal was made of the degree to which the concept 'consideration for others' truly summed up the views and the evidence on the basis of which that concept had been formulated. This process was meant also to establish, in a fairly practical way, a relevant mental set in those responsible for originating the Thurstone-type statements.

Main sources of statements. In chapter 2 are set out the several sources of the hypotheses that would be investigated, namely:

1 test-room work with boys and with parents of boys;
2 personal interviews with boys and their parents;
3 interviews with television production staff and others;
4 the ideas of the research team;
5 the existing literature dealing with television violence;
6 press clippings.

From these sources came a wealth of opinions and indications about specific ways in which attitudes might be changed through exposure to television violence. Quite a lot of this material consisted of potential attitude statements and these items were shaped into statements by the research team. In addition, team members themselves generated a large number of further statements.

For the eight attitudinal dimensions, the average number of statements was 42.

Challenging and modifying attitudinal statements. These statements were then subjected to a challenging procedure. This was intended: to eliminate statements that did not appear to relate principally to the attitudinal dimension in terms of which the measuring technique was to be developed; to eliminate or suitably modify statements wrongly referring to another dimension as well; to identify and then to modify statements that appeared to be ambiguous, unclear, over-long.

Clarity and simplicity of expression were particularly important in that the different statements had to be readily understood by 13-16 year old boys [2] many of whom could be expected to have reading and/or intellectual difficulties. To this end, the basic principles of question design were followed in drafting or re-drafting the statements [3]. After these two kinds of steps had been taken, the remaining statements were subjected to a trial rating process by research and administrative staff at the Centre with a view to detecting (and correcting) further weaknesses in them.

Following such challenging and checking procedures, there remained between 30 and 50 statements per attitudinal dimension and these totals were regarded as acceptable as a basis for the next step in the construction procedure, namely the rating of the statements on the Thurstone model.

The statements within one of the eight sets are listed below as an example.

List 7.1
Statements relating to one of the attitudinal dimensions

Concerning: RESPECT FOR AUTHORITY

1 Obedience and respect for authority are the most important things children should learn
2 What young people need most is strict discipline
3 Children should love and respect their parents
4 I ignore 'keep off the grass' signs
5 Boys deserve the punishment they get from teachers at school
6 There is no need to take any notice of what your parents tell you.
7 The police are thugs
8 The majority of policemen are decent people
9 People who are put in charge of things at school are usually creeps or goody-goodies
10 Playing tricks on the school caretaker is good fun
11 Being cheeky to the school caretaker can be good fun
12 I don't think the police deserve respect
13 Playing-up teachers at school is OK because most boys do it

14 People ought to help the police with their enquiries
15 I don't think that most school teachers deserve any respect
16 If you don't want to do as the school teacher tells you, don't do it
17 Swearing at teachers is OK
18 I don't see why we shouldn't swear at our parents
19 In sport, you should accept the referee's decision without cheeking him or swearing at him
20 The Church does good work and deserves our support
21 The Church is full of religious cranks who try to push religion down your throat
22 You should take notice of your parents' advice
23 It's quite a laugh to ring the police up and say there's a bomb about to go off
24 One should treat one's parents like any other adult
25 You shouldn't answer your parents back
26 Cheeking your parents is OK if in fun
27 Cheeking the teachers at school is OK if in fun
28 The referee's word is final
29 Traffic Wardens should be given more credit for the work which they do
30 Traffic Wardens are sometimes a little bit unfair
31 Bishops, vicars and Church officials do not practise what they preach; they are, in other words, hypocrites
32 The older generation are a lot of 'squares' and fuddy-duddies
33 Politicians are only concerned with their own interests
34 The police are unjust
35 Parents think they know best, but they're no better than anyone else really
36 I don't think my parents know what they are talking about half the time
37 Grown-ups should not be allowed to boss kids around
38 Most teachers are very helpful
39 If a law or rule is sensible, people should obey it
40 All rules have got good reasons behind them
41 Many adults are too stupid to deserve respect from children
42 Children should always be polite to grown-ups
43 It is unforgivable for a boy to hit his mother
44 There are some teachers who deserve it when a boy hits them back
45 The police have 'got it in' for teenagers

Judging the statements

The judges who would rate the attitudinal statements. Whereas Thurstone's technique is usually interpreted to require that a panel of intellectually superior persons should be responsible for the rating or grading or judging of the statements on the grading continuum, it was regarded as necessary, in this case, that the judges be ordinary boys aged 12-17 years and their parents.

There were two linked reasons for this decision. Since the statements relating to a given attitudinal dimension were to be used to interpret or measure the attitudes of 12-17 year old boys, it was necessary that the scale values attached to those statements should properly reflect their attitudinal significance in the world of 12-17 year old boys. For example, it is possible that a panel of school teachers would regard the statement 'Answering teachers back is OK' as reflecting a major degree of disrespect for authority – whereas boys in today's society may perhaps regard such a view as a minor (and perhaps even justified) departure from an overall pattern of respect for authority, including respect for teachers. One could of course overstate this sort of argument, but in general it is desirable that the values and the interpretations of the judges should be the same as those of the boys who would use the full procedure and be evaluated in terms of their interpretations of the statements.

The second reason for departing from the practice of using a panel of experts as judges is that the attitudinal hypotheses with which we are concerned were derived principally from questioning 12-17 year old boys and their parents. Hence it is *their* interpretations of the terms in the hypotheses that are the relevant ones and *their* gradings of the statements in terms of such concepts that, likewise, are the relevant ones.

In the circumstances, it was planned that the judges invited to take part should be sufficient in number to yield at least 50 judgements (from 25 boys and 25 adults) on each of the statements in each attitudinal dimension.

The recruitment of the judges. Boys and their parents were recruited (a) through a special recruitment 'survey' conducted in Greater London; through an arrangement with a market research organisation which brings large numbers of adult members of the public to a London centre for testing procedures; through an arrangement with a comprehensive school. Approximately 105 persons in all took part.

With respect to the special recruiting survey, the recruiters aimed to secure promises from London boys and their parents to attend evening judging sessions at the Centre. Recruiters were assigned to six areas of different socio-economic levels and each was given a quota in terms of the ages of the boys (i.e. an equal number for each year in the range 12-17 years). The recruiter was instructed to arrange that each participating boy be accompanied by one of his parents. Invitees were informed that the evening's activities would include a judging session and that their views about social issues involving young people would be asked for; that boys and parents would be in separate groups; that refreshments would be served on arrival; that fares would be refunded and that a fee of £1 each would be paid to parents and to sons. Those promising to attend were given an appointment card, a covering letter and a map for getting to the Survey Research Centre. Young boys almost always agreed to come with a parent, whereas many of the older boys preferred to come alone. All rating took part on Centre premises in groups.

The second source of judges was a comprehensive school in East London. Boys were selected from the school roll with a control over social class and age and through the school an invitation was issued to their parents to take part as well. The boys were processed in groups at the school during the day, while the co-operating parents went through the same form of group session on school premises at night.

The third set of judges, consisting of parents of boys aged 12-17 years, was drawn from Londoners attending evening research sessions conducted by Midas Research. These people went through the grading procedure in large group sessions at the Commonwealth Institute.

The materials used in the judging process. There were in all eight sets of statements, each numbering between 31 and 50. Each set was to be judged or graded in terms of a specific dimension.

For each dimension, the 31-50 statements relating to it were typed on individual small cards, making up a 31-50 item pack. For the eight dimensions there were thus eight packs of cards (each with statements relating to a different dimension) for each judge.

Another item of material used for the judging test was a set of continuous numerical rating scales, one for each of the attitudinal or reactive dimensions. The physical forms of two such scales are shown in diagram 7.1.

Key elements in each type of scale were:

1. *The question to judges set out above the scale.* The purpose of this question was both to identify the attitudinal or reactive dimension in terms of which the judging of statements was to be done and to orient the judge to the sorting of statement cards on the scale concerned.
2. The naming of the extremities of the scales and the identification of the mid-point in each.

Diagram 7.1 Forms of rating scale used

HOW ATTRACTIVE OR OTHERWISE DOES THIS BOY FIND VIOLENCE?

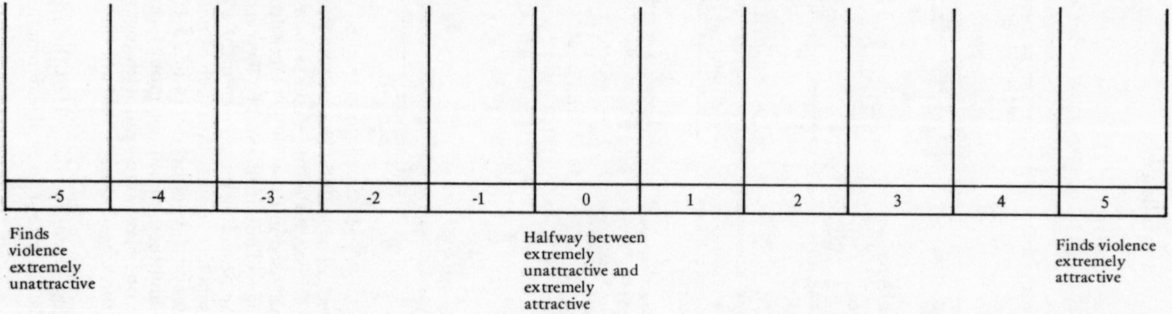

-5	-4	-3	-2	-1	0	1	2	3	4	5
Finds violence extremely unattractive					Halfway between extremely unattractive and extremely attractive					Finds violence extremely attractive

TO WHAT EXTENT DOES THE BOY SAYING THIS ACCEPT VIOLENCE AS A WAY TO SOLVE HIS PROBLEMS?

0	1	2	3	4	5	6	7	8	9	10
Definitely does not accept violence as a way to solve his problems					Halfway between fully accepts and definitely does not accept					Fully accepts violence as a way to solve his problems

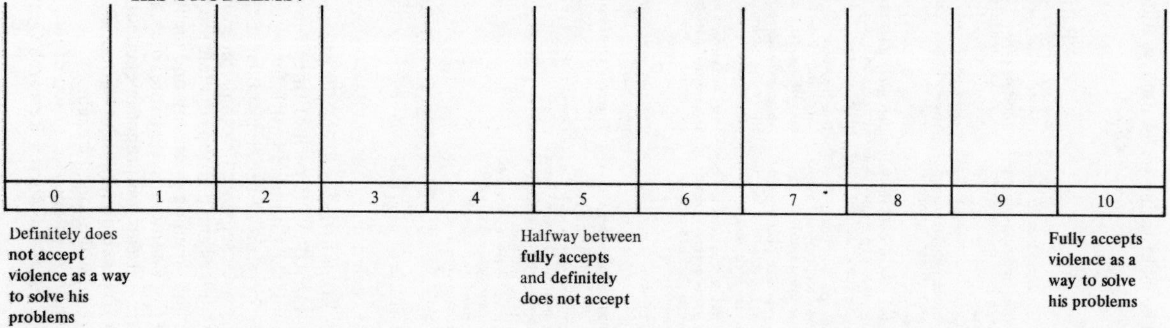

The eight rating scales used by judges were designated as follows.

Table 7.1
Rating scale designations

Orienting questions by type of attitudinal or reactive measure	Minus or zero extremity designations	Plus extremity designations	Scale in miniature
How much consideration has this boy got for other people?	Absolutely no consideration at all.	The highest possible consideration.	0 … 10
To what extent does the boy saying this accept violence as a way to solve his problems?	Definitely does not accept violence as a way to solve his problems.	Fully accepts violence as a way to solve his problems.	0 … 10
How angry and bitter does this boy feel (toward everything around him)?	This boy feels extremely angry and bitter towards everything around him.	This boy is extremely good-tempered or carefree.	- 5 … 0 … +5
How much respect does the boy saying this have for the authority mentioned?	Absolutely no respect at all for the authority mentioned.	The highest possible respect for the authority mentioned.	0 … 10
To what extent does the boy saying this accept violence as a normal part of human existence?	Does not accept violence as a normal part of human existence.	Accepts violence as a normal part of human existence.	0 … 10
How nervous is this boy?	This boy is extremely nervous.	This boy is extremely calm and relaxed.	- 5 … 0 … +5
How attractive does this boy find violence?	This boy finds violence extremely unattractive.	This boy finds violence extremely attractive.	- 5 … 0 … +5
If someone agrees with the statement on this card, how much do you think he objects to the idea of violence? Place each card in a space below to indicate how much the person objects to violence.	Doesn't object at all.	Strongly objects.	1 … 7 *

*Adopted as a 7-point scale from other parts of the enquiry.

The administration of the judging sessions. As stated on page 260, the judging procedure was carried out in each of three venues: the Survey Research Centre, a comprehensive school, the Commonwealth Institute. The procedure used in these three places differed only in terms of the steps taken at the reception stage. Thus at the Survey Research Centre boys were separated from parents on arrival, thereby providing on a given night a group of boy judges and a group of adult judges working in separate rooms. As much as possible, the boys coming in on any one night were of similar ages (i.e. either 13-14 or 15-16). At the Commonwealth Institute, only adults attended and they met in two groups, one per night. At the comprehensive school, boys from the one class were dealt with together by research personnel of the Centre. Parents came to the school at night and did their judging in groups of about 12 each.

The size of any one group of judges varied with the venue and day. Thus the groups working at the Survey Research Centre varied in size from four to twelve depending upon the outcome of the recruiting survey. At the comprehensive school, group size varied from between 10 and 15, while at the Commonwealth Institute group size was 30 (adults). Obviously larger groups were more difficult to process than smaller groups, but in all cases it was possible to exercise a high degree of control over the behaviour of the group members (i.e. the judges).

The administrator told the group in broad terms what they would be doing during the session, namely grading people on the basis of statements attributed to them. He then illustrated this procedure with an example of a physical kind. This example involved the grading of people for *physical strength* on the basis of what those people said about their own strength. The administrator personally delivered the illustration, aiming through it to demonstrate the following points.

(a) The line with the sections on it was a type of ruler or scale, such that the statements at its ends showed what its lowest and highest values were and the statement at its middle showed what its middle value was.

(b) The basic question throughout the judging operation would be: 'Suppose a boy said . . . (i.e. the *statement on a card*), where would you place him on this ruler or scale?'. Whatever point on the scale this was, the statement card considered was to be sorted there.

(c) A judge was fully at liberty to change the position of any sorted card as he worked through a given pack, it being likely that the sorting of some fresh card would require that a space be opened up between two cards at that time sorted next to each other.

The administrator next demonstrated the same operation in a psychological context, demonstrating the rating procedure on a scale of 'friendliness'. In this case, statement cards were sorted in response to the question 'How friendly is this boy?'

The judging operation. The judges were now prepared for their first rating operation. Each was given a giant-sized rating scale and a pack of statement cards relevant to that scale. They were told to read the question at the top of the rating card (e.g. How much consideration has this boy got for other people?) and then each of the three grading terms linked to the scale itself (i.e. the two extremity terms and the middle term). After this, they were instructed to take up the pack of statement cards and to start sorting them along the scale. They were reminded to read each statement carefully and then to place it at that point on the scale that best described or graded the boy who would make such a statement. They were also encouraged to use all the spaces along the scale and were reminded to re-sort any cards as often as they liked.

While the judges worked at their grading task, staff members moved about the room on the lookout for difficulties or obvious mistakes and attempted to clarify the procedure and the rules wherever necessary. They were not, however, to take over any grading activities *for* a judge.

Upon completing the grading of the pack of statement cards, a judge was to write on each sorted card the number of the scale position to which he had assigned it. He then put all the sorted cards back into a pack and fixed it with a rubber band ready for collection by a test room attendant.

As a judge finished with a single pack of statements and a specific scale, he was given the next pack of statement cards and the rating scale relevant to that pack and worked through the second of his grading procedures. This process was repeated for each new statement pack handed out.

The principal difficulties encountered by judges were: a tendency on the part of some of them to use the scale as if it had only three scalar positions on it (i.e. two end positions and a middle position); difficulties in grasping the scaling concept especially with respect to the bi-polar scales; reading difficulties. Special attention was given to detecting and to overcoming such problems.

The time taken by the judges to complete the rating operation for a single statement pack varied quite a lot but averaged out at something like fifteen minutes. Taking rest pauses into account, judges tended to process five statement packs per session. Over a period of approximately two months, the statement packs for all eight attitude dimensions were dealt with in this way by about 50 judges each (namely 25 boys and 25 adults).

Analysing results and selecting statements

For each statement in each statement pack, the judging operation had produced a distribution of at least 50 ratings on a relevant scale. The data was then processed through computer facilities to yield the following information about each statement:

1 Its median position on its rating scale for
   (a) boys alone
   (b) adults alone
   (c) boys and adults taken together.

2 Its semi-interquartile range on the rating scale, also for boys alone, for adults alone, for boys and adults taken together.

The results for boys and for adults were broadly similar.

For the 31-50 statements relating to a given attitudinal dimension, the following criteria were applied for selecting those 10-15 of them most suitable for providing a Thurstone-type measurement of the attitude concerned. Thus for a statement to be selected:

1 Its median value would be approximately the same for boys and for adults (i.e. not more than one scale unit apart), and its semi-interquartile range should, for both boys and adults, be less than 2.00 (later dropped to 1.50).

2 It had to contribute to the selected composite of statements in such a way that the median values [5] of selected statements were fairly evenly spread along the attitudinal continuum.

Two further adjustments to the selection procedure were made. If the selected statements included two that were fairly similar in subject matter, then if possible one of them was replaced by a statement with a similar median value but different subject matter. Secondly, certain of the selected statements, though meeting all the above criteria, appeared on intuitive inspection to relate substantially to some other attitude in addition to (or even instead of) that in terms of which it had been selected. Such statements were either replaced by others with acceptable median values and semi-interquartile ranges or (if there were no such statements available) were left out altogether.

The eight sets of statements selected in this manner were now ready for use in a pilot operation.

The responses to be offered to boys in measuring their attitudes

In using composites of statements for measuring attitudes, the usual procedure is to ask respondents to say of each statement whether he agrees or disagrees with it or is undecided. After this, the average of the median values of his endorsed statements is calculated to provide an index of the respondent's attitudes. However, a trial of the new attitude measuring composites, conducted on a wide range of boys at a Secondary Modern school, showed that many boys were agreeing with statements with which they were in fact in only *partial* agreement, and that this was leading to their endorsement of more than half of the statements in the system – thereby reducing its discriminative power. Accordingly, it was proposed that the response category 'agree' be given protection by splitting the response category 'disagree' into 'strongly disagree' and 'slightly disagree'. The offer of answers was thus

Strongly disagree/slightly disagree/agree/don't know

The scoring system remained unchanged however, with only the statements endorsed as 'agree' contributing to a boy's 'score'. [6]

The manner of presenting statements to boys

It still remained to devise a system or systems for presenting the different sets of statements to boys – that is, in conducting the measurements for which they had been devised.

Whereas Thurstone's scaling composites are commonly presented as a printed list, each statement with a choice of reply against it, it was regarded as essential that in the present case steps should be taken to make the attitude measuring operation as practical and as attention-getting and as interesting as possible. This view was taken (i) because of the youthfulness of many of the boys who were to be interviewed; (ii) because of the near-illiteracy that was expected to be found amongst at least 10 per cent of them, (iii) because attitude measurement (using the eight composites) was to be only *part* of an interview lasting for about three hours [7].

For each of the eight composites of statements, each statement was printed on a large card (8 in. by 5 in.), the cards for the different composites being in different colours. Four of the eight sets of cards were to be sorted into coloured bags fixed on the wall and labelled:

Strongly disagree/slightly disagree/agree/don't know

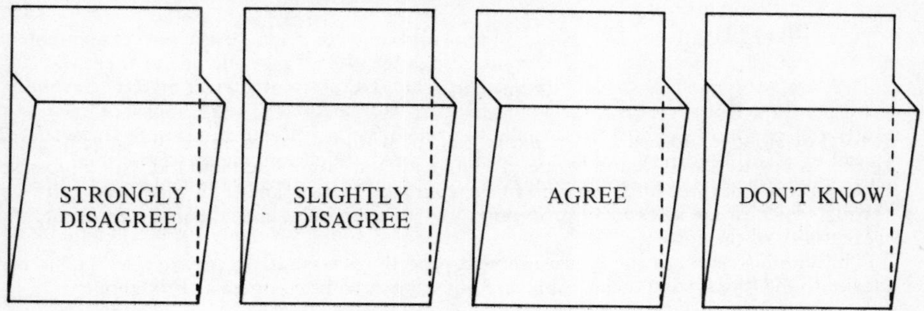

In dealing with a given set of cards, the boy read out what was on the first card and sorted it, read out what was on the next card and sorted it, and so on for all the cards in that particular pack. The interviewer listened in order to be sure that the statement was being correctly read by the boy.

The other four of the eight sets of cards were to be dealt with in a different way, simply to provide variety for the boy. Boys were seated in front of a display screen, with the interviewer on the other side of it. The interviewer showed one card at a time to the boy through a large rectangular aperture in the screen, without being seen himself. The boy was required to read out aloud what was on the card and then to press one of four 'buttons' on a small console in front of him, the buttons being labelled in the same way as were the bags used in the other system. Thus if the boy pushed the 'slightly disagree' button, one section of the screen lit up to display 'slightly disagree'. This told the interviewer what choice had been made by the boy (allowing him to code it) and it also served to catch the boy's attention.

These two methods of presentation were to be integrated within the total interview at the Survey Research Centre, but to be spaced out as necessary.

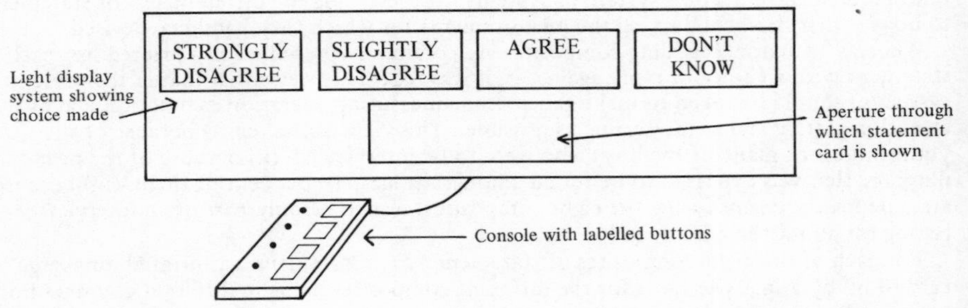

Piloting the procedure

A total of 30 boys took part in the *piloting* of the whole intensive interview, being brought to the Survey Research Centre by car after an earlier at-home interview and with a promise of £3 for the full three hour session. In the course of this session 25 of them were put through the attitude assessment procedures and an appraisal was made of the apparent workability of the system.

The administration of the 8 measurement procedures was satisfactory in that the interviewer found the system manageable and boys appeared to co-operate throughout.

In addition certain other critical procedures were at this stage brought to bear on the different measures. Thus:

(a) An analysis was made, for each of the measures, of the degree to which their constituent statements were endorsed, special note being made of the relative discriminative power of those statements.

(b) Further critical appraisal was made of the statements, with special reference to the undimensionality of the attitudinal concept as defined in the hypothesis; verbal ambiguities or difficulties; the semi-interquartile ranges of statements.

On the basis of this examination, certain changes were made. The most substantial of them involved the hypothesis that 'long-term exposure to television violence leads boys to accept violence as a normal part of human existence.' The evidence decisively pointed to the dependent variable in this hypothesis being two-dimensional in that it could be interpreted both as a view that violence is an intrinsic part of human nature and as a view that violence is widespread and usual amongst people (though not necessarily intrinsic to human nature). Both notions had been put forward in the hypothesis development stage of the work, but the more recurrently offered view had to do with violence being *intrinsic* to human nature. Accordingly the hypothesis was re-stated in terms of this concept. It also appeared that the dependent variable so defined was dichotomous in character: you either agreed or disagreed with the view that man is intrinsically violent. Accordingly a new set of statements was generated, some reflecting agreement with the view that man is intrinsically violent and the others reflecting disagreement. These statements were not to be given scalar values but were to be scored 2 or 1 or 0 according to whether they supported (2) or opposed (0) the view referred to in the hypothesis. The value (1) was allotted where the respondent endorsed the response 'don't know'.

Within the *other* scales, some of the statements were dropped for one or more of the following reasons: lack of simplicity or clarity; possible multi-dimensionality; a rather high interquartile range.

The eight sets of statements, as used in the different attitude measures, are set out in Appendix 1.

Scoring boys for attitude/reaction tendencies

The different attitude measures were administered to the sample of 1,565 boys and scores were calculated on the following patterns. For each of the seven Thurstone scales (relating to hypotheses 1-4, 6, 9-10 as set out on page 256), the median values of the endorsed statements were aggregated and this total was divided by the total number of those endorsed statements. This is the standard Thurstone method. For the measurement of 'acceptance of violence as an intrinsic part of human nature' (see hypothesis 5 on page 256 score was the weighted total of reactions to all nine statements: (2) for agreement with a statement supportive of such a view, (0) for disagreement, (1) for 'no opinion'. See scoring details in Appendix 1.

DERIVING AND USING MEASURES OF CALLOUSNESS

The technique used for constructing measures of various attitudes, as detailed on pages 257-64.

was in general applied also in constructing measures of boys' callousness in relation to violence going on in the world around them. There were to be two such measures, namely:

(i) callousness in relation to directly experienced 'near' violence, such as occurs in the home, on the street, in areas which boys frequent;

(ii) callousness in relation to indirectly experienced 'distant' violence mediated by a mass medium such as press, television, radio.

These were the two dependent variables featured in hypotheses 7 and 8 on page 256. Ordinarily the construction of techniques for measuring them would have been presented along with the description of the construction of the other attitude measures featured in this chapter. But there were certain differences and additional steps which make it desirable to describe their construction separately.

The general form of the proposed measures

It was intended that for each measure, the type of violence referred to in the callousness variable (e.g. 'near' violence) should be presented in specific forms (e.g. pictures of *specific acts* of violence) rather than in broad descriptive terms (e.g. 'violence that you see going on around you day by day'). It was also intended that boys' reactions to these presentations of violence should be assessed through their rejection or endorsement of statements expressing different degrees of callousness, for example:

'I would feel sorry for the person on the receiving end';
'What other people do is no concern of mine';
'I would think it a bit of a laugh';
'I would feel shocked by it';

So the construction process required:

(a) that there be developed or selected (i) a varied set of stimuli presenting 'near' violence and (ii) a varied set of stimuli presenting 'distant' violence as ordinarily presented through the mass media;

(b) that for each of the two sets of stimuli there be developed a set of statements empirically established as implying certain degrees of callousness and together constituting a scale running from a high degree of callousness to a complete absence of callousness.

The visual stimuli: 'near' violence

Following piloting and other selective procedures, six visual stimuli were used in the test procedure. The six depicted:

(i) a boy about to trip an old man who is walking with a cane;

(ii) a man in a nearby flat beating up a woman (in a form of domestic violence);

(iii) a boy being punched and pushed around by a gang in an alley;

(iv) a youth cutting the face of another youth with a broken bottle;

(v) a boy being held down while another boy kicks him in the ribs;

(vi) a man flogging a dog.

The first three were used on the first half of the sample and the second three on the remaining half. All six are shown in Appendix 3. The reason for this particular temporal arrangement was that the inclusion of all six in the one interview took more time to administer than was available in the one interview, bearing in mind that many other tests had also to be delivered. On the other hand, it was highly desirable to base the assessment of 'near-violence callousness' on a greater array of violent acts than could be presented by just three acts.

The visual stimuli: 'distant' violence

Six visual stimuli were used in the assessment of callousness regarding distant violence presented through the mass media. The six were:

(i) a picture of the wreckage of an air crash (under the caption 'Burst tyre blamed for air crash in which 72 Britons died');

(ii) a picture of police activity (under a headline 'Bid to kill Kray witness in London');

(iii) a picture of a ship on fire (under the caption '84 die trapped in ring of fire');

(iv) a picture of Vietnam children running from a bombed village (under the caption 'Flight from hell');

(v) a picture of Bangladesh troops in a public bayoneting of alleged collaborators with 'West Pakistan' forces;

(vi) a picture of a girl in Northern Ireland tied to a pole after having her head shorn and being tarred (under a caption 'The IRA's revenge on girls').

Here too the first three stimuli were used on the first half of the sample and the second three on the remaining half. All six are given in Appendix 3.

The selection of statements for use in measuring reaction to the visual stimuli

Near violence. In line with the Thurstone technique of scale construction, the first step in the construction process was the creation of a pool of statements thought to imply various degrees of callousness on the part of persons endorsing them as true. For 'near' violence, the pool included 25 statements as set out in Appendix 2. These were processed through the Thurstone judgement system in the same way as was done in developing the other scales featured in this chapter. More specifically, a panel of boys and adult judges, 54 in all, rated the 25 statements on a 7-point scale running from extreme callousness to a complete absence of callousness. For each of the 25 statements it was thus possible to calculate a 'mean value' on the callousness scale and a measure of the scatter of ratings along that scale (i.e. the semi-interquartile range of the ratings for that statement). These values are set against the 25 statements in Appendix 2.

On the basis of these median and range values, it was possible to select twelve statements which, as a set, were well spaced along the 7-point continuum and which excluded statements with large semi-interquartile ranges. The chosen twelve are marked with an asterisk in Appendix 2.

Distant violence. The same type of operation was carried out with respect to 'distant' violence. The original 26 statements are shown in Appendix 2 each with its median value and semi-interquartile range set against it. The 9 selected statements are marked with an asterisk.

Using the two techniques in the intensive interview

The administration of these two measures was sectionalised in the sense that the exposure of a boy to the six visual stimuli was not done all in the one sequence. Rather, exposure to stimulus 1 in the 'near-violence' set was followed by two quite different attitude tests before the interviewer returned to the presentation of further visual stimuli in the callousness testing sequence. This was done to avoid boring or tiring the boy with the repetitive sorting or examination of the same set of statements about reactions.

What follows is a general outline of the administrative procedure used in securing reactions to the first of the visual stimuli.

(a) The boy was shown the first of the 'near-violence' pictures (dealing with 'tripping an old man up'). He was asked to study the picture and to read out the statement that was printed on it:

> 'You are walking down the street when you happen to see a boy you don't know about to trip an old man who is walking with a cane.'

(b) The boy was then asked to tell the interviewer what he saw in the picture (the purpose of this being to try to force the boy into perceiving the different elements in the picture).

(c) The boy was then given the first of the statements in the 'near-violence' callousness test (reading: 'I would hope that somebody would do something to stop it') and told that his job was to decide whether or not that statement was what he himself would think if he came across what he saw in the picture. He was further told that if the statement *was* what he would feel, he should put the card bearing it into one of three bags on the wall, namely the one labelled 'agree', but to use the 'disagree' bags if what was on the card was *not* what he would feel. There was also a bag for 'don't know'. The instructional introduction was quite lengthy and included appeals for care and for absolute frankness. Following this, the boy was asked to look again at the picture, read out aloud the statement on the card and then to put the card into the bag that came nearest to what he believed.

(d) When this was done, the boy sorted each of the other cards in the 'near-violence' pack, being required, for each card, to look at the picture and to read aloud the statement on it before sorting it.

(e) The verbal procedure administered by the intensive interviewer is set out in full in Appendix 4 to this chapter.

(f) The same type of operation was administered with respect to the 'distant-violence' stimuli.

Scoring boys for callousness in relation to 'near' and 'distant' violence

The score for a given visual stimulus was based on the median values of the statements sorted into the 'agree' bag. For each boy, these were summed and divided by the total number of such cards (i.e. sorted as 'agree') in order to arrive at a Thurstone-type score. For the callousness score on 'near-violence', all three averages were converted into an overall average. Similarly for the three averages computed for the 'distant-violence' stimuli.

In recording the results from the two types of callousness test, eight separate scores were card punched: one for each of the six stimuli, one for the average of all three averages on the 'near-violence' measure and one for the average of all three averages on the 'distant-violence' measure.

Notes

[1] The main exception applied to the measure of 'regarding violence as an intrinsic part of human nature'. See special comments on pages 265-7.

[2] On whom the attitude measures would eventually be used.

[3] For example: statements were kept as short as possible, were limited in terms of their information content, were kept concrete, were expressed positively, were kept free of words that could easily sound like something else, were made up of words expected to be quite familiar to boys; qualifying clauses were avoided or, if that was not possible, were placed at the *beginning* of statements; very broad concepts were avoided where possible.

[4] See 'Respondent understanding of survey questions' in W.A. Belson, *Polls*, vol.3 (4) 1968.

[5] Median values for the combined distributions of boys and adults.

[6] As is normally done in many Thurstone scales.

[7] It was expected at that time to last three hours. In fact it ran for three and a half hours for most boys, and for some as long as four hours.

APPENDICES TO CHAPTER 7

Appendix 1	The statements making up the attitude composites in terms of which attitude scores were computed, showing median values and semi-interquartile ranges.
Appendix 2	The two sets of statements in terms of which callousness was mentioned.
Appendix 3	The twelve visual stimuli used in the callousness measure.
Appendix 4	Administration of the callousness measure.

Appendix 1

The statements making up the composite in terms of which attitude scores were computed

Entered against these statements are their median values and their semi-interquartile ranges, all of them established through the Thurstone judging or grading operation.

The median values have been adjusted (by subtracting 1.00 from each) so that the lowest point in the grading scale is 0.00 (rather than 1.00).

Statements	Scale value	Semi interquartile range
Consideration for others		
I do not care about other people in any way whatsoever.	0.04	0.27
If a new boy came to my school or where I work, I would do my best to help him get to know people.	9.52	0.75
One should put one's litter in a waste paper bin.	7.75	1.28
If I won the pools, I would give a lot of the money away to charity.	9.00	1.25
Being rude to old people is fun.	0.88	1.11
Knocking on people's doors and then running off is a good game.	1.81	1.31
It's fun to put on a comic voice and pretend to be somebody else when anyone rings me up.	3.97	1.16
It's OK to tell people to buzz off.	2.88	1.12
Boys should help their fathers with jobs in the house, flat, garden, or on the car.	8.28	1.37
Scale range: 0.00 – 10.00		
Violence to solve problems		
It's better to settle disagreements by talking rather than by fighting.	1.29	0.90
I would only use force to protect someone I loved or a member of my family.	4.27	1.42
A good way to impress girls is for them to see that you can push other blokes around.	8.04	1.07
When you are in a hurry to get somewhere, it is quite OK to push past people to make sure you catch your bus or train.	6.85	1.33
If a friend gets hit by a gang of blokes the best thing to do is to get your mates together and go after the other gang.	8.89	1.23
It is never OK to use violence or force.	0.16	0.33
Violence should only be used in a good cause.	5.34	1.00
It's manly to settle a quarrel with your fists.	7.58	1.39
It's OK to use violence to get what you want.	9.23	0.98
If a burglar broke into my house, I would try to knock him out with something.	6.25	1.47
Scale range: 0.00 – 10.00		

Statements	Scale value	Semi-interquartile range
Angry or bitter feelings		
I think we should be kind and understanding towards all people of other races.	0.29	1.03
If someone is rude to me I do not usually bother to answer back.	3.00	1.57
I sometimes disobey my parents just to annoy them.	7.36	1.40
I get on well with most people.	1.33	0.77
I am usually polite and obedient to teachers at school.	1.97	1.17
I get angry only if someone is unfair or mean, but not otherwise.	4.53	1.14
I get annoyed with people who do not agree with me.	8.04	1.09
If the team I support (in soccer, or other sports) loses, I feel like getting my revenge by having a go at the winning team's supporters.	8.98	0.86
I often get so angry that I smash things up or destroy things.	9.76	0.58
I feel jealous of some people.	5.94	1.00

Scale range: 0.00 – 10.00

Statements	Scale value	Semi-interquartile range
Respect for authority		
Most policemen are decent people	7.83	1.14
There is no need to take any notice of what your parents tell you.	0.47	1.09
I don't think the police deserve respect.	1.06	1.43
The police are unfair.	2.40	1.48
Cheeking the teachers at school is OK if in fun.	4.72	1.37
Swearing at teachers is OK.	0.61	1.04
I don't think my parents know what they are talking about half the time.	3.17	1.38
Cheeking your parents is OK if in fun.	5.67	1.33
Children should love and respect their parents.	9.53	0.84
The police are thugs.	0.43	0.89
Parents think they know best, but they're no better than anyone else really.	4.17	1.55
If you don't want to do as the school teacher tells you, don't do it.	1.50	1.44
In sport, you should accept the referee's decision without cheeking him or swearing at him.	8.19	1.21
People ought to help the police with their enquiries.	8.10	1.19

Scale range: 0.00 – 10.00

Statements	Scale value	Semi-interquartile range
Anxiety, nervousness, emotional instability		
I hardly ever worry about the future.	1.60	0.82
I find it very hard to make friends with people.	6.54	1.03
I always feel afraid that some maniac might attack me when I am alone, and murder me.	9.73	0.85
Nothing ever frightens me at all.	0.05	0.28
I feel a bit shy when I meet strangers.	5.32	0.89
I think it is natural to be suspicious of strangers.	4.62	1.01
I often feel that other people are staring at me.	7.94	0.95
I enjoy going out and making new friends.	1.00	1.13
There have been only a few times when I have been scared.	3.15	1.16
I am very easily upset.	8.94	0.95

Scale range: 0.00 – 10.00

Statements	Scale value	Semi-interquartile range
Attractiveness of violence		
Shooting people looks like fun.	9.85	0.33
I don't believe in watching or using violence of any kind.	0.18	0.58
I don't like people who are always fighting.	2.17	1.34
I admire people like boxers who use their fists to prove that they're better than the next person.	7.04	1.19
I think it's great when a player in the team I support hacks somebody down – especially if the ref. doesn't see it.	8.57	0.93
I enjoy watching wrestling but I would not like to take part.	4.41	1.38
I don't like rough games.	1.30	1.22
It must be horrible to be involved in a riot.	1.50	1.29
I enjoy playing sports like rugger, soccer, hockey.	5.20	0.77
I enjoy watching boxing.	5.67	1.21
I don't like wars, except in films on the TV.	3.40	1.63
Watching a good punch-up in the street or in the playground livens things up a bit.	7.81	1.20
Having a friendly fight with your mates is good fun.	6.39	0.92

Scale range: 0.00 – 10.00

Statements	Scale value	Semi-interquartile range
Objections to the idea of violence		
I don't have any opinions at all about the use of violence in the world.	2.82	1.42
It makes no sense here in England for anyone to be violent to anyone else.	4.81	1.31
Fist fights are a very poor way for people to sort out their differences.	4.24	0.71
It's a bit much if a group of boys pick on a boy who is on his own.	5.11	0.76
It's good for husbands and wives to have flaming rows occasionally as a way of letting off steam.	2.21	0.97
Violence between countries is often necessary but I don't approve of people inside this country being violent to each other.	3.59	1.26
It's OK to feel violent at times, but it is never OK to be violent.	3.29	0.86
Boxing should be banned.	5.78	0.56
Since police forces and governments use violent means to solve their problems, members of the public should have the right to do the same.	1.25	1.56
Since boys will be boys, I don't mind if the occasional phone kiosk gets smashed up.	0.71	1.05

Scale range: 0.00 – 6.00

Violence as an intrinsic part of human nature

Score for response			Statements
Agree	No opinion	Disagree	
2	1	0	Men will always enjoy boxing and wrestling
2	1	0	As long as there are human beings there will always be violence
0	1	2	Violence between human beings will eventually die out
0	1	2	The day will come when the world will be at peace
2	1	0	Every person has a violent streak in him
2	1	0	There will always be violence in the world
2	1	0	We are all savages just under the skin
0	1	2	People are slowly learning not to be violent
0	1	2	Countries will eventually stop fighting wars

Appendix 2

The statements generated in the process of developing systems for rating boys in terms of callousness

In this section are the original statements, as presented to raters, from which the 'callousness' scales were constructed

Scale values (medians) and semi-interquartile ranges are shown after each statement. The statements selected for use in the rating scales are marked with an asterisk (*).

		Scale value	Semi-interquartile range
	Callousness/near events scale		
1	Since I don't know how it started maybe the victim deserves to be punished this way.	5.38	1.09
2	It would depress me very much to see this.	1.46	0.84
3	I think it might be fun to stay around and watch what happens.	6.72	0.65
4	I would physically restrain him (or them) if I could.	2.08	1.26
5	I might try to talk him (or them) out of it.	2.47	0.87
6	I wouldn't pay any attention to it.	5.40	1.14
*7	This would make me angry.	2.42	1.21
8	I would hope nobody got seriously hurt.	3.12	0.83
*9	I would move off as quickly as I could.	5.00	1.21
*10	I would hope that somebody would do something to stop it.	3.50	1.15
*11	I think it is wrong for people to do things like this.	2.83	1.08
12	Although there would be nothing I could do, I would hope that somebody would do something to stop it.	3.46	0.85
*13	What other people do is no concern of mine.	5.70	1.03
*14	I think that the person on the receiving end probably deserves what he or she is getting.	6.40	0.72
*15	I would tell my mates so they could watch the excitement too.	6.76	0.55
*16	I would try and find a policeman or a teacher or an adult.	2.28	0.82
*17	I would feel sorry for the person on the receiving end.	2.62	1.23
*18	This sort of thing happens all the time; I might not take any notice of it.	5.02	0.78
19	It would upset me to see this.	2.26	0.93
20	I might join in myself, with the person doing it.	6.72	0.62
*21	I would try to stop it if I thought I could.	2.06	0.69
22	I would feel shocked about it.	2.56	0.97
23	I wouldn't have any particular feelings about it.	5.21	1.16
*24	I would not feel upset because of it.	5.50	0.90
25	Seeing this would make me feel sick.	1.81	0.75

*These statements were selected to make up the 'near-violence' callousness scale.

		Scale value	Semi-interquartile range
	Callousness/distant events scale		
*1	These things just happen; that's life.	4.50	1.23
2	I have no opinion; it's got nothing to do with me.	5.97	0.82
3	I'm not interested in stories like this.	6.06	1.03
4	So long as the people close to me are OK, I'm not too bothered about what happens far away.	5.20	1.40
*5	It's not my problem, so I'm not interested.	6.10	0.75
6	Life is dangerous, so people should look out for themselves.	5.16	1.31
7	That's their hard luck.	6.82	0.38
*8	Things I don't see for myself have no effect on me.	5.38	0.77
*9	I find reading about people's troubles amusing.	6.85	0.32
10	There's nothing I can do about it, so I don't get too concerned about things like this.	5.23	0.96
11	In some ways, their suffering is their own fault.	5.75	0.88
12	Well, it's too bad, but the people involved are not totally innocent victims.	5.16	0.72
13	Even if I could help out in some way, I probably wouldn't really.	5.65	0.83
14	I just think it's very sad that these things happen.	2.32	0.92
15	I would not feel upset after reading this.	5.80	0.96
16	I wouldn't have any particular feelings if I read this.	5.05	1.12
17	I would feel very upset if I read something like this.	1.31	0.67
*18	I feel a little shocked reading about these kinds of things.	2.45	0.75
19	It's quite a shock to read about these things going on.	1.95	0.69
*20	There must be some way to stop this from happening again.	1.77	0.94
*21	There is no excuse for this. It should not have happened.	2.94	1.63
22	I don't like hearing about these things.	2.39	0.88
23	It's terrible that things like this can happen.	1.61	0.68
*24	I really feel sorry for the people involved.	1.19	0.43
25	These things are very upsetting.	1.56	0.72
*26	I never really think very much about the victims when these things happen.	5.07	0.52

*These statements were selected to make up the 'distant-violence' callousness scale.

Appendix 3

The visual stimuli used in the assessment of callousness in relation to 'near' and 'distant' violence

'NEAR' VIOLENCE STIMULI

YOU ARE WALKING DOWN THE STREET WHEN YOU HAPPEN TO SEE A BOY YOU DON'T KNOW ABOUT TO TRIP AN OLD MAN WHO IS WALKING WITH A CANE.

YOU ARE STANDING ON THE BALCONY OF A FRIEND'S FLAT WHEN YOU HAPPEN TO SEE A MAN IN THE WINDOW OF A FLAT NEXT DOOR YELLING AND BEATING UP A WOMAN.

YOU SEE A BOY YOU DON'T KNOW, WHO HAS COME FROM OUT-OF-TOWN TO LONDON TO SEE HIS TEAM PLAY YOUR LOCAL CLUB. HE IS SURROUNDED AND STARTS GETTING PUSHED AROUND BY A GROUP OF BOYS.

'NEAR' VIOLENCE STIMULI

IMAGINE YOU ARE WALKING DOWN THE STREET AND YOU HAPPEN TO SEE A MAN YOU DON'T KNOW CUTTING ANOTHER MAN'S FACE WITH A BROKEN BOTTLE'

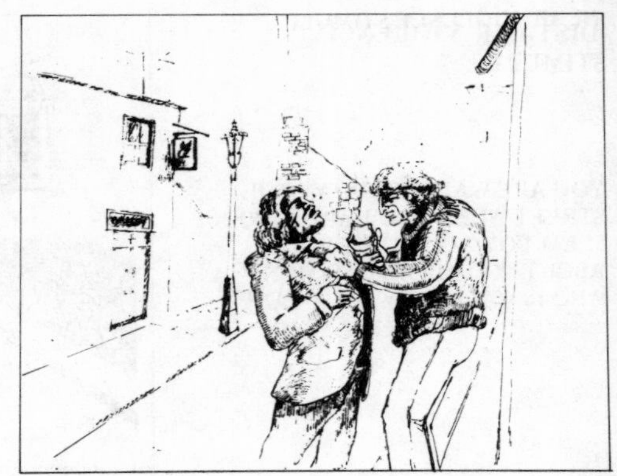

IMAGINE YOU ARE WALKING ACROSS A FIELD WHEN YOU SEE SOME BOYS YOU DON'T KNOW KICKING ANOTHER BOY IN THE RIBS.

IMAGINE YOU ARE ON YOUR WAY HOME AND YOU HAPPEN TO SEE A MAN YOU DON'T KNOW FLOGGING A DOG.

'DISTANT' VIOLENCE STIMULI

Burst tyre blamed for air crash in which 72 Britons died

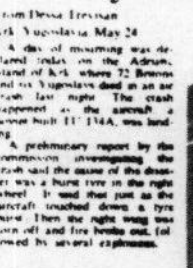

From Dessa Trevisan
Krk, Yugoslavia, May 24

A day of mourning was declared today on the Adriatic island of Krk, where 72 Britons and six Yugoslavs died in an air crash last night. The crash happened as the aircraft, a Soviet-built TU 134A, was landing.

A preliminary report by the commission investigating the crash said the cause of the disaster was a burst tyre in the right wheel. It said that just as the aircraft touched down a tyre burst. Then the right wing was torn off and fire broke out, followed by several explosions.

Part of the charred wreckage of the TU 134 A that crashed on landing in Yugoslavia with the loss of 78 lives on Sunday night

Car gangsters shoot twice in Fulham street

BID TO KILL KRAY WITNESS IN LONDON

By JOHN STEVENS and JILL PALMER

TWO BLASTS from a shotgun were fired from a car at Mr. Charles Mitchell, a key prosecution witness in the Kray gang trial three years ago, outside his Fulham home today.

Mr. Mitchell, aged 42 and 6ft. 3in. tall, was walking to his own car, parked outside his home in Ellerby Street when the gunman opened fire.

Sheet of flame kills all aboard British ship

84 DIE TRAPPED IN RING OF FIRE

By PHILIP MELLOR

A BRITISH freighter became a blazing tomb for all 74 people aboard when it crashed with an oil tanker yesterday.

There was a huge blast and flames engulfed both ships.

Crash . . then death in seconds

'DISTANT' VIOLENCE
STIMULI

FLIGHT FROM HELL

Horror of the village bombed by mistake

Revenge . . . the day the Mukti Bahini caught up with the people they said had collaborated with the West Pakistan forces

Indian move to end street execution of Razakars

From HAROLD JACKSON : New Delhi, December 21

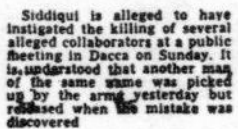

Siddiqui is alleged to have instigated the killing of several alleged collaborators at a public meeting in Dacca on Sunday. It is understood that another man of the same name was picked up by the army yesterday but released when the mistake was discovered

THE IRA's REVENGE ON GIRLS

Their crime: going out with soldiers

TWO young Ulster girls had their hair shorn off yesterday by the I.R.A.

They paid the cruel penalty for going out with British soldiers.

Lesson

SHORN

TARRED

BOARD 1
N1

Callousness: near events

N1. Tripping old man

What would he feel (or feel like doing) if he saw this particular event in real life (= tripping old man)?

NEAR EVENTS PICTURE N1 (tripping old man)

USE 3-CHOICE SYSTEM ON BOARD 1 (= AGREE, DISAGREE, DON'T KNOW)

TELL THE BOY:

"We would like you to do something different now."

TAKE THE BOY TO THE PICTURES ON THE WALL.

INSTRUCT THE BOY TO LOOK AT THE PICTURE LABELLED N1.

READ THE CAPTION TO THE BOY.

ASK HIM TO SAY WHAT HE SEES IN THE PICTURE.

THEN GIVE BOY ONE OF THE PACKS OF CARDS WHICH HAVE AN 'N' ON THE BOTTOM RIGHT HAND CORNER OF EACH CARD.

INFORM THE BOY:

"This pack of cards will help you to tell us what you would feel and what you would do if you saw this (POINT) in real life."

INSTRUCT HIM TO READ THE FIRST CARD OUT ALOUD. HELP HIM WITH ANY READING OR COMPREHENSION DIFFICULTIES. SAY:

"We want you to tell us if you would feel or do what it says on the card if you saw this (POINT TO PICTURE) in real life."

SHOW HIM SORTING BAGS, BOARD 1.

"If you *agree* that the card says what *you* feel or do, put the card in this bag (POINT) which says '*agree*'."

"If you *disagree* with what the card says – if it says something you would *not* feel or do – put the card in this bag (POINT) which says '*disagree*'."

"If you are *not sure* or *can't make up your mind* if you would feel or do what the card says, put the card in this bag (POINT) which says '*don't know*'."

SAY EMPHATICALLY

"One thing is very important. I am not asking you how you reckon you OUGHT to feel. What I want to know is how you *really and truly* would feel about what's in that picture. Please be absolutely honest with me."

"Now will you put this first card in one of the bags to tell me if you agree or disagree with what's on it, or if you don't know. *Be absolutely honest.*"

AFTER HE SORTS IT, SAY:

"Now look at the picture again. (PAUSE). Now read out what's on the next card. (HELP IF NECESSARY). Now put it into one of the bags to show how you *really would* feel if you saw this (POINT TO PICTURE) in real life."

NEXT SAY:

"Now go through the rest of the cards, one at a time. Look up at the picture, and read the card out aloud each time. Then put the card in one of the bags to show how you *really would* feel."

NOTE: THERE ARE 12 CARDS IN THE 'N' PACK. TRY TO ENSURE THAT EACH BOY READS EACH STATEMENT OUT ALOUD TO YOU AND UNDERSTANDS WHAT HE IS READING. HELP HIM WITH DIFFICULTIES.

CHAPTER 8

THE CONSTRUCTION OF MEASURES OF BOYS' PREOCCUPATION WITH, FEELING OF WILLINGNESS TO COMMIT, DESIRE TO COMMIT ACTS OF VIOLENCE OF THE PARTICULAR KIND FEATURED IN TELEVISION PROGRAMMES; SOME OTHER MEASURES.

Contents

8 THE CONSTRUCTION OF MEASURES OF BOYS' PREOCCUPATION WITH, FEELING OF WILLINGNESS TO COMMIT, DESIRE TO COMMIT ACTS OF VIOLENCE OF THE PARTICULAR KIND FEATURED IN TELEVISION PROGRAMMES; SOME OTHER MEASURES

INTRODUCTION

Hypotheses 9, 10 and 11 are to be contrasted with the earlier behavioural hypotheses. They took the following forms.

Hypothesis 9. High exposure to television violence increases the degree to which boys think about or are preoccupied with the different sorts of violence that are shown on television.

Hypothesis 10. High exposure to television violence increases the degree to which boys would like to commit the kinds of violence shown on television.

Hypothesis 11. High exposure to television violence increases the degree to which boys feel willing to commit the kinds of violence shown on television.

Measurement of the dependent variables in these three hypotheses called for preliminary technique development, details of which are set out in this chapter.

MEASURING 'FEELING OF WILLINGNESS TO COMMIT'

It is essential that this measure be seen solely as one of the *feeling* of 'willingness to commit' and *not* as one of *actual* willingness to commit. In a sense, the hypothesis here involved is connected with the possible weakening of boys' rejection of, or reaction against, such behaviour.

It was intended from the outset that this particular measure should be linked to each of a number of types of television violence (e.g. shooting someone, using a karate chop on someone). For each of them, the measure would involve the respondent in saying under which of a range of circumstances he feels willing to commit the act concerned. For example:

'Under which of the following conditions would you be willing to *shoot someone with a gun*?'

1 If my life depended on it
2 If the other person was an enemy of my country
3 If that other person had insulted my mother

and at the extreme level,

4 If that other person had annoyed me
5 If I was in a bad mood

6 If I was bored and wanted something to do.

On this system, *the list of circumstances* is meant to constitute a continuum or scale, running from circumstances which, if endorsed, would indicate a strong feeling of willingness to commit the act concerned (e.g. if I was in a bad mood) to circumstances that, if endorsed, would indicate a feeling of willingness to commit the act only under considerable pressure (e.g. if my life depended on it).

Such a technique may at first suggest the use of a Guttman type of scale. However, this is not what is needed because Guttman's technique is concerned with scaling a *single* dimension – whereas 'willingness to commit' appears to be multi-dimensional in character. Thus willingness to act violently may be related to the degree of threat to oneself (e.g. if my life depended on it), to the degree of threat to someone else, to the degree of personal anger, to the degree of patriotism, to desire for the possessions of the victim, to desire for 'a giggle' or a laugh. In other words, we are concerned here with a multi-dimensional concept.

One might of course have attempted to limit the measurement of 'how willing' a boy is to commit violence to some single one of the dimensions listed above [1] (e.g. self-protection) but this would have distorted the nature of the concept in the hypothesis – a concept that reflected the many different views on the basis of which the hypothesis was formulated.

Methods of construction of the measuring technique

The basic strategy. The construction strategies that went into the measuring technique in its final form [2] were as follows.

1 A large number of conditions under which one might be violent (e.g. if someone had insulted me) was generated by research staff at the Centre.

2 Rating techniques were used to select from the full set of conditions those which were subject to a fair measure of agreement between raters and which, as a collection of conditions, were spread along a continuum from 'least willing' to 'most willing'. We aimed to select approximately ten such 'conditions'.

3 A selection was made of 20 acts of violence of the kind that are either frequently or from time to time presented on television (e.g. stabbing someone with a knife; hitting someone with a bottle; hitting someone with your fist). It was intended that for each of these acts the survey respondents should say under which of the selected conditions (ten or so of them) they would feel willing to commit it.

4 A further rating operation was then carried out to develop scalar values for each 'condition' in relation to each act, with a view to using these scalar values for deriving 'willingness' scores in relation to all 20 acts taken together and in relation to each of the 20 considered separately.

Steps 2 and 4 might have been carried out as *one* step, but the volume of work that would have been involved for each rater was considered to be too great.

Deriving a pool of conditions under which violence might be committed. Centre staff were asked to volunteer motivating conditions under which violence of any kind might be committed. The suggestions made were challenged and modified to render each of them relatively clear and unitary. This process yielded the following 41 'conditions'.

List 8.1
The 41 conditions under which violence might be committed

1 If my life depended on it
2 If there was no other way out
3 If my happiness depended on it
4 If it would prevent someone else getting hurt
5 If I was in a bad mood
6 If it would make me happy
7 If I felt like it
8 If someone annoyed me
9 If I was given the opportunity
10 If I had nothing else to do
11 If I was bored
12 If someone forced me to
13 If there was no other alternative
14 If a group of blokes attacked me
15 If someone called me a coward
16 If someone called me something I didn't like
17 If someone attacked me
18 In a pretend sort of way during a game
19 Against someone in my family
20 To get pleasure
21 On my best friend(s)
22 To defend my property
23 If my life was in immediate danger
24 If my country was at war
25 To protect an animal
26 If it was expected of me
27 If I was very afraid
28 If I got angry with someone
29 For kicks or fun
30 To see what would happen
31 To get my own way in something
32 If someone was rude to me
33 If another boy insulted my girl friend
34 Against another boy
35 Against my girl friend
36 If I was fouled in a football game
37 To stop myself getting arrested by the police
38 In self defence
39 To protect someone
40 Against someone who tried to stop me getting what I wanted
41 Just for something to do

It is apparent that there is a considerable variety in the points of reference amongst the 41 conditions listed above, and also that there are amongst them different dimensions in terms of which willingness might be gauged. These dimensions appeared to include the following:

- if there is a threat to one's own person or property;
- if there is a threat to someone else/to my country;
- if one is in a bad mood or angry;
- for personal gain;
- if one is bored;
- to get fun or pleasure.

Rating the pool of conditions in terms of implied willingness to be violent. This was to be a generalised rating in the sense that the ratings were to be referred to 'violence in general' – rather than to some particular act of violence. It was expected that this first rating operation would whittle down the 41 conditions to about ten well balanced and appropriate items, and that 'willingness' ratings in terms of the 20 different TV acts would then become feasible.

Boys (64) in the age range 12-17 years at a Secondary Modern school were asked to rate the 41 conditions (see list 8.1) in terms of implied willingness to use violence. To these ratings were added those of 33 London boys in the same age range recruited through survey methods. The rating scale used took the following form.

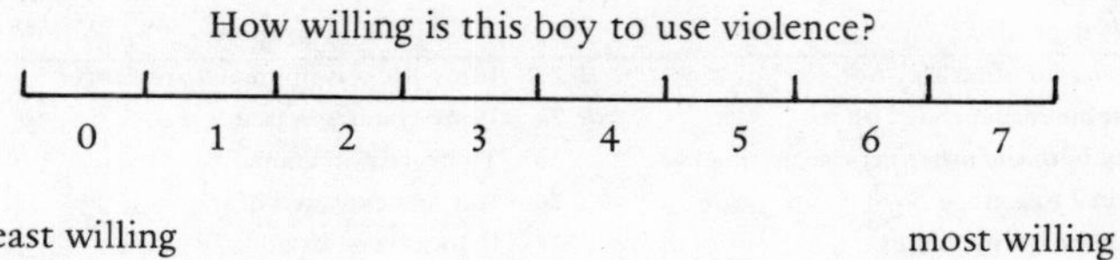

Each of the 41 conditions was rated on this scale using the Thurstone technique. That one amongst them that implied greatest willingness to be violent was to be rated as 7 and that one which implied least willingness to be violent was to be rated as 0. The others were to be graded between those extremes to indicate the level of willingness implied in them. It was then possible to derive for each of the 41 conditions a median value (on the willingness scale) and an index of disagreement between judges (i.e. semi-interquartile range).

These values were then used as an aid in selecting a limited number of conditions for inclusion in the enquiry. Their selection was carried out as follows.

1 The 41 conditions were separated into six groups according to the kind of dimension that seemed to be inherent in them (e.g. threat to oneself or one's property; personal boredom; for fun).

2 Within each of these six groups, the conditions were listed in order according to median value (each with its index of scatter entered against it).

3 A selection of 10 conditions was then made with a view to:

- securing a representative range of median values within each of the groups and over the whole 41 items;
- eliminating wherever possible conditions with high indices of scatter;
- maintaining the multi-dimensionality of the original 41 conditions.

In the course of this rating operation, it became clear that the wording of some of the conditions was proving difficult for the raters and hence changes were made. The final set of ten conditions is shown in table 8.1, along with approximate [3] median values. These values would of course be replaced in the final rating operation dealing with specific acts of violence, but they were needed for first selecting the ten basic 'conditions'.

Selecting 20 acts of violence of the kind shown on television. The final rating of 'willingness' to be violent were to be in terms of each of a number of acts of violence of the kind commonly presented on television. To secure realistic variety for this approach it was planned that there be 20 such acts. For each of them, boys would be asked (in the general survey) if they would be willing to commit the act if (*naming the act*) . . . for each of the 10 selected conditions considered in sequence. For each condition agreed, the boy would receive a 'willingness score' based on the median values *yet to be developed.*

Existing sources of information were investigated in a search for specific acts of

Table 8.1
The 10 items or conditions selected

	Approximate median ratings of 'conditions'
if I wanted some fun	6.07
if I was angry with the other person	5.54
if I was in a bad mood	5.41
if I was just bored	5.10
if it was necessary for protecting some other person	3.83
if the other person had insulted me	3.77
if the person concerned was a boy who had insulted a girl I was with	3.35
if the other person was an enemy of my country	2.66
if it was in self defence	1.78
if my life was threatened	0.42

violence presented on television, but without much success. Subsequently 30 members of the general London public attending a Survey Research Centre session for other purposes were asked to write down specific acts of violence seen by them on television. This was done also with a sample of boys in the age range 12-17 years.

The yield of acts from these two sources was content analysed to yield slightly generalised lists of TV presented acts of violence. From this list a selection of 20 was made with a view to ensuring that the list of 20 was varied in character and that it included the more frequently volunteered types of violent behaviour.

The list of 20 acts selected in this way was as follows.

List 8.2
20 acts of violence said by viewers to be of a kind presented on television

1 Stabbing someone with a knife
2 Kicking someone or putting the boot in
3 Shooting someone with a gun
4 Throwing a petrol bomb at someone
5 Being in a gang that was beating someone up
6 Slashing someone or cutting him with a razor
7 Pushing someone out of a window
8 Hitting someone with a piece of wood or a club or iron bar
9 Using a whip on someone
10 Using a karate chop on someone
11 Throwing acid in someone's face
12 Trying to throttle or strangle someone
13 Swearing at someone
14 Hitting someone with your fists
15 Threatening someone
16 Bashing up or fighting a coloured immigrant
17 Hitting someone with a bottle
18 Using judo on someone
19 Running down someone with a bike or motorbike or scooter or car
20 Torturing someone

Developing a scoring system for 'willingness to commit' the 20 violent acts. The scoring of boys for willingness to commit TV presented acts of violence required that each of the 10 conditions for 'being violent' be rated on a willingness continuum in relation to each of the 20 TV acts. Such a body of information would allow the derivation of both an overall 'willingness' score and a separate willingness score for each of the 20 acts. The required ratings were made as follows.

1 Boys (29) and parents (18) attended a judging session at the London School of Economics.

2 These people met in four groups of 10 to 14 each in the course of a week and went through a specialised judging procedure.

(a) The basic task of each respondent was to complete the following judging operation for each of the 20 acts of violence. Each respondent was asked to use the rating scale shown below to indicate how strong or weak a specified 'reason' was for committing the television-type act concerned.

Diagram 8.1

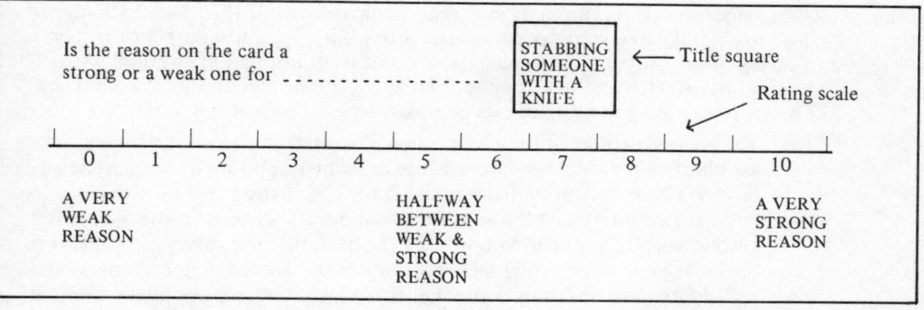

(b) In administering this system, a giant sized rating scale was used (2 feet across). All 20 acts, each on a 2 in. by 2 in. square of paper, were stapled in a pack to the title square at the top of the page. These were numbered 1 to 20. A 21st act was also included for control purposes, this one reading '*being violent*'.

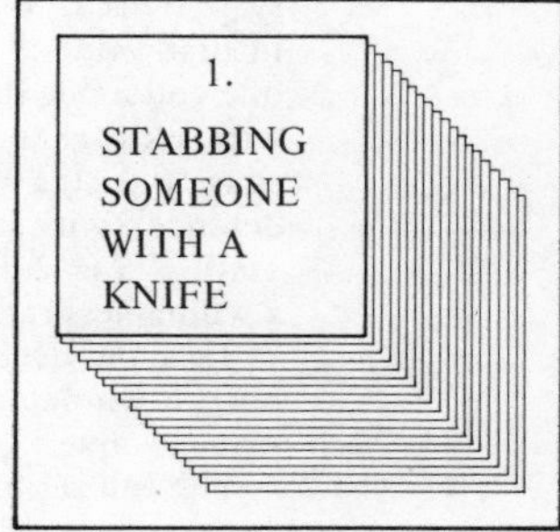

The judge was required to sort all 10 conditions (each on a separate small card) for being violent along the rating scale to indicate how weak or strong a reason each was for committing the TV-type act shown in the title square. The scale positions into which they were sorted were then entered on the 10 cards and the 'act' in the title square was torn off and put on top of the 10 'condition' cards relating to that act. These were clipped together and collected.

The respondent was then passed a second pack of 10 'condition' cards and was asked to rate these along the rating scale in terms of the second of the TV acts of violence (i.e. *kicking someone or putting the boot in*). Just as with the first TV-act, the 10 condition-cards were marked with the rating scale positions to which the judge had assigned them. They were then bundled together along with the slip of paper on which the TV-act concerned was printed. This process was continued for all 21 of the acts in the title square.

(c) The control exercised over the judging operation was 'tight'. There was an introductory explanation and illustration of the job to be done, with questions and answers. Then the judges were asked to work under conditions of no discussion and no comparisons. If they had difficulty of any kind, they were to attract the attention of the administrator or her assistant for personal explanation – but were not to call anything out. The administrator and her assistant explained these rules and went round the room looking for difficulties or misunderstandings of any kind.

(d) The judges' ratings of each 'condition' (in relation to each act) were analysed to provide measures of median values and semi-interquartile ranges. These data provided a basis (i) for eliminating any item that had too large a semi-interquartile range for meaningful inclusion in the measuring system and (ii) for scoring boys (on the basis of their survey responses) in terms of how willing they were to commit the acts of violence concerned.

Take the act 'stabbing someone with a knife' as an example of the scoring system used. For this act, the condition 'if I was in a bad mood' had a median value of 0.1 (on the 0-10 point scale used). That implied that anyone endorsing such a statement feels particularly willing to 'stab someone with a knife' and his willingness score (for that act and that condition) is thus 10.0 - 0.1 = 9.9. In the same way, the condition, 'if it was in self defence' (with its median value of 7.5) would warrant a willingness rating of 10.0 - 7.5 (= 2.5). If a boy rejected a 'condition' altogether, then he was given a willingness rating of zero for that condition (for that act).

To avoid decimal places, all scores were based on 100 and rounded to nearest whole number. Thus a willingness score of 10.00 - 0.58 (= 9.42) would convert to a score of 94.

The full set of willingness scores for all 20 acts is given in table 8.2.

Administering the 'willingness' measure in the survey

The technique devised for assessing feeling of willingness was administered within the

Table 8.2
Weights allotted to the different conditions for committing different acts of violence

	Type of act	Type of condition†									
		1	2	3	4	5 *	6	7	8	9	10
1	Stabbing someone with a knife	26	97	100	94		36	100	21	99	99
2	Kicking someone or putting the boot in	17	87	99	85		22	95	04	91	98
3	Shooting someone with a gun	18	99	100	97		26	100	13	99	99
4	Throwing a petrol bomb at someone	37	98	100	97		36	100	20	98	99
5	Being in a gang that is beating someone up	–	97	99	93		45	99	21	96	99
6	Slashing someone or cutting them with a razor	36	97	100	97		37	99	22	98	99
7	Pushing someone out of a window	25	98	99	95		33	99	20	98	99
8	Hitting someone with piece of wood or a club, or iron bar	19	96	99	95		27	99	10	97	99
9	Using a whip on somebody	19	95	99	94		29	100	15	98	99
10	Using a karate chop on somebody	06	91	99	86		19	99	05	96	98
11	Throwing acid in someone's face	41	99	100	99		57	99	23	99	99
12	Trying to throttle or strangle somebody	19	96	100	93		31	100	14	98	99
13	Swearing at someone	–	38	94	33		–	97	–	55	60
14	Hitting someone with your fists	04	79	98	74		07	98	04	80	97
15	Threatening someone	08	49	98	55		13	99	05	73	95
16	Bashing up or fighting with a coloured immigrant	10	72	99	88		17	99	06	87	99
17	Hitting somebody with a bottle	17	96	100	87		20	99	11	97	99
18	Using judo on somebody	04	89	97	88		11	98	05	90	97
19	Running down somebody with bike, etc.	28	98	99	98		25	95	12	98	99
20	Torturing somebody	49	98	99	98		47	99	20	98	99

*Not included in scoring system because semi-interquartile ranges for this condition were very large for most of the acts of violence.

†The ten conditions were as follows:

1 if it was in self defence
2 if the other person had insulted me
3 if I wanted some fun
4 if I was very angry with someone
5 if the other person was an enemy of my country
6 if it was necessary for protecting some other person
7 if I was just bored
8 if my life was threatened
9 if the person concerned was a boy who had insulted a girl I was going out with
10 if I was in a bad mood

– Not included in the scoring system because it was nonsensical in relation to this particular act.

intensive interview at the Centre and took the following form.

(a) Boys were given a sorting card on which was (i) a 'type of act' square (see diagram 8.2) in which would be placed a card saying, for example, 'I would be willing to stab someone if . . . '; (ii) a set of 10 squares in each of which was printed a single 'condition' for committing an act of violence (e.g. 'if it was in self defence'). They were also given a handful of blue discs and asked to put one in each of the 'condition' squares that was true for them in relation to the act of violence displayed in the 'type of act' square. All conditions marked with a disc were coded for that boy against the act concerned.

(b) The act of violence in the title square was then changed for 'act 2' and the boy used the same set of discs to indicate under which of the ten conditions he would commit *that* act.

(c) This procedure was continued for all 20 acts of violence.

The instructions for administering this procedure are given in Appendix 1.

Computing the willingness score

The willingness score for each boy for all 20 acts taken together and for each of the acts taken separately was derived through a computer programme and was fed into the 'data set' for the next stage in computer analysis.

MEASURING PREOCCUPATION WITH TV-TYPE ACTS OF VIOLENCE

In this case, what was required was a measure of the degree to which boys mentally dwelt upon the kinds of acts of violence presented from time to time on television.

The television acts considered. The same 20 acts of violence as were used to assess 'willingness' to commit TV-type acts of violence were re-used in this measure. But a method had to be derived to assess degree of preoccupation with each of them.

The measurement technique in summary form. In this case, a simple verbal rating scale was used. For each of the 20 acts the boy was asked *how often* thoughts about the act concerned came into his mind and he was offered a choice of reply between

Never in my whole life
Very rarely
Rarely
Now and then
Fairly often
Very often

The measuring technique in detail. The administration of this procedure was intended both to be attention-getting and to provide variety in terms of what the boy had to do during his long intensive interview.

(a) The boy was passed 20 cards, one at a time. On each of these cards was a

Diagram 8.2 The placement board used in the question concerning willingness to commit specific acts of violence with an example of the cards used

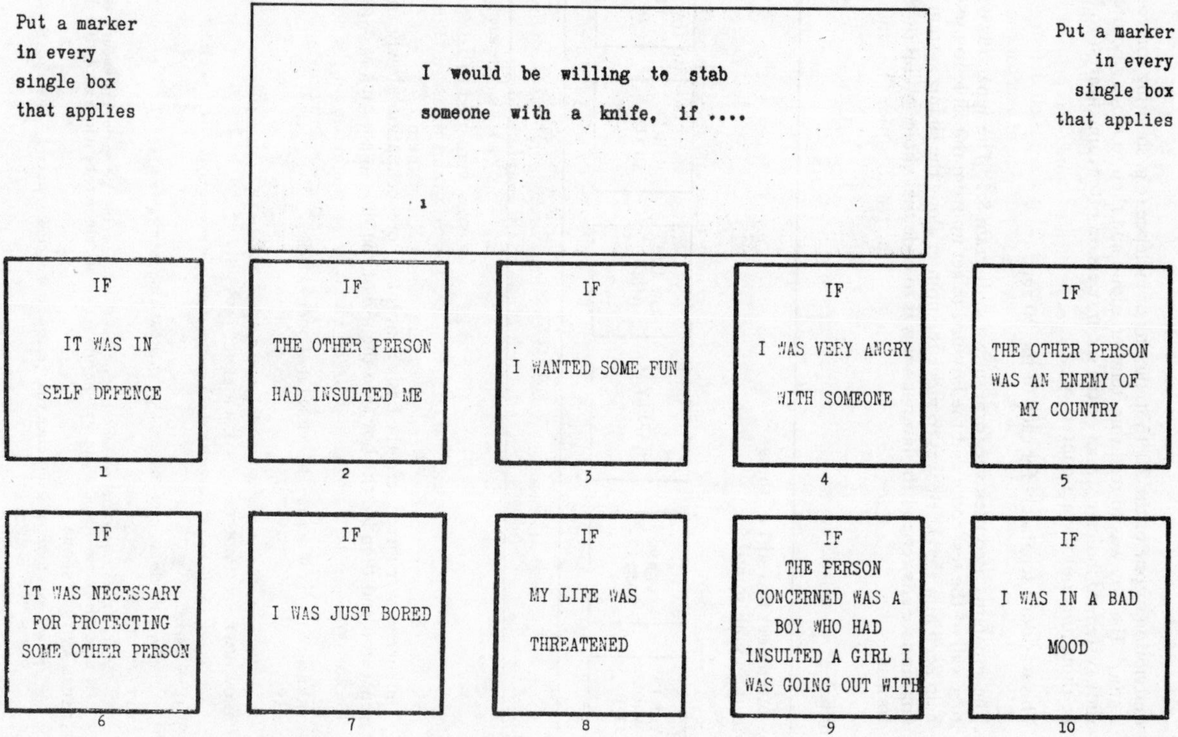

Put a marker
in every
single box
that applies

I would be willing to stab
someone with a knife, if ....

1

Put a marker
in every
single box
that applies

IF IT WAS IN SELF DEFENCE	IF THE OTHER PERSON HAD INSULTED ME	IF I WANTED SOME FUN	IF I WAS VERY ANGRY WITH SOMEONE	IF THE OTHER PERSON WAS AN ENEMY OF MY COUNTRY
1	2	3	4	5
IF IT WAS NECESSARY FOR PROTECTING SOME OTHER PERSON	IF I WAS JUST BORED	IF MY LIFE WAS THREATENED	IF THE PERSON CONCERNED WAS A BOY WHO HAD INSULTED A GIRL I WAS GOING OUT WITH	IF I WAS IN A BAD MOOD
6	7	8	9	10

description of one of the 20 TV-type acts of violence (e.g. shooting someone with a gun). The boy was to read this item out aloud and then to move a pointer on a slide system to indicate which of the six answers on offer came nearest to how often he thought about the act concerned.

(b) This was done separately for each of the 20 acts.

(c) The apparatus used took the form shown in diagram 8.3. The apparatus was fixed to a wall of the test room and the boy had to get up from the table to use it (to help keep him alert). He was to move the pointer along the sliding system to the appropriate answer and the interviewer was to code that choice on his or her coding form.

Diagram 8.3

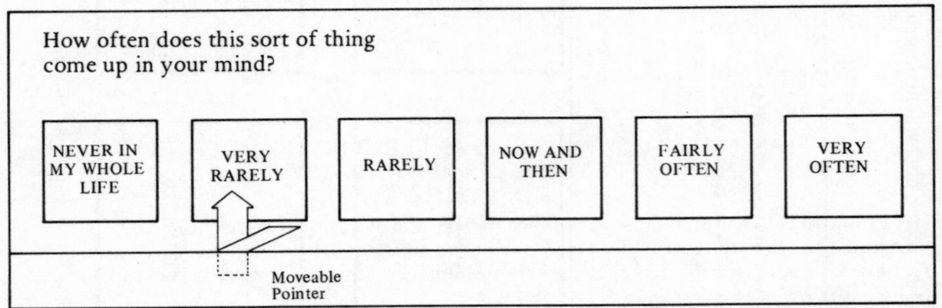

(d) The interviewer introduced the basic concept of 'preoccupation' slowly and with repetition and then led the boy into the use of the slide as a means of expressing his answer.

TAKE BOY TO SLIDE SCALES, SECTION 1 (PREOCCUPATION)

SAY:

> 'My questions now are about certain acts of violence. The acts are typed on these cards.'

SHOW HIM PACK MARKED: ACTS OF VIOLENCE (AV)

> 'I want you to answer a question about each of the acts of violence typed on these cards.'

PAUSE AND SAY:

> 'Here is the first of them (PASS CARD 1). Read it out for me please.' (WAIT).

SAY SLOWLY

> 'As you know, some boys see something or hear about it and then go on thinking about it from time to time. Perhaps they think about it all the time – they don't seem to be able to get if off their minds.'

PAUSE AND SAY SLOWLY

> 'What I want to know is how often you think about the act on your card – how often the idea of it comes into your mind.'

PAUSE AND THEN SAY EMPHATICALLY:

'It counts even if the idea just came and went in your mind. It would count even if you had no intention of doing it. It would count even if you were just remembering seeing it demonstrated somewhere. So you see what I am after is how often a thought about stabbing someone comes into your mind. (PAUSE). Think carefully about it before you answer.'

SAY:

'I want you to answer by moving this yellow pointer to one of those boxes. (POINT)

SAY:

'Read out aloud what's in those boxes.'

CORRECT AS NECESSARY.

SAY:

'Now move the pointer to show me how often you have thought about the act on the card – how often the idea of it or a thought about it has come into your mind. Look at the card and then move the pointer to where you think is right for you.'

CODE HIS CHOICE ON APPROPRIATE GRID.

SAY:

'The rest are done in the same way. But please be open and honest about it. I have to know what actually happens in your mind. Remember you have a false name and nobody else will ever know what you told me.'

The full verbal instructions are given in Appendix 2 to this chapter.

ASSESSING HOW OFTEN BOYS 'FEEL LIKE COMMITTING' TV-TYPE ACTS OF VIOLENCE

Here too, the TV featured acts of violence used in the assessment were the 20 acts developed for the study of 'willingness'. And the measure of the frequency with which boys feel like committing such acts was the same simple verbal rating scale that was used in the preoccupation assessment, namely

Never in my whole life
Very rarely
Rarely
Now and then
Fairly often
Very often

The method of administering this scale was the same as for the measurement of preoccupation. Thus 20 acts of violence were printed on 20 cards, each of which the boy read out aloud before moving a pointer on a wall scale to indicate how often he had felt like doing it. The verbal detail that went with this procedure was as follows.

TAKE BOY TO THE SLIDE SCALE, SECTION B (FEELING LIKE COMMITTING)

SAY:

'The next set of questions are about particular acts of violence. In fact they are the same acts of violence I asked you about before, but this time the question about them is different.'

PASS BOY FIRST CARD. SAY:

'This time I want to know how often you FEEL LIKE DOING the act on the card. I need to know how often you feel like doing what's on the card.'

SAY:

'Before you start, I want especially to ask you to be completely honest with your answers. Our work will be wasted if you are not completely straightforward when you choose your answers.'

SAY:

'Now go ahead and choose your answers from what's on the card.'

CODE HIS ANSWER IN APPROPRIATE GRID.

GO ON PASSING HIM THE CARDS ONE AT A TIME, CODING AS YOU GO.

THE ORDER OF PLACEMENT OF THE THREE MEASURES IN THE INTENSIVE INTERVIEW

The three measures dealt with in this chapter were spaced through the intensive interview. Thus of the 19 measuring procedures administered during the intensive interview, these three were ordered as follows:

6th: the measurement of preoccupation with acts of violence of the kind presented on television;

13th: the measure of frequency of 'feeling like committing such acts';

17th: the measure of willingness to commit such acts.

In between these came sequences calling for the use of different sorting and grading methods, the whole sequence being designed to maintain the interest of the boy being interviewed.

The presentation of the last of the three was different in that it involved a lengthy procedure coming at the end of a long interview. Hence where the interview had taken a very long time to administer and when it was so late at night that the interview had to be cut short, the 'willingness' measure was the one to be dropped. However, only 17 cases in all were lost to the willingness measurement in this way partly because it was possible to bring back most of the boys for whom the interview had been incomplete.

MEASURING 'SLEEP DISTURBANCE'

One of the 22 hypotheses investigated dealt with sleep disturbance in boys, namely:

'Long term exposure to television violence contributes to sleep disturbance in boys (as defined by: frequency of nightmares; sleeping with the light on; fear of going to bed; difficulty in getting to sleep)'.

Questions relating to the dependent variable (thus defined) were asked of both boy and his mother, as follows.

1 (Asked of boy). 'During the last year, how often have you lain awake at night for a long time, trying to get to sleep?'

2 (Asked of boy). 'During the last year, how often have you had nightmares?'

3 (Asked of mother). 'Over the past year, how often has your son needed to sleep with the light on all night?'

4 (Asked of mother). 'Over the past year, has your son been afraid to go to bed at night for any reason at all?' *If 'yes'*: 'How often?'

For each of these four questions, the respondent had the following choice of answers: *very often/fairly often/now and then/hardly ever/never.*

To derive an overall score for 'sleep disturbance', the available answers were given weights of 0 (= never), 1, 2, 3, 4 (= very often) and the individual respondent's four replies were added to give a numerical total.

It must be noted of course that this particular index of sleep disturbance could not detect or reflect sleep disturbances of which there was neither conscious nor visible evidence.

Notes

[1] This approach was for a time considered and some work was done towards its completion. It was dropped after discussion and operational difficulties and was replaced by a multi-dimensional approach.

[2] Certain other steps were tried out but were discontinued.

[3] 'Approximate' in the sense that some of the ten conditions were slightly modified after the median values had been established.

APPENDICES TO CHAPTER 8

PLACEMENT BOARD

Willingness to commit specific acts of violence

How willing is the boy to commit certain acts of violence

1 TAKE BOY TO FLAT SURFACE WHERE PLACEMENT BOARD IS LAID OUT

SAY:

"The next set of questions concerns how willing you would be to do certain kinds of things. In fact they are the acts you looked at earlier on."

SAY:

"We'll use *these* cards (SHOW ORANGE PACK) and *this* board (POINT)."

PUT FIRST ORANGE CARD ON BOARD ABOVE THE 10 SQUARES.

2 SAY:

"This one (POINT TO ORANGE CARD) SAYS: I would be willing to STAB SOMEONE WITH A KNIFE . . . *IF* . . . ."

STRESS 'IF' AND THEN SAY:

"And you have to choose your answers among *these* in the boxes (POINT TO ALL OF THEM).

You put one of these markers (SHOW DISC) on every answer that would be true in your own case."

PASS BOY ABOUT 12 MARKERS AND SAY:

"Try it."

SAY:

"Would you be willing to stab someone with a knife (POINT) if . . . it was in self defence (POINT)?"

IF HE SAYS 'YES', TELL HIM:

"Then put a blue marker in that square."

SHOW

IF NO, SAY:

"And would you be willing to stab someone with a knife if that other person had insulted you?"

GET HIM TO PLACE MARKER IN SQUARE IF 'YES'

*NOW TELL HIM

"Look at each of the others in turn. If it would be true for you, put a blue marker in the square. Go ahead."

CODE HIS CHOICES AS HE GOES.

WATCH HIM AND THEN SAY:

"Tell me when you have decided for *all* of them."

WHEN HE SEEMS TO HAVE FINISHED, ASK HIM ABOUT EACH HE HAS NOT MARKED WITH DISC. ASK IF THAT MEANS HE WOULD *NOT* KNIFE ANY-ONE FOR THAT REASON.
CORRECT AS NECESSARY

THEN CODE ALL ADDITIONAL MARKINGS.

3 THEN DEAL WITH THE NEXT ACT OF VIOLENCE. SAY:

"Now let's do the next one in the same way."

PLACE THE NEXT ORANGE CARD ON TOP OF THE FIRST ONE AND ASK BOY TO READ IT OUT AND THEN PUT A DISC ON ALL THAT APPLY

CODE AS HE GOES.

4 NOW DEAL WITH THE OTHER ORANGE CARDS, CODING FOR EACH AS HE GOES. BEFORE THE BEGINNING OF EACH OF THESE SEQUENCES, REMIND HIM TO CONSIDER ALL THE ANSWERS IN THE SQUARES.

5 WHEN THIS IS DONE, CODE THE CARDS IN THE SORTING BAGS ON BOARD 2. THESE ARE THE D5 CARDS.

Willingness to commit acts of violence

I would be willing to

1 stab someone with a knife
2 kick someone, or put the boot in
3 shoot someone with a gun
4 throw a petrol bomb at someone
5 be in a gang that is beating someone up
6 slash someone, or cut him with a razor
7 push someone out of a window
8 hit someone with a piece of wood, a club or an iron bar
9 use a whip on someone
10 use a karate chop on someone
11 throw acid in someone's face
12 try to throttle or strangle someone
13 swear at someone
14 hit someone with my fists
15 threaten someone
16 bash up or fight a coloured immigrant
17 hit someone with a bottle
18 use judo on someone
19 run someone down with a bike or motor bike or scooter or car
20 torture someone

Scale items

1 if it was in self defence
2 if the other person had insulted me
3 if I wanted some fun
4 if I was very angry with someone
5 if the other person was an enemy of my country
6 if it was necessary for protecting some other person
7 if I was just bored
8 if my life was threatened
9 if the person concerned was a boy who had insulted a girl I was going out with
10 if I was in a bad mood

SLIDE SCALES:
SECTION A &
CARDS AV

Preoccupation with different acts of violence

To find out to what extent boys are preoccupied with specific acts of violence

TAKE BOY TO SLIDE SCALES, SECTION A (PREOCCUPATION)

SAY:

"My questions now are about certain acts of violence. The acts are typed on *these* cards."

SHOW HIM PACK MARKED: ACTS OF VIOLENCE (AV)

"I want you to answer a question about each of the acts of violence typed on these cards."

PAUSE AND SAY:

"Here is the first of them (PASS CARD 1). Read it out for me please (WAIT).

SAY SLOWLY

"As you know, some boys see something or hear about it and then go on thinking about it from time to time. Perhaps they think about it all the time – they don't seem to be able to get it out of their minds."

PAUSE AND SAY SLOWLY

**"What I want to know is *how often* you think about the act on your card – how often the idea of it comes into your mind."

PAUSE AND THEN SAY *EMPHATICALLY:*

"It counts even if the idea just came and went in your mind. It would count even if you had no intention of doing it. It would count even if you were just remembering seeing it demonstrated somewhere. So you see what I am after is how often a thought about Karati chopping comes into your mind. (PAUSE). Think carefully about it before you answer."

SAY:

"I want you to answer by moving this yellow pointer to one of those boxes (POINT).

SAY:

"Read out aloud what's in those boxes."

CORRECT AS NECESSARY.

SAY:

"Now move the pointer to show me how often you have thought about the act on the card – how often the idea of it or a thought about it has come into your mind. Look at the card and then move the pointer to where you think is right for you."

CODE HIS CHOICE ON APPROPRIATE GRID

SAY:

"The rest are done in the same way. But please be open and honest about it. I have to know what actually happens in your mind. Remember you have a false name and nobody else will ever know what you told me.' '

PASS REST OF CARDS ONE AT A TIME, SAYING FOR EACH

"How often have you thought about *this* one. I mean how often has it come into your mind?" Read it out aloud for me and then answer by moving the pointer."

CODE EACH AS HE GOES.

CHAPTER 9

THE SURVEY PROCEDURE

Contents

9 THE SURVEY PROCEDURE

INTRODUCTION AND SUMMARY OF SURVEY METHODS

The survey procedures which were used to collect the required information were complex and lengthy. Because of this, it seemed desirable to precede the necessarily detailed description of them with a summary, this summary to be presented in the context of (i) a reminder about the different measuring techniques that were developed for use in the enquiry and (ii) an illustration of the way that these techniques and the survey would be used for investigating the different hypotheses.

The different measuring techniques used in the survey: a summary

The construction of measuring techniques for use in the enquiry extended over a period of sixteen months. It entailed the empirical development of procedures for making the following measurements.

1. The relative extent of boys' exposure to television violence from the year 1958.
2. The degree to which boys committed (a) acts of violence generally and (b) certain kinds of violence including
   - violence in the company of other boys,
   - irritating and annoying others,
   - violence in sport or play,
   - swearing at or abusing people.
3. The degree to which boys were preoccupied with acts of violence shown on television, felt like committing such acts, felt 'willing' to commit such acts.
4. The degree to which boys
   - were considerate towards others,
   - regarded violence as a way to solve their problems,
   - had angry or bitter feelings about 'people and things' in the world around them,
   - respected authority,
   - regarded violence as an intrinsic part of human nature,
   - exhibited symptoms of anxiety,
   - found the idea of violence attractive,
   - objected to the idea of violence,
   - had nightmares or disturbed sleep.

5 The degree to which boys were callous in relation to violent events around them and to violent events reported in the mass media.

6 The relative extent of boys' exposure to television output generally, to comics, to violent films, to newspapers.

The application of the measuring techniques in investigating the hypotheses: a summary

These eliciting procedures were used, in the context of a specialised research strategy, in a major social investigation. This was conducted in Greater London and was based on a representative sample of 1565 boys aged 12-17 years.

The purpose of the survey was to investigate each of the 22 hypotheses. Take hypothesis 1 as an example of what was done. This hypothesis was that:

> 'The long term exposure of boys to television violence increases the degree to which they themselves commit acts of violence.'

Through the investigation, assessments were made of each boy's exposure to television violence and of his personal involvement in violent behaviour. In addition, he and his parents provided a very large amount of background information about him and his up-bringing, the latter information to be used where applicable in the proposed matching procedure. Boys were separated into two groups, namely those with higher exposure scores and those with lower exposure scores. Those with lower exposure scores were then equated to the others in terms of the most relevant of 227 background variables. To be relevant, a background variable had *both* to be predictive of violent behaviour and to be a source of appreciable difference between the sub-groups which were to be matched. In fact, matching usually involved the equation of the two samples in terms of an empirically developed composite of about 20 relatively independent variables.

The violence scores of the higher exposure group and of the matched or modified lower exposure group were then compared. If there remained a significant difference between them after matching, then this particular test was regarded as providing evidence in support of the hypothesis. A similar check was made upon the reverse formulation of the hypothesis, to investigate the possibility that apparent support for the hypothesis was simply a reflection of the more violent boys being led, by that more violent disposition, to watch a greater amount of television violence.

Broadly the same strategy was used to investigate the possibility that level of violent behaviour was affected by: exposure to specific kinds of television violence; exposure to comics; exposure to violent films; exposure to newspapers.

Using this multiple testing system, many [1] separate 'testing by matching' operations were carried out. The overall strategy involved both in single tests and in the composite of tests is detailed in chapter 1.

The collection of the large amount of information required for the overall testing strategy summarised above called for an extended form of contact with each boy in the sample. In fact three steps in data collection were involved for each boy:

(a) an at-home interview with both the boy's mother and the boy himself;

(b) a phase of at-home information provision, by the boy and his parents, in the absence of the interviewer (i.e. a self-completion process which required the input of a lot of time by the boy and possibly by his parents);

(c) an extended and intensive interview with the boy at the Survey Research Centre, lasting for 3½ hours on average.

THE SURVEY METHODS IN DETAIL

SAMPLING

The total survey area

The enquiry was intended to be limited to Greater London, an area defined by the Ordnance Survey Map of 1966 [2], with a maximum east-west dimension of 36 miles, a maximum north-south dimension of 29 miles, and with an estimated population of 7,452,346. [3]

For strictly practical reasons connected with timing and costs [4], the survey area was limited to a region defined by a circle with diameter of approximately 24 miles centred on the survey headquarters in mid-London. In this part of Greater London, the population is 6,313,512, constituting 85 per cent of the whole of the Greater London population of 7,452,346. [3]

The type and size of sample required

What was required was a 1,600 person sample, representative of 12-17 year old boys living in this area – a requirement that was complicated by the fact that there is available nothing approaching a full listing of the names of such persons.

The requirement of representativeness is, of course, a standard one in survey research, but it was particularly important in the present case that such representativeness should extend to the matters under consideration in this particular enquiry: for example, extent and nature of TV viewing, degree to which boys are violent, degree to which they are callous, and so on.

The sampling method used

Stratified random sampling methods were used to secure a sample of 40 electoral wards from which to draw respondents, and the random principle was an integral feature of the method used for sampling boys within each of these wards.

Drawing a sample of 40 electoral wards

The selection of interviewing areas was conducted through a standard form of stratified random sampling. The whole of the survey area was first divided into 8 regions, as in table 9.1 and diagram 9.1. Within each of these regions the number of wards to be drawn (out of the required 40) was to be in direct proportion to its population size. Thus region C (north-west London) with its 784,980 inhabitants out of the total of 6,313,512 in the whole survey area, was to yield 5 wards [5], region D (northern London) with its population of 955,555 was to yield 6 wards, and so on.

The manner of drawing the required number of wards from each region was as follows.

1 All the electoral wards in the region were listed according to electorate size.

Table 9.1
Composition of the sample in terms of regions, London Boroughs and area units*

Regional sectors of Greater London	Constituent administrative areas (all London Boroughs)	Wards drawn
A. Inner London North	Hammersmith; Kensington & Chelsea; City of Westminster; Camden; Islington; Hackney; Tower Hamlets.	Wormholt Sherbrooks N/S Stanley Camden Thornhill Haggerston Defoe Poplar West
B. Inner London South	Wandsworth; Lambeth; Southwark; Lewisham.	Roehampton Shaftsbury/Latchmere Vassall Knight's Hall Thornton Bellenden Bricklayers Forest Hill
C. North-West	Harrow; Brent; Ealing.	Wealdstone Church End Kenton Walpole Perivale
D. Northern	Barnet; Haringey; Waltham Forest; Enfield (part)	Barnet Woodhouse West Hendon Alexandra Bowes High Cross Chingford Central
E. North-East	Redbridge; Newham; Barking	Ilford Bridge West Ham Hainault
F. South-West	Hounslow (part); Richmond upon Thames (part); Kingston upon Thames (part)	Central Twickenham East Sheen Malden Green
G. Southern	Merton; Sutton; Croydon (part)	Wimbledon East Mitcham North Wallington North East
H. South-East	Greenwich; Bromley (part)	Vanbrugh Bickley

*The number of wards drawn in each region was subject to rounding to maintain the total at 40 wards.

Diagram 9.1 Map of survey area (showing wards sampled and the regions within which these wards fell)

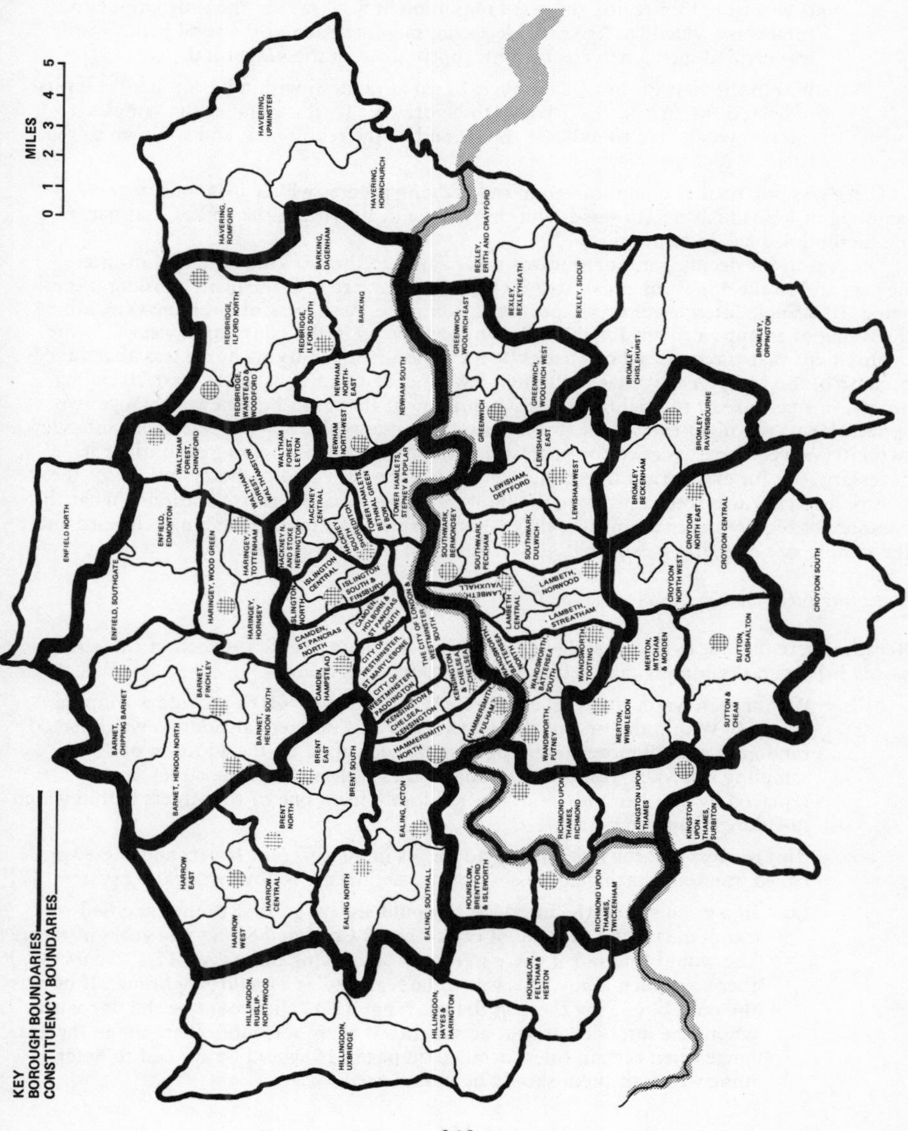

2 A cumulative count was then made, providing a cumulative total of persons in going from the ward with the smallest to that with the largest population.

3 If within a given region the ward requirement was (say) 5, then the cumulative total was divided by 5 to provide a sampling interval and the total list of wards was divided into 5 parts, each with approximately the same total.

4 Within the first of these, a number drawn at random within its cumulative limits indicated the first of the 5 wards to be drawn. To this number the sampling interval was added to indicate the second of the required 5, and so down to the fifth.

There was one further complication in the drawing process which arose out of the sampling of individuals *within* wards and this will be dealt with at the end of that part of the methodological description.

The reason for deciding upon 40 wards was related to the working potential of interviewers and to the appointment strategy which they were to use, the main considerations being: (i) a single interviewer was expected to complete 10 successful interviews (including the fixing of an appointment for the follow-up interview) in the course of a week; (ii) the requirement that three spaced call-backs be made before a qualifying home was abandoned because of 'no reply' meant that each interviewer needed a total list of at least 20 calling points; (iii) because of the tightly specific requirement that each interviewer arrange two appointments per night each night (for a period about a week after the placement interview), two interviewers were assigned to each ward with a view to their helping each other if necessary; (iv) for every ward the number of boys to be collected each day by car for the Centre interview was four, this being the limit imposed by safety considerations. What this complex of requirements meant was that 40 boys were to be interviewed in each ward and the sample size of 1,600 meant that 40 wards would thus be required.

Sampling boys within wards

Because there did not exist anything like a full list of young people for each of the 40 wards [6], special sampling tactics had to be developed, as follows.

1 Within each ward, the total electorate was divided by 40 to provide a sampling interval. Within the first of the 40 sections thus defined, an address was selected randomly and 39 more were progressively identified by the addition of 39 sampling intervals. If more than one of these fell into a single street, it was replaced by another address drawn randomly from one of the streets within which no address had been drawn.

2 This process had thus yielded 40 addresses in 40 different streets and these were called 'random starting addresses' for use within the following locating system. [7]

(a) In a given street, the interviewer would always go first to the specified 'random starting address'. Let this be 22 Cracknell Street in a given instance. She would find out if there were any boys living there aged 12-17 years. If there was such a boy, this was to be regarded as a *qualifying* home. If he was the only boy living there in the age range 12-17, he would be the one with whom the interview would be sought. If there was more than one in the age range, then certain rules, detailed on page 315 would be applied to determine which of them should be interviewed.

(b) If the random starting address in this street was *not* a qualifying one, then the interviewer was to call at the house with the next highest number on either side [8] of the first one (e.g. 24 Cracknell Street) and repeat the search there. If that house did not qualify, the interviewer called at the *next* highest, and so on, right along the street. If a qualifying home had not been found by then, the interviewer would work back down the other side of the street, and then back up the original side, eventually coming right back to the original 'random starting address'.

(c) In working through a street, the interviewer was to 'pick up' all available information about which homes in the street had in them boys aged 12-17. But they were also told it was vital that such information should *not* cause them to break their search system (e.g. by going straight to a house reputed to have 12-17 year old boys in it) for to do so could well be to overload the sample with boys who were well-known to the 'locals'. Rather, such information was to be used *solely* to identify possible qualifying homes at which the interviewer got no reply when she called there in the normal course of events. Taking short cuts by going *directly* to a home reputed to have boys in it would lead to dismissal (of the interviewer).

(d) The interviewer was told that in working to her basic search pattern she would at some time find herself in a position of getting no reply *and* of having no prior information that this was or was not a qualifying home. In such cases, she was to make a special effort to find out from other residents in the street if there was in fact a 12-17 year old boy normally resident there. Other boys, either in the street or in other homes, were of course a specially useful source of such information.

(e) The interviewer was told that in operating the stipulated search pattern, she was to regard each house she called at not only as a potential qualifying home, but also as a source of information about the residential whereabouts of boys aged 12-17 years.

(f) The interviewer was told that there were several important additional rules governing her search system.

  (i) A single 'random starting address' could lead to only *one* interview. Thus once the qualifying home was found and the interview completed there, the interviewer was to move on to another 'random starting address' in another street.

  (ii) If at a qualifying home there was more than one boy aged 12-17 years, the interviewer would use the following system to decide which boy should be interviewed.

    - At the first such home, the boy to be interviewed would be the one nearest in age to 12 (provided he was in the age range 12-17 years);
    - at the next such home, the boy to be interviewed would be the one closest to 18 years;
    - and so on, according to the pattern: nearest to 14, nearest to 13, nearest to 17, nearest to 15, nearest to 16, nearest to 12, nearest to 18, nearest to 14, nearest to 13, nearest to 17 and so on.

(iii) If at a qualifying home, the appropriate boy was away for a period, the interviewer was to enquire when he was due home and to 'earmark' that time for a return call to his home.

(iv) If the interviewer got an unbreakable refusal to take part, she was to resume her search in the street concerned, working to the specified search pattern.

(v) If the interviewer was to exhaust all the addresses in a given street without finding any qualifying home, then she was to ask for and would be given a substitute 'random starting point' in another street (by Head Office).

(vi) Two interviewers were to work in each ward, having 20 'random starting addresses' apiece.

(vii) Interviewers were to keep the following records of all calls made: street and house number; dates of all personal calls made at house; whether a qualifying house; source of information if not a qualifying house (i.e. a member of the household concerned, a neighbour, other); ages of all 12-17 year old boys in qualifying house; age of boy with whom interview sought; reason for failure to interview boy in qualifying house. A copy of the interviewer contact sheet is given in the Appendix to this chapter.

The success of the interviewers in carrying out their part of the sampling operation

Adherence to sampling instructions

Clearly the second part of the sampling operation was dependent for its success upon the interviewers carrying through their sampling instructions.

They operated under a system of tight control, continuing supervision and of follow-up checks. This control and checking system was directed at maintaining the quality of interviewing and rigour of the sampling system. With respect to sampling, the fieldwork controller was with few exceptions in daily telephone contact with each interviewer, passed out a substitute starting point for a new street only when the interviewer reported that some street had failed to yield a qualifying address, met interviewers on the job to discuss and clear up their sampling (and other) problems. Two 'checker' interviewers were employed to go over the routes claimed to have been traversed by interviewers, in order to find out if homes said to be non-qualifiers were *in fact* non-qualifiers, if contacts said to have been made with households had in fact been made with them, if reported refusals had in fact been refusals. The results of this check and of the supervision requirements indicated that the interviewers were in fact correctly reporting their calling system. A scrutiny of the interviewer contact sheets likewise was reassuring. The interviewers were of course made fully aware of the checking objectives and they knew that faulty work would lead to dismissal.

Percentage of eligible persons interviewed

An analysis of the contact sheets provided further evidence about the administration of the sampling system. Details are given in tables 9.2 and 9.3, their more salient indications being as follows.

1 On average, the number of addresses called at to find a qualifying address was ten; to find such an address and to conduct an interview there required, on average, calls at 13 addresses.

2 The total number of addresses called at in pursuit of the qualifying addresses was approximately 21,600.

3 The percentage of streets in which there was at least one qualifying address was 90 per cent and the percentage of these streets in which an interview was conducted was 93 per cent. The percentage of all qualifying addresses at which an interview was conducted was 82 per cent.

4 Of the 1,650 boys who were interviewed at home, 1,565 subsequently went through a second (intensive) interview at the Survey Research Centre. In terms of complete *double* interviews, the success rate was 78 per cent $(=\frac{1565}{2001})$.

Table 9.2

Success rates in locating qualifiers and interviewing them

Result of search and attempt to interview		No qualifier in street	One or more qualifiers in street
street:	n=	181	1685
qualifier asked to co-operate:	n=	0	2001
Interview conducted in qualifying home		N.A.	1650
Failure to conduct interview in qualifying home		N.A.	436
Reasons for failures to conduct interviews in qualifying homes:		N.A.	Per cent of failures
No contact made with family/with boy			5
Boy away long period			6
Boy ill/E.S.N.			4
Refusal by boy			36
– no reason given		14	
– too busy		8	
– working too late		6	
– not interested		8	
Refusal by parent(s)			39
Reason not clear			10

Percentage of all qualifier(s) interviewed at home = 82%

Percentage of qualifying streets where interview was conducted = 93%

Percentage of streets with at least one qualifying home = 90%

Table 9.3
Other sampling data

	Percentage of addresses
Origin of information about possibly qualifying homes	
Interviewer personally spoke to member of household	54
Interviewer informed by neighbour	31
Home not occupied	1
Not clear from interviewer's records	14
	n
Total number of addresses called at in identifying the 2001 qualifying addresses	21,615
Total number of qualifying addresses	2,001
Total number of boys interviewed at home	1,650 (= 82 per cent of 2,001)
Total number of boys interviewed both at home and at the Survey Research Centre	1,565 (= 78 per cent of 2,001)

THE INTERVIEW AT HOME

The foregoing description of sampling procedure brings us to the point where the interviewer had identified a given boy as a member of the target sample. From here on, and in very broad terms, the task of the interviewer was (i) to secure the agreement of the boy and his parents to complete certain information-giving tasks at home and (ii) to secure the agreement of the boy and his mother that the boy be brought to the Survey Research Centre for a follow-up interview. In doing this, the interviewer was urged to work closely to the printed instructions (see General Appendix).

On meeting the boy (and his mother) the interviewer was to tell him (i) that she was from the University and that she would like to interview him; (ii) that a fee of £2.00 was being paid to boys for this first interview *plus* a follow-up interview at the Survey Research Centre. To secure the interview, the interviewer was to explain as necessary (i) that the university enquiry was about the ways in which young people are influenced by various things – their reading, the films they see, the television they watch, the schooling they get, and so on; (ii) that the interview was strictly confidential. On securing agreement, the interviewer was to start the interview straight away, asking to come inside if not already there.

Once inside and ready to start interviewing, the interviewer (i) was to explain that she wanted to interview the mother first (for about 20 minutes); (ii) was to tell the boy briefly what sorts of things he would be asked about (e.g. his comic reading, newspaper reading, viewing, radio listening, his interests); (iii) was to tell him that for his second interview he would be called for by car to go to the Survey Research Centre and that he would get £2.00 at the end of that second interview.

The interview with the mother

The interview with the boy's mother was conducted through a fully structured questionnaire (see General Appendix). Through this questionnaire the mother was asked principally about:

- the boy's nature and behaviour when he was under 4 years of age (e.g. 'When your son was under 4 years of age, how often did he break up his toys or break up anything else?'/'When he was under 4, was he friendly towards strangers?');
- the ways in which she and her husband dealt with him in various situations when he was under 4 (e.g. 'When he was less than 4, how often did you cuddle him?'/'When he was less than 4, did you go to him if he cried?');
- the boy's illnesses if any and his general state of health;
- degree to which the boy has been scared to go to bed at night/has had to sleep with a light on.

In addition, she was asked for a lot of information about herself and her husband, including:

- their respective ages;
- household composition including the presence in the home of the boy's father, grandparents;
- the father's job and her own work history;
- television facilities in the home;
- education and religious background;
- country of birth.

These and the many other details provided by the mother were collected as possible matching variables. The reason for the limit 'under 4' was that this increased the likelihood of the behaviour and characteristic covered being stable in relation to television (see chapter 2). The boy was to be excluded from this part of the interview.

Where a mother was not available but a father was (as happened occasionally), this interview was conducted with the father.

At the end of this part of the interview, the interviewer asked the mother to complete a further questionnaire in the absence of the interviewer and to have the boy bring this completed questionnaire with him (in a sealed envelope – see later) on coming to the Centre for his interview. This questionnaire was a list of hobbies and topics and the mother was required to tick all those in the list that qualified as *her* interests. She was to put a single tick if 'fairly interested in it', a double tick 'if very interested in it', a cross if not interested in it and a double cross if she disliked it. For those of the items marked with a double tick, the mother was to indicate for how many years she had been interested in the items concerned. There was a similar list for the father to complete. The interviewer marked the two lists respectively as 'mother' and 'father'.

The purpose of this self-completion questionnaire was to gather evidence of the pre-television interests of the two parents, this information to be considered as possible matching material.

The 'interests' questionnaire is shown in the General Appendix.

The interview with the boy

The interview with the boy was aimed at setting him going on two self-completion tasks, one complex and the other very simple. The first concerned the boy's past viewing behaviour and it was completed as background to more intensive questioning at the Centre. The second concerned his use of the other mass media and various aspects of his personal background.

The past viewing of the boy

Details were presented, in chapter 4, of a technique for securing information about the boy's past viewing of both television generally (the control material) and more violent kinds of television. What was required was that each boy in the sample should provide certain information about his past viewing in relation to 117 different programmes. The two classes of information needed about each of the 117 programmes were: (i) whether the boy had *ever* viewed the programme concerned; (ii) the period of years between his first and last viewing of it.

As a procedure, that technique had emerged as highly reliable (see chapter 4). But having boys use the technique, in a self-completion context, called for a substantial programme of introduction and demonstration. The interviewer then worked through a 45-minute sequence which is best described by presenting the verbatim instructions to which she worked (presented also in the General Appendix).

(VERBATIM PROCEDURE, PAGES 7-9 OF ITEM 1 IN SECTION III OF THE GENERAL APPENDIX)

1. Explain that you want to demonstrate what he has to do with the booklet.

2.(a) Ask him to read aloud the first page of instructions and (you) flip through the booklet to show him the white instructions and the coloured programme sheets.

(b) Then ask him for what is not clear and clarify this for him (though be guided in this by an awareness that much detailed explanation is still to come).

3.(a) Tell him you want him to try it out using YOUR booklet.

(b) Take out his three envelopes to be used as markers, lay them out and then take out of YOUR booklet 10 programme sheets for him to sort, but be sure to take them out one at a time. These 10 are the first of the 20 which you will be using from your demonstration pack.

(c) Watch him sort these for any evidence of misunderstanding (noting that he must pile the sheets onto the SQUARES on the marker envelopes).

(d) Then challenge each sheet sorted into heap 1 by asking if he has EVER seen it. Then challenge each sheet sorted into heap 2, similarly by asking if he has EVER seen it. Then challenge each sheet in heap 3 by asking why he sorted it into heap 3. CORRECT ANY MISUNDERSTANDINGS and ask what else he is puzzled or confused about. Then stress the following three rules:

- he must put into heap 3 all programmes he is NOT SURE about;
- he must NOT GUESS because that will spoil the information he is giving us;
- he must be absolutely honest over where he sorts the sheets.

4. Now pass him 10 more programme sheets and watch him sort them. Take these out of your booklet one at a time. Clear up his mistakes or his stated problems.

5. Now tell him he has about 100 sheets to sort in all and flip through his own booklet to illustrate this.

6. NOW explain what happens when he has finished the sorting operation.

(a) Explain that at the end of his sorting of the 100 or so sheets he will find THIS card in his booklet. SHOW IT in his demonstration pack and ask him to read it out aloud for you. This is the sheet numbered 134, and beginning with the heading NEXT STEPS.

(b) Ask him to do what it says with the three heaps of sorted sheets (that is, put heap 3 into envelope 3, put heap 2 into envelope 2, turn heap 1 over). Correct him if he is wrong.

(c) (i) Ask him to read Instruction 135 (relating to his age on first and last seeing a programme in a given series) and then to try answering the first two age questions on the back of the topmost programme sheet in his heap 1.

(ii) When he has done this, tell him there's a way of making things easier for him. Ask him to turn to Instruction 136 and read it aloud.

(iii) Tell him that it helps to know when the programme actually started to be broadcast and when was the last time it was broadcast. Take the sheet for which he has just given 2 ages, remind him of when the programme was first shown and ask him if he now wants to change the age he gave for first looking at it. Enter the new age. Do the same thing with respect to the age of last seeing the programme.

(iv) Now tell the boy it can help even more if he is reminded about some of the things that were happening when he was younger. Show him his PERSONAL TIME CHART* and get his personal entries onto it. Then tell him to look at what was happening the year the series was first shown, what was happening the year he said he first watched it . . . and ask him what changes he now wants to make in his answer about his age the first time he watched the programme. Enter the change.

(v) Now tell the boy that the other ages should be worked out by him in the same way. He should always look to see what years the series started and finished and then he should use his Personal Time Chart to decide what age he was when he FIRST saw it and what age he was when he LAST saw it.

(vi) Now get him to work through the rest of the programme sheets on his heap 1. Throughout, help him to make use of the 2 aids available to him (i.e. dates of first and last broadcast; Personal Time Chart).

(vii) In doing the above (i.e. (i)-(vi)):

- encourage him to ask for help if he is puzzled at all;
- watch him for evidence of error or difficulty or misunderstanding;
- draw his attention to the NOTE at the bottom of each of the programme sheets.

7. Tell the boy that this is what he is being asked to do with all his heap 1 sheets.

8. Tell him also that when he finishes with the ages, he should put a rubber band round the heap 1 sheets and put this lot into the heap 1 envelope.

9. Now ask him to say what he is not clear about, and clear up the problem for him. Don't say 'Have you any doubts or uncertainties?'. Say instead 'What are the things about that job that are not clear yet?'.

10. Tell him he will find a pleasant surprise in the white pages.

11. Say his job is to complete the sorting of the sheets after you (the interviewer) leave him, getting it done as quickly as possible during the week and giving us the completed job when we collect him for his second interview.

12. Now take back all the demonstration pages, telling the boy that he must start afresh with his OWN booklet of programme sheets.

*See this in chapter 4.

The self-completion booklet about other media usage, interests, personal details

The boy was next introducted to a self-completion booklet. It was in fact a fully structured questionnaire designed for self-completion at home by boys in the sample. This is presented in full in the General Appendix.

The information requested in it was as follows.

1 *Comic reading.* On page 1 of the questionnaire, the boy was asked 'Which of the following comics or magazines have you ever *regularly* read or *regularly* looked through?'. There followed a list of 21 comics and comic books. The boy was required to put a tick after each to which the answer to the question was 'yes' and a cross against all the others (see chapter 5). There was also a question on this page about the *frequency* with which the boy reads a comic of any kind 'these days'.

2 *Newspapers read.* On page 2, a similar type of question was asked about each of 21 publications made up of the national dailies, the London evening papers, the Sunday nationals and three weekly publications. Also on this page was a question about general frequency of reading a daily newspaper 'these days' and similarly for frequency of reading a Sunday newspaper (see chapter 5 for details).

3 *Violent films.* On page 3 there was a question about whether or not the respondent had ever seen certain films at the cinema. A list of 22 violent films was presented for respondent consideration. Also on this page was a question

about the general frequency of attending a cinema 'these days', one about the boy's favourite film stars and another about the types of film the boy likes best.

4 *Interests.* On page 4 were questions about the boy's interest in a wide range of sports of the more active and/or violent kind and on pages 8-10 questions about his other interests.

5 *Musical tastes.* On page 5 was a list of 12 different kinds of music which boys were asked to tick if 'interested in' (e.g. Reggae, 'pop', folk) and two questions about instrument playing by the boy himself.

6 *Personal details.* On pages 6 and 7 were questions about a range of personal details needed as possible matching variables and including: age, place of birth, various details about schooling and exams, religious denomination and frequency of church attendance, whether left or right handed, the availability at school of special projects and of certain rough games or sports, whether discipline at school was considered tough, whether the boy was usually tired after a day at school, frequency of lying awake at night and of having nightmares, his speed compared with other boys in swimming and running, whether he shaves yet, his general state of health, hair colour, nail biting, choice of older or younger boys as friends, attendance at a youth club, membership of scouts, etc. (all of them contributing to the total list of over 200 possible matching variables).

Certain of the variables listed in 1-6 were required for grading the boy in terms of dependent and independent variables referred to in the hypotheses, but most were included as potential matching criteria. The self-completion questionnaire is presented in full in the General Appendix.

Making the appointment for interview at the Survey Research Centre

At the end of the interview the boy was asked to agree, with the consent of his parent(s), an appointment to come to the Survey Research Centre for interview at a specific time approximately a week hence. To aid his agreement he was told that:

- he would get £2 for the double interview (to be paid at the end of the second interview);
- he would also get a record token and could take part in a Treasure Hunt for which there were prizes;
- a lot of other boys would be taking part.

He was told that the interview would be at the Survey Research Centre in mid-London, and that a car would call for him. Stress was laid on the importance of his taking part and upon his being ready for collection by the driver at the time agreed for this.

He was reminded that he should bring with him in the large envelope provided for this purpose his own sorted programme sheets, his self-completion booklet, the interest sheets of his parents.

He was left an appointment card on which was the date and time of his agreed appointment (to be collected by car). He and his family were thanked for their co-operation. As the interviewer left she reminded them once more than the boy should be ready for collection by the driver at the appointed time.

Concerning the appointment making system. The appointment system was delicately balanced and difficult to maintain. What was needed for each of the sampling sub-areas was a supply of 4-5 interviewees per evening, delivered at the Centre on time. 'On time' meant at approximately 5.15 pm on four evenings of the week and 6.30 pm on the remaining evening. By scheduling a start to evening interviewing for 5.15 pm, it was expected that boys, many of whom were only 12 or 13, should be through the interview by about 8.45 pm and ready to go home by car at about 9.00 pm. The 'late start' evening (Thursday) was mainly for older boys or for boys whose commitments prevented them from starting earlier.

Since boys came from areas as far as 12 miles out from central London, the time of collection had to be varied according to the distance of the sampling area from the centre of town.

Two interviewers worked in each sampling area. Each was to interview 10 boys per week and was to arrange that these 10 boys be collected for the second interview a week after the first – two per night per interviewer. This sort of operation was going on simultancously in each of four interviewing areas, with the aim of spreading such interviews out at the level of sixteen per night.

Ordinarily one might expect some freedom of movement in such a system, for example by having an interviewer in one of the other areas make up a shortfall in an interviewer's appointments, or by making do with less than the maximum of 16 per night. To a minor degree this was done, but (i) car safety requirements put a limit of four upon the number of persons who could travel with the driver; (ii) it was not always possible to cut back on the number of intensive interviewers on duty on any one night; (iii) the field work had to be completed within six months.

In fact the interviewers who conducted the first interview (called 'Placement Interviewers' because they 'placed' the self-completion material in the homes of boys) kept remarkably well to these tight arrangements. However there was some free play in that another placement interviewer and another car driver were available to be called on, and in that it was usually possible to provide an extra intensive interviewer to cope with an occasional overbooking on some one night. Notwithstanding this, the appointment system was a tight and difficult one and it was within this system that the placement interviewers had to make their appointments.

COLLECTING BOYS FROM THEIR HOMES FOR INTERVIEW AT THE SURVEY RESEARCH CENTRE

The main collection task was carried through by three drivers employed by the Centre and by one or more drivers from car hire firms. Drivers were expected to be in their respective collection areas a half-hour ahead of time in order to familiarise themselves with the various collection points and then to complete their collections quickly, getting to the Centre with the boys as quickly as possible. This operation was beset by difficulties, namely: by some one or other of the boys in a given area not being ready on time; by the driver getting lost in getting to the area or not being able to find some one address; by the driver being held up by heavy traffic either going to the area or in getting through it back to the Centre.

The three drivers employed by the Centre generally did a very good job in spite of the difficulties. But the several hire car firms able to take part in this work, and tried out in sequence during the survey, repeatedly failed to get to their pick-up areas on time and/or to get to the Centre with the boys on time.

CHECKING IN AT THE CENTRE

On arrival at the Centre, boys were offered light refreshments (soft drinks, doughnuts, sandwiches). Following this they were checked in by the receptionist and given a false name (on a card) for use throughout the interview (e.g. Charlie, Bert, John, Fred, Peter, Bill). They were then taken by the receptionist through to one or the other of the Centre's 18 interviewing rooms.

THE INTENSIVE INTERVIEW

The principal procedures

As he entered his interviewing room he found his intensive interviewer waiting for him and was introduced to him by his (the boy's) false name. The boy was told by the interviewer that this false name was the only name he would be known by as far as he, the interviewer, was concerned. (The interviewer was introduced to the boy by his first name only). The intensive interviewer and the boy now began a 3½ hour interview, broken by rest pauses, by refreshment breaks as necessary, by the requirements of the Treasure Hunt and by a physical measurement session.

The general form of the intensive interview

The interview was basically structured, though it left – and depended upon – a considerable amount of directed 'free play' for interviewer initiative. The interview was fully tape-recorded so that the quality of the interviewer's work could be checked and controlled (see later for details).

In the typical interview the boy went through the following stages..

1 The self-completion materials brought in by the boy were checked for completeness.

2 The interviewer delivered a questioning technique designed to get estimates of the total number of times the boy had seen the programmes already classified by him as 'having definitely been seen' (see chapter 4 for details).

3 The interviewer delivered the eliciting procedure designed to provide a comparative estimate of the boy's involvement in violent behaviour.

4 The eight assessments of attitude/reactive tendencies were delivered in the same general sequence as were the assessments of the willingness of boys to commit TV featured acts of violence (and preoccupation with these).

5 A large number of personal details were collected from the boy – details of a kind that it was inappropriate to collect through the self-completion method at home. These were for use as possible matching criteria.

6 Various physical measurements were made (e.g. weight, height, grip strength).

Items 1-5 were always delivered in that order. Item 6 was delivered at different times for the different interviews, both to spread out the demand for physical measuring equipment and to allow interviewers to use the visit to these facilities for varying the routine of the interview for the boy. After making the various physical measurements, the interviewer passed the boy back to the receptionist who took him through the Treasure Hunt (a matter of sticking pins into a map of London to indicate where certain clues led the boy to think that 'treasures' were hidden). The treasure hunt did not of course provide data to be used in the investigation.

In the course of the interview and at the discretion of the interviewer the boy was taken out to the kitchen for refreshment. For some boys this was done more than once, its purpose being to break the long sequence of the interview, to allow the boy or the interviewer to go to the washroom, to keep the boy alert.

Another feature of the test room procedure was the deliberate variation of the type of task the boy was required to do. Thus whereas all the attitude measurements might have been conducted through ticking lists of statements, one list after the other, this was thought to be likely to make the whole task so boring as to produce meaningless results. Accordingly the equipment used to deliver these measuring procedures was varied, sorting boxes being used in one case, a slide system in another, buttons and lights in another and a disc system in yet another. Overall there was very considerable variation both in equipment and in the nature of the tasks to be performed. The reader will find pictorial presentations of these in chapters 1-9 of this volume.

Checking the boy's self-completion materials

Each boy was required to bring with him, in a large envelope provided for this purpose (i) his three envelopes containing programme sheets; (ii) his own self-completion booklet; (iii) the self-completion interest forms of his mother and his father.

The interviewer was to check through these items to find out (i) if all were present; (ii) if each item had been satisfactorily completed. In the event of the interest check lists being missing, the parents were to be approached to complete the old or fresh copies. If the boy's self-completion task was unfinished or if one of the self-completion documents was missing, the interviewer was required to collect that information before starting the interview. In fact it happened that in only very few cases were the required materials missing or incomplete.

Finalising the frequency of viewing check (see details of technique development in chapter 4)

The boy's work (at home) on the programme booklet had led him (i) to sort all 117 programmes as 'definitely seen' or 'never seen' or 'not sure'; (ii) to enter on the backs of all the 'definitely seen' programmes his estimates of his age on first watching it and also his age on last watching it.

The interviewer now proceeded first to check on the adequacy of the boy's sortings and estimates and then to get estimates of how many times each programme had been seen in the interval of time between his first and last seeing it. The procedure for doing this is detailed in verbatim form in Section C of the interviewer's instruction manual and may be examined in the General Appendix. In summary form, this procedure was as follows.

1. The intensive interviewer challenged the boy's sorting of all programmes in the 'definitely seen' envelope using a book of visual and memory aids to do this and challenging and probing systematically. The age limits on each card sorted as 'yes' were also challenged.

2 The intensive interviewer then dealt with the frequency of viewing the *first* of the programmes in the 'definitely seen' envelope, using the following lengthy procedure in order to teach the boy what he had to do and to develop in him an awareness of the need for care.

(a) The boy was reminded of the ages entered for his first and last viewing of the programme and was told by the interviewer that this represented a period of so many years.

(b) The boy was then told that in that period of (say 2) years, there were so many broadcasts of that particular programme. This number could be estimated by working from the yearly averages given in the interviewer's instruction manual for that programme – and for each of the 117 programmes. The interviewer specified the maximum.

(c) The interviewer then asked the boy to say how many out of that maximum (for the programme being considered) he had in fact seen, but much stress was put upon his taking a lot of care in giving this answer.

'I want you to tell me just how many of these . . . episodes you think you saw. BUT before you answer, I want to say that it is very important for you to make a real effort to remember how many times it was. If you answer carelessly, then our work will be wasted. It's very important for you to really try to remember how many times it was. Will you really try hard for me?' WAIT FOR HIS REPLY.

EMPHASISE WITH:

'Thank you. Your careful reply is absolutely necessary if our research is to be of any use.'

SAY:

'So you watched . . . (NAME THE PROGRAMME) over a period of . . . years. In that time, there were . . . (GIVE NUMBER) episodes of . . . . ' (NAME THE PROGRAMME).

WRITE NUMBER JUST UNDER NAME OF PROGRAMME AND LET BOY SEE IT. SAY:

'How many of those . . . episodes do you think you saw?'

WRITE HIS NUMBER IN THE SPACE JUST BELOW Q.2 ON THE BACK OF THE SHEET.

IF THE BOY SEEMS TO BE IN DIFFICULTY WITH THE QUESTIONS OR TO BE ANSWERING CARELESSLY, HELP HIM IN ONE OR MORE OF THE FOLLOWING WAYS:

- Use your visual and verbal aids.
- Tell him the time of day it was on.
- Remind him of how it differs from some other programmes.

(d) The interviewer was told to be ready to challenge any slipshod answering, saying such things as:

- You mean you saw just about every episode that was shown when you were a viewer of . . . .
- But that's more than were shown.
- So you saw only very few of the episodes of . . . that were broadcast in the period you were a viewer of it. Is that right? Only . . . . (GIVE HIS FIGURE)?

SAY:

'So you see I do need you to be careful about your answer. Think carefully before you give me the number of times. Now let's do the others.'

3 The intensive interviewer now dealt with the second programme sheet (in the 'definitely seen' pack of programme sheets) in less protracted fashion, namely:

'Let's take the next programme in your heap 1. It is . . . . You said you viewed that one from age . . . to . . . . That's . . . years you were a viewer of it.'

'In those . . . years, there were . . . episodes of . . . . '

ENTER THIS NUMBER ON HIS CARD JUST BELOW THE TITLE OF THE PROGRAMME.

'How many of those . . . episodes do you think you saw?'

ENTER REPLY.

4 Thereafter the same procedure was applied to each of the other sheets in the 'definitely seen' pack, but with the stipulation that if the boy seemed to be getting careless or seemed uncertain, the interviewer must administer the challenging procedure as set out under 2 above or some appropriate part of it. Throughout, the interviewer was required to use the visual aids to help recall and to challenge (i) any tendency to answer in the same manner for each programme (e.g. 'all of them', 'about half'); (ii) all large claims (e.g. 'Could you think carefully about that one again – I really need a careful and correct reply'; 'Do you really and truly mean that you saw just about all of them?')

5 All claims were entered on the back of the programme sheet concerned. The programme sheets were clipped together and put back into the 'definitely seen' envelope.

6 The programme sheets in the 'not sure' envelope were now taken out and an effort made to clear up whatever uncertainty had led to their being classified that way. If this could be done, the interviewer then got frequency estimates for these programmes, using the same technique as for the 'definitely seen' programmes.

Administering the procedure for eliciting information about boys' involvement in violent behaviour

This procedure has already been described in some detail in chapter 6. Accordingly all that need be done at this point is to outline (i) the preparatory steps taken to deliver it and (ii) the equipment used.

The boy was told that the next step was a very important one. He was made aware of the equipment that was to be centrally used in this procedure, namely the sorting screen, the book of instructions and the book of sorting cards. The screen was, up to this point, set up either on the floor or on the side table out of the way of the interviewer and the boy.

The boy was introduced to the procedure in the following way.

BASIC INSTRUCTIONS

STEP 1.

1 Tell boy we want him to sort some cards and that on each card is a description of one of the things that boys may get up to in their spare time.

2 Show him green card 1 as in example. Ask him to read out what is on it. (If he can't read, you will have to read all cards for him).

3 Tell him that you have about 50 more cards and that you need to know if he has done these things in the last six months. Say 'we' will be using 'this' screen and 'these' sorting boxes in the interview.

4 Explain that:

- if he did it in the last six months, he should put the card in the YES box;
- if he did not do it in the last six months, he should put the card in the NO box;
- if he is not sure he should put it face down in front of the screen.

5 Also explain:

- where you will sit and he will sit;
- the use of the slot at the bottom of the screen.

6 Check his grasp of instructions by asking him:

- what goes into the YES box;

– what goes into the NO box;

– what to do if NOT SURE.

STEP 2.

INITIAL SORTING TO TEACH THE RULES

TELL BOY YOU WILL SOON BE GOING BEHIND THE SCREEN AND WILL PASS HIS CARDS TO HIM ONE AT A TIME THROUGH THE SLOT. TELL HIM THE FIRST FEW WILL BE PRACTICE CARDS.

SEAT YOURSELF BEHIND SCREEN, SAY:

'You will see that the cards I pass you are about some of the rough and violent activities that boys sometimes get up to – some of the arguments, pranks or fights they get into. This is something a lot of boys do. We want to know how much of it you yourself do.'

'In your case it is only the LAST SIX MONTHS we are interested in. We want to know about things you did in the LAST SIX MONTHS.'

'Remember you have got a false name and I don't want to know your REAL name. That is so that you can tell us EVERYTHING. Is that all right?'

'We NEED to know EVERYTHING if our research is going to be useful. If you hold back anything then we will both be just wasting our time. Is that O.K?'

'And remember you have a false name. I will be calling you . . . (GIVE FALSE NAME).'

'I don't know you, you don't know me, and I don't suppose we will ever meet again. And everything you say is absolutely private.'

STEP 3.

SAY:

'Just before we start, I want you to think back to a time that was six months ago . . . That will be back in . . . .' (NAME THE MONTH).

PAUSE

'Round about that time . . . '

NAME 3-4 MAJOR NEWS ITEMS

THEN SAY:

'Can you remember anything YOU were doing round about that time?'

PAUSE AND ENCOURAGE HIM TO FIX SOME PERSONAL EVENTS.

THEN SAY:

'So when I ask you if you did something IN THE LAST SIX MONTHS, I mean the six months since (NAME THE MONTH) last when you were . . . (NAME HIS PERSONAL EVENTS OR, IF THERE WERE NOT ANY, THE PUBLIC EVENTS OF THAT TIME).

'Once you've sorted them all, I'll want to ask you some questions about some of them, so try to sort them carefully.'

After this, a series of five practice cards was used to reinforce the five basic rules, the system of instruction being that of question and answer. The verbal procedure for the first of the practice cards was as follows.

SAY:

'Now let's try sorting some of the cards.'

PASS CARD 1 (KICKING SOMEONE).

SAY:

'I WILL HOLD IT while you read it out aloud for me.'

SAY:

'Suppose a boy did that BY ACCIDENT – for example when he was playing football. What box should he put it in?'

CORRECT HIM IF WRONG (RIGHT ANSWER IS THE YES BOX).

'So the rule is: if you kicked someone even by accident it would go into the yes box.'

SAY:

'Now look at this card again and decide whether you have kicked someone in the last six months. Then put it into the box where it ought to go.'

PUSH THE CARD RIGHT THROUGH THE SLOT SO THAT HE CAN PICK IT UP AND SORT IT.

There then followed four more practice cards designed to teach the rules that:

- an act counts as 'yes' even if it was not very serious;
- an act does NOT count if it was done more than six months ago;
- the card should be placed face downwards if the boy is not sure where to sort it;
- an act counts even if it was done in self defence.

After this, the boy was tested to find out if he had grasped the rules and to re-teach him if he was in error or in doubt.

SAY:

'That's the end of the practice. Let's just make sure we've got all the rules.'

1 'If you did it by accident, what box would it go in?' (= 'YES' box).

CORRECT IF WRONG. PRAISE IF RIGHT.

2 'If it was not very serious, what box would you put it in?' (= 'YES' box).

CORRECT IF WRONG.

3 'If it was MORE THAN SIX MONTHS AGO that you did what was on the card, what box would you put the card in?' (= 'NO' box).

PRAISE IF RIGHT. CORRECT IF WRONG.

4 'If you can't remember whether you did it or not in the last six months where would you put the card?' (= 'FACE DOWN IN FRONT OF YOU').

IF THE BOY IS WRONG, TELL HIM:

'You would put the card face down in front of you.'

5 'Even if there was a good reason for doing what was on the card – like defending yourself – what box would you put the card in?' (= 'YES' box).

PRAISE IF RIGHT. CORRECT IF WRONG.

6 'You are allowed to ask me any questions to help sort the cards. Ask as much as you like. But if that doesn't help you, put the card face down in front of you.'

'Please ask me questions every time things are not clear to you.'

After a further reminder, the boy was processed through the rest of the 53 web-cards, with interspersed reminders and instructions as detailed in chapter 6.

After all 53 web-cards had been sorted, the boy was taken through his 'not sure' cards and as many of these as possible were resolved with the aid of the interviewer.

After this came the 'pretending game' with instructions as follows:

SAY:

'Now I want you to imagine something for me. I want you to imagine you have used violence on a boy and that this has damaged him very badly.'

PAUSE AND SAY:

'Just imagine you had done that' (PAUSE). 'Would you have admitted it to me?'

If the boy responded 'yes', he was to be questioned to find out 'why' and the interviewer was to report back to him the gist of his reasons in order to consolidate his willingness to make admissions. He was in addition required to offer several extra reasons for talking, as set out on a fold-out chart constituting part of the instruction booklet for interviewers (see page 53g of booklet in chapter 6), for example 'What you say is absolutely private'/'There's no name connected with it . . . in fact you've got a false name'/'In our report, all this will come out as tables, with lots of figures and absolutely no names.' (The interviewer was required to repeat the case for 'telling' and to be prepared to readminister arguments as he thought necessary). He was then to proceed with certain questions about each card sorted as 'yes' (see later).

If the boy replied 'no' (as did many of the boys), the interviewer was likewise to find out why. He was then to discuss that boy's reasons for not being willing to tell and to do this in a flexible manner. When he had identified the main reasons (and tried to deal with them) he was to use, as necessary, further arguments from a list of standard 'counter arguments' set out (for this purpose) on page 53g of the interviewers' instruction booklet. There were different counter arguments for different objections or fears. For example boys who feared that interviewers might 'tell someone' were eligible for counter arguments such as: 'If we did a thing like that, boys would not help us any more . . . . We'd be finished'; . . . 'If we talked, other boys in your area would get to know and we'd be finished'; . . . 'Anyhow, there were at least four boys came in together. I don't know their names. Even if I did, I wouldn't know which one you were'; . . . 'I wouldn't do a thing like that. Anyhow it would only be my word against yours . . . there are no witnesses . . . you could deny the whole thing'; . . . . The interviewer repeated relevant arguments and stored these to use throughout the rest of the interview as a device for disarming any remaining or resurgent wariness in the boy.

After this, the interviewer asked the boy to re-sort all his 'no' cards; going back behind the screen for this.

In the final and crucial part of the extraction procedure, the interviewer put the screen aside and questioned the boy in detail about each of the cards sorted as 'yes'. The interviewer worked to the following instructions for each of these cards.

SAY:

'Let's take the first card you sorted as 'YES'. It is . . . '

READ IT OUT AND HOLD IT IN FRONT OF BOY

'Exactly how many times did you do that in the last 6 months?'

FORCE A NUMERICAL ANSWER AND ENTER ON FRONT OF CARD.

THEN SAY:

'Tell me the different things you did on those occasions/that occasion.'

FOR EACH OF THEM, GET ENOUGH INFORMATION TO BE ABLE TO SPECIFY:

- The nature of the act (e.g. kicked, punched, pushed, cut, . . .)
- The object of the act (e.g. another boy, a cat, . . .)
- The implement if any (e.g. knife, stick, . . .)
- What led him to do it (e.g. the boy was rude to him, 'for fun', . . .)
- The circumstances (e.g. in football)

THEN ASK

'How many times did you do that sort of thing?'

ENTER NUMBER AFTER THE SPECIFIED ACT.

IF THE ACT SOUNDS LIKE A REPEAT OF A PREVIOUS ONE, CHECK THAT THIS IS SO AND IN THAT EVENT ENTER A MINUS SIGN AFTER IT.

NOW GO ON, GETTING HIM TO SPECIFY THE OTHER ACTS AND GETTING A NUMBER FOR EACH. MARK AS MINUS IF THE ACT HAS BEEN SPECIFIED ALREADY.

KEEP IT UP WHILE HIS OVERALL TOTAL IS STILL GREATER THAN THE SUM OF HIS SPECIFICS.

NOW DEAL WITH ALL OTHER 'YES' SHEETS IN THE SAME WAY.

BUT WORK QUICKLY.

This step brought to an end the questioning procedure for the violence statements. A typical entry might look as follows.

I have had a fight

5 times

Had a fist fight with a boy and punched him in the face and chest. He had insulted me when I was with a girl 1

With my gang I had a punch up with boys in another gang, using fists, boots and sticks. They're the lot from . . . Street and we don't like them 6

I have had a fight.

The assessment of attitude and reaction tendencies

After a break for food and talk, the interviewer began delivery of a series of attitude-type measurements concerned respectively with:

- callousness in relation to *near* events involving violence and to *distant* events involving violence;
- consideration for others;
- acceptance of violence as a way to solve problems;
- preoccupation with and willingness to commit certain TV-presented forms of violence; frequency of feeling like committing such acts;
- tendency to have angry or bitter feelings towards the 'world about one';
- respect for authority;
- a belief that violence in people is basic and inevitable;
- a general state of anxiety and/or emotional disturbance;
- tendency to object to the whole idea of violence;
- a tendency to be attracted by the idea of violence.

These measures have all been described in detail in earlier chapters and all that need be done in this chapter is to specify the order and some special features of their administration to boys.

1 Where a specific measure was made up of rather similar but independent parts which together would take a long time to deliver, those parts were delivered as separate sub-tests, with other attitude tests coming in between them. The purpose of doing this was to reduce boredom with what would otherwise be a long test and to safeguard the procedure as a whole against boredom. Thus the first element of attitude measurement dealt with one of the three units in the 'callousness towards near-violence' measurement, the second with consideration for others, the third with acceptance of violence as a way to solve problems, the fourth with the second of the units in the 'callousness towards near-violence' measurement and so on, as shown in diagram 9.1.

Diagram 9.1 Order and characteristics of attitude tests

Order of test	Type of test	Type of equipment used
1	First unit of measurement of callousness in relation to near violence	Visual stimulus on wall; various cards describing reactions to stimulus; bags on wall for sorting cards.
2	Consideration for others	Various cards carrying the different attitudinal statements; bags on wall for sorting cards to indicate whether boy agrees, disagrees or is undecided about them.
3	Acceptance of violence as a way to solve one's problems	Ditto 2.
4	Second unit of measurement of callousness in relation to near violence	Ditto 1.
5	Third unit of measurement of callousness in relation to near violence	Ditto 1.
6	Preoccupation with acts of violence seen on television	A pointer on a slide calibrated in terms of frequency; boy moves pointer along slide to indicate his personal frequency.
7	Tendency to have angry and bitter feelings towards the world about one.	A press button system in which boy responds to verbal stimuli. Response is indicated to boy and to interviewer by red light behind a blown-up version of his choice of response.
8	Respect for authority	Ditto 7.
9	View that human violence is inborn and inevitable	Ditto 7.
10	Feelings of anxiety and of emotional disturbance	Ditto 7.
11	First unit of measurement of callousness in relation to distant violence	Ditto 1.
12	Second unit of measurement of callousness in relation to distant violence	Ditto 1.
13	Frequency of feeling like committing any one of 20 acts of violence frequently shown on television	Ditto 6.
14	Attractiveness of violence to the boy	Ditto 2.
15	Tendency to object to the idea of violence	Ditto 2.
16	Third unit of the measurement of callousness in relation to distant violence	Ditto 1.
17	Willingness to do various forms of TV presented violence	A set of statements in squares, with boy placing discs in each to indicate agreement or disagreement in his case.

2 A second feature of this measurement sequence was that the equipment used was varied (even though this was not essential for test delivery) in order to keep the boy interested. Thus whereas most of the attitude testing *could* have been done by having the boy sort cards into bags to indicate agreement or disagreement with what was written on the cards, this equipment was replaced in some of the tests with a 'press button and lights' system, in others with a 'pointer on slide' system and in one case with a 'disc placement' system. This design for variability included the tactic of moving the boy around the room for the different tests, and of having him stand from time to time. Diagram 9.2 provides an indication of the different types of equipment used.

At the same time, basic procedure in most of the tests remained one of having the boy endorse statements as ones he agreed with or disagreed with or that he regarded as true or false.

Details of the administrative procedure for all the different tests are set out in chapter 7. One of the important features of these procedures was that the interviewer was required to work to printed instructions in delivering the various measures – a delivery which was fully tape recorded for quality control purposes.

Personal details for pool of matching variables

After the attitude testing phase of the interview, the boy was put through a lengthy questioning session designed principally to provide *some* of the items needed for the pool of matching variables. In this sequence there were groups of questions about each of family composition, size and nature of dwelling, household facilities and possessions, degree to which the neighbourhood was violent, family cohesiveness, various aspects of parental behaviour especially their treatment of the boy, living conditions for the boy at home, aspects of the boy's personality, his own social behaviour, aspects of school achievements and of school life including truancy, and so on. There was a special section on the punishments his parents administered to him.

Physical measurements

At some point during the interview, the interviewer took the boy to the reception area in order to carry out a number of basic measurements including those of height, weight, grip strength, cranial circumference, chest measurement (inflated, deflated). Skin colour was also recorded. This short sequence was fixed to occur at a different point in the interviewing sequence for the different interviewers (to avoid congestion over the measuring equipment).

Coding the responses in the interviewing sequence

Throughout the intensive interview the interviewer coded the replies of boys in a form designed for rapid data processing.

Checking out

At the end of this procedure, the boy was returned to reception, was paid his £2 and given his 50p record token. He had of course already taken part in the treasure hunt. Some boys (a small minority) who had opted to make their own way home were paid their fares for this. Most boys however were to go home by car. Those returning to any one area by car waited

Diagram 9.2

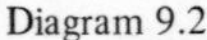

(a) The sorting bags used in tests 2, 3, 14, 15.

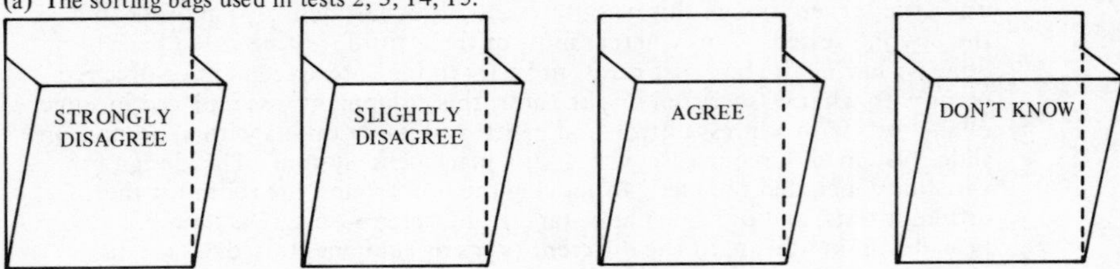

(b) The press button and lights system used in tests 7, 8, 9, 10.

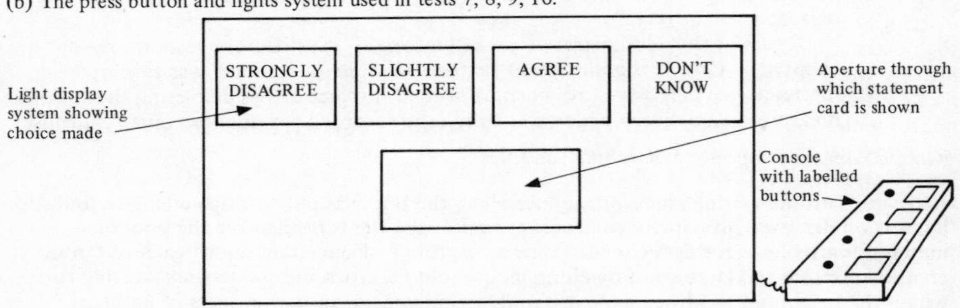

(c) The pointer on slide system used in tests 6, 13.

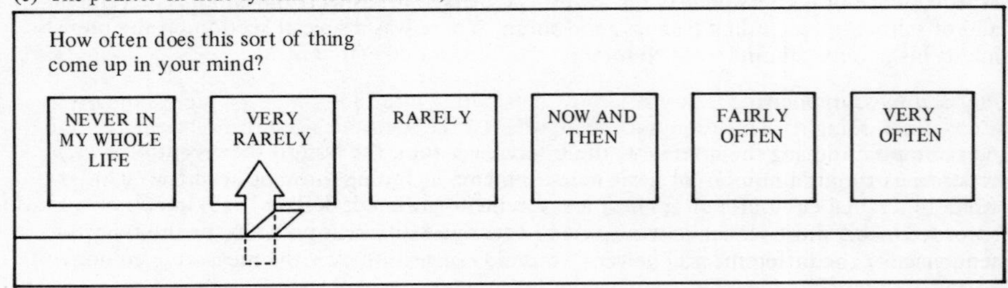

(d) The sorting bags used in the 'Callousness' tests (1, 4, 5, 11, 12, 16.)

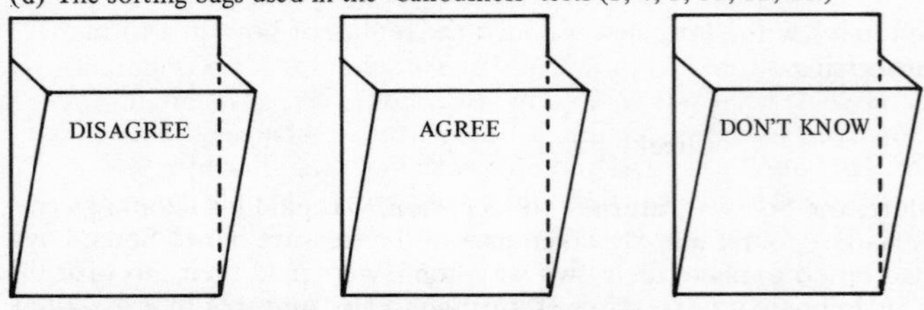

(e) 'Willingness' sorting board – see Chapter 8 page 14.

until the original four had all completed the interview and then went home together in a car provided by the Survey Research Centre. Whilst waiting to go home they could use various board games or could read journals or magazines or comics in the waiting room. Where boys had a telephone at home, their parents were alerted if the boys looked like being late home and also when they were about to leave for home.

If a boy was very late in finishing, the other boys went on home ahead of him. Occasionally a boy did not complete all parts of the intensive interview before the deadline of 11.00 pm and efforts were made in that case to get him back on a second evening, usually with success.

The tape recording of interviews

All interviews were fully tape recorded as a basis for controlling the quality of the interviewer performance. Obviously it was essential to see that the presence of the recorder did not distract or disturb the boy. The following steps were therefore taken: (a) the boy was told at the outset about the tape recorder and was given the opportunity to have it eliminated; (b) initially the recording was of routine questions so that there was no reason for alarm on the part of the boy at that stage, and certainly there was no evidence of this; (c) by the time the questioning about violence started the boy had been with his interviewer for some time and tended to have accepted him; (d) also by this time the tape recorder had for many 'sunk into the background'; (e) the boy was reminded that the meeting was private and that he had a false name and he was told that, if he so wished, the tape would be destroyed at the end of the interview; he was also told that the only purpose of the recording was to help those running the survey to see that the interviewers did their job of questioning properly. Interviewers were told to watch for any uneasiness on the part of boys and to seek to allay it then and there. In general, boys seemed to accept the tape recorder without worry and to be overlooking it after the first ten minutes or so of the interview (i.e. long before the questions about violent behaviour were asked).

The interviewers; selection, training and control

The intensive interviewing task was a most demanding one and required a high standard in the interviewers doing it. This requirement dominated the methods used for selection, training and control of the interviewer force. Another dominating factor was the requirement that interviewers should be available for evening work on at least two and preferably five nights a week.

Furthermore, those taking part would need to have been in some other form of employment as well (i.e. during the day up to 4.30 pm or perhaps 5.00 pm) because the payment for one 3½ hour interview per night could not provide a living wage.

Selection

In the circumstances, advertising was directed principally at the school teacher population. At the level of basic characteristics, what was wanted in interviewers was good intelligence, friendliness, a dependable manner, firmness, the use of unsophisticated language and accent, the ability in this situation to be morally neutral and unshockable. In addition, it was essential that interviewers employed in this work should be responsible people, good at dealing with adolescent boys, able to stick to interviewing instructions, honest and generally of good character.

Out of the initial applicants, 60 were interviewed and 40 invited to attend a 3-day selection-training course. They attended this course on the understanding that it *was* selective. Throughout the course, ratings were made of interviewer characteristics. The 40 eventually yielded 32 appointees, of whom 17 were able to work on the first day of the survey period – and 17-20 each night thereafter. As interviewing on the project progressed, there were inevitably losses and these had to be replaced. Here, too, selection was on a performance basis.

Initially it had been felt that female interviewers would be unsuitable for interviewing these boys when it came to extracting information about violent behaviour. However, the study of tape recorded performances and growing experience of interviewer performance made it clear that the women already working as interviewers were quite effective. Accordingly when replacements became necessary, as many women as men were employed, although in selecting women, special attention was given to the requirement that they be as unshockable and generally as durable as the male interviewers.

Training

During the three days of the selection-training course, the applicants were given an outline of the overall strategy of the enquiry, and a detailed description of the intensive interview. They were taken step by step through that interviewing procedure, with discussion breaks at frequent intervals. Those attending were seated in working groups and much of their time went into practice interviewing in which different people took turns at being 'boy' and 'interviewer'. In addition a number of boys were brought into the operation to make for more realistic practice. There was special emphasis in the course on the use of specialised challenging and probing methods when this was required, the need to follow instructions when these were given and to stick rigorously to the set wording of questions. In the training operation, self-criticism was stressed as necessary and was constantly encouraged.

Throughout the course, there was special emphasis on the need to be self-critical, unshockable, friendly but not matey, sympathetic without taking sides. Above all, there was emphasis on the need to remain morally neutral throughout.

For the successful applicant, there came a period of further practical training at the Centre, with boys specially brought in for that purpose (but not drawn from the actual sample to be used in the study).

Training was continued throughout the period of the enquiry. This was done mainly through the quality controllers and their advisers, working from the tape recordings of the interviews. They were concerned with matters such as: deviation from instructions, use of leading probes, a failure to probe and challenge where necessary, failure to secure sufficient information about the nature of the violent acts committed by boys, hurried or dreary administration, insensitive performance, moralistic utterances, unreadable or ambiguous or inaccurate entries. The quality controllers passed an evaluative statement to each interviewer each day, pointing to faults and to good features in the interview. They raised doubtful matters with the project director and took up points of failure personally with the interviewers concerned.

In the course of the enquiry, some interviewing positions fell vacant and had to be filled. This was done mainly through conducting further training courses of the kind already described. In some cases however replacement interviewers came in (on a trial basis) as 'apprentices' to some of the better interviewers and then tried several interviews alone but with tape recorder running. An evaluation of these performances led to a decision about whether to bring that interviewer into the team.

The most demanding aspect of interviewer administration was arranging that a full force of interviewers be available, *on time*, each night for the interviewing operation. To this end, interviewers were given weekly timetables of work geared to their availability. A limited number of interviewers tended to be available for additional work at short notice and were on call (for a small fee) if suddenly needed. When a boy or two boys did not turn up, the now inoperative interviewers were given coding tasks (and so helped the staff engaged full time on this activity).

Interviewers were required to be ready *in their interviewing rooms* from the time the first group of boys was expected. But they were asked to be at the Survey Research Centre somewhat earlier than this to allow time for discussion with the supervisory and quality control staff as necessary.

Notes

[1] Two for each of 22 principal hypotheses and for 150 sub-hypotheses, exclusive of those used in the context of the secondary control system and in investigating the possibility of an 'outlyer' effect.
[2] Map L 1568, published by the Director General of the Ordnance Survey, 1966.
[3] As in Census report for 1971.
[4] Thus boys were to be brought by car after school or work to the Survey Research Centre in mid-London for their second interviews. They had to arrive there by 6.30 pm at the latest if they were to have much chance of leaving for home by 10.30 pm – a relatively late hour for the younger boys. Previous experience with this sort of arrangement had shown that for areas further out than 12 miles, the journey in was unworkably long. Furthermore, the cost of hire-car transport both to and from the Centre was in excess of what was regarded as a reasonable limit in relation to the funds available for this project.
[5] $\frac{784{,}980}{6{,}313{,}512} \times \frac{40}{1} = 4.97 = 5$ to the nearest whole number.

[6] School lists were ruled out because (i) many schools would not make them available to a non-governmental enquiry; (ii) such lists are bound to be incomplete in that some boys will not be attending school in their own areas and many older boys will now be living in an area other than that at which they went to school. Another method that was considered was the use of an enumeration survey, but its expensiveness ruled it out.
[7] This system is fully detailed in 'Instructions for placement interviewers' in the General Appendix.
[8] Initially the rule had been 'the house with the next highest number' (i.e. 23 Cracknell Street). But this had led to unnecessary and sometimes hazardous street crossings.

APPENDIX TO CHAPTER 9

Appendix 1 Contact sheet used by placement interviewers

Contact sheet used by placement interviewers

Appendix 1

Area ....

Street ....

1. It is essential that the contact sheet be well kept. Study it carefully when first you receive it. It will be the basis both of our sampling record and of our standard checking procedure on interviewers.
2. Don't enter more than one street on one side of a contact sheet.

For all homes at which you should call						For qualifying homes only	
House number	Age of all boys in qualifying home X if not qualifying	Dates of all personal calls at the house 1st	2nd	3rd	If not a qualifying household, what is the basis of this conclusion? (Circle reply or enter as 'other reason')	If qualifier, give age of boy you tried to interview and say if successful (✓) or not (X)	If not successful with qualifier, what was the reason for failure? Give as fully as possible
					· spoke to member of household · told by neighbour · other reason		
					· spoke to member of household · told by neighbour · other reason		
					· spoke to member of household · told by neighbour · other reason		
					· spoke to member of household · told by neighbour · other reason		
					· spoke to member of household · told by neighbour · other reason		
					· spoke to member of household · told by neighbour · other reason		
					· spoke to member of household · told by neighbour · other reason		
					· spoke to member of household · told by neighbour · other reason		
					· spoke to member of household · told by neighbour · other reason		
					· spoke to member of household · told by neighbour · other reason		
					· spoke to member of household · told by neighbour · other reason		
					· spoke to member of household · told by neighbour · other reason		
					· spoke to member of household · told by neighbour · other reason		

INTERVIEW COMPLETED AND APPOINTMENT MADE WITH:

Name and address of boy ____________________

Time and date of appointment for Centre interview ____________________

What the collector should note ____________________

CHAPTER 10

A SHORT INTRODUCTION TO THE FINDINGS

Contents

STATISTICAL AND OTHER EVALUATIONS OF THE FINDINGS

The evaluation of the present set of findings is a complex and demanding affair involving a range of considerations which include: critical appraisal of the research design; the direction and the numerical size of differences; the comparison of differences; the statistical significance of differences; the existence of contradictory evidence. These and other considerations, taken together, can and should be used to challenge our interpretations and generally to reduce the uncertainties of any conclusions we may reach. Much has already been said about their use in this enquiry.

Estimating statistical significance

The application of one of these challenging methods is, in the specialised context of this enquiry, subject to certain problems, and it seems appropriate to present some of these problems in this introduction to the findings. I am referring to the application of a test of statistical significance to a difference between Qualifiers and *Modified* Controls with respect to the dependent variable.

Such problems include:

1 the need to calculate the variances for weighted samples;

2 the appropriateness of one-tail and of two-tail tests of significance.

There is in addition the broader problem of just how complete or crucial or final we should regard a significance of difference test to be.

Calculating the variance for weighted samples. The calculation of the significance of the difference between Qualifying and Weighted Control samples calls for the insertion of variance figures into the following equation.

$$\sigma_D = \sqrt{\frac{\sigma^2_Q}{N_Q} + \frac{\sigma^2_{MC}}{N_{MC}}} \qquad (1)$$

where σ^2_Q = variance for Qualifying sample

σ^2_{MC} = variance for Modified Controls

N_Q = cases in Qualifying sample

N_{MC} = cases in Modified Control sample

Complications arise over the calculation of the variance for the *weighted* Control sample and in this case the following formula was used.

$$\sigma^2_{MC} = \frac{1}{N_Q} \left[\Sigma_i w_i{}^2 \Sigma_j X^2_{ij} + \overline{X}^2_C \Sigma_i w_i{}^2 n_{c_i} - 2\overline{X}_C \Sigma_i w_i{}^2 n_{c_i} \overline{X}_{c_i} \right] \qquad (2)$$

where σ^2_{MC} = variance for weighted or Modified Controls

X_{ij} = score of the jth case ub tge i^{th} sub-group

N_Q = total size of Q sample

$\overline{X}_C$ = mean of unweighted Control sample

n_{c_i} = number in the ith sub-group of Controls

$\overline{X}_{c_i}$ = mean of ith sub-group of Controls

w_i = n_{Q_i}/n_{C_i}

For the Qualifiers, where no weighting was involved, a much simpler formula was appropriate, namely:

$$\sigma^2_Q = \frac{1}{N_Q} \left[\Sigma_i \Sigma_j X^2_{ij} - N_Q \overline{X}^2_Q \right] \qquad (3)$$

where σ^2_Q = variance of the Qualifying sample

X_{ij} = score of the jth case in the ith sub-group (see sub-groups in Table 6 in Chapter 3).

N_Q = number of cases in the total Qualifying sample.

$\overline{X}_Q$ = mean score of Qualifying sample.

Beyond this point, the Critical Ratio was calculated through the formula:

$$CR = \frac{M_Q - M_{MC}}{\sigma_D} \qquad (4)$$

where CR = critical ratio of the difference between means

M_Q = mean of Qualifying sample

M_{MC} = mean of Modified Control sample

σ_D = standard error of the difference between means

The use of one-tail or two-tail distributions in calculating P values. In this inquiry, an important consideration in calculating P values was the directional character of the hypotheses. Thus the hypotheses had been expressed in terms of 'exposure to television violence modifying behaviour or mental state' *in a particular direction.* Accordingly it is appropriate that the P values be based upon one-tail interpretation of the probability tables. The P values presented in the main body of the report have all been calculated on this basis. At the same time, there may well be many who would want to see presented the P values for a non-directional formulation of the hypotheses and these have been presented in the Technical Appendix. Such P values are of course simply twice the size of P values based upon the one-tail extractions.

The concept of 'an index of effect'

In order to produce a single index of the *degree* to which hypothesised changes had taken place, the following computation was made with respect to each hypothesis.

$$\frac{M_Q - M_{MC}}{M_{MC}} \times 100\% \qquad (5)\ [1]$$

This value was regarded as reflecting the degree to which viewers had shifted away from their pre-television condition.

The 'index of effect' cannot, of course, be considered in isolation from the statistical significance of that difference from which it, too was derived. Nor is a P value to be interpreted without consideration of the size of the 'index of effect'.

The relevance of a test of statistical significance

As already stated, the evaluation of hypotheses rested upon more than scrutiny of the P values. Also important were the size of the difference (in dependent variable scores) between samples, the relation of the Forward and the Reverse hypothesis results and the other factors already listed. What the statistical significance value tells us about is the degree of likelihood that our test results have arisen solely through sampling error. The statistical significance value warns us, as it were, against taking our results too much at face value – and this warning is important.

Having said this, I think it is highly desirable that certain misuses of significance values be warned against. The first of these is to regard a P value larger than .05 as of no statistical significance. Statistical significance is a matter of degree and it would be extreme folly to rule an hypothesis as untenable simply on the basis of a P value of .06. It is also most undesirable to interpret a highly significant P value (e.g. .001) as necessarily indicating an important trend – for it is obvious that even very small differences between samples can be associated with very significant P values simply because the number of cases studied was very large and/or because the standard deviations on the dependent variable were very small. On the other hand, it is quite possible for a real difference of quite substantial size to have a P value of little significance (because of small sample sizes and/or large standard deviations). The use in this study of an 'index of effect', reflecting the size of the difference between means (after matching), is meant partly to arrest or to counter misinterpretation of very small but highly significant differences (see later in this chapter). It is also meant to guard against the over-ready discounting of large differences between the Qualifying and the Modified Control samples solely on the basis of a large P value.

It is against this background and in this context that results have been interpreted on the system set out in table 10.1.

The implications of the correlation of the matching composite with the dependent variables

In my statement of findings in chapters 11-19, the various P values have *not* been adjusted to take account of the fact that the various matching composites are correlated with their corresponding dependent variables. The effect of such a correlation would have been to

Table 10.1
Showing system used for evaluating forward and reversed forms of hypotheses

Index of effect		P value	Evaluation of hypotheses (forward and reversed form)
Size	Interpretation		
0% or less	Nil or less	Any	No support for hypothesis
0%+ −3%	Extremely small	.05 or less	Virtually no support
		.05+ −.10	Virtually no support and slightly uncertain at that
		.10+ −.15	Virtually no support and uncertain at that
		.15+ −.20	Virtually no support and very uncertain at that
		.20+ or over	No meaningful support
3%+ −5%	Very small	.05 or less	Very little support
		.05+ −.10	Very little support and slightly uncertain at that
		.10+ −.15	Very little support and of an uncertain kind at that
		.15+ −.20	Very little support and of a very uncertain kind at that
		.20+ or over	No meaningful support
5%+ −10%	Small	.05 or less	A small degree of support
		.05+ −.10	A small degree of support of a slightly uncertain kind
		.10+ −.15	A small degree of support of an uncertain kind
		.15+ −.20	A small degree of support of a very uncertain kind
		.20+ or over	No meaningful support
10%+ −15%	Moderate	.05 or less	A moderate degree of support
		.05+ −.10	A moderate degree of support but of a slightly uncertain kind
		.10+ −.15	A moderate degree of support but of an uncertain kind
		.15+ −.20	A moderate degree of support but of a very uncertain kind
		.20+ or over	No meaningful support
15%+ −20%	Fairly large	.05 or less	A fairly large degree of support
		.05+ −.10	A fairly large degree of support but of a slightly uncertain kind
		.10+ −.15	A fairly large degree of support but of an uncertain kind
		.15+ −.20	A fairly large degree of support but a very uncertain kind
		.20+ or over	No meaningful support
20%+ −30%	Large	.05 or less	A large degree of support
		.05+ −.10	A large degree of support but of a slightly uncertain kind
		.10+ −.15	A large degree of support but of an uncertain kind
		.15+ −.20	A large degree of support but of a very uncertain kind
		.20+ or over	No meaningful support
30%+ or more	Very large	.05 or less	A very large degree of support
		.05+ −.10	A very large degree of support but of a slightly uncertain kind
		.10+ −.15	A very large degree of support but of an uncertain kind
		.15+ −.20	A very large degree of support but of a very uncertain kind
		.20+ or over	No meaningful support

‘shorten the odds’ that residual differences found between Qualifying and Modified Control groups are due simply to sampling accidents. Indeed, the application of stratified techniques in the derivation of the sample is likely to have a similar implication for significance testing.

Whereas in principle it is desirable to take account of such correlations in calculating P values, there are certain arguments and problems that stand in the way of so doing: (i) the post-facto nature of the application of the matching composite; (ii) the particular segmentation method used to develop the matching composite departs sharply from the normal requirements for calculating R; (iii) the unacceptability of interpreting the matching composite as a single variable and particularly as a continuous variable; (iv) the non-normal distribution of many of the dependent variables, especially the behavioural ones; (v) the special character of the double-criterion system used in collecting matching variables to make up the matching composite.

In the circumstances it seemed, in general, desirable to calculate P values without taking account of the ‘correlation factor’, and to regard such significance testing as constituting a somewhat more tougher (and more conservative) challenge to the hypotheses than might otherwise have been made. However, a decision of this sort could hardly be reached without some appraisal, however crude from the statistical viewpoint, of the *extent* of the difference it would make to the size of the P values. In other words, it was desirable to make a number of test comparisons of P values calculated *with* and *without* ‘correction’ for the ‘correlation factor’.

The method used for calculating the modified P values — which in the circumstances must be regarded as crude — was to calculate a new σD on the basis of ‘within-group’ variances alone, the groups in this case being the 30 or so different matching sub-groups. The two variance figures used in this calculation were, of course, those for the Qualifiers and the Modified Controls, the *weighted* character of the Modified Controls being taken into account.

The results of these test comparisons are set out in table 10.2.

The principal indications of table 10.2 are as follows.

1 As must be expected, the application of ‘correction’ for the correlation factor increases the size of the Critical Ratios and thereby increases the significance levels of the various findings. In other words, if the correlation factor had been taken into consideration through the method specified above, we could expect the significance of the findings throughout the enquiry to increase.

2 At the same time, it is clear that the increases in significance level shown in table 10.2 are not of any substantial order. Indeed, amongst the 60 conversions presented in table 10.2, there was only one instance where a P value over the 5 per cent level (.051) was thereby caused to drop *below* the 5 per cent level (.043) — and even in this case, the change could not have affected the interpretation of the findings involved.

In these circumstances — and bearing in mind the technical objections that may be made to the different correction procedures available to us, there is no strong case for applying a correction for the correlation factor throughout the enquiry. At the same time, it follows from the details in table 10.2 that the uncorrected P values are conservatively based and constitute a slightly tougher challenge to the tenability of the various hypotheses.

Nonetheless it was planned that when the size of the P value seemed critical in evaluating

Table 10.2

Showing the effect on P values of applying a correction to allow for the correlation between matching composite and dependent variables

Independent variable		Dependent variable 1 DV1†				Dependent variable 2 DV2				Dependent variable 3 DV3				Dependent variable 4 DV4				Dependent variable 4 with ceiling of 70 DV4 (70)			
		Correlation factor allowed for				Correlation factor allowed for				Correlation factor allowed for				Correlation factor allowed for				Correlation factor allowed for			
IV††	Direction	No		Yes		No		Yes		No		Yes		No		Yes		No		Yes	
		CR	P*	CR	P*	CR	P*	CR	P*	CR	P*	CR	P*	CR	P*	CR	P*	CR	P*	CR	P*
IV1	F	1.83	.034	2.01	.022	1.73	.042	2.30	.011	1.89	.029	2.01	.022	2.02	.022	2.10	.018	2.00	.023	2.12	.017
	R	3.40	<.001	4.03	<.001	3.09	.001	3.63	<.001	4.06	.001	4.66	<.001	0.63	.264	0.73	.233	0.63	.264	0.73	.233
IV27	F	1.06	.145	1.09	.138	1.64	.051	1.72	.043	1.36	.087	1.44	.075	2.16	.015	2.25	.012	1.89	.029	2.03	.021
	R	2.62	.004	2.84	.002	3.13	<.001	3.64	<.001	3.34	<.001	3.67	<.001	0.31	.378	0.35	.363	0.31	.378	0.35	.363
IV28	F	2.44	.007	2.57	.005	1.10	.136	1.13	.129	2.56	.005	2.67	.004	1.47	.071	1.60	.055	0.99	.161	1.07	.142
	R	1.65	.050	1.89	.029	1.81	.035	2.04	.021	2.67	.004	3.06	.001	2.84	.002	3.25	<.001	2.84	.002	3.25	<.001
IV29	F	2.57	.005	2.72	.003	2.83	.002	3.01	.001	3.00	.001	3.19	<.001	1.22	.111	1.23	.109	1.71	.044	1.82	.034
	R	1.39	.082	1.61	.054	2.78	.003	3.10	<.001	2.43	.008	2.84	.002	1.36	.087	1.58	.057	1.36	.087	1.51	.066
IV30	F	2.41	.008	2.49	.006	2.95	.002	3.14	<.001	2.64	.004	2.78	.003	−0.17	.433	−0.18	.429	0.40	.345	0.43	.334
	R	1.90	.029	2.03	.021	2.25	.012	2.50	.006	1.08	.140	1.19	.117	2.62	.004	2.96	.002	2.62	.004	3.00	.001
IV31	F	0.37	.356	0.41	.341	0.79	.215	0.85	.198	−0.07	.472	−0.08	.468	1.96	.025	2.05	.020	1.72	.044	1.85	.032
	R	0.81	.209	0.92	.179	0.93	.176	1.05	.147	2.62	.004	2.94	.002	−0.04	.484	−0.04	.484	−0.04	.484	−0.04	.484

*P is based on one-tail extractions, because the hypotheses are directional.

†DV = dependent variable: 1 = weighted score for violence; 2 = total all acts with ceiling of 50 on each type of act; 3 = all, less trivial acts; 4 = total of all serious acts; 4 (70) = total score, with ceiling of 70 on total.

††IV = independent variable: 1 = exposure to TV violence; 27 = exposure to TV generally, including TV violence; 28 = exposure to comics/comic books; 29 = exposure to violent films; 30 = exposure to newspapers; 31 = special score for non-violent exposure within context of TV generally.

the tenability of an hypothesis, the modified P values would be calculated simply to show how much difference the correction could have made.

HOW THE FINDINGS ARE TO BE INTERPRETED WITH SPECIAL REFERENCE TO THE FORWARD AND THE REVERSED HYPOTHESES

In chapter 3 I set out the general strategy for interpreting findings, with special reference to the findings for the forward and the reverse hypotheses. For the sake of the completeness of this 'introduction to the findings', I have repeated hereunder much of what was said on this particular point in chapter 3.

1 If the check on the forward version of the hypothesis does not support that hypothesis, then that forward version of the hypothesis may be regarded as being rendered less tenable by the evidence. This applies irrespective of the finding for the check on the hypothesis in its reversed form.

2 If *both* the forward and the reversed forms of the hypothesis are supported by the evidence then the forward version of the hypothesis is regarded as being rendered more tenable by the evidence, though the possibility exists that this positive finding for the forward version of the hypothesis is a reflection to some degree at least, of the working of the hypothesis in reverse. Where this type of finding emerges, it is also possible that: (a) there is in operation a circular process in which television violence leads to greater violence by boys, that when boys become more violent they elect to watch a greater amount of violent television, that this in turn makes them more violent, and so on; (b) that for *some* boys the forward hypothesis is true and that for others the reverse hypothesis is true. In the circumstances, where *both* the forward and the reversed forms of the hypothesis are supported by the findings, the interpretation adopted is that: the hypothesis is rendered more tenable by the evidence, but that tenability is less firm than would have been the case if the reversed form of the hypothesis had been *without* support.

3 If the evidence supports the forward form of the hypothesis but not the reversed form of the hypothesis, then that forward version of the hypothesis is regarded as being rendered more tenable by the evidence – and there is very little possibility that the positive finding for the forward hypothesis is simply a reflection of the working of the hypothesis in its reverse form.

4 These three arguments would apply equally to the tenability of the reversed form of the hypothesis were we to decide to consider that form in its own right.

5 There is of course the question of the *degree* of increased tenability. On this matter, the writer has worked in line with the system described in table 10.1.

THE SPECIAL CHARACTER OF THE RELATIONSHIP OF THE FORWARD AND THE REVERSE HYPOTHESES

The strategy of forward and reverse hypothesis testing may be subject to some degree of misunderstanding. Thus it might possibly be argued that if the forward form of the hypothesis is supported by the evidence then so must be its reverse form – in that the same population of boys is involved in both the forward and the reverse tests and that whatever the association between serious violence and exposure to television violence may be, that association lies as a common background to both the forward and the reverse forms of the hypothesis.

In fact that argument would hold only in the case where the relationship between exposure to television violence and involvement in violent behaviour was of a sloping and straight line kind with very little scatter along that straight line.

Figure 10.1

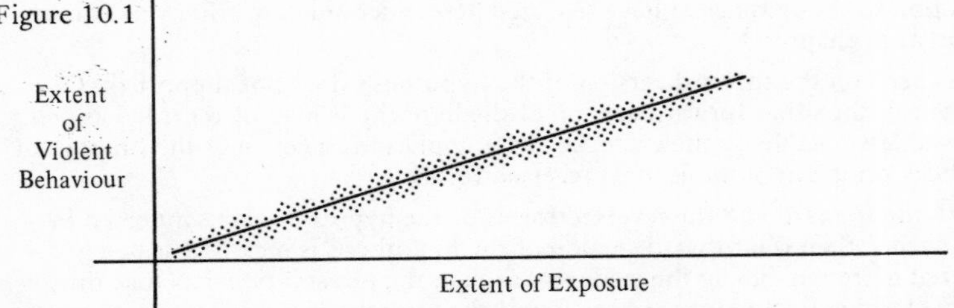

But if the relationship between exposure to television violence and level of violent behaviour is of an irregular kind, with a high degree of scatter of cases, then it is most unlikely that the forward and the reverse hypotheses will yield the same result. Indeed, it is precisely this situation that lies behind certain of the findings presented in chapter 12.

Let us look more closely at the situation where the relationship is of that irregular and scattered kind. In the fictitious case presented in figure 10.2, that half of the sample that had been more exposed to television violence has a higher score for serious violence than has the less exposed half of the sample. The ratio of scores is 17 : 12. But there is *no difference* between the exposure scores of the more and the less violent boys (503 : 503). In fact it is possible, simply by shifting the cases horizontally or vertically, to change the quantitative comparisons quite markedly. And in reality it would be a major coincidence if a comparison of high and low scorers on the vertical and the horizontal axes emerged as proportionately the same.

Of course figure 10.2 deals only with purely correlational data and not with the situation after massive matching. But the point that matters here is that matching can upset even further any theoretical expectation that the results of checking the forward and the reversed forms of the hypothesis will be the same.

The research methodologist may care to consider the implications of the situation I have just presented. It is that when the two variables postulated in a causal hypothesis have an irregular or scattered form of association, that very irregularity holds clues as to the direction of such causal association as exists between those two variables. A tightly straight-line association does not offer any such clues. The nature of the clues available from the scattered irregular association are best appreciated in the context of the hypothetico-deductive method as described in chapter 3.

Figure 10.2

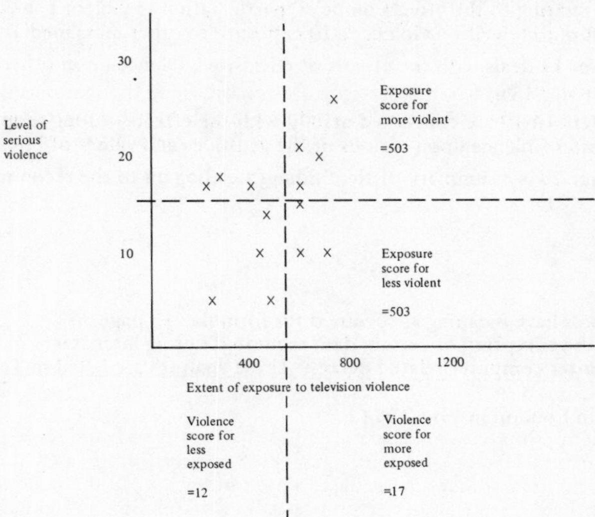

THE LOCATION IN THIS REPORT OF THE VARIOUS FINDINGS

A great volume of information has been derived from this enquiry, with its very volume raising problems of presentation. The following presentation strategy was adopted.

(a) Two technical appendices present, for *each* hypothesis and each sub-hypothesis, [2] the full matching composite used and the details of the matching itself (including the various mean scores, the 'index of effect', the Critical Ratio and the P value). This has been done separately for the forward and the reversed forms of each hypothesis. The total number of the hypotheses and sub-hypotheses involved is over 400. From this material, the statistically oriented reader will be in a position to carry out further analyses of the findings if he so wishes.

(b) In chapter 11, details are presented of the nature and the extent of violence committed by London boys. This information was collected principally to provide a factual basis for the investigation of the various causal hypotheses. But obviously it has value and social significance in its own right.

It has, in fact, been given some publication already in the form of a paper presented at the meeting of the British Association for the Advancement of Science and later, at the Annual Conference of the National Association for Maternal and Child Welfare. [3] However, chapter 11 presents these findings in greater detail than has previously been done.

(c) In chapter 12, I have presented the principal findings of the investigation, namely those relating to the effects on boys' participation in violent behaviour of (i) high exposure to television violence; (ii) exposure to other mass media.

(d) Chapter 13 deals with the effects of television violence upon other forms of the behaviour of boys.

(e) Chapters 14-19 are concerned mainly with the effects of long-term exposure to television violence upon various of the attitudes and values of boys.

(f) Chapter 20 is a summary of the findings (leading on to the recommendations of chapter 21).

Notes

[1] Symbols have meaning as specified for formula (4), page 342.

[2] With the exception of certain data requested during later stages of report writing and received after computer-related delays. These analyses are listed in Technical Appendix II.

[3] Held in London in June 1974.

CHAPTER 11

FINDINGS: THE NATURE AND DISTRIBUTION OF VIOLENCE AMONGST BOYS

Contents

11 FINDINGS: THE NATURE AND DISTRIBUTION OF VIOLENCE AMONGST BOYS

Though this study was not designed for the collection of information about the incidence of violence by London boys, it has nonetheless yielded a considerable amount of such information. This information is of several kinds.

1. The frequency of endorsement of each of the 53 stimulus items used in the elicitation procedure.
2. The incidence of violence at each of six levels of intensity
3. Violence scores derived as measures of the dependent variable in hypotheses relating exposure to television violence and violent behaviour.
4. The characteristics of boys related to the level of their violence.

The frequency of endorsement of items in the web of stimuli

A count was made of the number of boys who sorted the different stimulus cards into the 'yes' box (indicating that they had done the kind of thing on the card in the last six months). In addition, a count was made of the frequency with which 'what was on each card' was said to have been done (in the last six months). Neither of these two counts was used in its own right in the hypothesis testing process, or as a final measure of violence, but their indications are interesting and they are relevant to study of the incidence of different sorts of violence and to the situations in which violence occurs. Details are shown in table 11.1.

Table 11.1 must be interpreted warily because many of the stimulus items in it are very broad (deliberately so), because some are fairly specific acts of violence whilst others are no more than the situations in which violence can occur, and others again are nothing more than the motivation for being violent. This mixed character of the data arises out of the items on the cards constituting a special kind of evocation system — *a web of stimuli* — for getting boys to say enough about their violent behaviour for the interviewer to start asking questions about what *in particular* was done and *how often* each of these particular acts was done.

The main indications of the 'scene setting' data of table 11.1 appear to be as follows.

1. The different stimulus items evoked responses at widely different frequencies — as they were intended to do.
2. Nonetheless table 11.1 gives an early indication of an overall high frequency of violent behaviour.

Table 11.1
Claimed frequency of committing violence of the 'kind' indicated on the stimulus card

— = less than 0.5%

	Number and name of stimulus item	Did it in last 6 months %	How often in last 6 months: 1-9 times %	10 or more %
40	I have had an argument with somebody	95	52	43
1	I have kicked somebody	91	48	43
7	I have sworn at somebody or used bad language on them	90	31	59
13	I have teased somebody or 'taken the mickey out of' someone	90	41	49
16	I have lied to someone	90	46	44
49	I have lost my temper with somebody	89	64	25
2	I have tried to torment someone	81	43	38
17	I have fooled or larked around while I was out with some of my mates	79	46	33
36	I have thrown something at someone	79	56	23
4	I have tried to trip someone up	78	44	34
25	I have irritated, annoyed or played people up	78	42	36
23	I have twisted someone's arm	76	59	17
9	I have made rude finger signs at someone	73	35	38
28	I have played violent or dangerous games	68	39	29
42	I have tried to frighten someone	68	56	12
24	I have threatened somebody	65	51	14
41	I have done something to get my own back on somebody	65	53	12
5	I have had a fight	62	50	12
14	I have given someone a 'deadleg'	56	44	12
38	I have been rude to people in authority (like police, teachers, parents)	56	40	16
43	I have been violent in self-defence	55	49	6
53	I have been rough or tough or violent in sport or play	55	35	20
35	I have shot an airgun or catapult or arrow at someone or something	49	30	19
47	I have been violent because I have been excited or upset about something	45	42	3
50	I have been violent when I really didn't want to be	44	40	4
30	I have been violent at school or at work	42	31	11
26	I have been violent while doing sport	42	28	14
32	I have been violent during the breaks at school or at work	38	28	10
44	I have set something on fire	38	32	6
21	I have been violent while I was with some of my mates or friends	37	30	7
37	I have beaten someone up	33	30	3
15	I have been violent just for fun or for a laugh or for a dare	31	23	8
45	I have hurt a girl in some way	31	28	3
6	I have hurt an animal	30	25	5
29	I have hit someone with something (e.g. bottle, hammer, stick, brolly, etc.)	29	25	4
10	I have given someone a 'head butt'	28	24	4
8	I have taken part in wrestling or boxing or judo or karate	26	15	11
22	I have damaged places or things (like trains, buses, shops, cars, old houses, 'phone boxes, parking meters, electricity meters, gas meters, etc.)	25	21	4
27	I have tried to start a fight in some way	24	22	2
19	My mates and I have picked on or set about other people or boys	23	19	4
33	I have been in fights with boys from other schools	23	22	1
3	I have set a 'booby trap' of some kind	21	18	3
31	I have been violent on the way to or from school or work	18	16	2
18	I have been violent to impress my mates or girls or other people	15	12	3
46	I tried to make girls do things they don't want to do	12	10	2
51	I have damaged someone's car (but not in a road accident)	12	11	1
39	I have been violent to people in authority (like police, teachers, parents)	12	11	1
20	I have set my mates onto other people or boys	11	10	1
12	I have been violent while at a football ground	10	8	2
48	I have cut someone with a knife or a razor or glass	8	8	—
52	I have done damage to a train	8	7	1
11	I have been violent on the way to watch a football match	7	6	1
34	I have been violent while I was 'bunking off' from school or lessons	4	4	—

The incidence of violence at each of six levels of seriousness

The levels of seriousness

The questioning procedure that was used to elicit the information in table 11.1 was followed by a further stage designed to yield information about *specific* acts in the last six months and the incidence of their occurrence in that period. The resultant enormous yield was then sorted into six broad categories which differentiated between acts in terms of *how* violent they were, namely:

Only very slightly violent
A bit violent
Fairly violent
Quite violent
Very violent
Extremely violent

An illustrated scale of seriousness

This grading had been guided by an illustrated scale. In other words, each of the six categories listed above had been illustrated or exemplified by a widely varied set of examples of the kinds of acts that should go into it. This set of illustrations had been empirically developed through the ratings of members of the public. Details of its origination are given in chapter 6, but one of its features should be noted again at this point. We had gone to the public after clear evidence of major disagreement amongst our rating staff about where on the scale of seriousness different acts should be put. It was thought that an illustrated scale would anchor the system against major disagreements and that since the public had in fact been a principal source of the hypotheses being investigated, they should be used in developing the illustrations.

However, there was early evidence, once this operation was started, of sharp discord amongst the public, too, about how different acts should be rated. In the end, we settled for illustrative acts about which the public tended less to disagree and the rating of the thousands of acts of violence derived from boys was carried out against such illustrations.

This issue of disagreement is worthy of note in its own right, for it suggests an underlying lack of consensus in our society about the seriousness of different acts of violence and in all likelihood of greater permissiveness about violent behaviour on the part of some people than on the part of others. The following table 11.2 illustrates something of the nature of this disagreement. It is of course based on only the 43 cases used in establishing the illustrations.

The incidence of violence at each of six levels of seriousness or intensity

In table 11.3 I have presented (a) a shortened version of the illustrated scale; (b) for each of the six categories of the illustrated scale, the distribution of boys in terms of how often they had committed that category of violence; (c) the average number of such acts per boy.

1 The total amount of violence committed was considerable. Admittedly, much of

Table 11.2
Ratings by adult members of the public of several acts of violence (i.e. of 4 of the 116 acts rated by them)

Acts of violence	Ratings of the act						
	Not the least bit violent	Only very slightly violent	A bit violent	Fairly violent	Quite violent	Very violent	Extremely violent
	%	%	%	%	%	%	%
I chopped down a young tree that had been planted in the park	7	21	22	28	14	6	2
I broke open a parking meter	5	16	35	19	12	11	2
I scratched the paint on a new car with a knife	0	7	14	34	27	16	2
I deliberately cut someone with a razor	0	0	0	5	12	39	44

it was of a very minor kind, being no more than rough mischief. Nonetheless the incidence of violent behaviour remains high if this level of violence is omitted from the count. And at the serious level (made up of acts graded as quite violent or very violent) the average per boy was approximately 6 acts in the last 6 months.

2 There is a very sharp fall-off in terms of the 'average number of acts committed in the last 6 months' as we go from those rated 'fairly violent' (39 times in the last 6 months) to those rated 'quite' violent (4 in the last 6 months) and those rated 'very violent' (2 in the last 6 months).

3 Table 11.3 also gives us the claimed frequency of occurrence of acts within each of the six different 'intensity' categories. These distributions indicate an enormous variability in extent of violence by individual boys, with some boys doing relatively little and others a great deal. This applies all the way through the six categories and it is particularly marked for the top three combined. Thus we find that whereas half the sample had not operated at all at this upper level of violence, 12 per cent had committed ten or more acts of this kind, some of them very many more than ten times.

4 One more point about these frequencies. The very top category (i.e. 'extremely' violent acts) averages out at 0.035 acts per boy in six months. This average might be thought of as so small that it could be ignored. But that 0.035 figure represents 55 acts from our sample of 1,565 boys. At that level of seriousness, 55 acts are something to take careful note of, even though the extremes of possible sampling error are high (i.e. plus or minus 0.029). If one extrapolates that '55 acts' finding to the whole of London's boys in the 12-17 age range, the total number of acts of this 'extremely' violent kind could be of an order that many would regard as alarming.

Table 11.3
Distribution of violence in terms of its level of seriousness or intensity

Only very slightly violent	A bit violent	Fairly violent	Quite violent	Very violent	Extremely violent
Examples:	Examples:	Examples:	Examples:	Examples:	Examples:
One day after gym I kept flicking my towel at a boy when he came out of the shower	I hit a boy with bare fists in a fight	I gave a boy a hard head butt	I knocked a boy off his bike as he rode past me	I deliberately hit a boy on the face with a broken bottle	I fired a revolver at someone
I squirted water at a boy, wetting his clothes	I kept poking my brother with a ruler to make him say he was sorry	I twisted a boy's arm till he yelled with pain	I cut a boy's thumb with a knife during a school row	I tried to force a girl to have sexual intercourse with me	I set fire to a large building
I wrote in big letters on the wall of a building	I stuck matches in a parking meter to stop it working	I punched a boy in the stomach	I deliberately dropped a lighted cigarette into a shopper's bag	I fired an airgun at a boy passing in the street outside	I stabbed another boy
I threatened to give a boy a hiding	I deliberately smashed a school window	I shot hair pins at a boy from an elastic band	I shot a cat with a pellet from an air rifle	I loosened the screws on the handlebars of a boy's bike so that he would have a crash	I threw the cat into the fire
I played my Hi-Fi equipment loudly to annoy the neighbours	I played a boy up by throwing his school bag out of a window	I pulled the wings off flies	I busted the telephone in a telephone box	I half strangled a cat with my hands	
I called a boy a bastard while playing rugby	I called a coloured boy a wog	I broke down a young tree that had been planted in the park	I slashed the tyres of some cars in a car park	I took a hammer to a car and laid into it	
	With my mates I shouted abuse at some meths. drinkers in the park	I deliberately ripped a train seat	I threatened to kill my father	I broke into a house and smashed everything I could find	
	I told my teacher to get stuffed	I scratched the paint on a new car with my knife		I told a boy his mother had been killed in a car accident just to upset him	
		I sent obscene letters to someone			

Frequency of occurrence*	n	Frequency of occurrence	n	Frequency of occurrence	n	Frequency of occurrence	%	Frequency of occurrence	%	Frequency of occurrence	%
0	3	0	23	0	79	0	901	0	1264	0	1544
1-9	60	1-9	302	1-9	439	1-9	523	1-9	237	1	12
10-19	113	10-19	244	10-19	277	10-20	56	10-19	22	2	5
20-29	110	20-29	155	20-29	173	20-29	33	20-29	9	3	2
30-39	80	30-39	150	30-39	120	30-39	14	30-39	5	6	1
40-49	75	40-49	88	40-49	74	40-49	12	40-49	4	21	1
50-99	306	50-99	298	50-99	236	50-99	19	50-99	21		
100-199	354	100-199	219	100-199	129	100-199	6	100-199	3		
200-299	218	200-299	64	200-299	27	200-299	0	200-299	0		
300-499	169	300-499	15	300-499	3	300-499	0	300-499	0		
500 or more	77	500 or more	7	500 or more	1	500	1	500	0		
All = 1565 cases		All = 1565 cases		All = 1565 cases		All = 1565 cases		All = 1565 cases		All = 1565 cases	
†Average per boy in 6 month period		Average per boy in 6 month period		Average per boy in 6 month period		Average per boy in 6 month period		Average per boy in 6 month period		Average per boy in 6 month period	
158.8		59.4		39.3		4.1		2.0		0.035	

*Frequencies are condensed for convenience of presentation
†Averages are based on UNGROUPED data

Table 11.4
Frequency of acts of violence of the more serious kind
(i.e. combining 'quite', 'very', 'extremely' violent)

Times committed at this level in last 6 months	Number of boys n	%
0	840	53.7
1	186	11.9
2	110	7.0
3	62	4.0
4	44	2.8
5	45	2.9
6	33	2.1
7	25	1.6
8	22	1.4
9	10	0.6
10-39	121	7.7
40-69	47	3.0
70-99	7	0.5
100-199	9	0.6
200-500	4	0.3
All	1565	100.1%

The characteristics of boys related to the extent of their violence

For the purposes of hypothesis investigation, four separate measures of violent behaviour were taken. One of these has been dealt with already, namely the number of acts of the more violent kind that he commits. In this category are the acts which were rated as 'quite' violent or 'very' violent, or 'extremely' violent. Another of these four measures of violence was the sum total of all the boy's acts of violence, less those rated as 'only very slightly violent'. A third measure was the sum total including that bottom category. The fourth was the boys' score on a weighted system in which the following weights were allotted (on the basis of ratings by the public – see chapter 6) to acts of violence of different levels of seriousness:

Only very slightly violent	9
A bit violent	26
Fairly violent	44
Quite violent	63
Very violent	87
Extremely violent	100

The availability of these four sets of scores made it possible to assess the relationship of violence, at each of four different levels, to the characteristics of boys. One of these sets of analyses, incorporating the measure of serious violence, is presented in table 11.5. The others are presented in the Appendix to this chapter.

The main indications of table 11.5 are as follows

1 Violence in boys (at the serious level) is positively associated with: truancy; non-enjoyment of school; stealing sweets from a shop. It is negatively associated with: occupational level of father.

Table 11.5
The distribution of violence at its more serious level*, analysed by various characteristics of boys

CHARACTERISTICS OF BOYS	No. of cases	Frequency of occurrence of violent behaviour at this level in last 6 months				
		0 (837)	1 (186)	2-3 (170)	4-9 (179)	10 or more (187)
	n	%	%	%	%	%
All cases	(1559)†	54	12	11	11	12
Age of boy						
12-13 years	(623)	53	11	12	12	12
14-15 years	(584)	52	10	11	13	14
16-18 years‡	(349)	57	16	10	9	9
Type of school attended						
Secondary Modern	(379)	44	15	15	11	15
Comprehensive	(566)	54	10	11	14	13
Grammar	(330)	65	10	9	8	8
Public	(183)	58	11	9	11	11
Father's occupational level						
AB	(283)	71	10	7	6	7
C	(364)	59	13	9	12	8
D	(357)	48	14	12	13	12
E	(248)	45	11	17	12	15
F/G	(141)	40	12	10	15	23
Size of household						
2-3 people	(189)	60	11	12	11	7
4 people	(457)	56	12	10	10	13
5 people	(406)	57	12	11	11	9
6 people	(253)	51	13	10	11	15
7 people or more	(254)	43	12	14	15	16
Skin colour						
'Coloured'	(146)	42	16	18	15	9
White	(1356)	55	12	10	11	12
Truancy by boy						
Not at all	(1207)	60	12	10	9	9
Once a month	(126)	35	12	15	20	18
More than once a month	(181)	29	13	12	19	27
Has he enjoyed school?						
Yes	(1222)	58	12	10	11	10
No	(324)	37	13	14	15	20
Lots of spare time if still at school						
Yes	(531)	54	11	9	13	12
No	(870)	57	11	11	10	11
Average grip strength						
10-24 kilograms	(352)	52	13	11	13	11
25-30 kilograms	(433)	54	10	12	12	12
31-38 kilograms	(403)	54	12	10	11	13
39-60 kilograms	(353)	55	12	11	10	11
Ever stolen sweets from a shop?						
Yes	(686)	44	12	12	15	17
No	(870)	61	12	10	9	8
How long has mother worked since marriage?						
Not at all	(222)	43	17	11	14	15
For up to 2 years	(268)	55	13	9	10	13
For 3-5 years	(303)	57	12	11	8	12
For 6-10 years	(396)	55	10	12	13	10
Over 10 years	(305)	53	10	10	12	14
How often punished for violence/destructive behaviour when under age of 4						
Always	(240)	43	17	14	14	12
Mostly	(325)	53	13	8	14	13
Hardly ever	(284)	50	10	15	15	11
Not at all	(151)	50	9	14	14	14
Never violent	(522)	63	11	8	7	11

*In this table, categories 4, 5, 6 have been combined to form a single category – the more serious violence. Categories 4, 5 and 6 are respectively: quite violent acts; very violent acts; extremely violent acts.

†This figure is usually in excess of the total for the sub-groups set out under it – because for some cases usable data were not available for BOTH the variables involved in the cross-break.

‡A few boys had turned 18 between the first and the second interview.

2 For this sample, coloured boys were more involved than whites at the middle frequencies of violence (at this serious level), but less at the zero frequency and at the higher frequency levels.

3 There is some tendency for grammar school boys to be less violent than other boys.

4 In spite of a number of trends, the evidence of table 11.5 indicates that violent behaviour is widely spread across society.

This is not to say that other of the variables in table 11.5 are without association *within sample sub-groups* – but in terms of the *overall* sample, not to any appreciable degree.

It must be remembered, in examining the data in table 11.5, that they have to do with numerical association and *not necessarily with causal relationships.*

Other of the predictors of violence are given in the Appendix of chapter 3 and many more appear in the Technical Appendix.

APPENDIX TO CHAPTER 11

Appendix 1 Violent behaviour in the different sections of the boy population in London: Tables 11.A1-A3

Table 11.A1 Appendix 1

The distribution of violence, *expressed as a weighted score**, analysed by various characteristics of the boys

CHARACTERISTICS OF BOYS	No. of cases	Frequency of occurrence of violent behaviour at this level in last 6 months				
		0-12	13-24	24-45	46-84	85+
		316	316	318	317	292
	n	%	%	%	%	%
All cases	(1559)†	20	20	20	20	19
Age of boy						
12-13 years	(623)	22	22	20	19	17
14-15 years	(584)	18	17	20	24	21
16-18 years‡	(349)	20	22	22	18	17
Type of school attended						
Secondary Modern	(379)	20	24	18	18	20
Comprehensive	(566)	18	21	21	20	19
Grammar	(330)	23	16	22	23	17
Public	(183)	24	19	23	20	15
Father's occupational level						
A/B	(283)	26	23	17	19	16
C	(364)	19	21	22	22	16
D	(357)	20	18	20	22	20
E	(248)	17	23	22	19	20
F/G	(141)	18	18	19	22	23
Size of household						
2-3 people	(189)	24	19	20	19	18
4 people	(457)	19	22	19	21	20
5 people	(406)	22	19	21	22	16
6 people	(253)	21	18	20	23	19
7 or more	(254)	17	22	23	17	22
Skin colour						
'Coloured'	(146)	25	25	23	17	10
White	(1365)	20	20	20	21	20
Truancy by boy						
Not at all	(1207)	23	21	20	20	16
Once a month	(126)	10	18	19	28	25
More than once a month	(181)	9	17	21	19	34
Has he enjoyed school?						
Yes	(1222)	22	21	21	19	17
No	(324)	14	15	20	26	25
Lots of spare time if still at school						
Yes	(531)	16	17	23	22	22
No	(870)	23	22	19	20	16
Average grip strength						
10-24 kilograms	(352)	21	26	17	20	16
25-30 kilograms	(433)	23	20	21	18	18
31-38 kilograms	(403)	20	16	21	23	20
39-60 kilograms	(353)	18	19	22	21	20
Ever stolen sweets from a shop?						
Yes	(686)	10	19	21	24	26
No	(870)	28	21	20	17	13
How long has mother worked since marriage?						
Not worked at all	(222)	18	16	23	17	27
For up to 2 years	(268)	18	21	19	23	20
For 3-5 years	(303)	24	22	19	17	17
For 6-10 years	(396)	20	21	21	21	18
Over 10 years	(305)	19	21	19	24	18
How often punished for violent/destructive behaviour when under 4?						
Always	(240)	19	15	23	20	23
Mostly	(325)	18	17	24	22	19
Hardly ever	(284)	19	22	19	23	17
Not at all	(151)	17	25	16	20	22
Never violent	(522)	24	22	19	18	17

*Where the weights allocated were as follows:
Only very slightly violent = 9; A bit violent = 26; fairly violent = 44; quite violent = 63; very violent = 87; extremely violent = 100.

†This figure is usually in excess of that for the total of the sub-groups set out below it — because for some cases usable data were not available for BOTH the variables involved in the cross-break.

‡A few boys had turned 18 between the first and the second interview.

Table 11.A2

The distribution of violence, defined as total number of acts irrespective of how serious*, analysed by various characteristics of the boys

CHARACTERISTICS OF BOYS	No. of cases	Frequency of occurrence of violent behaviour at this level in last 6 months				
		0-54	55-124	125-234	235-424	425+
		241	337	338	341	302
	n	%	%	%	%	%
All cases	(1559)†	15	22	22	22	19
Age of boy						
12-13 years	(623)	20	25	20	20	16
14-15 years	(584)	13	19	22	25	22
16-18 years‡	(349)	11	21	25	21	22
Type of school attended						
Secondary Modern	(379)	18	22	21	19	20
Comprehensive	(566)	15	20	22	24	19
Grammar	(330)	14	22	20	24	21
Public	(183)	16	23	24	20	17
Father's occupational level						
A/B	(283)	17	24	22	19	17
C	(364)	13	21	24	24	17
D	(357)	15	21	21	24	20
E	(248)	16	23	22	21	19
F/G	(141)	15	22	20	21	22
Size of household						
2-3 people	(189)	19	18	23	22	19
4 people	(457)	12	24	19	24	21
5 people	(406)	17	23	21	22	17
6 people	(253)	19	16	23	25	17
7 or more	(254)	13	24	24	16	22
Skin colour						
'Coloured'	(146)	16	32	25	14	12
White	(1365)	16	21	21	23	20
Truancy by boy						
Not at all	(1207)	18	23	22	21	17
Once a month	(126)	7	18	25	25	25
More than once a month	(181)	8	16	19	26	31
Has he enjoyed school?						
Yes	(1222)	17	23	22	21	18
No	(324)	10	17	23	24	26
Lots of spare time if still at school						
Yes	(531)	12	17	23	25	22
No	(870)	19	25	20	20	16
Average grip strength						
10-24 kilograms	(352)	20	28	18	19	14
25-30 kilograms	(483)	19	20	22	22	17
31-38 kilograms	(403)	14	19	22	23	23
39-60 kilograms	(353)	9	20	24	24	23
Ever stolen sweets from a shop?						
Yes	(686)	8	18	23	24	27
No	(870)	21	25	21	20	13
How long has mother worked since marriage?						
Not worked at all	(222)	16	14	23	21	27
For up to 2 years	(268)	14	22	19	25	20
For 3-5 years	(303)	18	26	17	20	19
For 6-10 years	(396)	15	21	25	22	17
Over 10 years	(305)	14	21	24	22	19
How often punished for violent/destructive behaviour when under 4?						
Always	(240)	12	23	20	21	24
Mostly	(325)	15	17	23	27	18
Hardly ever	(284)	15	21	25	21	18
Not at all	(151)	15	26	19	21	21
Never violent	(522)	17	23	21	20	18

*To arrive at THIS violence score for any one boy, a count was made of all his acts of violence, irrespective of how violent these acts may have been. For each of the 53 categories in the web of stimuli, a ceiling of 50 acts was applied.

†This figure is usually in excess of that for the total of the sub-groups set out below it – because for some cases usable data were not available for BOTH the variables in the cross-break.

‡A few boys had turned 18 between the first and the second interviews.

Table 11.A3
The distribution of violence, defined as the total number of acts *less* those rated as only very slightly violent, and analysed by various characteristics of the boys

CHARACTERISTICS OF BOYS	No. of cases	Frequency of occurrence of violent behaviour at this level in last 6 months				
		0-14	15-34	35-74	75-164	165+
		213	308	362	370	306
	n	%	%	%	%	%
All cases	(1559)†	14	20	23	24	20
Age of boy						
12-13 years	(623)	12	21	24	22	20
14-15 years	(584)	12	16	23	26	23
16-18 years‡	(349)	18	23	22	23	14
Type of school attended						
Secondary Modern	(379)	12	24	20	21	23
Comprehensive	(566)	11	19	25	24	21
Grammar	(330)	16	18	23	27	15
Public	(183)	17	21	22	26	14
Father's occupational level						
A/B	(283)	20	20	24	20	16
C	(364)	15	19	25	25	16
D	(357)	11	19	22	26	22
E	(248)	9	23	23	23	23
F/G	(141)	13	14	26	25	23
Size of household						
2-3 people	(189)	18	20	20	23	19
4 people	(457)	14	19	24	23	20
5 people	(406)	14	20	23	25	17
6 people	(253)	14	19	23	26	19
7 or more people	(254)	9	21	25	21	24
Skin colour						
'Coloured'	(146)	14	25	24	25	12
White	(1356)	14	19	23	24	21
Truancy by boy						
Not at all	(1207)	15	21	24	23	17
Once a month	(126)	10	16	21	23	29
More than once a month	(181)	7	18	19	27	30
Has he enjoyed school?						
Yes	(1222)	15	20	24	22	18
No	(324)	9	17	19	30	25
Lots of spare time if still at school						
Yes	(531)	11	18	22	26	23
No	(870)	15	20	24	22	18
Average grip strength						
10-24 kilograms	(352)	13	21	26	23	18
25-30 kilograms	(433)	13	21	23	22	21
30-38 kilograms	(403)	15	16	23	25	21
39-60 kilograms	(353)	15	21	21	26	18
Ever stolen sweets from a shop?						
Yes	(686)	6	16	22	27	27
No	(870)	19	22	24	21	14
How long has mother worked since marriage?						
Not worked at all	(222)	12	18	23	19	27
For up to 2 years	(268)	13	18	25	26	19
For 3-5 years	(303)	17	22	22	22	17
For 6-10 years	(396)	13	20	23	25	20
Over 10 years	(305)	10	21	24	26	19
How often punished for violent/destructive behaviour when under 4						
Always	(240)	12	18	21	25	24
Mostly	(325)	10	19	24	26	21
Hardly ever	(284)	11	22	23	27	17
Not at all	(151)	12	16	28	19	25
Never violent	(522)	19	21	23	21	16

†This figure is usually in excess of that for the total of the sub-groups set out below it – because for some cases usable data were not available for BOTH the variables in the cross-break.

‡A few boys had turned 18 between the first and the second interviews.

CHAPTER 12

FINDINGS: THE TENABILITY OF HYPOTHESES ABOUT THE EFFECTS OF EXPOSURE TO TELEVISION VIOLENCE UPON THE EXTENT OF VIOLENT BEHAVIOUR BY BOYS (INVESTIGATING HYPOTHESES I-IV)

Contents

12 FINDINGS: THE TENABILITY OF HYPOTHESES ABOUT THE EFFECTS OF EXPOSURE TO TELEVISION VIOLENCE UPON THE EXTENT OF VIOLENT BEHAVIOUR BY BOYS

(INVESTIGATING HYPOTHESES I-IV)

THE NATURE OF THE HYPOTHESES

Whereas this enquiry dealt with the tenability of a large number of hypotheses, its central concern was with the hypothesis:

> 'High exposure to violence on television increases the degree to which boys commit acts of violence.'

There were four versions of this hypothesis, sub-hypotheses 1, 2, 3 and 4, dealing respectively with the following dependent variables.

1 Violence expressed as a weighted total (dependent variable I-DVI), where the weights were as follows:

Only very slightly violent	9
A bit violent	26
Fairly violent	44
Quite violent	63
Very violent	87
Extremely violent	100

2 Violence expressed as the total number of acts committed, irrespective of how serious they were (dependent variable 2-DV2).

3 Violence expressed as a total number of acts committed, less those rated as 'only very slightly' violent (DV3).

4 Violence expressed as the total number of acts of violence of the more serious kind, i.e. 'quite violent' plus 'very violent' plus 'extremely violent' (DV4).

The second, third and fourth of these dependent variables clearly form a rising sequence in terms of seriousness, while the first of them is a generalised measure of involvement in violence, based on all six levels, and referred to in this chapter as 'violence in general'.

These four versions of the central hypothesis were of course due for investigation in both their forward and their reversed forms.

In approaching a study of this nature it must be remembered that 'violence' was defined in line with the public's view of it, namely: 'any form of behaviour that produces hurt or harm for the object on the receiving end (whether animate or inanimate); for animate objects the hurt or harm may be either psychological or physical'. It must also be remembered that the principal independent variable in each of the four hypotheses was *extent of exposure to television violence over a period going back to 1959*; that the violence studied was limited to that committed in the six months prior to the interview. Further details about the independent variable and the dependent variables are given in chapters 4 and 6 respectively.

In addition, each of hypotheses 1 and 4 had linked to it various sub-hypotheses as detailed in the grid on pages 4 and 5. Thus for hypothesis 1 there were 25 sub-hypotheses, each linking its dependent variable with exposure to some particular kind of television violence, e.g. 'programmes featuring violence of a realistic kind'; 'programmes where the violence is performed by basically 'good guy' types who are also 'rebels' or 'odd-men-out'; and so on as set out in the grid (pages 4 and 5). The same 25 sub-hypotheses were linked to hypothesis 4. All 50 sub-hypotheses were due for investigation in both their forward and their reversed forms.

THE ADDITIONAL HYPOTHESES ADDED FOR CONTROL AND COMPARATIVE PURPOSES

To the complex shown in the grid of hypotheses, several other hypotheses were added. Two of these were included for control purposes – that is, as controls that went beyond the internal control system involved in the matching of the Control sub-group to the Qualifying sub-group. The first hypothesis in this 'secondary control' system was:

> 'High exposure to *television output (considered generally)* is less likely to increase the degree to which boys commit violence than is high exposure to television *violence* itself.'

The second hypothesis in this secondary control system was:

> 'High exposure to *non-violent television* is less likely to increase the degree to which boys commit violence than is (i) high exposure to television violence and (ii) high exposure to television output in general.'

In formulating these two control-hypotheses it was realised that there would be a large degree of overlap between their independent variables and the independent variable in the master hypothesis, [1] namely exposure to television violence generally (see table 12.8). Nonetheless it was expected that in going from exposure to television violence to exposure to television generally and then on to exposure to non-violent television, there would be an appreciable degree of fall-off in exposure to *violent* television programmes. [2]

Three more hypotheses were added for comparative purposes, relating respectively to violent comic books, violent films, newspapers. These were:

- 'High exposure to comics and comic books increases the degree to which boys commit acts of violence.'
- 'High exposure to violence on the cinema screen increases the degree to which boys commit acts of violence.'
- 'High exposure to newspapers increases the degree to which boys commit acts of violence.'

THE DIFFERENT HYPOTHESES AND SUB-HYPOTHESES INVESTIGATED (continued over)

The independent variables

1 High exposure to violence on television generally
2 High exposure to programmes containing fictional violence of a realistic kind
3 High exposure to programmes where violence is performed by basically 'good guy' types who are also 'rebels' or 'odd-man out'
4 High exposure to programmes in which much of the violence occurs in a domestic or family setting
5 High exposure to programmes which feature defiance of, or rudeness toward authority figures
6 High exposure to programmes where violence is shown as glorified, romanticised, idealised or ennobling
7 High exposure to programmes where violence is presented as 'fun and games' or like a game or as something to entertain
8 High exposure to programmes in which the violence is presented as being in a good cause
9 High exposure to programmes where the physical or mental consequences of violence, for the victim, are shown in detail
10 High exposure to programmes where the violence is related to racial or minority group strife
11 High exposure to programmes where the violence is performed by basically 'good guy' types or heroes who are also tough (i.e. who can endure physical violence and fight on)
12 High exposure to programmes where the violence is of a verbal kind
13 High exposure to programmes in which the violence is just thrown in for its own sake, or is not necessary to the plot
14 High exposure to programmes in which the violence is gruesome, horrific or scary
15 High exposure to fictional programmes about the English police at work which also feature the kinds of violence which go on in society

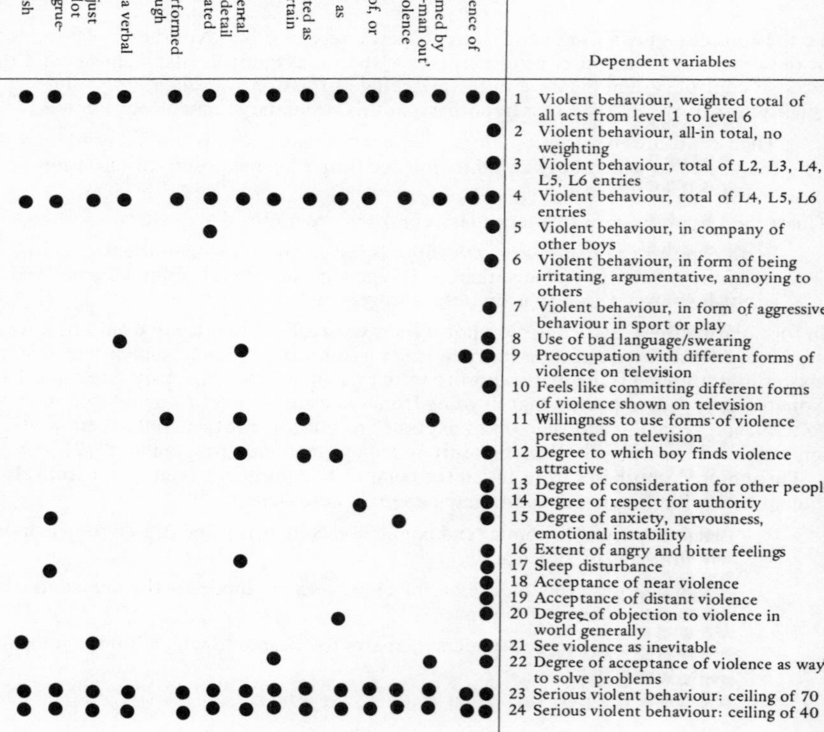

Dependent variables	1	2	3	4	5	6	7	8	9	10	11	12	13	14	15
1 Violent behaviour, weighted total of all acts from level 1 to level 6	●	●	●	●	●	●	●	●	●	●	●	●	●	●	●
2 Violent behaviour, all-in total, no weighting	●														
3 Violent behaviour, total of L2, L3, L4, L5, L6 entries	●														
4 Violent behaviour, total of L4, L5, L6 entries	●	●	●	●	●	●	●	●	●	●	●	●	●	●	●
5 Violent behaviour, in company of other boys	●									●					
6 Violent behaviour, in form of being irritating, argumentative, annoying to others	●														
7 Violent behaviour, in form of aggressive behaviour in sport or play	●														
8 Use of bad language/swearing	●											●			
9 Preoccupation with different forms of violence on television	●	●							●						
10 Feels like committing different forms of violence shown on television	●														
11 Willingness to use forms of violence presented on television	●		●				●		●		●				
12 Degree to which boy finds violence attractive	●					●	●		●						
13 Degree of consideration for other people	●														
14 Degree of respect for authority	●				●										
15 Degree of anxiety, nervousness, emotional instability	●			●										●	
16 Extent of angry and bitter feelings	●														
17 Sleep disturbance	●								●					●	
18 Acceptance of near violence	●														
19 Acceptance of distant violence	●														
20 Degree of objection to violence in world generally	●					●									
21 See violence as inevitable	●												●		●
22 Degree of acceptance of violence as way to solve problems	●		●					●							
23 Serious violent behaviour: ceiling of 70	●	●	●	●	●	●	●	●	●	●	●	●	●	●	●
24 Serious violent behaviour: ceiling of 40	●	●	●	●	●	●	●	●	●	●	●	●	●	●	●

THE DIFFERENT HYPOTHESES AND SUB-HYPOTHESES INVESTIGATED (continued over)

The independent variables

16 High exposure to a selection of 5 cartoon programmes in which the characters are violent to each other (i.e. Boss Cat, Popeye, Pugwash, Yogi Bear, Tom & Jerry)
17 High exposure to Tom and Jerry
18 High exposure to plays or films in which personal relationships are a major theme, and which feature verbal abuse (e.g. swearing, quarrelling) or physical violence
19 High exposure to violence through the news or newsreel programmes
20 High exposure to comedy programmes which feature 'slapstick' violence and/or verbal abuse between characters
21 Science fiction programmes involving violence (e.g. where creatures destroy people, where humans use super weapons to destroy men)
22 High exposure to 'Westerns' which include violence, for example, as between cowboys and Indians
23 High exposure to a selection of 3 sporting programmes which present violence by competitors or spectators (i.e. Sports View, Grandstand, Saturday Sports Time)
24 High exposure to wrestling and boxing
25 High exposure to films or series which feature gangs or gangsters engaged in violent organised crime
26 High exposure to programmes in which the violence is performed by adults
27 High exposure to television generally
28 High exposure to violent comic books
29 High exposure to violent films
30 High exposure to newspapers
31 High exposure to non-violent television

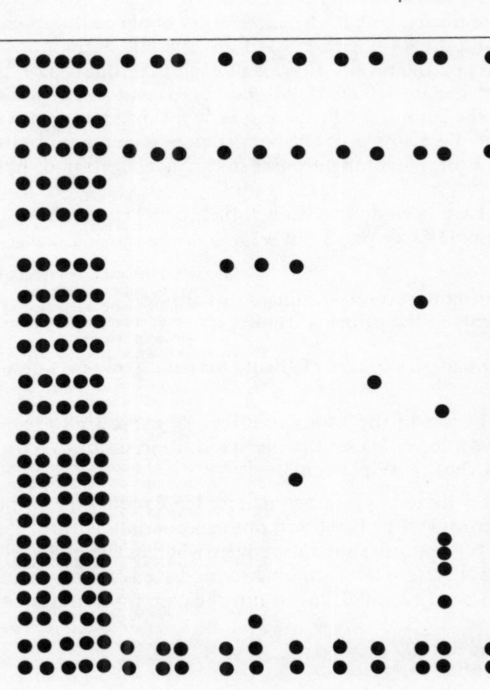

Dependent variables	16	17	18	19	20	21	22	23	24	25	26	27	28	29	30	31
1 Violent behaviour, weighted total of all acts from level 1 to level 6	●	●	●	●	●	●	●	●	●	●	●	●	●	●	●	●
2 Violent behaviour, all-in total, no weighting												●	●	●	●	●
3 Violent behaviour, total of L2, L3, L4, L5, L6 entries												●	●	●	●	●
4 Violent behaviour, total of L4, L5, L6 entries	●	●	●	●	●	●	●	●	●	●	●	●	●	●	●	●
5 Violent behaviour, in company of other boys												●	●	●	●	●
6 Violent behaviour, in form of being irritating, argumentative, annoying to others												●	●	●	●	●
7 Violent behaviour, in form of aggressive behaviour in sport or play						●	●	●				●	●	●	●	●
8 Use of bad language/swearing			●									●	●	●	●	●
9 Preoccupation with different forms of violence on television												●	●	●	●	●
10 Feels like committing different forms of violence shown on television												●	●	●	●	●
11 Willingness to use forms of violence presented on television				●								●	●	●	●	●
12 Degree to which boy finds violence attractive		●										●	●	●	●	●
13 Degree of consideration for other people												●	●	●	●	●
14 Degree of respect for authority												●	●	●	●	●
15 Degree of anxiety, nervousness, emotional instability						●						●	●	●	●	●
16 Extent of angry and bitter feelings												●	●	●	●	●
17 Sleep disturbance												●	●	●	●	●
18 Acceptance of near violence		●										●	●	●	●	●
19 Acceptance of distant violence		●										●	●	●	●	●
20 Degree of objection to violence in world generally		●										●	●	●	●	●
21 See violence as inevitable		●										●	●	●	●	●
22 Degree of acceptance of violence as way to solve problems							●					●	●	●	●	●
23 Serious violent behaviour: ceiling of 70	●	●	●	●	●	●	●	●	●	●	●	●	●	●	●	●
24 Serious violent behaviour: ceiling of 40	●	●	●	●	●	●	●	●	●	●	●	●	●	●	●	●

A PRELIMINARY BRIEF PRESENTATION OF THE PRINCIPAL FINDINGS AND OF THE PROBLEMS THEY RAISE FOR INTERPRETATION

Table 12.1 sets out the principal results of the investigation of hypotheses 1-4. With these are certain other findings: the results of investigating parallel hypotheses about each of three other mass media, namely comics, cinema, press; the results of applying the secondary control system to the investigation of hypotheses 1-4. Throughout the table, the results reported relate to both the forward and the reverse forms of the different hypotheses. I have reserved for a later chapter presentation of the results of testing the 50 sub-hypotheses of hypotheses 1 and 4, dealing with the effects (upon behaviour) of exposure to 25 *different sorts* of television violence.

PROBLEMS TO BE FACED IN INTERPRETING THE FINDINGS

It is essential that, before we attempt to reach conclusions about the tenability of hypotheses featured in table 12.1, there should be an appraisal of the meaningfulness of the different sets of information presented in it. (i) There are in table 12.1 certain seemingly discordant elements that need to be understood and explained. (ii) The Critical Ratios and P values presented in table 12.1 take no account of the correlation between dependent variable and matching composite, and the P values are based on 'one-tail' extractions from probability tables. (iii) The forward and the reversed forms of each hypothesis have to be interpreted in combination. In fact, chapter 10 dealt with points (ii) and (iii) at some length, but what was said there will be summarised here and brought into the context of the statement of 'findings'. (iv) There is also a point of importance to be made about the stability of one of the variables used for matching purposes in the investigation of hypothesis 1.

Only after these various matters have been dealt with will final conclusions about the tenability of hypotheses 1-4 be presented (see pages 389-92).

Problems relating to several seemingly discordant elements in the principal findings

There are in table 12.1 several seemingly discordant elements that are likely to worry or to puzzle the perceptive reader.

1. There is a major leap in the size of the 'index of effect' of exposure to television violence in going from hypotheses 1-3 on the one hand, to hypothesis 4 on the other (from about 12 per cent to 49 per cent).
2. Whereas for hypotheses 1-3 there is a proportionately large reduction in the index of effect as we go from IV1 to IV31 within the secondary control system, this tends not to happen for hypothesis 4. Moreover, whereas the index of effect for IV27 within the control system tends to be intermediate between that for IV1 and IV31 for hypotheses 1, 2 and 3, this is not the case for hypothesis 4.

The large increase in the size of the index of effect in going from hypotheses 1-3 to hypothesis 4

The evidence of table 12.1, as it relates to the forward tests of hypotheses 1-4 is set out in

Table 12.1

The principal findings for hypotheses 1, 2, 3 & 4 and for closely associated behaviour

Type of exposure involved in the hypotheses (all are independent variables)	Direction of the hypothesis	The hypotheses under investigation															
		H1 Violence as weighted total of all acts				H2 Violence as total of all acts (no weighting)				H3 Violence as total of all acts, less trivia				H4 Violence as total of serious acts			
		Means for: Qualifiers (M_Q) **	Mod controls (M_{MC}) **	% diff† $\frac{M_Q - M_{MC}}{M_{MC}}$	Signif. of Diff P ††	Means for: Qualifiers (M_Q)	Mod controls (M_{MC})	% diff $\frac{M_Q - M_{MC}}{M_{MC}}$	Signif. of Diff P††	Means for: Qualifiers (M_Q)	Mod controls (M_{MC})	% diff $\frac{M_Q - M_{MC}}{M_{MC}}$	Signif. of Diff P††	Means for: Qualifiers (M_Q)	Mod controls (M_{MC})	% diff $\frac{M_Q - M_{MC}}{M_{MC}}$	Signif. of Diff P††
Violence on TV	F*	56.76	51.01	11.27	.034	294.10	265.03	10.97	.042	114.10	100.85	13.14	.029	7.48	5.02	49.00	.022
as in H 1-4 (IV1)	R*	607.81	563.51	7.86	<.001	614.60	572.02	7.44	.001	602.96	551.29	9.37	<.001	582.65	574.14	1.48	.264
TV generally	F	55.58	52.19	6.50	.145	286.39	261.69	9.44	.051	111.83	102.51	9.09	.087	7.39	4.86	52.06	.015
(IV 27)	R	100.41	95.57	5.06	.004	100.98	94.94	6.36	<.001	99.93	93.96	6.66	<.001	96.63	96.03	0.62	.378
Non-violent TV	F	54.14	52.96	2.23	.356	277.17	266.28	4.09	.215	109.37	109.88	−0.46	.472ǂ	7.17	4.94	45.14	.025
(IV 31)	R	312.00	305.42	2.15	.209	312.40	304.66	2.54	.176	313.28	292.59	7.07	.004	297.47	297.80	−0.11	.484ǂ
Comics/comic	F	57.06	49.45	15.39	.007	276.49	260.89	5.98	.136	118.81	100.97	17.67	.005	7.99	5.94	34.51	.071
books (IV 28)	R	9.08	8.58	5.83	.050	8.79	8.24	6.68	.035	9.17	8.35	9.82	.004	9.59	8.64	11.00	.002
Violent films	F	56.95	49.11	15.96	.005	295.76	252.45	17.16	.002	114.81	94.68	21.26	.001	6.80	5.39	26.16	.111
(IV 29)	R	5.88	5.57	5.57	.082	6.05	5.43	11.42	.003	5.86	5.32	10.15	.008	5.63	5.35	5.23	.087
Newspapers	F	57.27	49.53	15.63	.008	289.54	249.69	15.96	.002	117.84	99.98	17.86	.004	6.84	7.08	−3.39	.496ǂ
(IV 30)	R	6.23	5.87	6.13	.029	6.27	5.84	7.36	.012	6.19	5.98	3.51	.140	6.39	5.88	8.67	.004

*F = Forward form of the hypothesis / R = Reverse form of the hypothesis

**M_Q = Mean score of Qualifiers on dependent variable / M_{MC} = Mean score of Modified Controls on dependent variable

†% Diff is referred to in the report as 'the index of effect'. It does not imply that the extent of the effect on behaviour is of the same size as the % difference, but the bigger the index, the bigger the probable change

††These P values have been computed as for one-directional hypotheses. By contrast, the P values in the Technical Appendix take no account of the direction of the hypothesised change and are therefore very conservative values, constituting a tough challenge to the hypothesis. The Critical Ratios have been calculated without adjustment for the 'correlation factor'.

ǂ Critical Ratio was very small but negative.

somewhat greater detail in table 12.2.

Table 12.2
Demonstrating the jump in size of the index of effect in going from hypotheses 1, 2, 3 to hypothesis 4

The hypotheses under investigation (All below are in the Forward form)	Measures relating to amount of violent behaviour			
	Means for		% Diff (= Index† of effect)	Signif. of differences
	Qualifiers M_Q	Modified controls M_{MC}	$\frac{M_Q - M_{MC}}{M_{MC}}$	P*
Hypothesis 1 (linking IV1 & DV1)	57.76	51.01	11.27	.034
Hypothesis 2 (linking IV1 & DV2)	294.10	265.03	10.97	.042
Hypothesis 3 (linking IV1 & DV3)	114.10	100.85	13.14	.029
Hypothesis 4 (linking IV1 & DV4)	7.48	5.02	49.00	.022

*Based on 'one-tail' extractions (because the hypotheses are directional). No adjustment made for 'correlation factor'.
†In general, the greater the size of the index the greater the probable effect of exposure to television violence.

A conservative estimate of the P values of these indices of change marks each finding as statistically meaningful and as increasing the tenability of the four hypotheses in their forward forms. However, what is remarkable about these findings is the sharp increase in the size of the 'index of effect' in going from hypotheses 1, 2 and 3 to hypothesis 4. It is such a large increase that one must consider how it arose and its possible implications.

1 The first thing to notice in this connection is that we are not dealing with different samples as we go from hypotheses 1-3 to hypothesis 4. In other words, though this big jump in the size of the index of change may have arisen from the internal oddities of the particular sample used, it does *not* arise from differences between *two* samples.

2 At the level of *internal oddities* of the sample, it seems possible that the very large size of the index of increase in serious violence has arisen from what is sometimes referred to as the 'outlyer' problem. In the present case, this would involve the presence, in the Qualifying group, of a limited number of boys with very large scores on 'serious violence' – compared with none (or very few) in the Control group. *Such a situation could be a genuine outcome of heavy exposure to television violence.* On the other hand, it *could* conceivably have risen out of (i) an oddity in the particular sample drawn and/or (ii) exaggerated claims about their serious violence on the part of a minority of boys in the heavy exposure group.

Despite the care taken in the development of the measuring technique and its use, and in spite of the 'ceiling' put upon claims about each class of violence, we cannot rule out such an eventuality – though it does not appear to have happened for the lesser levels of violent behaviour.

Several steps were taken to increase understanding of the jump in the 'index of effect' to 49 per cent.

(a) The heavy and the light exposee groups (i.e. the Qualifiers and the Controls) were compared in terms of the distribution of their scores for serious violence. The comparison is shown in table 12.3. It provides evidence that an 'outlyer' phenomenon was present to a certain degree. The single score of 500 for one boy is especially noteworthy (see later for evaluative comment).

Table 12.3
Distribution of serious violence 'scores' for the Qualifiers on the hypothesis (i.e. heavier viewers of violence) and the Controls (i.e. the lighter viewers of violence)

'Score' for involvement in serious violence	Exposees to TV violence	
	Heavier (Qualifiers)	Lighter (Controls)
	n	n
0	411	429
1	95	91
2-3	77	95
4-9	92	87
10-39	66	56
40-69	29	17
70-99	4	3
100-299	7	5
300-499	0	0
500*	1	0
All	782	783

*Obviously this one case calls for special attention in the analysis and in the interpretation of findings. See 2 (b) and also (d).

(b) To damp down the special effect of the 'outlyers', a ceiling of 70 was imposed on boys' scores for serious violence – bringing the scores of all who scored over 70 back to the level of 70. The whole matching process was then reapplied and a new 'index of effect' was computed. This step is particularly important in dealing with the '500 acts' case.

(c) The eliminating of any 'outlyer' effect was taken to an extreme by re-computing the 'index of effect' with a new ceiling of 40 imposed on the serious violence scores of boys.

The results of steps (b) and (c) are shown in table 12.4.

Clearly the size of the 'index of effect' falls off with each lowering of the 'ceiling' and obviously there would be a virtual disappearance of the 'index of effect' if the ceiling was dropped sufficiently low. What matters here however, is that even with a major lowering of the ceiling, the index of effect remained large and statistically meaningful.

(d) A question of importance is 'What would happen if we discounted wholly or partly the outstanding score of 500 that stemmed from one boy. Suppose we cut it back to the middle of the interval 200-299 at which there are already three cases . . . or to 70 . . . or if we eliminated it altogether from the count?' For these three situations, the 'index of effect' would be respectively: 43 per cent; 38 per cent; 36 per cent. In other words, whatever we may do about that special score of 500, the result for the forward version of hypothesis 4 is that the 'index of effect' remains large and statistically meaningful. Similarly if we cut back *all* scores to the ceiling of 70.

Table 12.4
Variations in the index of effect with the imposition of ceilings on boys' 'scores' for serious violence

The dependent variable in hypothesis 4 – as 'ceilings' are applied to individual scores	Measures relating to amount of violent behaviour			
	Means for		% Diff (= Index of effect)	Signif. of differences
	Qualifiers M_Q	Modified controls M_{MC}	$\frac{M_Q - M_{MC}}{M_{MC}}$	P*
No ceiling (on DV4)	7.48	5.02	49.00	.022
Ceiling of 70 (on DV4)	5.76	4.41	30.61	.023
Ceiling of 40 (on DV4)	4.77	3.88	22.94	.039

*P is based on 'one-tail' extractions (because the hypotheses are directional)

Having made these cautionary analyses and statements, I think it essential that I draw the reader's attention to the clear possibility that the various extreme scores for serious violence are in fact *accurate* measures of the violent behaviour of boys – so that cutting boys back to a ceiling 70 could well involve an understatement of the extent of television's effect on the general level of serious violence committed by boys.

Whereas it is essential that the researcher be wary about the special effects of outlyer scores, it is also important that they do not reject divergent evidence as somehow unacceptable. In the present case, the danger inherent in a small number of very large scores is that we could be led by the resultant averages into thinking that more *individuals* are markedly affected than is the case.

3 Another possible explanation of the large jump in the violence 'scores' in going from hypotheses 1-3 to hypothesis 4, is that serious violence (DV4) may be a different type of variable from those principally involved in hypotheses 1-3. If this were so, it would make that large jump less puzzling.

There are several sets of evidence bearing on this possibility. First the contribution of the dependent variable in hypothesis 4 (i.e. DV4) to the dependent variable scores for hypotheses 1, 2 and 3 (for DV1, DV2, DV3) is relatively small as shown in table 12.5.

Table 12.5
The contributions of 'serious violence' to the dependent variable scores in hypotheses 1, 2 and 3

Class of score	Average score per boy on the dependent variable on the hypothesis (a)	Average score per boy when serious violence is eliminated (b)	% Difference (i.e. a-b as % of a)
			%
*Weighted score** for all acts of violence (as in hypothesis 1)	5138.6	4702.8	8.5
Total *number* of acts of violence including trivia (as in H.2)	263.6	257.5	2.3
Total *number* of acts of violence excluding trivia (as in H.3)	104.8	98.7	5.8

*Sample averages and weights involved in these calculations are as follows:- 'only very slightly violent' . . . wt.9 and average 158.8; 'a bit violent' . . . wt.26 and average 59.4; 'fairly violent' . . . wt.44 and average 39.3; 'quite violent' . . . wt.63 and average 4.1; 'very violent' . . . wt.87 and average 2.0; 'extremely violent' . . . wt.100 and average 0.035.

Secondly, whereas the dependent variables in hypotheses 1, 2 and 3 (i.e. DV1, DV2 and DV3) are closely correlated with each other, the relationship of the dependent variable in hypothesis 4 (i.e. DV4) with any of them is relatively low – certainly low enough for DV4 to be considered appreciably independent of DVs 1, 2 and 3.

Table 12.6
The inter-correlation* of the different dependent variables

Dependent variables	DV1	DV2	DV3	DV4
DV1	1.000	.930	.973	.589
DV2	.930	1.000	.873	.389
DV3	.973	.873	1.000	.513
DV4	.589	.381	.513	1.000

*Pearson Product Moment coefficients

Furthermore, we should note that 'serious violence (i.e. DV4) is a minority event, its incidence over a six month period averaging out at about 6 times per boy, whereas the incidence of lesser forms of violence in the same period was approximately 258 times per boy.

Moreover, there were some appreciable differences between boys who committed 'serious violence' and the rest of the boy population. These differences were shown in table 11.6 in the preceding chapter.

To sum up: an examination of the evidence available provides no case for assuming that the large increase in the size of the 'index of effect' in going from hypotheses 1-3 to hypothesis 4 is an artifact or errór of some kind. It also indicates that DVs 1-3 and DV4 are sufficiently different for such a result to emerge.

Variation in the 'indices of effect' in going from one to another class of exposure to television violence within the 'secondary control system'.

The second of the oddities referred to as featured in table 12.1 concerns variation in the index of effect for serious violence in going from the hypotheses featuring independent variable 1 (= IV1) to those featuring independent variables 27 and 31 (IV27 and IV31).

Table 12.7
The results of using a secondary control system in the investigation of hypotheses 1-4

Secondary control sequence		'Indices of effect' for the four different hypotheses				
Type of exposure	Index of effect	H1	H2	H3	H4	H4 ceiling of 70
Exposure to television violence (IV1)	Index (P*)	11.27% (.034)	10.97% (.042)	13.14% (.029)	49.00% (.022)	30.61% (.023)
Exposure to television generally (IV27)	Index (P)	6.50% (.145)	9.44% (.051)	9.09% (.087)	52.06% (.015)	28.54% (.029)
Exposure to non-violent television (IV31)	Index (P)	2.23% (.356)	4.09% (.215)	−0.46% (− .472)†	45.14% (.025)	26.13% (.043)

*P is based on '1-tail' extractions and does not take account of extent of the correlation between the dependent variable and the matching composite.
†Critical ratio was very small but negative.

This oddity is a particularly challenging one, though as will be illustrated hereunder, it does in fact arise from the special nature of (i) what is being measured by the independent variables 27 and 31 and (ii) the equally special nature of the relationship between the extent of exposure to television violence and involvement in the more serious kinds of violent behaviour.

Each of hypotheses 1, 2, 3 and 4 had been subject to check through a 'secondary control system'. Thus IV1 is 'extent of exposure to TV violence', which is of course a vital part of each of hypotheses 1, 2, 3 and 4. On the other hand, IV31 was meant to be 'extent of exposure to *non-violent* television programmes'. On this thinking, one might reasonably expect the index of effect to diminish sharply [3] when IV31 is substituted (in any of the 4 hypotheses) for IV1. Still within this secondary control system, IV27 (which is 'amount of exposure to *television programmes generally*') appears to be intermediate between IV1 and IV31 with respect to extent of exposure to television violence and one might *on that basis* reasonably expect the size of the index of effect (for IV27) to lie *between* that for IV1 and IV31.

Whereas this expected pattern of findings does tend to emerge for hypotheses 1, 2 and 3, it does not do so for hypothesis 4 whether we assess DV4 with or without the ceiling of 70 applied. See table 12.7. This is the second of the two seemingly discordant elements in the findings and it, too, calls for careful consideration.

(a) *The nature of IV27 and IV31.* The first thing to note about IVs 31 and 27 is that *they are not what they could all too easily seem to be.* Thus boys who see a lot of non-violent television (IV31) could easily be thought to be boys who see very little *violent* television. In fact this is not so. Such is the generalised nature of viewing that a boy who scores high on exposure to *non-violent* programmes will automatically score high on exposure to *violent* programmes (IV1). Similarly, boys who score high on exposure to television generally (IV27) will automatically score high on exposure to television *violence* (IV1). The correlation grid of table 12.8 quantifies this overlap or duplication phenomenon.

Table 12.8
The extent of overlap between independent variables IV1, IV27 and IV31, shown through correlation coefficients*

Independent variables	IV1	IV27	IV31
Violent TV (IV1)	1.000	.873	.721
TV generally (IV27)	.873	1.000	.855
Non-violent TV (IV31)	.721	.855	1.000

*Pearson Product Moment coefficients

Nonetheless the table 12.8 data leave room for an assumption of a descending order of difference (in exposure to TV violence) between higher and lower scorers as we go from IV1 to IV27 to IV31. It was on the basis of such an assumption that IV27 and IV31 were linked with IV1 to make up a secondary control system. In fact, this assumption is borne out by the numerical details in table 12.9.

In developing this table, a calculation was made of the degree to which *high* scorers on IV31 and *low* scorers on IV31 had been exposed to television violence as measured by IV1. The mean exposure scores of these two groups were 721 and 438 units respectively, indicating a difference of 283 units of exposure to violence on television. The same kind of calculation was made for IV27 and IV1. The difference between means for amount of exposure to TV violence in going from IV1 to IV27 to IV31 was 400, 341, 283 – a descending series.

At the same time, those three figures make it clear that in going from IV1 to IV31, we are not going from a big difference (in exposure to TV violence) to no difference at all or even to some negative difference. In other words, the secondary control system can provide us with a comparison of three sets of information: (i) the relative levels of violent behaviour of boys who differ sharply in terms of how much television violence they have seen (IV1); (ii) the relative violence levels of two groups of boys who differ somewhat less in terms of the amount of television violence they have seen; (iii) the relative levels of violence of two groups of boys who differ less again in terms of the amount of television violence they have seen.

Table 12.9
The IV1 scores of the 6 sub-groups involved in the secondary control system

Type of exposure	Sample split into higher and lower scoring groups	Mean scores of sub-group pairs in terms of IV1	Difference between pairs in terms of means on IV1
Exposure to violence on television (IV1)	Higher scoring group on IV1	776	400
	Lower scoring group on IV1	376	
Exposure to television generally (IV27)	Higher scoring group on IV27	747	341
	Lower scoring group on IV27	406	
Exposure to non-violent television (IV31)	Higher scoring group on IV31	721	283
	Lower scoring group on IV31	438	

Let me take this distinction one step further. The data in tables 12.8 and 12.9 indicate that the phenomenon with which we are concerned in this section is really a difference in outcome *when we apply two control systems that are by no means equivalent* or equally discriminating, namely:

(i) the built-in control system which allows the estimation (after matching) of the difference in violence level of boys who have seen a lot of television violence (the Qualifiers) and of boys who have seen much less television violence (the Controls) – the difference between them in terms of exposure to television violence being 400 units;

(ii) the *secondary control system* which compares the estimated differences in violence level between groups of boys as we go from an exposure differential of 400 units (IV1) to an exposure differential of 341 (IV27) to an exposure differential of 283 units (IV31).

Having said all this, the fact remains that whereas for hypotheses 1, 2 and 3 the secondary control system does yield descending indices of effect, it does NOT do so to any meaningful degree for hypothesis 4. This particular point is taken up under (b) below.

(b) *What lies behind the hypothesis 4 outcome?* A close examination of the raw data, at a numerical level, brought out fairly clearly what lies behind the discordant element referred to in the previous paragraph and shown in table 12.7. As it happens, this examination also added to our knowledge about the relationship between exposure to television violence and participation in the *more serious* kinds of violent behaviour.

In the first place, the precise form of this relationship differs in a fundamental way in going from the dependent variables featured in hypotheses 1, 2 and 3 on the one hand to the dependent variable featured in hypothesis 4. For simplicity of presentation I have limited my comparison of these relationships or trends to the variables in hypotheses 1 and 4, but the reader may take it that the trends for hypotheses 1, 2 and 3 are closely similar to each other, the big difference being between hypotheses 1, 2 and 3 as a group and hypothesis 4. The differences between the trends for the variables in hypotheses 1 and 4 are shown in figure 12.1.

For violent behaviour considered generally (as in hypothesis 1) there is, *for the greater part of the sample*, a 'rising' [4] relationship between violent behaviour and exposure to television violence (see Line Chart 1). But this is not so for violent behaviour of the more serious kind (as in hypothesis 4). For the latter level of violent behaviour, the form of the line chart is fundamentally an irregular three-phase one. [4]

The nature of the association between violent behaviour and exposure to television violence (as presented in the line charts of figure 12.1) will determine, to a substantial degree, the outcome of the secondary control system, namely the *sequence* of 'indices of effect' which that system is designed to produce. In the present case, the secondary control system for the investigation of hypothesis 1 is geared to the form of association represented by Line Chart 1, whereas for hypothesis 4, the form of association is the markedly different one represented by Line Chart 2. So there is indeed room for quite genuine and informative differences in the way the secondary control system works for the investigation of hypotheses 1, 2 and 3 on the one hand and hypothesis 4 on the other.

This particular point can be taken further by superimposing on figure 12.1 the six mean scores (for exposure to television violence) presented in table 12.9. (See figure 12.2)

It would be wrong to attempt to derive corresponding estimates of violent behaviour by projection from the line charts to the vertical axis in figure 12.2. But the evidence in figure 12.2 makes it clear nonetheless that we can reasonably expect the secondary control system to yield a descending series of 'indices of effect' when applied to hypothesis 1 (Line Chart 1) – whereas we can have *no such expectation* when the secondary control system is applied to hypothesis 4 (Line Chart 2).

For his fuller consideration of this particular matter, the reader may wish to have certain further information. This consists of the form of the association between exposure to TV violence and (i) level of violence when a ceiling of 70 is applied to the violence score of each boy; (ii) level of violence when a ceiling of 40 is applied to the violence score of each boy. These forms of association are illustrated in figure 12.3.

The line chart linking extent of exposure to TV violence and violent behaviour is of course of great importance in its own right. It is discussed in a later part of this chapter.

The influence of exposure to television output considered generally (i.e. irrespective of whether violent or otherwise)

Despite the case presented on pages 375-9 it may be felt by some that the data in table 12.7 still leave open the possibility that it is *exposure to television irrespective of whether that television material is violent in character*, that increases involvement in serious violence. In view of such a possible situation, certain further analyses were made of the data which had

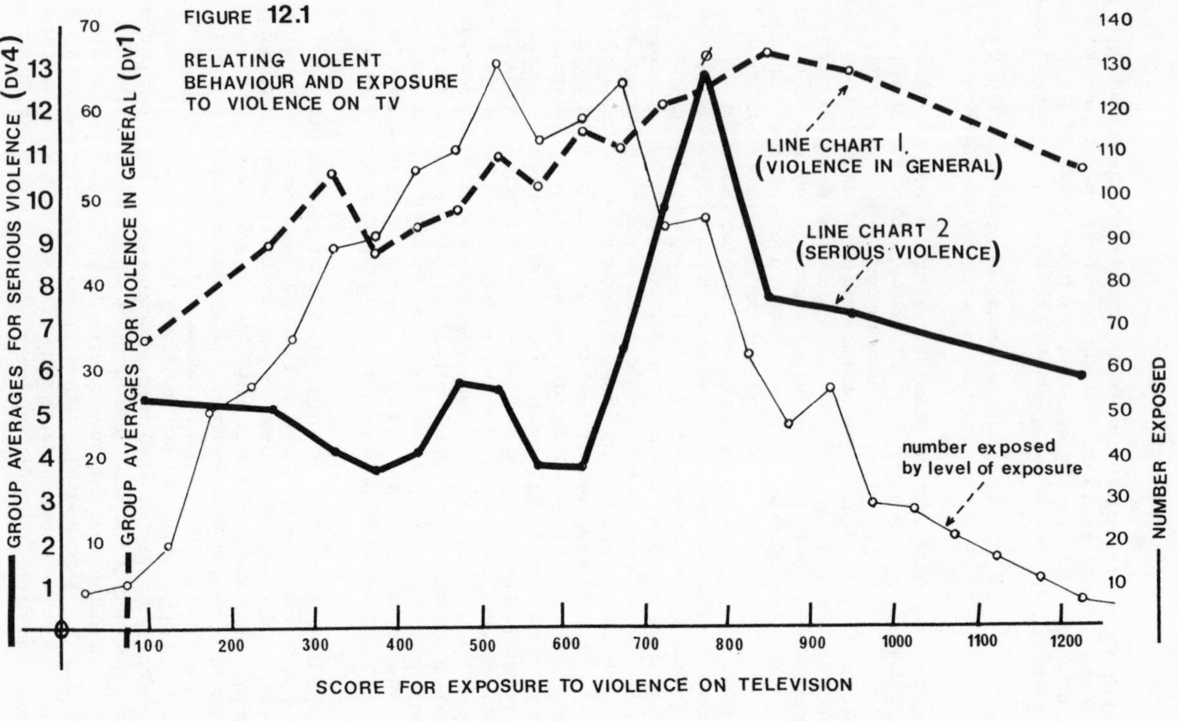

FIGURE 12.1

RELATING VIOLENT BEHAVIOUR AND EXPOSURE TO VIOLENCE ON TV

Ø ceiling of 250 on individual cases

Figure 12.2 (a)

Showing mean scores for violence exposure of:

(a) those who see much TV violence; ______ ______ ______

(b) those who see little TV violence; ___ ___ ___ ___

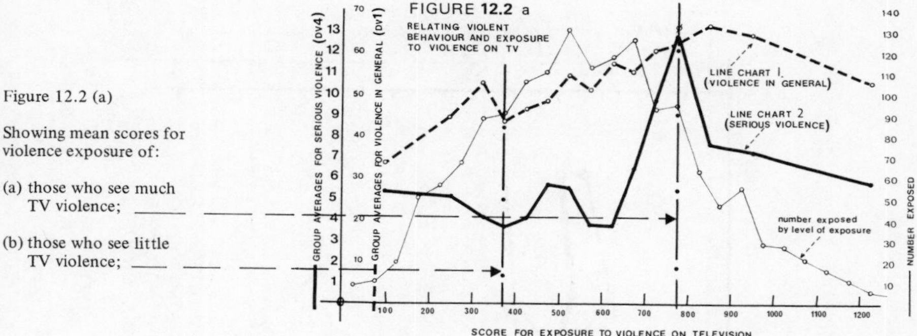

Figure 12.2 (b)

Showing mean scores for violence exposure of:

(a) those who see much television (irrespective of type); ______ ______ ______

(b) those who see little television (irrespective of type); ______ ______ ______

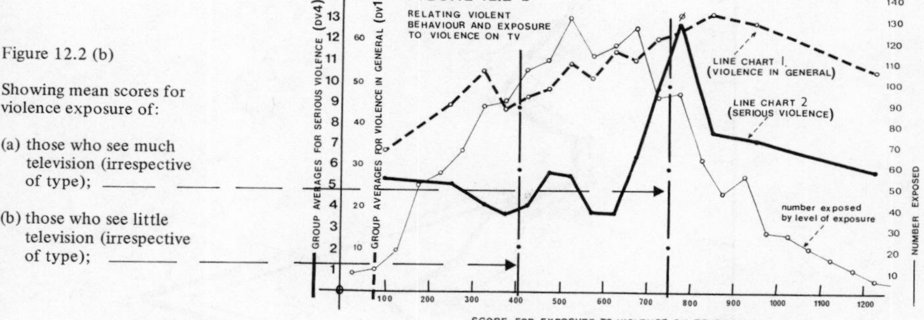

Figure 12.2 (c)

Showing mean scores for violence exposure of:

(a) those who see much non-violent television; ______

(b) those who see little non-violent television; ______

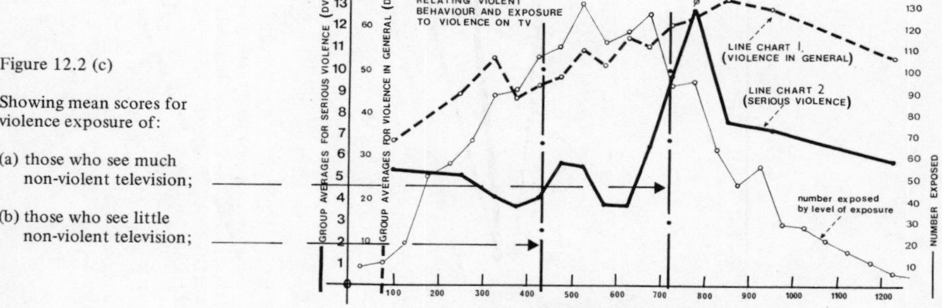

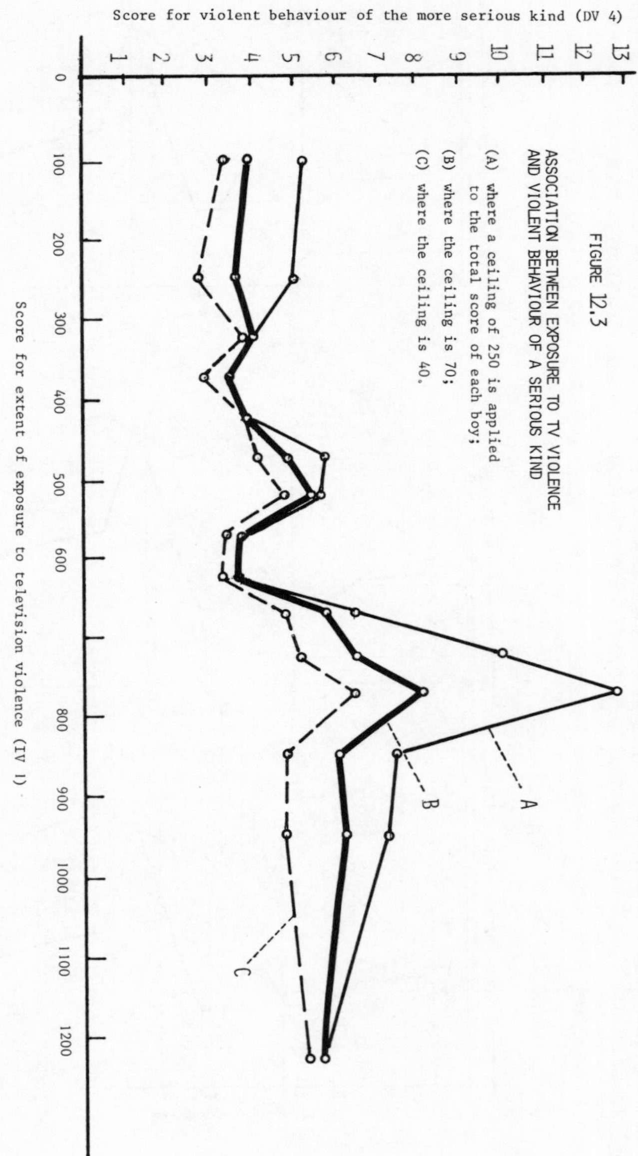

FIGURE 12.3

ASSOCIATION BETWEEN EXPOSURE TO TV VIOLENCE AND VIOLENT BEHAVIOUR OF A SERIOUS KIND

(A) where a ceiling of 250 is applied to the total score of each boy;

(B) where the ceiling is 70;

(C) where the ceiling is 40.

already produced the following table 12.10 (see also table 12.1 in this chapter).

Table 12.10

Heavier exposees to TV output (IV27) = Qualifiers (a)	Lighter exposees to TV output (IV27) = Controls (b)	Controls matched to Qualifiers = Modified Controls (c)	Difference between (a) and (c)		
			a-c	$\frac{a-c}{c}$ %	P a-c
7.39	4.81	4.86	2.53	52.06%	.02

These steps were designed to partial out of table 12.10 the differences found to exist between the Qualifiers and the Modified Controls in terms of extent of exposure to television *violence.* The steps were as follows.

1 Both the Control sample (lighter exposees to television output – IV27) and the Qualifier sample were split into the 37 matching sub-groups involved in the original matching of Controls to Qualifiers.

2 Within each of those 37 sub-groups, the Controls were equated to the Qualifiers in terms of the extent of exposure to television *violence (IV1).* The effect of this was to produce modified scores, for each Control sub-group, in terms of involvement in serious violence (DV4).

3 For each of the 37 matching sub-groups, the new Control scores for DV4 were multiplied by the number of cases in the equivalent Qualifier sub-groups and a new average for the (modified) Controls was computed. This third step was equivalent to matching the two groups in terms of the composite of matching variables used in the development of table 12.10. The results are shown in table 12.11

The 'index of effect' is extremely small and the P value indicates a non-significant result from the statistical viewpoint. In other words there is no meaningful difference (in terms of involvement in serious violence) between the Qualifiers and the Modified Controls after the double matching operation here involved. *The very strong indication of this finding is that it is not television viewing as such that produces serious violence in boys, but the violent content of television output.*

Table 12.11

Heavier exposees to TV output (IV27) = Qualifiers (a)	Lighter exposees to TV output (IV27) = Controls (b)	Controls matched to Qualifiers in terms of both IV1 and original matching composite (c)	Difference between a and c		
			a-c	$\frac{a\text{-}c}{c}$ %	P a-c
7.39	4.81	7.31	0.08	1.09%	.47

The relevance of the apparent conflict between the primary and the secondary control systems

One of the things that has been established through the foregoing analyses and discussion is that there is no real contradiction between the outcome of the secondary control system as here formulated and that from the primary control system. The seeming contradiction, as it applies to hypothesis 4, arises from: (i) the irregular nature of the association between exposure to television violence and involvement in serious violence and (ii) the high degree of positive association between exposure to television as such and exposure to violent television. On the other hand, the irregular character of the association between exposure to television violence and involvement in serious violence argues for a reformulation of hypothesis 4 in terms other than the more exposed *half* of the sample versus the less exposed *half*.

Summing up on the seemingly discordant elements in table 12.1

The upshot of the findings and the discussion presented on pages 370-84 may be stated as follows.

1 The considerable leap in the size of the 'index of effect' in going from hypotheses 1-3 on the one hand to hypothesis 4 on the other is still very much present when a ceiling of 70 is imposed upon total score for serious violence, and it does not appear to be an artifact of any kind. It may well spring from the 'serious violence' variable being basically a different kind of variable from 'violence of the less than serious' kind.

2 Whereas we might, on an 'outlyer' argument, challenge the applicability of the 49 per cent 'index of effect' found for hypothesis 4, the 'index' is most unlikely to be less than 31 per cent in size and even that minimum figure has to be considered as large and as statistically meaningful. It is of course unwise, in view of the measurement problems that had to be dealt with in this enquiry, to give much weight to a specific index figure: the important thing is that by all reasonable standards the 'index of effect' for hypothesis 4 is large and statistically meaningful.

3 There is no real contradiction between the seemingly discordant findings for the

two control systems used in connection with hypothesis 4. That seeming discrepancy springs in large part from (i) the fact that merely to watch television output is to watch both non-violent and violent material; (ii) the irregular nature of the association between exposure to violence on television and involvement in serious violence.

The efficiency of the reverse hypothesis testing procedure as it relates to hypotheses 1-4

The function of 'reverse hypothesis testing' has already been described in general terms in chapters 3 and 10. Two aspects of that form of testing must however be considered specifically in relation to hypotheses 1-4. These two aspects are:

1 the way in which the independent variable (violent disposition) was measured;

2 the use of 'infancy' correlates of violent behaviour for matching purposes in dealing with the forward form of each hypothesis.

The measure used for assessing violent disposition (as referred to in the reverse forms of hypotheses 1-4. Hypotheses 1, 2, 3 and 4 had each been postulated in the following form:

> 'High exposure to television violence causes boys to increase the amount of their violent behaviour.'

That was the forward or normal form of each of those four hypotheses, the dependent variables being respectively DV1, DV2, DV3, DV4 according to whether the reference was to hypothesis 1 or 2 or 3 or 4.

The *reverse* formulation of the forward hypothesis was:

> 'Violent boys, just because they are violent (by disposition), seek out violent television programmes to a greater degree than do boys who are less violent (by disposition).'

The measure of 'violent disposition' does, *in the reverse formulation*, refer to a disposition present in the boy during his growing up period – a description which it is being postulated led him to watch a greater amount of violence on television. Obviously a direct measure of the degree to which the boy had a violent disposition in his infancy and while growing up was beyond the scope of this enquiry. An *indicator* of the unavailable measure was therefore sought. In this context *present day level of violence* was regarded as an indicator or index of an underlying and long established tendency to be violent, and it was so regarded on the following grounds: (i) the reverse formulation of the hypothesis involves an assumption that *television* is not the cause of present-day violence – so that present day violence would have to have some other sources; (ii) it is not reasonable to conclude that present day violence is equally likely to erupt from boys with an early and enduring *gentle* disposition – versus boys with an early and enduring violent disposition. In other words, an assumption was made that the boys with (present-day) high levels of violent behaviour would (in the absence of a television effect) be the more violently disposed in their early childhood and during the extended period of their exposure to television violence.

Obviously the soundness of this assumption cannot be proved. But there is internal evidence in support of it. Thus there is a correlation between present day level of violent behaviour and each of a number of 'infancy states' (under 4 years) which might, between them, readily be interpreted as indices of an early disposition towards violence. These 'infancy states', all of them involving mother's claims about the boy when under 4 years of age, included: frequent loss of temper (positive), frequent temper tantrums (positive), a tendency to smash toys (positive), a tendency to yell when hurt (positive), toughness (positive), a tendency to be noisy (positive); a tendency to be shy (negative), gentle (negative).

Having said all this, let me repeat that there is a degree of assumption behind the practice or position adopted. But in this matter it is vital to bear in mind the nature of the investigatory strategy being used. This method is not the controlled experimental model of the laboratory or the agricultural experiment – it would be impossible to deal realistically with the problem of television's effects using such a method. We are using instead the Hypothetico-Deductive method. This method allows all manner of reasonable deductions/expectations from the hypothesis to be tested, some based on rigorously derived evidence and some based on reasonable assumptions. The penalty for using the Hypothetico-Deductive method is of course that we cannot speak of *proof* – only of the degree to which the evidence supports or does not support the hypothesis.

The use of 'infancy states' for matching Controls to Qualifiers in relation to the forward formulations of hypotheses. 'Infancy states' were involved in another aspect of the enquiry and this may by-pass, to some extent, dependence upon reverse hypothesis testing as an element in the investigating strategy being used. Thus the several 'infancy states' listed above (and many others) were included in the pool of 227 matching variables from which the matching composite for dealing with a *forward* hypothesis were drawn. The upshot of this situation was that after matching, the Modified Controls and the Qualifiers tended to be equal in terms of those 'infancy states' that were correlated with present-day violence. So if those 'infancy states' were in fact evidence of the extent to which there was an early disposition towards violence, then to some extent at least we will have by-passed our dependence upon *the testing of the reverse formulation* as part of the hypothesis-testing strategy. And the upshot of such a situation is of course that the present test of each of the forward forms of hypotheses 1-3 is more independent and final than would otherwise have been the case.

Recapitulation of several important points concerning the interpretation of the findings

1 *Concerning the 'correlation factor'.* The results as set out in this and subsequent chapters have NOT been corrected for what I have called the 'correlation factor'. For each hypothesis investigated, the Control sample had been equated to the Qualifying sample in terms of a composite of *correlates* of the dependent variable. The effect of doing this was to 'reduce the odds' that the residual difference between those two samples was the result simply of a sampling accident.

Whereas the general application of a statistically acceptable solution was baulked by a number of technical considerations (see chapter 10), I have made a number of test applications of a relatively crude correction procedure in order to assess the effect on the P-values of ignoring the correlation factor. The results of these test applications are shown in table 10.2 of chapter 10. They indicate that the application of the correction would in general increase the tenability of already tenable hypotheses, but not to any appreciable or important degree; that the correction would do little towards rendering tenable hypotheses that were not already tenable (in its absence).

In the circumstances it will generally be sufficient to regard the uncorrected P-values as constituting a somewhat conservative and somewhat tougher challenge to the hypotheses than is strictly warranted — but one which nonetheless is most unlikely to change evaluations of tenability.

2 *The joint implications of the index of effect and the P-value.* The results of each hypothesis test (whether for the hypothesis in its forward or reversed form) must be interpreted through the joint consideration of the index of effect and the P-value. The index of effect indicates the relative extent of the change stemming from exposure to the independent condition or variable, while the P-value warns us about the extent of the danger that such a change may in fact be the result simply of a sampling error. Table 10.1 of chapter 10 systematises interpretation of results in terms of those two classes of information. According to that table, an index of 14 per cent accompanied by a P-value of .07 would be interpreted as giving the hypothesis concerned a 'moderate degree of support, though of a slightly uncertain kind'. See table 10.1, chapter 10 for further details.

3 *Bringing together the indications of the forward and the reverse hypothesis results.* The strategy for interpreting the joint indications of the forward and the reverse hypothesis tests has been described in detail in chapter 3.

The stability of the matching variables used in investigating hypothesis 1

One feature of the testing of hypothesis 1 is the use of 'stealing sweets from a shop' as one of the items in the predictive composite. This variable proved to have useful predictive power. However, its 'stability' as a matching variable was questioned in an early critical appraisal of the methods which had been used in testing hypothesis 1. To be more specific, the suggestion was made that 'stealing sweets from shops' might in fact have been influenced by exposure to television violence — i.e. that it is not 'stable'.

This variable had been included in the matching pool in the first place because an earlier enquiry into causal factors in the development of stealing had provided evidence that militated strongly against television influencing (positively or negatively) the extent of boys' involvement in stealing. Furthermore, 'stealing sweets from shops' had been found through this earlier study to have a higher correlation with stealing in general than did other classes of theft amongst those studied.

Nonetheless, since this query had been made, a special analysis was carried out to assess its validity. The matching system for investigating hypothesis 1 was re-run, but this time with 'stealing sweets from a shop' excluded from the pool of possible matching variables. The results of this analysis are shown in column (b) in table 12.12.

Table 12.12 shows that the result of testing hypothesis 1 with 'stealing sweets' excluded is only slightly different from the result with it *included*. If one were to make anything of this difference, it would be to the effect that the exclusion of 'stealing sweets' from the matching composite increases slightly the statistical significance of a finding that is already

Table 12.12

The investigation of hypothesis 1 repeated with certain of the pool items excluded from the analysis on the grounds of their possibly being unstable

(a) With full pool of potential matching variables		(b) With 'stealing sweets from a shop' excluded from the pool		(c) With 'stealing sweets from a shop' and three other items* excluded from the pool	
(i) Items in the matching composite in order of their emergence from the analysis		(i) Items in the matching composite in order of their emergence from the analysis		(i) Items in the matching composite in order of their emergence from the analysis	
42	Ever stolen sweets from a shop	190	Boy's age at interview	190	Boy's age at interview
190	Boy's age at interview	27	Proportion of boys in district who are 'fairly violent'	226	District of residence
65	Grip strength (average of left and right hands)	61	Height	61	Height
27	Proportion of boys in district who are fairly violent	62	Weight	170	Father's age on finishing full-time education
61	Height	63	Grip strength (best of 3, left hand)	65	Grip strength (average of left and right hands)
62	Weight	224	Which placement interviewer	62	Weight
225	Which intensive interviewer	226	District of residence	227	Date of intensive interview
169	Mother's age on finishing full-time education	87	Was he 'calm' (when under 4)?	225	Which intensive interviewer
68	Chest measurement expanded	227	Date of interview	68	Chest measurement expanded
123	Mother tended to punish boy when he misbehaved (when under 4)	73	Frequency of breaking toys (when under 4)	115	Did mother tend to ignore his tantrums (when under 4)
227	Date of interview	182	Frequency of being slapped or spanked (when under 4)	121	Did mother tend to ignore him when he rebelled against her requirements (when under 4)?
218	Proportion of coloured people in district	68	Chest measurement expanded	114	Did mother tend to get angry with him when he cried?
153	Number of illnesses	117	Did mother tend to ignore his tantrums (when he was under 4)?	181	Frequency of being scolded (when under 4)
77	Frequency of yelling when hurt (when under 4)	121	Did mother tend to ignore him when he rebelled against her requests (when under 4)?	73	Frequency of breaking toys (when under 4)
122	Mother tended to punish him when he was violent or destructive (when under 4)	114	Did mother tend to get angry with him when he cried?	162	Father's job
162	Father's job	119	When boy lost temper (under 4) did mother tend to get angry too?	95	Was he competitive (when under 4)?
95	Was he competitive (when under 4)?	181	Frequency of being scolded (when under 4)	181	Frequency of being scolded (when under 4)
226	District of residence	225	Which intensive interviewer	187	Frequency of being punished (when under 4)
		186	Frequency with which privileges removed as a punishment (when under 4)	224	Which placement interviewer
		120	Mother tended to punish him when he rebelled (when under 4)	153	Number of illnesses
				186	Frequency with which privileges removed as a punishment (when under 4)

(ii) Mean scores for violent behaviour	(a)	(b)	(c)
Qualifiers (Q)	= 56.76	= 56.76	= 56.76
Controls (C)	= 46.79	= 46.79	= 46.79
Modified Controls (MC)	= 51.01	= 49.93	= 49.84
Percentage difference $\frac{M_Q - M_{MC}}{M_{MC}}$	= 11.27%	= 13.70%	= 13.89%
Critical ratio	= 1.83	= 2.17	= 2.20
P** value	= .034	= .015	= .014

*For (c), the variables eliminated from the pool were: stealing sweets from a shop (V.52); proportion of boys in district who are 'fairly' violent (V.37); has boy ever stolen money (V.53); did boy enjoy being at school (V.61).

**'One tail' extractions from probability tables. No adjustment made for 'correlation factor'.

statistically significant.

This kind of challenge was taken further by dropping from the pool three more matching variables which conceivably might be thought by some critics to be unstable. These were: proportion of boys in district who are thought by respondent to be violent; has the respondent ever stolen money; did the respondent enjoy being at school. The results (also shown in table 12.12) were virtually the same as those that emerged when only 'stealing sweets' was excluded. The general indication of this evidence is that the results of the analysis would have been virtually the same with 'stealing sweets' excluded and so the argument in terms of 'instability' of that variable carries no practical weight.

THE TENABILITY OF HYPOTHESES 1, 2, 3 AND 4

The foregoing appraisal, at the methodological level, of the evidence stemming from the investigation of hypotheses 1, 2, 3 and 4 leaves us in a position where we can be reasonably sure about the meaning of the evidence in table 12.1. It is not, it appears, simply an artifact produced by an 'outlyer' phenomenon; it is not negated by the evidence from the secondary control system; the large jump in the size of the 'index of effect' in going from hypotheses 1-3 to hypothesis 4 is compatible with the dependent variable in hypothesis 4 (i.e. serious violence) being only moderately correlated with the dependent variables in hypotheses 1, 2 and 3. The main findings are shown in table 12.13 along with relevant significance figures.

Concerning hypothesis 1

1 Hypothesis 1 relates *exposure to violence on television* and *a weighted score for violent behaviour.* For this hypothesis, the score for violent behaviour was based upon the total amount of a boy's violence (in the last six months), with each act given a weight according to its level of seriousness. Details of this system were set out in chapter 6 and summarised on page 366. The derived score is referred to here as an index of 'violence in general'.

2 The *forward* version of hypothesis 1 gets a moderate degree of support from the evidence in table 12.13; the index of effect is moderate in size (11.27 per cent) and the P-value is within the 5 per cent limit. In this sense, its general tenability is increased. However the *reverse* form of hypothesis 1 is also rendered more tenable, though the size of the 'index of effect' for it is smaller (7.86 per cent). In other words, the evidence supports (i) the view that high exposure to television violence moderately increases the degree to which boys engage in 'violence in general' and (ii) the view that to some small degree boys who engage in a lot of violence are thereby led to watch more violence on television.

3 One possible interpretation of this double finding is that there is in operation a circular process, with the more violent boys watching more violence on television and thereby becoming more violent. On the other hand it may simply be that some one section of the sample conforms to the reverse hypothesis and another section conforms to the forward hypothesis. *A further possibility arises directly out of the rationale used for testing reverse hypotheses and specified in chapter 3: it is possible that the positive finding for the forward form of the hypothesis is to*

Table 12.13
Results of investigating hypotheses 1, 2, 3 and 4

Hypothesis investigated	Direction of hypothesis	Measures relating to amount of violent behaviour			
		Means for		% Diff (= Index of effect)	Signif. of differences
		Qualifiers M_Q	Modified controls M_{MC}	$\frac{M_Q - M_{MC}}{M_{MC}}$	P*
Hypothesis 1 (involving IV1 & DV1)	F	56.76	51.01	11.27	.034
	R	607.81	563.51	7.86	<.001
Hypothesis 2 (involving IV1 & DV2)	F	294.10	265.03	10.97	.042
	R	614.60	572.02	7.44	.001
Hypothesis 3 (involving IV1 & DV3)	F	114.10	100.85	13.14	.029
	R	602.96	551.29	9.37	<.001
Hypothesis 4 (involving IV1 & DV4)	F	7.48	5.02	49.00	.022
	R	582.65	574.14	1.48	.264
Hypothesis 4 with ceiling of 70 on score	F	5.76	4.41	30.61	.023
	R	582.65	574.14	1.48	.264
Hypothesis 4 with ceiling of 40 on score	F	4.77	3.88	22.94	.039
	R	582.65	574.14	1.48	.264

*P values are 'one-tail' extractions from probability tables. No allowance has been made for the 'correlation factor' – though the effect of correcting for it would be to reduce the numerical size of the P value and hence to tender the results in table 12.13 more significant in the statistical sense.

some extent a reflection of the working of the hypothesis in reverse. In terms of that rationale we must conclude that though the hypothesis (forward form) gets support from the evidence, we cannot rule out the possibility that this support is to some extent a reflection simply of a reverse process being in operation.

Concerning hypothesis 4

1 Hypothesis 4 links exposure to television violence and violent behaviour of the more serious kind (DV4). The serious violence score (DV4) was a count of the number of a boy's acts of violence (in the last six months) that had been rated by the project analysts as 'quite violent' or 'very violent' or 'extremely violent'.

2 The evidence of table 12.13 gives a very large degree of support to hypothesis 4 in its forward form, namely that 'high exposure to television violence increases the degree to which boys engage in such violence'. The index of effect is large and statistically meaningful. Along with this, we find that the evidence does *not* support the hypothesis in its reverse formulation. In other words, the evidence both supports the hypothesis in its forward form and tends to rule out the possibility that this support is an artifact arising out of the *reverse* hypothesis being true. *This finding, for serious violence, is probably one of the most*

important results of the enquiry.

3 Nonetheless it is necessary that this finding be seen in proper perspective. Thus only half of London's boys were involved at all in this more serious form of violent behaviour in the six month period studied. Moreover, violence at this serious level accounts for an average of approximately 6 acts per boy in six months, compared with over 200 acts of the less violent kind (in that same period). However, having said this, we must take careful note of the fact that an average of 6 acts of this seriously violent kind over a six-month period aggregates to an enormous amount of serious violence in the London area in the course of a year. Furthermore, 12 per cent [5] of London's boys appear to be quite heavily involved at this level.

Concerning hypotheses 2 and 3

1 It will help put into perspective the findings for hypotheses 2 and 3 if my statement about them is preceded with a reminder of what these hypotheses are and how they relate to hypotheses 1 and 4. Hypothesis 2 is geared to the dependent variable DV2, which is the total number of acts of violence admitted by boys (with various ceilings applied to reduce the influence of such exaggeration as may have occurred), with no weighting for level of seriousness of the constituent acts. Since acts rated as 'only very slightly violent' make up by far the largest part of boys' totals, DV2 can be interpreted as reflecting principally involvement in acts of a trivial kind. Hypothesis 3 was also a total, but it *excluded* the acts rated as 'only very slightly violent'. This meant that its principal constituents were acts which had been rated as 'a bit violent' or 'fairly violent'. DV2 and DV3 are therefore regarded here as standing mainly for two levels of involvement, DV2 standing mainly for degree of involvement in trivial acts of violence and DV3 mainly for involvement in acts of a moderately violent kind.

2 The outcome for hypotheses 2 and 3 was closely similar to that for hypothesis 1, namely: for each of them, the forward form of the hypothesis gets a moderate degree of support from the evidence, with the P-value in each case within the 5 per cent limit; and for each of them, the reverse form of the hypothesis gets a degree of support which, though of a statistically highly significant kind, is at a slightly lower level (the indices being in the range 7-10 per cent). That the results should have been so similar to each other and to that for hypothesis 1 may not seem surprising, but it should be noted that it is in principle conceivable that rather different results might have emerged. For example, it could be that television's influence in the DV2-DV3 range is principally in terms of trivial rather than middle-range violence, or vice-versa. Results of a different kind did in fact emerge in going from DV1 to DV4. In the present case, however, the result was much the same for each of hypotheses 2 and 3, indicating a certain evenness of effect in that range.

3 At the same time, we must take careful note of the possibility raised by the finding that *both* the forward and reversed forms of these two hypotheses were supported by the evidence. That double finding means that it remains possible that the positive results for the forward hypotheses are to some extent reflections

of the working of those hypotheses in reverse. It is also possible that we have here, as for hypothesis 1, a circular process, with violent behaviour leading boys to watch more television, with television producing more violence, and so on. Be that as it may, the general effect of the evidence is to support hypotheses 2 and 3, but to leave open the possibility that this support is in part a reflection of a reverse process being in operation.

Concerning all four hypotheses

The overall indications of these findings are, then, that:

(a) The evidence increases the tenability of the hypothesis that high exposure to television violence increases the degree to which boys engage in acts of violence, and this applies irrespective of the level of violence concerned.

(b) For violent behaviour *below* the level of what has been defined in this study as 'serious violence', there exists a possibility that the positive finding for these lower levels of violence is to some extent a reflection of violent boys being led, by their more violent dispositions, to seek out violent material on television.

(c) But for *serious violence* such a possibility tends not to exist and the total pattern of the evidence may be regarded as giving strong support to the forward form of the hypothesis, namely: 'High exposure to television violence increases the degree to which boys engage in acts of violence of a serious kind'. Furthermore, the increase appears to have been of a substantial order.

(d) There are two other possible explanations of the finding, *for the lesser levels of violence*, that *both* the forward and the reverse hypotheses are given a degree of support by the evidence: (i) *both* forward and reverse processes occur; (ii) there is in operation a circular process whereby violent television makes boys behave more violently, this in turn leads them to watch a greater amount of violence on television, and so on.

SOME SPECULATIVE COMMENTS ABOUT THE NATURE OF THE RELATIONSHIP BETWEEN EXPOSURE TO TELEVISION VIOLENCE AND VIOLENT BEHAVIOUR

Concerning serious violence

The precise form of the association between extent of exposure to television violence and the extent of boys' involvement in violent behaviour at a serious level is a matter of very considerable importance to the whole issue of the influence of exposure to television violence.

If we assume that the *shape* of the curve defining this association (see figure 12.1) is broadly similar to that which defines the *influence* of television violence upon violent behaviour, then some interesting propositions emerge.

1 For exposures anywhere in the score range of 100 to 650, much the same degree of violent behaviour accrues;

2 For exposure in the score range 650-1100, there is a sharp increase in the general level of serious violence;

3 Beyond the 1100 score mark, further increases in exposure do not in general increase serious violence, but tend rather to decrease it towards the pre-650 level.

Taking this speculative approach further, it may well be that:

4 Exposure to television violence in the score range 0-650 has relatively little effect, the average of approximately 4.5 acts (in six months) being the level at which serious violence normally goes on in the absence of television violence.

5 Beyond the 1100 exposure level, boys are too 'satiated' with television, and their time too much taken up by it, to have the energy or the time for very much violence of the serious kind.

It might of course be argued that this decline is simply an 'ageing' effect: as boys get older, not only will they have accumulated a greater viewing hourage, but they will also have become less violent simply because of that increasing age. However the association between age and level of violence is only very small (see table 11.6, chapter 11) and so the 'ageing' explanation will not do.

Points 1, 2 and 3 are open to verification within the testing rationale used in this study and it is strongly recommended that such an investigation be made. Such a check should serve to maximise our knowledge about the ways in which exposure to television violence increases violent behaviour of the more serious kind. Certainly the possibility of an eventual reducing effect should be investigated — as should the present indication that quite a lot of television violence can be absorbed without the level of violence increasing (i.e. from levels 0-650.)

At the same time, it must be carefully noted that such further analysis can serve only to refine the present findings and not to negate them.

Concerning violence at the less serious level

I have already commented on the important difference in the shape of the relationship between (i) exposure to television violence and violent behaviour of the less serious kind and (ii) exposure to television violence and serious violence (see figure 12.1). For less serious violence, the relationship is basically a 'rising' one. Looked at in detail, however, we find (i) that the rise is an irregular one and (ii) that it is not maintained for the minority of boys with exposure 'scores' of over '850 units'. What this means in terms of *causal* relationships is open to investigation through the system of analysis already used throughout this enquiry. But here too, such further analyses can be expected only to refine the present findings and not to negate them.

One other point of importance must be made about the effects of television violence upon violent behaviour of the less serious kind. Further analyses and research are necessary to resolve the residual ambiguity about the support given by the evidence to the forward forms of the hypotheses. To some extent that may be done through further and more detailed analyses of the large body of data derived from the enquiry. And to some extent, further data collection may be necessary.

A comment on the correlation factor

It should be noted that the effect of applying an acceptable form of correction for the correlation factor would, in the present case, have been simply to increase slightly confidence that the findings in table 12.13 had not arisen out of sampling error. That in turn would serve to increase slightly further the tenability of the four hypotheses. See chapter 10, table 10.2, for tabular details.

DEGREE OF ASSOCIATION BETWEEN EXPOSURE TO TELEVISION VIOLENCE AND THE 53 DIFFERENT ITEMS IN THE WEB OF STIMULI

One special feature of this enquiry was the use of a web of stimuli to elicit from boys information about the nature and extent of any violent behaviour they had engaged in. There were 53 units or elements in this web, some being *specific acts* of violence, some being *situations* or places in which violence occurred, and others being *reasons* for being violent. For each boy, response details for each of the 53 web-items had been recorded and so there was opportunity to study the degree to which exposure to television violence (IV1) was associated with violence in each of those 53 categories. This was done because it seemed that the results might provide leads to the kinds of violent behaviour most likely to be evoked by exposure to television violence. I stress 'leads' (rather than firm conclusions) because: (i) *full* empirical matching for *each* of the 53 acts was not available because of limited computer facilities; (ii) few of the 53 web-items were highly specific in character.

On the other hand, something more than a mere 'association check' was available. Thus:

1. An all-purpose matching composite was developed, the criterion being the total number of acts of violence committed (IV2) and the matching variables all being drawn from the pool of 227 possible predictors. See figure 12.4.
2. This matching composite was then used in 53 separate matching operations, one for each of the 53 different 'web' items. This matching operation can be illustrated through what was done for one of the 53 items, namely 'I have done damage to a train' (see table 12.14).
   - (a) (As in all 53 checks). The Qualifiers were boys who had seen a relatively large amount of TV violence and the Controls were boys who had seen relatively little TV violence.
   - (b) The Qualifiers and the Controls were each split into the matching sub-groups defined by the matching composite.
   - (c) For each of these (matching) sub-groups, a calculation was made of (i) the mean score in terms of how often the boys in it had done damage to a train in the six-month qualifying period and (ii) the score variability for that (matching) sub-group.
   - (d) The different matching sub-groups of the Control sample were then weighted to equal the number in the corresponding (matching) sub-group in the Qualifying sample and an average for the whole modified Control group was thus calculated. A weighted variance figure was also calculated for the

Figure 12.4 Showing matching composites used for matching Controls to Qualifiers for investigating 53 sub-hypotheses linking (i) exposure to TV violence and (ii) each of the 53 items in the web of stimuli. Table 12.14 involves the use of this matching composite in relation to web item 52 (= 'I have done damage to a train')

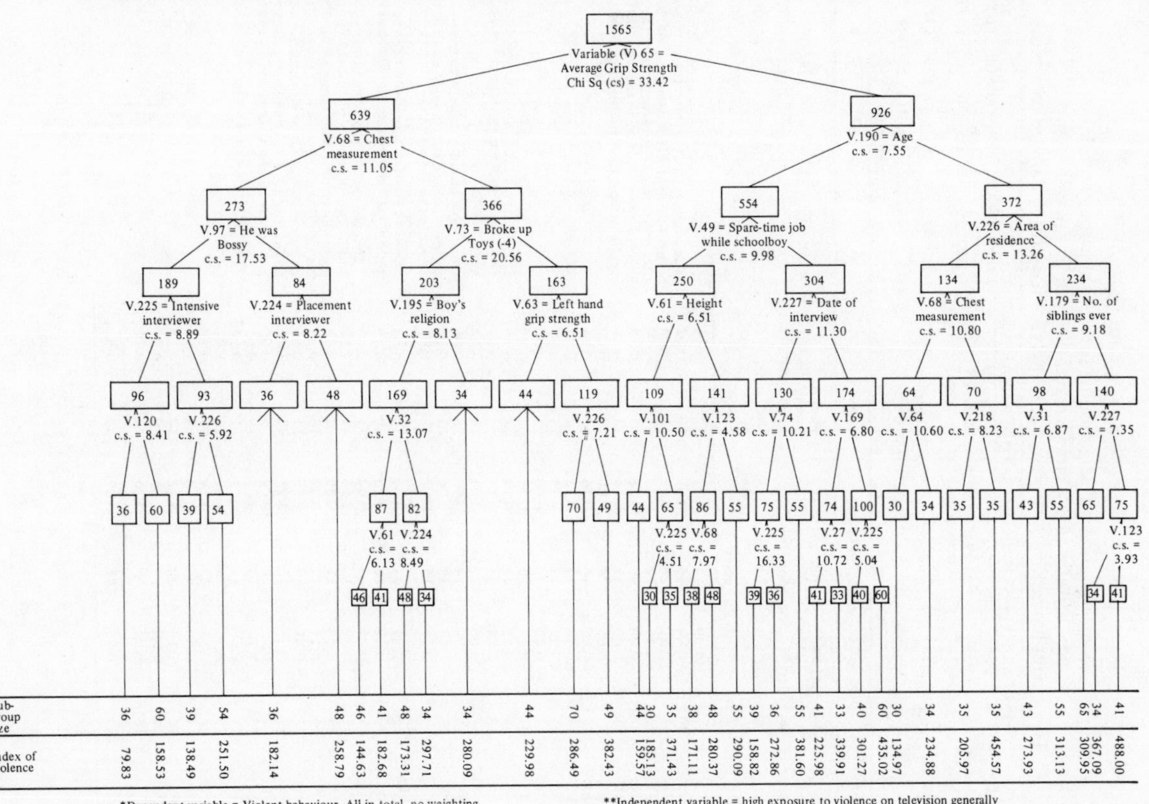

Sub-group size	36	60	39	54	36	48	46	41	48	34	34	44	70	49	44	30	35	38	48	55	39	36	55	41	33	40	60	30	34	35	35	43	55	65	34	41
Index of violence	79.83	158.53	138.49	251.50	182.14	258.79	144.63	182.68	173.31	297.71	280.09	229.98	286.49	382.43	159.57	185.13	371.43	171.11	280.37	290.09	158.82	272.86	381.60	225.98	339.91	301.27	435.02	134.97	234.88	205.97	454.57	273.93	313.13	309.95	367.09	488.00

*Dependent variable = Violent behaviour, All-in total, no weighting

**Independent variable = high exposure to violence on television generally

Table 12.14
Demonstrating investigation of forward hypotheses linking
(i) exposure to TV violence and (ii) each of the web items.
This example features web item 52, namely: 'I have done damage to a train'

All cases	INDEX OF BEHAVIOUR ON DEPENDENT VARIABLE (a) Average level of behaviour* for Qualifiers†	(b) Average level of behaviour for Controls††	(c) Modified average for Controls††	DIFFERENCE between (a) and (c) (a) −(c)	DIFFERENCE between (a) and (c) as % of (c) (a) −(c) x 100 / (c) (Index of change)	SIGNIFICANCE OF DIFFERENCE CR***	p**
1565	0.85	0.29	0.56	0.29	52%	0.75	0.45

Matching sub-groups	Average level for Qualifiers† No. of cases	Level	Average level for Controls†† No. of cases	Level	Modified average level for Controls†† No. of cases	Level
32	12	0.00	24	0.13	12	0.13
33	20	0.00	40	0.02	20	0.02
34	11	0.45	28	0.00	11	0.00
35	27	0.15	27	0.19	27	0.19
18	7	0.00	29	0.38	7	0.38
19	11	0.00	37	0.14	11	0.14
80	20	0.05	26	0.00	20	0.00
81	16	0.00	25	0.16	16	0.16
82	16	0.00	32	0.13	16	0.13
83	21	0.33	13	0.15	21	0.15
21	11	0.45	23	0.00	11	0.00
22	24	0.17	20	0.25	24	0.25
46	28	0.75	42	0.12	28	0.12
47	25	0.04	24	0.46	25	0.46
48	17	0.00	27	0.04	17	0.04
98	16	0.00	14	0.00	16	0.00
99	23	1.09	12	0.00	23	0.00
100	19	0.16	19	0.05	19	0.05
101	23	0.65	25	0.20	23	0.20
51	32	2.69	23	0.09	32	0.09
104	29	0.07	10	0.20	29	0.20
105	21	0.05	15	0.00	21	0.00
53	43	8.37	12	2.17	43	2.17
108	24	0.29	17	0.00	24	0.00
109	16	0.13	17	0.59	16	0.59
110	31	0.81	9	0.56	31	0.56
111	45	0.09	15	3.93	45	3.93
56	9	0.11	21	0.00	9	0.00
57	19	0.16	15	0.07	19	0.07
58	21	0.19	14	0.14	21	0.14
59	21	0.33	14	1.07	21	1.07
60	21	0.33	22	0.18	21	0.18
61	35	0.09	20	1.15	35	1.15
62	37	1.16	28	0.18	37	0.18
126	9	0.00	25	0.32	9	0.32
127	22	0.95	19	0.26	22	0.26
All	782	0.85	783	0.29	782	0.56

NOTE
The upper sections of this table presents the basic findings, that is the residual difference between the Qualifying and Control groups after matching. The lower part of the table, opposite, presents important working details that lie behind the basic findings.

*Level indicates average number of occasions of damaging train.

†Qualifying group = those who have been exposed to a relatively large amount of television violence.

††Control group = those who have been exposed to relatively little television violence.

**Two-tail extractions from probability table. In this case there was no initial hypothesis of a one-directional kind. Implicit in this check on the 53 web-items is the hypothesis that a change might occur in either direction – that is, for specific acts of violence. This makes it correct to use the two-tail type of extraction.

***No adjustment for 'correlation factor'.

modified Control group.

(e) The difference between the means for the Qualifiers and the Modified Controls was then calculated and this was expressed as a percentage difference between those two samples; that difference was also expressed as a Critical Ratio and its statistical significance was calculated.

In other words, the only difference between the computer processing used here and that employed on the many different hypotheses was that a separate matching composite was not developed for each of the 53 web items. At the same time this difference is important and makes it most necessary to regard the resulting 53 percentages and P values in a conservative fashion.

The results of this 53-item analysis are set out in table 12.15.

Some speculative comments based on table 12.15. The details in table 12.15 should form a basis for useful *speculation* about the kinds of violent behaviour that were most influenced by exposure to television violence. Most of the web items in the list of 53 are broad in character and all of them were used only as the first step in eliciting information about violent behaviour. Nonetheless, even at that broad level they could be useful starting points for speculation. In fact, they appear to provide some grounds for *speculating* as follows.

(a) High exposure to television violence is more likely to stimulate violent behaviour:
   (i) of the kind that is unplanned, spontaneous [6], unskilled;
   (ii) when the boy has a lot of time to fill in/time on his hands;
   (iii) when the violence presented on television offers scope for *easy* imitation by the boy.

(b) High exposure to television violence is *less* likely to stimulate violent behaviour:
   (i) where temper, tension or anxiety ordinarily help to trigger off violence;
   (ii) where the violent act carries its own deterrent or where ordinarily there are deterrents in the offing;
   (iii) where the requirement of actually viewing television works against the boy being present in the situations where the violence is likely to occur (e.g. at football matches).

It is not suggested that any single category of violence can be sorted into just one or another of these six categories. Thus 'swearing' could be regarded as purely spontaneous, unplanned and unskilled, but it might also be regarded as triggered off by bad temper or as being an imitation of swearing shown on television. Much depends on the nature of the swearing that is done. Furthermore, there are elements of findings in table 12.15 that, depending on their interpretation, might be seen as conflicting with one or another of the six generalisations offered above. On balance, the evidence in table 12.15 tends to support them.

However, it must be remembered that the six generalisations put forward are no more than *speculations* arising out of the findings: they are not the findings as such.

Table 12.15
Showing direction of change for the 53 web items

Item No.	Type of Web item	Mean score for: Qualifiers Q	Mean score for: Modified Controls MC	Difference $M_Q - M_{MC}$: As % of M_{MC} %	As CR	As P*
	A. Suggesting Increase					
34	Violence while truanting	0.25	0.11	+122	0.74	–
3	Set a booby trap	1.37	0.74	+84	2.20	.05
22	Damaged things/places	3.88	2.15	+80	1.15	–
31	While going to or from school	1.58	0.89	+78	1.35	.20
24	Threatened somebody	10.23	5.80	+76	2.15	.05
18	To impress mates/others	1.99	1.17	+70	0.85	–
13	Teased or took mickey	60.96	38.36	+59	3.54	.01
10	Gave head butt	1.83	1.20	+53	1.47	.20
52	Did damage to train	0.85	0.56	+52	0.75	–
7	Swore/bad language	170.88	114.69	+49	4.06	.01
28	Violent or dangerous games	14.81	10.55	+40	2.11	.05
37	Beat someone up	3.14	2.33	+35	0.74	–
9	Made rude finger signs	44.41	32.90	+35	1.97	.05
25	Irritated or annoyed	34.57	25.76	+34	1.78	.10
15	Violent for fun/laugh/dare	4.76	3.65	+30	1.22	–
26	While doing sport	8.27	6.61	+25	1.24	–
	B. Intermediate Items					
16	Lied to someone	36.32	30.52	+19	1.21	–
17	Violent while larking about with mates	25.83	21.90	+18	0.99	–
46	Tried to make girls do what they didn't want to do	1.22	1.05	+16	0.41	–
51	Damaged a car	0.72	0.63	+16	0.18	–
1	Kicked somebody	38.78	33.61	+15	0.93	–
53	Violent in sport or play	14.49	12.62	+15	0.58	–
44	Set something on fire	3.97	3.46	+15	0.37	–
42	Tried to frighten someone	5.77	5.13	+13	0.44	–
40	Had an argument	37.58	33.77	+11	0.74	–
23	Twisted someone's arm	10.45	9.79	+7	0.27	–
48	Cut somebody with knife	0.19	0.18	+4	0.10	–
8	Did some wrestling, boxing, karate, judo	4.25	4.34	−2	−0.12	–
2	Tried to torture somebody	32.74	33.78	−3	−0.23	–
36	Threw something at somebody	12.37	12.78	−3	−0.16	–
4	Tried to trip someone up	23.33	24.11	−3	−0.18	–
45	Hurt a girl	2.67	2.79	−4	−0.08	–
38	Rude to people in authority	12.91	13.59	−5	−0.19	–
29	Hit someone with something	1.73	1.84	−6	−0.22	–
32	During break at school/work	4.68	5.21	−10	−0.49	–
35	Shot airgun etc. at someone/something	30.02	33.21	−10	−0.46	–
43	Violent in self-defence	2.77	3.15	−12	−0.48	–
49	Lost my temper with someone	15.20	17.45	−13	−0.70	–
6	Hurt an animal	3.65	4.25	−14	−0.37	–
41	Did something to get own back	5.24	6.08	−14	−0.67	–
	C. Suggesting Decrease					
20	Set mates onto others	0.29	0.37	−21	−0.81	–
30	Violent at school or work	7.05	9.09	−22	−0.80	–
21	Violent when with mates	3.03	3.93	−23	−1.29	.20
47	Violent when excited/upset	1.89	2.59	−27	−1.36	.20
50	Violent when didn't want to be	1.40	1.99	−30	−1.68	.10
19	Mates and I set about others	1.86	2.69	−31	−1.06	–
5	Had a fight	4.95	7.51	−34	−2.13	.05
14	Gave someone a deadleg	4.43	7.17	−38	−1.43	.20
33	In fights with boys from other schools	0.59	0.96	−39	−1.73	.10
39	Violent to people in authority	0.54	0.91	−41	−1.05	–
12	Violent at a football match	0.76	1.44	−47	−1.59	.20
11	Violent on way to football match	0.39	0.83	−53	−2.10	.05
27	Tried to start a fight	0.92	2.49	−63	−2.72	.01

*Two-tail distributions used because no directional hypotheses formulated.
– = Not significant at the 20% level
.01 = Significant at the 1% level; .05 = Significant at the 5% level; .10 = Significant at the 10% level; .20 = Significant at the 20% level

THE TENABILITY OF THE THREE HYPOTHESES ABOUT THE INFLUENCE ON BOYS OF VIOLENCE IN OTHER OF THE MEDIA

The three hypotheses

For comparative purposes, a study was made of the tenability of several hypotheses concerned with the influence of other of the mass media on the violence levels of boys. These hypotheses were:

(i) 'High exposure to violent comics or comic books increases the degree to which boys commit acts of violence'.

(ii) 'High exposure to violence on the cinema screen increases the degree to which boys commit acts of violence'.

(iii) 'High exposure to newspapers increases the degree to which boys commit acts of violence'.

The method of investigating the three hypotheses

How exposure to the other mass media was assessed

The methods used to 'score' exposure to comics, violent films and newspapers were described in full in chapter 5 *and so are presented only in summary form in this chapter.*

Exposure to violent films. Some 22 films were selected as examples of violent films. They spanned the years 1958-1971, most had been graded as A or U and all had been graded as violent by a panel of judges. A boy's score was the number of these films (out of 22) that he claimed he had seen. This score must not be seen as being the total number of violent films seen – a boy's lifetime total is likely to be far in excess of his score out of those 22 films. The list of 22 was simply a discriminant to be used for *grading* boys in terms of extent of exposure.

The sample of 22 was as follows:

Dr No
Spartacus
From Russia with Love
The Great Escape
The Longest Day
How the West was Won
Lawrence of Arabia
Goldfinger
Zulu
The Long Ships
The Fall of the Roman Empire
Thunderball
Nevada Smith
You Only Live Twice
The Green Berets
Planet of the Apes
Where Eagles Dare
The Battle of Britain
On Her Majesty's Secret Service
Butch Cassidy and the Sundance Kid
Cromwell
Little Big Man

The distribution of boys in terms of claimed exposure to these films is shown in table 12.16.

Table 12.16

Number of films (in the sample) claimed to have been seen	% of boys	Number of films (in the sample) claimed to have been seen	% of boys
0	9	11-12	7
1-2	19	13-14	4
3-4	19	15-16	2
5-6	16	17-18	—
7-8	14	19-20	—
9-10	10	21-22	—

— = less than 0.5%

For general background purposes, boys were also asked to say how often they visited a cinema 'these days'. The distribution of responses is shown in table 12.17.

Table 12.17

	%
Two or more times a week	1
About once a week	5
About once a fortnight	9
About once a month	20
About once in two months	23
Less often	38
Not at all	4
No information	—

– = less than 0.5%

Exposure to comics and comic books. Twenty one comics or comic books were selected as a basis for scoring boys on exposure to comics or comic books. The methods for getting this information are given in detail in chapter 5. In brief, these were the 21 which the evidence suggested were amongst the more frequently read of the 45 comics/comic books considered. Since all 45 contained violence in some form or another, no attempt was made to separate them, for selection purposes, into violent and non-violent. Accordingly, we are concerned here with effect of exposure to comics/comic books, though this automatically means exposure to *violence* through their content.

The 21 comics/comic books used for scoring purposes were as follows:

Dandy	Superman (comic book)	Victor
Hornet	Tiger (and Jag)	Sparky
Batman with Robin (comic book)	Cor!!	Smash
Beano	Wizard	Hotspur
Topper	Goal (magazine)	Beezer
Valiant (and TV21)	Scorcher	Shoot
Buster (and Jet)	Lion (and Thunder)	Score

The distribution of boys in terms of the number of these they claimed they had ever 'regularly read' or ever 'regularly looked through' was as shown in table 12.18.

Table 12.18

Number of comics or comic books claimed as *ever* regularly read or ever regularly looked through	%	Number of comics or comic books claimed as *ever* regularly read or ever regularly looked through	%*
0	6	11-12	9
1-2	10	13-14	6
3-4	14	15-16	5
5-6	14	17-18	4
7-8	12	19-20	5
9-10	12	21	4

*Total 101% because of 'rounding'.

Information was also collected about the frequency with which boys claimed to read a comic/comic book. [7] Details are given in table 12.19.

Table 12.19

How often† does boy read a comic/comic book	%*
Once a week	39
Once a fornight	11
Once a month	11
Less often	37
Never	1
No information	2

†'These days, how often do you read a comic?'
*Total 101% because of 'rounding'.

Exposure to newspapers. The different newspapers available to boys in London tend to present at least some degree of violence – in that they report violent events and news. The possibility of distinguishing between them, in terms of the degree to which violence is presented through them, is both difficult and unrealistic. Exposure to newspapers was regarded as automatically involving some degree of reported violence.

The 21 publications selected as a basis for scoring boys (on exposure to newspapers) were as follows.

Daily Telegraph	Daily Mail	Evening News	Sunday Telegraph
The Sun	The Times	Weekend	Observer
Daily Mirror	The Morning Star	Reveille	Sunday Times
Daily Express	Financial Times	Titbits or Saturday Titbits	The People
The Guardian	Evening Standard	Sunday Express	News of the World
			Sunday Mirror

The distribution of boys in terms of the number of these they claimed *ever* to have 'regularly read or regularly looked through' [8] is shown in table 12.20.

Table 12.20

Number of papers so claimed†	%	Number of papers so claimed†	%
0	2	11-12	5
1-2	13	13-14	2
3-4	23	15-16	1
5-6	24	17-18	1
7-8	19	19-20	—
9-10	10	21	—

— = less than 0.5%
†'Which of the following papers have you ever regularly read or regularly looked through?'

In addition and as general background boys were asked: 'These days, how often do you read a daily paper?' and 'These days, how often do you read a Sunday paper?' Response distributions are shown in table 12.21.

Table 12.21

'These days, how often do you read a daily newspaper?'	%*	'These days, how often do you read a Sunday paper?'	%†
Every day	53	Every Sunday	71
Most days	27	Once in two Sundays	15
Once or twice a week	14	Once a month	4
Once a month	2	Less often	8
Less often	4	Never	—
Never	—	No information	1
No information	1		

*101% because of 'rounding'
†99% because of 'rounding'

Research design

To establish Qualifying and Control groups with respect to seeing violent films, boys were separated into a higher and a lower scoring group in terms of the number of films seen out of those listed for discriminatory purposes. The same thing was done quite separately in establishing Qualifying and Control groups with respect to exposure to comics and comic books. Similarly with respect to newspapers.

Separately for each hypothesis, the Controls were matched to the Qualifiers in terms of a composite of variables which together maximised the power in the forward pool of matching variables to predict the dependent variable. For each hypothesis, the violence score for the Qualifiers was compared with the violence score for the modified Controls. This comparison yielded an index of effect and the statistical significance of the difference between Qualifiers and Modified Controls was calculated. The same process was repeated for the reverse form of each hypothesis.

The matching composites and the matching processes involved in these operations are shown in full in the Technical Appendices to this report. One such composite of predictors and one such matching process are presented as examples in figure 12.5 and in table 12.22.

Findings

Table 12.23 presents the findings in summary form.

The principal indications of table 12.23 are as follows.

1 *Comics/comic books*

(a) *In relation to DV1 (i.e. violence in general).* The evidence in table 12.23 gives a fairly large degree of support to the hypothesis that *exposure to comics or comic books increases the degree to which boys are violent in the general sense* (i.e. when violence is assessed as a weighted score based on all the different levels of violence committed). In other words, the evidence increases the tenability of that hypothesis in its forward form. At the same time, the evidence also gives a small degree of support to the hypothesis in its reversed form. According to the basic rationale of the hypothesis evaluation method, this finding leaves open the possibility that the positive result for the forward hypothesis is to *some extent* (small, in this case) a reflection of the working of the hypothesis in reverse.

(b) *In relation to DV4 (serious violence).* As it relates to the hypothesis that *exposure to comics/comic books increases boys' violence at the serious level*, the evidence in table 12.23 gives to that hypothesis a very large degree of support (34.51 per cent) which is nonetheless of a slightly uncertain kind (P = .071). When, as a safeguard against the occurrence of an 'outlyer effect' (see pages 373-4 of this chapter), a ceiling (70) is placed on the maximum DV4 score allowable to any boy, the size of the index of effect falls to 15 per cent and the P value to about .16. Along with this situation, the evidence gives a moderate degree of support to the hypothesis in reverse (an 'index of effect' of approximately 11 per cent and a P-value beyond the .01 level).

On balance, I would regard the evidence as generally adding to the tenability of the hypothesis, but as warning us against over-certainty because of the possibility that the 'index of effect' shown in table 12.25 may have sprung out of the normal accidents of sampling and because of the possibility that a reverse process may be in operation.

On the other hand, it would be serious folly simply to reject the result of the test of the forward version of this hypothesis because of the elements of doubt that I have presented. What table 12.23 tells us is that (i) the evidence gives support to the forward hypothesis; (ii) it remains possible nonetheless that this support is a reflection to at least some extent of the reverse process being in operation (i.e. of a violent disposition in boys leading them to do more reading of comics than do other boys) and/or some sampling oddity (because P = .07).

(c) *In relation to DV2 and DV3.* The position for the sub-hypotheses involving DV2 and DV3 calls for special comment. DV2 is the sum of all acts of

FIGURE 12.5 Showing the composite of predictors of violent behaviour (DV1) and of exposure to violent films (IV 29) developed for studying the influence of exposure to violent films upon the violence levels of boys.

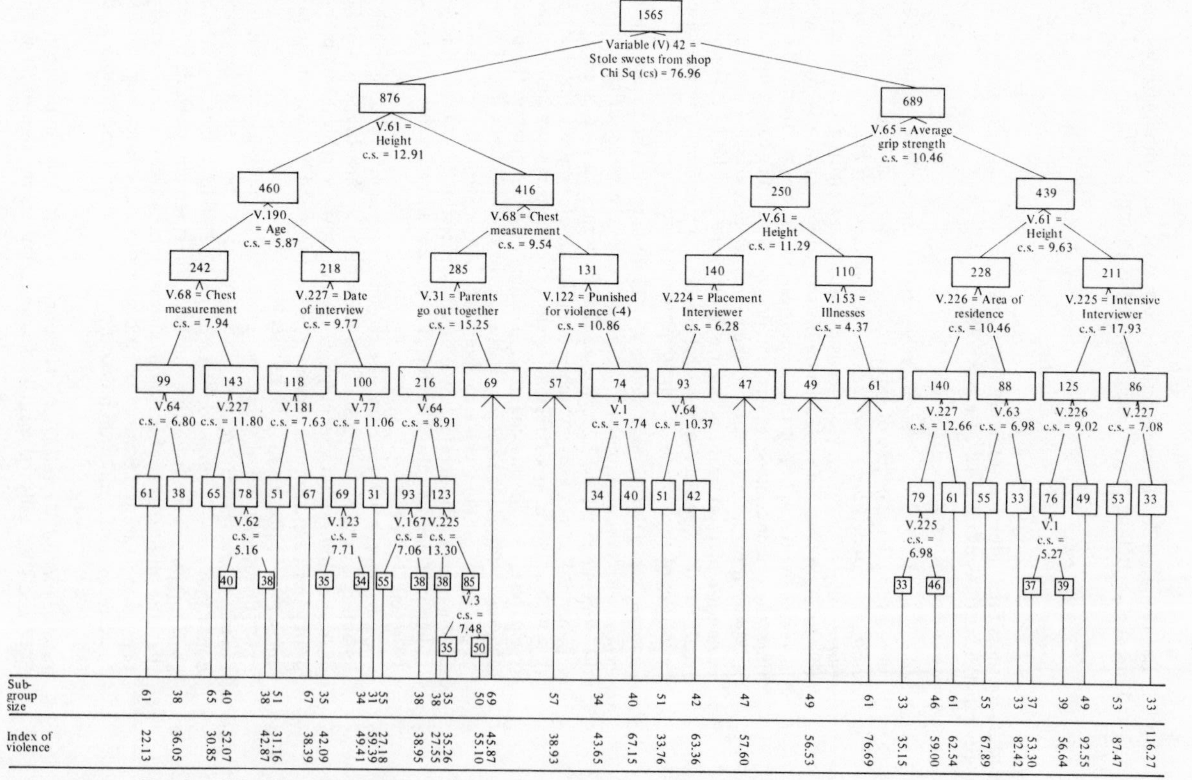

*Dependent variable = Violent behaviour, weighted total of all acts Level 1 to Level 6; **Independent variable = high exposure to violent films.

Table 12.22
Showing the matching of Controls to Qualifiers in terms of the matching composite shown in figure 12.5
This table relates to the Forward version of the hypothesis linking Independent Variable 29** and Dependent Variable 1*

ıl cases	Index of behaviour or attitude on dependent variable (a) Average index for Qualifiers†	(b) Average index for Controls††	(c) Modified average index for Controls††	Difference between (a) and (c) a − c	Difference between (a) and (c) as % of (c) $\frac{a - c \times 100}{c}$	Significance of Difference Cr	P≁
1565	56.95	45.94	49.11	7.84	15.96%	2.57	.005

Matching sub-groups	Average index of violence for Qualifiers† No. of cases	Index	Average index of violence for Controls†† No. of cases	Index
1	27	19.44	34	24.26
2	17	37.18	21	35.14
3	32	43.84	33	18.24
4	17	49.94	23	53.65
5	20	44.80	18	40.72
6	27	30.74	24	31.62
7	26	39.46	41	37.71
8	15	57.40	20	30.60
9	21	43.38	13	59.15
10	16	72.50	15	45.40
11	21	43.19	34	17.29
12	21	45.00	17	31.47
13	15	26.00	23	28.57
14	13	40.23	22	32.32
15	23	67.13	27	44.85
16	45	50.78	24	36.67
17	32	35.75	25	43.00
18	21	42.95	13	44.77
19	19	82.79	21	53.00
20	24	41.75	27	26.67
21	29	70.17	13	48.15
22	21	58.43	26	56.92
23	26	75.92	23	34.61
24	31	76.13	30	77.27
25	22	41.23	11	23.00
26	24	61.21	22	56.59
27	39	63.79	22	60.32
28	32	65.59	23	71.09
29	20	76.25	13	91.92
30	26	63.46	11	29.27
31	26	59.19	13	51.54
32	28	90.50	21	95.29
33	35	81.31	18	99.44
34	18	125.22	15	105.53
ALL	829	56.95	736	45.94

NOTE

The upper section of this table presents the basic findings, that is the residual difference between the Qualifying and Control groups after matching. The lower part of the table, opposite, presents important working details that lie behind the basic findings.

Footnotes

**Independent variable 29 = high exposure to violent films.

*Dependent variable 1 = violent behaviour, weighted total of all acts from level 1 to level 6.

†Qualifying group = those who have been exposed to a relatively large amount of film violence.

††Control group = those who have been exposed to relatively little film violence.

≁Using the one-tail extraction system.

Table 12.23

Results of investigating hypotheses about the effects of the other mass media upon violent behaviour by boys (in contrast with the results of exposure to television violence)

Type of exposure involved in the hypotheses	Direction of hypothesis	H1 (with DV1)		H2 (with DV2)		H3 (with DV3)		H4 (with DV4)		H4(70) (with ceiling of 70 on DV4		H4(40) (with ceiling of 40 on DV4)	
		Index of effect % θ	Signif. of diff P*	Index of effect % θ	Signif. of diff P*	Index of effect % θ	Signif of diff P*	Index of effect % θ	Signif. of diff P*	Index of effect % θ	Signif. of diff P*	Index of effect % θ	Signif. of diff P*
Comics/comic books	F	15.39	.007	5.98	.136	17.67	.005	34.51	.071	15.21	.161	14.86	.134
	R	5.83	.050	6.68	.035	9.82	.004	11.00	.002	11.00	.002	11.00	.002
Violent films	F	15.96	.005	17.16	.002	21.26	.001	26.16	.111	25.62	.044	21.20	.054
	R	5.57	.082	11.42	.003	10.15	.008	5.23	.087	5.23	.087	5.23	.087
Newspapers	F	15.63	.008	15.96	.002	17.86	.004	−3.39	.496	6.04	.344	9.13	.289
	R	6.13	.029	7.36	.012	3.51	.140	8.67	.004	8.67	.004	8.67	.004
Television violence	F	11.27	.034	10.97	.042	13.14	.029	49.00	.022	30.61	.023	22.94	.039
	R	7.86	<.001	7.44	.001	9.37	<.001	1.48	.264	1.48	.264	1.48	.264

θ Index of effect = $\frac{M_Q - M_{MC}}{M_{MC}} \times 100\%$

*P is a one-tail extraction from probability tables.

violence without regard to how serious any one of those acts may have been. Nonetheless, those scores are largely made up of acts of the 'only very slightly violent' grade – simply because such acts are so common and constitute an overwhelming part of the DV2 scores. The DV3 score, on the other hand, excludes the 'only very slightly violent' acts and is principally composed of acts graded as 'a bit violent' or 'fairly violent'.

For the DV2 measure of violence (principally representing trivial acts of violence), the evidence gives the hypothesis only a small degree of support, and it is in any case of an uncertain kind from the standpoint of statistical significance.

For the DV3 measure (principally reflecting a moderate level of violence), the evidence gives a fairly large degree of support to the hypothesis in its forward form. At the same time, the evidence gives a degree of support to the hypothesis in reverse as well, so that there exists the possibility that the support for the forward version of the hypothesis rests partly upon the hypothesis working in its reverse form.

On balance, the indications of table 12.23 are as follows.

(a) The hypothesis in its forward form has been rendered more tenable for violence considered generally (DV1), and for violence of the moderately serious kind (DV3), but not for the more trivial forms of violence. For the hypotheses dealing with DV1 and DV3, there does however exist the possibility that the support for the forward form is to some degree an artifact due to the hypotheses being true in reverse.

(b) For serious violence (DV4), the index of effect is large but there are reasons (partly the .071 P-value, partly the results of the outlyer check and partly the reverse-hypothesis finding), for maintaining a degree of wariness about the tenability of that hypothesis.

2 *Violent films*

(a) *In relation to DV1 (i.e. violence in general).* The evidence in table 12.23 gives a fairly large degree of support to the hypothesis that exposure to violent films increases the degree to which boys are violent in the general sense (i.e. where violence is assessed as a weighted score based on all the different levels of violence that boys commit). But that table also gives a small degree of support to the hypothesis in its reversed form and this raises the possibility that the forward working of the hypothesis is to some extent (a small extent in this case), a reflection of the working of the hypothesis in reverse. However, on balance the evidence in table 12.23 gives support to the hypothesis dealing with the effect of television violence upon DV1.

(b) *In relation to DV4 (serious violence).* As it relates to the hypothesis that exposure to violent films increases boys' violence at the serious level, the evidence in table 12.23 gives that hypothesis a large degree of support, the index of effect being over 20 per cent. At the same time, the P-value for DV4 is .111, and though it becomes .044 and .054 as different ceilings are applied to combat any possible outlyer effect, that .111 figure warns against over-certainty in reaching a decision about the degree to which the evidence supports the hypothesis. There is also a possibility that such evidence is to some small degree a reflection of a process which is the reverse of that hypothesised.

(c) *For the intermediate levels of violence*, as represented by DV2 and DV3, the evidence in table 12.23: (i) gives a fairly large degree of support to the hypotheses in their forward forms; (ii) raises the possibility that to some degree the findings for the forward hypotheses are really only reflections of that hypothesis working in reverse.

On balance, the indications of table 12.23 are as follows.

(a) The evidence renders more tenable the hypothesis that high exposure to violent films increases the degree to which boys are violent (irrespective of the level to which they are violent).

(b) However, for both serious and less than serious violence by boys, there are grounds for regarding the above conclusion with a degree of caution – either in relation to a reverse hypothesis finding or in relation to the P-value for one of the forward hypotheses.

3 *Newspapers*

(a) *In relation to DV1 (i.e. violence in general)*. The evidence in table 12.23 gives a fairly large degree of support to the hypothesis that exposure to newspapers increases the degree to which boys engage in violence in the general sense (i.e. where violence is assessed as a weighted score based upon all the different levels of violence that boys commit). The evidence also raises the possibility that the support given to the forward version of the hypothesis is to some small degree simply a reflection of the hypothesis working in reverse.

(b) *For serious violence (DV4)*. The evidence in table 12.23 gives no meaningful support to the hypothesis that exposure to newspapers increases boys' involvement in serious violence (as measured through DV4). On the other hand, the evidence gives a small degree of support to the hypothesis in its reverse form. According to the rationale used here for investigating hypotheses, this joint finding strongly militates against the forward version of the hypothesis as it relates to serious violence (i.e. DV4).

It is doubtful that the evidence linking newspaper exposure and DV4 (70)/DV4 (40) should in the circumstances be drawn on, but if so, then that evidence can indicate only a small degree of support (for the hypothesis) – *of a very uncertain kind at that.*

(c) *For the intermediate levels of violence,* as represented by DV2 and DV3, the evidence in table 12.23 is supportive of the hypothesis in the same way as for DV1.

On balance, the outcome of the investigation was as follows.

(a) For the less serious forms of violence, and for violence considered generally, the evidence gives a fairly large degree of support to the hypotheses, though there exists a possibility that this support stems to some small degree from the hypotheses working in reverse.

(b) The evidence does not give meaningful support to the hypothesis as it relates to serious violence.

Comparing the results for exposure to violence on television with the results for exposure to violence in the other mass media

It is important to consider the effects of exposure to television violence in the context of the effects of the other mass media and this can be done through tables 12.24 and 12.25. The main indications of the evidence are as follows.

1 *At the level of boys' violence, considered generally (DV1).* At this level, all four of the media hypotheses were supported by the evidence. For each of them there exists a possibility that to some small extent the support they receive is a reflection of the hypothesis working in reverse. But on balance, the tenability of each is advanced by the evidence. If anything, the support given to the TV violence hypothesis is a trifle less strong than that given to the hypotheses involving comics, violent films and newspapers respectively.

2 *At the level of 'serious violence' by boys (DV4).* With regard to serious violence by boys, the hypothesis featuring exposure to *television* violence got considerably more support from the evidence than did the hypothesis involving comics on the one hand or that involving violent films on the other. That involving newspapers can hardly be said to have been supported at all (i.e. at *this* level of violent behaviour by boys).

The degree to which the exposure levels to the different mass media are independent of each other

In table 12.25 I have presented evidence about the intercorrelations of the four mass media variables, namely, exposure to violence on television, exposure to comics and comic books, exposure to violent films, exposure to newspapers.

The main indications of this table are as follows.

1 Exposure to television violence is very little correlated with exposure to the other mass media and so it is unlikely that the results as they relate to television violence are really only indirect evidence of the effects of exposure to the other media.

2 Amongst the other media, association between degree of exposure is also limited, the highest being 0.45 (between exposure to comics/comic books and exposure to newspapers) which translates into a relationship of approximately 20 per cent only.

SOME CORRELATES OF EXPOSURE TO THE MASS MEDIA FEATURED IN THIS CHAPTER

Table 12.26 presents the degree of association between exposure to the different types of mass media being dealt with in this section and the characteristics of boys. The trends in

Table 12.24

Results of investigating hypotheses about the effect of four different mass media upon the violence level of boys

Type of exposure involved in the hypothesis	Direction of hypothesis	Indices of effects of exposure: Weighted total for violence (DV1)					Total number of acts of serious violence				
		M_Q	M_{MC}	$\frac{M_Q - M_{MC}}{M_{MC}}$ as %	CR	P*	M_Q	M_{MC}	$\frac{M_Q - M_{MC}}{M_{MC}}$ as %	CR	P*
Violence on television (IV1)	Forward	56.76	51.01	11.27	1.83	.034	7.48	5.02	49.00	2.02	.022
	Reverse	607.81	563.51	7.86	3.40	.001	582.65	574.14	1.48	0.63	.264
Comics or comic books (IV28)	Forward	57.06	49.45	15.39	2.44	.007	7.99	5.94	34.51	1.47	.071
	Reverse	9.08	8.58	5.83	1.65	.050	9.59	8.64	11.00	2.84	.002
Violent films (IV29)	Forward	56.95	49.11	15.96	2.57	.005	6.80	5.39	26.16	1.22	.111
	Reverse	5.88	5.57	5.57	1.39	.082	5.63	5.35	5.23	1.36	.087
Newspapers (IV30)	Forward	57.27	49.53	15.63	2.41	.008	6.84	7.08	−3.39	−0.01	.496
	Reverse	6.23	5.87	6.13	1.90	.029	6.39	5.88	8.67	2.62	.004

*One-tail extractions from probability tables.
No adjustment made for 'correlation factor'.

Table 12.25

Showing degree of association* between independent variables

Independent variables	1	28	29	30
1 (Television violence)	1.00	.08	.31	.15
28 (Comics)	.08	1.00	.08	.45
29 (Violent films)	.31	.08	1.00	.19
30 (Newspapers)	.15	.45	.19	1.00

*Product-moment coefficients

Table 12.26
Exposure to different kinds of media analysed by characteristics of boys

Some characteristics of boys		All	Amount of exposure to TV violence			Amount of exposure to comics			Amount of exposure to violent films			Amount of exposure to newspapers		
			Low	Med	High	Low	Med	High	Low	Med	High	Low	Med	High
		Level of exposure	0-504	505-634	635-1433	0-5	6-9	10-21	0-3	4-6	7-21	0-4	5-9	10-21
		No. of cases	615	317	627	546	405	608	609	367	583	584	375	600
		n	%	%	%	%	%	%	%	%	%	%	%	%
Grip strength:	10-30 Kgs	785	50	21	29	29	24	47	47	25	28	41	24	36
	31-60 Kgs	756	29	20	51	42	28	31	31	22	47	35	24	41
Skin colour:	Coloured	146	53	16	32	22	21	56	53	23	24	26	21	53
	White	1365	38	21	41	37	26	37	38	24	39	39	25	37
Size of household:	2-4 persons	646	36	19	46	39	27	34	34	22	44	41	25	34
	5 persons	406	41	23	36	38	26	36	38	25	37	38	25	37
	6+ persons	507	43	21	37	27	25	48	46	25	29	33	22	45
Ever stolen sweets:	Yes	686	35	19	46	29	28	42	34	26	41	31	26	44
	No	870	43	21	36	39	24	37	43	22	35	43	23	34
Job in spare time (if still at school)	Yes	531	36	19	45	35	29	37	36	25	39	35	24	42
	No	870	45	22	34	36	24	41	43	24	34	41	24	34
Enjoyed school:	Yes	1222	41	20	39	35	27	37	39	23	37	39	24	38
	No	324	34	20	46	34	22	44	37	25	38	34	25	41
Truancy:	Never	1207	41	21	38	36	26	38	41	24	36	40	24	36
	Once a month	126	36	21	42	29	25	45	36	28	37	26	27	47
	More than once a month	181	37	17	47	30	25	46	34	22	44	28	24	48
How often punished for violence or destruction when under 4 years:	Always or mostly	565	38	20	42	33	25	41	40	23	37	36	26	38
	Hardly ever	284	44	20	36	31	24	45	38	28	35	36	23	42
	Not at all	151	40	21	39	33	23	44	44	21	34	38	19	43
	Never violent	522	38	20	42	39	29	32	37	23	40	41	24	35
Father's occupation*:	A/B/C	647	41	20	39	47	26	27	39	22	39	43	24	33
	D	357	39	20	40	30	29	40	40	22	38	38	21	41
	E/F/G	389	40	19	41	22	24	54	41	26	33	31	25	43
How long has mother worked since marriage:	Not at all	222	43	24	33	39	21	39	43	21	35	39	24	38
	0-5 years	571	41	20	39	33	29	39	39	26	35	39	23	37
	6+ years	701	38	19	44	36	26	38	37	22	41	36	24	40
Age of boy:	12-13 years	623	54	22	24	30	24	45	51	22	28	44	22	34
	14-15 years	584	35	22	44	34	27	39	35	27	39	35	26	39
	16-18 years	349	21	15	63	45	27	28	26	21	53	30	24	47
Type of school attended:	Secondary modern	379	36	20	43	29	22	49	39	23	37	34	25	42
	Comprehensive	566	40	18	42	31	28	40	42	23	34	38	24	38
	Grammar	330	33	23	43	42	31	28	34	25	41	40	25	35
	Public	183	54	19	27	41	25	34	36	22	41	35	26	38

*A, B, C = Professional, semi-professional, executive, highly skilled.
D = Skilled.
E, F, G = Moderately skilled, semi-skilled, unskilled.

this table can be studied at the reader's leisure, but it may be helpful to him to have his attention drawn to some of the principal indications.

1 *Coloured* boys undergo greater exposure (than other boys) to comics and to newspapers and less exposure to television violence and violent films. These trends are all of a fairly marked character.

2 The trends for boys from large households (over 6 persons) are similar to those for coloured boys but not as marked.

3 Boys who *frequently truant* from school undergo more exposure (than other boys) to all four classes of media content.

4 The situation for boys *who have stolen sweets* is the same (as for truanting boys) – they undergo greater exposure than do other boys to all four types of media content.

5 Stronger boys undergo greater exposure (than do other boys) to television violence, to violent films and to newspapers and less exposure to comics.

6 Those who did *not enjoy school* underwent somewhat more exposure to television violence, to comics, to newspapers.

7 *Older* boys undergo greater exposure to television violence, to violent films, to newspapers and less exposure to comics.

8 *Public school* boys undergo markedly less exposure to television violence (than other boys); public and grammar school boys undergo less exposure (than other boys) to comics/comic books.

Notes

[1] See pages 376-84 for analysis of outcome.

[2] See pages 376-84 for analysis of outcome.

[3] But not completely, as we can reasonably expect high exposure to non-violent programmes to be positively associated with total amount of viewing and with viewing of television violence.

[4] Adopting a 'best fit' interpretation.

[5] Evidence from chapter 11, table 11.4.

[6] 'Spontaneous' does not necessarily imply a state of 'temper' (see (b) (i) on page 397

[7] 'These days, how often do you read a comic?'

[8] 'Which of the following papers have you ever *regularly read* or *regularly looked through?*'

CHAPTER 13

THE TENABILITY OF HYPOTHESES ABOUT THE EFFECTS OF EXPOSURE TO DIFFERENT KINDS OF TELEVISION VIOLENCE UPON THE EXTENT OF VIOLENT BEHAVIOUR BY BOYS

Contents

13 THE TENABILITY OF HYPOTHESES ABOUT THE EFFECTS OF EXPOSURE TO DIFFERENT KINDS OF TELEVISION VIOLENCE UPON THE EXTENT OF VIOLENT BEHAVIOUR IN BOYS

In this chapter I have presented evidence relating to the effects, on boys' behaviour, of long-term exposure to *different kinds* of television violence.

THE DIFFERENT KINDS OF TELEVISION VIOLENCE INVESTIGATED

Hypothesis 1 and hypothesis 4 each had linked to it 25 sub-hypotheses. These specified that *particular kinds* of television violence increased violent behaviour by boys exposed to them. The full set of 25 types was as follows.

2 [1] Programmes containing fictional violence of a realistic kind.

3 Programmes where violence is performed by basically 'good guy' types who are also rebels or 'odd-men-out'.

4 Programmes in which much of the violence occurs in a domestic or family setting.

5 Programmes which feature defiance of or rudeness towards authority figures.

6 Programmes where violence is shown as glorified, romanticised, idealised or ennobling.

7 Programmes where violence is presented as 'fun and games' or like a game or as something to entertain.

8 Programmes in which the violence is presented as being in a good cause.

9 Programmes where the physical or mental consequences of violence, for the victim, are shown in detail.

10 Programmes where the violence is related to racial or minority group strife.

11 Programmes where the violence is performed by basically 'good guy' types or heroes who are also tough (i.e. who can endure physical violence and fight on.)

12 Programmes where the violence is of a verbal kind.

13 Programmes in which the violence is just thrown in for its own sake or is not necessary to the plot.

14 Programmes in which the violence is gruesome, horrific or scary.

15 Fictional programmes about the English police at work which also feature the kinds of violence which go on in society.

16 A selection of (5) cartoon programmes in which the characters are violent to each other (i.e. Boss Cat, Popeye, Pugwash, Yogi Bear, Tom and Jerry).

17 Tom and Jerry.

18 Plays or films in which personal relationships are a major theme and which feature verbal abuse (e.g. swearing, quarrelling) or physical violence.

19 Violence through the news or newsreel programmes.

20 Comedy programmes which feature 'slap-stick' violence and/or verbal abuse between the characters.

21 Science fiction programmes involving violence (e.g. where creatures destroy people, where humans use super weapons to destroy men).

22 Westerns which include violence, for example, as between Cowboys and Indians.

23 A selection of (3) sporting programmes which present violent behaviour by competitors or spectators (i.e. Sportsview, Grandstand, Saturday Sportstime).

24 Wrestling and boxing.

25 Films or series which feature gangs or gangsters engaged in violent organised crime.

26 Programmes in which the violence is performed by adults.

Each of the 25 was separately geared to the dependent variable of hypothesis 1, e.g.

> 'High exposure to programmes that contain fictional violence of a realistic kind increases the degree to which boys commit acts of violence'.

Similarly, each was geared to the dependent variable in hypothesis 4, for example:

> 'High exposure to television programmes where the physical or mental consequences of violence (for the victim) are shown in detail, increases the degree to which boys engage in violent behaviour of the more serious kind'.

THE METHODS OF INVESTIGATION USED

The research strategy

Each of the above 50 sub-hypotheses (i.e. all 25 programme types linked to hypothesis 1 and all 25 linked to hypothesis 4) was subjected to the same type of challenging procedure as were hypotheses 1-4. Each was tested in its forward and in its reversed form. The reader should study the detailed description of this investigatory strategy as presented in chapter 3, as commented on in chapter 10 and as illustrated in chapter 12.

Measurement of boys' exposure to different kinds of television output

In chapter 4 I set out in detail the methods used to assess the degree to which boys had been exposed to the different kinds of television programmes featured in the sub-hypotheses. For all twenty-five of them, exposure was related to the period between 1959 and the time of interview in 1972.

THE FINDINGS

The results of investigating the 50 sub-hypotheses are set out in full in the Appendix to this chapter and are summarised in table 13.1.

At first sight, these findings may well be puzzling: the evidence renders most of the sub-hypotheses in the DV1 part of the table more tenable; similarly, but more decisively so, for the majority of the sub-hypotheses in the DV4 part of the table.

The reason for this outcome may possibly be found in the correlation matrix presented in

Table 13.1
Results of investigating 50 sub-hypotheses about the effects of exposure to different kinds of television violence

(a)

Type of programme (IV)		Dependent variable for H1 (= DV1) % Diff	P*
2	F	17.52	.003
	R	6.24	.005
3	F	10.04	.068
	R	8.56	.002
4	F	12.81	.034
	R	9.04	<.001
5	F	8.30	.092
	R	5.89	.005
6	F	11.20	.038
	R	7.37	.003
7	F	14.05	.013
	R	6.25	.012
8	F	14.36	.012
	R	4.90	.020
9	F	18.04	.003
	R	7.05	<.001
10	F	12.51	.025
	R	9.23	<.001
11	F	8.59	.090
	R	5.87	.011
12	F	16.79	.004
	R	8.05	.001
13	F	13.17	.019
	R	7.65	.001
14	F	17.39	.004
	R	6.54	.005
15	F	5.46	NS
	R	5.42	.036
16	F	14.66	.009
	R	6.58	<.001
17	F	11.39	.071
	R	4.06	.005
18	F	12.01	.029
	R	6.16	.011
19	F	11.48	.031
	R	3.98	.034
20	F	12.63	.019
	R	7.35	<.001
21	F	6.28	NS
	R	3.53	.040
22	F	13.51	.014
	R	8.62	.007
23	F	8.25	.095
	R	10.63	.002
24	F	1.81	NS
	R	12.57	<.001
25	F	11.66	.031
	R	6.57	.007
26	F	13.37	.019
	R	6.96	.005

(b)

Type of programme (IV)		Dependent variables for H4: DV4 % Diff	DV4 P*	DV4 (70) † % Diff	DV4 (70) † P*
2	F	66.15	.006	45.75	.003
	R	0.04	NS	0.04	NS
3	F	41.43	.041	23.84	.056
	R	−1.18	NS	−1.18	NS
4	F	32.54	NS	34.06	.025
	R	−0.17	NS	−0.17	NS
5	F	38.31	.047	18.92	NS
	R	−1.37	NS	−1.37	.100
6	F	46.03	.023	24.31	.061
	R	0.05	NS	0.05	NS
7	F	26.85	NS	11.39	NS
	R	−0.26	NS	−0.26	NS
8	F	63.01	.006	θ	θ
	R	0.76	NS	0.76	NS
9	F	53.51	.012	38.03	.009
	R	−0.06	NS	−0.06	NS
10	F	57.32	.010	39.72	.007
	R	2.95	.093	2.95	.093
11	F	55.99	.010	32.50	.018
	R	−1.10	NS	−1.10	NS
12	F	37.04	.093	30.17	.038
	R	2.05	NS	2.05	NS
13	F	70.07	.003	43.42	.004
	R	0.64	NS	0.64	NS
14	F	49.41	.025	32.13	.021
	R	0.79	NS	0.79	NS
15	F	39.13	.075	53.57	.001
	R	1.80	NS	1.80	NS
16	F	18.20	NS	8.14	NS
	R	−0.31	NS	−0.31	NS
17	F	8.46	NS	6.04	NS
	R	−0.70	NS	−0.70	NS
18	F	79.16	.001	56.66	<.001
	R	3.78	.095	3.78	.095
19	F	40.12	.038	23.60	.054
	R	0.64	NS	0.64	NS
20	F	22.12	NS	14.56	NS
	R	0.06	NS	0.06	NS
21	F	9.79	NS	4.52	NS
	R	−1.94	NS	−1.94	NS
22	F	61.76	.007	49.47	.001
	R	4.38	NS	4.38	NS
23	F	−2.32	NS	−5.27	NS
	R	7.48	.027	7.48	.027
24	F	35.10	.049	37.22	.009
	R	7.80	.020	7.80	.020
25	F	56.78	.011	32.48	.022
	R	0.44	NS	0.44	NS
26	F	41.48	.034	24.25	.054
	R	−0.65	NS	−0.65	NS

For note to table see over.

NOTES TO TABLE 13.1

For identity of programmes see table 13.3.

*One-tail tests

(a) = results relating to hypothesis 1 (involving DV1); (b) = results relating to hypothesis 4 (DV4 and DV4 (70)).

†DV4(70) = score for serious violence with ceiling of 70 on total score available.

NS = P>.100.

θ = Not provided by computing agency.

table 13.2. All the independent variables in the sub-hypotheses (i.e. IV2-IV26) are positively correlated with IV1 and for fifteen of them that correlation was over +0.90. In other words, for many of the different types of television violence under study, high exposure tended markedly to go along with high exposure to television violence generally — and vice-versa. As one might expect from this, there is also a high degree of correlation between exposure levels for many of the different *kinds* of television violence.

What all this means of course is that it is extremely difficult to sort out the effect of exposure to, say, Westerns, from exposure to television violence generally (r = +0.84) or from exposure to violence committed in a good cause (r = +0.82) or from violence of a verbal kind (r = +0.83) and so on. This is because in the normal state of affairs, viewers do not expose themselves to Westerns *only*. In terms of the findings shown in table 13.1, it means that the 'index of effect' for Westerns could be very much mixed up with the 'index of effect' for other kinds of violent programmes and for violent programmes generally.

However, one must not make too extreme an interpretation of the data in table 13.2. In the first place, a correlation of just under +0.90 allows for a 20 per cent non-relationship between the variables concerned. Secondly, many of the correlations between programme types fell far below the +0.90 level, about one in four of them being under r = .50 and about half of them being below r = .70.

In these circumstances it seems reasonable to interpret table 13.1 in a *comparative way* in order to identify the types of television violence more likely to produce violent behaviour and those *less likely* to do so. The ground work for doing this has been completed in the data display of table 13.3.

One seeming oddity about the content of table 13.3 is that the rank order of the programme types listed in sectors (a) and (b) are by no means the same. Thus 'cartoon violence' (considered generally) is fifth on the DV1 list and 22nd on the DV4 list; programmes presenting verbal violence are fourth on the DV1 list and 17th on the DV4 list; programmes presenting violence just as something to entertain are 7th on the DV1 list and 20th on the DV4 list; and so on. The difference between the results for DV1 and DV4 no doubt relates to those two variables having a considerable degree of independence of each other — in fact, being different variables.

With respect to the relative potency of the different programme types in stimulating violence in boys, there are numerous indications in table 13.3. However I have for the present limited my commentary to a consideration of the types of programmes that appear to influence the development of *serious* violence in boys. I have done this for the sake of brevity, clarity, and above all to focus attention upon what seem to me to be the more important of the table 13.3 data. The reader may wish to study table 13.3 for further indications, especially as these relate to the stimulation in boys of the *less* serious forms of violence.

In terms of the stimulation of *serious* violence by boys, the main indications of table 13.3

Table 13.2

The numerical association between exposure to different kinds of television violence

TYPE OF TELEVISION VIOLENCE	1*	2	3	4	5	6	7	8	9	10	11	12	13	14	15	16	17	18	19	20	21	22	23	24	25	
1	1.00																									
2	.97	1.00																								
3	.95	.93	1.00																							
4	.92	.92	.86	1.00																						
5	.95	.95	.94	.88	1.00																					
6	.97	.94	.97	.85	.93	1.00																				
7	.94	.91	.92	.85	.92	.95	1.00																			
8	.98	.96	.96	.88	.96	.98	.95	1.00																		
9	.97	.97	.93	.93	.95	.92	.90	.94	1.00																	
10	.93	.92	.85	.87	.89	.86	.86	.89	.92	1.00																
11	.97	.94	.96	.87	.93	.99	.94	.99	.92	.87	1.00															
12	.98	.96	.93	.95	.93	.94	.94	.96	.95	.92	.95	1.00														
13	.96	.93	.93	.86	.92	.98	.94	.99	.91	.87	.99	.94	1.00													
14	.96	.93	.90	.86	.91	.96	.92	.97	.91	.92	.96	.94	.97	1.00												
15	.71	.77	.62	.76	.68	.60	.59	.66	.75	.68	.62	.70	.63	.64	1.00											
16	.63	.59	.59	.59	.62	.59	.60	.63	.62	.54	.61	.60	.61	.57	.50	1.00										
17	.40	.39	.36	.39	.41	.37	.36	.41	.41	.35	.39	.38	.40	.37	.38	.85	1.00									
18	.79	.82	.68	.89	.74	.67	.68	.73	.82	.76	.69	.80	.70	.73	.94	.54	.39	1.00								
19	.59	.52	.46	.52	.55	.47	.49	.53	.57	.78	.48	.55	.49	.60	.43	.35	.26	.51	1.00							
20	.70	.66	.63	.74	.67	.64	.66	.68	.69	.61	.65	.72	.67	.64	.57	.88	.83	.67	.40	1.00						
21	.67	.64	.58	.58	.67	.61	.61	.68	.66	.57	.64	.65	.66	.61	.44	.53	.42	.49	.36	.57	1.00					
22	.84	.84	.86	.79	.79	.83	.79	.82	.84	.76	.82	.83	.77	.74	.54	.49	.27	.59	.38	.52	.48	1.00				
23	.47	.44	.42	.45	.43	.40	.40	.42	.47	.46	.40	.45	.39	.41	.38	.31	.21	.43	.36	.34	.27	.40	1.00			
24	.48	.46	.45	.45	.46	.45	.46	.46	.45	.50	.46	.48	.45	.47	.30	.29	.16	.36	.37	.30	.28	.39	.36	1.00		
25	.94	.93	.89	.86	.90	.95	.89	.96	.89	.85	.95	.91	.97	.96	.73	.59	.41	.78	.48	.66	.60	.70	.39	.43	1.00	
26	.93	.91	.92	.83	.91	.96	.87	.96	.88	.83	.96	.89	.96	.93	.57	.57	.37	.64	.46	.62	.60	.79	.38	.44	.94	1.00

*See full list of programme types as detailed in table 13.3 and on pages

Table 13.3
Results of investigating hypotheses about the effects on boys' behaviour of long term exposure to *different kinds* of television violence: entries in order with respect to sub-hypothesis tenability

(a)

Type of programme (IV)		Dependent variable for H1 (= DV1) % Diff	P*
9	F	18.04	.003
	R	7.05	<.001
2	F	17.52	.003
	R	6.24	.005
14	F	17.39	.004
	R	6.54	.005
12	F	16.79	.004
	R	8.05	.001
16	F	14.66	.009
	R	6.58	<.001
8	F	14.36	.012
	R	4.90	.020
7	F	14.05	.013
	R	6.25	.012
22	F	13.51	.014
	R	8.62	.007
26	F	13.37	.019
	R	6.96	.005
13	F	13.17	.019
	R	7.65	.001
4	F	12.81	.034
	R	9.04	<.001
20	F	12.63	.019
	R	7.35	<.001
10	F	12.51	.025
	R	9.23	<.001
18	F	12.01	.029
	R	6.16	.011
25	F	11.66	.031
	R	6.57	.007
19	F	11.48	.031
	R	3.98	.034
17	F	11.39	.071
	R	4.06	.005
6	F	11.20	.038
	R	7.37	.003
3	F	10.04	.068
	R	8.56	.002
11	F	8.59	.090
	R	5.87	.011
5	F	8.30	.092
	R	5.89	.005
23	F	8.25	.095
	R	10.63	.002

(b)

Type of programme		Dependent variables for H4			
		DV4		DV4 (70)	
(IV)		% Diff	P*	% Diff	P*
18	F	79.16	.001	56.66	<.001
	R	3.78	.095	3.78	.095
13	F	70.07	.003	43.42	.004
	R	0.64	NS	0.64	NS
2	F	66.15	.006	45.75	.003
	R	0.04	NS	0.04	NS
8	F	63.01	.006	θ	θ
	R	0.76	NS	0.76	NS
22	F	61.76	.007	49.47	.001
	R	4.38	NS	4.38	NS
10	F	57.32	.010	39.72	.007
	R	2.95	.093	2.95	.093
25	F	56.78	.011	32.48	.022
	R	0.44	NS	0.44	NS
11	F	55.99	.010	32.50	.018
	R	−1.10	NS	−1.10	NS
9	F	53.51	.012	38.03	.009
	R	−0.06	NS	−0.06	NS
14	F	49.41	.025	32.13	.021
	R	0.79	NS	0.79	NS
6	F	46.03	.023	24.31	.061
	R	0.05	NS	0.05	NS
3	F	41.43	.041	23.84	.056
	R	−1.18	NS	−1.18	NS
26	F	41.48	.034	24.25	.054
	R	−0.65	NS	−0.65	NS
19	F	40.12	.038	28.60	.054
	R	0.64	NS	0.64	NS
15	F	39.06	.075	53.57	.001
	R	1.80	NS	1.80	NS
5	F	38.31	.047	18.92	NS
	R	−1.37	NS	−1.37	.100
12	F	37.04	.093	30.17	.038
	R	2.05	NS	2.05	NS
24	F	35.10	.049	37.22	.009
	R	7.80	.020	7.80	.020
4	F	32.54	NS	34.06	.025
	R	−0.17	NS	−0.17	NS
7	F	26.85	NS	11.39	NS
	R	−0.26	NS	−0.26	NS
20	F	22.12	NS	14.56	NS
	R	0.06	NS	0.06	NS
16	F	18.20	NS	8.14	NS
	R	−0.31	NS	−0.31	NS

Table 13.3 (cont.)

(a)

Type of programme (IV)		Dependent variable for H1 (= DV1) % Diff	P*
21	F	6.28	NS
	R	3.53	.040
15	F	5.46	NS
	R	5.42	.036
24	F	1.81	NS
	R	12.57	<.001

(b)

Type of programme		Dependent variables for H4			
		DV4		DV4 (70)	
(IV)		% Diff	P*	% Diff	P*
21	F	9.79	NS	4.52	NS
	R	−1.94	NS	−1.94	NS
17	F	8.46	NS	6.04	NS
	R	−0.70	NS	−0.70	NS
23	F	−2.32	NS	−5.27	NS
	R	7.48	.027	7.48	.027

Code to programme content

2 Fictional violence of a realistic kind.

3 Violence by good guy who is also rebel or odd-man-out.

4 Violence in a domestic or family setting.

5 Featuring defiance or rudeness towards authority figures.

6 Violence is glorified, romanticised, idealised, ennobling.

7 Violence presented as 'fun and games'/like a game/as something to entertain.

8 Violence presented as being in a good cause.

9 Physical or mental consequences for victim of violence are shown in detail.

10 Violence is related to racial or minority group strife.

11 Violence is by good guy type or hero who is also tough.

12 Violence of a verbal kind.

13 Violence is thrown in for its own sake/not necessary to the plot.

14 Where the violence is gruesome, horrific or scary.

15 Fictional programmes about the English police at work, which also feature the kinds of violence which go on in society.

16 Cartoon programmes (a group of 5) in which the characters are violent to each other.

17 Tom and Jerry.

18 Where personal relations are a major theme and which feature verbal abuse or physical violence.

19 Violence in news or newsreel programmes.

20 Comedy featuring slapstick violence and/or verbal abuse.

21 Science fiction involving violence.

22 Westerns involving violence.

23 Sporting programmes which present violence by competitors/spectators.

24 Wrestling and boxing.

25 Showing gangs or gangsters engaged in violent organised crime.

26 Where the violence is performed by adults.

are as follows.

1 Programme types that are the *more* likely to stimulate *serious* violence in boys are specified in (a)-(e) below. The examples given with these different programme types are all drawn from the sample of the programmes broadcast in the period 1959-1971. *Inevitably many of them will now be out of date and non-current*, but that is in no way an invalidating situation because we are dealing here with the cumulative build-up in boys of the influence of *past* exposures. The non-current examples are simply illustrations of past input (into boys) of different types of television violence. The reader who wants *current* examples of those different types could get them by having current programmes so rated by a panel of experienced viewers on the lines adopted in this enquiry (see chapter 4).

(a) Plays or films in which personal relationships are a major theme and which feature verbal abuse, swearing, quarrelling, physical violence. The emphasis in this category of programmes is largely upon personal relationships of a non-domestic and non-humorous kind. Examples have been: 'Crane'; 'Softly Softly'; some of the Wednesday plays; 'The Power Game'; 'The Human Jungle'.

(b) Programmes in which the violence is just thrown in for its own sake or is not necessary to the plot. Examples: 'Man from Uncle'; 'Cinema'; 'Danger Man'.

(c) Programmes presenting fictional violence of a realistic kind. Examples: 'Hawaii 5-0'; 'The Informer'; 'Ironside'; 'Softly Softly'.

(d) Programmes in which the violence is presented as being in a good cause. Examples: 'The Saint'; 'Danger Man'; 'The Untouchables'.

(e) Westerns which include violence. Examples: 'Wayne in Action'; 'Gunsmoke'; 'High Chaparral'.

2 Programme types that are *less* likely to produce *serious* violence in boys are as follows. [2]

(a) Sporting programmes that present violent behaviour by competitors or spectators. Examples have been: 'Sportsview'; 'Grandstand'; 'Saturday Sportstime'.

(b) 'Tom and Jerry' and other cartoon programmes. Examples: 'Popeye'; 'Boss Cat'.

(c) Science fiction programmes involving violence. Examples: 'Quatermas and the Pit'; 'Lost in Space'; 'Dr Who'.

(d) Comedy programmes that present slapstick violence and/or verbal abuse between characters. Examples: 'Steptoe and Son'; 'Whacko'; 'Till Death Us Do Part'.

(e) Programmes that present violence as 'fun and games' or 'like a game' or as something to entertain. Examples: 'High Adventure'; 'Please Sir'; 'Thunderbirds'.

It is vital in considering the ten groups of programme types set out above to keep it in mind that many programmes do to some degree fall into more than one of those groups. I will be commenting on the implications of this later in the chapter.

SOME INDICATIONS OF THE FINDINGS FOR THE CONTROL OF TELEVISION VIOLENCE

Some hypotheses about the features of television violence that stimulate serious violence by boy viewers

Whereas table 13.3 does, in my opinion, provide much material for hypothesising about the ways in which television violence affects boys, *it is essential to keep it in mind that any such hypothesising must be entered into with great wariness and with scientific humility.* Above all, we must not develop pet speculations which would then be allowed to harden into theory without rigorous test and challenge.

With these dangers in mind, what I have done in the present situation is to formulate a series of *hypotheses* on the basis of the special character and contrasts of table 13.3, drawing also upon the definitional detail of table 4.6 in chapter 4. These hypotheses concern those features of television violence that relate to the stimulation of serious violence in boys. They are set out in two groups. The first group concerns programme features that are *more* likely to stimulate serious violence and the second group concerns programme features that are *less* likely to do so.

Group 1 hypotheses. Serious violence by boys is *more* likely to be stimulated by television output of the following kinds.

(a) Programmes where violence of a nasty kind appears to be sanctioned by showing it being done in a good cause or with seeming legality. Though this point arises out of the detail of table 13.3, it should also be linked up with the finding of a strong tendency by boys to regard their own violent acts (and those of others) as somehow not violent if those acts were 'justified'.

(b) Programmes that make it easy for boys to identify with the person or persons being violent.

(c) Programmes where the subject matter is of a kind which tends to demand that the constituent violence be on a large scale, possibly with mass killings. Westerns have tended to be of this kind, as have many programmes (usually films) of the epic variety.

(d) Programmes where the law enforcer, in order to defeat the villains does himself commit considerable violence, perhaps of a kind that is tougher and nastier than that used by the villains.

(e) Programmes in which violence is presented in a context where personal relationships are a major theme. In real life, priority has been given, through training and sanctions, to the protection of our working relationships with other people against the outbreak of serious violence. Presumably the presentation by television of nastiness and violence as a normal element in such relationships tends to reduce in boys such barriers as society has built up in them against being seriously violent in the personal relations context.

(f) Programmes where violent television of a serious kind is taken out of its developmental context (as when it is just 'thrown in') (i) so that it can be made more violent than its developmental background would warrant it being and (ii) so that boys are not in a position to regard that developmental background as unlikely to apply to them.

(g) Programmes where the violence is presented with such realism that it us unlikely to be rejected as mere fiction, but instead is given the weight of believability and of normality.

Where a programme has built into it *several* of the negative elements listed above, it is likely to be more potent in stimulating serious violence. Some programmes have *heavy* loadings of this violent kind. For example, (see table 4.6 of chapter 4), 'Wayne in Action', which had a high violence loading as a Western, had high loadings also as 'violence in a good cause', as 'fictional violence of a realistic kind', and as 'violence in the context of personal relationships'. 'Hawaii 5-0' is not only an example of 'realistic violence' but also qualifies as 'violence in a good cause'. The reader may wish to appraise other programmes in the same way, starting, say, with the modern programmes such as 'Starsky and Hutch', 'The Professionals', 'Target'.

Group 2 hypotheses. Serious violence by boys is *less* likely to be stimulated by television output of the following kinds.

(a) Programmes where the violence shown is obviously far beyond the capabilities and/or the opportunities of the viewer, as are many forms of science fiction and cartoon programmes.

(b) Programmes where the violence shown is so ridiculous or far fetched that it is passed off by boys as having nothing to do with real life.

(c) Where the programme is humorous – in that a humorous presentation or theme is likely to make it harder for the programmer to introduce into it really nasty violence. This is not the same thing as saying that a humorous context somehow lessens the effects of such violence as is inherent in it.

(d) Programmes where the violence presented is of the purely verbal kind rather than being all or partly of the physical kind. Such programmes are less likely to stimulate serious violence. (At the same time, the evidence indicates that they do produce violence of the *less serious* kind, particularly swearing and the use of bad language.

(e) Programmes where the television experience leaves the boy satisfied and good tempered – as distinct from tense or irritated or bored (see also chapter 18).

(f) Actuality programmes where the televised violence is, as it were, closely contained within a special environment – as for the sporting event where the televised violence is in fact an accurate representation of the specialised violence that is intrinsic to that particular sport.

(g) Programmes where the process of watching a televised event is likely to keep boys out of a situation in which violence is likely to occur (for example, a televised major soccer match).

(h) In actuality broadcasting, provided it is not markedly selective and is not edited to highlight its more violent elements. This is mainly because actuality tends to put a limit upon the excesses of the occasional producer who has an innovative fixation on the production of nasty or epic violence.

A provisional guideline system for the programmer

The programmer may well wish to use the foregoing hypotheses as *provisional guidelines of a preventive nature* for controlling the presentation of violence through television. I consider that they do provide the beginning of a meaningful guideline system for reducing the degree to which exposure to television stimulates serious violence by boys. At the same time I recommend that steps be taken as soon as possible to subject each guideline to further investigation both to challenge it and to tighten up its guideline capabilities.

I must add that this guideline system would be very incomplete, even at the provisional level, if we did not build into it the principal finding of this enquiry, namely that high exposure to television violence promotes serious violence by boys. At this stage, the most effective and basic step would be to cut back sharply on the *total amount* of violence on television. The other guidelines would be built 'on top of' this basic requirement – about which there is an extended commentary in chapter 20.

THE FORM OF INVESTIGATION NEEDED FOR FURTHERING GUIDELINE DEVELOPMENT

Investigation of the present and other guideline hypotheses is open to the skilled researcher through a range of techniques which the writer has used on past occasions. These techniques include the following.

1 Trained introspection by boys following experimental exposure to television material, this process being designed to challenge, and as necessary to modify, our hypothesising about the mechanics of reaction to specific kinds of violence on television.

2 Controlled studies, within an experimental design, of changes and developments in boys' mental content following exposure to selected forms of television violence.

3 Fairly complex further analyses of the present body of information, principally to isolate and identify those programme characteristics that have been more potent/less potent in producing changes in the behaviour of boys.

Notes

[1] 'Type' 1 = TV violence generally.

[2] See the qualification, within item 1 of page 441, about the examples given. This qualification applies equally to the examples given below item 2.

APPENDIX TO CHAPTER 13

Table A1	Principal numerical results of challenging 25 sub-hypotheses of hypothesis 1.
Table A2	Principal numerical results of challenging 25 sub-hypotheses of hypothesis 4 (no additional ceiling on total score).*
Table A3	Principal numerical results of challenging 25 sub-hypotheses of hypothesis 4, with additional final ceiling of 70 on total score.*

*See details of the scoring system as set out in chapter 6.

Table 13.A1
Summary of findings for various sub-hypotheses of hypothesis 1
(see summary of this table in table 13.1)

Sub-hypotheses of hypothesis 1, relating DV1 and:	Direction of hypothesis	Means for Qualifiers (Q), Controls (C) and Modified Controls (MC)			Differences between Q and MC means		Significance of difference	
		M_Q	M_C	M_{MC}	$M_Q - M_{MC}$	As % of M_{MC}	CR	P*
IV2†	F	57.08	46.48	48.57	8.51	17.52	2.73	.003
	R	2171.11	1960.48	2043.56	127.55	6.24	2.56	.005
IV3	F	56.64	46.93	51.47	5.17	10.04	1.49	.068
	R	865.85	775.41	798.30	67.55	8.56	2.95	.002
IV4	F	58.05	45.49	51.46	6.59	12.81	1.82	.034
	R	677.96	599.99	621.83	56.13	9.04	3.53	<.001
IV5	F	55.96	47.60	51.67	4.29	8.30	1.33	.092
	R	1035.25	944.60	977.71	57.54	5.89	2.56	.005
IV6	F	57.10	46.45	51.35	5.75	11.20	1.78	.038
	R	2005.30	1799.60	1867.57	137.73	7.37	2.76	.003
IV7	F	57.39	46.18	50.32	7.07	14.05	2.23	.013
	R	921.91	832.00	867.64	54.27	6.25	2.27	.012
IV8	F	57.01	46.55	49.85	7.16	14.36	2.26	.012
	R	2369.33	2155.62	2258.62	110.71	4.90	2.06	.020
IV9	F	57.45	46.10	48.67	8.78	18.04	2.80	.003
	R	1049.70	952.79	980.55	69.15	7.05	3.18	<.001
IV10	F	56.83	46.71	50.51	6.32	12.51	1.96	.025
	R	669.29	608.54	609.97	56.32	9.23	4.06	<.001
IV11	F	57.04	46.53	52.53	4.51	8.59	1.34	.090
	R	2174.65	1963.29	2054.05	120.60	5.87	2.28	.011
IV12	F	57.93	45.61	49.60	8.33	16.79	2.66	.004
	R	1236.88	1098.61	1144.76	92.12	8.05	3.09	.001
IV13	F	56.70	46.84	50.10	6.60	13.17	2.08	.019
	R	1194.86	1081.67	1110.00	84.86	7.65	3.03	.001
IV14	F	57.79	45.76	49.23	8.56	17.39	2.67	.004
	R	948.87	856.73	890.65	58.22	6.54	2.60	.005
IV15	F	54.62	48.97	51.79	2.83	5.46	0.88	.189
	R	65.77	61.14	62.39	3.38	5.42	1.80	.036
IV16	F	55.14	48.52	48.09	7.05	14.66	2.37	.009
	R	98.19	91.43	92.13	6.06	6.58	3.77	<.001
IV17	F	54.00	43.74	48.48	5.52	11.39	1.47	.071
	R	8.98	8.52	8.63	0.35	4.06	2.58	.005
IV18	F	56.22	47.24	50.19	6.03	12.01	1.89	.029
	R	94.94	85.40	89.43	5.51	6.16	2.30	.011
IV19	F	55.35	48.11	49.65	5.70	11.48	1.86	.031
	R	61.68	58.39	59.32	2.36	3.98	1.82	.034
IV20	F	56.18	47.19	49.88	6.30	12.63	2.08	.019
	R	108.34	100.10	100.92	7.42	7.35	4.18	<.001
IV21	F	54.85	48.76	51.61	3.24	6.28	1.03	.152
	R	88.29	83.63	85.28	3.01	3.53	1.75	.040
IV22	F	56.36	47.16	49.65	6.71	13.51	2.19	.014
	R	88.67	77.51	81.63	7.04	8.62	2.45	.007
IV23	F	56.55	49.28	52.24	4.31	8.25	1.31	.095
	R	12.38	10.91	11.19	1.19	10.63	2.82	.002
IV24	F	55.54	48.01	54.55	0.99	1.81	0.29	.386
	R	55.09	47.42	48.94	6.15	12.57	3.25	<.001
IV25	F	56.96	46.63	51.01	5.95	11.66	1.87	.031
	R	240.51	219.14	225.68	14.83	6.57	2.45	.007
IV26	F	57.14	46.41	50.40	6.74	13.37	2.08	.019
	R	194.78	175.80	182.10	12.68	6.96	2.60	.005

For note to table see page 429

Table 13.A2
Summary of findings for various sub-hypotheses of hypothesis 4
(see summary of this table in table 13.1)

Sub-hypotheses of hypothesis 4, relating DV4 and:	Direction of hypothesis	Means for Qualifiers (Q), Controls (C) and Modified Controls (MC)			Differences between Q and MC means		Significance of difference	
		M_Q	M_C	M_{MC}	$M_Q - M_{MC}$	As % of M_{MC}	CR	P*
IV2†	F	7.56	4.67	4.55	3.01	66.15	2.52	.006
	R	2090.48	2046.12	2089.58	0.90	0.04	0.02	.492
IV3	F	7.34	4.89	5.19	2.15	41.43	1.74	.041
	R	828.67	814.39	838.56	−9.89	−1.18	−0.42	.337
IV4	F	7.78	4.43	5.87	1.91	32.54	1.18	.119
	R	651.28	628.96	652.41	−1.13	−0.17	−0.07	.472
IV5	F	7.22	5.00	5.22	2.00	38.31	1.68	.047
	R	992.81	988.14	1006.60	−13.79	−1.37	−0.57	.284
IV6	F	7.55	4.67	5.17	2.38	46.03	1.99	.023
	R	1916.69	1891.75	1915.73	0.96	0.05	0.02	.492
IV7	F	7.37	4.85	5.81	1.56	26.85	1.18	.119
	R	883.05	872.39	885.37	−2.32	−0.26	−0.09	.464
IV8	F	7.58	4.64	4.65	2.93	63.01	2.53	.006
	R	2268.02	2259.34	2250.88	17.14	0.76	0.33	.371
IV9	F	7.43	4.79	4.84	2.59	53.51	2.26	.012
	R	1007.04	996.99	1007.68	−0.64	−0.06	−0.03	.488
IV10	F	7.74	4.48	4.92	2.82	57.32	2.31	.010
	R	652.54	624.80	633.87	18.67	2.95	1.32	.093
IV11	F	7.55	4.67	4.84	2.71	55.99	2.34	.010
	R	2081.90	2059.45	2105.14	−23.23	−1.10	−0.42	.337
IV12	F	7.77	4.45	5.67	2.10	37.04	1.32	.093
	R	1193.18	1146.87	1169.22	23.96	2.05	0.80	.212
IV13	F	7.50	4.71	4.41	3.09	70.07	2.72	.003
	R	1141.71	1136.16	1134.41	7.30	0.64	0.25	.401
IV14	F	7.65	4.57	5.12	2.53	49.41	1.96	.025
	R	917.13	891.15	909.93	7.20	0.79	0.32	.375
IV15	F	6.72	5.51	4.83	1.89	39.13	1.44	.075
	R	61.62	65.07	60.53	1.09	1.80	0.53	.298
IV16	F	6.56	5.67	5.55	1.01	18.20	0.83	.203
	R	92.14	97.16	92.43	−0.29	−0.31	−0.15	.443
IV17	F	6.28	5.71	5.79	0.49	8.46	0.38	.352
	R	8.56	8.93	8.62	−0.06	−0.70	−0.39	.348
IV18	F	7.66	4.53	4.27	3.38	79.16	3.02	.001
	R	90.40	90.04	87.11	3.29	3.78	1.31	.095
IV19	F	6.74	5.47	4.81	1.93	40.12	1.77	.038
	R	61.03	59.20	60.64	0.39	0.64	0.28	.389
IV20	F	6.90	5.29	5.65	1.25	22.12	1.01	.156
	R	102.70	105.60	102.64	0.06	0.06	0.03	.488
IV21	F	6.40	5.83	5.82	0.57	9.79	0.48	.316
	R	84.63	87.14	86.30	−1.67	−1.94	−0.94	.174
IV22	F	7.15	5.07	4.42	2.73	61.76	2.45	.007
	R	84.80	81.70	81.24	3.56	4.38	1.24	.108
IV23	F	6.75	5.77	6.91	−0.16	−2.32	−0.11	.456
	R	11.94	11.40	11.10	0.83	7.48	1.92	.027
IV24	F	7.39	4.83	5.47	1.92	35.10	1.66	.049
	R	55.39	47.74	51.38	4.01	7.80	2.05	.020
IV25	F	7.40	4.83	4.72	2.68	56.78	2.29	.011
	R	229.29	230.45	228.29	1.00	0.44	0.16	.436
IV26	F	7.47	4.75	5.28	2.19	41.48	1.82	.034
	R	187.05	183.92	188.27	−1.23	0.65	−0.24	.405

For note to table see page 429

Table 13.A3
Summary of findings for various sub-hypotheses of hypothesis 4, with ceiling of 70 on total score for any boy
(see summary of this table in table 13.1)

Sub-hypotheses of hypothesis 4 (70), relating DV4 (7) and:	Direction of hypothesis	Means for Qualifiers (Q), Controls (C) and Modified Controls (MC)			Differences between Q and MC means		Significance of difference	
		M_Q	M_C	M_{MC}	$M_Q - M_{MC}$	As % of M_{MC}	CR	P*
IV2	F	5.83	4.14	4.00	1.83	45.75	2.75	.003
	R	2090.48	2046.12	2089.58	0.90	0.04	0.02	.492
IV3	F	5.61	4.36	4.53	1.08	23.84	1.59	.056
	R	828.67	814.39	838.56	−9.89	−1.18	−0.42	.337
IV4	F	6.19	3.79	4.61	1.57	34.06	1.96	.025
	R	651.28	628.96	652.41	−1.13	−0.17	−0.07	.472
IV5	F	5.53	4.45	4.65	0.88	18.92	1.28	.100
	R	992.81	988.14	1006.60	−13.79	−1.37	−0.57	.284
IV6	F	5.83	4.15	4.69	1.14	24.31	1.55	.061
	R	1916.69	1891.75	1915.73	0.96	0.05	0.02	.492
IV7	F	5.68	4.30	5.09	0.58	11.39	0.72	.236
	R	883.05	872.39	885.37	−2.32	−0.26	0.09	.464
IV8	F**							
	R	2268.02	2259.34	2250.88	17.14	0.76	0.33	.371
IV9	F	5.88	4.09	4.26	1.62	38.03	2.38	.009
	R	1007.04	996.99	1007.68	−0.64	−0.06	−0.03	.488
IV10	F	5.98	3.99	4.28	1.70	39.72	2.46	.007
	R	652.54	624.80	633.87	18.67	2.95	1.32	.093
IV11	F	5.83	4.15	4.40	1.43	32.50	2.10	.018
	R	2081.90	2059.45	2105.14	−23.23	−1.10	−0.42	.337
IV12	F	6.04	3.93	4.64	1.40	30.17	1.78	.038
	R	1193.18	1146.87	1169.22	23.96	2.05	0.80	.212
IV13	F	5.78	4.19	4.03	1.75	43.42	2.69	.004
	R	1141.71	1136.16	1134.41	7.30	0.64	0.25	.401
IV14	F	5.88	4.09	4.45	1.43	32.13	2.04	.021
	R	917.13	891.15	909.93	7.21	0.79	0.32	.375
IV15	F	5.59	4.40	3.64	1.95	53.57	3.07	.001
	R	61.62	65.07	60.53	1.09	1.80	0.53	.298
IV16	F	5.05	4.93	4.67	0.38	8.14	0.58	.281
	R	92.14	97.16	92.43	−0.29	−0.31	−0.15	.443
IV17	F	5.09	4.71	4.80	0.29	6.04	0.35	.363
	R	8.56	8.93	8.62	−0.06	−0.70	−0.39	.348
IV18	F	5.99	3.96	3.83	2.17	56.66	3.39	.001
	R	90.40	90.04	87.11	3.29	3.78	1.31	.095
IV19	F	5.29	4.68	4.28	1.01	23.60	1.61	.054
	R	61.03	59.20	60.64	0.39	0.64	0.28	.390
IV20	F	5.43	4.52	4.74	0.69	14.56	0.98	.164
	R	102.70	105.60	102.64	0.06	0.06	0.03	.488
IV21	F	5.09	4.89	4.87	0.22	4.52	0.33	.371
	R	84.63	87.14	86.30	−1.67	−1.94	0.94	.174
IV22	F	5.68	4.30	3.80	1.88	49.47	3.04	.001
	R	84.80	81.70	81.24	3.56	4.38	1.24	.108
IV23	F	5.21	4.87	5.50	−0.29	−5.27	−0.39	.348
	R	11.94	11.40	11.10	0.83	7.48	1.92	.027
IV24	F	6.12	3.86	4.46	1.66	37.22	2.38	.009
	R	55.39	47.74	51.38	4.01	7.80	2.05	.020
IV25	F	5.67	4.31	4.28	1.39	32.48	2.01	.022
	R	229.29	230.45	228.29	1.00	0.44	0.16	.436
IV26	F	5.79	4.19	4.66	1.13	24.25	1.61	.054
	R	187.05	183.92	188.27	−1.23	−0.65	−0.24	.405

For note to table see page 429

NOTES TO TABLES 13.A1, 2 and 3

*P based on one-tail extractions from probability tables.

†See pages 414-5 of this chapter for identity of these independent variables.

**Figures not supplied by computing agency.

CHAPTER 14

THE TENABILITY OF HYPOTHESES ABOUT THE EFFECTS OF EXPOSURE TO TELEVISION VIOLENCE UPON FOUR SPECIFIC FORMS OF BEHAVIOUR: VIOLENCE IN THE COMPANY OF OTHER BOYS; VIOLENCE IN THE FORM OF ANNOYING, IRRITATING, ARGUMENTATIVE BEHAVIOUR; VERBAL VIOLENCE; VIOLENCE IN SPORT OR PLAY (HYPOTHESES 5-8)

Contents

14 THE TENABILITY OF HYPOTHESES ABOUT THE EFFECTS OF EXPOSURE TO TELEVISION VIOLENCE UPON FOUR SPECIFIC FORMS OF BEHAVIOUR: VIOLENCE IN THE COMPANY OF OTHER BOYS; VIOLENCE IN THE FORM OF ANNOYING, IRRITATING, ARGUMENTATIVE BEHAVIOUR; VERBAL VIOLENCE; VIOLENCE IN SPORT OR PLAY (HYPOTHESES 5-8)

THE NATURE OF THE HYPOTHESES

Chapters 12 and 13 dealt with the investigation of four principal hypotheses, each concerned with the effects of television violence upon violent behaviour by boys. However, the enquiry dealt also with four additional behavioural hypotheses. These took the following forms.

Hypothesis 5	High exposure to television violence increases the degree to which boys are violent in the company of other boys.
Hypothesis 6	High exposure to television violence increases the degree to which boys engage in behaviour in the form of being irritating, argumentative, annoying to others.
Hypothesis 7	High exposure to television violence increases the degree to which boys engage in aggressive behaviour in sport or play.
Hypothesis 8	High exposure to television violence increases the degree to which boys engage in bad language or swearing.

An investigation was also made of a number of sub-hypotheses of each of the above four, on the following pattern:

(a) The degree to which boys are violent in the company of other boys is increased by high exposure to:

- television programmes in which the violence is presented in the context of racial or minority strife (IV10);
- comics or comic books (IV28);

- violent films (IV29);
  newspapers (IV30).

- violent films (IV29);
- newspapers (IV30).

(b) The degree to which boys are irritating, argumentative, or annoying to others is increased by high exposure to:

- comics or comic books (IV28);
- violent films (IV29);
- newspapers (IV30).

(c) The degree to which boys are aggressive in sport or play is increased by high exposure to:

- Westerns (IV22);
- sporting programmes which feature violence by competitors or spectators (i.e. Sportsview, Grandstand, Saturday Sportstime, but excluding wrestling and boxing) (IV23);
- programmes presenting wrestling or boxing (IV24);
- comics or comic books (IV28);
- violent films (IV29);
- newspapers (IV30).

(d) The degree to which boys use bad language/swear is increased by high exposure to:

- programmes where there is violence of the verbal kind (IV12);
- plays or films in which personal relationships are a major theme and which feature verbal abuse (e.g. swearing, quarrelling) or physical violence (IV18);
- comics or comic books (IV28);
- violent films (IV29);
- newspapers (IV30).

The background to these hypotheses is given in chapter 2. IV = independent variable. See full list of dependent and independent variables in table 2.7 of chapter 2.

THE METHODS OF INVESTIGATION USED

The basic research strategies for investigating these causal hypotheses

The methods used for investigating the tenability of hypotheses 5-8 were in principle the same as those used on hypotheses 1-4. Thus for each of hypotheses 5-8, three basic steps were involved and these were applied quite separately in challenging the forward and then the reversed forms of the hypotheses. These three steps, which are detailed fully in chapter 3, were as follows.

(i) First came the development of a composite of predictors of the dependent and independent variables considered jointly.

(ii) This composite was then used to equate the Controls to the Qualifiers in terms of the correlates of the dependent and the independent variables.

(iii) A calculation was then made of the significance of the *residual* difference between the means of the Qualifiers on the one hand and of the Modified Controls on the other.

Let me emphasise that this three-stage process was used separately for the forward and the reversed forms of each hypothesis. Also, it was used separately for the forward and the reversed forms of each of the various sub-hypotheses.

The reader who has skipped straight to this chapter will need to go back to chapter 3 if he is to understand the three steps referred to above.

Measuring the different dependent variables featured in hypotheses 5-8

Hypothesis 5: concerning violence in the company of other boys. Three 'web' items were used as a basis for scoring boys in terms of 'violent behaviour in the company of other boys'. These 'web' items were:

- I have (been violent while I) fooled or larked around with some of my mates (Item 17, chapter 6, page 207);
- My mates and I have picked on or set about other people or boys (Item 19, chapter 6, page 207);
- I have been violent while I was with some of my mates or friends (Item 21, chapter 6, page 207).

For each of these, the usual probing and challenging checks had been made to determine the number of separate acts of violence claimed for the last six months. A ceiling of 30 (acts) was placed upon each of the three in order to eliminate distortion through massive claiming. Scoring was independent of the *level* of violence of the different acts, the only exclusion being of acts that had been rated as 'not violent'. The total for all 3 groups was regarded as an index of amount of violence carried out in the company of 'mates', and it was to be used in a comparative fashion.

Hypothesis 6: concerning involvement in 'irritating, argumentative, annoying behaviour'. Another five of the web items were used as a basis for scoring a boy in terms of 'degree to which he had been irritating, argumentative, annoying to others'. These items were:

- I have made rude finger signs at someone (Item 9, chapter 6, page 207);
- I have teased or taken the mickey out of someone (Item 13, chapter 6, page 207);
- I have irritated or annoyed or played people up (Item 25, chapter 6, page 207);
- I have been rude to people in authority (like police, teachers, parents) (Item 38, chapter 6, page 207);
- I have had an argument with somebody (Item 40, chapter 6, page 207).

For each of these five items, the usual probing and challenging tactics were applied to secure the boy's estimate of frequency of occurrence (at any level of violence) in the last six months. For each of them a ceiling of fifty acts was set. The resulting five scores were then added to yield a total which was regarded as an *index* of 'involvement in irritating, argumentative, annoying behaviour'.

Hypothesis 7: concerning 'aggressive behaviour in sport or play'. Three of the web items were used as a basis for scoring a boy in terms of degree to which he had been engaged in 'aggressive or violent behaviour in sport or play'. These items were:

- I have been violent while doing sport (Item 26, chapter 6, page 207);
- I have played violent or dangerous games (like slaps, knuckles, bulldog) (Item 28, chapter 6, page 207);
- I have been rough or tough or violent in sport or play (Item 53, chapter 6, page 207).

For each of these three items, the usual probing and challenging was applied to secure the boy's estimate of number of occurrences in the last six months. For each of the items a ceiling of 30 was imposed on the highest score possible. The only acts excluded from this count were those rated as 'not violent'. The aggregate from the three items was regarded as an *index* of involvement in 'aggressive or violent behaviour in sport or play'.

Hypothesis 8: concerning 'use of bad language/swearing'. In this case the assessment in terms of the dependent variable was made through only one of the web items, namely:

- I have sworn at somebody or used bad language on them (Item 7, chapter 6, page 207).

A ceiling of 300 was put upon the score available through this item. That score was regarded as an *index* of level of involvement in bad language/swearing.

Cross analyses made with respect to the dependent variables

A range of cross analyses was made to determine differences between population sectors in terms of the four dependent variables of hypotheses 5-8.

FINDINGS

The characteristics of boys with high and low scores on the dependent variables featured in hypotheses 5, 6, 7 and 8

In tables 14.1, 14.2 and 14.3 the results are presented of analysing violence scores by the characteristics of boys.

1 *Characteristics according to level of involvement in violent behaviour in the company of other boys.* Details are given in table 14.1.

The principal indications of table 14.1 are as follows.

(a) There is relatively little relationship between 'being violent in the company of other boys' and:

(i) size of household;
(ii) how long mother has worked since marriage;
(iii) frequency of punishment for violence/destructive behaviour when under four years (statement by parent).

Table 14.1
Distribution of indices of violence 'in the company of boys'

BACKGROUND AND CHARACTERISTICS OF BOYS	Index of violence 'in company of other boys'					
	All	0	1-2	3-7	8-27	28-90
Cases (n)	1559	269	304	340	340	306
% across	101%	17%	20%	22%	22%	20%
Father's occupational level	n	%	%	%	%	%
Professional, semi-professional, executive	283	26	25	18	18	14
Highly skilled	364	16	18	25	23	19
Skilled	357	17	18	23	21	21
Moderately skilled	248	11	22	22	28	17
Semi-skilled/unskilled	141	18	12	21	22	27
Age of boy						
12-13 years	623	21	20	24	19	15
14-15 years	584	16	19	20	23	22
16 + years	349	13	19	21	24	23
Type of school last attended						
Secondary modern	379	12	20	25	23	21
Comprehensive	566	16	18	23	23	20
Grammar	330	22	20	20	19	19
Public	183	24	26	17	19	15
Size of household						
2-3	189	13	19	19	25	24
4	457	16	20	23	21	19
5	406	21	21	22	17	19
6	253	17	19	21	26	18
7+	254	17	18	23	23	19
Skin colour						
Coloured	146	25	19	23	17	16
White	1365	16	19	22	22	20
Truancy						
Never	1207	20	21	23	20	17
About once a month	126	6	17	22	24	30
More than once a month	181	8	15	15	30	31
Enjoyed school						
Yes	1222	19	20	22	20	18
No	324	9	17	21	27	25
How long mother has worked since marriage						
Not at all	222	12	21	22	21	25
Up to two years	268	16	16	24	24	19
3-5 years	303	21	18	21	21	18
6-10 years	396	17	19	22	24	18
More than 10	305	18	21	20	20	20
How often punished for violence/destruction when under four years						
Always	240	16	20	20	23	21
Mostly	325	17	16	23	25	20
Hardly ever	284	21	19	22	19	19
Not at all	151	16	18	21	23	23
Never violent when under 4	522	17	23	22	21	17
Spare time job (if still at school)						
Yes	531	12	17	21	25	25
No	870	22	22	22	15	15
Strength of grip						
10-24 kilograms	352	21	20	24	21	14
25-30 kilograms	433	19	23	21	20	16
31-38 kilograms	403	15	19	21	23	22
39-60 kilograms	353	14	15	21	24	26

(b) There is a substantial relationship between 'being violent in the company of other boys' and:

 (i) occupational level of boy's father (a negative relationship);
 (ii) frequency of truancy (a positive relationship);
 (iii) boy's claim that he enjoyed school (a negative relationship);
 (iv) having a spare-time job while still at school (a positive relationship).

2 *Characteristics, according to level of involvement in irritating, annoying, argumentative behaviour* Details are presented in table 14.2.

The principal indications of table 14.2 are as follows:

(a) There is relatively little relationship between 'irritating, annoying, argumentative behaviour' and:

 (i) how long mother has worked since her marriage;
 (ii) frequency of punishment for violent/destructive behaviour when under four years (statement by parent);

(b) There is a substantial relationship between being 'irritating, annoying, argumentative' and:

 (i) age of boy (a positive relationship);
 (ii) skin colour of boy (white boys are more 'irritating, etc.' than coloured boys);
 (iii) sweet stealing (sweet stealers are more 'irritating, etc.' than non sweet stealers);
 (iv) truancy (a positive relationship);
 (v) spare time job while still at school (if yes, more behaviour of the 'irritating, etc.' kind);
 (vi) strength of grip (a positive relationship);
 (vii) occupational level of boy's father;
 (viii) size of household.

3 *Characteristics according to level of involvement in aggressive behaviour in sport or play.* Details are presented in table 14.3.

The principal indications of table 14.3 are as follows.

Violent behaviour in sport or play has a large degree of association with 'sweet stealing' and a moderate one with skin colour (whites are more aggressive in sport or play). Apart from these two trends, violence in sport or play is very evenly spread across the society of London boys.

4 *Characteristics according to level of involvement in swearing and bad language.* Details are presented in table 14.4.

The principal indications of table 14.4 are as follows.

(a) There is little or no relationship between 'use of swearing/bad language' and:

 (i) occupational level of fathers of boys;
 (ii) how long mother has worked (if at all);
 (iii) frequency of being punished for violent/destructive behaviour when under four years (statement by parent).

Table 14.2
Characteristics of boys, according to level of involvement in irritating, annoying, argumentative behaviour

BACKGROUND AND CHARACTERISTICS OF BOYS	No. of cases	Score for being irritating, argumentative, annoying 0-10	11-30	31-64	65-120	121-250
		297	329	321	376	286
	n	%	%	%	%	%
Father's occupational level						
Professional/semi-professional, executive	283	17	21	24	19	19
Highly skilled	364	15	20	23	23	20
Skilled	357	19	22	21	23	15
Moderately skilled	248	23	22	19	21	16
Semi-skilled/unskilled	141	26	24	19	15	16
Age of boy						
12-13 years	623	26	27	20	16	11
14-15 years	584	17	18	19	24	21
16-18 years	349	9	17	23	24	27
Type of school						
Secondary modern	379	26	23	17	19	15
Comprehensive	566	19	21	21	24	15
Grammar	330	11	18	23	22	27
Public	183	19	23	24	16	19
Size of household						
2-3 people	189	18	17	19	24	22
4 people	457	17	21	17	23	21
5 people	406	18	22	23	20	16
6 people	253	21	21	20	20	17
7+ people	254	22	22	26	16	15
Skin colour						
Coloured	146	26	27	23	18	5
White	1365	18	21	20	21	19
Ever stolen sweets						
Yes	686	12	19	22	23	25
No	870	25	23	20	19	13
Truancy						
Never	1207	21	23	20	20	16
Once a month	126	13	13	26	24	24
More than once a month	181	14	17	20	22	28
Enjoyed school						
Yes	1222	20	21	21	22	16
No	324	15	20	21	19	26
How long has mother worked since her marriage						
Not at all	222	18	17	23	24	18
Up to 2 years	268	18	19	22	21	20
3-5 years	303	23	22	16	22	17
6-10 years	396	19	20	22	21	17
Over 10 years	305	17	23	19	20	21
How often punished for violence/destruction when under four years						
Always	240	19	23	22	18	19
Mostly	325	18	21	19	22	20
Hardly ever	284	20	18	25	19	18
Not at all	151	23	22	16	25	14
Never violent	522	18	22	20	21	18
Had spare time job while still at school						
Yes	531	13	21	19	25	22
No	870	24	23	21	17	15
Strength of grip						
10-24 kilograms	352	29	25	19	18	8
25-30 kilograms	433	23	24	20	19	15
31-38 kilograms	403	16	17	25	21	22
39-60 kilograms	353	9	18	19	26	28

Table 14.3
Characteristics of boys related to amount of aggressive behaviour in sport or play

BACKGROUND AND CHARACTERISTICS OF BOYS	No. of cases	Score for aggressive behaviour in sport or play				
		0	1-4	5-11	12-30	31-90
		250	323	318	355	313
	n	%	%	%	%	%
Father's occupational level						
Professional/semi-professional, executive	283	18	23	18	21	20
Highly skilled	364	17	20	19	23	21
Skilled	357	15	21	20	22	22
Moderately skilled	248	15	20	22	25	18
Semi-skilled/unskilled	141	14	21	23	24	18
Age of boy						
12-13 years	623	13	23	22	24	17
14-15 years	584	13	19	21	25	22
16-18 years	349	25	20	16	17	22
Type of school						
Secondary modern	379	15	22	21	24	18
Comprehensive	566	14	22	21	21	21
Grammar	330	19	17	19	24	22
Public	183	17	21	22	21	19
Size of household						
2-3	189	18	21	18	25	18
4	457	18	18	21	23	20
5	406	15	22	22	22	20
6	253	14	23	16	25	22
7+	254	15	22	22	21	20
Skin colour						
Coloured	146	15	25	26	21	13
White	1365	16	20	20	23	21
Ever stolen sweets						
Yes	686	11	20	18	25	26
No	870	20	21	22	21	16
Truancy						
Never	1207	16	22	21	22	19
Once a month	126	13	22	18	24	23
More than once a month	181	17	14	20	29	19
Enjoyed school						
Yes	1222	17	21	20	23	19
No	324	13	20	21	21	25
How long has mother worked since marriage						
Not at all	222	13	24	19	22	22
Up to 2 years	268	14	19	21	23	22
3-5 years	303	17	22	19	21	22
6-10 years	396	18	21	20	26	16
Over 10 years	305	15	20	21	22	21
How often punished for violence/destruction when under four years						
Always	240	15	19	20	25	21
Mostly	325	13	22	21	23	21
Hardly ever	284	19	17	16	25	23
Not at all	151	14	21	25	25	15
Never violent	522	17	22	21	20	20
Had spare time job while still at school						
Yes	531	12	19	20	26	23
No	870	17	22	21	23	18
Strength of grip						
10-24 kilograms	352	15	23	22	24	17
25-30 kilograms	433	15	22	20	24	18
30-38 kilograms	403	16	19	22	21	22
39-60 kilograms	353	18	19	18	22	23

Table 14.4
Characteristics of boys analysed by use of swearing and bad language

BACKGROUND AND CHARACTERISTICS OF BOYS	No. of cases	Amount of bad language/swearing				
		0-1	2-8	9-30	31-190	191-300
		296	323	343	325	272
	n	%	%	%	%	%
Father's occupational level						
Professional/semi-professional, executive	283	17	24	23	21	16
Highly skilled	364	19	19	20	23	18
Skilled	357	18	20	24	20	18
Moderately skilled	248	22	19	23	20	16
Semi-skilled/unskilled	141	21	23	20	19	17
Age of boy						
12-13 years	623	26	26	23	16	9
14-15 years	584	15	19	22	23	21
16-18 years	349	13	13	20	27	27
Type of school						
Secondary modern	379	25	23	18	17	17
Comprehensive	566	18	19	23	24	16
Grammar	330	17	18	24	20	21
Public	183	16	21	26	22	14
Size of household						
2-3	189	14	17	23	25	20
4	457	19	18	23	24	17
5	406	18	23	24	18	17
6	253	21	22	18	19	21
7+	254	24	22	20	20	15
Skin colour						
Coloured	146	25	23	29	18	5
White	1365	19	21	21	21	19
Ever stolen sweets						
Yes	686	10	18	24	23	25
No	870	26	23	21	19	11
Truancy						
Never	1207	21	23	23	21	13
Once a month	126	15	17	20	17	32
More than once a month	181	11	12	18	24	35
Enjoyed school						
Yes	1222	20	22	23	20	16
No	324	16	17	20	24	24
How long has mother worked since marriage						
Not at all	222	17	21	18	19	25
Up to 2 years	268	21	18	21	21	18
3-5 years	303	21	25	21	18	15
6-10 years	396	18	22	24	20	15
Over 10 years	305	16	16	25	25	18
How often punished for violence/destruction when under four years						
Always	240	20	19	21	23	17
Mostly	325	14	19	27	22	17
Hardly ever	284	21	18	21	23	18
Not at all	151	17	23	23	17	21
Never violent	522	21	24	20	19	17
Had spare time job while at school						
Yes	531	15	17	24	24	20
No	870	22	25	22	19	12
Strength of grip						
10-24 kilograms	352	26	29	23	15	7
25-30 kilograms	433	24	21	22	20	13
30-38 kilograms	403	16	19	23	21	21
39-60 kilograms	353	11	13	21	27	28

(b) On the other hand, there is a substantial degree of relationship between 'use of swearing and bad language' and:

(i) age of boy;
(ii) skin colour (white boys 'swear etc.' more than coloured boys);
(iii) sweet stealing (a positive relationship);
(iv) truancy (a positive relationship);
(v) strength of grip (a positive relationship);
(vi) having a spare time job while at school (a positive relationship).

The tenability of hypotheses 5, 6, 7 and 8 and of their sub-hypotheses

The tenability of hypothesis 5 and its sub-hypotheses

In table 14.5 are the results of using the standard hypothesis challenging procedure on *hypothesis 5* and its associated sub-hypotheses.

Table 14.5
Dealing with the tenability of the hypothesis that exposure to television violence increases the degree to which boys commit violence in the company of other boys; the tenability of several sub-hypotheses

Hypothesis and sub-hypothesis investigated	Direction of hypothesis	Means for Qualifiers (Q) Controls (C) and Modified Controls (MC)			Differences between Q and MC means		Significance of difference	
		M_Q	M_C	M_{MC}	M_Q-M_{MC}	As % of M_{MC}	CR	P*
Hypothesis 5 relating DV5 and IV1†	F	13.92	10.02	13.17	0.75	5.69	0.70	.242
	R	614.99	539.60	571.63	43.36	7.59	3.11	.001
A sub-hypothesis of hypothesis 5, relating DV5 and IV10	F	14.06	10.37	13.33	0.73	5.48	0.66	.255
	R	673.54	598.76	628.70	44.84	7.13	3.22	.001
Hypotheses involving the other mass media								
(a) DV5 and IV28	F	13.35	11.07	11.64	1.71	14.69	2.01	.022
	R	8.93	8.23	8.21	0.72	8.77	2.30	.011
(b) DV5 and IV29	F	13.84	10.39	11.44	2.40	20.98	2.72	.003
	R	5.97	4.99	5.39	0.58	10.76	2.62	.004
(c) DV5 and IV30	F	13.05	11.36	12.47	0.58	4.65	0.67	.251
	R	6.12	5.75	5.95	0.17	2.86	0.88	.189

*P is a one-tail extraction from the probability tables.
†DV5 is the dependent variable 'violence in the company of other boys'. For the identity of the different independent variables (IV's), see pages 432-3 and table 2.7, chapter 2.

The principal indications of table 14.5 are set out below. The form in which they are expressed is based on the logic and the systematisation set out in chapters 3 and 10.

The central hypothesis (relating DV5 and IV1). Hypothesis 5 postulated that:

> 'High exposure to television violence increases the degree to which boys are violent in the company of other boys'.

The evidence in table 14.5 (line 1) tends not to give this hypothesis any meaningful support: the 'index of effect' is 'small' (5.69 per cent) and the P-value is .242.

The programme-type sub-hypotheses. A sub-hypothesis of hypothesis 5 postulated that:

> 'High exposure to programmes about racial and minority group violence increases the degree to which boys commit violence in the company of other boys'.

The situation for this sub-hypothesis is closely similar to that for the central hypothesis: the evidence tends not to give it any meaningful support.

The other-media sub-hypotheses. Table 14.5 also presents evidence about the tenability of hypotheses relating increase in 'violence committed by boys in the company of other boys' to exposure to: comics or comic books; violent films; newspapers.

(a) The evidence gives a 'moderate' degree of support to the hypothesis that exposure to comics/comic books (IV28) increases the degree to which boys engage in violent behaviour in the company of other boys: the index of effect is 14.69 per cent and the P-value is .022 (line 5). At the same time, the evidence gives a 'small' degree of support to the hypothesis in its reversed form.

(b) The evidence of table 14.5 gives a 'large' degree of support to the hypothesis that exposure to violent films (IV29) increases the degree to which boys are violent in the company of other boys: the index of effect is 20.98 per cent and the P-value is .003. At the same time the evidence gives a 'moderate' degree of support to the hypothesis in its reversed form.

(c) On the other hand, the evidence tends not to give meaningful support to the hypothesis that exposure to newspapers increases boys' involvement in violence in the company of other boys: the index of effect is 'small' and the P-value is .251.

To sum up about the other 'mass media' hypotheses: (i) the evidence gives no meaningful support to the hypothesis featuring newspapers; (ii) the evidence gives support to the hypotheses featuring comics and violent films but we cannot rule out the possibility that this support is in part a reflection of a reverse process being in operation.

The tenability of hypothesis 6 and its sub-hypotheses

In table 14.6 are the results of using the standard hypothesis challenging procedure on hypothesis 6 and its associated sub-hypotheses.

The principal indications of table 14.6 are set out below. The form in which they have been expressed is based on the logic and the systematisation set out in chapters 3 and 10.

The central hypothesis (relating DV6 and IV1). Hypothesis 6 postulated that:

> 'High exposure to television violence increases the degree to which boys engage in irritating, annoying, argumentative behaviour'.

The evidence in table 14.6 gives no meaningful support to this hypothesis: the index of effect is 3.33 per cent and the P-value is .271 (see line 1 of table 14.6).

Table 14.6

Dealing with the tenability of the hypothesis that exposure to television violence increases the degree to which boys engage in irritating, annoying, argumentative behaviour; the tenability of several sub-hypotheses

Hypothesis and sub-hypothesis investigated	Direction of hypothesis	Means for Qualifiers (Q), Controls (C) and Modified Controls (MC)			Differences between Q and MC means		Significance of difference	
		M_Q	M_C	M_{MC}	M_Q-M_{MC}	As % of M_{MC}	CR	P*
Hypothesis 6, relating DV6 and IV1†	F	72.02	56.55	69.70	2.32	3.33	0.61	.271
	R	618.73	538.95	576.41	42.32	7.34	2.92	.002
Hypotheses involving the other mass media								
(a) DV6 and IV28	F	60.12	68.45	62.45	−2.33	−3.73	−0.69	.245
	R	8.09	9.09	8.46	−0.37	−4.37	−1.12	.131
(b) DV6 and IV29	F	73.51	53.89	59.83	13.68	22.86	4.10	<.001
	R	6.08	4.93	5.58	0.50	8.96	2.09	.018
(c) DV6 and IV30	F	67.52	60.95	67.83	−0.31	−0.46	−0.09	.464
	R	6.10	5.78	5.89	0.21	3.57	1.11	.134

*P is a one-tail extraction from the probability tables.

†DV6 is the dependent variable 'extent of irritating, annoying, argumentative behaviour. For the identity of the different independent variables (IVs), see pages 432-3 and table 2.7, chapter 2.

Table 14.7

The tenability of the hypothesis that exposure to television violence increases the degree to which boys engage in violence in the form of aggressive behaviour in sport or play; the tenability of several sub-hypotheses of hypothesis 7

Hypotheses investigated	Direction of hypothesis	Means for Qualifiers (Q), Controls (C) and Modified Controls (MC)			Differences between Q and MC means		Significance of difference	
		M_Q	M_C	M_{MC}	M_Q-M_{MC}	As % of M_{MC}	CR	P*
Hypothesis 7 relating DV7 and IV1†	F	18.92	14.74	16.44	2.48	15.08	1.80	.036
	R	604.65	553.60	559.33	45.32	8.10	3.53	<.001
Sub-hypotheses of hypothesis 7 relating								
(a) DV7 and IV22	F	18.43	15.22	16.35	2.08	12.72	1.93	.027
	R	87.65	78.74	79.30	8.35	10.53	3.06	.001
(b) DV7 and IV23	F	20.21	15.06	15.59	4.62	29.63	3.87	<.001
	R	12.86	10.47	11.53	1.33	11.54	2.75	.003
(c) DV7 and IV24	F	18.49	15.16	16.27	2.22	13.65	1.99	.023
	R	55.77	46.91	48.39	7.38	15.25	3.84	<.001
Hypotheses involving the other mass media								
(a) DV7 and IV28	F	17.56	16.09	16.42	1.14	6.94	1.04	.149
	R	9.10	8.10	8.08	1.02	12.62	3.27	<.001
(b) DV7 and IV29	F	18.80	14.61	15.75	3.05	19.37	2.65	.004
	R	5.97	5.05	5.43	0.54	9.94	2.43	.008
(c) DV7 and IV30	F	18.45	15.16	16.16	2.29	14.17	2.10	.018
	R	6.29	5.60	5.97	0.32	5.36	1.64	.051

*P is a one-tail extraction from the probability tables.

†The dependent variable (DV7) is the degree to which boys engage in aggressive behaviour in sport or play. The various independent variables (IVs) are identified on pages 432-3 and table 2.7, chapter 2.

The other-media sub-hypotheses. The evidence gives no support to the hypotheses that involvement in irritating, annoying, argumentative behaviour is increased by (a) high exposure to comics or comic books; (b) high exposure to newspapers.

On the other hand, the evidence in table 14.6 gives a 'large' degree of support to the hypothesis that such behaviour is increased by exposure to violent films: the index of effect is 22.86 per cent and the P-value is smaller than .001. Moreover the index of effect for the reverse form of the hypothesis is 'small'.

On balance, the evidence in table 14.6 gives support to the hypothesis featuring violent films but not to the hypotheses featuring (a) comics/comic books and (b) newspapers.

The tenability of hypothesis 7 and its sub-hypotheses

In table 14.7 are the results of using the standard hypothesis challenging procedure on hypothesis 7 and its associated sub-hypotheses.

The principal indications of table 14.7 are set out below. The form in which they are expressed is based on the logic and the systematisation presented in chapters 3 and 10.

The central hypothesis (relating DV7 and IV1). Hypothesis 7 postulated that:

> 'High exposure to television violence increases the degree to which boys engage in violence in the form of aggressive behaviour in sport or play'.

The evidence in table 14.7 gives a 'fairly large' degree of support to this hypothesis: the index of effect is 15.08 per cent and the P-value is .036.

At the same time, the reversed form of the hypothesis gets a 'small' degree of support from the evidence, so that the possibility exists that the support given to the forward form of the hypothesis is to some extent a reflection simply of a reverse process being in operation. Nonetheless, we must remember that this is but one of the possible implications of the support given to the reverse hypothesis. [1]

The programme-type sub-hypotheses. Several of the sub-hypotheses of hypothesis 7 linked 'being violent in the form of aggressive sport or play' to exposure to different types of programmes, namely:

(a) Westerns (IV22);

(b) sporting programmes (i.e. Sportsview, Grandstand, Saturday Sportstime) (IV23);

(c) programmes presenting boxing/wrestling (IV24).

The evidence in table 14.7 gives a 'moderate' degree of support to the hypotheses which feature Westerns and programmes about boxing/wrestling, and a 'large' degree of support to that featuring sporting programmes.

In each of these three cases, the reverse form of the hypothesis is also supported by the evidence, so that here too we must conclude that the support given by the evidence to the forward form of the hypothesis may be only a reflection of a reverse process being in operation. On balance, the strongest of the three hypotheses is that which features sporting programmes (i.e. Sportsview, Grandstand, Saturday Sportstime).

Other-media sub-hypotheses. The evidence of table 14.7 gives a 'fairly large' degree of support to the hypothesis that 'involvement in violence in the form of aggressive sport or play' is increased by exposure to violent films (index of effect is 19.37 per cent and the P-value is .004) and a 'moderate' degree of support to the hypothesis that this form of violence is increased by exposure to newspapers (index of effect is 14.17 per cent and the P-value is .018). In each case, the reversed form of the hypothesis is also supported by the evidence, though not to the same degree as was the forward form.

The sub-hypothesis featuring comics or comic books gets only 'small' support (index of effect is 6.94 per cent) of an 'uncertain' kind (P-value is .150). In addition, the reversed form of the hypothesis gets a larger degree of support than does the forward form of the hypothesis. In the circumstances, it would be unwise to regard the evidence as giving much in the way of support to this hypothesis.

The tenability of hypothesis 8 and its sub-hypotheses

In table 14.8 are the results of using the standard hypothesis challenging procedure on hypothesis 8 and its associated sub-hypotheses.

Table 14.8
Dealing with the tenability of the hypothesis that exposure to television violence increases the degree to which boys use bad language/swear; the tenability of several sub-hypotheses of hypothesis 8

Hypothesis and sub-hypotheses investigated	Direction of hypothesis	Means for Qualifiers (Q), Controls (C) and Modified Controls (MC)			Differences between Q and MC means		Significance of difference	
		M_Q	M_C	M_{MC}	M_Q-M_{MC}	As % of M_{MC}	CR	P*
Hypothesis 8, relating DV8 and IV1†	F	86.57	57.85	73.71	12.86	17.45	1.90	.029
	R	627.56	531.12	577.55	50.01	8.66	3.39	<.001
Sub-hypotheses of hypothesis 8 relating								
(a) DV8 and IV12	F	87.81	56.58	69.39	18.42	26.55	2.78	.003
	R	1282.17	1056.92	1176.37	105.80	8.99	3.04	.001
(b) DV8 and IV18	F	87.01	57.11	65.74	21.27	32.36	3.58	<.001
	R	96.61	83.95	89.55	7.06	7.88	2.74	.003
Hypotheses involving the other mass media								
(a) DV8 and IV28	F	72.02	72.39	66.25	5.77	8.71	1.05	.147
	R	8.48	8.70	8.24	0.24	2.91	0.76	.224
(b) DV8 and IV29	F	85.44	57.29	75.75	9.69	12.79	1.13	.149
	R	6.26	4.76	5.39	0.87	16.14	3.29	<.001
(c) DV8 and IV30	F	84.10	59.96	70.81	13.29	18.77	2.19	.014
	R	6.26	5.63	5.84	0.42	7.19	2.12	.017

*P is a one-tail extraction from the probability tables.
†The dependent variable (DV8) is 'degree to which boys use bad language/swear'. The various independent variables (IVs) are identified on pages 432-3 of this chapter and in table 2.7, chapter 2.

The principal indications of table 14.8 are set out below. The form in which they are expressed is based on the logic and the systematisation presented in chapters 3 and 10.

The central hypothesis (relating DV8 and IV1). Hypothesis 8 postulated that:

'High exposure to television violence increases the degree to which boys use bad language or swear'.

This hypothesis gets a 'fairly large' degree of support from the evidence in table 14.8 (the index of effect is 17.45 per cent and the P-value is .029). However the reversed form of the hypothesis gets a 'small' degree of support, so that the possibility exists that the support for the forward hypothesis is in part a reflection of a reverse process being in operation.

The programme-type sub-hypotheses. Two of the sub-hypotheses of hypothesis 8, were that boys' use of bad language and swearing were being increased by exposure to:

(a) programmes where the violence is of a verbal kind (IV12);

(b) plays and films in which personal relations are a major theme and which feature verbal violence (e.g. swearing, quarrelling) or physical violence (IV18).

The evidence in table 14.8 provides a 'large' to 'very large' degree of support to these two sub-hypotheses. In each case the reverse form of the hypothesis is also supported by the evidence, but to a much lesser degree than is the forward hypothesis.

Other-media sub-hypotheses. The evidence in table 14.8 gives a 'small' degree of support to the hypothesis that bad language and swearing are increased by exposure to comics or comic books (index of effect is 8.71 per cent) but this support is of an 'uncertain' kind (P = .147).

Table 14.8 provides a moderate but 'uncertain' degree of support for the hypothesis that exposure to violent films increases the degree to which boys use bad language/swear (the index of effect is 12.79 per cent and the P-value .129). The uncertainty of the support for this hypothesis is further increased by the fact that its reverse form gets a somewhat larger degree of support of a highly significant kind (in the statistical sense). On balance it would be unwise to treat the outcome of this testing operation (as reported in lines 9 and 10 of table 14.8) as warranting confidence in the sub-hypothesis concerned.

There is in the evidence a 'fairly large' degree of support for the hypothesis that high exposure to newspapers increases the degree to which boys use bad language/swear (the index of change is 18.77 per cent and the P-value is .014). The reverse form of this hypothesis also gets a degree of support but of a much smaller kind than went to the forward version (7.19 per cent). On balance, the evidence is supportive of this sub-hypothesis.

Summing up on the investigation of the four hypotheses (5-8)

Hypotheses 7 and 8 each got a 'fairly large' degree of support from the evidence gathered. However, the evidence from the reverse hypothesis tests means that we cannot rule out the possibility that this support is to some extent a reflection of a reverse process being in operation.

The evidence does not give meaningful support to either of hypotheses 5 or 6.

Note

[1] For a listing of these three, see pages 389-90.

CHAPTER 15

THE TENABILITY OF THE HYPOTHESES THAT SEEING PARTICULAR ACTS OF VIOLENCE ON TELEVISION INCREASES: BOYS' PREOCCUPATION WITH SUCH ACTS; BOYS' FEELING OF WILLINGNESS TO COMMIT SUCH ACTS; BOYS' DESIRE TO COMMIT SUCH ACTS (HYPOTHESES 9, 10, 11)

Contents

15 THE TENABILITY OF THE HYPOTHESES THAT SEEING PARTICULAR ACTS OF VIOLENCE ON TELEVISION INCREASES: BOYS' PREOCCUPATION WITH SUCH ACTS; BOYS' FEELING OF WILLINGNESS TO COMMIT SUCH ACTS; BOYS' DESIRE TO COMMIT SUCH ACTS

(HYPOTHESES 9, 10, 11)

THE NATURE OF THE HYPOTHESES

In chapter 13, I dealt with the influence of 25 different categories of programme output upon the behaviour of boys, for example, fictional violence of a realistic kind, violence in the news, science fiction violence, cartoon violence. However, boys and their parents and others of those interviewed in the hypothesis making stage of the enquiry had suggested that boys could be specially influenced by the presentation of particular acts of violence that are shown with some recurrence on television. I refer to acts of the kind: stabbing someone with a knife, kicking someone or putting the boot in, shooting someone, using judo on someone, threatening someone, and so on, as listed in chapter 8 and on page 450 of this chapter.

Against this background, the following hypotheses had been developed.

> *Hypothesis 9* [1]. 'High exposure to television violence increases the degree to which boys think about or are preoccupied with the different sorts of violence that are shown on television.'
>
> *Hypothesis 10*. 'High exposure to television violence increases the degree to which boys would like to commit the kinds of violence shown on television.'
>
> *Hypothesis 11*. 'High exposure to television violence increases the degree to which boys feel willing to commit the kinds of violence they see on television.'

An investigation was also made of a number of sub-hypotheses of those three, on the following pattern:

(a) Preoccupation with acts of violence frequently shown on television is increased by exposure to:

- fictional violence of a realistic kind (IV2) [2] ;

- programmes where the physical or mental consequences of violence are shown in detail (IV9);
- comics/comic books (IV28);
- violent films (IV29);
- newspapers (IV30).

(b) The feeling of willingness to use TV-type violence is increased by exposure to:
- programmes where the violence is performed by basically 'good guy' types who are also rebels or 'odd-men-out' (IV3);
- programmes where the violence is presented as 'fun and games' or like a game or as something to entertain (IV7);
- programmes that show violence as being done in a good cause (IV8);
- programmes where the physical or mental consequences of violence, for the victim, are shown in detail (IV9);
- programmes where the violence is performed by basically 'good guy' types or by heroes who are also tough (i.e. who can endure physical violence and fight on) (IV11);
- programmes where the violence is presented through television news or through newsreel programmes (IV19);
- comics or comic books (IV28);
- violent films (IV29);
- newspapers (IV30).

(c) The feeling that one would like to commit TV-type acts of violence is increased by exposure to:
- comics or comic books (IV28);
- violent films (IV29);
- newspapers (IV30).

The background to these hypotheses and sub-hypotheses is given in chapter 2.

THE METHODS OF INVESTIGATION USED
(being a summary of details presented in chapters 3 and 8)

The basic research strategies for investigating these causal hypotheses

The methods used for investigating the tenability of hypotheses 9-11 were in principle the same as those used on hypotheses 1-4. Thus for each of hypotheses 9-11, three basic steps were involved and these were applied quite separately in challenging the forward and the reversed forms of the hypotheses. These three steps, which are detailed fully in chapter 3, were as follows.

(i) First came the development of a composite of predictors of the dependent and independent variables considered jointly.

(ii) This composite was then used to equate the Controls to the Qualifiers in terms of the correlates of the dependent and the independent variables.

(iii) A calculation was then made of the significance of the *residual* difference between the means of the Qualifiers on the one hand and of the Modified Controls on the other.

Let me emphasise that this three-stage process was used separately for the forward and the reversed forms of each hypothesis. Also, it was used separately for the forward and the reversed forms of each of the various sub-hypotheses.

The reader who has skipped straight to this chapter will need to go back to chapter 3 if he is to understand the three steps referred to above.

The formulation and measurement of the independent variables (see chapter 8 for details)

Overall strategy

In chapter 8, I have presented a full description of the basic characteristics of the three dependent variables and of the methods used to measure them. These details are summarised below.

(a) All the measurements of boys' views and reactions in relation to TV acts of violence were made in relation to 20 separate TV acts identified as such through interviews with members of the viewing public and with boys in the age range 12-17 years.

(b) Boys' reactions to each of these kinds of violence were measured in terms of (i) preoccupation with it; (ii) his views about how often he has felt like committing it himself; (iii) his feeling of willingness to commit it himself.

The twenty TV-type acts

The twenty TV-type acts centrally involved in each of the three measurements were as follows.

1 Stabbing someone with a knife
2 Kicking someone or putting the boot in
3 Shooting someone with a gun
4 Throwing a petrol bomb at someone
5 Being in a gang that is beating someone up
6 Slashing someone or cutting him with a razor
7 Pushing someone out of a window
8 Hitting someone with a piece of wood or a club or iron bar
9 Using a whip on somebody
10 Using a karate chop on somebody
11 Throwing acid in someone's face
12 Trying to throttle or strangle somebody
13 Swearing at someone
14 Hitting someone with your fists
15 Threatening someone
16 Bashing up or fighting with a coloured immigrant

17 Hitting someone with a bottle
18 Using judo on somebody
19 Running someone down with a bike or motor-bike or scooter or car
20 Torturing somebody

Measuring level of preoccupation with the TV acts of violence

For this measure, boys used a slide-type rating procedure (see chapter 8) to indicate how often 'this sort of thing comes into your mind'. The ratings available and the weights given them were as follows.

Never in my whole life	0
Very rarely	1
Rarely	2
Now and then	3
Fairly often	4
Very often	5

Four of the 20 TV acts were deleted from the list of 20 (i.e. numbers 13, 14, 15, 18) as indicating relatively low degrees of violence. For the remaining 16 acts, the frequency ratings given to these were added and divided by the total number of acts so rated (usually 16, but sometimes less). The resulting figure was then multiplied by 10 to give a decimal-free score. This was the score used as an overall index of 'preoccupation'. At the same time, the ratings for each of the 20 acts were coded and punched onto cards so that the distribution of these could be analysed in their own right.

Measuring the degree to which boys feel like committing the TV-type acts of violence

This score was based on the same 16 acts. Here again the boy rated each in terms of how often he had 'felt' like committing it, using the same slide-type rating scale, with the following class of replies available, each being given a weight, as shown below, for the derivation of an overall score.

Never in my whole life	0
Very rarely	1
Rarely	2
Now and then	3
Fairly often	4
Very often	5

Overall score was the sum total of the weights of the chosen replies, divided by the number of the acts so rated. This result was then multiplied by 10 to yield a decimal-free score.

Here, too, the ratings for each of the 20 TV-type acts were coded and card-punched for the derivation of a distribution of reactions for each.

Measuring willingness to commit the listed TV-type acts

Score for willingness to commit the TV-type acts of violence has to be carefully interpreted. It relates to boys' *feelings* of willingness and does not necessarily indicate that they would in fact commit such acts.

Full details of the method used to measure this variable are given in chapter 8 and what follows is simply a summary.

1 For each of the 20 TV-type acts, each boy was asked to consider 10 different circumstances in which he might or might not feel willing to commit the act concerned (e.g. if my life was threatened; if the other person had insulted me).

2 These 10 circumstances had been selected (through preliminary research) from a larger array using Thurstone-type rating procedures and criteria of selection and a panel of 94 boy-raters. The ten circumstances were as follows:
   1 If my life was threatened
   2 If it was in self-defence
   3 If it was necessary for protecting some other person
   4 If the other person was an enemy of my country
   5 If I was very angry with someone
   6 If the person concerned was a boy who had insulted a girl I was going out with
   7 If the other person had insulted me
   8 If I was in a bad mood
   9 If I wanted some fun
   10 If I was just bored

3 Still at this instrument making stage, these ten were subjected to a further rating sequence in which boys and their parents considered each circumstance in relation to each act and made a rating in terms of 'how strong or weak a reason the circumstance indicated was for committing the act concerned'.

   One of the ten circumstances (i.e. if the other person was an enemy of my country') was rejected at this stage because its semi-interquartile range was large and because it did not act as an effective discriminant. This process yielded a set of 20 x 9 median values (less 4 [3]) which were then converted for scoring purposes on the following system. For a given circumstance in relation to a given act, the index of 'willingness' was 10—median score. Thus if 'stabbing someone with a knife' because 'I was bored' received a rating of .01 (as it did) then the boy who said, in the final test, that he was willing to do just that, would be regarded as 'very willing to be violent' and would be given a score of 9.9 for such an admission. All willingness scores were multiplied by 10 to yield decimal free indices.

For all 9 indices in relation to all 20 acts, the willingness indices were as shown in table 8.2 of chapter 8. [4]

If a boy rejected some reason, whatever the TV-type acts concerned, he was given a zero score for that reason or circumstance. His total score was the aggregate of all these weighted indices as indicated by his endorsements and rejections.

The aggregate for each boy was coded and punched onto a card for processing. A second aggregate, based upon the 16 TV-type acts of violence identified for use in scoring pre-occupation, was also calculated and card-punched for use as the dependent variable in hypothesis 11. Finally, a separate 'willingness' score was computed for each of the 20 TV-type acts of violence and card-punched.

Cross analyses made with respect to independent variables

A range of cross-analyses was made to determine differences between population sectors in terms of the dependent variables of hypotheses 9, 10 and 11.

FINDINGS

Findings have been set out under three main headings.

1 The distribution of responses in terms of the three dependent variables.
2 The distribution of responses analysed by the characteristics of boys.
3 The tenability of the different hypotheses.

The first two categories of findings are presented as background to the investigation of the hypotheses and should provide useful information about the attitudinal positions taken by boys in relation to TV-type acts of violence.

The distribution of responses in terms of the dependent variables

Preoccupation with acts of violence (TV-type)

In table 15.1 are presented the distributions, for each of the 10 acts, of boys' preoccupation ratings.

The principal indications of table 15.1 data on preoccupation levels are best seen by direct study of that table. The reader may, however, wish to note the high level of the combined percentages for 'fairly often' and 'very often' with respect to quite serious acts of violence.

The frequency of 'feeling like committing' the TV-type acts

Table 15.1 also presents distributions of frequency ratings in relation to each of the 20 TV-type acts of violence.

Here too, the indications of table 15.1 are mainly at the level of detail which the reader should extract for himself. At the more general level, it is noteworthy that:

1 The percentage in the 'never' column increases in going from the 'preoccupation' to the 'feel like committing' section of table 15.1. Nonetheless there is for most of the acts a large percentage of boys who say they have at some time felt like committing the act concerned.
2 There is a small but noteworthy minority of boys who say they often feel like committing even quite violent acts (of this TV-type).

Feeling of willingness to commit TV-type acts of violence under specified conditions: frequency of endorsement of circumstances

Table 15.2 presents the percentages of boys who said they would feel 'willing' to commit the different TV-type acts under the circumstances specified in the testing procedure.

The principal indications of table 15.2 are as follows:

1 Many boys appear 'unwilling' to use the TV-type of violence even in extreme circumstances, e.g. 'if my life was threatened'. To some extent this may be because the boy does not know how to commit the act concerned, but this finding fits in with another finding of this enquiry, namely that 28 per cent of boys agree that 'It's never OK to use violence or force'.

Table 15.1

Acts of violence: preoccupation and pre-disposition in relation to acts of violence shown on television*

(1565 cases)

	ACTS OF VIOLENCE	How often boy thinks about the act							How often boy feels like committing the act						
		Never in my whole life	Very rarely	Rarely	Now and then	Fairly often	Very often	D.K. or N.I.	Never in my whole life	Very rarely	Rarely	Now and then	Fairly often	Very often	D.K. or N.I.
		%	%	%	%	%	%	%	%	%	%	%	%	%	%
1	Stabbing someone with a knife	20	39	18	17	5	2	–	53	29	8	7	2	1	1
2	Kicking someone or putting the boot in	8	27	20	28	13	4	–	17	31	20	20	7	3	1
3	Shooting someone with a gun	34	27	16	12	7	4	–	54	22	12	8	3	2	1
4	Throwing a petrol bomb at someone	59	22	8	5	3	2	–	75	16	5	2	1	1	1
5	Being in a gang that is beating someone up	36	33	15	10	5	2	–	47	29	11	8	2	2	1
6	Slashing someone or cutting him with a razor	47	30	11	7	3	2	–	63	21	8	4	2	1	1
7	Pushing someone out of a window	53	29	9	6	2	2	–	61	21	10	5	1	1	1
8	Hitting someone with a piece of wood or a club or iron bar	24	32	19	15	6	3	–	32	30	16	14	5	2	1
9	Using a whip on someone	48	30	11	7	3	2	–	58	23	10	6	2	1	1
10	Using a karate chop on somebody	23	24	19	21	10	4	–	28	24	19	17	8	4	1
11	Throwing acid in someone's face	63	24	6	3	2	2	–	78	14	5	1	1	–	1
12	Trying to throttle or strangle someone	34	31	17	11	4	2	–	44	28	13	10	3	1	1
13	Swearing at someone	4	11	10	25	26	24	1	4	11	12	24	24	23	1
14	Hitting someone with your fists	1	11	16	31	23	17	1	2	14	16	32	20	15	1
15	Threatening someone	7	18	21	30	17	8	–	8	22	21	27	14	6	1
16	Bashing up or fighting a coloured immigrant	37	28	15	10	6	4	–	46	26	12	9	4	3	1
17	Hitting someone with a bottle	37	33	15	9	3	2	–	46	27	15	8	2	1	1
18	Using Judo on someone	30	24	17	16	9	5	–	30	24	16	16	9	5	1
19	Running down someone with a bike or motorbike or scooter or car	48	26	12	9	3	2	1	59	21	10	6	2	1	1
20	Torturing someone	42	28	13	9	4	3	1	56	22	9	7	3	2	1

*Totals across may not equal 100 because of rounding process.

– = less than .5%

Table 15.2
Acts of violence: willingness to commit*
(1565 cases)

	ACTS OF VIOLENCE	I WOULD COMMIT THE ACT IF:–									
		My life was threatened	It was in self-defence	It was necessary for protecting some other person	The other person was an enemy of my country	I was very angry with someone	The person concerned was a boy who had insulted a girl I was going out with	The other person had insulted me	I was in a bad mood	I wanted some fun	I was just bored
		%	%	%	%	%	%	%	%	%	%
1	Stabbing someone with a knife	78	76	59	41	5	8	3	2	–	–
2	Kicking someone or putting the boot in	81	91	76	44	36	36	26	11	4	2
3	Shooting someone with a gun	79	80	61	53	5	7	3	2	–	–
4	Throwing a petrol bomb at someone	70	64	51	47	6	7	3	2	1	1
5	Being in a gang that is beating someone up	60	NA	49	35	16	19	12	6	4	3
6	Slashing someone or cutting them with a razor	76	75	56	40	8	11	5	3	–	1
7	Pushing someone out of a window	76	75	56	40	7	8	4	2	–	–
8	Hitting someone with a piece of wood, or a club, or iron bar	85	88	72	49	19	19	12	5	1	1
9	Using a whip on somebody	75	76	60	38	13	15	9	3	2	1
10	Using a karate chop on somebody	84	91	76	50	29	31	22	7	4	2
11	Throwing acid in someone's face	67	61	43	33	4	5	3	1	–	–
12	Trying to throttle or strangle somebody	79	77	57	42	10	12	7	3	–	1
13	Swearing at someone	NA	NA	NA	NA	80	62	75	55	17	14
14	Hitting someone with your fists	84	94	81	51	55	53	48	21	5	4
15	Threatening someone	74	68	67	44	54	52	50	22	7	5
16	Bashing up or fighting with a coloured immigrant	79	85	64	45	23	34	28	8	4	3
17	Hitting somebody with a bottle	81	85	65	44	15	17	11	6	1	1
18	Using Judo on somebody	85	93	77	52	33	37	28	11	6	4
19	Running someone down with a bike or motorbike or scooter or car	73	61	53	40	7	9	5	3	1	1
20	Torturing somebody	63	49	44	38	10	12	8	5	2	1

*Totals across may not equal 100 because of rounding process
– = less than .5%
NA = not applicable

2 There is, for most of the acts, a sharp fall-off in the percentage endorsing any one circumstance as we go from the four most compelling circumstances to the rest of the circumstances listed across the table. This is fairly obviously due to the different levels of pressure in the different circumstances, but it is noteworthy nonetheless. For the lesser levels of violence (in the TV act) that fall-off is in general less marked.

3 Perhaps the most noteworthy feature of table 15.2 is the percentage of boys who say they feel willing to commit quite serious acts of violence for what to many readers will seem to be minor or weak reasons: 26 per cent would feel willing 'to put the boot in' if the other person 'insulted me'; 3 per cent would feel willing to slash someone or cut them with a razor if 'in a bad mood'. Even the small percentages in the 'if I was bored' column do represent a lot of boys.

The reader must of course be careful in interpreting the word 'willing'. The evidence does not necessarily mean that boys who say that they would be 'willing' to do certain things would in fact go out and do them. The evidence means no more than what it says – that the boys so professing themselves had a 'feeling of willingness'. The reader may care to think of this as indicating a certain permissiveness of approach at the 'doing' level.

The distribution of responses analysed by the characteristics of boys

In the following tables, the scores on the 3 dependent variables (as defined in the three hypotheses) have been analysed according to the characteristics of the boys. Table 15.3 de deals with *preoccupation* with TV-type acts of violence, table 15.4 with frequency of *feeling like committing* such acts and table 15.5 with '*feeling willing*' to commit them.

The principal indications of tables 15.3, 15.4 and 15.5 are as follows.

For table 15.3, dealing with preoccupation with TV-type acts of violence

There is relatively little association between preoccupation with TV-type acts of violence and the following variables: occupational level of boy's father; age of the boy; type of school last attended; skin colour of boy; how long mother has worked since marriage; how often the boy was punished for violence/destructive behaviour when under 4 years of age; whether boy had a spare time job (if still at school); strength of grip.

On the other hand, there is moderate to substantial association between 'preoccupation' and: truancy level (positive); whether boy enjoyed school (negative); whether boy has ever stolen sweets (positive).

For table 15.4, dealing with frequency with which boys feel like committing TV-type acts of violence

The principal indications here are the same as for 'preoccupation' scores, as detailed above for table 15.3.

For table 15.5, dealing with the degree to which boys feel 'willing' to commit TV-type acts of violence

There is relatively little association between 'willingness' scores and: age of boy; size of household; skin colour of boy; how long boy's mother has worked since marriage; how often

Table 15.3
Distribution of indices of 'preoccupation with TV violence' according to characteristics of boys

BACKGROUND AND CHARACTERISTICS OF BOYS	Index of preoccupation with TV type violence					
	All	0-3	4-8	9-13	14-19	20-24
	Cases(n)	214	374	365	330	276
	% across	14%	24%	23%	21%	18%
Father's occupational level	n	%	%	%	%	%
Professional, semi-professional, executive	283	11	27	28	21	13
Highly skilled	364	16	23	23	21	17
Skilled	357	12	22	24	21	20
Moderately skilled	248	17	25	20	18	21
Semi-skilled/unskilled	141	15	20	23	26	16
Age of boys						
12-13 years	623	17	23	21	21	18
14-15 years	584	12	25	23	23	16
16+ years	349	11	23	28	19	19
Type of school last attended						
Secondary modern	379	13	23	24	22	18
Comprehensive	566	14	25	21	20	19
Grammar	330	14	25	24	21	15
Public	183	14	24	26	22	14
Size of household						
2-3 persons	189	15	29	23	19	14
4 persons	457	15	20	27	23	15
5 persons	406	12	26	24	20	18
6 persons	253	12	26	21	21	21
7 + persons	254	15	23	19	22	22
Skin colour						
Coloured	146	15	29	20	12	24
White	1365	14	23	24	22	17
Truancy						
Never	1207	15	25	23	21	16
About once a month	126	10	22	24	25	20
More than once a month	181	8	18	24	24	25
Enjoyed school						
Yes	1222	15	24	24	20	16
No	324	9	22	20	25	24
How long has mother worked since marriage						
Not at all	222	13	23	19	24	21
Up to 2 years	268	13	22	24	24	17
3-5 years	303	16	26	26	17	16
6-10 years	396	12	26	26	20	16
More than 10 years	305	15	22	21	24	19
How often punished for violence/destruction when under four years						
Always	240	15	23	23	22	18
Mostly	325	11	23	22	25	18
Hardly ever	284	14	24	23	21	18
Not at all	151	17	26	23	20	15
Never violent when under four years	522	14	25	25	19	17
Spare time job (if still at school)						
Yes	531	11	24	23	24	17
No	870	16	25	23	19	17
Strength of grip						
10-24 kilograms	352	17	24	21	22	16
25-30 kilograms	433	14	24	22	21	19
31-38 kilograms	403	13	24	23	20	20
39-60 kilograms	353	10	24	28	22	15
Ever stolen sweets?						
Yes	686	8	22	24	24	22
No	870	18	26	22	19	15

Table 15.4
Distribution of indices of 'feeling like committing TV type violence', analysed by characteristics of boys

BACKGROUND AND CHARACTERISTICS OF BOYS	Indices of 'feeling like committing TV type violence'					
	All	0-1	2-4	5-9	10-16	17-43
	Cases(n)	249	315	375	354	266
	% across	16%	20%	24%	23%	17%
	n	%	%	%	%	%
Father's occupational level						
Professional, semi-professional, executive	283	11	27	28	21	13
Highly skilled	364	16	23	23	21	17
Skilled	357	12	22	24	21	20
Moderately skilled	248	17	25	20	18	21
Semi-skilled/unskilled	141	15	20	23	26	16
Age of boys						
12-13 years	623	17	23	21	21	18
14-15 years	584	12	25	23	23	16
16+ years	349	11	23	28	19	19
Type of school last attended						
Secondary modern	379	13	21	22	23	20
Comprehensive	566	17	17	23	25	17
Grammar	330	19	22	24	22	14
Public	183	16	21	32	18	13
Size of household						
2-3 persons	189	17	19	28	22	14
4 persons	457	16	21	25	24	14
5 persons	406	16	20	24	22	17
6 persons	253	14	23	21	21	21
7+ persons	254	17	16	22	26	19
Skin colour						
Coloured	146	20	21	24	18	17
White	1365	16	20	24	23	17
Truancy						
Never	1207	18	22	24	22	15
About once a month	126	11	17	28	26	18
More than once a month	181	7	12	23	27	31
Enjoyed school						
Yes	1222	18	22	24	22	15
No	324	10	14	23	27	25
How long has mother worked since marriage						
Not at all	222	17	20	22	22	19
Up to 2 years	268	15	19	26	23	16
3-5 years	303	20	22	23	20	15
6-10 years	396	11	21	24	26	18
More than 10 years	305	18	17	23	23	18
How often punished for violence/destruction when under four years						
Always	240	14	18	23	25	20
Moderately	325	14	21	22	24	18
Hardly ever	284	18	15	27	20	20
Not at all	151	14	23	26	25	13
Never violent when under four years	522	18	23	23	22	15
Spare time job (if still at school)						
Yes	531	13	20	27	23	18
No	870	19	21	23	22	16
Strength of grip						
10-24 kilograms	352	19	25	19	24	13
25-30 kilograms	433	15	19	26	20	21
31-38 kilograms	403	16	18	25	22	19
39-60 kilograms	353	14	20	26	26	14
Ever stolen sweets?						
Yes	686	10	17	24	26	23
No	870	21	23	24	20	13

Table 15.5
Distribution of indices of 'willingness to commit TV type violence', analysed by characteristics of boys

BACKGROUND AND CHARACTERISTICS OF BOYS	All	Indices of 'willingness to commit TV type acts'				
		0-604	605-964	965-1324	1325-2074	2075-8293
	Cases(n) % across	306 20%	317 20%	321 21%	315 20%	300 19%
	n	%	%	%	%	%
Father's occupational level						
Professional, semi-professional, executive	283	24	23	25	18	9
Highly skilled	364	20	22	21	21	16
Skilled	357	18	20	20	23	20
Moderately skilled	248	17	19	20	18	26
Semi-skilled/unskilled	141	21	15	13	23	28
Age of boy						
12-13 years	623	19	21	19	18	23
14-15 years	584	19	18	21	23	19
16 + years	349	22	22	23	19	13
Type of school last attended						
Secondary modern	379	15	16	20	23	26
Comprehensive	566	21	18	20	20	21
Grammar	330	24	27	22	18	8
Public	183	21	21	20	18	20
Size of household						
2-3 persons	189	22	19	19	26	14
4 persons	457	21	23	21	19	17
5 persons	406	20	21	21	20	18
6 persons	253	17	19	22	21	21
7 + persons	254	19	17	20	18	27
Skin colour						
Coloured	146	17	21	14	23	25
White	1365	20	20	21	20	19
Truancy						
Never	1207	21	22	22	19	16
About once a month	126	16	19	13	26	25
More than once a month	181	13	13	15	24	35
Enjoyed school						
Yes	1222	21	22	21	19	17
No	324	15	15	18	23	30
How long has mother worked since marriage						
Not at all	222	22	15	21	22	21
Up to 2 years	268	19	22	19	17	24
3-5 years	323	19	24	17	21	18
6-10 years	396	20	22	20	19	19
More than 10 years	305	20	16	23	24	18
How often punished for violence/destruction when under four years						
Always	240	16	20	16	23	24
Moderately	325	18	19	22	18	23
Hardly ever	284	18	25	18	18	20
Not at all	151	15	21	25	21	19
Never violent when under four years	522	25	19	22	20	14
Spare time job (if still at school)						
Yes	531	18	22	21	20	19
No	870	22	20	20	20	18
Strength of grip						
10-24 kilograms	352	18	18	22	19	23
25-30 kilograms	433	18	21	19	20	23
31-38 kilograms	403	21	20	21	22	17
39-60 kilograms	353	23	23	21	20	14
Ever stolen sweets?						
Yes	531	18	22	21	20	19
No	870	22	20	20	20	18

punished for violent/destructive behaviour when under 4 years; whether boy has a spare time job (if still at school); whether boy has ever stolen sweets.

There is moderate to substantial association between 'willingness' and: occupational level of boy's father (negative); truancy level (positive); whether boy enjoyed school (negative); whether boy attended a grammar school rather than some other kind of school (such boys are less 'willing' to commit TV-type acts of violence).

Occupational level of father and boy's grammar school status are discriminating in relation to 'willingness' but not in relation to either 'preoccupation' or 'frequency of feeling like committing' TV-type acts of violence. Why did they not emerge as discriminants in tables 15.3 and 15.4? Quite possibly, a feeling of willingness to so act is more likely to be inhibited by cultural training and surround than are the other two conditions. The issue is well worth further scrutiny and speculation.

The tenability of hypothesis 9 and of its sub-hypotheses

Hypothesis 9 postulated that:

> 'High exposure to television violence increases the degree to which boys think about or are preoccupied with the different acts of violence they see on television'.

In table 15.6, I have presented the results of using the standard hypothesis challenging procedure on hypothesis 9 and on its associated sub-hypotheses.

The principal indications of table 15.6 are set out hereunder.

1 *The central hypothesis (relating DV9 and IV1)*

The evidence in table 15.6 gives no support to the central hypothesis.

2 *The programme-type sub-hypotheses*

The two sub-hypotheses of hypothesis 9 concerned the effect, on preoccupation with TV-type acts of violence, of exposure to:

(a) programmes representing fictional violence of a realistic kind;

(b) programmes where the physical or mental consequences of violence, for the victim, are shown in detail.

Neither of these sub-hypotheses is supported to any meaningful degree by the evidence in table 15.6.

3 *The media-type sub-hypotheses*

The bottom six lines of table 15.6 relate to the effect of the other mass media upon preoccupation (by boys) with types of violence presented on television. The mass media concerned are comics/comic books, violent films, newspapers, in that order.

The evidence does not give support of any meaningful kind to the sub-hypotheses involving comics or newspapers. For that involving violent films, the support is of only a very small and uncertain kind.

Table 15.6
Dealing with the tenability of the hypothesis that exposure to television violence increases boys' preoccupation with different forms of violence presented on television

Hypothesis investigated*†	Direction of hypothesis	Means for Qualifiers (Q) Controls (C) and Modified Controls (MC)			Difference between Q and MC means		Significance of difference	
		M_Q	M_C	M_{MC}	$M_Q - M_{MC}$	As % of M_{MC}	CR	P*
Hypothesis 9, relating DV9‡ & IV1	F	12.52	12.10	12.57	−0.05	−0.40	−0.10	.460
	R	592.92	566.19	573.38	19.54	3.41	1.49	.068
Sub-hypotheses of hypothesis 9 relating								
a) DV9 & IV2	F	12.64	11.98	12.46	0.18	1.44	0.42	.337
	R	2124.07	2015.31	2043.18	80.89	3.96	1.73	.042
b) DV9 & IV9	F	12.65	11.97	12.45	0.20	1.61	0.46	.323
	R	1026.20	979.69	988.34	37.86	3.83	1.74	.041
Hypotheses involving the other mass media								
a) DV9 & IV28	F	12.69	11.93	12.39	0.30	2.42	0.68	.248
	R	8.99	8.23	8.31	0.68	8.18	2.23	.013
b) DV9 & IV29	F	12.58	12.01	12.06	0.52	4.31	1.22	.111
	R	5.88	5.16	5.47	0.41	7.50	1.83	.034
c) DV9 & IV30	F	12.64	11.97	12.51	0.31	1.04	0.29	.386
	R	6.17	5.73	5.97	0.20	3.35	1.05	.147

*DV = dependent variable
IV = independent variable
†For identity of each IV, see pages 448-9, (shown also in table 2.7, chapter 2).
‡DV9 is dependent variable in hypothesis 9 (i.e. preoccupation with acts of violence shown on television)

The tenability of hypothesis 10 and its sub-hypotheses

Hypothesis 10 postulated that:

> 'High exposure to television violence increases the degree to which boys would like to commit the kinds of violence shown on television'.

In table 15.7, I have presented the results of using the standard hypothesis challenging procedure on hypothesis 10 and its sub-hypotheses.

The principal indications of table 15.7 are set out hereunder.

1 *The central hypothesis (relating DV10 and IV1)*

The evidence in table 15.7 gives no meaningful support to the central hypothesis.

2 *The media-type sub-hypotheses*

(a) The hypothesis that exposure to comics/comic books increases the frequency with which boys feel like committing certain acts of violence of the sort commonly shown on television gets a 'small' degree of support from the

Table 15.7

Dealing with the tenability of the hypothesis that exposure to television violence increases the degree to which boys would like to commit the different forms of violence shown on television

Hypothesis investigated*†	Direction of hypothesis	Means for Qualifiers (Q) Controls (C) and Modified Controls (MC)			Difference between Q and MC means		Significance of difference	
		M_Q	M_C	M_{MC}	$M_Q - M_{MC}$	As % of M_{MC}	CR	P*
Hypothesis 10 relating DV10‡ & IV1	F	9.42	8.88	9.38	0.04	0.43	0.09	.464
	R	600.03	551.46	567.03	33.00	5.82	2.54	.006
Hypotheses involving the other mass media								
a) DV10 & IV28	F	9.61	8.68	8.92	0.69	7.74	1.64	.051
	R	9.00	8.18	8.45	0.55	6.51	1.75	.040
b) DV10 & IV29	F	9.66	8.57	8.69	0.97	11.16	2.41	.008
	R	5.80	5.20	5.42	0.38	7.01	1.80	.036
c) DV10 & IV30	F	9.64	8.64	9.10	0.54	5.93	1.30	.097
	R	6.16	5.72	5.79	0.37	6.39	2.08	.019

*DV = dependent variable
IV = independent variable
†For identity of each IV, see pages 448-9, (shown also in table 2.7, chapter 2).
‡DV10 is dependent variable in hypothesis 10 (i.e. degree to which boys feel they would like to commit acts of violence shown on television).

evidence in table 15.7 (index of effect = 7.74 per cent). The reverse form of the hypothesis gets about the same degree of support from the evidence – so that the possibility exists that the support given the forward hypothesis is only a reflection of the operation of a reverse process. In any case it is important to note that the degree of support given to the forward version of the hypothesis is only 'small'.

(b) The hypothesis in this case is that exposure to violent films increases the degree to which boys feel like committing TV-type acts of violence. This hypothesis gets a 'moderate' degree of support from the evidence in table 15.7 (the index of effect is 11.16 per cent and the P value .008). The *reversed* form of the hypothesis also gets a degree of support, though at a lower level (7.01 per cent).

(c) The third of the media-type hypotheses postulated that exposure to newspapers increases the degree to which boys feel like committing the TV-type acts of violence. This hypothesis gets a 'small' degree of support from the evidence (index of effect = 5.93 per cent), but from a statistical viewpoint, this support is of a slightly uncertain kind (P = .097). Since in addition this hypothesis in reverse also gets a 'small' degree of support from the evidence, it would be unwise to regard the total body of evidence as giving much in the way of support to this sub-hypothesis.

The tenability of hypothesis 11 and of its sub-hypotheses

Hypothesis 11 postulated that:

> 'High exposure to television violence increases the degree to which boys feel willing to commit the kinds of violence they see on television'.

The television-type violence involved in this hypothesis consists of the same 20 acts as are featured in hypotheses 9 and 10. I wish to repeat here that 'willingness to commit' various acts of violence does not necessarily imply anything more than a *feeling* of willingness. Indeed, 'willingness' to commit is probably best interpreted simply as a pre-disposition to commit.

In table 15.8, I have presented the results of using on hypothesis 11 the standard hypothesis challenging procedure that was used on all the other hypotheses dealt with in this enquiry.

The principal indications of table 15.8 are set out hereunder:

1 *The central hypothesis (relating DV11 and IV1)*

The evidence in table 15.8 gives no meaningful support to the central hypothesis, namely that exposure to television violence increases boys' feeling of willingness to use the TV-type acts of violence studied: the index of effect is 'very small' (1.77 per cent) and the difference between the willingness scores of the Qualifiers and Modified Controls is not statistically meaningful (P = .337).

2 *The programme-type sub-hypotheses*

Various sub-hypotheses of hypothesis 11 were also challenged. These each postulated some particular kind of television programme as increasing the degree to which boys feel willing to commit TV-type acts of violence. The programme types involved were:

(a) those where the violence is performed by basically 'good guy' types who are also rebels or 'odd-men-out' (IV3);

(b) those where violence is represented as 'fun and games' or like a game or as something to entertain (IV7);

(c) those that show violence being done in a good cause (IV8);

(d) those where the physical or mental consequences of violence, for the victim, are shown in detail (IV9);

(e) those where the violence is performed by basically 'good guy' types or by heroes who are also tough (i.e. who can endure physical violence and fight on) (IV11);

(f) those where the violence is presented through the news or through newsreel programmes (IV19).

The evidence of table 15.8 does not give support of any meaningful kind to sub-hypotheses (a) and (c); only minor support of an uncertain kind to sub-hypotheses (b) and (e); a 'small' degree of support to sub-hypotheses (d) and (f) – though in each case that support was of a slightly uncertain kind (P's = .052 and .092 respectively).

Table 15.8
Dealing with the tenability of the hypothesis that exposure to television violence increases boys' willingness to use forms of violence presented on television

Hypothesis investigated*†	Direction of hypothesis	Means for Qualifiers (Q) Controls (C) and Modified Controls (MC)			Differences between Q and MC means		Significance of difference	
		M_Q	M_C	M_{MC}	$M_Q - M_{MC}$	As % of M_{MC}	CR	P*
Hypothesis 11 relating DV11‡ & IV1	F	1410.80	1391.49	1386.21	24.60	1.77	0.42	.337
	R	582.07	575.56	566.73	15.34	2.71	1.18	.119
Sub-hypotheses of hypothesis 11 relating								
a) DV11 & IV3	F	1408.97	1393.33	1381.42	27.25	1.97	0.43	.337
	R	826.32	815.70	817.42	8.90	1.09	0.38	.352
b) DV11 & IV7	F	1433.52	1368.88	1369.49	64.03	4.68	1.07	.142
	R	888.01	866.06	850.71	37.90	4.46	1.60	.059
c) DV11 & IV8	F	1419.54	1382.76	1430.08	−10.54	−0.74	−0.17	.433
	R	2274.24	2252.49	2295.31	−21.07	−0.92	0.39	.349
d) DV11 & IV9	F	1446.60	1355.74	1351.12	95.48	7.07	1.63	.052
	R	1005.39	997.91	980.24	25.15	2.57	1.12	.131
e) DV11 & IV11	F	1411.57	1390.74	1356.69	54.88	4.05	0.95	.170
	R	2086.10	2053.62	2071.98	14.12	0.68	0.27	.394
f) DV11 & IV19	F	1428.48	1373.13	1354.16	74.32	5.49	1.33	.092
	R	59.95	60.14	60.13	−0.18	0.30	−0.14	.444
Hypothesis involving the other mass media								
a) DV11 & IV28	F	1546.71	1255.01	1380.80	165.91	12.02	2.56	.052
	R	9.41	7.77	8.22	1.19	14.48	3.77	<001
b) DV11 & IV29	F	1406.21	1395.43	1365.61	40.60	2.97	0.71	.239
	R	5.57	5.44	5.27	0.30	5.69	1.44	.075
c) DV11 & IV30	F	1461.18	1339.31	1450.52	10.66	0.73	0.18	.429
	R	6.12	5.76	5.86	0.26	4.44	1.43	.076

*DV = dependent variable
IV = independent variable
†For identity of each IV, see pages 448-9, (shown also in table 2.7 of chapter 2)
‡DV11 is dependent variable in hypothesis 11 (i.e. feeling of willingness to commit acts of violence shown on television)

3 *The media-type sub-hypotheses*

The initial hypothesis was restated in three forms, each with a different mass medium substituted for television violence. The results were as follows.

(a) *For comics/comic books (IV28)* the results in table 15.8 give a moderate degree of support to the hypothesis that exposure to comics and comic books increases boys' feeling of willingness to commit TV-type acts of violence: the 'index of effect' is 12.02 per cent and the P value (one-tail extraction) is .052. At the same time, the reversed hypothesis also gets a moderate degree of support (with an index of effect of 14.48 per cent and a P value of .001). This leaves us with the possibility that the support given to the forward form of the hypothesis rests upon the hypothesis working in reverse.

(b) *For violent films* the evidence in table 15.8 provides no meaningful support for the sub-hypothesis.

(c) *For newspapers*, the evidence in table 15.8 gives no meaningful support to the hypothesis relating to newspapers: the index of effect is negligible and the statistical significance (P) of the residual difference between the Qualifiers and the Modified Controls is .429.

For all the hypotheses and sub-hypotheses represented in table 15.8, the majority outcome is one of non-support by the evidence. The exception are those hypotheses that have the following variables as their causal factor (i.e. independent variables):

- exposure to programmes where the physical or mental consequences of violence, for the victim, are shown in detail (DV9) (a small degree of support);
- exposure to television news and newsreel programmes (DV19) (with a small degree of support of an uncertain kind);
- exposure to comics/comic books (DV28) (a moderate degree of support, but with the reversed form of the hypothesis getting at least as much support from the evidence).

The tenability of the central elements in hypotheses 9, 10, 11

In table 15.9, I have put together the findings related to the central elements of hypotheses 9, 10 and 11.

Table 15.9
Showing the results for the central element of each of hypotheses 9, 10 and 11

Hypotheses	Direction of hypothesis	Means for Qualifiers (Q), Controls (C) and Modified Controls (MC)			Difference between Q and MC means		Significance of difference	
		M_Q	M_C	M_{MC}	M_Q-M_{MC}	As % of M_{MC}	CR	P*
H9, linking DV9 and IV1	F	12.52	12.10	12.57	−0.05	−0.40	−0.10	.460
	R	592.92	566.19	573.38	19.54	3.41	1.49	.068
H10, linking DV10 and IV1	F	9.42	8.88	9.38	0.04	0.43	0.09	.464
	R	600.03	551.46	576.03	33.00	5.82	2.54	.006
H11, linking DV11 and IV1	F	1410.80	1391.49	1386.21	24.60	1.77	0.42	.337
	R	582.07	575.56	566.73	15.34	2.71	1.18	.119

*DV = dependent variable
IV = independent variable
IV1 = extent of exposure to television violence
DV9 = preoccupation with acts of violence shown on television
DV10 = degree to which boys feel they would like to commit acts of violence shown on television
DV11 = feeling of willingness to commit acts of violence shown on television

For all three hypotheses, the central element got no meaningful support from the evidence. Where such a finding emerges, the results for the reverse hypothesis cease to be of direct relevance to the study of the tenability of the hypothesis. However, it is worth noting that for hypothesis 10, the reverse hypothesis is associated with a 'small' index of effect and that the P value is highly significant.

Notes

[1] Hypotheses numbered as in table 2.7, chapter 2.
[2] IV = independent variable; the numeral (2 in this case) identifies the independent variable involved.
[3] Excluded because the 'reason' was nonsensical in relation to the act concerned (e.g. swearing at someone in defence of my country).
[4] Less deletions as shown.

CHAPTER 16

THE TENABILITY OF TWO HYPOTHESES TO THE EFFECT THAT EXPOSURE TO TELEVISION VIOLENCE MAKES BOYS MORE CALLOUS IN RELATION TO REAL LIFE VIOLENCE – BOTH VIOLENCE GOING ON AROUND THEM AND VIOLENCE THAT THEY HEAR ABOUT THROUGH THE NEWS (HYPOTHESES 18, 19)

Contents

16 THE TENABILITY OF TWO HYPOTHESES TO THE EFFECT THAT EXPOSURE TO TELEVISION VIOLENCE MAKES BOYS MORE CALLOUS IN RELATION TO REAL LIFE VIOLENCE – BOTH VIOLENCE GOING ON AROUND THEM AND VIOLENCE THAT THEY HEAR ABOUT THROUGH THE NEWS

(HYPOTHESES 18, 19)

THE NATURE OF THE HYPOTHESES

In the hypothesis developing stage of this investigation, a view that was frequently encountered was that long term exposure to television violence hardens boys so that they tend not to react to real life violence with sympathy or shock or horror. It was against this background that two related hypotheses were formulated, one of them dealing with violence of the sort that boys might encounter personally in their own neighbourhoods and the other dealing with violence as reported in the news and occurring beyond the immediate surround of the boy, quite possibly in another country. These two categories of violence were referred to as 'near' violence and as 'distant' violence, respectively.

The two hypotheses were worded as follows:

Hypothesis 18 [1]. 'High exposure to television violence hardens boys (i.e. renders them more callous) in relation to directly experienced violence such as occurs in the home, or street, or areas which boys frequent (i.e. 'near' violence).'

Hypothesis 19 [1]. 'High exposure to television violence hardens boys (i.e. renders them more callous) in relation to indirectly experienced 'distant' violence presented by forms of mass media such as press, television, radio.'

The background to the development of these hypotheses is given in chapter 2.

An investigation was also made of a number of sub-hypotheses of hypotheses 18 and 19.

1 Callousness in relation to 'near' violence is increased by high exposure to:

(a) violence presented through television newsreel programmes and through television news (IV19 [2])

(b) comics and comic books (IV28)

(c) violent films (IV29)

(d) newspapers (IV30)

2 Callousness in relation to 'distant' violence is increased by high exposure to: (a), (b), (c), (d) as detailed within (1) above.

THE METHODS OF INVESTIGATION USED
(being a summary of details presented in chapters 3 and 7)

The basic research strategies for investigating these causal hypotheses

The methods used for investigating the tenability of hypotheses 18 and 19 were in principle the same as those used on hypotheses 1-4. Thus for each of hypotheses 18 and 19, three basic steps were involved and these were applied quite separately in challenging the forward and then the reversed forms of the hypotheses. These three steps, which are detailed fully in chapter 3, were as follows.

(i) First came the development of a composite of predictors of the dependent and independent variables considered jointly.

(ii) This composite was then used to equate the Controls to the Qualifiers in terms of the correlates of the dependent and the independent variables.

(iii) A calculation was then made of the significance of the *residual* difference between the means of the Qualifiers on the one hand and of the Modified Controls on the other.

Let me emphasise that this three-stage process was used separately for the forward and the reversed forms of each hypothesis. Also, it was used separately for the forward and the reversed forms of each of the sub-hypotheses of each of the hypotheses.

The reader who has skipped straight to this chapter will need to go back to chapter 3 if he is to understand the three steps referred to above.

Measuring the different dependent variables

Full details of the procedures used for measuring the two dependent variables are set out in chapter 7. What follows is no more than a summary of that methodology.

Both measures involved securing the reactions of boys to a set of pictures, three depicting near (or local) type violence and three depicting distant or media-presented violence.

1 *Measuring the degree to which boys are callous in relation to near violence*

(a) For each of the three [3] pictures of a (near) violent happening, the boy first studied the depiction (e.g. boy tripping an old man) and then sorted, as 'agree' or 'disagree', a set of 12 cards on each of which was a verbalised reaction to the depicted violence. Each of these twelve statements had been allotted a value derived through the Thurstone evaluation system (i.e. its median value). Some examples from the twelve follow.

Statement judged	*Median value* [4]
I would feel sorry for the person on the receiving end	2.62
What other people do is no concern of mine	5.70
I would tell my mates so that they could watch the excitement too	6.76

(b) An individual boy's score was the aggregate of the median values of all the statements he agreed with (out of the 36 offered between the three pictures) divided by the total number of them he had agreed with. The range of possible scores was 1.00-7.00 and the higher the score, the more callous the boy may be regarded as being. [5]

2 *Measuring the degree to which boys are callous in relation to 'distant' violence*

(a) For each of the three [6] pictures of a (distant) violent happening, the boy first studied the depiction (e.g. report of a fatal aircraft crash) and then sorted, as 'agree' or 'disagree', a set of nine cards on each of which was a verbalised reaction to the depicted violence. Each of these nine statements had been allotted a value derived through the Thurstone evaluation system (i.e. its median value). Some examples from the nine follow.

Statements	*Median values* [7]
I really feel sorry for the people involved	1.19
There must be some way to stop this from happening again	1.77
It's not my problem, so I'm not interested	6.10

(b) An individual boy's score was the aggregate of the median values of all the statements he agreed with (out of the 27 offered between the three pictures) divided by the total number of them he had agreed with. The range of possible scores was 1.00-7.00 and the higher the score, the more callous the boy may be taken to be in relation to distant violence. [8]

Cross analyses made with respect to the dependent variables

A range of cross-analyses was made to determine differences between population sectors in terms of the dependent variables featured in hypotheses 18 and 19.

FINDINGS

The findings have been set out under two headings, namely:

1 the distribution of scores for callousness, according to the characteristics of boys;

2 the tenability of the hypotheses being dealt with in this chapter.

The first section may be regarded as providing basic information about the dependent variables, whilst the second is the key element of the findings.

Distribution of scores for callousness, according to characteristics of boys

Callousness scores in relation to 'near' and 'distant' violence were calculated through the methods briefly described in this chapter and detailed in chapter 7. These scores were then analysed according to the background and the characteristics of the boys studied. Details are shown in tables 16.1 and 16.2.

The principal indications of tables 16.1 and 16.2 are as follows.

1 *Concerning 'near' violence*

(a) There was but little association between callousness for near violence and: size of household; skin colour; how long mother has worked since marriage; how often boy was punished for violence or destruction when under four years of age; whether boy has a spare-time job (if still at school).

(b) On the other hand, there was substantial association between callousness for near violence and: frequency of truancy (positive); whether boy enjoyed being at school (negative).

2 *Concerning 'distant' violence*

(a) There was but little association between callousness for 'distant' violence and: age of boy; how long mother had worked since marriage; whether boy had spare-time job (if still at school); strength of grip.

(b) On the other hand, there was substantial association between callousness for distant violence and: occupational level of boy's father (negative); frequency of truancy (positive); grammar school education (less callous).

3 *Concerning the degree to which callousness is common to the different sample sectors*

Perhaps the really important thing about tables 16.1 and 16.2 is the degree to which callousness or the absence of it is spread across the different social, economic, educational, experiential, racial sectors of the sample. In general, these different population sectors are much more similar than they are different.

The tenability of hypothesis 18 and its sub-hypotheses

In table 16.3, I have presented the results of using the standard hypothesis challenging procedure on hypothesis 18 and its associated sub-hypotheses.

The principal indications of table 16.3 are set out hereunder.

1 *The central hypothesis (relating DV18 and IV1)*

The evidence in table 16.3 gives no support at all to hypothesis 18, which links callousness in relation to 'near' violence to extent of exposure to television violence. The index of effect is minutely negative and the P-value is far from being statistically significant.

2 *The sub-hypotheses of hypothesis 18*

A check was also made on the tenability of the hypothesis that long-term exposure to *television newsreel programmes and to television news* increases the

Table 16.1
Distribution of indices of acceptance of 'near' violence analysed according to characteristics of boys

BACKGROUND AND CHARACTERISTICS OF BOYS	All	Index of acceptance of 'near' violence				
		0-263	264-278	279-298	299-332	333-530
	Cases(n)	300	285	323	330	321
	% across	19%	18%	21%	21%	21%
Father's occupational level	n	%	%	%	%	%
Professional, semi-professional, executive	283	16	23	24	19	17
Highly skilled	364	21	17	20	24	18
Skilled	357	20	16	21	20	23
Moderately skilled	248	21	17	18	21	23
Semi-skilled/unskilled	141	18	19	18	20	26
Age of boys						
12-13 years	623	24	17	23	21	15
14-15 years	584	15	18	20	22	24
16+ years	349	17	22	17	19	25
Type of school last attended						
Secondary modern	379	18	16	19	23	24
Comprehensive	566	22	18	19	22	18
Grammar	330	16	21	21	22	20
Public	183	16	22	31	15	16
Size of household						
2-3 persons	189	15	21	23	21	20
4 persons	457	21	19	20	19	21
5 persons	406	19	17	23	23	18
6 persons	253	17	20	17	22	24
7 + persons	254	21	15	20	21	22
Skin colour						
Coloured	146	20	16	21	14	29
White	1365	19	19	21	22	19
Truancy						
Never	1207	21	19	21	21	18
About once a month	126	13	16	22	25	24
More than once a month	181	12	17	18	20	34
Enjoyed school						
Yes	1222	20	19	21	21	18
No	324	17	13	19	21	30
How long has mother worked since marriage						
Not at all	222	17	16	20	25	22
Up to 2 years	268	18	18	19	24	21
3-5 years	303	19	20	22	19	19
6-10 years	396	20	19	21	19	20
More than 10 years	305	20	17	21	20	22
How often punished for violence/destruction when under four years						
Always	240	18	16	20	27	20
Mostly	325	18	19	21	20	22
Hardly ever	284	20	15	21	20	24
Not at all	151	19	25	21	19	17
Never violent when under four years	522	21	19	22	20	19
Spare time job (if still at school)						
Yes	531	18	17	22	22	20
No	870	21	19	20	21	18
Strength of grip						
10-24 kilograms	352	27	16	20	24	13
25-30 kilograms	433	17	19	23	21	20
31-38 kilograms	403	17	18	20	20	25
39-60 kilograms	353	18	21	20	19	22
Ever stolen sweets?						
Yes	686	15	17	20	23	25
No	870	22	19	21	20	17

Table 16.2
Distribution of indices of acceptance of 'distant' violence analysed according to characteristics of boys

BACKGROUND AND CHARACTERISTICS OF BOYS	Index of acceptance of 'distant' violence					
	All	0-214	215-254	255-304	305-364	365-528
	Cases (n)	323	373	411	296	156
	% across	21%	24%	26%	19%	10%
	n	%	%	%	%	%
Father's occupational level						
Professional, semi-professional, executive	283	22	30	28	16	5
Highly skilled	364	23	26	26	16	8
Skilled	357	22	23	24	20	11
Moderately skilled	248	16	20	29	23	13
Semi-skilled/unskilled	141	17	13	31	25	14
Age of boys						
12-13 years	623	24	23	24	18	11
14-15 years	584	18	23	27	21	10
16+ years	349	19	26	30	17	8
Type of school last attended						
Secondary modern	379	17	21	28	23	11
Comprehensive	566	20	23	25	20	12
Grammar	330	26	29	26	12	6
Public	183	21	25	27	20	7
Size of household						
2-3 persons	189	26	22	26	14	12
4 persons	457	22	24	26	17	11
5 persons	406	21	24	25	20	9
6 persons	253	15	26	28	21	9
7 + persons	254	19	22	28	22	9
Skin colour						
Coloured	146	17	21	25	27	11
White	1365	21	24	27	18	10
Truancy						
Never	1207	23	25	26	17	9
About once a month	126	17	20	23	31	10
More than once a month	181	12	21	28	21	18
Enjoyed school						
Yes	1222	21	25	27	18	9
No	324	18	19	25	25	13
How long has mother worked since marriage						
Not at all	222	25	21	24	20	9
Up to 2 years	268	19	23	32	17	9
3-5 years	303	20	25	24	19	11
6-10 years	396	20	26	24	19	11
More than 10 years	305	21	23	30	19	8
How often punished for violence/destruction when under four years						
Always	240	18	20	25	25	12
Mostly	325	20	23	25	21	11
Hardly ever	284	21	21	29	19	10
Not at all	151	19	27	28	17	10
Never violent when under four years	522	23	27	26	15	9
Spare time job (if still at school)						
Yes	531	19	25	27	17	11
No	870	22	24	25	20	9
Strength of grip						
10-24 kilograms	352	25	26	27	16	7
25-30 kilograms	433	17	24	24	22	14
31-38 kilograms	403	23	22	26	19	10
39-60 kilograms	353	18	25	30	19	8
Ever stolen sweets?						
Yes	686	18	22	26	22	12
No	870	23	26	26	17	8

Table 16.3
Dealing with the tenability of the hypothesis that high exposure to television violence increases the degree of callousness of boys in relation to 'near' violence

Hypothesis*† investigated	Direction of hypothesis	Means for Qualifiers (Q) Controls (C) and Modified Controls (MC)			Difference between Q and MC means		Significance of difference	
		M_Q	M_C	M_{MC}	$M_Q - M_{MC}$	As % of M_{MC}	CR	P**
Hypothesis 18 relating DV18‡ & IV1	F	301.19	301.07	302.45	−1.26	−0.42	−0.53	.298
	R	581.42	576.20	588.37	−6.95	−1.18	−0.52	.302
Sub-hypotheses of hypothesis 18 relating DV18 & IV19	F	300.46	301.81	301.92	−1.46	−0.48	−0.60	.274
	R	60.10	59.99	60.66	−0.56	−0.92	−0.45	.326
Hypotheses involving the other mass media								
a) DV18 & IV28	F	302.03	300.23	301.68	0.35	0.12	0.14	.444
	R	8.88	8.30	8.66	0.22	2.54	0.70	.242
b) DV18 & IV29	F	303.31	298.67	299.01	4.30	1.44	1.74	.041
	R	5.43	5.58	5.72	−0.29	−5.07	−1.33	.092
c) DV18 & IV30	F	303.21	298.98	301.03	2.18	0.72	0.88	.189
	R	6.02	5.86	5.97	0.05	0.84	0.26	.397

*DV = dependent variable
IV = independent variable
†For identity of each IV, see pages 468-9 (shown also in table 2.7, chapter 2)
‡DV18 is dependent variable in hypothesis 18 (i.e. callousness in relation to 'near' violence)
**P based on one-tail extractions from probability tables.

degree to which boys are callous with regard to 'near' violence. The evidence in table 16.3 gives no support at all to this hypothesis.

3 *The effects of exposure to the other mass media.*

(a) *Comics/comic books.* The evidence gives no meaningful support to the hypothesis that exposure to comic books and comics increases the degree to which boys become more callous in relation to 'near' violence.

(b) *Violent films.* For the hypothesis that exposure to violent films makes boys more callous (in relation to near events), the index of effect is extremely small (1.44 per cent). This finding, in spite of the P-value being statistically significant (.041), must mean that the hypothesis gets virtually no support from the evidence.

(c) *Newspapers.* The hypothesis linking newspaper exposure to increased callousness in boys (with regard to 'near' violence) gets virtually no support from the evidence.

The tenability of hypothesis 19 and its sub-hypotheses

In table 16.4 are presented the results of using the standard hypothesis challenging procedure on hypothesis 19 and its sub-hypotheses.

The principal indications of table 16.4 are set out hereunder.

1 *The central hypothesis (relating DV19 and IV1)*

The evidence in table 16.4 gives no support at all to hypothesis 19 which links callousness in relation to 'distant' violence to extent of exposure to television violence. More specifically the 'index of effect' is virtually zero.

2 *The sub-hypotheses of hypothesis 19*

It was also hypothesised that high exposure to a specific type of television output, namely newsreel programmes and the news, increases boys' callousness in relation to 'distant' violence. The evidence in table 16.4 gives no support at all to this hypothesis.

3 *Hypotheses relating to the other mass media*

The three hypotheses linking certain other mass media – comics and comic books, violent films, newspapers – to the development of callousness in relation to 'distant' violence, get either no support or no meaningful support from the evidence in table 16.4

It is noteworthy that for newspapers, the *reverse* form of the hypothesis (namely that callousness, in relation to 'distant' violence, *increases* exposure to newspapers) got a small degree of support from the evidence in table 16.4: the index of effect was of the order of 7 per cent and the P-value was highly significant in the statistical sense.

Summing up on the challenging of hypotheses 18 and 19

Neither hypothesis 18 nor hypothesis 19 gets any support from the evidence of this enquiry. In other words, the present body of evidence does not support the view that high exposure

Table 16.4
Dealing with the tenability of the hypothesis that high exposure to television violence increases the degree to which boys are made more callous with respect to 'distant' violence

Hypothesis investigated*†	Direction of hypothesis	Means for Qualifiers (Q) Controls (c) and Modified Controls (MC)			Difference between Q and MC means		Significance of difference	
		M_Q	M_C	M_{MC}	M_Q-M_{MC}	As % of M_{MC}	CR	P**
Hypothesis 19 relating DV19‡& IV1	F	268.66	267.49	268.74	−0.08	−0.03	−0.02	.492
	R	574.31	583.29	580.61	−6.30	−1.09	−0.49	.312
Sub-hypotheses of hypothesis 19 relating DV19 & IV19	F	270.34	274.65	273.62	−3.28	−1.20	−0.95	.171
	R	60.23	59.86	60.16	0.07	0.12	0.05	.480
Hypotheses involving the other mass media								
a) DV19 & IV28	F	273.14	271.80	274.92	−1.78	−0.65	−0.44	.330
	R	8.99	8.20	8.65	0.34	3.93	1.07	.142
b) DV19 & IV29	F	273.75	271.03	270.96	2.79	1.03	0.80	.212
	R	5.52	5.49	5.39	0.13	2.41	0.62	.268
c) DV19 & IV30	F	273.16	271.76	275.29	−2.13	−0.77	−0.58	.281
	R	6.17	5.71	5.74	0.43	7.49	2.39	.008

*DV = dependent variable
IV = independent variable
†For identity of each IV, see pages 468-9 (shown also in table 2.7, chapter 2)
‡DV19 is dependent variable in hypothesis 19 (i.e. callousness in relation to 'distant' violence)
**P based on one-tail extractions from probability tables

to television violence increases boys' callousness in relation to either 'near' or 'distant' violence.

The outcome was the same for the sub-hypothesis linking exposure to newsreel programmes/television news to callousness of either kind – it got no support.

Nor does the evidence give support to the view that exposure to newspapers or violent films, or comics/comic books increases either kind of callousness in boys.

Notes

[1] Hypotheses numbered as in chapter 2.

[2] IV = independent variable; the numeral identifies the independent variable involved.

[3] There was a change-over of the pictures for the second half of the sample, a new set of three pictures then being substituted for the first set. This arrangement was meant both to vary the stimulus material and to limit the testing load of any one boy. The two halves of the sample were designed to be equivalent.

[4] Median values are all in terms of how callous or non-callous the statement indicated the endorsee to be.

[5] Averages were all expressed on a base of 1,000 to allow the computer averages to be expressed as whole numbers without loss of precision (e.g. 5.74 would become 574).

[6] As [3] above.

[7] As [4] above.

[8] As [5] above.

CHAPTER 17

THE TENABILITY OF A GROUP OF HYPOTHESES DEALING WITH THE EFFECTS OF EXPOSURE TO TELEVISION VIOLENCE UPON BOYS' ATTITUDES TOWARDS THE CONCEPT OF VIOLENCE AND TOWARDS ITS USE (HYPOTHESES 12, 20, 21, 22)

Contents

17 THE TENABILITY OF A GROUP OF HYPOTHESES DEALING WITH THE EFFECTS OF EXPOSURE TO TELEVISION VIOLENCE UPON BOYS' ATTITUDES TOWARDS THE CONCEPT OF VIOLENCE AND TOWARDS ITS USE (HYPOTHESES 12, 20, 21, 22)

THE NATURE OF THE HYPOTHESES

In this chapter I have grouped together a number of hypotheses in which the dependent variables are either attitudes towards some aspect of the concept of violence or attitude towards a particular use of violence. There are four of these hypotheses in all and they take the following forms.

Hypothesis 12: 'High exposure to television violence increases the degree to which boys find violence attractive.'

Hypothesis 20: 'High exposure to television violence increases the degree to which boys object to the idea of violence.'

Hypothesis 21: 'High exposure to television violence increases the degree to which boys see violence as a basic part of human nature and as inevitable.'

Hypothesis 22: 'High exposure to television violence increases the degree to which boys accept violence as a way to solve problems.'

The background to the development of these hypotheses is given in chapter 2. An investigation was also made of a number of sub-hypotheses of the principal hypotheses and of the influence of certain of the mass media upon the dependent variables. Details follow.

For hypothesis 12: 'The degree to which boys find violence attractive' is increased by:

(a) exposure to programmes where violence is shown as glorified, romanticised, idealised, or ennobling (IV6)

(b) exposure to programmes where violence is presented as fun and games or like a game or as something to entertain (IV7)

(c) exposure to programmes where the physical and mental consequences of violence, for the victim, are shown in detail (IV9)

(d) exposure to 'Tom and Jerry' programmes (IV17)

(e) exposure to comics/comic books (IV28)

(f) exposure to violent films (IV29)

(g) exposure to newspapers (IV30)

For hypothesis 20: 'The degree to which boys object to the "idea of violence" ' is increased by:

(a) as in (a) above (IV6)

(b) exposure to violence through television newsreel programmes and television news (IV19)

(c) exposure to certain mass media, as in (e), (f), (g) of hypothesis 12 (IVs 28, 29, 30)

For hypothesis 21: 'The degree to which boys see violence as inevitable' is increased by:

(a) exposure to programmes in which the violence is just thrown in for its own sake or is not necessary to the plot (IV13)

(b) exposure to fictional programmes about the English police at work, which also feature the kinds of violence that go on in society (IV15)

(c) exposure to television newsreel programmes and to television news (IV19)

(d) exposure to certain mass media as in (e), (f), (g) of hypothesis 12 (IVs 28, 29, 30)

For hypothesis 22: 'The degree to which boys regard violence as a way to solve problems' is increased by:

(a) exposure to programmes where violence is performed by basically 'good guy' types who are also rebels or 'odd-men-out' (IV3)

(b) exposure to programmes in which the violence is presented as being in a good cause (IV8)

(c) exposure to Westerns which include violence, for example, as between cowboys and Indians (IV22)

(d) exposure to certain mass media as in (e), (f), (g) of hypothesis 12 (IVs 28, 29, 30)

The background to the development of the four central hypotheses and of their sub-hypotheses is given in full in chapter 2.

THE METHODS OF INVESTIGATION USED
(being a summary of details presented in chapter 7)

The basic research strategies for investigating these causal hypotheses

The methods used for investigating the tenability of hypotheses 12, 20, 21, 22 and their sub-hypotheses were in principle the same as those used on hypotheses 1-4. Thus for each of hypotheses 12, 20-22, three basic steps were involved and these were applied quite separately in challenging the forward and then the reversed forms of the hypotheses. These three steps, which are detailed fully in chapter 3, were as follows.

(i) First came the development of a composite of predictors of the dependent and independent variables considered jointly.

(ii) This composite was then used to equate the Controls to the Qualifiers in terms of the correlates of the dependent and the independent variables.

(iii) A calculation was then made of the significance of the *residual* difference between the means of the qualifiers on the one hand and of the Modified Controls on the other.

Let me emphasise that this three-stage process was used separately for the forward form and the reversed form of each hypothesis. Also, it was used separately for the forward form and the reversed form of each of the *sub-hypotheses.*

The reader who has skipped straight to this chapter will need to go back to chapter 3 if he is to properly understand the three steps referred to above.

Measuring the different dependent variables featured in hypotheses 12, 20-22

All four dependent variables dealt with in this chapter were measured through Thurstone-type rating scales, the construction and full form of which are given in detail in chapter 7. What follows is an illustrated summary of the four measuring processes.

Measuring the degree to which boys find violence attractive (DV12) [1]

1 Each boy completed a 13-statement Thurstone-type rating scale. Each of the 13 statements in that scale had already been allocated a median value derived through the Thurstone evaluation system in the range of 0-10. Some examples follow:

Statements	*Median values*
I don't like rough games	1.30
I don't like wars except in films on the TV	3.40
I admire people like boxers who use their fists to prove that they are better than the next person	7.04

2 An individual boy's score was the aggregate of the median values of all the statements he agreed with, divided by the total number of such statements. The range of possible scores was 0.00-10.00 and the higher the score the more the boy may be taken to find violence attractive. [2]

For full details of this scale — of its construction and use — see chapter 7.

Measuring the degree to which boys object to 'the idea of violence' (DV20) [3]

1 Each boy completed a 10-statement Thurstone-type rating scale. Each of the 10 statements in that scale had already been allocated a median value derived through the Thurstone evaluation system in the range 0-6. Some examples follow:

Statements	*Median values*
Since boys will be boys, I don't mind if the occasional phone kiosk gets smashed up	0.71
It's good for husbands and wives to have flaming rows occasionally as a way of letting off steam	2.21
Boxing should be banned	5.78

2 An individual boy's score was the aggregate of the median values of all the statements he agreed with, divided by the total number of such statements. The range of possible scores was 0.00-6.00 and *the higher the score the more that boy may be taken to object to the idea of violence.*

For full details of this scale – of its construction and use – see chapter 7.

Measuring the degree to which boys regard violence as inevitable (i.e. as a basic part of human nature) (DV21) [4]

1 Each boy considered nine statements putting different views about the degree to which violence is a basic part of human nature. Responses endorsing a specific view that this *is* the case were allotted a score of 2, those denying it a score of 0 and those expressing no opinion a score of 1. The nine statements were as follows.

	Agree	*No opinion*	*Disagree*
We are all savages just under the skin	2	1	0
There will always be violence in the world	2	1	0
Every person has a violent streak in him	2	1	0
As long as there are humans in the world, there will always be violence	2	1	0
Men will always enjoy boxing and wrestling	2	1	0
People are slowly learning *not* to be violent	0	1	2
Countries will eventually stop fighting wars	0	1	2
Violence between human beings will eventually die out	0	1	2
The day will come when the world will be at peace	0	1	2

2 An individual boy's score was the aggregate of the values of all the answers he selected, divided by the total number of such answers (9 in this case). The maximum range of scores was 0.00-2.00 and the higher a boy's score, the more that boy may be taken as believing that violence is inevitable (i.e. a basic part of human nature).

For full details of this measure – of its construction and use – see chapter 7.

Measuring the degree to which boys accept violence as a way to solve problems (DV22) [5]

1 Each boy completed a 10-statement Thurstone-type rating scale. Each of the 10 statements in that scale had already been allocated a median value derived through the Thurstone evaluation system in the range 0-10. Some examples follow:

Statements	*Median values*
It's better to settle disagreements by talking rather than by fighting	1.29
Violence should only be used in a good cause	5.34
It's OK to use violence to get what you want	9.23

2 An individual boy's score was the aggregate of the median values of all the statements he agreed with, divided by the total number of such statements. The range of possible scores was 0-10.00 and *the higher a boy's score the more he may be taken to accept violence as a way to solve problems.* [6]

For full details of this scale – of its construction and use – see chapter 7.

Cross-analyses with reference to the dependent variables

A range of cross-analyses was made to determine differences between population sectors in terms of the four dependent variables featured in hypotheses 12, 20, 21 and 22.

FINDINGS

The findings have been set out under several headings.

1 The percentages of boys who agreed with the different attitude statements within the different scales

2 The distribution of averaged scores, for each of the four attitudinal variables, according to the characteristics of boys

3 The investigation of the hypotheses dealt with in this chapter.

The first two sections may be regarded as providing basic information about the dependent variables, whilst the third is the key element of the findings.

Percentages of boys agreeing with the different attitude statements within the four different attitudinal measures

For each of those four measures of attitude, each boy examined a set of statements, sorting each statement into one or another bag to indicate whether he agreed or disagreed with it. These four administrations were separated by other assessment processes, the separation being designed to reduce boredom and the influence of one set of statements upon the boy's processing of the next set.

The percentages of boys endorsing the different statements are set out in tables 17.1-17.4.

The indications of tables 17.1-17.4 are numerous and will best be noted by careful study of the tables themselves. However, there are several comments of a general nature that seem

Table 17.1
The attractiveness of violence: distribution of opinions
(1565 cases)

ATTITUDE STATEMENT	Scale value*	Reaction to statement Agree %	Disagree %	DK or NI %
I don't believe in watching or using violence of any kind	0.18	18	75	7
I don't like rough games	1.30	20	75	5
It must be horrible to be involved in a riot	1.50	63	25	12
I don't like people who are always fighting	2.17	56	38	5
I don't like wars, except in films on the TV	3.40	77	18	5
I enjoy watching wrestling but I would not like to take part	4.41	59	34	7
I enjoy playing sports like rugger, soccer, hockey	5.20	84	14	2
I enjoy watching boxing	5.67	72	25	3
Having a friendly fight with your mates is good fun	6.39	70	25	5
I admire people like boxers who use their fists to prove that they're better than the next person	7.04	27	64	9
Watching a good punch-up in the street or in the playground livens things up a bit	7.81	34	59	7
I think it's great when a player in the team I support hacks somebody down – especially if the Ref. doesn't see it	8.57	13	82	5
Shooting people looks like fun	9.85	5	91	4
ITEM ADDED AFTER FIRST RATING SESSION†				
I would not take part in a violent demonstration	0.87	61	26	13

*Mean value of statement on a scale running from 0-10
†Not used in assessment of attitude

Table 17.2
Concerning 'objections' to the idea of violence: distribution of opinions
(1565 cases)

ATTITUDE STATEMENT	Scale value*	Reaction to statement Agree %	Disagree %	DK or NI %
Since boys will be boys, I don't mind if the occasional phone kiosk gets smashed up	0.71	13	81	6
Since police forces and governments use violent means to solve their problems, members of the public should have the right to do the same	1.25	19	72	9
It's good for husbands and wives to have flaming rows occasionally as a way of letting off steam	2.21	35	51	14
I don't have any opinions at all about the use of violence in the world	2.82	15	74	11
It's OK to feel violent at times, but it is never OK to be violent	3.29	48	42	10
Violence between countries if often necessary but I don't approve of people inside this country being violent to each other	3.59	43	43	14
Fist fights are a very poor way for people to sort out their differences	4.24	60	35	5
It makes no sense here in England for anyone to be violent to anyone else	4.81	51	39	10
It's a bit much if a group of boys pick on a boy who is on his own	5.11	89	9	2
Boxing should be banned.	5.78	5	89	6
ITEM ADDED AFTER FIRST RATING SESSION†				
I think it does a boy good to be in a punch-up once in a while	1.65	45	47	8

*Mean value of statement on a scale running from 0-6
†Not used in assessment of attitude

Table 17.3
Violence as a basic part of human nature: distribution of opinions
(1565 cases)

ATTITUDE STATEMENT	Reaction to statement		
	Agree %	Disagree %	DK or NI %
We are all savages just under the skin	16	68	16
There will always be violence in the world	60	25	15
Every person has a violent streak in him	76	17	8
As long as there are human beings there will always be violence	70	21	9
Men will always enjoy boxing and wrestling	64	22	14
People are slowly learning NOT to be violent	44	41	16
Countries will eventually stop fighting wars	33	46	21
Violence between human beings will eventually die out	15	68	17
The day will come when the world will be at peace	25	52	23

Table 17.4
Violence as a way to solve problems: distribution of opinions
(1565 cases)

ATTITUDE STATEMENT	Scale value*	Reaction to statement		
		Agree %	Disagree %	DK or NI %
It is never OK to use violence or force	0.16	28	64	8
It's better to settle disagreements by talking rather than fighting	1.29	82	14	4
I would ONLY use force to protect someone I loved or a member of my family	4.27	54	38	9
Violence should only be used in a good cause	5.34	71	22	7
If a burglar broke into my house, I would try to knock him out with something	6.25	67	17	15
When you are in a hurry to get somewhere it is quite OK to push past people to make sure you catch your bus or train	6.85	19	75	6
It's manly to settle a quarrel with your fists	7.58	18	74	9
A good way to impress girls is for them to see that you can push other blokes around	8.04	8	88	5
If a friend gets hit by a gang of blokes the best thing to do is to get your own gang together and go after the other gang	8.89	32	58	11
It's OK to use violence to get what you want	9.23	6	90	4
ITEMS ADDED AFTER FIRST RATING SESSION†				
It's wrong to hit out when boys deliberately insult you	1.00	24	67	9
I would only hit someone if it was in self-defence	3.45	59	34	7

*Mean value of statement on a scale running from 0-10
†Not used in assessment of the attitude

to apply.

About a quarter of the boys took the view that 'it is never OK to use violence or force', while at least one in six seemed willing to condone the use of violence without much provocation. Between those limits, the condoning of violence seems to depend on circumstances and these circumstances are particularly worth study (see tables 17.1, 17.2 and 17.4).

Distribution of attitudinal scores according to the characteristics of boys

Scores for the four attitudinal variables were calculated through the methods described briefly in this chapter and detailed in chapter 7. These scores or indices were then analysed according to the background and characteristics of the boys studied. Details are given in tables 17.5-17.8.

The principal indications of tables 17.5-17.8 are as follows.

1. *Concerning the degree to which boys find violence attractive.* There is a substantial degree of association between 'finding violence attractive' and: occupational level of boy's father (negative); truancy (positive); whether boy enjoyed school (negative); whether boy has ever stolen sweets (positive). There is also a large difference in 'finding violence attractive' in going from boys with Secondary Modern school background to those with Public school background, the former tending more to find violence attractive.
2. *Concerning 'objecting to the idea of violence'.* There is a substantial degree of association between 'objecting to the idea of violence' and: occupational level of boy's father (positive); Grammar school background (positive); truancy (negative); enjoyment of school (positive).
3. *Concerning 'seeing violence as inevitable'.* There is a substantial degree of association between 'seeing violence as inevitable' and: age of boy (positive); skin colour (whites have greater tendency to see violence as inevitable); enjoyment of school (negative); strength of grip (positive).
4. *Concerning 'acceptance of violence as a way to solve problems'.* There is a substantial degree of association between 'acceptance of violence as a way to solve problems' and: occupational level of boy's father (negative); truancy (positive); enjoyment of school (negative); type of school last attended (negative); skin colour (black boys tend more to accept violence as a way to solve their problems).

The tenability of hypothesis 12 and its sub-hypotheses

In table 17.9 are presented the results of using the standard hypothesis challenging procedure on hypothesis 12 and its sub-hypotheses.

The principal indications of table 17.9 are set out hereunder.

The central hypothesis (relating DV12 and IV1). The central hypothesis in this group postulated: 'High exposure to television violence increases the degree to which boys find violence attractive'.

The evidence in table 17.9 gives very little support to hypothesis 12: though the P-value indicates a residual difference of a *highly significant* kind between the Qualifiers and the Modified Controls, the *index of effect is very small* (3.85 per cent).

Table 17.5
Distribution of indices of degree to which boys find violence attractive, analysed according to characteristics of boys

BACKGROUND AND CHARACTERISTICS OF BOYS	Index of degree to which boys find violence attractive					
	All	0-354	355-414	415-484	485-554	555-722
	Cases(n) % across	280 18%	389 25%	349 22%	328 21%	213 14%
	n	%	%	%	%	%
Father's occupational level						
Professional, semi-professional, executive	283	23	31	19	18	8
Highly skilled	364	19	26	23	19	12
Skilled	357	18	23	20	22	17
Moderately skilled	248	13	23	25	24	15
Semi-skilled/unskilled	141	15	18	26	21	21
Age of boys						
12-13 years	623	19	29	23	19	10
14-15 years	584	16	21	23	21	18
16-18 years	349	19	25	20	23	12
Type of school last attended						
Secondary modern	379	13	22	24	24	17
Comprehensive	566	17	24	23	22	13
Grammar	330	22	25	20	20	13
Public	183	22	31	21	14	13
Size of household						
2-3 persons	189	19	31	23	17	10
4 persons	457	20	23	21	24	12
5 persons	406	19	26	21	18	16
6 persons	253	16	21	23	23	16
7 + persons	254	14	25	26	21	13
Skin colour						
Coloured	146	18	27	22	19	13
White	1365	18	24	22	21	14
Truancy						
Never	1207	19	29	22	20	10
About once a month	126	13	14	23	27	22
More than once a month	181	15	12	18	25	30
Enjoyed school						
Yes	1222	19	28	22	21	10
No	324	14	15	22	23	27
How long has mother worked since marriage						
Not at all	222	15	24	25	22	14
Up to 2 years	268	17	22	25	21	15
3-5 years	303	21	29	20	19	10
6-10 years	396	18	24	21	22	15
More than 10 years	305	17	26	22	20	15
How often punished for violence/destruction when under four years						
Always	240	12	29	23	20	17
Mostly	325	18	22	25	20	15
Hardly ever	284	17	21	25	25	12
Not at all	151	19	19	25	25	13
Never violent when under four years	522	21	29	20	18	12
Spare time job (if still at school)						
Yes	531	14	24	25	21	16
No	870	21	27	21	20	11
Strength of grip						
10-24 kilograms	352	22	30	22	19	8
25-30 kilograms	433	17	25	25	20	13
31-38 kilograms	403	18	22	21	23	17
39-60 kilograms	353	16	24	22	22	16
Ever stolen sweets?						
Yes	686	12	21	22	24	21
No	870	23	28	22	19	8

Table 17.6
Distribution of indices of degree to which 'boys object to the idea of violence' analysed by characteristics of boys

BACKGROUND AND CHARACTERISTICS OF BOYS	Indices of degree to which boys object to the idea of violence, analysed by characteristics of boys					
	All	0-314	315-374	375-414	415-444	445-545
	Cases(n)	234	339	331	365	290
	% across	15%	22%	21%	23%	19%
Father's occupational level	n	%	%	%	%	%
Professional, semi-professional, executive	283	8	18	22	25	26
Highly skilled	364	13	19	22	26	20
Skilled	357	15	21	21	23	19
Moderately skilled	248	19	25	22	20	15
Semi-skilled/unskilled	141	24	26	21	18	11
Age of boys						
12-13 years	623	15	23	20	25	17
14-15 years	584	17	22	21	22	18
16-18 years	349	12	19	23	23	22
Type of school last attended						
Secondary modern	379	20	26	18	20	16
Comprehensive	566	15	23	22	24	15
Grammar	330	8	14	22	26	30
Public	183	13	19	25	26	17
Size of household						
2-3 persons	189	13	21	23	25	19
4 persons	457	13	20	19	25	23
5 persons	406	13	23	19	23	22
6 persons	253	20	23	21	21	16
7 + persons	254	19	22	28	22	9
Skin colour						
Coloured	146	21	23	25	18	14
White	1365	14	21	21	24	19
Truancy						
Never	1207	11	20	23	26	20
About once a month	126	25	28	15	18	13
More than once a month	181	31	29	16	12	12
Enjoyed school						
Yes	1222	12	21	23	25	20
No	324	28	26	13	19	15
How long has mother worked since marriage						
Not at all	222	17	25	20	23	15
Up to 2 years	268	16	23	24	20	18
3-5 years	303	16	18	17	26	22
6-10 years	396	15	21	17	25	22
More than 10 years	305	15	22	26	21	16
How often punished for violence/destruction when under four years						
Always	240	18	29	15	24	14
Mostly	325	19	17	22	23	18
Hardly ever	284	17	19	21	26	18
Not at all	151	15	25	21	23	17
Never violent when under four years	522	10	22	23	22	22
Spare time job (if still at school)						
Yes	531	15	24	20	25	17
No	870	14	20	22	24	20
Strength of grip						
10-24 kilograms	352	14	21	19	27	18
25-30 kilograms	433	16	25	21	22	15
31-38 kilograms	403	14	19	24	24	19
39-60 kilograms	353	15	21	20	21	24
Ever stolen sweets?						
Yes	686	20	23	20	20	17
No	870	11	21	22	26	20

Table 17.7
Distribution of indices of 'degree to which boys see violence as inevitable', analysed according to characteristics of boys

BACKGROUND AND CHARACTERISTICS OF BOYS	Indices of degree to which boys see violence as inevitable					
	All	0-84	85-114	115-154	155-174	175-200
	Cases(n)	288	354	380	287	250
	% across	18%	23%	24%	18%	16%
	n	%	%	%	%	%
Father's occupational level						
Professional, semi-professional, executive	283	19	20	25	21	14
Highly skilled	364	21	21	24	20	15
Skilled	357	16	24	25	18	18
Moderately skilled	248	19	24	23	17	18
Semi-skilled/unskilled	141	16	28	26	18	13
Age of boys						
12-13 years	623	23	25	26	13	12
14-15 years	584	16	23	23	21	18
16-18 years	349	15	18	24	24	20
Type of school last attended						
Secondary modern	379	18	25	26	12	19
Comprehensive	566	19	23	23	19	16
Grammar	330	18	19	25	23	15
Public	183	20	25	24	15	16
Size of household						
2-3 persons	189	14	23	23	21	19
4 persons	457	16	24	25	18	17
5 persons	406	18	23	25	18	16
6 persons	253	21	22	24	19	14
7 + persons	254	24	21	23	17	15
Skin colour						
Coloured	146	29	27	19	14	11
White	1365	18	22	25	19	17
Truancy						
Never	1207	20	23	25	19	14
About once a month	126	17	18	24	15	25
More than once a month	181	13	23	21	19	24
Enjoyed school						
Yes	1222	20	24	25	17	15
No	324	12	19	22	25	21
How long has mother worked since marriage						
Not at all	222	21	20	22	23	14
Up to 2 years	268	18	22	24	20	16
3-5 years	303	24	23	24	15	14
6-10 years	396	15	23	27	17	17
More than 10 years	305	16	27	21	18	18
How often punished for violence/destruction when under four years						
Always	240	15	25	26	18	16
Mostly	325	14	24	22	22	18
Hardly ever	284	22	23	25	18	12
Not at all	151	23	22	26	14	15
Never violent when under four years	522	19	21	24	19	17
Spare time job (if still at school)						
Yes	531	16	22	24	22	16
No	870	22	23	26	16	14
Strength of grip						
10-24 kilograms	352	26	25	26	11	12
25-30 kilograms	433	18	24	23	20	15
31-38 kilograms	403	15	21	25	20	18
39-60 kilograms	353	15	20	23	22	19
Ever stolen sweets?						
Yes	686	16	21	23	21	19
No	870	21	24	26	16	14

Table 17.8
Distribution of indices of degree to which boys 'accept violence as a way to solve their problems', analysed by characteristics of boys

BACKGROUND AND CHARACTERISTICS OF BOYS	Indices of 'acceptance of violence as a way to solve problems'					
	All	0-324	325-394	395-474	475-554	555-890
	Cases(n)	204	348	351	332	324
	% across	13%	22%	23%	21%	21%
	n	%	%	%	%	%
Father's occupational level						
Professional, semi-professional, executive	283	19	29	22	18	12
Highly skilled	364	12	27	24	20	17
Skilled	357	11	18	22	23	26
Moderately skilled	248	13	20	19	25	24
Semi-skilled/unskilled	141	9	15	18	27	31
Age of boys						
12-13 years	623	13	23	23	21	20
14-15 years	584	12	20	22	23	23
16-18 years	349	16	25	22	19	17
Type of school last attended						
Secondary modern	379	9	19	25	25	23
Comprehensive	566	12	21	22	24	21
Grammar	330	18	26	19	16	21
Public	183	16	26	25	17	16
Size of household						
2-3 persons	189	13	23	29	20	15
4 persons	457	12	23	21	23	21
5 persons	406	16	24	24	18	18
6 persons	253	12	21	20	19	27
7 + persons	254	11	19	21	27	22
Skin colour						
Coloured	146	66	18	21	27	27
White	1365	14	23	23	21	20
Truancy						
Never	1207	14	24	24	20	18
About once a month	126	7	18	17	29	29
More than once a month	181	10	17	15	25	33
Enjoyed school						
Yes	1222	14	24	24	20	18
No	324	9	15	17	28	31
How long has mother worked since marriage						
Not at all	222	9	20	24	23	24
Up to 2 years	268	16	21	21	23	20
3-5 years	303	12	26	24	19	18
6-10 years	396	15	22	21	21	20
More than 10 years	305	12	22	23	20	23
How often punished for violence/destruction when under four years						
Always	240	9	20	20	24	27
Mostly	325	10	23	22	21	24
Hardly ever	284	14	23	23	20	21
Not at all	151	11	21	26	21	22
Never violent when under four years	522	17	24	23	21	15
Spare time job (if still at school)						
Yes	531	10	23	20	22	25
No	870	16	23	25	20	17
Strength of grip						
10-24 kilograms	352	11	26	23	20	20
25-30 kilograms	433	13	19	24	22	22
31-38 kilograms	403	12	20	23	22	22
39-60 kilograms	353	16	24	20	22	19
Ever stolen sweets?						
Yes	686	10	20	21	21	28
No	870	16	24	24	21	15

Table 17.9
Dealing with the tenability of the hypothesis that exposure to television violence increases the degree to which boys find violence attractive
(Hypothesis 12)

HYPOTHESIS INVESTIGATED*†	Direction of hypothesis	Means for Qualifiers (Q) Controls (C) and Modified Controls (MC)			Differences between Q and MC means		Significance of difference	
		M_Q	M_C	M_{MC}	M_Q-M_{MC}	As % of M_{MC}	CR	P*
Hypothesis 12 relating DV12 & IV1	F	448.88	427.10	432.24	16.64	3.85	2.78	.003
	R	601.36	556.24	565.37	35.99	6.37	2.80	.003
Sub-hypotheses of hypothesis 12 relating								
a) DV12 & IV6	F	449.53	426.45	442.23	7.30	1.65	1.19	.117
	R	1978.58	1827.92	1933.07	45.51	2.35	0.83	.203
b) DV12 & IV7	F	448.47	427.54	441.98	6.49	1.47	1.01	.156
	R	914.05	840.55	895.45	18.60	2.08	0.78	.218
c) DV12 & IV9	F	450.58	425.40	431.36	19.22	4.46	3.16	$<.001$
	R	1035.62	967.64	994.43	41.19	4.14	1.80	.036
d) DV12 & IV17	F	438.79	433.50	432.93	5.86	1.35	0.70	.242
	R	8.79	8.72	8.73	0.06	0.63	0.39	.348
Hypotheses involving the other mass media								
a) DV12 & IV28	F	452.65	423.26	437.05	15.60	3.57	2.49	.006
	R	9.30	7.88	8.17	1.13	13.83	3.60	.001
b) DV12 & IV29	F	444.90	430.19	432.47	12.43	2.87	2.07	.019
	R	5.83	5.18	5.48	0.35	6.39	1.53	.063
c) DV12 & IV30	F	451.78	423.77	437.02	14.76	3.38	2.45	.007
	R	6.30	5.58	5.86	0.44	7.51	2.34	.010

*DV = dependent variable
IV = independent variable
†For identity of DVs and IVs, see pages 479-80 and table 2.7, chapter 2.

Along with this, we should note that the reverse form of the hypothesis gets a small degree of support from the evidence, so that there exists a possibility that even the minor support given hypothesis 12 is to some extent a reflection of the hypothesised process working in reverse.

The sub-hypotheses of hypothesis 12. A check was also made on four sub-hypotheses relating increase in the degree to which boys find violence attractive to exposure to certain kinds of television programmes, namely:

(a) those where violence is shown as glorified, romanticised, idealised or ennobling (IV6)

(b) those where violence is presented as fun and games, or like a game or as something to entertain (IV7)

(c) those where the physical and mental consequences of violence, for the victim, are shown in detail (IV9)

(d) those showing Tom and Jerry (IV17)

The evidence in table 17.9 gives virtually no support to the sub-hypotheses featuring programme types (a) and (b) and no meaningful support to (d).

For the sub-hypothesis featuring programme type (c), the index of effect is very small (4.46 per cent). It is true, of course, that the P-value indicates that the difference between Qualifiers and Modified Controls is very unlikely to be the product simply of sampling error. But that in no way changes the import of the very small size of the index of effect (or of the difference on which it is based) and so we must conclude that the hypothesis featuring programme type (c) gets only very little support from the evidence.

The effects of exposure to the other mass media. As stated on pages 479-80, a study was also made of the tenability of three further sub-hypotheses of hypothesis 12. These postulated that the attractiveness (to boys) of violence would be increased by exposure to:

(a) comics or comic books (IV28)

(b) violent films (IV29)

(c) newspapers (IV30)

Table 17.9 shows that for all three media, the index of effect is either very small or extremely small (though it also appears that this particular level of effect is unlikely to have arisen from sampling error). On the basis of the very small size of the index, we must conclude that these three sub-hypotheses get, at best, only 'very little' support from the evidence.

On the other hand, the evidence in table 17.9 gives a moderate degree of support to the hypothesis that boys who find violence attractive are thereby led, to some degree, to do more reading of comics and comic books. Furthermore, the findings in table 17.9 give a small degree of support to the hypotheses that such boys are also led to do more newspaper reading and/or to see a greater number of violent films.

Table 17.10
Dealing with the tenability of the hypothesis that exposure to television violence increases the degree to which boys object to the idea of violence in the world (Hypothesis 20)

HYPOTHESIS INVESTIGATED*†	Direction of hypothesis	Means for Qualifiers (Q) Controls (C) and Modified Controls (MC)			Differences between Q and MC means		Significance of difference	
		M_Q	M_C	M_{MC}	$M_Q - M_{MC}$	As % of M_{MC}	CR	P*
Hypothesis 20 relating DV20 and IV1	F	382.00	383.91	379.23	2.77	0.73	0.57	.284
	R	566.51	591.16	590.10	−23.59	−4.00	−1.83	.034
Sub-hypotheses of hypothesis 20 relating								
a) DV20 & IV6	F	382.63	383.29	383.82	−1.19	−0.31	−0.24	.405
	R	1847.35	1959.47	1964.33	−116.98	−5.96	2.33	.010
b) DV20 & IV19	F	381.49	384.46	383.04	−1.55	−0.40	−0.33	.371
	R	59.64	60.46	61.31	−1.67	−2.72	1.28	.100
Hypotheses involving the other mass media								
a) DV20 & IV28	F	375.98	389.96	379.37	−3.39	0.89	0.61	.271
	R	7.92	9.27	8.52	−0.60	−7.04	−1.84	.032
b) DV20 & IV29	F	377.98	388.57	388.24	−10.26	−2.64	−2.20	.014
	R	5.32	5.69	5.58	−0.26	−4.66	−1.14	.127
c) DV20 & IV30	F	377.75	388.32	381.73	−3.98	−1.04	−0.75	.227
	R	5.73	5.15	5.99	0.26	−4.34	1.33	.092

*DV = dependent variable
IV = independent variable

†For identity of DVs and IVs, see pages 479-80 and table 2.7, chapter 2.

The tenability of hypothesis 20 and its sub-hypotheses

In table 17.10 are presented the results of using the standard hypothesis challenging procedure on hypothesis 20 and its sub-hypotheses.

The principal indications of table 17.10 are set out hereunder.

The central hypothesis (relating DV20 and IV1). The central hypothesis in this group stated that 'High exposure to television violence increases the degree to which boys object to the idea of violence in the world.'

The evidence in table 17.10 gives no meaningful support to the central hypothesis.

The several sub-hypotheses of hypothesis 20. A check was also made on the tenability of 2 sub-hypotheses relating increase in the degree to which boys object to the 'idea of violence in the world' to exposure to certain kinds of television programmes, namely:

(a) those where violence is shown as glorified, romanticised, idealised, ennobling (IV6)

(b) television newsreel programmes and television news (IV19)

In each case, the evidence gives no support at all to the hypothesis. Nor does it give meaningful support to the view that such exposure *reduces* the degree to which boys object to the idea of violence in the world.

With regard to the *reverse* hypotheses (i.e. that boys who object to the idea of violence in the world are thereby led to watch more television violence of the sort specified in the sub-hypotheses above), it is perhaps not surprising to see that neither is supported by the evidence. On the other hand, there would be a small degree of support for the view that boys who object to the idea of violence in the world are thereby led to do less viewing of programmes that present violence as glorified, idealised, romanticised or ennobling.

The effects of exposure to the other mass media. Three of the sub-hypotheses were concerned with the effects of exposure to certain of the mass media upon the degree to which boys object to the idea of violence in the world. These mass media were: comic books and comics; violent films; newspapers.

None of these three hypotheses gets support from the evidence, the various indices of effect being either minute or negative in direction. Moreover, even those indices that are negative in direction are at best only extremely small.

The tenability of hypothesis 21 and its sub-hypotheses

In table 17.11 are presented the results of using the standard hypothesis challenging procedure on hypothesis 21 and its sub-hypotheses.

The principal indications of table 17.11 are set out hereunder.

The central hypothesis (relating DV21 and IV1). The central hypothesis in this group stated that: 'High exposure to television violence increases the degree to which boys see violence as a basic part of human nature.' The evidence gives no meaningful support to hypothesis 21: the index of effect is negligible and in any case, P is far from being statistically meaningful.

Table 17.11
Dealing with the tenability of the hypothesis that exposure to television violence increases the degree to which boys see violence as inevitable (i.e. as a basic part of human nature)

HYPOTHESIS INVESTIGATED*†	Direction of hypothesis	Means for Qualifiers (Q) Controls (C) and Modified Controls (MC)			Differences between Q and MC means		Significance of difference	
		M_Q	M_C	M_{MC}	M_Q-M_{MC}	As % of M_{MC}	CR	P*
Hypothesis 21 relating DV21 & IV1	F	127.47	122.01	126.72	0.75	0.59	0.31	.378
	R	598.29	556.13	579.89	18.40	3.17	1.34	.090
Sub-hypotheses of hypothesis 21 relating								
a) DV21 & IV13	F	126.17	123.30	127.85	−1.68	−1.31	−0.71	.239
	R	1175.71	1095.68	1141.40	34.31	3.01	1.23	.109
b) DV21 & IV15	F	128.22	121.31	125.12	3.10	2.48	1.29	.099
	R	66.22	60.28	62.97	3.25	5.16	1.61	.054
c) DV21 & IV19	F	126.60	122.83	126.59	0.01	0.01	0.004	.484
	R	61.19	58.71	60.04	1.15	1.92	0.90	.184
Hypotheses involving the other mass media								
a) DV21 & IV28	F	122.67	126.81	123.89	−1.22	−0.98	−0.51	.305
	R	8.29	8.94	8.65	−0.36	−4.16	−1.18	.119
b) DV21 & IV29	F	126.85	122.36	124.04	2.81	2.26	1.16	.123
	R	5.70	5.28	5.54	0.16	2.89	0.73	.234
c) DV21 & IV30	F	125.38	124.07	124.03	1.35	1.09	0.58	.281
	R	5.93	5.95	5.85	0.08	1.37	0.41	.341

*DV = dependent variable
IV = independent variable

†For identity of DVs and IVs, see pages 479-80 and table 2.7, chapter 2

The several sub-hypotheses of hypothesis 21. A check was also made of the tenability of three sub-hypotheses relating increase in the degree to which boys see violence as a basic part of human nature to exposure to certain kinds of television programmes, namely:

(a) those where the violence is just thrown in for its own sake or is not necessary to the plot (IV13)

(b) fictional programmes of the English police at work which also feature the kinds of violence which go on in society (IV15)

(c) television newsreel programmes and television news (IV19)

The evidence in table 17.11 gives no support to the sub-hypothesis featuring programme-type (a). For the second sub-hypothesis, the evidence provides virtually no support, and for the third, no meaningful support.

The evidence thus militates strongly against taking seriously any of these three sub-hypotheses.

The effects of exposure to the other mass media. A check was also made of the tenability of three hypotheses relating increase in the degree to which boys regard violence as a basic part of human nature to exposure to different mass media. These media were:

(a) comics or comic books (IV28)

(b) violent films (IV29)

(c) newspapers (IV30)

The evidence in table 17.11 gives no support to the hypothesis involving comics, virtually none to that involving violent films, and no meaningful support to that involving newspapers.

The tenability of hypothesis 22 and its sub-hypotheses

In table 17.12 are presented the results of using the standard hypothesis challenging procedure on hypothesis 22 and its sub-hypotheses.

The principal indications of table 17.12 are set out hereunder.

The central hypothesis (relating DV22 and IV1). The central hypothesis in this group postulated that 'High exposure to television violence increases the degree to which boys accept violence as a way to solve problems.'

The evidence in table 17.12 does not give meaningful support to the central hypothesis.

The several sub-hypotheses of hypothesis 22. Several sub-hypotheses of hypothesis 22 postulated that exposure to particular types of television programming increased boys' acceptance of violence as a way to solve problems. These programme types were as follows:

(a) programmes where violence is performed by basically good guy types who are also rebels or odd-men-out (IV3)

(b) programmes in which the violence is presented as being in a good cause (IV8)

Table 17.12
Dealing with the tenability of the hypothesis that exposure to television violence increases the degree to which boys accept violence as a way to solve problems
(Hypothesis 22)

HYPOTHESIS INVESTIGATED*†	Direction of hypothesis	Means for Qualifiers (Q) Controls (C) and Modified Controls (MC)			Differences between Q and MC means		Significance of difference	
		M_Q	M_C	M_{MC}	M_Q-M_{MC}	As % of M_{MC}	CR	P*
Hypothesis 22 relating DV22 & IV1	F	450.32	443.84	447.65	2.67	0.60	0.34	.367
	R	577.60	579.95	572.62	4.98	0.87	0.39	.348
Sub-hypotheses of hypothesis 22 relating								
a) DV22 & IV3	F	450.07	444.09	446.47	3.60	0.81	0.45	.326
	R	820.24	821.72	812.33	7.91	0.97	0.35	.363
b) DV22 & IV8	F	450.80	443.56	446.74	3.86	0.86	0.48	.316
	R	2251.23	2274.63	2236.72	14.51	0.65	0.28	.390
c) DV22 & IV22	F	450.63	443.50	442.34	8.29	1.87	1.08	.140
	R	83.65	82.67	82.31	1.34	1.63	0.48	.316
Hypotheses involving the other mass media								
a) DV22 & IV28	F	459.61	434.49	447.40	12.21	2.73	1.51	.066
	R	9.20	8.03	8.57	0.63	7.35	1.89	.029
b) DV22 & IV29	F	446.52	447.70	453.34	−6.82	−1.50	−0.87	.192
	R	5.54	5.47	5.38	0.16	2.97	0.74	.230
c) DV22 & IV30	F	454.12	439.82	450.10	4.02	0.89	0.52	.302
	R	6.18	5.72	6.07	0.11	1.81	0.57	.284

*DV = dependent variable
IV = independent variable

†For identity of DVs and IVs, see pages 479-80 and table 2.7, chapter 2.

(c) Westerns which include violence, for example, as between cowboys and Indians (IV22)

Sub-hypotheses (a) and (b) got no meaningful support from the evidence in table 17.12 and sub-hypothesis (c) virtually no support.

The effects of exposure to certain of the other mass media. Three sub-hypotheses of hypothesis 22 stipulated that exposure to certain mass media tends to increase boys' acceptance of violence as a way to solve problems. These media were:

(a) comic books and comics (IV28)

(b) violent films (IV29)

(c) newspapers (IV30)

Sub-hypothesis (b) got no support from the evidence, (a) got virtually no support and (c) got no meaningful support.

Summing up on the tenability of hypotheses 12, 20, 21 and 22

The central hypotheses

The evidence collected in this enquiry gives no meaningful support to hypotheses 20, 21 or 22. These postulated that

'High exposure to television violence increases the degree to which:

(a) boys object to the idea of violence (hypothesis 20);

(b) boys see violence as a basic part of human nature and as inevitable (hypothesis 21);

(c) boys accept violence as a way to solve problems (hypothesis 22).'

Hypothesis 12 links high exposure to television violence to 'the degree to which boys find violence attractive'. It gets no more than a very small degree of support from the evidence and even this support is subject to some degree of doubt (because of the greater strength of the reverse form of that hypothesis).

The 'other mass-media' hypotheses

Checks were made on the tenability of a range of hypotheses which separately linked exposure to comics, violent films and newspapers to the four independent variables listed above – making up 12 sub-hypotheses in all. The evidence gives very minor support to only two of them and none to four of them. In general, the evidence provides no grounds for continuing to take these hypotheses seriously.

The programme-type sub-hypotheses

Of the twelve sub-hypotheses featuring different types of television programmes, only one gained any degree of support from the evidence, namely that featuring programmes that show in detail the mental or physical consequences of violence for the victim. But even that degree of support was of a very small kind.

Notes

[1] DV12 = dependent variable 12.

[2] Averages were all expressed on a base of 100 to allow the computed average to be expressed as a whole number (e.g. an average of 3.80 would be expressed as 380) without loss of precision.

[3] DV20 = dependent variable 20.

[4] DV21 = dependent variable 21.

[5] DV22 = dependent variable 22.

[6] Averages were all expressed on a base of 100 to allow the computer averages to be expressed as whole numbers (e.g. an average of 1.32 was expressed as 132) to avoid loss of precision.

CHAPTER 18

THE TENABILITY OF THE HYPOTHESIS THAT EXPOSURE TO TELEVISION VIOLENCE PRODUCES PROBLEMS OVER SLEEP (HYPOTHESIS 17)

Contents

18 THE TENABILITY OF THE HYPOTHESIS THAT EXPOSURE TO TELEVISION VIOLENCE PRODUCES PROBLEMS OVER SLEEP

THE NATURE OF THE HYPOTHESIS

This chapter is principally concerned with the hypothesis that:

> 'High exposure to television violence increases the degree to which boys are involved in problems over sleep.'

The original hypothesis had been worded solely in terms of 'sleep disturbance'. The statements out of which the hypothesis was developed did, however, relate to the fuller concept of 'problems over sleep' and for this reason the hypothesis was later restated in that form.

Several sub-hypotheses were also derived, namely that boys' problems over sleep are increased by exposure to:

(a) television programmes where the physical and mental consequences of violence, for the victim, are shown in detail (IV9);

(b) television programmes in which the violence is gruesome, horrific or scary (IV14);

(c) comic books and comics (IV28);

(d) violent films (IV29);

(e) newspapers (IV30).

THE METHODS OF INVESTIGATION USED
(being a summary of details presented in chapters 3 and 8)

The basic research strategies for investigating the causal hypothesis

The methods used for investigating the tenability of hypothesis 17 were in principle the same as those used on hypotheses 1-4.

Thus for the investigation of hypothesis 17, three basic steps were involved and these were applied quite separately in challenging the forward form and then the reversed form of the hypothesis. These three steps, which are detailed fully in chapter 3, were as follows.

(i) First came the development of a composite of predictors of the dependent and independent variables considered jointly.

(ii) This composite was then used to equate the Controls to the Qualifiers in terms of the correlates of the dependent and the independent variables.

(iii) A calculation was then made of the significance of the *residual* difference between the means of the Qualifiers on the one hand and of the Modified Controls on the other.

Let me emphasise that this three-stage process was used separately for the forward and the reversed forms of the hypothesis. Also, it was used separately for the forward and the reversed forms of each of the sub-hypotheses.

The reader who has skipped straight to this chapter will need to go back to chapter 3 if he is to understand the three steps referred to above.

Measuring the dependent variable

The assessment of 'problems over sleep' called for a range of questions dealing with the different aspects of that matter that had been raised during the hypothesis developing phase of the enquiry.

Obviously boys themselves could answer questions about such of their sleep problems as they were aware of, but it seemed desirable that a parent should also be questioned, in that parents may well know of aspects of such problems that their sons might not happen to mention.

With respect to each boy, four questions were asked, two being addressed to the boy's mother and two to the boy himself. The four questions asked were:

1 (Asked of mother) 'Over the past year, how often has your son needed to sleep with a light on at night?'

2 (Asked of mother) 'Over the past year, has your son been scared to go to bed at night for any reason at all?' (YES/NO). If 'YES', ask: 'How often?'

3 (Asked of boy) 'Over the last year, how often have you lain awake at night for a long time, trying to sleep?'

4 (Asked of boy) 'During the last year, how often have you had nightmares?'

For each of these four questions, the offer of answer was: *Very often/fairly often/now and then/hardly ever/never.*

The four questions were combined to form a general indicator of the existence of problems over sleep. Obviously more information (about the effects of exposure to television violence) would have been secured if the four questions had been formulated as the dependent variables in four separate hypotheses. The high cost of analysis stood in the way of this but the data for such an analysis is available for processing in such an operation.

The method for combining the four questions was: (i) to give a weight to each of the replies on offer, as shown below; (ii) to sum the weights of the replies chosen and to divide this sum by the number of those replies. The resulting average was multiplied by 100 to remove decimals from the results, without losing precision.

Never	0
Hardly ever	1
Now and then	2
Fairly often	3
Very often	4

Cross-analyses made with reference to the dependent variable

A range of cross-analyses was made to determine differences between population sectors in terms of the dependent variable in hypothesis 17.

FINDINGS

Findings have been set out under several headings, namely:

1. the distribution of replies to the four questions making up the dependent variable;
2. the distribution of scores for the dependent variable according to the characteristics of the boys;
3. the tenability of the hypothesis.

The distribution of replies to the four questions relating to problems over sleep

Table 18.1 presents the distribution of replies to the four questions specified on page 502.

Table 18.1
Showing frequency of reported problems over sleep

	Nature of sleep problems over the past year	Never %	Hardly ever %	Now & then %	Fairly often %	Very often %	No information %
Q.1	How often has boy needed to sleep with light on? (Mother's reply)	95	2	1	–	2	–
Q.2	How often has boy been scared to go to bed at night? (Mother's reply)	91	4	3	1	1	–
Q.3	How often has boy lain awake for long periods trying to get to sleep? (Boy's reply)	16	38	30	9	7	1
Q.4	Frequency of nightmares? (Boy's reply)	52	33	11	2	1	1

The principal indications of table 18.1 are as follows:

(a) Some 16 per cent of boys claimed that over the past year they have often lain awake for long periods trying to get to sleep (fairly often or very often).

(b) Relatively few boys claimed that over the past year they have had nightmares often (3 per cent), and for only about 2 per cent did mothers claim that their sons *often* needed to sleep with the light on or often were scared to go to bed.

Distribution of scores on the dependent variable, analysed by the characteristics of boys

The aggregate scores for the dependent variable were analysed by the usual set of

Table 18.2
Distribution of indices of sleep disturbance, analysed by characteristics of boys

	Indices of degree to which boys are subject to sleep disturbance					
	All	0	1-34	35-54	55-104	105-400
	Cases(n)	184	369	357	472	177
	% across	12%	24%	23%	30%	11%
	n	%	%	%	%	%
Father's occupational level						
Professional, semi-professional, executive	283	11	28	24	29	8
Highly skilled	364	15	24	26	26	9
Skilled	357	10	23	23	31	13
Moderately skilled	248	16	23	18	32	10
Semi-skilled/unskilled	141	8	19	26	35	11
Age of boys						
12-13 years	623	11	19	23	31	16
14-15 years	584	11	25	23	31	9
16-18 years	349	15	28	22	28	7
Type of school last attended						
Secondary Modern	379	11	21	24	32	13
Comprehensive	566	15	24	20	29	12
Grammar	330	9	27	23	33	8
Public	183	9	27	28	26	10
Size of household						
2-3 persons	189	9	26	24	32	9
4 persons	457	14	24	25	28	9
5 persons	406	11	24	19	30	15
6 persons	253	8	24	23	34	10
7+ persons	254	14	19	24	30	13
Skin colour						
Coloured	146	12	18	25	34	10
White	1365	12	25	22	30	12
Truancy						
Never	1207	13	24	24	29	11
About once a month	126	9	27	21	33	11
More than once a month	181	8	21	21	36	14
Enjoyed school						
Yes	1222	13	24	23	29	11
No	324	9	23	21	32	15
How long has mother worked since marriage						
Not at all	222	14	20	20	33	14
Up to 2 years	268	10	27	23	29	10
3-5 years	303	13	24	25	29	9
6-10 years	396	13	24	23	30	10
More than 10 years	305	10	22	23	30	16
How often punished for violence/destruction when under four years						
Always	240	12	23	23	34	9
Mostly	325	10	22	20	34	13
Hardly ever	284	10	22	24	30	13
Not at all	151	13	24	26	27	11
Never violent when under four years	522	14	26	23	27	10
Spare time job (if still at school)						
Yes	531	13	24	24	29	10
No	870	11	23	22	31	12
Strength of grip						
10-24 kilograms	352	11	21	21	30	17
25-30 kilograms	433	11	21	24	31	12
31-38 kilograms	403	13	24	22	31	12
39-60 kilograms	353	12	30	24	30	4
Ever stolen sweets?						
Yes	686	9	23	23	34	11
No	870	14	24	23	27	12

characteristics and background details of boys and these are presented in table 18.2.

The principal indications of table 18.2 are as follows.

1 Older boys tend to have somewhat less trouble over sleep;
2 Those who truant more often tend to have somewhat more trouble over sleep;
3 The strongest of the boys (top quartile) tend to have somewhat less trouble over sleep.

The tenability of hypothesis 17 and its sub-hypotheses

The results of the investigation of the tenability of the hypothesis and its sub-hypotheses are set out in table 18.3.

Table 18.3
Dealing with the tenability of the hypothesis that exposure to television violence increases the degree to which boys are involved in sleep disturbance
(Hypothesis 17)

HYPOTHESIS INVESTIGATED*†	Direction of hypothesis	Means for Qualifiers (Q), Controls (C) and Modified Controls (MC)			Differences between Q and MC means		Significance of difference	
		M_Q	M_C	M_{MC}	M_Q-M_{MC}	As % of M_{MC}	CR	P*
Hypothesis 17 relating DV17 & IV1	F	56.97	63.98	59.61	−2.64	−4.43	−1.10	.136
	R	569.68	585.36	562.84	6.84	1.22	0.53	.289
Sub-hypotheses of hypothesis 17 relating								
a) DV17 & IV9	F	56.65	64.30	59.99	−3.34	−5.57	−1.40	.081
	R	983.64	1014.54	985.57	−1.93	−0.20	−0.09	.464
b) DV17 & IV14	F	57.86	63.09	59.63	1.77	−2.97	−0.75	.227
	R	896.66	907.85	876.97	19.69	2.25	0.89	.187
Hypotheses involving the other mass media								
a) DV17 & IV28	F	64.89	56.03	60.74	4.15	6.83	1.46	.072
	R	9.30	8.09	8.42	0.88	10.45	2.72	.003
b) DV17 & IV29	F	59.44	61.65	60.67	−1.23	−2.03	−0.48	.316
	R	5.40	5.58	5.53	−0.13	−2.35	−0.59	.278
c) DV17 & IV30	F	62.00	58.92	62.16	−0.16	−0.26	−0.06	.476
	R	6.11	5.82	5.87	0.24	4.09	1.27	.102

*DV = dependent variable
IV = independent variable

†For identity of DVs and IVs, see page 501 and table 2.7, chapter 2.

The principal indications of table 18.3 are presented below.

The central hypothesis (linking DV17 and IV1). The evidence in table 18.3 gives no support to the central hypothesis, namely that high exposure to television violence increases the degree to which boys have problems over sleeping.

Several sub-hypotheses of hypothesis 17. It had been hypothesised that boys' problems over sleep would be increased by high exposure to:

(a) television programmes where the physical and mental consequences of violence, for the victim, are shown in detail (IV9);

(b) television programmes in which the violence is gruesome, horrific or scary (IV14).

For neither of these programme types is the hypothesis supported by the evidence in table 18.3.

The influence of the other mass media. The evidence in table 18.3 gives no support to the hypotheses that boys' problems over sleep are increased by exposure to violent films or by exposure to newspapers.

On the other hand, there is a small degree of support for the hypothesis as it relates to comic books/comics. But that support is of a slightly uncertain kind (P = .07) and, in addition, the reverse hypothesis is more strongly supported. Accordingly, it would be unwise to conclude that the present tests have done much to support this particular hypothesis.

The tenability of two related hypotheses

Two other hypotheses that bore on the general peace of mind or tranquillity of boys had also been proposed for investigation. In their original form these concerned the effects of high exposure to television upon (i) the existence in boys of angry/bitter feelings; (ii) the degree to which boys are subject to anxiety, nervousness, emotional instability.

In the event, the construction of the tools or techniques for measuring those two dependent variables was subject to difficulties which, in the writer's opinion, rendered them of doubtful relevance for that purpose. They appear to have yielded measurements of related but nonetheless different dependent variables. Accordingly I have limited the tabular presentation of the findings for those two hypotheses to the technical appendix of this report.

In the circumstances, the reader should note that though the tabular findings give no support to the hypotheses as investigated, we must not conclude that the hypotheses in their *original* forms are thereby invalidated. They remain for further investigation, though such an investigation would have to be preceded by a major programme of work on the development of appropriate measuring tools.

CHAPTER 19

THE TENABILITY OF THE HYPOTHESES ABOUT THE EFFECTS OF EXPOSURE TO TELEVISION VIOLENCE UPON CONSIDERATION FOR OTHERS AND UPON RESPECT FOR AUTHORITY (HYPOTHESES 13 AND 14)

Contents

19 THE TENABILITY OF THE HYPOTHESES ABOUT THE EFFECTS OF EXPOSURE TO TELEVISION VIOLENCE UPON CONSIDERATION FOR OTHERS AND UPON RESPECT FOR AUTHORITY (HYPOTHESES 13 AND 14)

THE NATURE OF THE HYPOTHESES

In this chapter I have grouped together two hypotheses which, at least superficially, seem to be of a similar kind:

Hypothesis 13: 'High exposure to television violence reduces the extent to which boys show consideration for other people.';

Hypothesis 14: 'High exposure to television violence reduces boys' respect for authority.'

An investigation was also made of the tenability of a number of sub-hypotheses of those two, one of them relating to a particular type of programme and the rest to other of the mass media. These several sub-hypotheses are specified below.

For hypothesis 13: 'Boys' consideration for other people is likely to be reduced by exposure to:

(a) comics or comic books (IV28);

(b) violent films (IV29);

(c) newspapers (IV30).'

For hypothesis 14: 'Boys' respect for authority is likely to be reduced by:

(a) high exposure to programmes which feature defiance of or rudeness towards authority figures (IV5);

(b) exposure to comics or comic books (IV28);

(c) exposure to violent films (IV29);

(d) exposure to newspapers (IV30).'

The background both to the central hypotheses (13 and 14) and to the various sub-hypotheses is given in detail in chapter 2.

THE METHODS OF INVESTIGATION USED

The basic research strategies for investigating these causal hypotheses

The methods used for investigating the tenability of hypotheses 13 and 14 were in principle the same as those used on hypotheses 1-4.

Thus for each of hypotheses 13 and 14, three basic steps were involved and these were applied quite separately in challenging the forward and then the reversed forms of the hypotheses. These three steps, which are detailed fully in chapter 3, were as follows.

(i) First came the development of a composite of predictors of the dependent and independent variables considered jointly.

(ii) This composite was then used to equate the Controls to the Qualifiers in terms of the correlates of the dependent and the independent variables.

(iii) A calculation was then made of the significance of the *residual* difference between the means of the Qualifiers on the one hand and of the Modified Controls on the other.

Let me emphasise that this three-stage process was used separately for the forward and the reversed forms of each hypothesis. Also, it was used separately for the forward and the reversed forms of each of the sub-hypotheses of each of the hypotheses.

The reader who has skipped straight to this chapter will need to go back to chapter 3 if he is to understand the three steps referred to above.

Measuring the different dependent variables featured in hypotheses 13 and 14

The two dependent variables featured in this chapter were measured through Thurstone-type scales, the construction and full form of which are given in detail in chapter 7. What follows is an illustrative summary of the two measuring processes.

Measuring the degree to which boys are considerate towards other people

1 Each boy completed a 9-statement Thurstone-type rating scale. Each of the 9 statements in that scale had already been allocated a median value derived through the Thurstone evaluation system in the range 0–10. Some examples of its items follow.

Statements	*Median values*
Knocking on people's doors and then running off is a good game	1.81
One should put one's litter in a waste-paper bin	7.75
Boys should help their fathers with jobs in the house, flat, garden or on the car	8.28

2 An individual boy's score was the aggregate of the median values of all the statements he agreed with, divided by the total number of such statements. The range of possible scores was 0.00–10.00 and the higher the score the more the boy may be taken to be considerate towards others. [1]

For full details of this scale – of its construction and use – see chapter 7.

Measuring the degree to which boys have respect for authority (DV14)

1 Each boy completed a 14-statement Thurstone-type rating scale. Each of the 14 statements in this scale had already been allocated a median score derived through the Thurstone evaluation system (0-10). Some examples of items follow:

Statement	*Median values* (scale of 0-10)
The police are thugs	0.43
Cheeking your teachers at school is OK if in fun	4.72
Children should love and respect their parents	9.53

2 An individual boy's score was the aggregate of the median values of all the statements he agreed with, divided by the total number of such statements. The range of possible scores was 0.00–10.00 and the higher the score the greater the boy's 'respect for authority'. [2]

For full details of this scale – of its construction and use – see chapter 7.

Cross-analyses with reference to the dependent variables

A range of cross-analyses was made to determine differences between population sub-groups in terms of the dependent variables featured in hypotheses 13 and 14.

FINDINGS

The findings here have been set out under several headings, namely:

1 the percentage of boys who agreed with the different attitude statements within the different scales;

2 the distribution of averaged scores, for each of the two attitude variables, according to the characteristics of boys;

3 the tenability of the hypotheses dealt with in this chapter.

The first two sections may be regarded as providing basic information about the dependent variables, whilst the third is the key element of the findings.

Percentages of boys agreeing with the different attitude statements within the two different attitude measures or scales

For each of the two attitude measures, each boy had examined a set of statements, sorting each statement into one or another bag to indicate whether he agreed or disagreed with it. These two administrations were separated by other processes to reduce boredom and the influence of one set of statements upon the boy's processing of the next set.

The percentages of boys endorsing the different statements are set out in tables 19.1 and 19.2.

The indications of tables 19.1 and 19.2 are best grasped from a direct study of the details set out in them. Perhaps noteworthy amongst these details are the following:

1 *For table 19.1*

(a) the percentages of boys who were undecided about the different statements;

(b) 31 per cent disagreed that it is 'wrong to shout in the street when it is very late at night';

(c) 46 per cent disagreed that 'it's not fair to other people to play your transistor radio when you sit in a crowded place';

(d) 12 per cent disagreed that 'one should put one's litter in a waste-paper bin'.

2 *For table 19.2*

(a) the percentages of boys in the undecided column;

(b) 82 per cent felt that 'people ought to help the police with their enquiries';

(c) 28 per cent disagreed that 'in sport, you should accept the referee's decision without cheeking him or swearing at him'.

Distribution of attitude scores according to the characteristics of boys

Scores for the two attitude measurements were calculated through the methods outlined on pages 4 and 5 of this chapter. These scores were then analysed according to the usual set of background variables. Details are given in tables 19.3 and 19.4.

The principal indications of tables 19.3 and 19.4 are as follows.

1 *Table 19.3, concerning 'consideration for other people' (DV13).* There was moderate to substantial association between 'consideration for other people' and: age of boy (negative); truancy (negative); enjoyment of school (positive); strength of grip (negative); sweet stealing (negative).

2 *Table 19.4, concerning 'respect for authority' (DV14).* There is marked to substantial association between 'respect for authority' and: age of boy (negative); truancy (negative); enjoyment of school (positive); strength of grip (negative); sweet stealing (negative). The large extent of the negative association between truancy and respect for authority is particularly noteworthy.

The tenability of hypothesis 13

In table 19.5 are presented the results of using the standard hypothesis challenging procedure on hypothesis 13 and its sub-hypotheses.

The principal indications of table 19.5 are set out hereunder.

The central hypothesis (relating DV13 and IV1). The central hypothesis in this group

Table 19.1
Consideration for others: distribution of opinions
(1565 cases)

ATTITUDE STATEMENT	Scale value*	Reaction to statement		
		Agree %	Disagree %	DK or NI %
I do not care about other people in any way whatsoever	0.04	3	91	6
Being rude to old people is fun	0.88	3	94	3
Knocking on people's doors and then running off is a good game	1.81	17	78	5
It's OK to tell people to buzz off	2.88	33	58	9
It's fun to put on a comic voice and pretend to be somebody else when anyone rings me up	3.97	36	52	12
One should put one's litter in a waste paper bin	7.75	84	12	4
Boys should help their fathers with jobs in the house, flat, garden, or on the car	8.28	75	21	5
If I won the pools, I would give a lot of the money away to charity	9.00	23	54	24
If a new boy came to my school or where I work, I would do my best to help him get to know people	9.52	78	11	11
ITEMS ADDED AFTER FIRST RATING SESSION†				
It's not fair to other people to play your transistor radio when you sit in a crowded place	8.25	44	46	10
When we have sweets we should offer them to any friends who are with us	8.60	81	15	4
If your friend has a headache you should not be noisy	8.68	73	22	5
It's wrong to shout in the street when it is very late at night	8.85	65	31	4

*Mean value of statement on a scale running from 0–10.
†Not used in assessment of attitude.
DK or NI = Don't know or no information

Table 19.2
Respect for authority: distribution of opinions
(1565 cases)

ATTITUDE STATEMENT	Scale value*	Reaction to statement		
		Agree %	Disagree %	DK or NI %
The police are thugs	0.43	6	87	6
There is no need to take any notice of what your parents tell you	0.47	2	97	2
Swearing at teachers is OK	0.61	4	93	3
I don't think the police deserve respect	1.06	6	90	4
If you don't want to do as the school teacher tells you, don't do it	1.50	10	83	7
The police are unfair	2.40	8	83	9
I don't think my parents know what they are talking about half the time	3.17	9	86	5
Parents think they know best, but they're no better than anyone else really	4.17	18	73	9
Cheeking the teachers at school is OK if in fun	4.72	38	56	6
Cheeking your parents is OK if in fun	5.67	33	64	4
Most policemen are decent people	7.83	76	18	6
People ought to help the police with their enquiries	8.10	82	11	7
In sport, you should accept the referee's decision without cheeking him or swearing at him	8.19	67	28	4
Children should love and respect their parents	9.53	87	9	4

*Mean value of statement on a scale running from 0–10
DK or NI = Don't know or no information.

Table 19.3
Distribution of indices of 'consideration for others', analysed according to the characteristics of boys (DV13)

BACKGROUND AND CHARACTERISTICS OF BOYS	Index of 'consideration for others'					
	All	0-594	595-694	695-784	785-854	855-953
	Cases(n)	298	329	317	333	282
	% across	19%	21%	20%	21%	18%
	n	%	%	%	%	%
Father's occupational level						
Professional, semi-professional, executive	283	16	20	25	22	17
Highly skilled	364	20	22	18	23	16
Skilled	357	22	17	22	22	17
Moderately skilled	248	17	23	18	19	23
Semi-skilled/unskilled	141	16	27	19	16	22
Age of boys						
12-13 years	623	15	18	19	24	24
14-15 years	584	24	23	17	20	16
16-18 years	349	19	23	28	19	12
Type of school last attended						
Secondary modern	379	21	20	17	19	22
Comprehensive	566	17	22	22	22	17
Grammar	330	21	22	21	22	14
Public	183	18	19	23	21	19
Size of household						
2-3 persons	189	19	15	26	29	12
4 persons	457	18	22	21	21	18
5 persons	406	21	21	20	17	21
6 persons	253	20	23	16	25	15
7 + persons	254	16	22	20	20	21
Skin colour						
Coloured	146	17	18	18	20	26
White	1365	19	22	20	22	17
Truancy						
Never	1207	17	20	20	24	19
About once a month	126	29	21	23	13	14
More than once a month	181	22	31	23	13	12
Enjoyed school						
Yes	1222	16	21	21	23	19
No	374	30	23	18	17	13
How long has mother worked since marriage						
Not at all	222	21	16	22	21	20
Up to 2 years	268	19	25	16	22	17
3-5 years	303	16	20	22	22	19
6-10 years	396	20	22	21	19	18
More than 10 years	305	21	19	21	23	16
How often punished for violence/destruction when under four years						
Always	240	21	22	15	25	17
Mostly	325	19	20	21	21	19
Hardly ever	284	22	18	18	22	20
Not at all	151	14	21	25	19	23
Never violent when under four years	522	18	23	22	21	16
Spare time job (if still at school)						
Yes	531	20	25	20	19	15
No	870	17	19	20	24	21
Strength of grip						
10-24 kilograms	352	11	17	19	23	30
25-30 kilograms	433	20	21	19	24	15
31-38 kilograms	403	22	22	19	21	16
39-60 kilograms	353	22	24	25	18	12
Ever stolen sweets?						
Yes	686	26	23	19	17	14
No	870	13	19	21	25	21

Table 19.4
Distribution of indices of 'respect for authority' analysed according to the characteristics of boys

	Index of 'respect for authority'					
	All	0-624	625-724	725-804	805-844	845-954
	Cases(n)	296	329	360	344	230
	% across	19%	21%	23%	22%	15%
	n	%	%	%	%	%
Father's occupational level						
Professional, semi-professional, executive	283	14	19	25	25	16
Highly skilled	364	17	24	21	23	15
Skilled	357	20	21	21	21	17
Moderately skilled	248	24	15	29	21	12
Semi-skilled/unskilled	141	21	27	22	16	13
Age of boys						
12-13 years	623	14	15	23	31	17
14-15 years	584	20	24	23	18	15
16-18 years	349	26	27	24	13	11
Type of school last attended						
Secondary modern	379	22	20	24	20	15
Comprehensive	566	19	22	24	19	16
Grammar	330	17	22	23	25	14
Public	183	16	18	23	27	16
Size of household						
2-3 persons	189	14	27	23	25	11
4 persons	457	18	21	27	20	15
5 persons	406	19	20	20	24	17
6 persons	253	21	22	22	20	15
7 + persons	254	23	19	22	22	15
Skin colour						
Coloured	146	20	22	20	23	15
White	1365	19	21	24	22	15
Truancy						
Never	1207	14	20	24	26	16
About once a month	126	29	26	16	12	17
More than once a month	181	44	23	19	6	9
Enjoyed school						
Yes	1222	15	21	25	25	15
No	374	36	23	15	12	14
How long has mother worked since marriage						
Not at all	222	21	21	23	21	14
Up to 2 years	268	16	18	26	23	18
3-5 years	303	20	22	18	25	14
6-10 years	396	20	21	22	21	15
More than 10 years	305	19	24	24	19	14
How often punished for violence/destruction when under four years						
Always	240	18	21	23	22	16
Mostly	325	20	20	26	18	16
Hardly ever	284	24	19	24	22	11
Not at all	151	20	25	21	15	20
Never violent when under four years	522	15	21	22	27	14
Spare time job (if still at school)						
Yes	531	18	22	25	20	15
No	870	16	19	23	26	16
Strength of grip						
10-24 kilograms	352	14	14	23	31	17
25-30 kilograms	433	15	19	24	27	16
31-38 kilograms	403	22	24	24	17	13
39-60 kilograms	353	26	27	22	13	12
Ever stolen sweets?						
Yes	686	26	23	23	15	13
No	870	13	20	23	27	16

Table 19.5
Dealing with the tenability of the hypothesis that exposure to television *reduces* the degree of consideration that boys have for other people
(Hypothesis 13)

HYPOTHESIS INVESTIGATED*†	Direction of hypothesis	Means for Qualifiers (Q) Controls (C) and Modified Controls (MC)			Differences between Q and MC means		Significance of difference	
		M_Q	M_C	M_{MC}	M_Q-M_{MC}	As % of M_{MC}	CR	P*
Hypothesis 13 relating DV13 & IV1	F	703.79	726.61	714.02	−10.23	−1.43	−1.20	.115
	R	555.73	602.95	581.28	−25.55	−4.40	−1.94	.026
Hypotheses involving the other mass media								
a) DV13 & IV28	F	721.40	708.99	709.16	12.24	1.73	1.51	.066
	R	8.76	8.41	8.51	0.25	2.94	0.79	.215
b) DV13 & IV29	F	700.10	732.23	725.58	−25.48	−3.51	−3.23	<.001
	R	5.03	6.00	5.61	− 0.58	−10.34	−2.53	.006
c) DV13 & IV30	F	709.92	720.65	710.20	− 0.28	−0.04	−0.03	.488
	R	5.83	6.05	5.96	− 0.13	−2.18	−0.68	.248

*DV = dependent variable
IV = independent variable

†For identity of DVs and IVs, see page 508 and table 2.7, chapter 2.

postulated: 'High exposure to television violence reduces the extent to which boys show consideration for other people (DV13).'

The evidence in table 19.5 (line 1) gives virtually no support to this hypothesis, the index of effect being only −1.43 per cent and the P value .12 (see evaluation system in chapter 10).

The effects of exposure to the other mass media. Hypotheses had also been formulated about the effects (on consideration for others) on exposure to comics/comic books, violent films, newspapers.

The evidence in table 19.5 gives no meaningful support to the hypothesis featuring newspapers and no support to that featuring comics or comic books. It gives very little support to the hypothesis featuring violent films (index of effect = −3.51) and in this case, the reverse hypothesis is supported to a moderate degree, namely that boys who have consideration for others are thereby influenced to see fewer violent films.

The tenability of hypothesis 14

In table 19.6 are presented the results of using the standard hypothesis challenging procedure on hypothesis 14 and its sub-hypotheses.

The principal indications of table 19.6 are set out hereunder.

The central hypothesis (relating DV14 and IV1). The central hypothesis in this group postulated: 'High exposure to television violence reduces boys' respect for authority (DV14).'

The evidence in table 19.6 (line 1) gives no support to this hypothesis.

The programme type sub-hypothesis. A check was also made on the sub-hypotheses that respect for authority is reduced by high exposure to programmes that feature defiance of or rudeness towards authority figures (IV5).

The evidence in table 19.6 (line 3) gives no support to this hypothesis.

The other mass media. It had also been hypothesised that a loss in respect for authority figures would follow exposure to comics/comic books, to violent films, to newspapers.

The evidence in table 19.6 gives virtually no support to these three media-linked hypotheses. Nor would it give any support to hypotheses postulating *increase* in respect for authority as a result of media exposure.

It is noteworthy that the evidence in table 19.6 would give a moderate degree of support to an hypothesis that boys who respect authority tend, because of this, to be less exposed to violent films.

Summing up on the central hypotheses

The evidence presented in this chapter tends not to support the hypothesis that high exposure to television violence:

(a) tends to make boys less considerate of others;

(b) tends to make boys have less respect for authority figures.

Similarly for the hypotheses that exposure to other of the mass media has such an effect.

Table 19.6
Dealing with the tenability of the hypothesis that exposure to television violence *reduces* the degree to which boys respect authority
(Hypothesis 14)

HYPOTHESIS INVESTIGATED*†	Direction of hypothesis	Means for Qualifiers (Q) Controls (C) and Modified Controls (MC)			Differences between Q and MC means		Significance of difference	
		M_Q	M_C	M_{MC}	$M_Q - M_{MC}$	As % of M_{MC}	CR	P*
Hypothesis 14 relating DV14 & IV1	F	715.09	735.17	713.32	1.77	0.25	0.21	.417
	R	549.58	607.27	569.34	−19.76	−3.47	−1.49	.068
A sub-hypothesis of hypothesis 14 relating DV14 & IV5	F	721.34	728.93	707.55	13.79	1.95	1.67	.048
	R	955.35	1024.33	970.80	−15.45	−1.59	−0.67	.251
Hypotheses involving the other mass media								
a) DV14 & IV28	F	718.79	731.51	727.76	−8.97	−1.23	−1.13	.129
	R	8.64	8.55	8.57	0.07	0.82	0.20	.421
b) DV14 & IV29	F	713.74	737.98	720.65	−6.91	−0.96	−0.86	.195
	R	5.01	5.98	5.57	−0.56	−10.05	−2.56	.005
c) DV14 & IV30	F	715.77	734.78	723.04	−7.27	−1.01	−0.92	.179
	R	5.58	6.29	5.89	−0.31	−5.26	−1.63	.052

*DV = dependent variable
IV = independent variable

†For identity of DVs and IVs, see page 508 and table 2.7, chapter 2.

Notes

[1] Averages were all expressed on a base of 100 to allow the computed averages to be expressed as whole numbers (e.g. 3.80 was expressed as 380) without loss of precision.

[2] As [1] above.

CHAPTER 20

THE PRINCIPAL FINDINGS AND A COMMENTARY ON THEM

Contents

20 THE PRINCIPAL FINDINGS AND A COMMENTARY ON THEM

The findings from this enquiry, as they relate to the tenability of the hypotheses that were investigated, are numerous and varied. The better to grasp such trends and principles as appear to feature the total array of findings, I have set out hereunder what I consider are the principal results. Subsequently I have commented on what I consider are their indications.

PRINCIPAL FINDINGS

1 The most noteworthy of the findings presented in this report is that relating to *hypothesis 4*, namely that *high exposure to television violence increases the degree to which boys engage in serious violence*: the evidence gave this hypothesis a very large degree of support and that support was the more firm because the *reverse* formulation of the hypothesis got 'no meaningful' support from the evidence.

2 Broadly the same type of result emerged for many of the 25 sub-hypotheses of hypothesis 4, namely sub-hypotheses about the effects, on involvement in serious violence, of high exposure to certain kinds of television output. On the evidence of this enquiry, five types of television violence appear to be the more potent in releasing serious violence by boys, namely:

(a) plays or films in which violence occurs in the context of close personal relations;

(b) violent programmes in which the violence appears to have been 'just thrown in for its own sake' or is not necessary to the plot;

(c) programmes presenting fictional violence of a realistic kind;

(d) programmes in which the violence is presented as being in a good cause;

(e) Westerns of the violent kind.

By contrast, there was but little or no support for the hypotheses that exposure to the following kinds of programme output increases serious violence by boys.

(a) sporting programmes presenting violent behaviour by competitors or spectators (excluding programmes on boxing and wrestling);

(b) violent cartoons including Tom and Jerry;

(c) science fiction violence;

(d) slapstick comedy presenting violence or verbal abuse.

3 Hypotheses 1, 2 and 3 dealt with the effects of high exposure to television violence upon violent behaviour (principally) of the 'less than serious' kind. All

three hypotheses were supported by the evidence to a 'moderate' degree. However, in each case the reverse hypothesis also got a degree of support from the evidence, and so we cannot rule out, for any of them, the possibility that the support given to the forward form of the hypothesis is to some extent a reflection of a reverse process being in operation.

4 The evidence gave a 'fairly large' degree of support to two other behavioural hypotheses, namely that high exposure to television violence increases the degree to which boys: (i) are aggressive in sport or play (hypothesis 7); (ii) swear or use bad language (hypothesis 8). We must note however that in each case the reversed formulation of the hypothesis got a 'small' degree of support as well – so that here too we cannot rule out the possibility that to some extent the support given to the hypothesis is a reflection of a reverse process being in operation.

5 At a more generalised level, the evidence indicated that certain broad categories of violent behaviour were more likely (than were other categories) to be produced by high exposure to television violence, namely violent behaviour that is unskilled, spontaneous, unplanned; television-type acts of violence that offer scope for *easy* imitation. The opposite applied with acts that appeared to carry their own deterrents or where deterrents were 'in the offing' (e.g. picking a fight).

6 On the basis of a major set of purely correlational data (see figure 12.1, chapter 12), it appears that the association between involvement in serious violence and extent of exposure to television violence is of an irregular kind – with the level of serious violence tending to increase only after quite a lot of television violence has been seen. Such evidence raises questions concerning margins of safety and long term effects (see later for discussion). On the other hand, for less serious forms of violence by boys, the association is more regular in character, being suggestive of a rising curve.

7 There is a major difference in the character of the findings in going from the behavioural to the attitudinal hypotheses: the evidence gives very little support indeed to the various hypotheses relating to conscious attitudes or outlook or states of mind. More specifically:

(a) The evidence gave no meaningful support to the hypotheses that high exposure to television violence:

- (i) leads to preoccupation with acts of violence frequently shown on television;
- (ii) leads boys to feel more willing to commit such acts.

(b) The evidence gave no meaningful support to the hypothesis that high exposure to television violence 'hardens boys' (i.e. makes them more callous) in relation to violence in the world around them.

(c) Similarly there was no meaningful support for the hypothesis that high exposure to television violence:

- (i) causes boys to see violence as a basic part of human nature;
- (ii) causes boys to accept violence as a way to solve their problems;
- (iii) leads in general to sleep disturbances; [1]
- (iv) leads to a reduction in boys' consideration for others or in boys' respect for authority.

8 Some of the hypotheses investigated dealt with the influence of high exposure to comics, violent films, newspapers.

(a) *Concerning violence considered generally.* For all three media, the evidence gives a fairly large degree of support to the hypotheses that high exposure increases boys' involvement in violence considered generally (DV1) [2] – though for each it remains possible (on the evidence of reverse hypothesis testing) that this support is to some extent the reflection of a process, opposite in character to that hypothesised, being in operation.

(b) *Concerning serious violence.* The evidence gives no meaningful support to the hypothesis that high exposure to newspapers increases boys' involvement in serious violence. With respect to exposure to comics and violent films, the index of effect is in both cases large (34.51 per cent and 26.16 per cent respectively). We must exercise scientific wariness in our interpretation of these indices because of the joint indication of the statistical significance levels and of the reverse hypothesis test results. However, scientific wariness does not mean that we should disregard the positive indications of those large indices of effect.

COMMENTARY ON THE FINDINGS

I want to present two different kinds of commentary on the findings of this enquiry: (1) comments and suggestions about the principles and processes that appear to lie behind the changes indicated by the findings; (2) comments about the implications of the results for the control, by programme management, of the presentation of violence on television.

The underlying principles and processes

Whereas I regard it as essential for the researcher to study his findings for any indications of underlying principles and processes and whereas I have attempted to do this, I would like it to be quite clear that what I have to say here about such underlying principles or processes is in the form of hypotheses – as distinct from theories or firm conclusions.

There is of course an abundance of *existing* hypotheses about such processes, these being known by terms such as: imitation, catharsis, identification, triggering, desensitisation, attitude change, inhibition, disinhibitory learning, stimulation. Some of these hypothesised processes are briefly defined in the notes at the end of this chapter. [3] To some of them I will be referring in commenting on the implications of the *present evidence* for underlying processes. But there is no intention here of making this chapter an occasion for presenting a general review or appraisal of the many competing hypotheses that different researchers and theorists have put forward. That has already been done by others. [4] The reader should also study the hypotheses listed in chapter 2, table 2.4.

1 The evidence supports the view that whereas television violence has increased the degree to which boys commit violent acts, it has made relatively little difference to their conscious attitudes and opinions about violence. Odd as this finding may seem at first, it is not inconsistent with a situation in which society and the mass media continue to give verbal opposition to violence – to cry out against it – whilst at the same time television bombards its viewers with presentations of violent behaviour as a form of entertainment. If what society and the media *said*

or preached about violence was on a par with television's presentation of violent behaviour, then possibly attitudes and opinions would also have changed negatively. But even in the absence of overt condemnation of violence by society and the media, I see no good reason for assuming that a long drawn out modification of boys' behavioural conditioning in relation to violence will necessarily be accompanied by parallel changes in their conscious opinions about violence.

Whatever we may say about the underlying processes involved, the findings are suggestive of a situation in which boys are unaware of the changes that have taken place in them.

2 In my opinion the evidence is strongly suggestive of a disinhibition process. By this I mean a process through which those inhibitions against being violent that are ordinarily built up in boys by parents and other socialising agencies are progressively broken down by the continuous presentation of violence on television, so that eventually *such violent urges as are present in boys* are rendered much more likely to 'spill out' as it were, in the form of violent behaviour.

The evidence supporting this view or hypothesis is broadly as follows:

(a) As exposure to television violence continues, there is a progressive build-up in the degree to which boys engage in minor forms of violence and it is only when exposure is well advanced that the extent of *serious* violence also begins to increase. It is as though a break-down process releases minor forms of violence fairly readily but that the breakdown has to be well advanced for the release of the more serious forms of violence.

(b) The kinds of violence that tend most to be released appear to be spontaneous, unplanned and unskilled in character and to be of the sort that boys can easily use or adopt. This situation seems to me to suggest that the boys concerned have become subject to a fairly blind and automatic release process in which the normal irritations and pressures of existence lead to fairly unbridled reactions.

(c) It is particularly noteworthy that there does not appear to be a television-induced preoccupation with the kinds of acts of violence frequently shown on television or a feeling of increased willingness or desire to commit such acts. In other words, whatever is guiding the release of violence by boys, it does not appear to be a conscious fixation upon the acts of violence that are frequently shown on television. And this leaves open the possibility that the kinds of release stimulated by exposure to television violence are reflections of the violent dispositions inherent in the boys — that television's role is to facilitate the release of whatever tendencies to be violent the boys may have.

(d) The kinds of acts that exposure to television does *not* appear to increase include those that tend to carry their own deterrents or potential deterrents (e.g. picking a fight). This situation would hold up a 'disinhibition' process, but it is in the same broad explanatory category as is 'disinhibition', namely the category of de-conditioning/conditioning.

(e) The indication that behavioural changes occur without any parallel changes in attitude towards violence is suggestive of a slow and unconscious mechanism of behavioural change.

In no way am I suggesting that the evidence presented *establishes* a 'disinhibition' principle. I submit only that the evidence presented provides sufficient support for such an hypothesis to warrant its experimental investigation.

3 The formulation of a 'disinhibition' hypothesis is not meant to imply that other processes (supporting or opposing or independent) do not also occur. Indeed the most likely situation as I see the matter is that *various* processes are in operation, some more dominant than others and some specific to certain types of TV output, to certain types of violent behaviour, to certain types of boys, to certain types of situation.

4 One of the more frequently postulated views about how television violence exerts its influence is what is known as the imitation hypothesis – namely that boys copy the violence they see on television.

During the hypothesis development stage of this enquiry it had become quite clear that many boys and their parents were convinced that boys often took over certain of the violent behaviour they had seen on television, for example swearing and bad language from a wide range of programmes, gun play from Westerns. At later group discussion sessions (conducted for other purposes) during the Kung Fu period, parents had been full of stories about the imitation by their sons of Kung Fu type violence. Such is the frequency and the vigour of claims about imitation that I would consider it very strange indeed if a theorist refused to consider an imitation hypothesis. Certainly too this present enquiry provided evidence that is consistent with an imitation process being in operation in certain circumstances. Thus:

(a) high exposure to programmes involving a lot of swearing and verbal abuse was associated with an increase in the degree to which boys swore or used bad language;

(b) high exposure to sporting programmes presenting violence was associated with an increase in the degree to which boys were themselves violent in sport or play.

On the other hand, we must consider the limitations that certain of the evidence, already presented in *support* of the disinhibition hypothesis, puts upon the operation of the imitation process, thus:

(a) There is an absence of support for the hypotheses that exposure to television violence,

    (i) causes preoccupation with its acts of violence;
    (ii) produces in boys a willingness/desire to commit such acts.

(b) The findings indicate that it is violence of the unplanned, spontaneous, unskilled and 'easy to adopt' kind that tends to be produced by exposure to television violence. This is not to say that certain individuals don't from time to time take over the working details of TV presentations of complex acts of violence. What is being said is that this is not what normally happens.

On the basis of the evidence available, my impression of the imitation process – and I do not put the matter higher than 'impression' – is that in the television context (i) imitation tends to relate to simple acts of the sort that boys can perform almost automatically; (ii) the imitation or adoption of simple television acts may well be facilitated by a disinhibition process.

Of course, one may ask why it is that large scale imitation of TV acts of violence — both sophisticated and simple acts — does not take place. Certainly a great many boys would have the ability to consciously copy even very complicated violence shown on television. But at the risk of stating the obvious, the likelihood of this happening is inversely dependent upon both the perceived likelihood of getting caught for such behaviour and the existence in the boy of anti-violence conditioning — a fact of life that tends not to be properly represented in laboratory type studies of the imitation process.

5 In some ways the results are relevant to the 'catharsis' hypothesis. In the television context this is the hypothesis that viewers tend to 'get violence out of their systems' through seeing violence acted out for them on the screen.

The results of the present enquiry do of course raise major problems for the catharsis hypothesis interpreted in any overall or general sense, for the overall indication of the findings was that exposure to television violence *increases* the amount of violence that boys commit. However, one might attempt a more limited interpretation of the 'catharsis' hypothesis by postulating that only certain types of violence are subject to the catharsis effect. In that case, the evidence in the lower part of table 12.15, chapter 12, is well worth consideration in the context of the catharsis hypothesis. That evidence is suggestive of reductions in the incidence of certain kinds of violence (e.g. tried to start a fight, violent on the way to a football match, being violent to someone in authority, giving someone a 'deadleg').

That sort of evidence might be consistent with a modified catharsis hypothesis. But it is also consistent with a 'displacement' hypothesis — in that there is only so much a boy can do in the time available to him. Nonetheless, it does seem worthwhile giving further consideration to the possible operation of a catharsis process of a fairly specialised and individual kind and I think it desirable to do this in the context of disinhibition, imitation and displacement hypotheses.

6 The findings for hypotheses 18 and 19 (chapter 16) bear on the 'desensitisation' hypothesis, namely the hypothesis that continued exposure to television violence dulls the emotional reactivity of the exposees to the spectacle of real life violence. The evidence derived from the present study gives no support to the 'desensitisation' hypothesis. Of course, the measurements made of attitudes tended to be at the conscious level only, whereas desensitisation may have occurred *below* the conscious level. I think too that it is desirable to keep it in mind that in our society there is considerable verbal condemnation of *real life* violence, and that the news media usually express shock and sympathy in reporting natural disasters and tend to condemn personal violence. Quite possibly, this situation has worked against the emergence or operation of desensitisation. However, whatever the subtleties of the situation, the two hypotheses postulating desensitisation do not get support from the evidence of this enquiry.

7 The evidence seems also to provide some grounds for an 'inertia' or 'satiation' hypothesis. It is noteworthy that with *extreme* levels of exposure to television violence, some of the increases in boys' violence tend to fall away: certainly there

is an *overall* increase in violence by such boys – but not to the same extent as those subjected to only *substantial* exposure. See figure 12.1, chapter 12. However, we must also note that this particular item of evidence is of an uncorrected correlational kind and must therefore be regarded warily. Whereas the evidence available leads me to doubt very much that extensive empirical matching will change the indications of the trend data, that matching operation must be carried out if we are to pursue the interpretation of this aspect of the findings much further. In the meantime it seems reasonable to ask if perhaps the acquisition of a *very high* degree of exposure to television violence has left such boys with very little time – and perhaps little energy – for carrying out violence of their own.

Summing up. The principal hypothesis put forward in this section is that exposure to television violence serves to reduce such inhibitions as have been built up in boys against being violent, and that this happens without boys being aware of the changes they have undergone. As this breakdown or erosion goes on, boys slip more easily and spontaneously than formerly into violent forms of reaction to the stimuli of their environment. Imitation seems also to be involved under certain circumstances and it may be operating within the context of the disinhibition process. The evidence is not inconsistent with the limited operation of a catharsis process, but that evidence could equally well support a 'displacement' hypothesis. The evidence does not support the 'desensitisation' hypothesis – though it remains possible that desensitisation is nonetheless occurring at the sub-conscious level.

Indications for the control, by programme management, of the presentation of violence on television

1 The evidence of this enquiry gives support to the hypothesis that exposure to television violence has led to an increase in violence by boys. This support is very strong with respect to violent behaviour of the more serious kind. *The principal indication of this finding is that there should be a substantial cut-back in the amount of violence presented through television.*

2 The extent and the nature of the cut-back are obviously of importance.

(a) *Concerning the extent of the necessary reduction in the amount of violence being presented on television.* According to the evidence of chapter 12, it appears that as the amount of exposure to television violence increases, so does the degree to which boys commit violence of a relatively non-serious kind (see chapter 12, page 389). However, as the amount of exposure goes on increasing, there comes a point at which *serious* violence begins to be produced (perhaps liberated) in boys and the amount of this production increases as the amount of exposure to television violence goes on increasing. (At the extreme levels of exposure, it appears that some of the increase in violence is lost, possibly through an inertia factor).

For a control strategy, the implications of this situation appear to be as follows.

(i) As far as *serious* violence is concerned, there is a very well supported case for a major reduction in the total amount of violence shown on television (see chapter 12).

(ii) At the same time, if we are interested *solely* in the reduction of *serious* violence by boys, the cut-back in television violence does not necessarily have to be complete, for the increase in serious violence by boys does not appear to occur until the accumulated input has gone beyond a certain level. In other words, there appears to be scope for the presentation of a certain amount of violence without the production of serious violence in boy viewers. But that relatively safe level is far below the level at which violence has been presented on London's television service over the years.

(iii) However, if we are interested in reducing the degree to which television stimulates the *relatively non-serious forms of violence* in boys, then the cut-back in television violence would have to be very drastic indeed, for there is a steady increase in violence of this kind as exposure to TV violence increases. Of course, from a practical point of view, it is hard to see how there could ever be a *total* ban on television violence, if for no other reason that it is an intrinsic feature of some of our news. Moreover, producers might reasonably object that anything like the total elimination of violence is both unrealistic and impossible. Indeed, to attempt it would be to emasculate programming. But it is equally obvious from the evidence that there should be a substantial reduction in the violent content of television's output.

(b) *Concerning the nature of the violence that it is most necessary to eliminate.* If the amount of television violence is to be reduced, then someone has to decide upon criteria for reducing it. At a purely commonsense level, this should not be difficult once production staff accept television violence first and foremost as potentially damaging rather than regarding it principally as potential entertainment. Their priorities should be in this order and not the reverse. With this approach alone, linked to a responsible outlook, it should be possible to achieve a considerable reduction of the total amount of violence presented on television.

At the same time it is clear that the cutting back process can be more efficiently handled if we know which sorts of television violence are the *more* harmful and which are the *less* harmful. The investigation had yielded data that could be used for the development of *provisional* guidelines of the sort required, provided certain analytical procedures were applied to them. More specifically, the data available made it possible to investigate the tenability of a large number of hypotheses linking exposure to specific types of television violence to violent behaviour by boys, for example: 'High exposure to television programmes featuring fictional violence of a realistic kind increases the degree to which boys engage in serious violence'. There was scope for formulating (and investigating) many such hypotheses involving 25 different categories of television violence.

The outcome of this part of the investigation led to the development of the set of provisional guidelines set out on pages 422-3 of chapter 13 and repeated in chapter 1. In my recommendations (chapter 1), I have called for specialised research to examine, to extend and generally to develop the provisional guidelines so that they become of maximum use to programme staff in making their decisions about whether or not to present certain kinds of violence on television.

The degree to which the findings are applicable beyond London

Strictly speaking the results of this enquiry apply to London and they do not necessarily apply elsewhere. However I would be willing to hypothesise a similar outcome in cities where the nature of the television programming and the nature of the culture are broadly similar to those of London.

On these grounds, I would expect the results to have a considerable degree of relevance to other large cities in Britain. Much of the television presented to London boy viewers over the years has been similar to that presented to American boy viewers – partly because many of Britain's violent programmes have been imported from the USA. Certainly many of the programmes in the sample of programmes drawn for the London study were of USA origin. Culturally, there are of course many differences between the two countries, but in terms of those aspects of a culture that tend to be associated with violent behaviour, there is much that is similar in the cities of the two countries. So I would expect the findings of the London study to apply to many USA cities as well. On the same general argument, it seems reasonable to hypothesise an appreciable degree of applicability to other large cities in other countries where the television experience and the cultural situation are broadly similar to those of London.

Nonetheless it is highly desirable that, where opportunity exists, studies of the present kind should be carried out in other towns and countries, with all available benefit being taken from an examination of the research strategies and the measurement systems that were used in this London enquiry.

Notes

[1] This is not to say that television violence does not produce sleep disturbances for some boys. The finding as reported simply means that there is no overall increase – the average does not increase. Indeed, the figures suggest a very small (but statistically uncertain) *reduction* in the average.

[2] A weighted score in which 'less than serious' violence dominates.

[3] There has been a considerable build-up of hypotheses about the nature of the mechanisms or processes whereby exposure to television violence affects the outlook and/or the behaviour of those exposed to it. These hypotheses, as they relate to the television context, include the following.

1. *The 'catharsis' hypothesis.* This is the hypothesis that there will be a 'drawing off' of the aggressive energies of those who watch violence being acted out on the television screen. For discussion, see S. Feshbach (1961) 'The stimulating versus cathartic effects of a vicarious aggressive activity', *Journal of Abnormal and Social Psychology*, vol.63; R. Goranson (1969), 'The catharsis effect: two opposing views', *Mass Media and Violence*, R. Baker and S. Ball (eds), US Government Printing Office, USA. Feshbach distinguishes between situations in which he postulates the 'catharsis' process will and will not be produced.

2 *The 'imitation' hypothesis.* This is the hypothesis that viewers copy behaviour and pick up outlooks that have been presented on television. This hypothesis is often tied in with the further hypothesis that 'imitation' is more likely to occur if the behaviour/outlook concerned are those of some person with whom the viewer can identify. See A. Bandura, D. Ross and S.A. Ross (1961), 'Transmission of aggression through imitation of aggressive models', *Journal of Abnormal and Social Psychology*, vol.63; D.J. Hicks (1965), 'Imitation and retention of film-mediated aggressive peer and adult models', *Journal of Personality and Social Psychology*, vol.2, no.1.

3 *The 'identification' hypothesis.* A common form of this hypothesis is that if young viewers can identify with certain positive characteristics of a television personality, this state will tend to facilitate the adoption of the aggressive behaviour of that personality. For discussion, see W. Schramm, J. Lyle, E.B. Parker (1961), *Television in the Lives of our Children*, Stanford University Press.

4 *The 'triggering' hypothesis.* A common form of this hypothesis is that television can set up, in some viewers, linkages between a TV stimulus and a TV response and that a similar stimulus in real life may, in an unstable mind, set off the TV-type response. For discussion, see R. Walters and D. Willows (1968) 'Imitative behaviour of disturbed and non-disturbed children following exposure to aggressive and non-aggressive models', *Child Development*, vol.39.

5 *The 'desensitisation' hypothesis.* This is the hypothesis that constant exposure to television violence dulls the emotional reactions of the exposees to the spectacle of real life violence. For discussion, see S.M. Berger (1962), 'Conditioning through vicarious instigation', *Psychological Review*, vol.69.

[4] R.E. Goranson (1969) in 'A review of recent literature on psychological effects of media portrayals of violence' in *Mass Media and Violence* (a report to the National Commission on the causes and prevention of violence), by D.L. Lange, R.L. Baker and S.J. Ball, US Government Printing Office, Washington DC; D. Howitt and G. Cumberbatch (1975), *Mass Media Violence and Society*, Paul Elak (Scientific Books) Ltd., London.